A BIBLIOGRAPHY OF
DR. JOHN DONNE

JOHN DONNE

He was of stature moderately tall; of a straight and equally proportioned body, to which all his words and actions gave an unexpressible addition of comelinesse.

His aspect was cheerfull, and such as gave a silent testimony of a cleere knowing soule, and of a conscience at peace with it selfe.

His melting eye shewed he had a soft heart, full of noble pity, of too brave a spirit to offer injuries, and too much a Christian, not to pardon them in others.

His fancie was un-imitable high, equalled by his great wit, both being made usefull by a commanding judgement.

His mind was liberall, and unwearied in the search of knowledge, with which his vigorous soule is now satisfied, and employed in a continuall praise of that God that first breathed it into his active body, which once was a Temple of the holy Ghost, and is now become a small quantity of Christian dust. But I shall see it re-inanimated.

1640   *Izaak Walton*

A BIBLIOGRAPHY OF
Dr. John Donne

DEAN OF SAINT PAUL'S

BY

GEOFFREY KEYNES Kt.

M.A. M.D. D.Litt. LL.D.

FOURTH EDITION

OXFORD
AT THE CLARENDON PRESS
1973

Oxford University Press, Ely House, London W. 1

GLASGOW NEW YORK TORONTO MELBOURNE WELLINGTON
CAPE TOWN IBADAN NAIROBI DAR ES SALAAM LUSAKA ADDIS ABABA
DELHI BOMBAY CALCUTTA MADRAS KARACHI LAHORE DACCA
KUALA LUMPUR SINGAPORE HONG KONG TOKYO

*Printed in Great Britain
at the University Press, Oxford
by Vivian Ridler
Printer to the University*

GENERAL PREFACE

THE first edition of this Bibliography of Dr. John Donne was printed in an edition of three hundred copies in 1914 at the Cambridge University Press as the second (and last) publication of the Baskerville Club. It was distributed to the thirty-seven members of the Club after the outbreak of the first World War and I received my copy while serving with the Royal Army Medical Corps in France. The remainder of the edition was marketed by Messrs. Bernard Quaritch Ltd. The second edition of three hundred and fifty copies was published by the Cambridge University Press in 1932 and, after being out of print for some years, was produced in a third Cambridge edition of seven hundred and fifty copies in 1958. The issue of these three 'limited' editions, each revised and enlarged, has failed to satisfy the ever-growing interest in Donne and his works, and it is believed that in the quatercentenary year of his birth a still larger and better edition will be welcomed. The Syndics of the Cambridge University Press have surrendered the publication rights to the Delegates of the Clarendon Press, though the general style and character of the book have been maintained, while incorporating much revision and rewriting with a very greatly enlarged section of Biography and Criticism.

In a very careful review[1] of the 1958 edition of this Bibliography the late Professor R. C. Bald found a good deal to criticize. His own thirty years' study of Donne's life and works had naturally given him the advantage of some detailed knowledge which had escaped my own investigations, and this, coupled with disagreement on a few technical points, led him to conclude that 'the book cannot yet be regarded as the definitive bibliography of Donne'. This opinion suggests the doubt whether any bibliography should ever be labelled 'definitive', that is, a bibliography complete and perfect in every detail. The term is hardly applicable to a book, which from its very nature, is always capable of improvement and extension as knowledge accumulates and literary records multiply. Professor Bald in arriving at his conclusion generously set out in his review every smallest particular in which he thought my work was deficient, so

[1] *The Library*, NS. v, xiv, 1959, 54–8.

that I have been able, with his help, to bring the book a step nearer the unattainable summit of perfection. His splendid *Life of Donne* published by the Clarendon Press in 1970 has been the source of further improvement in detail.

At the same time efforts have been made to increase the value of the book to students. In the first place the self-defeating convention of quasi-facsimile has been circumvented by providing an actual facsimile of every title-page of importance within the range of Donne's published work. Secondly the coverage of the Appendix entitled 'Biography and Criticism' has been greatly enlarged, not only in the field of twentieth-century criticism, but also in that of the seventeenth and eighteenth centuries. This, much larger than might have been expected, has resulted from a close and very pleasant collaboration with Professor Wesley Milgate of Canberra University over a long period. Distance has been no bar to communication and has been fortified by his friendship during two periods when he visited this country. The list of books from Donne's library has been increased, again with the help of Mr. John Sparrow, from 197 to 213 titles. Others will no doubt come to light as time passes. Mr. Robert S. Pirie of Hamilton, Massachusetts, has shared with me his knowledge of Donne's books, having formed during recent years the only private collection of original editions which can rival my own. I am grateful to Professor Dame Helen Gardner for advice and encouragement.

Some recent critics or editors will not find their work recorded here because the printer's deadline had to be fixed at 1 June 1971. This is to be regretted, but was unavoidable. The illustrations, reproduced by the photolitho process instead of collotype, have been varied. As before, the numbering of entries up to 104, covering all the original editions of Donne's works, has remained unaltered. None of the entries recorded under 'Biography and Criticism' is numbered, being arranged either chronologically with references in the General Index, or alphabetically without index references to the names of authors.

GEOFFREY KEYNES

May 1972

CONTENTS

Note. The numbering of the entries in this bibliography is the same as in the last edition up to no. 104. Any additional items are signified by the addition of letters, though some of these letters were also used in the previous editions. After no. 104 the numbering is different, but all the *original editions* of Donne's works come before this point and so have the same numbers as before.

ILLUSTRATIONS

LINE DRAWING

REPRODUCTIONS BY OFFSET LITHOGRAPHY

ABBREVIATIONS

ALFORD   *The Works of John Donne*. With a memoir of his life. By Henry Alford. London, 1839. 6 vols. [no. 33.]

BALD   *John Donne*. A Life by R. C. Bald. Oxford, 1970.

CHAMBERS   *Poems of John Donne*. Edited by E. K. Chambers. London, 1896. 2 vols. [no. 93.]

GOSSE   *The Life and Letters of John Donne*. By Edmund Gosse. London, 1899. 2 vols.

GRIERSON   *The Poems of John Donne*. Edited by H. J. C. Grierson. Oxford, 1912. 2 vols. [no. 96.]

POTTER and SIMPSON   *The Sermons of John Donne*. Edited by George R. Potter and Evelyn M. Simpson. Berkeley and Los Angeles, 1953 [etc.]. 10 vols. [no. 33*h*.]

SIMPSON   *A Study of the Prose Works of John Donne*. By Mrs. E. M. Simpson. Oxford, 1924.

AUL   Aberdeen University Library

BJ   Johns Hopkins University Library, Baltimore

BM   British Museum.

BLO   Bodleian Library, Oxford.

DWL   Dr. Williams's Library, London.

FSLW   Folger Shakespeare Memorial Library, Washington, D.C.

GUL   Glasgow University Library

HCL   Harvard College Library.

HEH   H. E. Huntington Library, California.

LCW   Library of Congress, Washington, D.C.

LUL   London University Library

NLC   Newberry Library, Chicago, Ill.

NLS   National Library of Scotland.

NYPL   New York Public Library.

PUL   Princeton University Library.

TCD   Trinity College, Dublin.

TSP   Theological Seminary, Princeton, N.J.

ULC   University Library, Cambridge.

ULD   University Library, Durham.

ULE   University Library, Edinburgh.

YUL   Yale University Library.

PSEUDO-MARTYR

BIBLIOGRAPHICAL PREFACE

DONNE'S *Pseudo-Martyr* belongs to the year 1609, and, though written after *Biathanatos*, was the first controversial work by him to be printed. It was entered on the Stationers' Register on 2 December 1609, though dated 1610 on the title-page. According to Walton (*Life*, 1658, pp. 37–8) it was written by Donne at the command of King James, and was completed within six weeks. Gosse pointed out, however, that this story is probably untrue. In his dedication Donne writes—'Of my boldnesse in this addresse, I most humbly beseech your Maiestie, to admit this excuse, that having observed, how much your Maiestie had vouchsafed to descend to a conversation with your Subiects, by way of your Bookes, I also conceiv'd an ambition, of ascending to your presence, by the same way'; it is unlikely that he would have written in this manner, had the book been composed expressly at the King's command. Further, a passage in the Advertisement shews that the Table of the Chapters had been in circulation for a considerable period before the completion of the book, and, though the last two chapters mentioned in it were never written, Donne still allowed their headings to appear in the Table.

I have abstained [he writes] from handling the two last Chapters upon divers reasons; whereof one is, that these Heads having beene caried about, many moneths, and thereby quarrelled by some, and desired by others, I was willing to give the Booke a hasty dispatch, that it might cost no man much time, either in expecting before it came, or in reading, when it was come. But a more principall reason was, that since the two last Chapters depend upon one another, and have a mutuall Relation, I was not willing to undertake one, till I might persevere through both. And from the last chapter it became me to abstaine, till I might understand their purposes, who were formerly engaged in the same businesse.

These are the summaries of the missing chapters:

Ch. xiii: *That all which his Maiefty requires by this Oath, is exhibited to the Kings of Fraunce, And not by vertue of any Indult, or Concordate, but by the inhærent right of the Crowne.*

Ch. xiiii: *Laſtly, that no pretence of Conuerſion at firſt, Aſsiſtance in the Conqueſt, or Acceptation of any Surrender from any of our Kings, can giue the Pope any more right ouer the Kingdome of England, then ouer any other free State whatſoever.*

Pseudo-Martyr is not a work of theological controversy, for it deals only with the question of the King's supremacy in order to shew, as the title-page states, 'That those which are of the Romane Religion in this Kingdome, may and ought to take the Oath of Allegeance'. The 'pseudo-martyrs' are the Catholic recusants who have brought punishment upon themselves by their refusal to recognize their lawful sovereign. As Mrs. Simpson remarked, '*Pseudo-Martyr* is a striking example of an almost unreadable book written by a man of genius.' It has been supposed that Donne had served his apprenticeship in the study of controversial literature while assisting Dr. Thomas Morton, then Dean of Gloucester, in the composition of his *Apologia Catholica* and other books published in the years 1605–9. Bald, however, has pointed out that, although Donne had certainly read part of the manuscript of Morton's *Catholic Appeale* some months before its publication, there is no real evidence that he had acted as assistant in the composition of *Apologia Catholica*, *A Catholic Appeale*, or any other book by Morton. The supposition rested originally on an unsupported statement by Dr. Jessopp (1897). Mrs. Simpson (*Prose Works*, pp. 179–80) did not question this, but Bald's detailed examination of the matter in his chapter ix, 'Controversy and Conflict', has effectively disposed of it. The same conclusion is reached by T. S. Healy in his Appendix C, *Ignatius his Conclave*, 1969, pp. 168–73 (see no. 11c). Donne's knowledge of authorities is fully deployed in *Pseudo-Martyr* and most of it now makes dull reading, so that it has never been reprinted.[1] The more interesting part of the book is the 'Preface to The Priestes, and Iesuites, and to their Disciples in this Kingdome', wherein he explains his own attitude and shortcomings in writing the book, and the stages by which he reached his present position.

They who have descended so lowe, as to take knowledge of me, and

[1] In the *Times Lit. Sup.* of 12 June 1953 was a letter from Professor Itrat-Husain of Dacca University announcing the preparation of a definitive edition of *Pseudo-Martyr*, and asking for news of the copy of the book given by Donne to King James, who received it on the evening of 24 January 1610. Itrat-Husain has since died and the projected new edition has not appeared.

to admit me into their considerations, know well that I used no inordinate
hast, nor precipitation in binding my conscience to any locall Religion.
I had a longer worke to doe then many other men; for I was first to blot
out, certaine impressions of the Romane religion, and to wrastle both
against the examples and against the reasons, by which some hold was
taken; and some anticipations early layde upon my conscience, both by
Persons who by nature had a power and superiority over my will, and
others who by their learning and good life, seem'd to me iustly to claime
an interest for the guiding, and rectifying of mine understanding in these
matters. And although I apprehended well enough, that this irresolution
not onely retarded my fortune, but also bred some scandall, and en-
dangered my spirituall reputation, by laying me open to many mis-
interpretations; yet all these respects did not transport me to any violent
and sudden determination, till I had, to the measure of my poore wit and
iudgement, survayed and digested the whole body of Divinity, contro-
verted betweene ours and the Romane Church.

Donne's book was perhaps too closely reasoned and written with too
studied a moderation to admit of a reply being easily framed, and none
was published until 1613; in that year was published a work by Thomas
Fitzherbert in which a long reply to *Pseudo-Martyr* is to be found. This
book, not recorded by Donne's earlier biographers, has the following title:

A ſupplement to the diſcuſſion of M. D. Barlowes anſwere To the Iudgment of
a Catholike Engliſhman etc. interrupted by the death of the Author F. Robert
Perſons of the Society of Ieſus . . . And By the way is briefly cenſured M. Iohn
Dunnes Booke, intituled Pſeudo-martyr . . . By F. T. . . . Permiſſu Superiorum.
M.DC.XIII. *⁴ A–Z⁴ Aa–Zz⁴ Aaa–Eee⁴; 4 ll., pp. 400, 4 ll. [*STC* 11021]
Copies: BM, BLO, ULC, G. L. Keynes.

The answer to *Pseudo-Martyr* occupies pp. 80–110 (Chap. II, §§ 18–78).
In it the author attempted to refute Donne by argument, and also by casting
aspersions on his learning and accuracy:

I hope some or others will, ere it be long, display *M. Dunns* ignorance
to the world, yea & make him understand, that it had byn much more
for his reputation to haue kept himselfe within his compasse, and not to
haue passed *ultra crepidam*, that is to say, beyond his old occupation of

making Satyres (wherein he hath some talent, and may play the foole without controle) then to presume to write bookes of matters in cōtrouersy, which are to be scanned and sifted by learned men, and require much more substance, then his scambling studyes, and superficiall knowledg can affoard (p. 107).

Some of the evidence of Donne's learning, apart from that so amply afforded by his own writings, will be found in a later section of this Bibliography, where are listed all the books and pamphlets bearing evidence of Donne's ownership.

Pseudo-Martyr is also referred to by John Boys, Dean of Canterbury, in his work—*An expoſition of the Dominicall Epiſtles and Goſpels vſed in our Engliſh Liturgie. Together with a reaſon why the Church did chuſe the ſame* ... *London* ... 1610. (*The Spring-part*, p. 118. *STC* 3458) 'I will not meddle', he wrote, 'with the cobwebs of learning in the Schoole, which have more wit then Art, yet more Art then use; nor with the distorted and idle glosses of the Canonists: he that list may burthen his memory with a shipfull of their fooleries, accurately collected by the penner of Pseudomartyr, cap. 10.' Also in *Works* (London, 1622–30), p. 277.

Pseudo-Martyr is not a common book at the present time, but, although it is a characteristic product of Donne's brain, it has not the same attractions as most of his other writings, and the demand has therefore been more easily satisfied. The Bridgewater Library contained a copy of the book[1] in its original limp vellum binding with a letter from Donne to Lord Chancellor Ellesmere pinned to the fly-leaf:

All Ryuers, though in there Course they are content to serue publique uses, yett there end ys, to returne into the Sea, from whence they issued. So, though I should haue much Comfort, that thys Booke might giue contentment to others, yet my Direct end in ytt was, to make yt a testimony of my gratitude towards yo[r] Lp. and an acknowledgement, that those poor sparks of Understandinge or Judgement w[ch] are in mee, were deriued and kindled from yo[u], and owe themselves to yo[u]. All good

[1] Sold at Sotheby's 19 March 1951, lot 109 (Quaritch, £450); collotype facsimile of the letter in the catalogue. Acquired by Allerton C. Hickmott, Hartford, Conn., and now in the collection of R. S. Pirie.

that ys in ytt, yor Lp may be pleasd to accept as yo^rs; and for the Errors, I cannot despayr of yor Pardon, since yo^u haue longe since pardond greater faults in mee.

yor Lps
humble and fayth-
full Seruant
J. Donne

Donne had been secretary to Lord Ellesmere in the years 1596–1601. Another presentation copy, now in the library of Mr. John Sparrow, was given by Donne to his friend Rowland Woodward. At the top of the title-page, here reproduced, is written the Spanish motto: *De juegos el mejor es con la hoja* (of games the best is with the leaf).[1]

1 PSEUDO-MARTYR [*STC* 7048] 4° 1610

Title (within rules double except below): Pſeudo-Martyr. . . . London Printed by W. Stansby for Walter Burre. 1610. [*see facsimile*]

Collation: A⁴ ¶² B–Z⁴ Aa–Zz⁴ Aaa–Ggg⁴ Hhh²; 216 leaves.

Contents: A1 title; A2*a*–A3*b* dedication *To the High and Mightie Prince Iames* . . . signed *Iohn Donne*; A4*a*–*b* *A Table of the Chapters*; ¶1*a*–¶2*a* *An advertiſement to the Reader*; ¶2*b* errata; B1*a*–E2*a* *A Preface to The Prieſtes and Ieſuits, and to their diſciples in this Kingdome*; E2*b* blank; E3*a*–Hhh2*b* (pp. 1–392) text.

Note: The *Table of the Chapters* gives the headings of fourteen chapters; the book, however, contains only twelve of these, the last two never having been written for reasons which the author explains in the *Advertisement* (see my preface). The book is very carelessly printed and contains a large number of misprints. The more serious ones are recorded by Donne in the errata, and he disarms complaint by putting above his list the following ingenuous statement: 'Thoſe literall and punctuall Errors which doe not much endanger the ſenſe, I have left to the diſcretion and favour of the

---

[1] A short account of Woodward will be found in Pearsall Smith's *Life and Letters of Sir Henry Wotton*, Oxford, 1907, II, 481. See also a note on him by M. C. Deas in *Rev. Eng. Stud.* VII, 1931, 454–7. Donne addressed poems to him and to other members of his family, and he may have owned the Westmoreland MS. of the Poems (see Grierson, II, lxxxi). Another book from his library, one volume of *Memoires de l'Estat de France sous Charles Neufiesme*, 2nd edn., 1578, is in the possession of Mr. Desmond Flower. It has the signature and motto and carries the hand-written bookplate of the Earl of Westmoreland, 1856.

PSEVDO-
MARTYR.

Wherein
OVT OF CERTAINE
Propofitions and Gradations, This
Conclufion is euicted.

THAT THOSE WHICH ARE
of the Romane Religion in this Kingdome,
may and ought to take the Oath of
Allegeance.

DEVT. 32. 15.

But he that fhould haue beene vpright, when he waxed fatte, fpurned with his heele: Thou art fat, thou art groffe, thou art laden with fatneffe.

IOB. 11. 5.

But oh that God would fpeake and open his lips againft thee, that he might fhew thee the fecrets of wifedome, how thou haft deferued double according to right.

2. CHRO. 28. 22.

In the time of his tribulation, did he yet trefpaffe more againft the Lord, for he facrificed vnto the gods of Damafcus, which plagued him.

LONDON
Printed by *W. Stansby* for *Walter Burre.*
1610.

Title-page of no. 1

Reader, as he shall meete with them. The rest he may be pleased to mend thus.'
The *Advertisement* was clearly written after the rest of the book had been set up
in type, and the position of these two leaves is variable. In one of the BM copies sign.
¶ is found with the leaves reversed between the two leaves of Hhh, implying that
these four leaves were imposed together. The pagination of sheets Y and Aa is faulty;
133, 136, 137, 140, 154 are printed 121, 124, 125, 128, 156. Various corrections
were made as the book passed through the press (Simpson, p. 186). *Pseudo-Martyr*
is listed in W. Jaggard's *Catalogue of such English books as lately have been, or now are,
in printing for publication*, London, 1618, 4° (*STC* 14341).

The book had been entered at Stationers' Hall on 2 December 1609 and was published
shortly afterwards; a copy was bought for the Earl of Rutland on 25 January 1609/10
for 3*s*. 6*d*.[1] Another copy was sent by J. Beaulieu to William Trumbull on 31 January
1609/10.[2]

Copies: BM (2), BLO, ULC (2), ULD (2), DWL, NLS; HCL, HEH, FSLW
(Britwell Court—Harmsworth copy), NYPL, TSP, YUL.

Cambridge Colleges: Caius, Emmanuel, Magdalene, Queens', St. John's (2),
Trinity (3).

Oxford Colleges: Corpus Christi, New College, St. John's, Trinity (Pope's copy with
his index), Queen's, Wadham, Worcester.

Lincoln's Inn Library; Chapter Library, Windsor; Lambeth Palace Library.

Dublin, Marsh Library.

Cathedral Libraries: Exeter, Hereford, Peterborough, St. Paul's, Salisbury.

G. L. Keynes; R. S. Pirie (Bridgewater copy); J. Sparrow (presentation copy to
R. Woodward; Gosse copy).

[1] *Historical Manuscripts Commission*, Rutland MSS., IV, 1905, p. 465.
[2] Ibid., Downshire MSS., II, 1936, p. 227 (Bald, p. 222).

CONCLAVE IGNATI

BIBLIOGRAPHICAL PREFACE

DONNE'S *Conclave Ignati* or *Ignatius his Conclave*, an attack on Bellarmine and the Jesuits, the third of his controversial writings, though the second to be published, was composed in 1610 and published early in 1611. Neither of the Latin editions is dated, but Gosse inferred from the references to Galileo and Kepler that the book was to be referred to about the year 1611 (I, 257). Mrs. Simpson fixed the date more accurately by noting that a quotation from Kepler is from a work published in 1610 and that the London edition was entered to Walter Burre in the Stationers' Register on 24 January 1610/11. Robert Burton wrote on the title-page of his copy now in Christ Church Library: *John Donne 1610*; a copy was bought by the Earl of Northumberland before 2 February 1611 and another was bought in that month in Paris by Pierre L'Estoile.[1]

Conclave Ignati is a vigorous, amusing, and sometimes scurrilous satire, but it received little notice from Donne's biographers until it was discussed in Gosse's book (loc. cit.). It was more fully considered by Mrs. Simpson (pp. 191–202), in Professor C. M. Coffin's *John Donne and the New Philosophy*, Columbia, 1937, in Bald's *Life of Donne*, 1970, and in great detail in T. S. Healy's scholarly edition of both Latin and English texts, Oxford, 1969. It has been suggested[2] that the form of the satire was to some extent derived from the *Satyre Ménippée*, 1594, and its supplement, *Le Supplément du Catholicon, ou nouvelles des régions de la lune*, 1595. Although the book was anonymous until 1634 there is in the epistle, *The printer to the Reader*, a veiled reference to *Pseudo-Martyr*: 'He chooses and desires, that his other book should testify his ingenuity, and candor, and his disposition to labour for the reconciling of all parts.' Burton's inscription in his copy of the first edition shews that the authorship was in fact known at the time of publication.

Two Latin editions were printed in 1611. One of these, a duodecimo, has no imprint, but was printed in London for Walter Burre as already mentioned; it is uncommon, only twelve copies having been recorded. The

---

[1] I. A. Shapiro, *Times Lit. Sup.*, 6 February 1953, p. 96.
[2] See C. M. Coffin, *John Donne and the New Philosophy*, pp. 201–3.

other is a thin quarto printed abroad, possibly at Hanau; this is still more uncommon and was first recorded in 1914. The first edition of the English version was also published in 1611, having been translated, in Healy's opinion, by Donne himself. The rendering was free, but the book, having been thought out and composed in Latin, was not readily recast, so that the English version has lost some of its edge. Two more English editions were published in 1626 and 1634–5, and it was reprinted under the date 1653 with the *Juvenilia* in the volume of 1652. The Latin version was reprinted in 1680, but not again until 1969 in Healy's edition. The English version has been reprinted in full only in John Hayward's Nonesuch *Complete Poetry and Selected Prose*, 1929 (see no. 97), by the Facsimile Text Society, 1941 (no. 11*b*), and by Healy.

Donne himself, as is implied in his preface, regarded the book as too undignified a production to be publicly acknowledged, though his name appeared on the title-pages of the English editions published after his death; it is omitted, however, from the Latin reprint of 1680. In the volume of 1652 the editor, John Donne the younger, described *Ignatius his Conclave* on the general title-page as 'lately found among his [the author's] own Papers', and appears to ignore the previous issues, but this was evidently for the purposes of sale.

Healy has suggested that Walton's account of how *Pseudo-Martyr* came to be written could be applied more appropriately to *Conclave Ignati*. It seems unlikely that the former could have been written in six weeks, whereas the other, slighter, book could easily have been done in a short time.

Conclave Ignati contains three passages in verse; near the beginning are two lines, followed soon after by six more, and near the end is a third passage of six lines. All of these are rendered in the same number of lines in the English version.

In the British Museum is a curiosity in the form of an English version of *Conclave Ignati* entitled 'Ignatius his Closet' (MS. Harl. 1019). The translator's name is not known nor the time at which he worked. If he made his translation before the appearance of Donne's own English version, registered 18 May 1611, he must have worked quickly. This was discovered by the late R. C. Bald (*Life of Donne*, p. 228). Another recent discovery is a Latin epigram of fourteen lines occasioned by the canonization of Loyola in 1622.

This was found by Professor P. G. Stanwood of the University of British Columbia in 1967 written in an early manuscript preserved in the library of Durham Cathedral. It was first printed in the *Times Literary Supplement*[1] and was reprinted with an English rendering by T. S. Healy in 1969.[2] Both authorities regard the lines as probably composed by Donne himself and Bald did not dissent.[3] The manuscript attribution was: *Dr. Dun Deane of Paules*.

Donne's book was mentioned by Robert Burton in *The Anatomy of Melancholy*, 1621.

2 CONCLAVE IGNATI [*STC* 7026] first Latin edition   12° [1611]
Title: Conclaue Ignati . . . [*no imprint; see facsimile*]

Collation: A–D¹² E⁶; 54 leaves.

Contents: A1 title; A2*a*–3*b Typographus Lectori*; A4*a*–E2*b* (pp. 1–94) text, addressed: *Angelis tutelaribus, Confiftorio Papali, & Collegio Sorbonæ Præfidentibus*; E3*a*–5*a Apologia pro Iefuitis*; E5*b* errata, 25 lines, headed: *Lectori. Iefuitarum Dæmonem credo operæ infediffe: unde alias tot errata? Noftra autem hic corrigimus: fed quando Iefuitæ fua*; E6 blank.

Note: The book was entered in the Stationers' Register on 24 January 1610/11: 'Walter Burre. Entred for Copy vnder thandes of Doctor Moreton, Doctor Mokett and master Adames warden, A booke in Latyne called, *Conclave Ignatij*, . . . [etc.] vj*ᵈ*.' The ornament used on A4 and E3 of this book is the same as is found on the title-page and other leaves of no. 3, which was perhaps printed at Hanau (see note), but the same one was also used by the London printers, and the late F. S. Ferguson identified the printer as William Hall (1598–1614), who used the ornaments and initials in several other books (personal communication). The YUL copy, lacking E6 blank, is untrimmed, measuring 155 × 87 mm.

Copies: BM, BLO, NLS, ULC; HCL, YUL.
   Cambridge: Trinity College.
   Oxford Colleges: Balliol, Corpus Christi (Twynne Collection), Christ Church (Burton copy).
   Westminster Abbey Library. G. L. Keynes.

3 CONCLAVE IGNATI continental Latin edition   4° [1611]
Title: Conclaue Ignati: . . . [*no imprint; see facsimile*]
Collation: A–D⁴ E²; 18 leaves.

---

[1] 'A Donne Discovery', *Times Lit. Sup.*, 19 October 1967, p. 984.
[2] *Ignatius his Conclave*, 1969, pp. 174–5.   [3] *Life of Donne*, p. 228 n.

Contents: A1 title; A2*a–b* (pp. 3–4) *Typographus Lectori*; A3*a*–E1*b* (pp. 5–34) text; E1*b*–E2*a* (pp. 34–5) *Apologia pro Iesuitis* (errata, headed *Lectori*, etc., at bottom of E2*a*); E2*b* blank.

Conclaue Ignati:

Siue
EIVS IN NV-
PERIS INFERNI
COMITIIS
Inthronisatio.

Vbi varia
De Iesuitarum Indole,
De nouo inferno creando,
De Ecclesia Lunatica instituenda,
per Satyram congesta sunt.

Accessit & Apologia
pro Iesuitis.

Omnia
Duobus Angelis Aduersariis,
qui Consistorio Papali, & Col-
legio Sorbonæ præsi-
dent, dedicata.

Title-page of no. 2

Note: This edition had not been noticed before 1914. Each of the two ULC copies is bound up with other tracts which were printed at Hanau, *apud Thomam Villerianum* (possibly a fictitious imprint), and it is probable, for typographical reasons, that this edition of *Conclave Ignati* was issued from the same press. The list of *errata* is faithfully reprinted except for the last four words, three of which have been corrected.

CONCLAVE IGNATI.

Siue

EIVS IN NVPERIS
INFERNI COMITIIS
INTHRONISATIO.

Vbi varia

De Iesuitarum Indole,
De nouo inferno creando,
De Ecclesia Lunatica instituẽda,

per Satyram congesta sunt.

ACCESSIT ET APOLOGIA
PRO IESVITIS.

Omnia

Duobus Angelis Aduersariis, qui Consistorio Papali, & Collegio
Sorbonæ præsident, dedicata.

Title-page of no. 3

c

Copies: BM (Breslau Stadtsbibliothek duplicate), ULC (2, Acton collection).
　　Breslau Public Library.[1]
　　G. L. Keynes.

4, 5 IGNATIUS HIS CONCLAVE [*STC* 7027] first English edition,
　　　alternative titles　　　　　　　　　　　　　　　　12° 1611

Title (within single rule): Ignatius his Conclaue . . . London Printed by
　　N. O. for Richard More, and are to be fold at his fhop in S. Dunftones
　　Church-yard. 1611. [*see facsimiles*]

Collation: A–G¹² (± G12); 84 leaves.

Contents: A1 blank; A2 title; A3*a*–A5*b* *The printer to the Reader*; A6*a*–G5*a* (pp. 1–
　　143) text; G5*b* blank; G6*a*–G7*b* *An Apology for Iefuites*; G8*a* errata, 19 lines;
　　G8*b*–G11 blank; G12 first title.

Note: Printed by Nicholas Okes (1606–*c.* 1635). Entered in the Stationers' Register
　　on 18 May 1611: 'Richard Moore. Entred for his Copy vnder th'andes of Doctor
　　Mokett, and Th'wardens, A booke called, *Ignatius his Conclaue* . . . [etc.] vj^d.' The
　　title was first printed on G12 enclosed in an ornamental border in an erroneous form;
　　this has usually been cancelled, but has survived in two copies. These shew that *of
　　Iefuits* in line 8 was misprinted *of fuits* (BM copy; see facsimile) or *ofefuites* (Windsor
　　copy),[2] and that the line *Tranflated out of Latine* had been omitted. In all copies except
　　one, which is defective, a reprinted title is found as A2; this is not an inserted leaf as
　　was proved in my copy, unbound when I acquired it, and shewing part of the stub of
　　G12 with portions of the ornamental border. The pagination is correct except that
　　p. 59 is numbered 39.

Copies: BM, ULC; HCL (2 copies, one, the J. C. Williams copy, lacking A1, G9–12),
　　HEH.
　　Cambridge: Emmanuel College.
　　Windsor, Chapter Library (at present lost). G. L. Keynes.

6 [IGNATIUS HIS CONCLAVE spurious title　　　　12° 1611

Title: Ignatius his Conclaue: or The Enthronifation of Loyola in Hell.
　　Imprinted At London in 1611.

Note: In the first edition of this bibliography I recorded an issue of *Ignatius his Conclave*
　　with the title as given above. The copy from which this was transcribed I had not

　　[1] Presumably, since a duplicate was sold. No answer has been received to inquiries.
　　[2] This copy was seen by Mrs. Simpson before 1948 (*Prose Works*, p. 195 n.), but when asked
for by T. S. Healy, S.J., in 1967 it could not be found (*Ignatius his Conclave*, 1969, p. xlvi). No
answer has been received to recent inquiries.

Ignatius his Conclaue:
OR
His Inthronifation in a late
Election in Hell:
Wherein many things are min-
gled by way of Satyr;
Concerning
The Difpofition of fuits,
The Creation of a new Hell, (Moore.
The eftablifhing of a Church in the
There is alfo a ded an Apology
for Iefuites.
All dedicated to the two Aduer-
fary Angels, which are Protectors
of the Papall Confiftory, and of
the Colledge of Sorbon.

LONDON,
Printed by N.O. for Richard More,
and are to be fold at his fhop
in S. Dunftones Church-
yard. 1611.

Ignatius his Conclaue:
OR
His Inthronifation in a late
Election in Hell:
Wherein many things are min-
gled by way of Satyr;
Concerning
The Difpofition of Iefuits,
The Creation of a new Hell, (Moore.
The eftablifhing of a Church in the
There is alfo added an Apology
for Iefuites.
All dedicated to the two Aduerfary
Angels, which are Protectors of the
Papall Confiftory, and of the
Colledge of Sorbon.
Tranflated out of Latine.
LONDON,
Printed by N.O. for Richard More,
and are to be fold at his fhop in
S. Dunftones Church-
yard. 1611.

First title-page of no. 5 (cancelled)   Second title-page of no. 4

myself seen; it was then in the library of the late W. A. White of New York and is now in the Harvard College Library. Mr. George P. Winship informed me that the book is really a copy of no. 4 lacking the title-page, which has been supplied by a modern reprint as above.]

7 IGNATIUS HIS CONCLAVE [*STC* 7028] second edition
12° 1626

Title (*within single rule*): Ignatius his Conclaue . . . London, Printed by M. F. for Richard More, and are to be fold at his fhop in S. Dunftans Church-yard. 1626. [*see facsimile*]

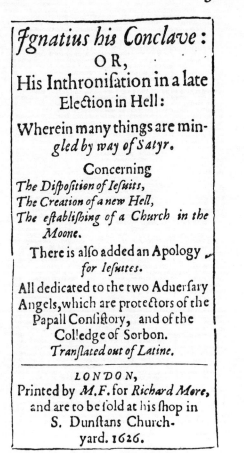

Title-page of no. 7   Title-page of no. 8

Collation: A–G¹²; 84 leaves.

Contents: A1–A2 blank; A3 title; A4a–A6b *The printer to the Reader*; A7a–G6a (pp. 1–143) text; G6b blank; G7a–G8b *An Apology for Iesuites*; G9–G12 blank.

Note: Printed by Miles Fletcher (1611–64).

Copies: BM, ULC, ULE.[1]
   King's College, Cambridge.

1 From the library of Drummond of Hawthornden.

8 IGNATIUS HIS CONCLAVE [*STC* 7029] third edition

12° 1634

Title (within single rule): Ignatius his Conclave . . . London, Printed for Iohn Marriott, and are to be fold by W. Sheares at the Harrow in Britains Burffe. 1634. [*see facsimile*]

Collation: A–F¹²; 72 leaves.

Contents: A1 title; A2*a*–A3*a The printer to the Reader;* A3*b* blank; A4*a*–F11*a* (pp. 1–135) text; F11*b*–F12*b An Apologie for Iefuites.*

Copies: BM, BLO, NLS, ULC; HCL, HEH, FSLW, YUL.
Jesus College, Oxford.
Peterborough Cathedral Library.
G. L. Keynes; H. Bradley Martin; R. S. Pirie.

9 IGNATIUS HIS CONCLAVE [*STC* 7030] third edition, variant title
12° 1635

Title (within single rule): Ignatius his Conclave: . . . [etc. as in no. 8].
London, . . . 1635.

Collation, Contents: As in no. 8.

Note: This issue consists of the same sheets as no. 8 with the date altered on the title-page, which is, however, not a cancel. Presumably the alteration was made while the book was in the press.

Copies: BM (Castle Howard copy), BLO, TCD; BJ, HCL, FSLW (Harmsworth copy), NLC, TSP, YUL, WLT.
Corpus Christi College, Oxford.
Lambeth Palace Library; Chapter Library, Windsor; Peterborough Cathedral Library; Innerpeffray Library, Perthshire; Carlisle Cathedral; York Minster.
G. L. Keynes; R. S. Pirie; I. A. Shapiro.

10 IGNATIUS HIS CONCLAVE [Wing D 1863] fourth edition
12° 1653

Subtitle (within single rule): Ignatius his conclave: . . .
Printed at London, 1653. [*see facsimile*]

Collation, Contents: See no. 45, *Paradoxes, Problems*, etc., 1652.

11 CONCLAVE IGNATII [Wing B 837] fifth edition   8° 1680

General title (within double rules): Lucii Cornelii Europaei Monarchia Solipforum. Et Conclave Ignatii: Sive Ejus in Nuperis Inferni Comitiis

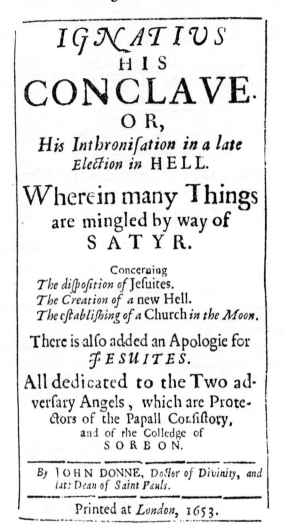

IGNATIUS
HIS
CONCLAVE.
OR,
*His Inthronisation in a late
Election in* HELL.

Wherein many Things
are mingled by way of
SATYR.

Concerning
The disposition of Jesuites.
The Creation of a new Hell.
The establishing of a Church *in the Moon.*

There is also added an Apologie for
JESUITES.

All dedicated to the Two ad-
versary Angels, which are Protectors of the Papall Consistory,
and of the Colledge of
SORBON.

By JOHN DONNE, *Doctor of Divinity, and
late Dean of Saint Pauls.*

Printed at *London,* 1653.

Sub-title of no. 10

Intronisatio. [*rule*] Londini, Prostat venalis apud Jacobum Collins, in
Vico vulgò vocato Essex -Street. 1680.

Collation: A–O⁸; 112 leaves.

Contents: A1 title; A2*a–b Timotæus Cursantius Leoni Allatio S.*; A3*a*–I2*b* (pp. 1–128)
Monarchia Solipsorum; I3*a*–I4*b Syllabus*; I5 subtitle to *Conclave Ignatii* (see fac-

CONCLAVE
IGNATII:
SIVE
Ejus in nuperis Inferni Comitiis Inthronisatio.

UBI VARIA

De {
Jesuitarum Indole,
Novo inferno creando,
Ecclesia Lunatica Instituenda,
}

PER SATYRAM

CONGESTA SUNT.

Accessit & Apologia pro
JESUITIS.

Omnia

*Duobus Angelis Adversariis, qui con=
sistorio Papali, & Collegio Sorbonæ
præsident, dedicata.*

LONDINI,
Anno Domini, 1680.

Sub-title of no. 11

Note: This book usually occurs bound up with a later work by Thomas Barlow, Bishop of Lincoln, *Papiſmus Regiæ Poteſtatis Everſor*, dated 1681, the general title-page being as follows:

Papiſmus Regiæ Poteſtatis Everſor. Reverendus admodum Epiſcopus Lincoln. Anglicè ſcripſit. Robertus Grovius S.T.B. De Angelicano Latinum fecit:. . . Quibus ab alio adjunguntur Monarchia Solipſorum et Conclave Ignatii. Londini, . . . apud Jacobum Collins, & Samuelem Lowndes, . . . 1682.

Copies: BM, BLO, ULE.
All Souls College, Oxford. Chetham's Library, Manchester.
Salisbury Cathedral Library.
G. L. Keynes (Duke of Beaufort copy).

11*a* IGNATIUS HIS CONCLAVE   8° 1929

In John Donne . . . Complete Poetry and Selected Prose Edited by John Hayward . . . 1929. (See no. 97.)

11*b* IGNATIUS HIS CONCLAVE ED. COFFIN   8° 1941

Ignatius his Conclave by John Donne Reproduced from the First Edition With a Bibliographical Note by Charles M. Coffin.
Published for the Facsimile Text Society [no. 53] New York: Columbia University Press. London: H. Milford. M.CM.XLI. 18 cm, pp. xxiii, xv, 143.

Reviewed: Times Lit. Sup., 9 August 1941, 387; Bower, F., *Mod. Lang. Notes*, LVII, 1942, pp. 468–73; Freeman, R., *Rev. Eng. Stud.* XIX, 1943, pp. 83–4; Spinka, M., *Church Hist.* X, 1941, p. 187; Tobin, J. E., *Thought*, XVII, 1942, p. 140.

11*c* IGNATIUS HIS CONCLAVE ED. HEALY   8° 1969

John Donne Ignatius His Conclave An Edition of the Latin and English Texts with Introduction and Commentary by T. S. Healy, S. J. Oxford At the Clarendon Press, 1969. 21.5 cm, pp. lii, 175, [1].

Note: After his commentary the editor has added four Appendices:
A. Differences between the Two Texts.
B. A Note on Sources.
C. Donne's Collaboration with Thomas Morton.
D. A Donne Discovery (the Latin poem on Loyola mentioned in the Bibliographical Preface with an English rendering).

SERMONS

BIBLIOGRAPHICAL PREFACE

DONNE had taken orders at the instigation of King James on 23
January 1614/15; he was appointed Dean of St. Paul's in November 1621, and in this capacity became one of the most celebrated
preachers of his time. The earliest of his sermons that has survived with a
date was preached on 30 April 1615; his last sermon was preached before
King Charles on 25 February 1630/1, and was soon afterwards printed under
the title of *Death's Duell*.[1]

Six of Donne's sermons were printed during his lifetime between 1622
and 1627; seven more, including *Death's Duell*, were printed soon after
his death, and later, in 1640, 1649, and 1660, three folio volumes containing 154 sermons were issued by his son, John Donne, D.C.L.[2] These
volumes included the seven posthumous sermons just mentioned, but the
remaining 147, with the exception of one which had been issued anony-
mously in 1638, had not been printed before.

Those sermons which were printed by Donne during his lifetime were
also collected by him in successive volumes containing *Three Sermons*
(1623), *Foure Sermons* (1625), and *Fiue Sermons* (1626); these volumes were
not reprints in the ordinary sense, but consisted of the sheets of the individual sermons as first issued bound up together, with a general title-page
prefixed to, or substituted for, the title-page of the first sermon. The
sermons also occur bound up together by their original owners; one such
volume in the library of Pembroke College, Cambridge, containing all the
sermons issued in quarto up to 1634, was evidently collected by Izaak
Walton, whose autograph appears in it in two places.[3] Another, now in the
H. E. Huntingdon Library, was formerly in the library at Bridgewater
House. It contains the first issue of *Death's Duell*, the sermon on *Judges
v. 20*, *Encaenia*, and *The First Sermon Preached to King Charles*. The last
two of these are inscribed *J. Bridgewater ex dono authoris* and dated

---

[1] This is stated by Walton to have been preached on the first Sunday in Lent. Gosse stated
that this fell on 12 February 1630/1, but Mrs. Simpson believed it was on 25 February, and Professor Shapiro that it was 27 February.

[2] See pp. 61–73 of the present work.   [3] See nos. 26 and 27.

respectively *20 June 1623* and *12 March 1625/6*, having been given to the first Earl of Bridgewater, son of Sir Thomas Egerton (afterwards Lord Ellesmere), whom Donne had served as secretary in the years 1596–1601. Bridgewater's wife, Frances, has put her initials, *F. B.*, on the fly-leaf and title-page of the sermon on *Judges v. 20.* A third volume, now in my library and formerly at Draycot House, Wilts., contains *Death's Duell*, the *Sermon preached to the King, 1625*, and the *Six Sermons, 1634.* A fourth, in the collection of R. S. Pirie, is formed of *Three Sermons, Six Sermons*, and *Death's Duell.*

According to Walton, Donne did not read his sermons from the pulpit, but, like other preachers of the period, as John Sparrow has shewn, committed them to memory or used short notes. Afterwards he would write them out or 'exscribe' them, as he called the process in a letter to Sir Robert Karre, in a form ready for publication.[1] It might take him eight hours to copy out a sermon, as he told Goodere in a letter of 30 August 1611 (*Letters*, p. 154). An idea of the manner in which he recast his sermons may be gained by comparing the text of the sermon printed by Milbourne in 1638 from an unauthorized copy with that of the same sermon as it was printed in the folio of 1660.[2] Walton's description of Donne's delivery of the first sermon, which he preached before the King, must be accepted as a true estimate of his great power as a preacher.

> Preaching the word so [Walton writes] as shewed his own heart was possest with those very thoughts, and joyes that he laboured to distil into others. A Preacher in earnest, weeping sometimes for his Auditory, sometimes with them; alwaies preaching to himself like an Angell from a cloud, but in none; carrying some, as St. Paul was, to Heaven in holy raptures, and inticing others by a sacred art and Courtship to amend their lives; here picturing a vice so as to make it ugly to those that practised it; and a vertue so, as to make it be loved even by those that lov'd it not, and all this with a most particular grace and an unexpressible addition of comelinesse. [Walton's *Life of Donne*, 1658, pp. 47–8.]

[1] See also p. 31 of the present work, and John Sparrow, *Essays and Studies by Members of the English Association*, XVI, 1931, 144, 'John Donne and Contemporary Preachers'.

[2] This sermon also exists in MS. Differences between the various versions have been described by Mrs. Simpson (see her *Prose Works*, pp. 263–8) and by John Sparrow (loc. cit.).

In spite of Walton's statement (*Life*, 1658, p. 88) that Donne 'left also sixscore of his sermons all written with his own hand', none is known to have survived in that form, but several collections are extant, copied out by the hands of various scribes. These are as follows:

(*a*) M, the Merton MS., given to the Bodleian Library by Dr. E. S. de Beer in 1959, was formerly known as the Collier MS., as it was believed to have been in the possession of John Payne Collier, described by him in his *History of Dramatic Poesy*, 1831, ii, pp. 431–3. This was questioned by Potter and Simpson (*Sermons*, I, pp. 33–8) because it does not now contain poems stated by Collier to have been in the volume. Further examination of the manuscript since it left the library of the late Wilfred Merton convinced Mrs. Simpson that this objection is not valid and it is conceded that the Merton and Collier MSS. are one and the same (*Sermons*, x, pp. 427–8). It is a folio volume with the initials HF on the cover and begins with sermons by Dr. John King and others, followed by sixteen sermons by Donne:

1. Eccles. 12: 1 (*XXVI Sermons*, 19)
2. Luke 23: 34 (*Fifty Sermons*, 34)
3. John 5: 22 (*Fifty Sermons*, 12)
4. John 7: 15 (*Fifty Sermons*, 13)
5. Ps. 144: 15 (*LXXX Sermons*, 74)
6. Matt. 21: 44 (*Fifty Sermons*, 35)
7. Ps. 38: 9
8. Col. 1: 24 (*Fifty Sermons*, 16)
9. Amos 5: 18 (*LXXX Sermons*, 14)
10. Prov. 8: 17 (*XXVI Sermons*, 18)
11. 1 Tim. 3: 16 (*XXVI Sermons*, 4)
12. Mark 16: 16 (*LXXX Sermons*, 76)
13. 1 Cor. 15: 26 (*LXXX Sermons*, 15)
14. Gen. 2: 18 (*Fifty Sermons*, 2)
15. Hos. 2: 19 (*Fifty Sermons*, 3)
16. 2 Cor. 4: 6 (*XXVI Sermons*, 25)

Of these no. 7 was not printed in the folios, but was first printed by Merton in 1921 (see no. 33*b*) from the version in the Dowden MS.

(*b*) D, the Dowden MS., a 4to volume formerly in the possession of Wilfred Merton, is not to be confused with the manuscript volume of Donne's poems, also known as 'the Dowden MS.' also from Merton's library (see p. 185 of the present work). The Dowden MS. of sermons belonged to Professor Edward Dowden of Dublin and was sold with his library at Hodgson's, 16 December 1913, lot 55, being bought by P. J. Dobell for Merton. It contains nine sermons, eight of which are by Donne, these being the same as nos. 1, 3–8, 10 in the Merton MS. This was also given to the Bodleian Library by Dr. E. S. de Beer in 1959.

(*c*) The Lothian MS., a 4to volume of sermons, formerly belonged to David Laing, who in 1851 lent it to William Pickering. It was catalogued with the Pickering library (Sotheby's, 8 August 1854, lot 1196), but was withdrawn by Laing. In 1855 Laing gave it to Dr. Jessopp, who had intended to bid up to £100 for it at the sale. In 1898 Jessopp presented it to the ninth Marquess of Lothian for the library at Newbattle Abbey. The volume was said at one time to be in Donne's hand, but this is no longer believed, though the resemblance is close. The first leaf became detached (probably by Dr. Jessopp) and was for a time in my possession, but I afterwards restored it to its proper place, and the whole manuscript is now, with the Newbattle Abbey books, in the National Library of Scotland. The volume, according to Potter and Simpson, contains thirty-nine sermons, of which eight, in the first section of nine, are by Donne. The ninth was thought by Sparrow[1] to be by Donne, but the latest editors of Donne's sermons did not agree.[2] The eight by Donne are the same as those in the Dowden MS.

(*d*) P, the St. Paul's Cathedral Library MS., is a 4to volume containing five sermons, four of which are by Donne. These are the same as nos. 5, 11, 15, 16 in the Merton MS. They were written out in 1625 by Knightley Chetwood, whose name appears on the first leaf and at the end.[3]

(*e*) Do., the Dobell MS., now in the Houghton Library at Harvard, was bought by the late P. J. Dobell at Sotheby's sale 10–12 June 1914. It is a folio volume bound in tooled morocco, and contains an important collection of Donne's poems (see p. 186) together with three of his sermons and other miscellaneous material. The sermons are the same as those in the Merton MS., nos. 1, 6, 7.

(*f*) A, in Ashmole 781, a commonplace book, in the Bodleian Library, is one sermon by Donne, the Valediction sermon, Merton MS., no. 1.

(*g*) E, the Ellesmere MS., acquired by myself at the sale of the remaining portion of the Bridgewater Library, Sotheby's 19 March 1951, lot 174, is a 4to volume of miscellaneous manuscripts bound up together in seventeenth-century calf with the Bridgewater crest stamped on the sides. Scattered among the contents[4] are eight of Donne's sermons, namely

---

[1] Loc. cit.

[2] It has been printed in *Sermons*, x, pp. 249–53.   [3] See Potter and Simpson, I. 41.

[4] See *Times Lit. Sup.*, 28 May 1954, for a full description by myself.

Merton MS., nos. 1, 3, 4, 8, 15, 10, 2, 13. The book has an intimate association with the Egerton family in that it contains a Latin letter and exercise written by young Thomas Egerton, who acted the second brother in *Comus* in 1634, as a New Year's gift for his father, the first Earl of Bridgewater.

It will be noticed that the only sermons known in manuscript versions are all contained in the Merton MS., though there are variations in the other texts. Only one individual who transcribed the sermons has been identified. In the course of litigation with Francis Bowman, the printer, concerning the *LXXX Sermons* and *Fifty Sermons* the younger Donne stated that the texts had been transcribed by two old servants of his father, Thomas Roper and Robert Christmas,[1] but these manuscripts have not survived for comparison.

The great majority of the sermons were reprinted by Dean Alford in his edition of 1839 (see no. 33*a*), but in a modernized form. No further extensive reprint was attempted until recently, a complete collection, fully edited by the late George Potter and Evelyn M. Simpson, having been published by the University of California Press in ten volumes, 1954 to 1962 (see no. 33*j*). These editors give a list of sermons reprinted in whole or in part in vol. 1, pp. 29–32.[2] Ten sermons were reprinted under my editorship by the Nonesuch Press in 1923. A volume of selected passages was made for the Oxford University Press by Logan Pearsall Smith in 1919, and a more extensive selection was included in John Hayward's Nonesuch edition of Donne, 1929.

Five Sermons, *Death's Duell*, and *LXXX Sermons* have been printed in facsimile by Scolar Press Ltd., Menston, Ilkley, Yorks.

12 SERMON ON JUDGES, xx. 15 (v. 20) [*STC* 7053] first edition
4° 1622

Title (within rules, double at sides): A Sermon Vpon The xv. Verſe Of The xx. Chapter Of The Booke Of Iudges . . . London Printed by William Stansby

---

[1] See 'Bowman *v.* Donne', by J. Milton French, *Times Lit. Sup.*, 12 December 1936.

[2] To this may be added *LXXX Sermons*, no. 66, printed in Sidney Dark's *The World's Great Sermons*, London, 1933.

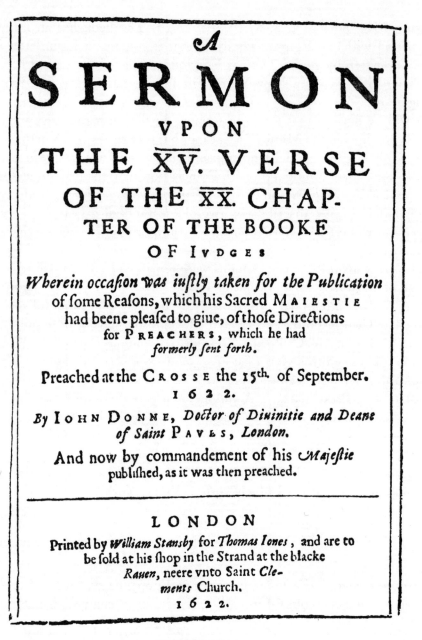

A

SERMON

VPON

THE XV. VERSE

OF THE XX. CHAP-

TER OF THE BOOKE

OF IVDGES

Wherein occasion was iustly taken for the Publication
of some Reasons, which his Sacred MAIESTIE
had beene pleased to giue, of those Directions
for PREACHERS, which he had
formerly sent forth.

Preached at the CROSSE the 15th. of September.
1 6 2 2.

By IOHN DONNE, *Doctor of Diuinitie and Deane*
of Saint PAVLS, *London.*

And now by commandement of his *Majestie*
published, as it was then preached.

LONDON

Printed by *William Stansby* for *Thomas Iones*, and are to
be sold at his shop in the Strand at the blacke
Rauen, neere vnto Saint *Cle-*
ments Church.
1 6 2 2.

Title-page of no. 12

for Thomas Iones, and are to be ſold at his ſhop in the Strand at the blacke
Rauen, neere vnto Saint Clements Church. 1622. [*see facsimile*]

Collation: A–I⁴ K²; 38 leaves.

Contents: A1 blank; A2 title; A3*a*–A4*a* dedication *To the right honourable, George,
Marqueſſe of Buckingham*; A4*b* errata, 5 lines; B1*a*–K2*b* (pp. 1–68) text.

Note: The reference to the text given on the title-page of this book is a mistake for
Judges 5: 20; this was not corrected until the third issue of the sermon (see no. 14).
Not reprinted in the folios; but it is printed by Alford, VI, 191. One of the FSLW
copies lacks the errata list, but they have not been corrected in the text.

A contemporary commentator, John Chamberlain, wrote of this sermon on 25
September 1622: 'On the 15th of this present the Dean of Paules preached at the
Crosse to certifie the Kings goode intention in the late orders concerning preachers
and preaching, and of his constancie in the true reformed religion, which the people
(as shold seeme) began to suspect; his text was the 20th verse of the 5th chapter of the
booke of Judges, somewhat a straunge text for such a business, and how he made yt
hold together I know not, but he gave no great satisfaction, or as some say spake as yf
himself were not so well satisfied.' (*Chamberlain's Letters*, 1939, II, 518. See p. 283.)

The book was entered at Stationers' Hall on 31 October 1622, and was published
before 16 November.[1]

Copies: BM, DWL, NLS; HCL, HEH, FSLW (2, one Harmsworth), YUL.
Christ Church, Oxford.
Cathedral Libraries: Carlisle, Lambeth Palace, St. Paul's.
G. L. Keynes (2, one in *Five Sermons*), R. S. Pirie (with one erratum corrected).

13 SERMON ON JUDGES, xx. 15 (v. 20) [incl. in *STC* 7053] first
edition, second issue   4° 1622

Title (within rules, double at sides): A Sermon Vpon The xv. Verſe Of The xx.
Chapter Of The Booke Of Iudges . . . [as in no. 12]. London Printed by
William Stansby for Thomas Iones, . . . 1622.

Collation: A–I⁴ K²; 38 leaves.

Contents: A1 blank; A2 title; A3*a*–A4*a* dedication; A4*b* blank; B1*a*–K2*b* (pp. 1–68)
text.

Note: A second issue of no. 12. The list of errata noted on A4*b* of the first issue has been
omitted. The first four have been corrected, but the fifth and the misprint on the
title-page remain as before.

[1] See Chamberlain's *Letters*, 1939, II, 464.

Copies: BLO, ULC; HCL, FSLW.

Trinity College, Cambridge (in *Three Sermons*, 1623).
Christ Church, Oxford.
J. Sparrow; G. L. Keynes (unbound and untrimmed).

14 SERMON ON JUDGES, v. 20 [*STC* 7054] second edition

4° 1622

Title (within double rules): A Sermon Vpon The xx. Verſe Of The v. Chapter Of The Booke Of Iudges . . . London, Printed for Thomas Jones, and are to bee ſold at his Shop in the Strand, at the blacke Rauen, neere vnto Saint Clements Church. 1622. [*see facsimile*]

Collation: A² B–I⁴ K², 36 leaves.

Contents: A1 title; A2 dedication; B1*a*–K2*b* (pp. 1–68) text.

Note: In this, the third, printing of the sermon most of the sheets B–K are the same as in no. 13, though there are a large number of minor changes throughout; sheets F and G have been completely reset. A new first quire of two leaves has been substituted for the original A 1–4. The text is now given correctly on the title-page, which also shews other minor alterations.

Copies: BM, TCD, ULD; HCL, HEH, FSLW (5, one in *Foure Sermons*, one in *Fiue Sermons*), LCW (in *Fiue Sermons*), NLC, YUL (2, one in *Fiue Sermons*).

Cambridge Colleges: Magdalene, Pembroke, Jesus (in *Fiue Sermons*), Trinity (in *Three Sermons*, 1624).

Cathedral Libraries: Christ Church, Oxford, Exeter, St. Paul's.

G. L. Keynes (2, one in *Foure Sermons*), R. S. Pirie (3, 2 in *Three Sermons* and *Fiue Sermons*).

15 SERMON ON ACTS, i. 8 [*STC* 7051] first edition   4° 1622

Title (within double rules): A Sermon Vpon The viii. Verſe Of The i. Chapter Of The Acts Of The Apoſtles. . . . London. Printed by A. Mat: for Thomas Iones and are to [be] ſold at his Shop in the Strand, at the blacke Rauen, neere vnto Saint Clements Church. 1622. [*see facsimile*]

Collation: A–G⁴; 28 leaves.

Contents: A1 blank; A2 title; A3*a–b* dedication *To the honourable company of the Virginian Plantation*; A4*a*–G4*a* (pp. 1–49) text (errata, 5 lines, at bottom of G4*a*); G4*b* blank.

Note: Issued again in 1624 (see no. 18), but not reprinted in the folios. It is given by Alford, vi, 225, and in my *Ten Sermons*, 1923. This and several of the succeeding

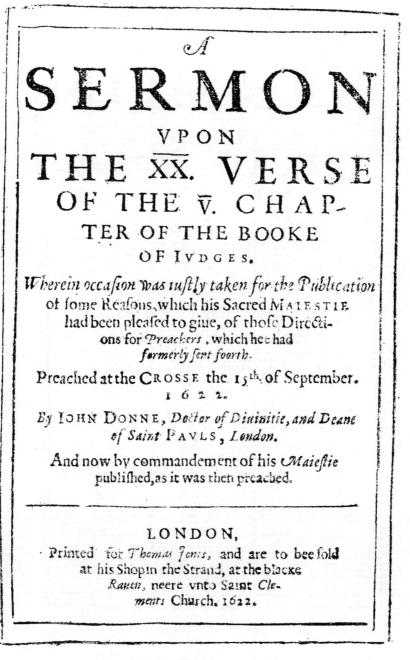

A

SERMON

VPON

THE XX̄. VERSE

OF THE V̄. CHAP-
TER OF THE BOOKE
OF IVDGES.

Wherein occasion was iustly taken for the Publication
of some Reasons, which his Sacred MAIESTIE.
had been pleased to giue, of those Directions for *Preachers*, which hee had
formerly sent foorth.

Preached at the CROSSE the 15th. of September.
1 6 2 2.

By IOHN DONNE, *Doctor of Diuinitie, and Deane*
of Saint PAVLS, *London.*

And now by commandement of his *Maiestie*
published, as it was then preached.

LONDON,
Printed for *Thomas Jones*, and are to bee sold
at his Shop in the Strand, at the blacke
Rauen, neere vnto Saint *Cle-*
ments Church. 1622.

Title-page of no. 14

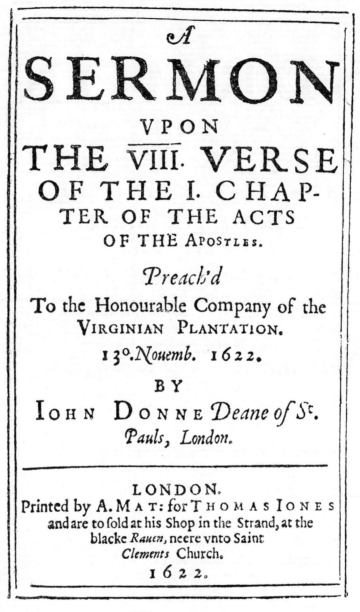

A

SERMON

VPON

THE VIII. VERSE

OF THE I. CHAP-

TER OF THE ACTS

OF THE Apostles.

Preach'd

To the Honourable Company of the
VIRGINIAN PLANTATION.
13º. *Nouemb.* 1622.

BY

IOHN DONNE *Deane of St.*
Pauls, London.

LONDON.
Printed by A. Mat: for THOMAS IONES
and are to fold at his Shop in the Strand, at the
blacke *Rauen*, neere vnto Saint
Clements Church.
1622.

Title-page of no. 15

sermons were printed by Augustin Matthewes (1619–53). Below the errata is the note: 'Other errors there are in miſ-printing, or in transpoſing letters, or in miſplacing Citations in the Margin, which will not (I think) hinder any willing Reader.'

Copies: BM, TCD, ULC; HCL, HEH, FSLW (Kay–Harmsworth copy), NYPL, LCW, PUL, YUL (O'Flahertie copy).

Magdalene College, Cambridge.

Christ Church, Oxford.

R. S. Pirie (in *Three Sermons*).

16 ENCÆNIA [*STC* 7039]   4° 1623

Title (*within double rules*): Encænia. The Feaſt Of Dedication. Celebrated At Lincolnes Inne, in a Sermon there vpon Aſcenſion day, 1623. . . . London, Printed by Aug. Mat. for Thomas Iones, and are to bee ſold at his Shop in the Strand, at the blacke Rauen, neere vnto Saint Clements Church. 1623. [*see facsimile*]

Collation: A⁴ (–A4) B–F⁴ G²; 26 leaves.

Contents: A1 title; A2*a–b* dedication *To the Maſters of the Bench, and the reſt of the Honourable Societie of Lincolnes Inne*; A3*a–b* *The Prayer before the Sermon*; [A4 cancelled]; B1*a*–G1*a* (pp. 1–41) text; G1*b*–G2*b* blank.

Note: On John 10: 22. Not reprinted in the folios, or by Alford. A4 has been cancelled in all the copies known to me, including those bound up in *Three Sermons*, etc. Notwithstanding the fact that the catchword on A3*b* corresponds with the first word on B1*a*, it is evident from the sewing that the signatures A2 and A3 have not been misprinted; presumably the cancelled leaf was a blank.

Copies: BM (2), BLO, ULC, ULD, DWL; HCL (2), HEH (2), FLSW (3, Harmsworth copy, *Foure Sermons, Fiue Sermons*), LCW, NLC, PUL, YUL (2, one in *Fiue Sermons*).

Cambridge Colleges: Pembroke, St. John's, Jesus, Trinity.

Oxford Colleges: Merton (2), Queen's (defective).

Lincoln's Inn Library (2).

G. L. Keynes (2, in *Foure Sermons* and *Fiue Sermons*).

R. S. Pirie (3, one separate lacks A2–4, one in *Three Sermons*, one in *Fiue Sermons*, lacks A3, 4, G1, 2).

17 THREE SERMONS [*STC* 7057] first issue   4° 1623

Title (*within double rules*): Three Sermons Vpon Speciall Occaſions. . . . London, Printed for Thomas Iones, and are to [be] ſold at his Shop in

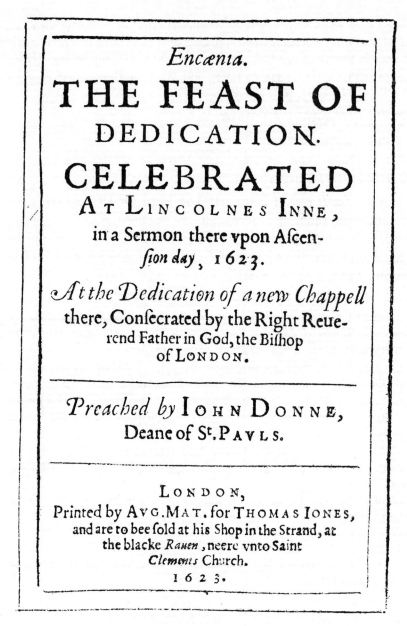

Encænia.

THE FEAST OF

DEDICATION.

CELEBRATED

AT LINCOLNES INNE,

in a Sermon there vpon Ascen-
sion day, 1 6 2 3.

At the Dedication of a new Chappell
there, Consecrated by the Right Reuerend Father in God, the Bishop
of LONDON.

Preached by IOHN DONNE,
Deane of St. PAVLS.

LONDON,
Printed by AVG. MAT. for THOMAS IONES,
and are to bee sold at his Shop in the Strand, at
the blacke *Rauen*, neere vnto Saint
Clements Church.
1 6 2 3.

Title-page of no. 16

THREE
SERMONS
VPON
SPECIALL
OCCASIONS.

Preached by IOHN DONNE
Deane of St. *Pauls* London.

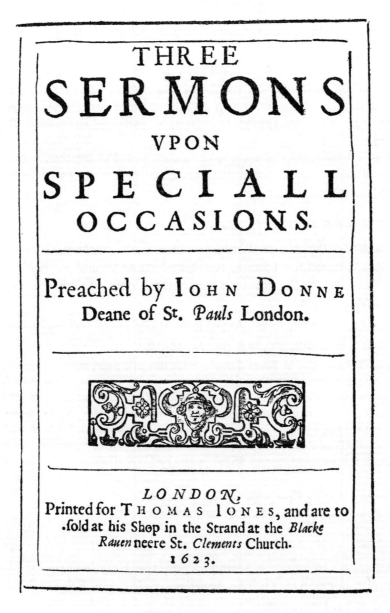

LONDON,
Printed for THOMAS IONES, and are to
.fold at his Shop in the Strand at the *Blacke*
Rauen neere St. *Clements* Church.
1 6 2 3.

Title-page of no. 17

the Strand at the Blacke Rauen neere St. Clements Church. 1623. [*see facsimile*]

Collation: A–I⁴ (±A1) K², A–G⁴, A–F⁴ G²; 38+28+26 = 92 leaves.

Contents: A1 general title; A2–K2 *A sermon vpon the xv verse of the xx chapter of the Booke of Iudges*, 1622 (as in no. 13); A1–G4 *A sermon vpon the viii. verse of the i. chapter of the Acts of the Apoſtles*, 1622 (as in no. 15); A1–G2 *Encænia*, 1623 (as in no. 16).

Note: This volume consists of nos. 13, 15, and 16, bound up together, with a general title-page as above substituted for the original A1 blank of no. 13.

Copy: Trinity College, Cambridge.

17a THREE SERMONS [*not in STC*] second issue   4° 1624

Title (*within double rules*): Three Sermons Vpon Speciall Occasions . . . London, Printed for Thomas Iones, and are to be ſold at his Shop in the Strand at the Blacke Rauen neere Saint Clements Church, 1624. [*see facsimile*]

Collation: π¹ A² B–I⁴ K², A–G⁴, A⁴ (–A4) B–F⁴ G²; 1+36+28+25 = 90 leaves.

Contents: π1 general title, etc., as in nos. 14, 15, 16.

Note: The Trinity copy of *Three Sermons* with this title-page, entirely reset and dated 1624 (first described in 1958), is imperfect, containing only the first sermon (no. 14). The other, complete, copy was acquired by R. S. Pirie from the Long Island Historical Society. The book is listed in *Catalogus Universalis, Pro Mundinis Francofurtensibus* (Frankfurt, 1624), under 'A Catalogue of such Bookes as have beene published, and (by authoritie) printed in English, since the last Vernall Mart, which was in Aprill 1624. till this present October 1624' (noted by G. R. Potter).

Copies:
Cambridge: Trinity College (imperfect, no. 14 only).
R. S. Pirie (nos. 14, 15, and 16, bound with nos. 24 and 27).

18 SERMON ON ACTS, i. 8 [*STC* 7052]   4° 1624

Title (*within double rules*): A Sermon Vpon The Eighth Verſe Of The Firſt Chapter Of The Acts Of The Apoſtles. . . . London, Printed for Thomas Iones. 1624. [*see facsimile*]

Collation: A–G⁴; 28 leaves.

Contents: A1 blank; A2 title; A3*a–b* introductory address *To the honourable companie of the Virginian Plantation*; A4*a*–G4*a* (pp. 1–49) text; G4*b* blank.

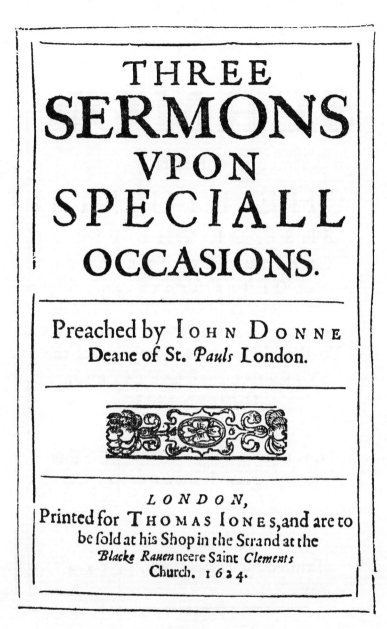

THREE
SERMONS
VPON
SPECIALL
OCCASIONS.

Preached by IOHN DONNE
Deane of St. *Pauls* London.

LONDON,
Printed for THOMAS IONES, and are to
be sold at his Shop in the Strand at the
Blacke Rauen neere Saint *Clements*
Church. 1624.

Title-page of no. 17*a*

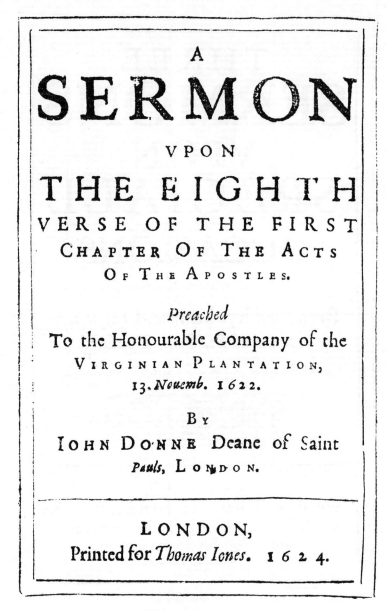

A SERMON

VPON

THE EIGHTH

VERSE OF THE FIRST
CHAPTER OF THE ACTS
OF THE APOSTLES.

Preached

To the Honourable Company of the
VIRGINIAN PLANTATION,
13. *Nouemb.* 1622.

BY

IOHN DONNE Deane of Saint
Pauls, LONDON.

LONDON,
Printed for *Thomas Iones.* 1624.

Title-page of no. 18

Note: A reprint of no. 15, in which the errata (noted on G4*a* of the first issue) have been corrected. The majority of the copies known to me occur in the *Foure Sermons* of 1625 and the *Fiue Sermons* of 1626. In most of these, by an error of the printer, the first page of the text and the second page of the introductory address have been transposed. In the FSLW and YUL copies of the *Fiue Sermons*, these pages are in their right positions. The Lincoln's Inn and YUL copies have THE EIGHT VERE on the title-page.

Copies: DWL; HCL, HEH (in *Fiue Sermons*) FSLW (3, Harmsworth copy, *Foure Sermons, Fiue Sermons*), LCW, YUL (in *Fiue Sermons*).
   Cambridge Colleges: Jesus, Pembroke.
   Exeter Cathedral Library; Lincoln's Inn Library (in *Fiue Sermons*).
   G. L. Keynes (2, in *Foure Sermons* and *Fiue Sermons*), R. S. Pirie (in *Fiue Sermons*).

19 FIRST SERMON PREACHED TO KING CHARLES

[*STC* 7040]   4° 1625

Title (*within double rules*): The Firſt Sermon Preached To King Charles, ... London, Printed by A. M. for Thomas Iones, and are to bee ſold at his Shop at the Signe of the Blacke Rauen in the Strand. 1625. [*see facsimile*]

Collation: A–H⁴; 32 leaves.

Contents: A1 blank; A2 title; A3*a*–H4*a* (pp. 1–59) text (errata, 1 or 2 lines, at bottom of H4*a*); H4*b* blank.

Note: On Ps. 11: 3. Not reprinted in the folios, or by Alford. The errata at the bottom of H4*a* consist sometimes of one line, sometimes of two. The second line runs: 'pa. 43, l. 20 for *Syllagismus* r. *Syllogismus*.' The addition was made while the book was in the press. The copy in Pembroke College Library has two lines transposed on p. 36.

Copies: BM, BLO, DWL (2 ll. errata), EUL[1], NLS; HCL (4), HEH, FSLW (4, Harmsworth copy, *Foure Sermons, Fiue Sermons*), LCW, NLC, YUL (3, one in *Fiue Sermons*).
   Cambridge Colleges: Emmanuel, Pembroke, St. John's, Trinity, Magdalene, Jesus.
   Cathedral Libraries: Exeter, St. Paul's.
   G. L. Keynes (2, in *Foure Sermons*, 1 l. errata, and *Fiue Sermons*, 2 ll. errata), R. S. Pirie (2, both 2 ll. errata, one in *Fiue Sermons*).

20 FOVRE SERMONS [*STC* 7042]

4° 1625

Title (*within double rules*): Foure Sermons Vpon Speciall Occaſions. . . . London, Printed for Thomas Iones, and are to be ſold at his Shop in the

[1] From the library of Drummond of Hawthornden.

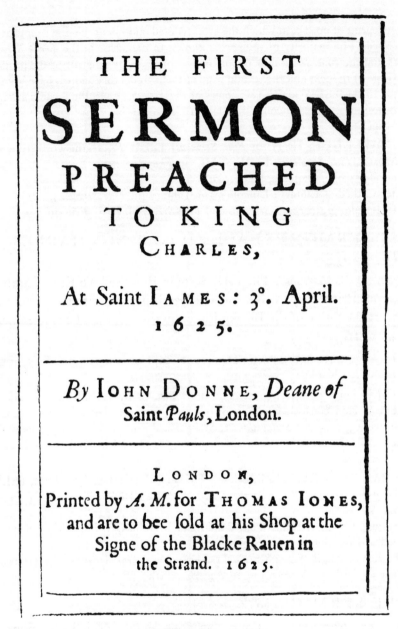

THE FIRST
SERMON
PREACHED
TO KING
CHARLES,

At Saint IAMES: 3°. April.
1 6 2 5.

By IOHN DONNE, *Deane of*
Saint *Pauls*, London.

LONDON,
Printed by *A. M.* for THOMAS IONES,
and are to bee fold at his Shop at the
Signe of the Blacke Rauen in
the Strand. 1 6 2 5.

Title-page of no. 19

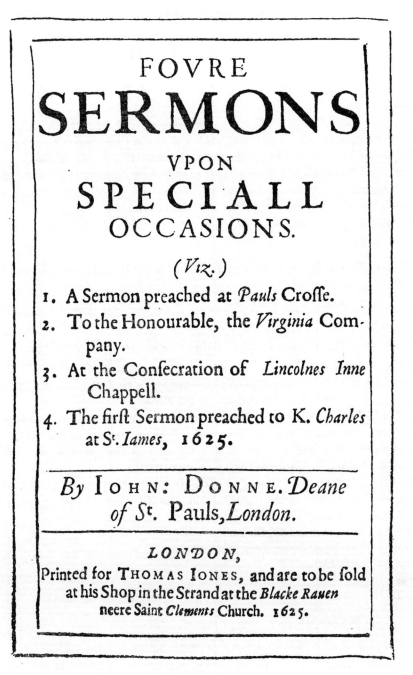

FOVRE
SERMONS
VPON
SPECIALL
OCCASIONS.

(*Viz.*)

1. A Sermon preached at *Pauls* Croſſe.
2. To the Honourable, the *Virginia* Company.
3. At the Conſecration of *Lincolnes Inne* Chappell.
4. The firſt Sermon preached to K. *Charles* at St. *Iames*, 1625.

By IOHN: DONNE. *Deane of* St. Pauls, *London.*

LONDON,
Printed for THOMAS IONES, and are to be ſold at his Shop in the Strand at the *Blacke Rauen* neere Saint *Clements* Church. 1625.

Title-page of no. 20

Strand at the Blacke Rauen neere Saint Clements Church. 1625. [*see facsimile*]

Collation: π¹ A² (−A1) B–I⁴ K², A–G⁴, A–F⁴ G², A–H⁴; 36+28+26+32 = 122 leaves.

Contents: π1 general title; A2–K2 *A sermon vpon the xx verse of the v. chapter of the Booke of Iudges*, 1622 (as in no. 14); A1–G4 *A sermon vpon the eighth verse of the first Chapter Of The Acts Of The Apostles*, 1624 (as in no. 18); A1–G2 *Encænia*, 1623 (as in no. 16); A1–H4 *The first sermon preached to King Charles*, 1625 (as in no. 19).

Note: This volume consists of nos. 14, 18, 16, and 19, bound up together, a general title-page having been substituted for the original title-page of no. 14.

Copies: FSLW (Gosse–Harmsworth copy), NYPL, University of Michigan. G. L. Keynes.

21 SERMON PREACHED AT WHITEHALL, 1625
  [*STC* 7050]   4° 1626

Title (*within double rules*): A Sermon, Preached To The Kings M^tie. At Whitehall, 24. Febr. 1625. . . . London, Printed for Thomas Iones, dwelling at the Blacke Rauen in the Strand. 1626. [*see facsimile*]

Collation: A–G⁴ H²; 30 leaves.

Contents: A1 blank; A2 title; A3a–A4b dedication *To his sacred Maiestie*; B1a–H1b (pp. 1–50) text (errata, 2 lines, on H1b); H2 blank.

Note: On Isaiah, l. 1. Not reprinted in the folios, or by Alford. Page 24 is misnumbered 26. There are variations in the marginal references. Perhaps printed by Augustin Matthewes; the initial letter on A3a is the same as that on X3a of Markham's *Booke of Honour*, A. Matthewes and J. Norton, 1625.

Copies: BLO, BM, DWL, NLS (2), ULC; HCL (2), HEH (2, one given by Donne to the first Earl of Bridgewater, one in *Fiue Sermons*), FSLW (3, one in *Fiue Sermons*), LCW, PUL, YUL (2, one in *Fiue Sermons*).
  Cathedral Libraries: Exeter, St. Paul's.
  Cambridge Colleges: Jesus, Pembroke.
  Christ Church, Oxford.
  Innerpeffray Library, Perthshire.
  G. L. Keynes (in *Fiue Sermons*), R. S. Pirie (2, one in *Fiue Sermons*).

22 FIVE SERMONS [*STC* 7041]   4° 1626

Title (*within double rules*): Fiue Sermons Vpon Speciall Occasions. . . . London, Printed for Thomas Iones, and are to bee sold at the Signe of the Blacke Rauen in the Strand. 1626. [*see facsimile*]

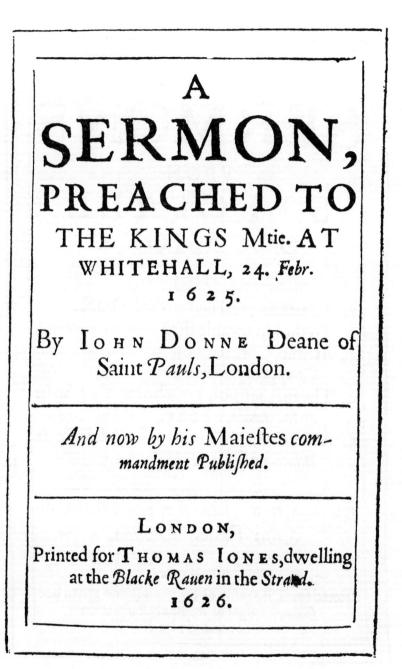

A SERMON,

PREACHED TO

THE KINGS Mtie. AT
WHITEHALL, 24. *Febr.*
1 6 2 5.

By Iohn Donne Deane of
Saint *Pauls*, London.

And now by his Maieſtes *com-
mandment Publiſhed.*

LONDON,
Printed for Thomas Iones, dwelling
at the *Blacke Rauen* in the *Strand.*
1 6 2 6.

Title-page of no. 21

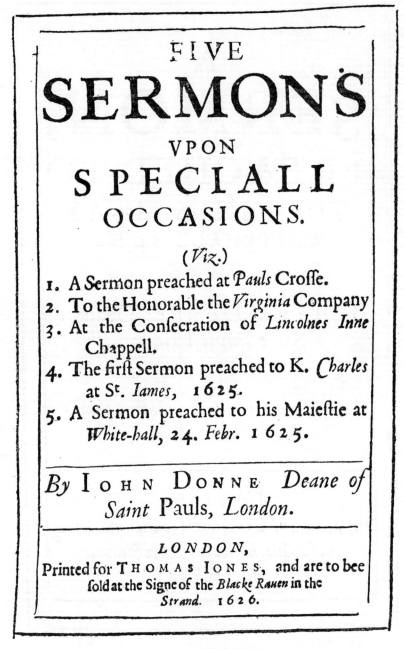

FIVE
SERMONS
VPON
SPECIALL
OCCASIONS.

(*Viz.*)

1. A Sermon preached at *Pauls* Croſſe.
2. To the Honorable the *Virginia* Company
3. At the Conſecration of *Lincolnes Inne* Chappell.
4. The firſt Sermon preached to K. *Charles* at Sᵗ. *Iames*, 1625.
5. A Sermon preached to his Maieſtie at *White-hall*, 24. *Febr.* 1625.

By IOHN DONNE *Deane of Saint* Pauls, *London.*

LONDON,
Printed for THOMAS IONES, and are to bee ſold at the Signe of the *Blacke Rauen* in the *Strand.* 1626.

Title-page of no. 22

Collation: π¹ B–I⁴ K², A–G⁴, A–F⁴ G², A–H⁴, A–G⁴ H²; 1 + 34 + 28 + 26 + 32 + 30 = 151 leaves.

Contents: π1 general title; B1–K2 *A fermon vpon the xx verfe of the v. chapter of the Booke of Iudges*, 1622 (as in no. 14 but lacking the first quire of two leaves); A1–G4 *A fermon vpon the eighth verfe of the firft Chapter Of The Acts Of The Apoftles*, 1624 (as in no. 18); A1–G2 *Encænia*, 1623 (as in no. 16); A1–H4 *The firft fermon preached to King Charles*, 1625 (as in no. 19); A1–H2 *A fermon, preached to the Kings Mtie. at Whitehall*, 1626 (as in no. 21).

Note: This volume usually consists of nos. 14, 18, 16, 19, and 21, bound up together. The first quire, 2 leaves, of no. 14 has been omitted and a general title-page has been substituted. My copy, however, consists of nos. 12, 18, 16, 19, and 21, and the general title-page has been inserted before the first (blank) leaf of no. 12.

Copies: BM (imperfect, no. 14 only with general title), TCD; HCL, HEH, FSLW (Gosse–Kay–Harmsworth copy), NYPL (Bliss copy), LCW, YUL.
Jesus College, Cambridge.
Merton College, Oxford; Lincoln's Inn Library.
G. L. Keynes, R. S. Pirie.

23 SERMON OF COMMEMORATION [*STC* 7049]   12° 1627

Title (within double rules): A Sermon Of Commemoration Of The Lady Dāuers, . . . London, Printed by I. H. for Philemon Stephens, and Chriftopher Meredith, and are to be fold at their fhop at the golden Lion in Pauls Church yard. 1627. [*see facsimile*]

Collation: A–H¹² I⁶; 102 leaves.

Contents: A1 title; A2a–A6b *The prayer before the Sermon*; A7a–H7b (pp. 1–170) text; H8 blank; H9a–I5a (pp. 1–17) *Memoriæ Matris Sacrum* [Latin and Greek verses by George Herbert]; I5b–I6b blank.

Note: On 2 Pet. 3: 13. Not reprinted in the folios, but it is printed by Alford, vi, 244, and by Pickering with the *Devotions*, 1840 (see no. 41). The printer, I. H., is probably to be identified with John Haviland (1621–38). Entered at Stationers' Hall, 7 July 1627. A few press corrections were detected by Potter and Simpson, *Sermons*, vol. vii, p. 375. See also pp. 3–9 for a description of the sermon.

Copies: BM (2, one in Ashley Library), BLO, ULC; HCL, FSLW (Powis¹–Harmsworth copy).
St. John's College, Cambridge.
Merton College, Oxford.

¹ Sold at Sotheby's, 20 March 1923, lot 85.

G. L. Keynes (Britwell Court copy);[1] R. S. Pirie, R. H. Taylor (Princeton, Izaak Walton's signature on the title-page).

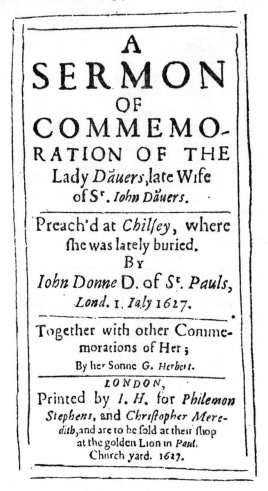

A

SERMON

OF

COMMEMO-

RATION OF THE

Lady *Dăuers*, late Wife

of S^r. *Iohn Dăuers.*

Preach'd at *Chilſey*, where

ſhe was lately buried.

B y

Iohn Donne D. of S^t. *Pauls,*

Lond. 1. *Ialy* 1627.

Together with other Comme-

morations of Her;

By her Sonne G. *Herbert.*

LONDON,

Printed by *I. H.* for *Philemon*

Stephens, and *Chriſtopher Mere-*

dith, and are to be ſold at their ſhop

at the golden Lion in *Paul.*

Chnrch yard. 1627.

Title-page of no. 23

24 DEATH'S DVELL first edition   4° 1632

Title (*within double rules*): Deaths Duell, . . . London, Printed by Thomas Harper, for Richard Redmer and Beniamin Fiſher, and are to be ſold at the ſigne of the Talbot in Alderſ-gate ſtreet. M.DC.XXXII. [*see facsimile*]

[1] Sold at Sotheby's, 30 March 1927, lot 607.

Corporis hæc Animæ fit Syndon Syndon Jesu.
Amen.

Martin D. scup. And are to be sould by R R and Ben: ffisher

DEATHS
DVELL,
OR,

A Confolation to the Soule, againft
the dying Life, and liuing
Death of the Body.

Deliuered in a Sermon at White Hall, before the
KINGS MAIESTY, *in the beginning
of Lent,* 1630.

By that late learned and Reuerend Diuine,
IOHN DONNE, Dr. in Diuinity,
& Deane of S. *Pauls*, London.

Being his laft Sermon, and called by his Maiefties houfhold
THE DOCTORS OWNE FVNERALL SERMON:

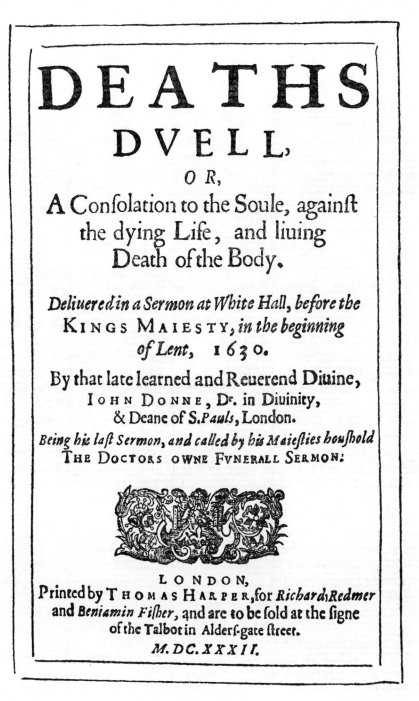

LONDON,
Printed by THOMAS HARPER, for *Richard Redmer*
and *Beniamin Fiſher*, and are to be ſold at the ſigne
of the Talbot in Alderſ-gate ſtreet.
M. DC. XXXII.

Title-page of no. 24

Collation: A–G⁴; 28 leaves.

Contents: A1*a* signature with ornament; A1*b* blank; A2*a* blank; A2*b* frontispiece; A3 title; A4*a–b* *To the Reader* signed *R.*; B1*a–*G2*a* (pp. 1–43) text; G2*b* blank; G3*a–*G4*a* (pp. 45–7) *An elegie, On Dr. Donne, Deane of Pauls* [by Henry King], and *An Epitaph on Dr. Donne* [by Edward Hyde]; G4*b* blank.

Frontispiece: On A2*b* (not an insertion). A head of Donne in a shroud, engraved by Martin Droeshout, after the drawing on a board made before Donne's death, which was also used for the effigy in St. Paul's.[1] The head is in an oval 13 × 10·5 cm, round the edge of which is inscribed:

EFFIGIES REUERENDISS: UIRI IOHANNES DONNE NUPER ECCLES: PAULINÆ DECANI.

Below is engraved:

Corporis hæc Animæ fit Syndon, Syndon Jesu
Amen.

Martin ₽ *fcup. And are to be fould by RR and Ben: ffifher.*

The plate-mark measures 16·5 × 11 cm.

Note: Death's Duell, a sermon on Ps. 68: 20, was preached on 25 February 1630/1,[2] five weeks all but a day before Donne's death on 31 March. It was reprinted as the last sermon in *XXVI Sermons*, 1660 (no. 31), and by Alford, VI, 278. It was also printed by Pickering with the *Devotions*, 1840 (see no. 41), in *Ten Sermons*, 1923, and in *Complete Poetry and Selected Prose*, ed. Hayward, 1929. The two elegies are unsigned, but were reprinted with a few changes in the text in the *Poems of 1633* (nos. 167 and 169); the first is by Henry King, the second by Edward Hyde. John Sparrow suggests that the Preface, signed *R*, may have been written by Izaak Walton. He points out that its third sentence contains the words 'there remained nothing for him to do, but to dye', which occurs in slightly different words in Walton's *Life of Donne*, 1658, p. 115. The manner of the whole Preface is also Walton's.

A copy in the Folger Shakespeare Memorial Library at Washington (formerly the Harmsworth copy) contains an extra leaf inserted between A3 and A4, with a dedicatory letter, *To his dearest sister Mrs. Elizabeth Francis of Brumstead in Norff.*, signed *Rich: Redmer.* I have seen no other copy with this leaf, which may have been specially printed for the publisher's sister.

It will be noticed that the frontispiece of Donne in his shroud is not an insertion, but was printed on the verso of the second leaf, though this has occasionally remained blank, as in my copy. Dame Helen Gardner[3] has pointed out that the hexameter,

---

[1] See Walton's account, Gosse, II, 281.

[2] This is stated by Walton to have been preached on the first Friday in Lent. Mrs. Simpson has pointed out to me that this fell on 25 February in 1630/1, and not, as stated by Gosse, on 12 February. [3] *The Divine Poems*, Oxford, 1952, pp. 112–13.

Corporis hæc animæ sit Syndon, Syndon Jesu, inscribed below the portrait, presents some difficulty both in sense and scansion. She interprets its meaning as being: 'May this shroud of the body be the shroud of the soul: the shroud of Jesus', and expresses the belief that it was composed by Donne himself, perhaps as 'a tortured rendering' of two lines in *The Second Anniversary* (ll. 113–14):

> Thinke that they shroud thee up, and think from thence
> They reinvest thee in white innocence.

John Sparrow suggests[1] as an alternative explanation that the words were transposed by Donne, or by a puzzled copyist, to improve the scansion, the correct order being, *Corporis hæc Syndon, Syndon animæ sit Jesu*, that is, 'This is my body's shroud, may my soul's shroud be that of Jesus.' Mr. Sparrow adds that Donne was certainly familiar with Alfonso Paleoti's treatise[2] on the *Sindon*, or winding sheet of Christ, preserved at Turin, and suggests that possibly a play upon words—*John Donne: sin done*—may also have been in Donne's mind.

Dame Helen further suggests that the title of *Death's Duell* with the frontispiece facing it was so arranged and worded by Donne's own wish, plans for the publication being his last activities before his death, so that he might yet speak from beyond the grave. On the other hand the book was not entered at Stationers' Hall until 30 September 1631, six months after his death, and not published until some time in 1632, which suggests that the plans were not made until afterwards. Moreover, a contemporary writer, Walter Colman, an observant friar educated at Douay, complained in doggerel at the end of his sole work, *La Dance Machabre or Death's Duel* [1633], that the title was stolen from him by one Roger Muchill, that is, Roger Mitchell, a bookseller at the Bull's Head, St. Paul's Churchyard, from 1627 to 1631, in which year he died. Colman's lines are headed: *The Author's Apologie for the title of his Booke iniuriously conferd by Roger Muchill, upon a Sermon of Doctor Donnes*, and he followed them with an abusive epitaph on 'Muchill', who died, it seems, before the publication of either book, the rights in Donne's sermon passing to Richard Redmer.[3]

It has been assumed that Bishop Henry King, as Donne's intimate friend and executor, was responsible for the first printing of *Death's Duel*. This assumption seemed to Potter and Simpson to give additional authority to the form of the first printing of *Death's Duel* in 1632. There are a large number of changes in detail when it was reprinted by the younger Donne in the folio of 1640. These editors have therefore preferred to give the text of 1632 in their collected *Sermons of John Donne*,

---

[1] *Times Lit. Sup.*, 13 March 1953.

[2] *Iesu Christi Crucifixi Stigmata Sacræ Sindoni impressa* (Venice, 1610), f°.

[3] See an article by me, quoting the lines and epitaph in full, in *Times Lit. Sup.*, 24 September 1938. My attention was drawn to Colman's book by Franklin B. Williams of Harvard University. There are copies of *La Dance Machabre* in BM, BLO; HEH, and Victoria and Albert Museum, Dyce Collection.

vol. x, 1962, pp. 230–48; the quarto had additional attractions as being nearer to Donne himself, who may even have left instructions as to its being printed. Potter and Simpson record all the changes made in 1640 in their notes.

Copies: BM (2), BLO, DWL (3, one lacking portrait), NLS (imperfect); HCL, HEH (lacking portrait), FSLW (3, Gosse, Britwell Court–Harmsworth copies, and Harmsworth copy noted above), YUL.

Cambridge Colleges: Jesus, St. John's, Trinity (2, no portraits).

Magdalen College, Oxford.

Cathedral Libraries: Exeter, Hereford (no portrait), Lincoln.

S. G. Dunn; G. L. Keynes (A2*b* blank); R. S. Pirie.

25 DEATH'S DUELL [incl. in *STC* 7032] first edition, second issue

4° 1633

Title (within double rules): Deaths Duell, . . . London Printed by B. Alſop, and T. Fawcet, for Beniamin Fiſher, and are to be ſold at the Signe of the Talbot in Alderſgate-ſtreet. M.DC.XXXIII. [*see facsimile*]

Collation: A⁴ (±A3) B–G⁴, 28 leaves.

Contents, frontispiece: The same sheets as in no. 24, with cancel title.

Note: The title-page of the second edition (see next entry) seems to have been inserted in the unsold copies of the first edition.

Copies: BM.

St. Paul's Cathedral Library.

26 DEATH'S DUELL [*STC* 7032] second edition   4° 1633

Title (within double rules): Deaths Duell . . . [etc. as in no. 25] M.DC.XXXIII. [*see facsimile*]

Collation: A–F⁴; 24 leaves.

Contents: A1 sign. & ornaments; A2 frontispiece; A3 title; A4*a–b To the Reader*; B1*a*–E4*b* (pp. 1–32) text; F1*a*–F3*a* (pp. 33–7) *An elegie, on Doctor Donne, Deane of Pauls* and *An epitaph on Doctor Donne* (colophon as on the title-page at bottom of F3*a*); F3*b*–F4*b* blank.

Frontispiece: As in no. 24.

Note: pp. 24, 30, 31, are numbered 22, 31, 30. The device on the title-page of this edition is a copy of one of those used by Gryphius (1529–50). It was first used by T. Creede in 1602, and probably passed to Bernard Alsop (1602–52) in 1617 (see no. 339 in McKerrow's *Printers' and Publishers' Devices*, London, 1913).

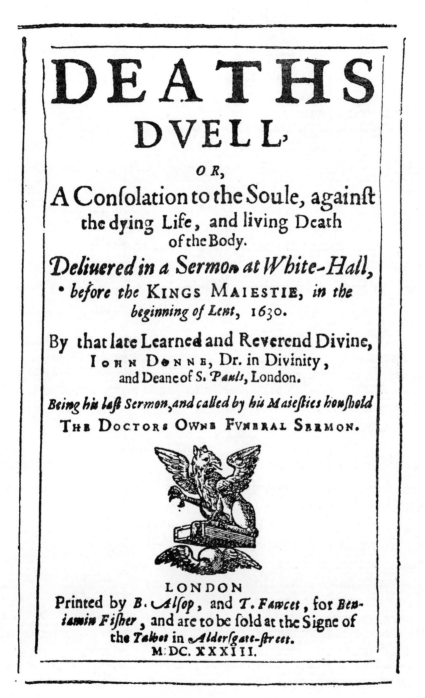

DEATHS

DVELL,

OR,

A Confolation to the Soule, againft
the dying Life, and living Death
of the Body.

Deliuered in a Sermon at White-Hall,
before the KINGS MAIESTIE, *in the*
beginning of Lent, 1630.

By that late Learned and Reverend Divine,
IOHN DONNE, Dr. in Divinity,
and Deane of S. Pauls, London.

Being his laft Sermon, and called by his Maiefties houfhold
THE DOCTORS OWNE FVNERAL SERMON.

LONDON
Printed by *B. Alfop,* and *T. Fawcet,* for *Ben-*
iamin Fifher, and are to be fold at the Signe of
the *Talbot* in *Alderfgate-ftreet.*
M:DC.XXXIII.

Title-page of nos. 25 and 26

Copies: BM (Ashley Library); HCL (O'Flahertie copy), HEH, FSLW, NLC, TSP, YUL.

Pembroke College, Cambridge (Izaak Walton's copy, part of whose signature is on the title-page).

Exeter Cathedral Library.

G. L. Keynes, R. S. Pirie (2, one lacking portrait).

26a DEATH'S DVELL [*STC* 7032*a*] second edition, variant title

4° 1633

Title (within double rules): Deaths Duell, . . . London, Printed by B. Alſop, and T. Fawcet, for Benjamin Fiſher, and are to be ſold at the Signe of the Talbot in Alderſgat-ſtreete. MDC.XXXIII. [*see facsimile*]

Collation: A–F⁴; 24 leaves.

Contents: A1 blank; A2 frontispiece; A3 title; A4*a–b To the Reader;* B1*a*–F4*b* as in no. 26.

Frontispiece: As in no. 24.

Note: The first sheet is a different setting from that of no. 26. The address *To the Reader* has a different head-piece and contains several errors. Potter and Simpson (1, 23 n.) suggest that this is really an earlier state than the corrected sheet found in all other known copies. This seems likely since on the second page lines 5–6 read: 'as being spoken most freely, and with least affection', instead of: '. . . feelingly, . . . affectation'.

Copy: G. L. Keynes.

27 SIX SERMONS (*STC* 7056]   4° 1634

Title (within ornamental border): Six Sermons Upon Severall Occaſions, . . . ¶ Printed by the Printers to the Univerſitie of Cambridge: [rule] And are to be ſold by Nicholas Fuſſell and Humphrey Moſley, at their ſhop in Pauls Church-yard. 1634. [*see facsimile*]

Collation: A–Z⁴; 92 leaves.

Contents: A1*a* ornament; A1*b* blank; A2 general title;
A3 subtitle to *Two ſermons preached before King Charles, Upon the xxvi verſe of the firſt Chapter of Geneſis;* A4*a*–F2*a* (pp. 1–37) text of first sermon; F2*b* blank;
F3 subtitle to *The ſecond ſermon preached before King Charles* . . .; F4*a*–L3*b* (pp. 1–40) text;
L4 subtitle to *A ſermon Upon the xix verſe of the ii Chapter of Hoſea;* M1*a*–O4*b* (pp. 1–24) text;

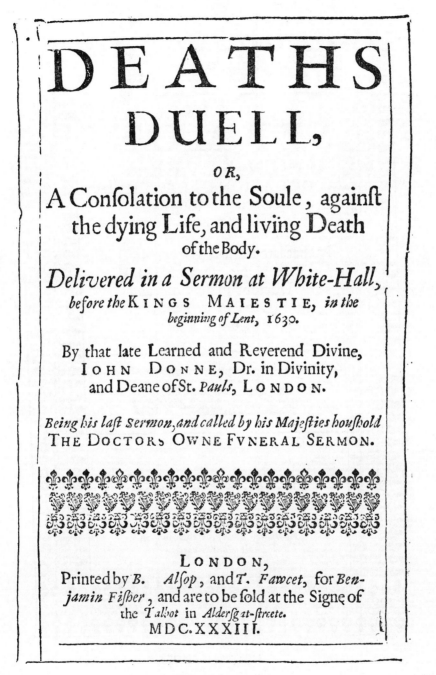

DEATHS
DUELL,

OR,

A Consolation to the Soule, against
the dying Life, and living Death
of the Body.

Delivered in a Sermon at White-Hall,
before the KINGS MAIESTIE, *in the*
beginning of Lent, 1630.

By that late Learned and Reverend Divine,
IOHN DONNE, Dr. in Divinity,
and Deane of St. *Pauls,* LONDON.

Being his last Sermon, and called by his Majesties houshold
THE DOCTORS OWNE FVNERAL SERMON.

LONDON,
Printed by B. *Alsop,* and T. *Fawcet,* for *Ben-*
jamin Fisher, and are to be sold at the Signe of
the *Talbot* in *Aldersgat-streete.*
MDC.XXXIII.

Title-page of no. 26*a*

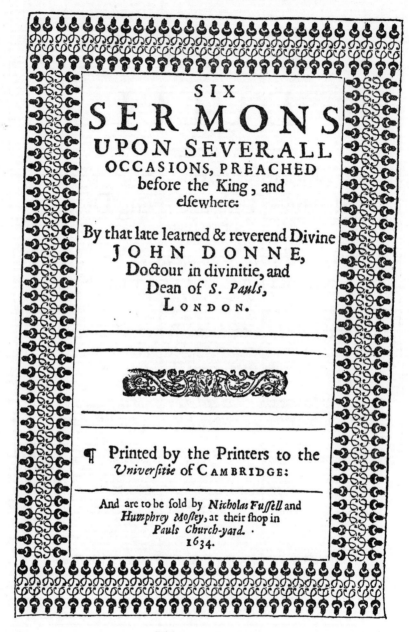

SIX
SERMONS
UPON SEVERALL
OCCASIONS, PREACHED
before the King, and
elsewhere:

By that late learned & reverend Divine
JOHN DONNE,
Doctour in divinitie, and
Dean of *S. Pauls*,
LONDON.

¶ Printed by the Printers to the
Universitie of CAMBRIDGE:

And are to be sold by *Nicholas Fussell* and
Humphrey Mosley, at their shop in
Pauls Church-yard.
1634.

Title-page of no. 27

P1 subtitle to *A ſermon Upon the xliiii verſe of the xxi Chapter of Matthew*; P2*a*–S2*b* (pp. 1–26) text;

S3 subtitle to *A ſermon Upon the xxii verſe of the v Chapter of John*; S4*a*–X3*a* (pp. 1–23) text; X3*b* blank;

X4 subtitle to *A ſermon Upon the xv verſe of the viii Chapter of John*; Y1*a*–Z4*b* (pp. 1–16) text.

Note: The University Printers were Thomas Buck and Roger Daniel. These sermons were all reprinted in the *Fifty Sermons*, 1649 (no. 30), where they are numbered 28, 29, 3, 35, 12, and 13 respectively. They are also printed by Alford, IV, 490, 512, 30; V, 28; VI, 191, 206. The fourth is stated in the *Fifty Sermons* to have been preached on 21 February 1611; but this is obviously a mistake, since Donne had at that date not yet taken orders. These sermons sometimes occur separately or two together, and they may have been so issued, though it seems unlikely, since the signatures run in one alphabet. For a list of copies of one or two of the sermons see Potter and Simpson, I, 25.

Copies: BM, BLO, GUL, LUL, ULC (2); HCL (2), HEH (last three sermons only), FSLW (2, one Harmsworth copy), TSP, YUL.

Cambridge Colleges: Jesus, Magdalene, Pembroke (Izaak Walton's copy, with signature on A1*b*), Trinity (2).

Oxford Colleges: Brasenose, Christ Church, Merton.

Cathedral Libraries: Lincoln, St. Paul's.

G. L. Keynes (2); J. Sparrow; R. S. Pirie (2).

28 SERMON ON ECCLES. xii. 1. [*STC* 17918] 8° 1638

Title (within double rules): Sapientia Clamitans, . . . London, Printed by I. Haviland, for R. Milbourne at the Unicorne neere Fleet-bridge. 1638. [*see facsimile*]

Collation: A² B–X⁸; 162 leaves.

Contents: A1 blank (?); A2 title; B1*a*–G8*a* (pp. 1–95) sermon I; G8*b* blank; H1 subtitle to sermon II; H2*a*–R5*b* (pp. 99–250) sermon II; R6 subtitle to sermon III; R7*a*–X8*a* (pp. 253–319) sermon III; X8*b* blank.

Sermon: The third sermon (pp. 251–319) is by Donne.

Subtitle (within double rules): *Mans timely remembring of his Creator; or An expoſition delivered in a Sermon upon Eccleſiaſtes* 12: 1.

Remember now thy Creator in the days of thy youth

[ornament between rules] *London, Printed by John Haviland, for Robert Milbourne* 1638.

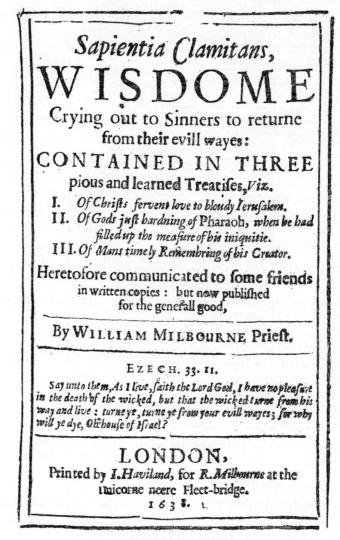

Sapientia Clamitans,

WISDOME

Crying out to Sinners to returne
from their evill wayes:

CONTAINED IN THREE

pious and learned Treatises, *Viz.*

I.   *Of Chrifts fervent love to bloudy Ierufalem.*
II. *Of Gods juft hardning of* Pharaoh, *when be had
        filled up the meafure of his iniquitie.*
III. *Of Mans timely Remembring of his Creator.*

Heretofore communicated to fome friends
in written copies : but now publifhed
for the generall good,

By WILLIAM MILBOURNE Prieft.

EZECH. 33. 11.

*Say unto them, As I live, faith the Lord God, I have no pleafure
in the death of the wicked, but that the wicked turne from his
way and live : turne ye, turne ye from your evill wayes ; for why
will ye dye, O houfe of Ifrael?*

LONDON,

Printed by *I. Haviland,* for *R. Milbourne* at the
lnicorne neere Fleet-bridge.
1 6 3 8. L

Title-page of no. 28

Note: These sermons do not seem to have been identified before 1914. The first two are
by Dr. Jackson;[1] the third, by Donne, was reprinted as sermon 19 in *XXVI Sermons,*
1660 (no. 31), where it has the title: *A Sermon of Valediction at my going into Germany, at Lincolnes-Inne, April* 18. 1619. The text of 1660 differs very considerably

[1] Thomas Jackson, Dean of Peterborough. See his *Works,* ed. Todd, 1844, XI, 361, and IX, 448.

from that of 1638;[1] probably the sermon was rewritten by Donne for publication after the first written copy had been 'communicated to some friends'. There is a manuscript copy of this sermon in the Bodleian Library (Ashmol. 781, ff. 1–11). It is also in all the manuscript collections except the St. Paul's MS.

William Milbourne, Priest, whose name appears on the title-page, was curate of Brancepeth, near Durham. He wrote a letter to his rector, John Cosin, expressing annoyance with his brother Robert, the publisher, 'because it is so printed upon the title page as that men being unacquainted with the matter take mee as the authour, and not as the publisher onlie'.[2] He is here using the term 'publisher' in the sense of 'editor'. His name was removed from a later issue of the book (see no. 28*a*).

Copies: BLO, ULC; HEH.
John Sparrow; Dulwich College.

28*a* SERMON ON ECCLES. xii. 1. [*STC* 17920] second issue

8° 1639

Title (within double rules): Wiſdome crying out to Sinners . . . London, Printed by M.P. for Iohn Stafford, dwelling in Black-horse Alley neere Fleetſtreet. 1639. [*see facsimile*]

Collation, Contents: A² (±A1) B–X⁸.

Note: A reissue by a different publisher of no. 28 (*Sapientia Clamitans*) with cancel title-page, from which the name of William Milbourne is omitted. In some copies the date on the title-page has been altered to 1640. The printer was probably Marmaduke Parsons (1607–40).

Copies: ULC (1639), DWL (1639); FSLW (no t.p.).
Emmanuel College, Cambridge (1640), Lambeth Palace Library (1640).

29 LXXX SERMONS [*STC* 7038] F° 1640

Title (within double rules): LXXX Sermons . . . London, Printed for Richard Royston, in Ivie-lane, and Richard Marriot in S. Dunſtans Church-yard in Fleetſtreet. M DC XL. [*see facsimile*]

Collation: A–B⁶ C⁴, B–Z Aa–Zz Aaa–Zzz Aaaa⁶, Bbbb⁴ Cccc⁸; 442 leaves.

Contents: A1 blank; A2 title; A3*a*–A4*a* The Epiſtle Dedicatorie To his moſt ſacred Maieſtie Charles . . . signed by *Jo: Donne* [jun.]; A4*b* blank; A5*a*–C1*a* The life and death of Dr. Donne by *Iz: Wa:* [*Izaak Walton*]; C1*b* Donne's epitaph; C2*a*–C4*a* table of the texts of the sermons; C4*b* Imprimatur, *Tho: Broun. Novemb.* 29. 1639;

[1] See Simpson, *Prose Works*, pp. 279–86.
[2] In *The Correspondence of John Cosin D.D.*, Surtees Soc. LII, 221–3; quoted by R. C. Bald in *Rev. Eng. Stud.* XXIV, 1948, 321–3, and by Potter and Simpson, I, 26.

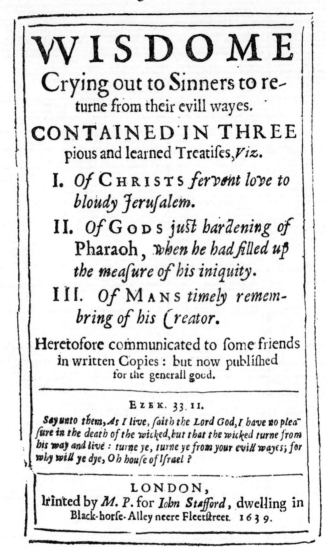

WISDOME

Crying out to Sinners to returne from their evill wayes.

CONTAINED IN THREE

pious and learned Treatifes, *Viz.*

I. *Of* CHRISTS *fervent love to bloudy Jerufalem.*

II. *Of* GODS *juft hardening of* Pharaoh, *when he had filled up the meafure of his iniquity.*

III. *Of* MANS *timely remem-bring of his Creator.*

Heretofore communicated to fome friends
in written Copies : but now publifhed
for the generall good.

EZEK. 33. 11.

Say unto them, As I live, faith the Lord God, I have no plea-
fure in the death of the wicked, but that the wicked turne from
his way and live : turne ye, turne ye from your evill wayes; for
why will ye dye, Oh houfe of Ifrael ?

LONDON,
Printed by *M. P.* for *Iohn Stafford,* dwelling in
Black-horfe-Alley neere Fleetftreet. 1639.

Title-page of no. 28*a*

B1 subtitle to *Sermons Preached upon Chriftmas-day*; B2*a*–Aaaa6 (pp. 1–826) sermons and subtitles; Bbbb1*a*–Bbbb2*b* table of scripture references; Bbbb3*a*–Bbbb4*b*
table of authors; Cccc1*a*–Cccc7*b* table of principal contents (errata, 14 lines, at bottom
of Cccc7*b*); Cccc8 blank.

Bee Wise as serpents
but innosent as Dous.

LXXX.
SERMONS
PREACHED BY THAT LEAR.
NED AND REVEREND DIVINE
IOHN DONNE. Dᴿ IN DIVINITIE
LATE DEANE OF Yᵉ CATHEDRALL
CHVRCH OF Sᵗ PAVLES
LONDON.

M. Merian Iun.

LXXX
SERMONS

PREACHED
BY THAT LEARNED AND
REVEREND DIVINE,

IOHN DONNE,

Dr IN DIVINITY,

Late Deane of the Cathedrall

Church of S. P A U L S *London.*

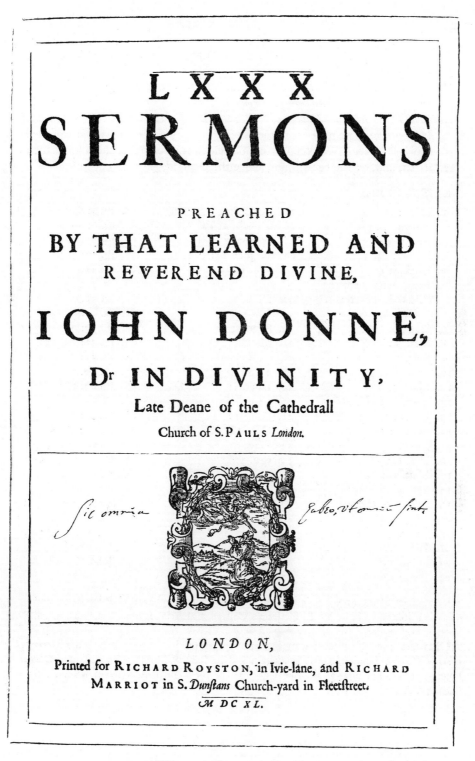

LONDON,

Printed for R I C H A R D R O Y S T O N, in Ivie-lane, and R I C H A R D
M A R R I O T in S. *Dunstans* Church-yard in Fleetstreet.
ᴍ ᴅᴄ xʟ.

Title-page of no. 29 (reduced)

Frontispiece: Inserted between A1 and A2. A bust of Donne in an oval, 9 × 6·5 cm, surrounded by an elaborate monumental design; in the upper part is inscribed: *Bee Wife as ſerpents | but inoſent as Dous*, and in the lower part: *LXXX | Sermons | Preached by that Lear-|ned and Reverend Divine | Iohn Donne. Dr in Divinitie | Late Deane of Yᵉ Cathedrall | Church of St Paules | London.* The engraving is signed below *M Merian Iun:*. The plate-mark measures 31 × 19·5 cm. In most copies of the book is found a later state of the engraving, on which is inscribed at the sides of the oval: *Ætat:* 42, and, on the background above the head, *A*, partially erased.[1]

Texts of the sermons:

1. Col. 1: 19, 20
2. Esaiah. 7: 14
3. Gal. 4: 4, 5
4. Luke 2: 29, 30
5. Exod. 4: 13
6. Lord, who hath be- leeved our report? [Esaiah. 53: 1]
7. John 10: 10
8. Matt. 5: 16
9. Rom. 13: 7
10. Rom. 12: 20
11. Matt. 9: 2
12. Matt. 5: 2
13. Job 16: 17–19
14. Amos 5: 18
15. 1 Cor. 15: 26
16. John 11: 35
17. Matt. 19: 17
18. Acts 2: 36
19. Apoc. [Rev.] 20: 6
20. John 5: 28, 29
21. 1 Cor. 15: 29
22. Heb. 11: 35
23. 1 Cor. 13: 12
24. Job 4: 18

25. Matt. 28: 6
26. 1 Thess. 4: 17
27. Ps. 89: 47 [48]
28, 29. John 14: 26
30. John 14: 20
31. Gen. 1: 2
32. 1 Cor. 12: 3
33. Acts 10: 44
34. Rom. 8: 16
35. Matt. 12: 31
36, 37. John 16: 8–11
38. 2 Cor. 1: 3
39. 1 Pet. 1: 17
40. 1 Cor. 16: 22
41. Ps. 2: 12
42. Gen. 18: 25
43. Matt. 3: 17
44. Rev. 4: 8
45. Apoc. 7: 2, 3
46. Acts 9: 4
47. Acts 20: 25
48. Acts 28: 6
49. Acts 23: 6, 7
50. Ps. 6: 1
51. Ps. 6: 2, 3
52, 53. Ps. 6: 4, 5

54. Ps. 6: 6, 7
55. Ps. 6: 8–10
56. Ps. 32: 1, 2
57. Ps. 32: 3, 4
58. Ps. 32: 5
59. Ps. 32: 6
60. Ps. 32: 7
61. Ps. 32: 8
62. Ps. 32: 9
63. Ps. 32: 10, 11
64. Ps. 51: 7
65. Ps. 62: 9
66. Ps. 63: 7
67. Ps. 64: 10
68. Ps. 65: 5
69. Ps. 66: 3
70. Prov. 25: 16
71, 72. Matt. 4: 18–20
73. John 14: 2
74. Ps. 144: 15
75. Esay. [Esaiah] 32: 8
76. Mark 16: 16
77, 78. 1 Cor. 15: 29
79. Ps. 90: 14
80. John 11: 21[2]

[1] Examples of the earlier state of the plate to be found in the BM Print Room and in the following libraries: HCL, YUL, St. John's College, Cambridge, Jesus College, Oxford, G. L. Keynes, G. Goyder.

[2] Passages from this sermon were inaccurately printed in Clement Barksdale's *Memorials of Worthy Persons*, London, 1661, pp. 5–22, and in John Wilford's *Memorials and Characters*, London, 1741, pp. 292–3, as 'The Character of Sir William Cockayne, Kt. . . . by John Donne . . .'.

Note: The sermons were all reprinted by Alford, I–VI. For an account of Walton's *Life of Donne* as here printed see pp. 240–1. The device used on the title-page both of this volume and of the *Fifty Sermons*, representing Daniel praying, was first used by G. Simson in 1597. It probably passed to Miles Fletcher (1611–64) in 1624, and was also used by his son James (1649–67). It is recorded as no. 308 in McKerrow's *Printers' and Publishers' Devices*, London, 1913. The portrait on the frontispiece appears to have been copied from Isaac Oliver's miniature (see *Iconography*, p. 372). The book was entered on the Stationers' Register on 3 January and, together with *Fifty Sermons* (no. 30), on 19 February 1639/40 to Miles Fletcher and John Marriott. On the second date a third share was assigned to Richard Royston.

Signature Ii2 is misprinted I2; pp. 73, 622, 642, 653 are misnumbered 75, 623, 632, 643; pp. 201, 580, 581 are misnumbered 120, 578, 579 in some copies (Potter and Simpson, 1, 5). The printing of this volume was the source of litigation between the younger Donne and the printer, Francis Bowman (see 'Bowman v. Donne', by J. Milton French, *Times Lit. Sup.*, 12 December 1936).

Copies: AUL, BM, BLO (2, one with annotations by S. T. Coleridge), EUL, LUL, NLS, ULC (2), ULD (2); HCL (5, one from Wordsworth's library with annotations by S. T. Coleridge), HEH (2, one a presentation copy from Walton with inscription on title-page)[1], NLC, NYPL (imperfect), LCW, PUL, YUL (2).

Cambridge Colleges: Christ's, Emmanuel, King's, Pembroke, Peterhouse, St. John's, Trinity.

Oxford Colleges: All Souls, Christ Church, Merton, New College, Jesus, Queen's, Wadham, Worcester.

Cathedral Libraries: Carlisle, Lincoln, Peterborough, Salisbury (with Walton's signature on title-page), Worcester, Exeter, Gloucester, Hereford, Durham, St. David's, Winchester.

Lambeth Palace Library; Chapter Library, Windsor; Innerpeffray Library, Perthshire.

G. L. Keynes (2), R. S. Pirie.

30 FIFTY SERMONS [Wing D 1862] F° 1649

Title (within double rules): Fifty Sermons, . . . London, Printed by Ja. Flesher for M. F. J. Marriot, and R. Royston. M DC XLIX. [*see facsimile*]

Collation: A⁴ B–Z⁶ Aa–Qq⁶ Rr⁴; 236 leaves.

Contents: A1 title; A2a–b dedication *To the right honourable Basil, Earle of Denby* signed by *Jo. Donne [jun.]*; A3a *For the right honourable Bolstred Whitlock, Richard Keeble,*

[1] *For my very deare sister mrˢ Debora Floud From her moste affectionate brother Izaak Walton.*

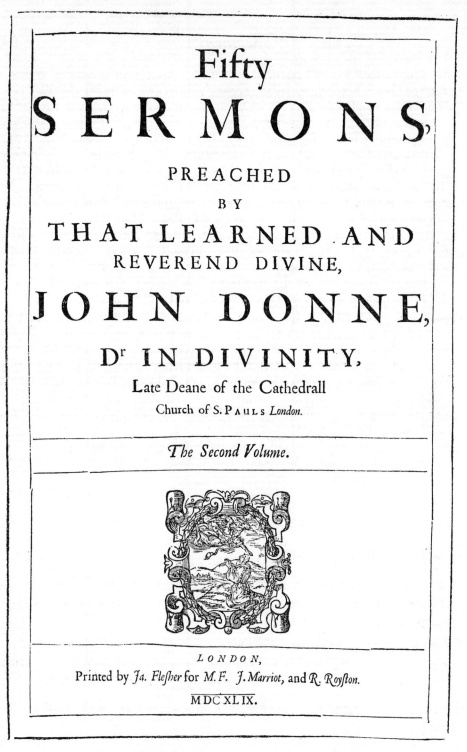

Fifty
SERMONS,

PREACHED

BY

THAT LEARNED AND
REVEREND DIVINE,

JOHN DONNE,

D^r IN DIVINITY,

Late Deane of the Cathedrall
Church of S. PAULS *London.*

The Second Volume.

LONDON,
Printed by *Ja. Flesher* for *M.F. J. Marriot,* and *R. Royston.*
MDC XLIX.

Title-page of no. 30 (reduced)

John Leile signed by *Jo. Donne* [*jun.*]; A3*b*–A4*b* table of the texts of the sermons; B1*a*–Rr4*b* (pp. 1–289, 300–474) sermons.

Texts of the sermons:

1. Matt. 22: 30	16. Col. 1: 24	35. Matt. 21: 44
2. Gen. 2: 18	17, 18. Matt. 18: 7	36–8. John 1: 8
3. Hos. 2: 19	19. Ps. 38: 2	39. Phil. 3: 2
4. Rev. 7: 17	20. Ps. 38: 3	40. 2 Cor. 5: 20
5. Eph. 5: 25–7	21–3. Ps. 38: 4	41. Hos. 3: 4
6. 1 John 5: 7, 8	24, 25. Ezek. 34: 19	42. Prov. 14: 31
7. Gal. 3: 27	26. Esai. 65: 20	43. Lam. 4: 20
8. Cant. 5: 3	27. Mark 4: 24	44. Matt. 11: 6
9, 10. Mic. 2: 10	28, 29. Gen. 1: 26	45. Deut. 25: 5
11. Gen. 28: 16, 17	30. Job 13: 15	46. Ps. 34: 11
12. John 5: 22	31. Job 36: 25	47. Gen. 3: 24
13. John 8: 15	32. Apoc. 7: 9	48. Lam. 3: 1
14. Job 19: 26	33. Cant. 3: 11	49. Gen. 7: 24
15. 1 Cor. 15: 50	34. Luke 23 [not 33]: 24	50. 1 Thess. 5: 16

Note: Sign. T3 is misprinted S3; pp. 28, 89, 150, 151, 165, and 212 are numbered 24, 98, 158, 159, 166, and 312; pp. 290–9 are omitted in the pagination. There are other misnumberings which are variable (see Potter and Simpson, 1, 7). The text is said (ibid.) to have been less carefully printed than the *LXXX Sermons*, though corrections were made while the book was in the press, especially in sheets Nn, Oo. One copy in the ULC has A3*b* blank and lacks A4; this may indicate an earlier issue of the volume. The sermons were all reprinted by Alford, I–VI. Mrs. Simpson noted that this volume was entered on the Stationers' Register on 19 February 1639/40, the same day as the second entry was made for the *LXXX Sermons*, though not published until nine years later. The *Fifty Sermons* is a considerably scarcer book than the *LXXX Sermons*.

Copies: BM, BLO, NLS, ULC (2); HCL, HEH, NYPL, LCW, PUL, YUL (2).
Cambridge Colleges: Christ's, Emmanuel, King's.
Oxford Colleges: Christ Church, Merton, New College, Wadham, Worcester.
Cathedral Libraries: Peterborough, St. Paul's, Carlisle, Worcester, Exeter, Winchester, Durham; Lambeth Palace Library.
G. L. Keynes; J. Sparrow; R. S. Pirie.

31 XXVI SERMONS [Wing D 1872] F° 1660

Title (within double rules): XXVI. Sermons . . . London: Printed by T. N. for James Magnes in Ruffel-ftreet near the Piazza in Covent-Garden. 1660/1. [*see facsimile*]

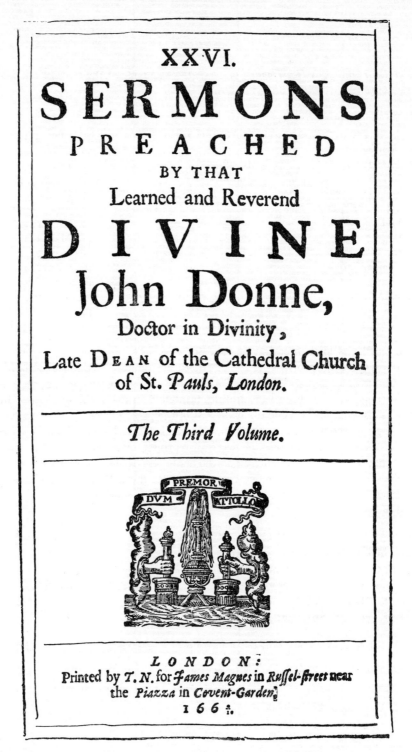

XXVI.
SERMONS
PREACHED
BY THAT
Learned and Reverend
DIVINE
John Donne,
Doctor in Divinity,
Late D E A N of the Cathedral Church
of St. *Pauls*, London.

The Third Volume.

LONDON:
Printed by *T. N.* for *James Magnes* in *Ruffel-ftreet* near
the *Piazza* in *Covent-Garden,*
1 6 6 ⅔.

Title-page of no. 31 (reduced)

Collation: A² B² π², B–Q⁴ S–Z⁴ Aa–Mm⁴ NnOo⁶ Pp–Zz⁴ Aaa–Ccc⁴ Ddd⁶ Fff⁴ Ggg⁴; 212 leaves.

Contents: A1 title; A2*a–b* dedication to King Charles II signed by *John Donne [jun.]*; B1*a*–B2*a To the reader* and *Postscript*; B2*b* letter from the Bishop of Peterborough to John Donne jun. on receiving the first volume of the sermons, dated 20 July 1640; π1*a*–π2*b* table of the texts of the sermons; B1*a*–Ggg4*a* (pp. 1–411) sermons; Ggg4*b* blank.

Texts of the sermons:

1. Luke 23: 40	10. Eccles. 5: 12, 13 [13, 15]	19. Eccles. 12: 1
2. Ezek. 33: 32	(two parts)	20. Rom. 13: 11
3. Jas. 2: 12	11. Esai. 52: 3	21. Exod. 12: 30
4. 1 Tim. 3: 16	12. Gen. 32: 10	22. Esther 4: 16
5. Matt. 6: 21	13, 14. 1 Tim. 1: 15[1]	23. Deut. 12: 30
6. Eccles. 8: 11	15. Acts 7: 60	24. Prov. 22: 11
7. Ps. 55: 19	16. Matt. 6: 21	25. 2 Cor. 4: 6
8. Matt. 9: 13	17. Jas. 2: 12	26. Ps. 68: 20
[9. omitted]	18. Prov. 8: 17	

Note: This volume was very carelessly edited and printed. It actually contains only twenty-three, instead of twenty-six, sermons; sermon 9 is left out altogether, but two of the sermons are printed twice over, nos. 16 and 17 being merely repetitions of nos. 5 and 3.[2] The collation, printed above, will be seen to be very erratic; three of the quires, Nn, Oo, and Ddd, contain six, instead of four, leaves, and two signatures, R (? with sermon 9) and Eee are omitted altogether. The pagination is very faulty, although the right number of pages, 411, is finally arrived at. The numbering runs as follows: B1–Q4 are numbered 1–120; S1–Aa4*a*, 129–183 (Aa4*b* is blank and has no pagination); Bb1–Kk4, 177–232; Ii1–Oo4, 241–296; Pp1–Ddd6, 285–392; Fff1–Ggg3*a*, 397–411. There are in addition several minor misprints in the pagination. There are also variable irregularities in some of the signatures. Potter and Simpson (I, 6) note that a large number of corrections were made while the book was passing through the press. They also note a change in type and style after sheet Aa, and infer, no doubt correctly, that the two parts of the book were printed simultaneously at two different presses. Sermon no. 26 was first published as *Death's Duell*, 1632 (no. 24). The sermons were all reprinted by Alford, I–VI.

The editor has added a Postscript to the preface on B2*a* as follows: 'By the Dates of these *Sermons*, the Reader may easily collect, that although they are the last that are

---

[1] Sermon no. 14 is dated differently in different copies of the book. See Potter and Simpson, I, 142 n., II, 466 n., III, 391.

[2] In the first two editions of this Bibliography I stated that under sermon 10 are included two sermons on the same text. Potter and Simpson, however, regard these as being two parts of a single sermon.

published, they were the first that were Preached; and I did purposely select these from amongst all the rest, for, being to finish this Monument, which I was to erect to his Memory, I ought to reserve those materials that were set forth with the best Polish: The Impression consists onely of Five hundred, which will somewhat advance the Price; but the buyer being at liberty, he can receive no prejudice.' This note was not altogether truthful, for the sermons, said to be 'the first that were preached', include *Death's Duell* and several others of Donne's last years. The statement that only 500 copies were printed explains the fact that the *XXVI Sermons* is considerably rarer than the two volumes of 1640 and 1649; it is also a smaller volume than these two, usually measuring about 29 × 19 cm as compared with 34 × 23 cm. Some copies, however, were printed on large paper, uniform in size with the other volumes; six such copies are noted below, one of them probably being the dedication copy, having the arms of King Charles II on the binding and his autograph initials on the fly-leaf. The book was printed by Thomas Newcomb (1649–81), and was twice reissued with new title-pages in 1661 (see nos. 32 and 32*a*). The curious device of two hands actuating pumps, with motto *Dum premor, attollor*, which is used on the title-pages of all the issues of this volume, is not mentioned by McKerrow in his *Printers' and Publishers' Devices*, London, 1913; but it was used *for J. Partridge* in 1630, *by J. R. for G. Thomason and O. Pullen* in 1645, and again *by T. N.* in 1670.

Copies:

(a) *Small paper:* BLO, ULC; HCL, NLC, YUL.
  Christ's College, Cambridge. Worcester College, Oxford.
  Cathedral Libraries: Winchester, Worcester; Lambeth Palace Library.
  G. L. Keynes.

(b) *Large paper:* HCL (Charles II's copy).
  St. Paul's Cathedral Library.
  Keynes Library, King's College, Cambridge (Aldenham House–Tredegar copy).
  G. L. Keynes (Beeching copy), the late E. M. Simpson, R. S. Pirie.

32 XXVI SERMONS [Wing D 1873] variant title　　　　　　　Fº 1661

Title (within double rules): XXVI. Sermons (Never before Publiſh'd) . . . London. Printed by Thomas Newcomb, and are to be ſold at the ſeveral Book-Sellers-ſhops in London, and at Weſtminſter-Hall. 1661. [*see facsimile*]

Collation: A² (±A1), etc. *Contents, Texts of the sermons:* As in no. 31.

Note: Both this book and no. 32*a* consist of the same sheets as no. 31 with cancel title-pages.

XXVI.

SERMONS

(Never before Publish'd)

PREACHED

BY THAT

Learned and Reverend.

DIVINE

John Donne,

Doctor in Divinity,

Late D E A N of the Cathedral Church
of St *Pauls,* London.

The Third Volume.

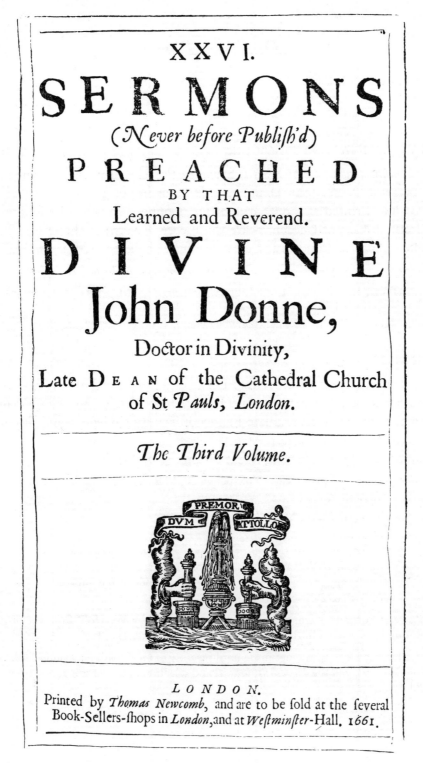

LONDON.
Printed by *Thomas Newcomb,* and are to be fold at the feveral
Book-Sellers-fhops in *London,* and at *Weftminfter*-Hall. 1661.

Title-page of no. 32 (reduced)

Copies: BM, ULC; YUL.
Sion College.
G. L. Keynes, R. S. Pirie.

32*a* XXVI SERMONS variant title   Fº 1661

Title (within double rules): XXVI. Sermons Preached By That Learned and
Reverend Divine John Donne, . . . [etc., as in no. 32]
London, Printed at the Charge of Dr. Donne, and are to be ſold at his
Houſe in Covent-Garden, neare the Fleece-Tavern; at the ſeveral Book
ſellers-ſhops in London and at Weſtminſter-hall, 1661. [*see facsimile*]

Collation: A² (±A1), etc. *Contents, Texts of the sermons:* As in no. 31.

Copies: DWL, Harmsworth Trust Library (Sotheby's 20 March 1950, lot 6637).
Carlisle Cathedral Library.
G. L. Keynes (Thomas Zouch–Dowden copy), I. A. Shapiro, R. S. Pirie.

33 SERMONS, ETC.   6 vols. 8º 1839

Title: The Works of John Donne, D.D., Dean of Saint Pauls 1621–1631,
With a memoir of his life. By Henry Alford, M.A., Vicar of Wymes-
wold, Leicestershire, and late Fellow of Trinity College, Cambridge. In
six volumes. Vol. 1. [etc.]
London: John W. Parker, West Strand. M.DCCC.XXXIX.

Collation: Vol. I, pp. xxxii, 587. Vol. II, pp. iv, 588. Vol. III, pp. iv, 614. Vol. IV,
pp. iv, 590. Vol. V, pp. iv, 623. Vol. VI, pp. iv, 569.

Contents: Vol. I, pp. ix–xxviii, Life of Dr. Donne.
Vol. I, p. 1–Vol. III, p. 491, Sermons I–LXXX.
Vol. III, pp. 493–614, Devotions upon Emergent Occasions.
Vol. IV, p. 1–Vol. VI, p. 298, Sermons LXXXI–CLVIII.
Vol. VI, pp. 299–441, Letters to several persons of honour.
Vol. VI, pp. 443–569, Poems.

Frontispiece: Portrait of Donne, 11·5 ×9 cm, engraved by W. Holl 'from the original
painting by Vandyke in the possession of F. Holbrooke, Esq.'[1]

Note: This was the only attempt made until recently to reprint all the sermons. The text
is modernized, and the *Devotions*, letters, and selection of poems are very imperfectly
edited.

---

[1] See *Iconography*, p. 376 of present work.

XXVI.

SERMONS

PREACHED

BY THAT

Learned and Reverend

DIVINE

John Donne,

Doctor in Divinity,

Late DEAN of the Cathedral Church
of St. *Pauls*, London.

The Third Volume.

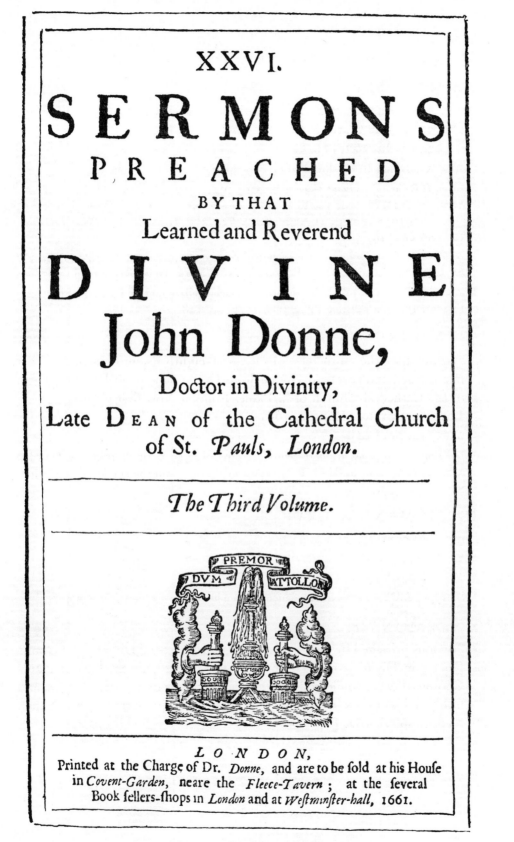

LONDON,
Printed at the Charge of Dr. *Donne*, and are to be fold at his Houfe
in *Covent-Garden*, neare the *Fleece-Tavern* ; at the feveral
Book fellers-fhops in *London* and at *Weftminfter-hall*, 1661.

Title-page of no. 32*a* (reduced)

33*a* SERMONS, SELECTED PASSAGES   8° 1919

Donne's Sermons Selected Passages with an essay by Logan Pearsall Smith
   Oforxd At the Clarendon Press MDCCCCXIX
   19 cm, pp. lii, 263, [1].

Frontispiece: Donne in his shroud after Droeshout.

Reviewed: Bailey, J., *Quart. Rev.* CCXXXIII, 1920, 317–28; Bredvold, L. I., *Journ.
   Eng. Germ. Philol.* XXI, 1922, 347–53; Gosse, Sir E., *Sunday Times* (Lond.), 12
   October 1919; Summers, M., *Mod. Lang. Rev.* XVII, 1922, 88–90; *Times Lit. Sup.*,
   30 October 1919.

Note: Passages from Donne's sermons will also be found in Pearsall Smith's *Treasury of
   English Prose*, London, 1919, Boston and New York, 1920. Reprinted in 1954.

Translated: Sermoni. Tr. di Margherti Guïdacci della scelta di L. P. Smith, 1920.
   Firenzi: Libreria Editrice Fiorentina, 1946. pp. 148.

33*b* SERMON ON PSALM xxxviii. 9.   4° 1921

A Sermon upon the ninth verse of the thirty-eighth Psalm Preached by that
   late learned and reverend Divine John Donne Doctor in Divinity, Dean
   of the Cathedral Church of S. Pauls, London Now first printed
   London, Privately Printed, 1921
   21·5 cm, pp. [44].

Note: Thirty-two pages are here reproduced in collotype facsimile from the Dowden
   MS. (see p. 29) now in BLO. Fifty copies were printed for the late Wilfred Merton.
   See also no. 33*h*.

33*c* SERMONS XV & LXVI   8° 1921

Donne Sermons XV and LXVI
   Cambridge At the University Press 1921
   16 cm, pp. vi, 56.

Note: From *LXXX Sermons*. Introductory note by 'Q.' Issued in paper wrappers at 1*s*.

33*d* X SERMONS ED. KEYNES   F° 1923

X Sermons preached by that late Learned and Reverend Divine John Donne
   Doctor in Divinity once Dean of the Cathedral Church of Saint Paul's
   Chosen from the whole body of Donne's Sermons by Geoffrey Keynes and
   published MDCCCCXXIII by the Nonesuch Press 30 Gerrard Street Soho
   29 cm, pp. vi, 162, [2].

Texts of the sermons:

Ps. 89: 48 (80 *Sermons*, 27)   Mark 16: 16 (80 *Sermons*, 76)   John 11: 21 (80 *Sermons*, 80)
Ps. 32: 9 (80 *Sermons*, 62)   Isa. 7: 14 (80 *Sermons*, 2)   Mark 4: 24 (50 *Sermons*, 27)
Job 19: 26 (50 *Sermons*, 14)   Ps. 65: 5 (80 *Sermons*, 68)   Ps. 68: 20 (26 *Sermons*, 26)
Acts 1: 8 (*Five Sermons*)

Note: 725 copies were printed in Garamond type at the Kynoch Press on Dutch mould-made paper. There is a Bibliographical Note at the end by the editor.

Reviewed: Saintsbury, G., *Nat. & Athen.* xxxiv, 1924, 901–2.

33e SERMONS, SELECTED PASSAGES

In John Donne . . . Complete Poetry and Selected Prose Edited by John Hayward . . . 1929 (see no. 97), pp. 555–760.

33f SERMON OF VALEDICTION [Ed. Simpson]   8° 1932

Donne's Sermon of Valediction at his going into Germany preached at Lincoln's Inn April 18 1619 Printed from the Original Version in the Lothian and Ashmole Manuscripts and from XXVI Sermons Edited by Evelyn Mary Simpson London: The Nonesuch Press, 1932
29 cm, pp. [iv]. 79, [5].

Note: 750 copies were printed on Auvergne hand-made paper in Fell types at the Oxford University Press.

Reviewed: *Times Lit. Sup.*, 6 April 1933, 244.

33g SERMON AT LINCOLN'S INN [Ps. xxxviii, 9] [Ed. Potter]
8° 1946

A Sermon Preached at Lincoln's Inn by John Donne on the Ninth Verse of Psalm xxxviii . . . Edited, with Introduction and Notes, by George Reuben Potter . . .
Stanford University Press . . . London: Geoffrey Cumberlege Oxford University Press [1946]
23 cm, pp. viii, 71, [1].

Note: The text is based on that in MS. Do (Houghton Library, MS. 966. 4); it is another version of no. 33b.

Reviewed: Allen, D. C., *Mod. Lang. Notes*, LXII, 1947, 58–9; *Durham Univ. Journ.* XXXIX, 1946, 38; Freeman, R., *Rev. Eng. Stud.* XXIII, 1947, 360–2; Levy, B. M., *Church Hist.* xv, 1946, 139–40; *Times Lit. Sup.*, 21 December 1946, p. 633.

33h SERMONS ED. POTTER & SIMPSON   8° 1953–5

The Sermons of John Donne Edited with Introductions and Critical
Apparatus, by George R. Potter and Evelyn M. Simpson In Ten
Volumes I. [etc.] University of California Press Berkeley and Los
Angeles 1953–62
24 cm.

Vol. I, 1953, pp. xiv, 354. Vol. II, 1955, pp. x, [ii], 466, [2 blank]. Vol. III, 1957,
pp. ix, [i], 434. Vol. IV, 1959, pp. vii, [iii], 419, [3 blank]. Vol. V, 1959, pp. vi, [ii],
430, [2 blank]. Vol. VI, 1953, pp. vi, [ii], 374, [2 blank]. Vol. VII, 1954, pp. vi, [ii],
463, [1]. Vol. VIII, 1956, pp. vi, [ii], 396. Vol. IX, 1958, pp. vi, [ii], 444, [4 blank].
Vol. X, 1962, pp. xvii, [iii], 497, [1 blank].

    Each volume has a frontispiece; vol. v has an Appendix on Donne's Tenure of the
Rectory of Blunham with two illustrations of church plate given by Donne; vol. VI
has two illustrations of Old St. Paul's.

Reviewed: Times Lit. Sup., 28 August 1953, p. 548: 'The Preacher of Paradox'; Allen,
D. C., *Mod. Lang. Notes*, LXIX, 1954, 116–20; Battenhouse, R. W., *Journ. Relig.*
XXXIII, 1953, 291–3; Coffin, C. M., *Kenyon Rev.* XVI, 1954, 292–8: 'Donne's
Divinity'; Ellrodt, R., *Études Angl.* IX, 1956, 348–9; Gardner, H., *New Statesman
& Nat.* XLVI, 1953, 572, 574: 'The Art of Preaching'; Garrison, W. E., *Christ.
Cent.* LXX, 1953, 576: 'For Court and Commons'; G[arrison], W. E., *Christ. Cent.*
LXX, 1953, 1327; Hanford, J. H., *Amer. Scholar*, XXII, 1953, 364, 366; Legouis, P.,
Études Angl. VIII. 1955, 342–4; Leishman, J. B., *Rev. Eng. Stud.* N.S. VI, 1955,
417–27; McDonald, G. D., *Lib. Journ.* LXXVIII, 1953, 1236. Nes, W. H., *Anglican
Theol. Rev.* XXXV, 1953, 280–2; *San Francisco Chron.*, 21 June 1953, p. 18; *San
Francisco Chron.*, 29 November 1953, p. 9; *Times Lit. Sup.*, 14 January 1955, p. 26:
'Donne as Preacher'; *Times Lit. Sup.*, 9 September 1955, p. 529: 'Donne in the
Pulpit'; *Times Lit. Sup.*, 11 January 1957, p. 25: 'The Autumn of John Donne';
Times Lit. Sup., 9 August 1957, p. 478: 'Donne and his Congregation'; *Times Lit.
Sup.*, 24 October 1958, p. 613: 'Sermons of an aging Donne'; *Times Lit. Sup.*, 6
November 1959, p. 646: 'Homiletic Genius'; *Times Lit. Sup.*, 22 February 1963,
p. 130: 'The Divine Paradox'; *U. S. Quart. Book Rev.* IX, 1953, 171–2.

33i ANTHOLOGY OF SERMONS   8° 1955

John Donne and the Christian Life. An Anthology of Selected Sermons
Preached by Donne. Ed. R. P. Sorlien. Ann Arbor University, Michigan.
1955.

33*j* SELECTED SERMONS ED. GILL   8° 1958

The Sermons of John Donne, selected and introduced by Theodore A. Gill. Living Age Books. New York. Meridian Books. 1958.
8°, pp. 288 (nine sermons, 1618 to 1630).

33*k* SELECTED SERMONS ED. SIMPSON   8° 1963

John Donne's Sermons on the Psalms and Gospels. With a Selection of Prayers and Meditations. Ed. with an Introduction by E. M. Simpson. Berkeley and Los Angeles. 1963.
20 cm, pp. [viii], 244, [2].

33*l* SELECTED SERMONS ED. FULLER   8° 1964

The Showing forth of Christ. Sermons of John Donne. Selected and Edited with an Introduction by Edmund Fuller. New York, Evanston, and London. 1964. pp. xviii, 230.
Reviewed: Carrithers, G. H., *Seventeenth Century News*, xxiii, 1965, 31.

DEVOTIONS

BIBLIOGRAPHICAL PREFACE

IN the winter of 1623 Donne was seized with an acute illness, described by Walton as 'a dangerous sicknesse, which turned to a spotted Feaver, and ended in a Cough, that inclined him to a Consumption'. His life was evidently at one time in danger, but his mental activity continued unabated, and he was a close observer of his own symptoms and mental reactions. The result was the volume of meditations known as his *Devotions*, put together during his convalescence from notes made during his illness. In January or February 1623/4 he wrote a letter to Sir Robert Karre, then gentleman of the bedchamber to the Prince of Wales, regarding a proposed dedication to the Prince.

> Though I have left my bed [he wrote] I have not left my bed-side; I sit there still, and as a Prisoner discharged, sits at the Prison doore, to beg Fees, so sit I here, to gather crummes. I have used this leisure, to put the meditations had in my sicknesse, into some such order, as may minister some holy delight. They arise to so many sheetes (perchance 20.) as that without staying for that furniture of an Epistle, That my Friends importun'd me to Print them, I importune my Friends to receive them Printed. . . . If you allow my purposes in generall, I pray cast your eye upon the Title and the Epistle, and rectifie me in them: I submit substance, and circumstance to you, and the poore Author of both.[1]

The proposed Dedication was duly prefixed to the *Devotions*, which consist of twenty-three *Stationes, sive Periodi in Morbo*, each followed by a Meditation, Expostulation, and Prayer. Donne's estimate of twenty sheets was exceeded, as the book eventually contained nearly twenty-seven. It was entered on the Stationers' Register to Thomas Jones on 9 January 1623/4.

Mrs. Simpson considered that 'as a manual of devotions this curious book compares unfavourably with the *Devotions* of Bishop Andrewes or the *Holy Living* of Jeremy Taylor'. Nevertheless, it is a deeply interesting record of the states through which Donne's extraordinary mind passed during this crisis in his life.

[1] *Letters*, 1651, no. 90.

Several letters from Donne, sent with gift-copies of the book, have survived; these were addressed to the Queen of Bohemia (Tobie Matthew collection, no. 5), to a lady of the court of Bohemia (Gosse, no. 22), to the Duke of Buckingham (Tobie Matthew collection, no. 10), and to another Lord (ibid. no. 11). The book seems to have been a popular one, and it passed through three editions (five issues) during Donne's lifetime; two more editions with frontispieces engraved by Marshall were published during the seven years succeeding his death. The *Devotions* were reprinted by Dean Alford in 1839, by Pickering in 1840, and by Talboys in 1841, but the book was not adequately edited until 1923, when a full collation of the texts was undertaken by John Sparrow, then a scholar of Winchester College, and the result embodied in a handsome edition by the Cambridge University Press. This is now the standard text of the *Devotions*. The Meditations were printed in Hayward's *Complete Poetry and Selected Prose* (London, 1929) (see no. 97), and again in an American reprint of this text (New York, 1941) (see no. 102). I do not know of any translation or foreign edition of the *Devotions*, but the following statement is made by Morhof in his *Polyhistor* in the course of his short account of Donne's works: 'Scripsit et *Meditationes* super morbo suo *sacras*, quæ in Linguam Belgicam conversæ et Amstelodami 1655 in 12° editæ sunt.'[1] This statement is sufficiently definite to make it probable that such a translation does exist; if so, it is probably by Sir Constantine Huygens, who had already translated some of Donne's poems (see no. 105).

The text of each section of the *Devotions* is preceded by Latin lines headed *Stationes, sive Periodi in Morbo, ad quas referuntur Meditationes sequentes*. Dr. Grosart found an English verse rendering of these lines inscribed on the fly leaves of a copy[2] of the third edition, 1627, and he believed the hand to be Donne's, though there is certainly no justification for this belief. They are reprinted in the Abbey Classics edition of the *Devotions* (see no. 42*b*).

[1] *Polyhistor*, 1714, lib. vi, cap. iv, § 18. See no. 133.

[2] This copy, in contemporary vellum, gilt, with the initials A. G. on the cover, was afterwards in the Thorn-Drury library, and was sold at Sotheby's, 23 November 1921, lot 1738. It was next in the Richard Jennings library, sold at Sotheby's, 28 April 1952, lot 161, and now belongs to John Sparrow.

John Chamberlain read the book immediately after publication and reported to Dudley Carleton that it contained curious conceits, but much piety.[1] The earliest borrower from *Devotions* was Sir Francis Bacon, who in 1625 incorporated in his *Essay* 'Of Goodness', with variations in the words, Donne's passage from Meditation 17 beginning 'No Man is an Island' (see p. 285 in the present work). Bacon had been quick in the uptake, but his plagiarism was not noticed until 1960.[2] Donne's book has not been frequently reprinted in recent years, but a passage, again from Meditation 17, has become famous through another medium—'Perchance hee for whom this *Bell* tolls, may bee so ill, as that he knowes not it *tolls* for him.'[3]

34 DEVOTIONS [*STC* 7033] first edition   12° 1624

Title (within double rules): Deuotions Vpon Emergent Occasions, . . . London, Printed by A. M. for Thomas Iones: 1624. [*see facsimile*]

Collation: A⁶ B–C¹² (±C2) D–Z¹² Aa–Dd¹² Ee⁴; 322 leaves.

Contents: A1 title; A2*a*–A4*b* (both A2 and A3 with sign. A3) *The Epiſtle Dedicatorie To the moſt excellent Prince, Prince Charles*; A5*a*–A6*a Stationes, ſiue Periodi in Morbo, ad quas referuntur Meditationes ſequentes*; A6*b* errata (7 lines); B1*a*–Ee3*b* (pp. 1–630) text; Ee4 blank.

Note: Leaf C2 (pp. 27–8) is a cancel, and I have not yet seen an example of the leaf it replaces, but Mrs. Simpson noted (*Rev. Eng. Stud.*, IX, 1933, 107) that the copy at Magdalen College, Oxford, has the stub of the original C2 with fragmentary words shewing that the endings of the first nine lines on p. 28 were identical with those in the cancel. Those of lines 10 and 11 are illegible, but lines 12–14 end differently; the remaining endings, lines 15–18, and the catchword are again identical. Mrs. Simpson suggested, therefore, that the resetting began in line 11 with 'hee that hath no more' down to 'that earth which hee is' in line 15. The first page number on this leaf is misprinted 393 for 27; the next number, 28, is correct; p. 168 is numbered 180 and the pagination of sign. Q is erratic. This edition of the *Devotions* and all the subsequent editions up to 1638 were printed by Augustin Matthewes (1619–53).

Copies: BM, BLO, ULC, DWL; HCL (2), HEH, FSLW (Harmsworth copy), YUL. Trinity College, Cambridge (2). St. Andrews University Library.

[1] See p. 283 under Chamberlain, *Letters*, 1965.
[2] John Crossett, *Notes and Queries*, N.S. VII, 1960, 386.
[3] Hemingway's novel, *For Whom the Bell Tolls*, 1941, and the film version which followed. Another book title borrowed from Donne is Dorothy Parker's *After Such Pleasures*, London, 1934 ('Farewell to love', line 23).

Oxford Colleges: All Souls, Magdalen, Worcester (imperfect).
Cathedral Libraries: Durham, Peterborough.
G. L. Keynes; J. Sparrow (imperfect); R. S. Pirie.

35 DEVOTIONS [*STC* 7033*a*] first edition, variant title   12° 1624

    Title (within double rules): Deuotions Vpon Emergent Occaſions . . . London,
         Printed for Thomas Iones. 1624. [*see facsimile*]

    Collation, contents: As in no. 34.

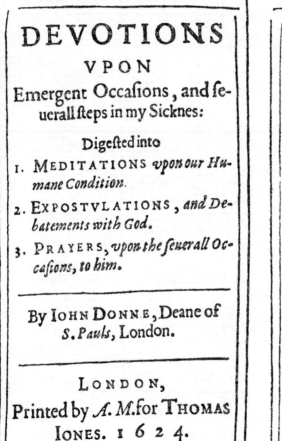

Title-page of no. 34   Title-page of no. 35

IV

Will: Marshall. Sculpsit.

Note: This variant title-page omits the printer's initials, *A.M.* Only two copies with this form of imprint are known. It has been suggested (Leo Kirschbaum, *Shakespeare and his Stationers*, 1955, pp. 43–4) that this was due to the fact that sometimes the printer was paid in books rather than in money, his name or initials appearing in these copies, but not in the copies sold by the holder of the copyright. This seems to be unlikely in the present instance since, if it is true, it would appear that nearly all the extant copies were not sold by the copyright holder, Thomas Jones. It is more likely that the omission was a press correction made early in the series, when only very few copies had been printed.

Copies: HEH (Beverley Chew copy).

G. L. Keynes (from the library of Lord North; section M omitted by the binder).

36 DEVOTIONS [*STC* 7034] second edition   12° 1624

Title (within double rules): Devotions Vpon Emergent Occasions ... London, Printed by A. M. for Thomas Iones, ... 1624. [*see facsimile*]

Collation: A–Z¹² Aa–Bb¹²; 300 leaves.

Contents: A1 blank; A2 title; A3*a*–A4*b The Epiſtle Dedicatorie*; A5*a*–*b Stationes*, etc.; A6*a*–Bb12*a* (pp. 1–589) text; Bb12*b* colophon.

Note: The errata recorded in the first edition have been corrected. pp. 7 and 323 are numbered 10 and 233; the pagination in sigs. I, M, and S is erratic.

Copies: BLO, ULC; HCL, HEH, FSLW (2, one Britwell Court–Harmsworth copy), NLC, YUL.

Oxford Colleges: Christ Church, Worcester.

St. Paul's Cathedral Library; Lambeth Palace Library.

G. L. Keynes; R. S. Pirie (Jennings copy).

37 DEVOTIONS [*STC* 7035] third edition   12° 1626

Title (within double rules): Devotions Vpon Emergent Occasions, ... London, Printed for Thomas Iones, ... 1626. [*see facsimile*]

Colophon: London Printed for Thomas Iones, and are to be ſold at the black Rauen, in the Strand. 1627.

Collation: A–Z¹² Aa–Bb¹²; 300 leaves.

Contents: A1 blank; A2 title; A3*a*–A4*b The Epiſtle Dedicatory*; A5*a*–*b Stationes*, etc.; A6*a*–Bb12*a* (pp. 1–589) text; Bb12*b* colophon.

Note: The two dates on the title-page and colophon suggest that the composition of this edition was begun in 1626 and finished in 1627. Later the date on the title-page was altered to 1627 (see no. 38). There are a number of minor errors in the pagination.

Copies: BM; HCL, PUL.
Lincoln Cathedral Library.
G. L. Keynes (in contemporary Lyonese binding, with goffered edges); J. Sparrow (2, one the Thorn Drury–Jennings copy described on p. 82, n.); R. S. Pirie (2).

38   DEVOTIONS [*STC* 7035*a*] third edition, variant title   12° 1627

    Title (*within double rules*): Devotions Vpon Emergent Occasions ... London, Printed for Thomas Iones ... 1627.

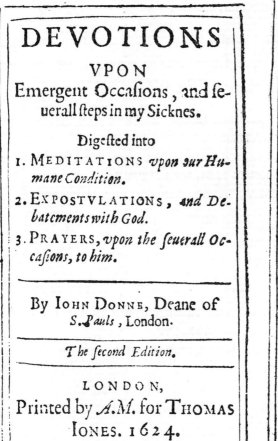

Title-page of no. 36   Title-page of no. 37

Colophon, Collation, Contents: As in no. 37.

Note: The same sheets as in no. 37, with the date altered on the title-page, presumably while the book was in the press, since the title-page is not a cancel.

Copies: BLO; HCL (Gosse copy, in contemporary binding with initials I.D. stamped in gold on the front cover; possibly Donne's own copy), FSLW (2, one Harmsworth copy), PUL, YUL.

> Corpus Christi College, Oxford; Sheffield University Library.
>
> Exeter Cathedral Library. Dublin, Marsh Library.
>
> G. L. Keynes; R. S. Pirie (contemporary Oxford binding).

39 DEVOTIONS [*STC* 7036] fourth edition   12° 1634

Title: Devotions Vpon Emergent Occasions, . . . London, Printed by A. M. and are to bee fold by Charles Greene, 1634. [*see facsimile*]

Colophon: London, Printed by A. M. and are to bee fold by Charles Greene. 1634.

Collation: A–Y¹²; 264 leaves.

Contents: A1 title; A2*a*–A3*b* dedication; A4*a–b Stationes*, etc.; A5*a*–Y10*a* text; Y10*b* colophon; Y11–Y12 blank.

Frontispiece: Inserted before A1. The effigy of Donne in a niche wrapped in his winding sheet; above his head is a skull wreathed with laurel. On either side are two biblical scenes with their texts inscribed below and above as follows: *Gen: Cap:* 3. *v.* 6. 24, *Ps:* 41. *v:* 3, *Iob:* 10. 9., *Mat:* 26. *v:* 41.

> Below is a shield inscribed: *Devotions | By John Donne late | Deane of S^t. Paules. | London. | Printed by Aug: Mathewes.* 1634 | *Will: Marshall Sculpsit.*
> The engraving measures 9·5 × 5 cm (see plate IV, enlarged).

Note: The volume has no pagination.

Copies: HCL, FSLW.

> Cambridge Colleges: Pembroke, Trinity. Worcester College, Oxford (no frontispiece).
>
> G. L. Keynes (no frontispiece; in a Cambridge binding of doeskin with gilt ornament and initials E D stamped on both covers); J. Sparrow; R. S. Pirie (no frontispiece).

40 DEVOTIONS [*STC* 7037] fifth edition   12° 1638

Title: Devotions Upon Emergent occafions, . . . London, Printed by A. M. and are to be fold by Richard Royfton in Ivie lane. 1638. [*see facsimile*]

Collation: A–T¹²; 228 leaves.

Contents: A1 title; A2*a–b* dedication; A3*a–b Stationes* etc.; A4*a*–T10*b* text; T11*a Imprimatur. Guil. Bray. Novemb.* 23. 1637.; T11*b*–T12 blank.

Frontispiece: As in no. 39, with the date altered to 1638.

Note: As in the edition of 1634, there is no pagination.

Copies: BM (no frontispiece), NLS; HEH.
　　St. John's College, Cambridge (no frontispiece).
　　Chetham's Library, Manchester; Aberdeen Public Library (no frontispiece).
　　G. L. Keynes (with one leaf, G11, in facsimile), R. S. Pirie (no frontispiece).

40*a* DEVOTIONS　　　　　　　　　　　　　　　　8° 1839

In The Works of John Donne. Ed. Henry Alford, M.A. London, 1839.
　　6 vols. 8° (see no. 33*a*).

Vol. III, pp. 493–614. *Devotions.*

DEVOTIONS
VPON
Emergent occafions, and
feverall fteps in my
Sicknefle.

Digefted into
1. MEDITATIONS, *upon our
humane Condition.*
2. EXPOSTVLATIONS, *and
Debatements with God.*
3. PRAYERS, *upon the feverall Occafions, to him.*

By IOHN DONNE, Deane
of S. *Pauls*, London.

The fourth Edition.

LONDON,
Printed by *A. M.* and are
to be fold by *Charles Greene*,
1 6 3 4.

Title-page of no. 39

DEVOTIONS
VPON
Emergent occafions,
and feverall fteps in
my Sicknefle.

Digefted into
1. MEDITATIONS, *upon our
humane Condition.*
2. EXPOSTVLATIONS, *and
Debatements with God.*
3. PRAYERS, *upon the feverall occafions to him.*

By Jo: DONNE, late Deane
of St. *Pauls*, London.

The fifth Edition.

LONDON,
Printed by *A M.* and are to be
fold by *Richard Royfton* in
Ivie lane. 1 6 3 8.

Title-page of no. 40

41 DEVOTIONS 8° 1840

Devotions by John Donne D.D. Dean of St Pauls with two sermons
    I On the decease of Lady Danvers mother of George Herbert
    II Deaths duel—his own funeral sermon
to which is prefixed his life by Izaak Walton.
London: William Pickering M DCCC XL.
17 cm, pp. cviii, 227, [1]; brown cloth with printed label on spine.

Frontispiece: Engraved reproduction (enlarged to 11·7 × 6·2 cm) of Marshall's frontispiece to the fourth edition of the *Devotions*, 1634 (no. 39).

Note: For the original editions of the two sermons, see nos. 23 and 24.

42 DEVOTIONS 12° 1841

Donne's Devotions.
Oxford: D. A. Talboys. 1841.
15 cm, pp. xiv, 292; black cloth, with gothic design in gold on the spine.

Note: The book is decorated with numerous woodcut headpieces, tailpieces, and initials. These combine inspirations derived from the Gothic revival and Victorian sentimentality, and must be some of the most inept illustrations ever invented. This edition has become very scarce.

42a DEVOTIONS 4° 1923

Devotions upon Emergent Occasions By John Donne Late Dean of Saint Paul's Edited by John Sparrow, Scholar of Winchester College, with a Bibliographical Note by Geoffrey Keynes, Fellow of the Royal College of Surgeons
Cambridge At the University Press MDCCCCXXIII
22 cm, pp. xxx, [viii], 160; half brown buckram paper boards.

Frontispiece: Collotype reproduction of the portrait in the National Portrait Gallery, here reproduced for the first time. (See *Iconography*, p. 372.)

Note: The text is based on a collation of the first three editions of 1624, 1624, and 1626. There are an introduction and explanatory notes by the editor.

Reviewed: Kendon, F., *Lond. Mercury*, 1923, pp. 432–4; Saintsbury, G. E. B., *Nat. & Athen.* XXXIV, 1924, 15, 547; *Times Lit. Sup.*, 27 December 1923, pp. 901–2.

42*b* DEVOTIONS 8° 1925

Devotions upon Emergent Occasions together with Death's Duel. By John
Donne, Dean of St. Paul's, London With an Introduction by William H.
Draper, M.A., Master of the Temple, Ornamented by Martin Travers
Simpkin, Marshall, Hamilton, Kent & Co., Ltd., London, E.C.4. [1925]
17 cm, pp. lxvii, [i], 192. The Abbey Classics, xx.

Note: The editor's introduction is preceded by Walton's *Life of Donne* and a list of
editions of the *Devotions*. At the end is an English version of the *Stationes*, erroneously
attributed to Donne (see bibliographical preface).

Reviewed: Times Lit. Sup., 11 March 1926, p. 178.

42*c* DEVOTION 17 1941

The Tolling Bell a Devotion by John Donne Stanford Conn, Printed at
The Overbrook Press 1941
19 cm.

Note: 540 copies printed, with a wood engraving by Rudolph Ruzick.

42*d* 'No man is an island' John Donne Peekskill Waten Hill Press 1946
21 cm, 4 ll.

42*e* The Bell: a Devotion by John Donne . Moylan, Pa. The Rose Valley Press
1946
15 cm, pp. vi, 21 (150 copies printed).

42*f* 'No man is an island', for mixed voices, a cappella by Jean Pierre Berger.
Bryn Mawr, Pa. T. Dresser [*c.* 1953]
20 cm, pp. 10.

42*g* MEDITATIONS

In Divine Poems Devotions Prayers The Peter Pauper Press New York
1953 (see no. 148).

42*h* DEVOTIONS AND DEATH'S DUEL 8° 1959

John Donne Devotions upon Emergent Occasions Together with Death's
Duel Ann Arbor Paperbacks. The University of Michigan Press [1959]
20·5 cm, pp. li, [i], 189, [5].

Note: With *The Life*, taken from Walton. There is no statement as to editor or source of
text, though it was taken from no. 42*a*. Third printing, 1965.

JUVENILIA

BIBLIOGRAPHICAL PREFACE

DONNE'S *Juvenilia* are clever and entertaining trifles, most of which were probably written before or soon after 1600 during his youth. His own opinion of them was expressed in a letter written probably to Sir Henry Wotton in 1600:

> Only in obedience I send you some of my paradoxes; I loue you & myself & them to well to send them willingly for they carry with them a confession of there lightnes. & your trouble & my shame. but indeed they were made rather to deceaue tyme then her daughth^r truth: although they haue beene written in an age when any thing is strong enough to overthrow her: if they make you to find better reasons against them they do there office: for they are but swaggerers: quiet enough if you resist them. if perchance they be pretyly guilt, that is there best for they are not hatcht: they are rather alarums to truth to arme her then enemies: & they haue only this advantadg to scape from being caled ill things that they are nothings: therfore take heed of allowing any of them least you make another.[1]

Owing to their rather free nature they could not be published during Donne's lifetime, but in 1632, shortly after his death, part of them was licensed by Sir Henry Herbert. The licences were granted on 25 October 1632, but on 14 November an order of inquiry was delivered at the King's command by the Bishop of London calling upon Sir Henry Herbert to explain before the Board of the Star Chamber his reasons 'why hee warranted the booke of D. Duns paradoxes to bee printed'.[2] The inquiry, however, was ineffectual in preventing the publication of the book, the title-page of which is dated 1633. It is not known through what channels the publisher, Henry Seyle, obtained possession of the text, which had been circulating for over thirty years in a number of manuscripts, but it is probable that the publication was quite unauthorized, and took place even without the

---

[1] Simpson, p. 316.
[2] *Calendar of Domestic State Papers*, Charles I, ccxxv, 20. See Gosse 1, 16–17, and the Grolier Club *Catalogue, Wither to Prior*, 1, 1905, 234.

knowledge of John Donne, jun., who, in his edition of 1652, makes no reference to any previous issues. Demand for the *Juvenilia* encouraged the publication of a second edition in the same year, 1633. Insertion of the licences in the first edition had been erratic, one or both being sometimes omitted. In the second edition they were omitted altogether, and twenty-three lines were added to the first problem, 'Why have bastards best fortune', which was particularly insulting to the court. The second edition is now more uncommon than the first. One or other is sometimes found included in contemporary bindings with the *Poems*, 1633.

In 1652 the younger Donne, in the course of his exploitation of his father's writings, issued an authorized edition of the *Juvenilia*, although he had previously, in 1637, pretended that the book was not by his father, and had obtained an injunction[1] from Archbishop Laud to prevent its publication. In the edition of 1652 he increased the number of the paradoxes from eleven to twelve and that of the problems from ten to seventeen, even the offensive passages in the first problem being now allowed to remain. To these he added two 'Characters', one already printed in the eleventh edition (1622) of Sir Thomas Overburie's *The Wife*,[2] 'An Essay of Valour' from the same source, 'A Sheaf of Miscellany Epigrams', a reprint of *Ignatius his Conclave*, and, finally, the *Essayes in Divinity*. The Epigrams purport to have been written by Donne in Latin and to have been translated into English by Jasper Mayne, D.D.[3] They may have been printed by the younger Donne in good faith, as it seems to be certain that Donne's *epigrammata mea Latina* once existed, for he mentions them in a Latin letter to Sir Henry Goodere (*Poems*, 1633, p. 352); but the epigrams attributed to him in this volume are certainly spurious and may well have been composed as well as translated by Jasper Mayne, who was an unprincipled and witty divine (see

[1] Calendar of Domestic State Papers, Charles I, cccLxxiv, 4. Printed by Grosart, *Poems*, ii, 1892, lii (see no. 98), and by Grierson, ii, lxvi.

[2] See Mrs. Simpson's 'John Donne & Sir Thomas Overburie's Characters', *Mod. Lang. Rev.* xviii, 1923, 413.

[3] The Epigrams were originally advertised by the publisher Mosely in a catalogue of his books as *Fasciculus Poematum et Epigrammatum Miscellaneorum Authore Johanne Dome* [sic] *D.D. Englished by Jasper Maine, Doctor in Divinity*, and were actually entered to Moseley as a 'small tract' in the Stationers' Register, 15 March 1650 (Simpson, p. 134). The book is also listed in W. London's *Catalogue of the most vendible Books in England*, 1658, Gg1a. This may account for the fact that Lowndes incorrectly records a separate issue of the Epigrams, dated 1632.

Gosse, 1, 16). The *Essayes in Divinity* had been printed in 1651 for a different publisher, but, as is explained elsewhere (see p. 126), they rarely occur as a separate volume; perhaps they had not sold well, and the younger Donne then sought to temper the secularity, and even obscenity, of the *Juvenilia* by issuing them in company with the *Essayes in Divinity* and in this way to invest the volume with an altogether fictitious respectability. This fact had not been noticed before the first edition of this bibliography, although it is laboured by the editor in his preface:

> I humbly here prefent unto your Honor, Things of the leaft and greateft weight, that ever fell from my Father's Pen; which yet, are not fo light that they feem vain; nor of fuch weight, that they may appear dull or heavy unto the Reader. The Primrofes and Violets of the Spring entertain us with more Delight, than the Fruits of the Autumn; and through our Gardens we pafs into our Groves and Orchards; preferving, and candying the Buds and Bloffomes of fome Trees, admitting them amongft our Delicacies & Sweetmeats; when as, the riper Fruit ferves onely to quicken and provoke our Appetite to a coarfer Fare. . . . They are the Effays of two Ages, where you may fee the quicknefs of the firft and the firmnefs of the latter. . . . Here then you have the entertainment of the Authors Youth; and the Affumption of his wit when it was employed in more Heavenly things.

Beyond the facts that the volumes usually occur bound up together and that the original dedication of the *Essayes in Divinity* has been cancelled in whole or in part, there is nothing in the bibliographical constitution of the whole to shew that they actually form one volume; but the passages quoted above make quite evident the editor's intention.

Manuscript versions of the *Juvenilia* are numerous, most of them being found with the following MSS. of the poems: A18, A25, B, Do, N, O'F. P, S, TCC, TCD, W (see pp. 185–6). Mrs. Simpson has found others in the following:

Ash. 826. Ashmole MS. 826, Bodleian Library.
Bur. Burley MS., now destroyed (see p. 133).
S962. Stowe MS. 962, British Museum.
Tan. Tanner MS. 299, Bodleian Library.

Wy. Wyburd MS., Bodleian Library (1935).

Long Island Historical Society, Brooklyn, N.Y.

Mrs. Simpson observed (*Prose Works*, p. 144) that Seyle used a poor copy of Donne's manuscript in 1633, thus perpetuating a number of blunders in the text.

Even in 1652 the *Paradoxes and Problemes* were not printed entire. Another Probleme entitled 'Why was Sir Walter Raleigh thought the fittest Man to write the Historie of these Times?' is found in eleven manuscripts, of which Tan. alone gives an introductory sentence: ''Tis one of Dr. Donne's problems (but so bitter, that his son Jack Donne LL.D. thought fit not to print it with the rest).'[1] Another Probleme, 'Why doth *Johannes Sarisburiensis* writing *de Nugis Curialium*[2] handle the providence and omnipotency of God?' is found, according to Mrs. Simpson, in four manuscripts (B, Dob, O'F, and S96) together with a longer form of Probleme 13, 'Why do women delight much in Feathers?', and a different conclusion to Probleme 4.[3] Ash. 826, identified by Mr. Percy Simpson, also added to Problemes 4, 8, and 9.[3]

The *Juvenilia* and their evident relation to Donne's poems and other writings are fully discussed by Mrs. Simpson in her *Study of the Prose Works*, 1948. Professor R. E. Bennett has noted that 'An Essay of Valour' was printed in *Cottoni Posthuma*, 1651, p. 323, as 'Valour Anatomised in a Fancie. By Sir Philip Sidney, 1581.' (See p. 292 under Howell.) I have also found eight of the Paradoxes reprinted without acknowledgement of Donne's authorship in John Dunton's *Athenian Sport: or Two Thousand Paradoxes merrily argued*, 1707 (see no. 46*a*).[4] Otherwise there was no reprint of the *Juvenilia* until the Nonesuch edition of 1923.

A curious discovery was published by the late Professor R. C. Bald[5] in 1964. It appears that thirteen of the *Problemes* were translated into Latin by a medical student, Louis Rouzée, and printed at Leyden in 1616.

---

[1] This text was first printed by Gosse, II, 52, and it was added to the Nonesuch edition, 1923 (see no. 46*b*).

[2] Donne inserted a quotation from this work on the title-page of *Biathanatos* (see no. 47).

[3] These were printed by Mrs. Simpson in the *Rev. Eng. Stud.* III, 1927, 129.

[4] This reprint was also noted independently in 1940 by the late Professor G. R. Potter (see p. 356.

[5] *Modern Philology*, LXI, 1964, 198–203.

Rouzée was a Fleming by birth, but was educated in France and had lived in England for ten years. He matriculated at Leyden aged 29 on 27 October 1615 and took his M.D. degree on 24 September 1616. Later he returned to England and, having been incorporated at Oxford in 1625, became a British subject in 1630. His book is entitled:

Problematum Miscellaneorum, Antaristotelicorum, centuria dimidiata, ad Dominos Studiosos in Academia Leydensi, A Ludovico Rovzæo Directa [device] Lugduni Batavorum, Ex Officina Godefridi Basson. Anno Domini 1616. (*¹² A–D¹²)

Bald found that Rouzée had used a source closely related to Ashmole MS. 826 (designated Y¹⁰ by Mrs. Simpson). His translations of Donne's *Problemes* were incorporated with others from various sources, some being by himself. Bald characterizes the translations as somewhat verbose. The following list gives the numbers as listed in 1633 and 1652 with Rouzée's numbers in brackets preceding his Latin titles.

1. (45) *Cur spurii aliis fortunatiores sunt?*
3. (29) *Qua de causa non ante hæc nostra tempora Iesuitas apparere fecit Diabolus?*
4. (1) *Cur plures viridis varietates sunt, quam aliorum colorum?*
6. (36) *Cur anima rationalis à commune opinione mulieribus attribuitur?*
7. (35) *Quare inter mulieros quæ pulcherrimæ ut plurimum sunt falsissimæ?*
8. (28) *Cur umbram sola efficit Veneris stella?*
9. (22) *Cur Veneris aster est πολυώνυμος, & vocatur tum Hesperus, tum Vesper?*
11. (4) *Unde sit quod lues venerea nasum corrodere tantoperè affectat?*
12. (50) *Cur nulli nunc ex amoris vehementia moriuntur?*
13. (38) *Cur plumis tantoperè delectantur mulieres?*
14. (12) *Cur aurum non coinquinat manus?*
15. (47) *Cur Magnates ex omnibus, qui à se dependent, praecipuè Lenones suos promovent?*
16. (20) *Quare Aulici magis, quam alius vitæ generis homines, athei sunt?*

Bald does not state where he found a copy of Rouzée's book for his description.

43 JVVENILIA [*STC* 7043] first edition   4° 1633

Title: [*double rule*] Iuuenilia: ... London, Printed by E. P. for Henry Seyle, and are to be fold at the figne of the Tygers head, in Saint Pauls Church-yard, Anno Dom. 1633. [*see facsimile*]

Collation: [A]⁴ B–H⁴; 32 leaves.

Contents: [A]1 blank; [A]2*a* title; [A]2*b* list of *Paradoxes*; [A]3*a*–F1*a Paradoxes* I–XI; F1*b* Licence, granted by Henry Herbert, 25 October 1632; F2*a* subtitle to *Problems*; F2*b* list of *Problemes*; F3*a*–H4*a Problemes* I–X; H4*b* Licence.

Paradoxes:

    I. A Defence of Womens Inconftancy.
    II. That Women ought to Paint.
    III. That by Difcord things increafe.
    IV. That Good is more common than Euill.
    V. That all things kill themfelues.
    VI. That it is poffible to find fome vertue in fome Women.
    VII. That Old men are more fantaftike than Young.
    VIII. That Nature is our worft guide.
    IX. That only Cowards dare dye.
    X. That a Wife man is known by much laughing.
    XI. That the gifts of the Body are better than thofe of the Minde.

Problemes:

    I. Why haue Baftards beft Fortunes?
    II. Why Puritans make long Sermons?
    III. Why did the Diuell referue Iefuites till thefe latter Dayes?
    IV. Why is there more Variety of Greene, than of any other Colour?
    V. Why doe Young Lay-men fo much ftudy Diuinity?
    VI. Why hath the Common Opinion afforded Women Soules?
    VII. Why are the Faireft falfeft?
    VIII. Why Venus Starre only doth caft a fhadow?
    IX. Why is Venus Starre Multinominous, called both Hefperus and Vefper?
    X. Why are new officers leaft oppreffing?

Note: The Licences are as follows:

Thefe eleuen [*ten*] *Paradoxes* [*Problemes*], *may bee printed: this fiue and twentieth of October, Anno Domini, one thoufand fix hundred thirty and two*

                                        Henry Herbert

Although it may be regarded as normal to find these two Licences on F1*b* and H4*b*, their occurrence is erratic. Of my two copies one lacks the first Licence and the other

IVVENILIA:

OR

CERTAINE

PARADOXES,

AND

PROBLEMES,

WRITTEN BY

I. DONNE.

LONDON,

Printed by *E. P.* for *Henry Seyle*, and are to be sold at the figne of the Tygers head, in Saint Pauls Church-yard, *Anno Dom.* 1633.

Title-page of no. 43

both. One of the HCL copies also lacks both and I have seen two others. One of the FSLW copies lacks the second. YUL has three forms, with neither, with both, and with the first only. Both this and the second edition were printed by Elizabeth Purslowe (1633–46). The device used on the title-pages of both editions is a copy of one of those used by the family Estienne of Paris. It was first used by G. Purslowe (1614–32) in 1618 and passed to Elizabeth Purslowe in 1632–3. It is recorded as no. 311 in McKerrow's *Printers' and Publishers' Devices*, London, 1913.

Copies: BM (3, one Ashley Library), BLO (2), ULC, ULD; HCL (2), HEH, FSLW (2, one Harmsworth copy), LCW, NLC, YUL (3).
     Cambridge Colleges: Emmanuel, Trinity.
     Oxford Colleges: All Souls, Wadham.
     Cathedral Libraries: Lincoln, St. Paul's, Winchester.
     John Rylands Library, Manchester; St. Andrew's University.
     G. L. Keynes (2); R. S. Pirie.

44 JVVENILIA [*STC* 7044] second edition   4° 1633

Title: Iuuenilia . . . London, Printed by E. P. for Henry Seyle, and are to be fold at the figne of the Tygers head, in St. Pauls Church-yard, Anno Dom. 1633. [*see facsimile*]

Collation: [A]⁴ B–F⁴; 24 leaves.

Contents: [A]1 blank; [A]2*a* title; [A]2*b* list of *Paradoxes*; [A]3*a*–D4*a* (pp. 1–27) *Paradoxes* I–XI; D4*b* blank; E1*a* subtitle to *Problemes*; E1*b* (p. 30) list of *Problemes*; E2–F4 (pp. 31–44) *Problemes* I–X.

Paradoxes and Problemes: As in the previous edition, with the addition of twenty-three lines to Probleme I.

Note: Sir Henry Herbert's *Licences* are omitted from this edition (see bibliographical preface).

Copies: HCL, HEH, FSLW (Harmsworth copy), NLC, YUL.
     Cambridge Colleges: Jesus, Pembroke, St. John's (imperfect).
     Oxford Colleges: Corpus Christi, Queen's.
     University Libraries: Durham, Liverpool.
     G. L. Keynes; I. A. Shapiro; R. S. Pirie.

45 PARADOXES, PROBLEMS, ESSAYES [Wing D 1866] third edition, first (or second?) issue   12° 1652

Title (within ornamental acorn border): Paradoxes, Problems, Effayes, Characters, . . . [rule] London, Printed by T. N. for Humphrey Mofeley at the Prince's Armes in St Paul's Church yard, 1652. [*see facsimile*]

IVVENILIA

OR
CERTAINE
PARADOXES
AND
PROBLEMES,
WRITTEN BY
I. DONNE.

The second Edition, corrected.

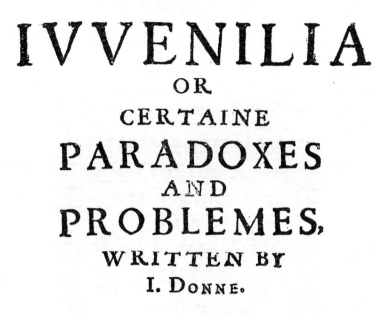

LONDON,

Printed by *E.P.* for *Henry Seyle*, and are to be sold at the signe of the Tygers head, in St. *Pauls* Church-yard, *Anno Dom.* 1633.

Title-page of no. 44

Collation: A⁸ B–K¹² L⁴; A⁶ (±A2–6) π² (±π2) B–K¹² L⁴; 120, 116 leaves.

Contents: A1 title; A2a–A5b dedication *To the Right Honourable Francis Lord Newport, Baron of Higharcale,* signed *Jo. Donne, From my house in Cov. Gard. March 2. 1652;* A6a–A8a *The table;* A8b *Ben. Johnson to the Author* (12 lines); B1a–D8b (pp. 1–64) *Paradoxes and Problemes;* D9a–D12a (pp. 65–71) *Characters;* D12b–E4a (pp. 72–9)

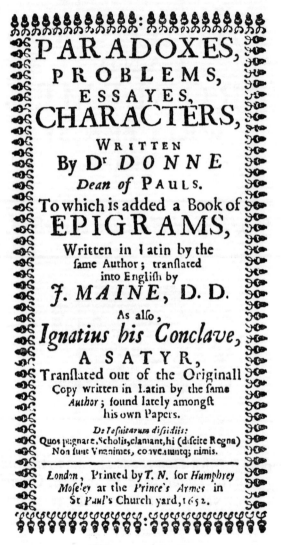

Title-page of no. 45

An Essay of Valour; E4*b* blank; E5*a*–E8*a* (pp. 81–7) *Paradox XII*; E8*b*–F4*a* (pp. 88–103) *A sheaf of Miscellany Epigrams*; F4*b* blank; F5 subtitle to *Ignatius his Conclave, 1653*; F6*a*–L2*a* (pp. 107–219) text; L2*b*–L4*b* blank; A1–L4 *Essayes in Divinity* (as in no. 50 with cancellations in the first quire).

Paradoxes: I–XI as in the editions of 1633.

      XII. That Virginity is a Vertue [placed after *An Essay of Valour*, E5–E8].

Problemes:

  I–X. as in the second edition of 1633.

   XI. Why doth the Pox so much affect to undermine the Nose?

   XII. Why die none for Love now?

  XIII. Why doe women delight much in Feathers?

  XIV. Why doth not Gold soyle the Fingers?

   XV. Why doe Great men of all dependants, choose to preserve their little Pimps?

  XVI. Why are Courtiers sooner Atheists, then men of other conditions?

 XVII. Why are Statesmen most incredulous?

Characters: The Character of a Scot at the first sight.

      The True Character of a Dunce.

Essay: An Essay of Valour.

Epigrams: A Sheaf of Miscellany Epigrams:

    1. Upon one who for his wives fault took it ill to be called Cuckold.

    2. Upon One Roger a Rich Niggard, familiarly unacquainted with the Author.

  3–4. Upon a Whore barren and not barren.

  5–7. On an old Bawd.

    8. On a Bawdy-house.

 9–10. Upon an old rich scolding Woman who being married to a poor young man upbraided him daily with the smallness of his Fortune. The Husbands complaint.

11–13. On her unpleasing kisses.

14–15. On the same old Wife.

16–19. Upon one who saw the Picture of his scolding wife in a Painters shop.

20–2. Upon a Pipe of Tobacco mis-taken by the Author for the Tooth-ach.

23–6. To the Tobacco-seller.

27–31. Upon a Town built in the place where a wood grew; From whence 'tis called the Dukes-Wood, or the Burse.

32–6. Upon navigable River cut through a Town built out of a Wood.

37–41. Upon the Medows over-flown there.

42–6. Upon a piece of ground ore-flown, where once a Leaguer quartered.

47–51. A Dutch Captain of Foot, having with his Soldiers entred a Breach, and there a while fought valiantly with a Two-handed Sword; In the very point of Victory, being mortally wounded, spake thus:

52. His Will.
53–5. To the Prince of Aurange, on his famous Victory over the Spaniards in Dukes-Wood.
56. A Panegyrick on the Hollanders being Lords of the Sea. Occafioned by the Authors being in their Army at Dukes-Wood.
57. To Sleep, ftealing upon him as he ftood upon the Guard in the corner of a running Trench, at the fiege of Duke's-Wood.
58. To his Fellow Sentinels.
59. In Comædam celeberrimam *Cinthiam* dictam ad inftantiam alterius fecit. Idem Anglicè verfum.
   On one particular paffage of her action, when fhe was to be ftript of her cloaths by Fulvio, but not without much refiftance. Videns excogitavit.

Ignatius his Conclave: As in the editions of 1611 et seq. (subtitle dated 1653) but without the leaves *The printer to the Reader*. See no. 10.

Essayes in Divinity: See no. 50 (title-page dated 1651).

Note: Printed, with the exception of the *Essayes in Divinity*, by Thomas Newcomb (1649–81). The lines by Ben Jonson on A8*b* are from his *Epigrams*, 1616; they were also printed in Donne's *Poems* of 1650 (no. 82); pp. 65, 68 are misnumbered 56, 86.

Copies: BM, DWL; HCL, HEH, YUL.
   Trinity College, Cambridge.
   New College, Edinburgh.
   G. L. Keynes; R. S. Pirie (Jennings copy).

46 PARADOXES, PROBLEMES, ESSAYES [Wing D 1867] third edition, second (or first?) issue   12° 1652

Title (within ornamental border): Paradoxes, Problemes, Effayes, Characters, Written By Dr Donne Dean of Pauls: . . . London, Printed by T:N: for Humphrey Mofeley at the Prince's Armes in St Pauls Churchyard, 1652. [*see facsimile*]

Collation: As in no. 45.

Contents: A1 title; A2*a*–A6*a* dedication; A6*b*–A8*a* The table; A8*b* Ben. Johnfon to the Author; B1–L4, *A*1–*L*4 as in no. 45.

Paradoxes, etc.: As in no. 45.

Note: In this issue the first quire of eight leaves has been reset, but the other sheets have been left untouched. There are certain minor alterations in the title-page, and the dedication, which is printed in a different type, contains an additional adulatory passage on A3*b*. Mrs. Simpson suggested (p. 136) that this may be the earlier issue of the two, the passage having been expunged from no. 45 on account of its possible misinterpretation.

Copies: BM (2, both lacking *Essayes*), BLO, NLS (Signet Library copy); HCL, FSLW, NLC, NYPL.

Oxford Colleges: Christ Church, Queen's.

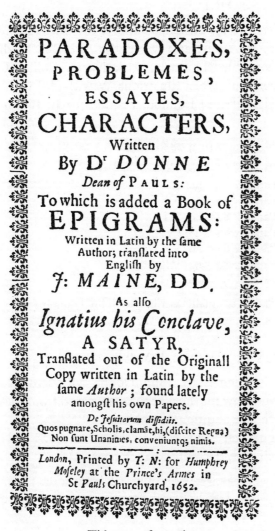

PARADOXES,
PROBLEMES,
ESSAYES,
CHARACTERS,
Written
By Dr *DONNE*
Dean of PAULS:
To which is added a Book of
EPIGRAMS:
Written in Latin by the same
Author; translated into
Englilh by
J: MAINE, DD.
As allo
Ignatius his Conclave,
A SATYR,
Tranflated out of the Originall
Copy written in Latin by the
fame *Author* ; found lately
amongft his own Papers.

De Jefuitarum diffidiis.
Quos pugnare, Scholis, clamāt, hi, (difcite Regna)
Non funt Unanimes, conveniuntq; nimis.

London, Printed by *T: N:* for *Humphrey Mofeley* at the *Prince's Armes* in
St *Pauls* Churchyard, 1652.

Title-page of no. 46

Cathedral Libraries: Cashel, Lambeth Palace, Worcester.

G. L. Keynes (2, one in elaborately tooled morocco, g.e., silk ties, but lacking *A*2–5 of the first book and *A*1–6 of the second); R. S. Pirie (Tollemache copy).

Thomas Otway possessed a copy inscribed: *Sum e libris Tho:Otway | ex AEde Christi Oxon | 1671.* (Sotheby's, 25 November 1957, lot 19.)

46*a* ATHENIAN SPORT   8° 1707

Title (within double rule): Athenian Sport: or, Two Thousand Paradoxes merrily argued to Amuse and Divert the Age: . . . With Improvements from the Honourable Mr. Boyle, Lock, Norris, Collier, Cowley, Dryden, Garth, Addison, and other Illustrious Wits. [rule] By a Member of the Athenian Society. [rule] London, Printed for B. Bragg in Paternoster-Row. 1707.

Collation: A⁸ a⁸ B–Z⁸ Aa–Mm⁸; 288 leaves.

Contents: p. 307 Paradox 61—no. IX.
            p. 308 Paradox 62—no. X.
            p. 314 Paradox 66—no. XI.
            p. 389 Paradox 82—no. III.
            p. 395 Paradox 84—no. IV.
            p. 399 Paradox 87—no. VI.
            p. 401 Paradox 89—no. VII.
            p. 402 Paradox 90—no. VIII.

Note: This compilation is usually ascribed to John Dunton (1659–1733), bookseller and literary hack.

46*b* PARADOXES & PROBLEMES   12° 1923

Paradoxes and Problemes by John Donne with two Characters and an Essay of Valour Now for the first time reprinted from the editions of 1633 and 1652 with one additional Probleme
Soho The Nonesuch Press 30 Gerrard Street 1923
22 cm, pp. viii, 80; decorated paper boards.

Note: 645 numbered copies were printed in Fell types at the Oxford University Press on hand-made paper. The additional *Probleme* is from the Bodleian Tanner MS. There is a Bibliographical Preface by Geoffrey Keynes.

Reviewed: McCarthy, D., *New Statesm.* XXII, 1923, 17.

46c DEFENCE OF WOMEN 1925

Jack Donne A Defence of Women for their Inconstancy & their Paintings made by Jack Donne & Printed now with five decorations by Norman Lindsay and published by the Fanfrolico Press
London [1925]
19 cm, pp. [12]; cloth.

Note: 370 copies printed. A reprint of Paradoxes I and II, with very unpleasant decorations.

46d JUVENILIA 4° 1936

Ivvenilia Or Certaine Paradoxes and Problems by John Donne Reproduced from the First Edition With a Bibliographical Note by R. E. Bennett
Published for the Facsimile Text Society By Columbia University Press
New York: M.CM.XXXVI.
19 cm, pp. [viii], [62]; cloth.

46e PROBLEME XI 1943

Headed: John Donne Why doth the pox soe much affect to undermine the nose?

Colophon: Pox. Populi. Press. MCMXLIII
21·5 cm, a single leaf folded.

Note: Privately printed by Charles D. O'Malley[1] at the White Knights Press, San Francisco, California.

[1] Late Professor of Anatomy, University of California, School of Medicine.

BIATHANATOS

BIBLIOGRAPHICAL PREFACE

BIATHANATOS is the earliest of Donne's controversial writings. His neurotic temperament had for many years been fascinated by the thought of suicide, and he had touched on the subject in two of his Paradoxes— V, 'That all things kill themselves', and IX, 'That only Cowards dare dye'. Later, probably in 1608, he sought by the most ingenious casuistry to justify the act of self-destruction.

> Whensoever any affliction assailes me [he wrote in the preface to *Biathanatos*] mee thinks I have the keyes of my prison in mine owne hand, and no remedy presents it selfe so soone to my heart, as mine own sword. Often Meditation of this hath wonne me to a charitable interpretation of their action, who dy so: and provoked me a little to watch and exagitate their reasons, which pronounce so peremptory judgments upon them. . . . And though I know, that the malitious prejudged man, and the lazy affectors of ignorance, will use the same calumnies and obtrectations towards me, (for the voyce and sound of the Snake and Goose is all one) yet because I thought, that as in the poole of Bethsaida, there was no health till the water was troubled, so the best way to find the truth in this matter, was to debate and vexe it, I abstained not for feare of mis-interpretation from this undertaking. Our stomachs are not now so tender, and queasie, after so long feeding upon solid Divinity, nor we so umbragious and startling, having been so long enlightened in Gods path, that wee should thinke any truth strange to us, or relapse into that child-ish age, in which a Councell in France forbad *Aristotles Metaphysiques*, and punished with Excommunication the ex[s]cribing, reading, or having that booke.

Mrs. Simpson (p. 159) observed that the title should properly be *Biaio-thanatos*, that is, 'dying a violent death', but that Donne used it in an altered form, 'Biothanatum, a Selfe Murderer', in *Pseudo-Martyr*, p. 208, and as '*peccatum Biathanaton*, a sin that murders it self', in a sermon preached in 1615.[1]

---

[1] *XXVI Sermons*, 1660, p. 157.

Donne was unwilling either to publish or to destroy this curious and characteristic product of his brain, and it was therefore handed round to a few friends in manuscript. One such copy, not in Donne's autograph, but with marginal annotations in his hand, he gave to Sir Edward Herbert, afterwards Lord Herbert of Cherbury, who in 1642 passed it on to the Bodleian Library, where it still is (MS. e Musaeo 131). Donne sent with the manuscript a letter, still extant, in which he wrote:

S[r]

I make account that thys Booke hath inough perform'd that which yt undertooke, both by Argument and Example. Itt shall therfore the lesse neede to bee yttselfe another Example of the Doctrine. Itt shall not therfore kyll yttselfe; that ys, not bury itselfe. for if ytt should do so, those reasons by which that Act should bee defended or excus'd, were also lost with ytt. Since ytt ys content to liue, ytt cannot chuse a whol-somer ayre then your Library, where Autors of all complexions are preserud. If any of them grudge thys Booke a roome, and suspect ytt of new, or dangerous Doctrine, you, who know us all, can best Moderate. To these Reasons, which I know your Loue to mee wyll make in my fauor, and dischardge, you may add thys, That though thys Doctrine hath not beene tought nor defended by writers, yet they, most of any sorte of Men in the world, haue practisd ytt.

> your uery true and earnest frinde and
> Seruant and Louer
>
> J: Donne[1]

At a later date, in 1619, before going to Germany, Donne seems to have forgotten about Herbert's copy and he sent another to Sir Robert Karre with a letter in which he wrote:

. . . But besides the Poems, of which you took a promise, I send you another Book to which there belongs this History. It was written by me many years since; and because it is upon a misinterpretable subject, I have always gone so near suppressing it, as that it is onely not burnt: no hand hath passed upon it to copy it, nor many eyes to read it: only to

---

[1] Simpson, p. 161, from the original MS.; also in *Letters*, 1651, no. 7.

some particular friends in both Universities, then when I writ it, I did communicate it: And I remember, I had this answer, That certainly, there was a false thread in it, but not easily found: Keep it, I pray, with the same jealousie; let any that your discretion admits to the sight of it, know the date of it; and that it is a Book written by *Jack Donne*, and not by D. *Donne*: Reserve it for me, if I live, and if I die, I only forbid it the Presse, and the Fire: publish it not, but burn it not; and between those, do what you will with it.[1]

In spite of Donne's wish thus expressed his son assumed the responsibility of making it public with a dedication to Lord Herbert's son, and it was duly licensed on 20 September 1644. This has usually been taken to be the date of publication, which is not given on the title-page, though the printer has left a space for it. Mrs. Simpson pointed out, however (p. 149), that the book was not entered on the Stationers' Register until 25 September 1646, so that 1646 or 1647 must be the year of publication. It seems certain, however, that 1647 is the correct date. Donne dated his letter to the Earl of Denbigh 16 November 1647 (see below), and Thomason's copy in the British Museum is dated by him 2 December 1647. The book was then entered to Henry Seyle or Seale, who had published the *Juvenilia* in 1633. The incomplete title-page suggests that the book was set up in type and, perhaps, most of it printed, in 1644, but that publication was delayed for some reason unknown. When the book was actually published three years later the printer forgot to make the necessary addition to the title-page. This edition is not very uncommon, but the majority of copies contain the title-page which was substituted for the original one in 1648. Seyle's rights were transferred to Humphrey Moseley on 13 June 1649, and, in anticipation of this, Moseley's name appears on the title-page of 1648.

A number of copies of *Biathanatos* were given by the younger Donne to his friends and patrons, sometimes accompanied by letters, and the following are known:

1. Inscribed to: 'Ye Rt. Honourable the Kinsmoll', i.e. Lady Kingsmell.
    (Formerly in the possession of Prof. S. G. Dunn.)

---

[1] *Letters*, 1651, no. 8.

2.   For his much honored frinde Mr Lee at the Cockpitt
     S^r

I take the bouldnesse to present to your hands this booke, hopinge that it may bee welcome to you, euen for the Patrones sake, who has receaued it soe nobly, that, I cannot doubt, but that all his frinds, will entertaine it as somethinge that belongs to my Lorde Herbert, and, has lyen still these fiftie last years, to expect a Patrone noble inough to entertaine a Peece that is an absolute Originall, and, I thinke, drawen by noe very ill a hande.

S^r your most humble Seruant
Jo: Donne[1]

Couent Garden
     October 26

(Cambridge University Library, G. 11. 8)

3.   For ye R^t w^{ll} Edward Carter Esq.
     S^r

I haue, here, sent you a Booke, that may, peraduenture, giue you some entertainement out of the noueltie of the subiect, but that is not all my reason of presentinge it to you, at this time; For, since I liued in this Parish I haue published a Volume of 80 Sermons preached by my Father, and haue prepared 60 more, which are licensed, and entered in the Printers halle, which is, as farr as I can driue them vntill the times allter;[2] I was encouradged to vndertake this worke, by the learnedest men in the kingdome, of all professions, and was often told, that I shoud deserue better by doinge soe, then by keeping them to my owne vse, for by this meanes, I did not only preach to the present adge, but to our childrens children; S^r, I write this to you, that you may iudg what a sad condition a Scholler is in, when at a publicke vestry, in this Parish, I was told by a pittifull ignorant Baker, I was an idle man and neuer preached

your humble seruant
Jo: Donne[3]
(Cambridge University Library, H.*6. 46(E)

[1] First printed in Walton's *Lives*, ed. Zouch, 4° 1796, and 8° 1807.
[2] See p. 69 of the present book.
[3] First printed in Walton's *Lives*, ed. Zouch, 4° 1796, and 8° 1807. Also by Simpson, p. 165.

4.   For ye R^t Honb^{le} the Earle of Denby.

    My Lorde

       Havinge with fower yeares care, and some arte, procured this Boocke to bee printed, which, beeinge writ upon a misinterpretable Doctrin, was in a daunger of beinge called in, and my Impression seazed on: In your Lo^{ps} absence from this towne, I was faine to begg for it anothers Protection. If your Lordship will bee pleased, at your leasure, to loock vpon it, I doubt not, but you will thinck it was very fitt to bee preserued by mee, with all industry, and that I am not ye less fitt by hauinge had that care to bee

       My Lorde

          Your Lo^{ps} most humble and obedient Seruant

                     Jo: Donne

    Nouember i6
      i647

(Pennant colln., Newnham Paddox, Rugby, sold at Christie's 4 July 1938, lot 61. Now in HCL.)

5.   To Sr Constantine Huygens Knight.[1]

    Sr.

       Beeinge lately told, by a gentleman of our Nation, that the Author of this Booke, had sometimes bin numbered amongst yr other Seruants, when you were in England, and, that you had an inclination to see this Paradox; I thoght, I might take the boldnesse, to put it into your hands, hearinge, you are soe great a fauorer of the languadge, it is writ in, as to vnderstande it; I did for manie years suppresse it, and had still kept to that resolution, but that, I thought it had enough performed, that, which it vndertoke, both by Argument, and Example, and therefore, the less needed to bee another Example of the Doctrine, and kill itselfe: that is, burie itselfe in a priuate and obscure Studdio; For, if it had done soe, those Reasons, by which that Act, should been Defended, or Excused, would bee allsoe lost with it. But, S^r, since it is content to liue, I presume it cannot chose a wholsomer ayre, then your Studio, where I beeleeue, Authors of all Complexions are preserued. If anie of them,

---

[1] Translator of Donne's poems into Dutch. See no. 108.

grudg this a roome, and suspect it, of daungerous and new Doctrine, you who know them all, can best moderate; To those reasons, which your loue to the Author will make, in his beehalfe, you may add this; That though this Doctrin hath not bin tought, nor defended by Writers, yet, thay, most of anie men in the worlde, haue practised it.

Sr Your most humble Seruant
John Donne[1]

Couent Garden
  London Julio 29
    1649

6. Given to the 'Lord Marquesse of Newcastle'. Now in HCL. (Formerly in Dr. Grosart's library, which is now in the Princeton Theological Seminary, U.S.A.)
7. Given to 'J. Marckham' with a letter (not recorded). (Cat. of Heber Library, pt. viii, no. 728.)
8. Given to the Earl of Oxford, with a long inscription on the fly-leaf. (Kay Library, sold at Sotheby's, 27 May 1930, lot 284. Tredegar Library, sold at Sotheby's, 1 June 1943, lot 207. Now FSLW.)
9. Inscribed 'A Present from Doctor John Dunne', but with no name. (Offered by Elkin Mathews Ltd., cat. 35, April 1931.)
10. Given to William Hodges (Heber–Britwell Court–Kern copy). R. S. Pirie.

Thus the younger Donne is seen quoting his father's letter to Herbert in his own less literate form and seeking patronage wherever he could find it.

No reasoned answer to Donne's 'paradox' was framed during the years immediately succeeding its publication, but his attitude was challenged in a volume of pietistic verses by Sir William Denny—*Pelecanicidium or the Christian Adviser against Self-Murder. London, for Thomas Hucklescott* (1653). [A–X⁸Y², with an allegorical frontispiece by F. Barlow.] In the *Proeme* Denny wrote (A5 *a–b*):

But mine Eares do tingle, to hear so many sad Relations, as even since March last concerning Severall Persons of diverse Rank, and Quality,

---

[1] Printed by R. M. Frye in *Notes and Queries*, cxcvii, 1952, 495. The book with the letter was in the possession of Dr. A. B. Grosart in 1863 (*Notes and Queries*, n.s. iii, iv, 1863, 295).

inhabiting within and about so Eminent a Citty, as late-fam'd London, that have made away and Murder'd Themselves. . . . Hence arose the Occasion of this Poeme . . . Lest the frequency of such Actions might in time arrogate a Kind of Legitimation by Custom, or plead Authority from some late-publisht Paradoxes, That Self-homicide was Lawfull.

Biathanatos attracted no further attention until the end of the century, when it was mentioned in Ezra Pierce's *Discourse of Self-Murder*, 1692, and was fully examined in J. Adams's *An Essay Concerning Self-Murther* . . . *With Some Considerations upon What is pretended . . . by the Author of a Treatise, intituled, Biathanatos, and Others*, London, 1700. Donne and Adams are associated in a reference by John Cockburn in his *Discourse of Self-Murder*, London, 1716, p. 30: '. . . that Copious, Learned and Laborious *Answer* of the Reverend Dr. Adams, to the most Imprudent as well as most Dangerous Book that ever was publish'd, I mean that of *Self-Murder*, which Dr. Donne's son set forth, as he says, according to his Father's Manuscript, but not much for his Father's Credit'. *Biathanatos* was again examined in Charle Moore's *A full enquiry into the subject of suicide*, 1790.[1] For other references to *Biathanatos* consult the sections of Biography and Criticism.

47 BIAΘANATOΣ [Wing D 1858] first edition   4° [1647]

Title (within double rules): BIAΘANATOΣ. . . . London, Printed by John Dawſon. [*see facsimile*]

Collation: ¶4 (*) *A*4 A–Z4 Aa–Dd4 Ee2; 120 leaves.

Contents: ¶1 blank; ¶2 title; ¶3*a*–¶4*b* dedication *To the Right Honourable the Lord Phillip Harbert* signed *Io: Donne. From my house in Covent-Garden. 28.*; (*) 1*a*–(*)2*b Authors cited in this Booke*; *A*1*a*–*A*4*b* (*A*2 with sign. ¶2) *Contents*; A1*a*–B4*b* (pp. 1–16) *Contents*; C1*a*–C4*b* (pp. 17–24) *The Preface, Declaring the Reaſons, the Purpoſe, the way, and the end of the author*; D1*a*–Ee2*b* (pp. 25–218 [should be 220]) text; at bottom of Ee2*b Imprimatur. Io: Ruſhworth. 20. Sept. 1644.*

---

[1] Another treatise was written, but never saw the light. John Sparrow has noted the following entry under the date 14 November 1705, in *Hearne's Collections*, vol. 1, Oxford, 1885, p. 73: 'Mr Kannell [*note:* this Mr. Kannell died in 1710] (Joseph) of Lincoln Col. writ a short Discourse against *Self-Murther* in opposition to Dr. *Donne*. He made some Application a little while since to get it printed, but could not prevail with anyone to undertake it, being a Book for wch. there is no manner of occasion. I am inform'd he is now quite off publishing it, being laugh'd at by some in the College, who entitle the Book, *Dr. Donne undone*.'

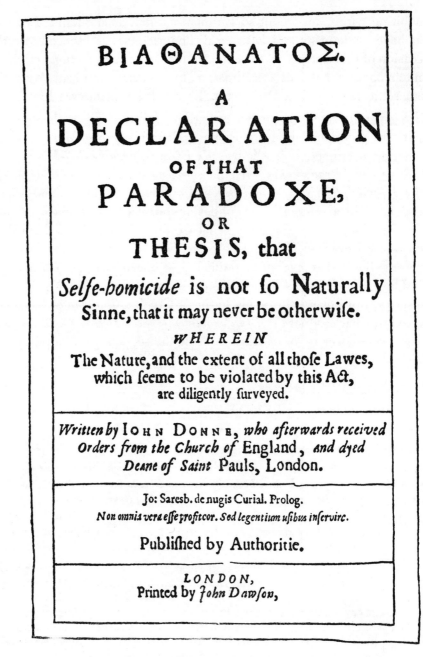

ΒΙΑΘΑΝΑΤΟΣ.

A
DECLARATION
OF THAT
PARADOXE,
OR
THESIS, that

Selfe-homicide is not so Naturally
Sinne, that it may never be otherwise.

WHEREIN
The Nature, and the extent of all those Lawes,
which seeme to be violated by this Act,
are diligently surveyed.

Written by IOHN DONNE, *who afterwards received*
Orders from the Church of England, *and dyed*
Deane of Saint Pauls, London.

Jo: Saresb. de nugis Curial. Prolog.
Non omnia vera esse profitcor. Sed legentium usibus inservire.

Published by Authoritie.

LONDON,
Printed by *John Dawson,*

Title-page of no. 47

Note: The late F. S. Ferguson pointed out to me that the conjugate leaves with sign. (*)
were originally imposed with Ee; occasionally they were left in that position.[1] P. 59 is
numbered 56, and numbers 192, 193 occur twice over, so that the number of
pages is two more than appears. The pagination begins very oddly on the fifth leaf of
the *Contents* list.

Some copies were printed on larger and finer paper than the bulk of the edition.
These have a 'bunch of grapes' watermark; the ordinary copies have a 'pot' watermark. At least three of the presentation copies (nos. 2, 4, and 10 above) are on the
larger paper, $7\frac{5}{8} \times 6$ in. as compared with $7\frac{5}{16} \times 5\frac{5}{8}$ in., and it is probable that
the special printing was made mainly for presentation (see R. S. Pirie, *The Book
Collector*, Autumn 1965, p. 362).

Copies: BM (2, one Ashley Library), BLO, ULC (3); HCL (4)[2], Chapin Library
(Gosse copy, in original sheep binding with printed label on back), HEH, NLC,
NYPL, LCW, PUL, TSP, YUL.
Cambridge Colleges: Emmanuel, St. John's.
Jesus College, Oxford.
New College, Edinburgh.
Cathedral Libraries: Peterborough, Winchester.
Inner Temple Library.
G. L. Keynes, R. S. Pirie (2)[3], J. Sparrow.

48 ΒΙΑΘΑΝΑΤΟΣ [Wing D 1859] first edition, second issue   4° 1648

Title (in red and black within ornamental border): ΒΙΑΘΑΝΑΤΟΣ... London,
Printed for Humphrey Moſeley, and are to be ſold at his ſhop at the
Princes Armes in St Pauls Churchyard. 1648. [*see facsimile*]

Collation, Contents: As in no. 47.

Note: The same sheets as in no. 47, with cancel title-page.

Copies: BM (2), BLO (with the name of Donne's daughter, Margaret Bowles, on the
title-page), NLS, TCD; HCL, HEH, NYPL, LCW, YUL.
Cambridge Colleges: Clare, King's, Magdalene (Pepys Library), Pembroke,
St. Catharine's, Trinity (4).
Oxford Colleges: All Souls, Christ Church, Corpus Christi, St. John's, Worcester.
Cathedral Libraries: Lincoln, St. Paul's.
John Rylands Library, Manchester; Lincoln's Inn Library.
G. L. Keynes, R. S. Pirie, J. Sparrow.

---

[1] As in a copy carrying the signature of Andrew Fletcher of Saltoun offered by Messrs. Robinson, cat. 84, April 1954.

[2] 2 copies presentation on large paper, nos. 4 and 6 above.

[3] 1 copy presentation on large paper, no. 10 above.

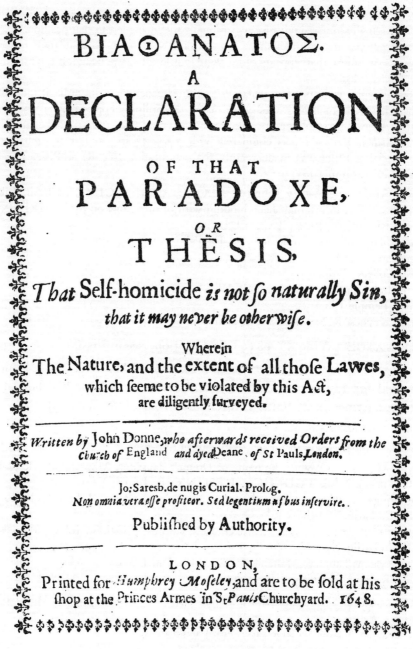

ΒΙΑΘΑΝΑΤΟΣ.
A
DECLARATION
OF THAT
PARADOXE,
OR
THESIS,

That Self-homicide *is not so naturally Sin,*
that it may never be otherwise.

Wherein
The Nature, and the extent of all those Lawes,
which seeme to be violated by this Act,
are diligently surveyed.

Written by John Donne, *who afterwards received Orders from the*
Church of England *and dyed* Deane *of* St Pauls London.

Jo: Saresb. de nugis Curial. Prolog.
Non omnia vera esse profiteor. Sed legentium usbus inservire.

Published by Authority.

LONDON,
Printed for *Humphrey Moseley,* and are to be sold at his
shop at the Princes Armes in St Pauls Churchyard. 1648.

Title-page of no. 48

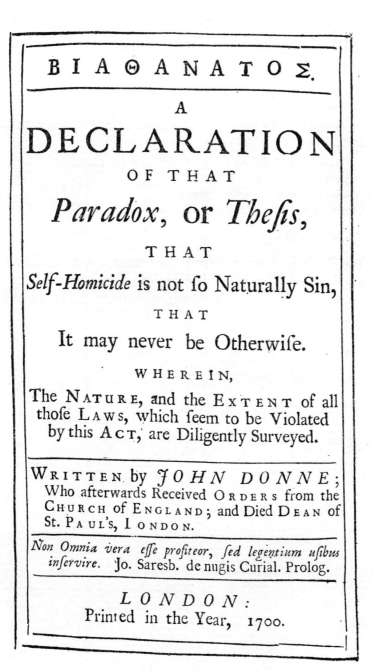

ΒΙΑΘΑΝΑΤΟΣ.

A
DECLARATION
OF THAT

Paradox, or Thesis,

THAT

Self-Homicide is not so Naturally Sin,

THAT

It may never be Otherwise.

WHEREIN,

The NATURE, and the EXTENT of all those LAWS, which seem to be Violated by this ACT, are Diligently Surveyed.

WRITTEN by *JOHN DONNE*; Who afterwards Received ORDERS from the CHURCH of ENGLAND; and Died DEAN of St. PAUL'S, LONDON.

Non Omnia vera esse profiteor, sed legentium usibus inservire. Jo. Saresb. de nugis Curial. Prolog.

LONDON:
Printed in the Year, 1700.

Title-page of no. 49

49 ΒΙΑΘΑΝΑΤΟΣ [Wing D 1860] second edition   8° 1700

Title (within double rules): ΒΙΑΘΑΝΑΤΟΣ. . . . London: Printed in the Year, 1700. [*see facsimile*]

Collation: a⁸ A–N⁸ O⁴; 116 leaves.

Contents: a1 title; a2*a–b* dedication; a3*a–b* authors; a4*a*–A8*b* contents; B1*a*–B4*b* (pp. I–VIII) preface; B5*a*–O3*b* (pp. 1–190) text; O4 blank.

Copies: BM, BLO, ULD, NLS; HCL, FSLW, PUL, YUL.
Christ's College, Cambridge.
Oxford Colleges: Christ Church, Merton.
G. L. Keynes; J. Sparrow, R. S. Pirie, Wilmarth S. Lewis (Horace Walpole's copy).

49*a* BIATHANATOS   8° [1930]

Biathanatos By John Donne Reproduced from the first edition With a bibliographical note by J. William Hebel
New York: The Facsimile Text Society. Oxford: B. H. Blackwell
19·5 cm, pp. 218.

ESSAYES IN DIVINITY

BIBLIOGRAPHICAL PREFACE

DONNE'S *Essayes in Divinity* were formerly believed to have been written about the years 1614–15. The editor, John Donne the younger, stated in his preface *To the Reader*, 'that they were the voluntary sacrifices of severall hours, when he had many debates betwixt God and himself, whether he were worthy, and competently learned to enter into Holy Orders', but Gosse (II, 63) regarded them as nothing more than scholastic exercises and conjectured that 'they were written to be laid before the Archbishop as proof of the soundness of the author's orthodoxy and the breadth of his learning'. Probably, however, this view was further from the truth than the younger Donne's, the *Essayes* being a genuine record of their author's uncertainties in his transition from a lay to a clerical life. Mrs. Simpson in the introduction to her edition of 1952 (no. 51*a*) supported this belief, regarding Gosse's inference as inconclusive, since several dates between 1611 and January 1615 could fit the statement. She believed in 1952 that the *Essayes* were written later than *Ignatius*, and indeed after the *Anniversaries*, to which they were very closely related, as well as to the early sermons. Later she told Dame Helen Gardner that she had changed her mind, placing them just before the poems. Her ground for the change was her observation that Donne's biblical references in the *Essayes* were based primarily on the Geneva version. Had they been composed after the publication of the Authorized Version in 1611 he would surely have used this instead.[1]

Gosse tended to underrate the value and interest of the *Essayes*, though admitting that the four Prayers with which the volume ends, noted by Izaak Walton in his copy of the book as 'Prayers used before his Sermons', have a more obvious emotional and biographical value than the *Essayes* themselves. Mrs. Simpson in her careful analysis of the text concluded that, though the book consists of desultory thoughts rather than being a consecutive and organized work, it has, nevertheless, many passages of great value and beauty. It was, after all, a posthumous publication, never worked over and polished by its author.

[1] See R. E. Hughes, *The Progress of the Soul*, 1969, p. 290, note.

The *Essayes* were printed by Thomes Maxey for Richard Marriot and published in 1651, but the book is usually found bound up with the *Juvenilia* of 1652 (nos. 45 and 46) under the title *Paradoxes, Problemes, Essayes, Characters*, without any specific mention of *Essayes in Divinity*. The reasons for this have been suggested on p. 95. The *Juvenilia* were printed in a different shop (Thomas Newcomb) for a different publisher (Humphrey Moseley), but already some copies of the *Essayes in Divinity* had been bound and sold separately as recorded below. As further evidence that they were first published as a separate book it may be remarked that Thomason dated his copy, now in the British Museum (E. 1362. 371), 'January 1ˢᵗ [1651/2],[1] and his copy of the *Juvenilia* (E. 1359. 267) 'November 8ᵗʰ [1652]'.[2] Moreover, the *Essayes* were advertised as a separate book in Humphrey Moseley's list of 1651 and by William London in his *Catalogue of the most vendible Books in England*, 1658 (f. M2a).

When the younger Donne decided to make the *Juvenilia* more respectable by adding the *Essayes in Divinity* he felt he must try to suppress his dedication to Sir Henry Vane the younger with the confusing results detailed on p. 128. It seems probable that the address to Vane (1613–62), republican and regicide, came to be regarded as impolitic when he was dedicating the composite volume to Francis Lord Newport (1619–1708), a consistent royalist.

One of the copies with the dedication intact must have been available to Dr. Jessopp, who included it in his scarce edition of 1855. He also modernized the spelling and punctuation. The original text is faithfully reproduced in Mrs. Simpson's Oxford edition of 1952 together with full annotations and a list of Donne's sources.

The *Essayes in Divinity* have been printed in facsimile by the Scolar Press Ltd., Menston, Ilkley, Yorks.

50 ESSAYES IN DIVINITY   12° 1651

Title (within ornamental border): Essayes in Divinity . . . London, Printed by T. N. for Richard Marriot, and are to be fold at his Shop in Sᵗ Dunstan's Church-yard Fleet-ſtreet. 1651. [*see facsimile*][3]

[1] In a modern binding, with leaves A2, 5 cancelled, leaving A3, 4, 6, which is unusual if it was bought separately.   [2] In a modern binding without the *Essayes*.

[3] In the sixth line *S Paul's* should be *Sᵗ Paul's*, but the small superior *t*, being very imperfectly inked in all copies, cannot be shewn in the reproduction.

Collation: A^6 ($\pm$A2–6) π^2 ($\pm\pi$2) B–K^{12} L^4; 120 leaves.

Contents: A1 title; A2*a*–6*b* dedication to Sr *H. Vane Junior* signed *John Donne* (A2 with sig. A3, A2–6 usually cancelled in whole or in part); π 1*a*–*b To the Reader*, unsigned; π 2 blank (usually cancelled); B1*a*–K11*a* (pp. 1–213) *Essayes in Divinity*; K11*b*–L4*b* (pp. 214–24) *Prayers*.

Note: The *collation* and *contents* were wrongly given in the previous editions of this bibliography. The true constitution was greatly confused by the binders, who were

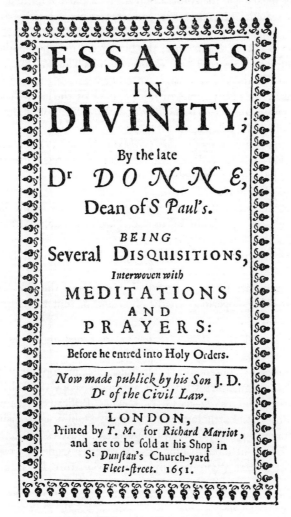

Title-page of no. 50

themselves confused by having been instructed to cancel the whole of the dedication (*A*2–6) when it was decided to issue the book as an adjunct to the *Juvenilia* of 1652, thus leaving the title-page as a detached leaf. This was further complicated by the leaf, *To the Reader*, being an insertion conjugate with a blank, which should normally have been removed, leaving only a stub, though sometimes left in position folded so as to come before its fellow. The truth became clear to me when I re-examined my complete and unsophisticated copy of the first separate issue of the book in its original binding. In this 'ideal copy' the constitution as given above is quite plain, though I did not at first appreciate it. The copies sold as a separate book usually have the dedication intact. In the composite volume the cancellation was often very carelessly done. Sometimes only *A*2–5 were removed; the binder did not then bother to reduce *A*6 to a stub, but left it and placed *To the Reader* with its blank (as in one of my copies of no. 46) between *A*6 and the title-page. In other copies *A*3–4 and 6 have been left. Occasionally, as in one of my copies of no. 45, none of the leaves has been cancelled, even the blank conjugate with *To the Reader*, being folded round the whole gathering so as to come before the title-page.[1]

The book was printed by Thomas Maxey (1637–57) for Richard Marriot. Mrs. Simpson was the first to detect the fact that some press corrections were made:

(i) *A*3 verso, lines 3–4: 'was obliged in a civil / business', altered to read: 'was obliged in Civill / business'.

(ii) π1 verso, lines 4–6: 'are now publish'd, both / to testifie his modest Va- / luation of himself, and /. . .', altered to read: 'are now publish'd both / to testifie his modest Va- / luation of himself and / . . .'.

(iii) H2 recto, last two lines: '. . . tribute ju- / ly . . .', altered to read: ' . . . tribut just- / ly . . .'.

These corrections are likely to be found in copies of the first separate issue, the corrected sheets being uppermost in the shop and so sent to the booksellers before those not corrected.

Copies: (*a*) With *Paradoxes, Problemes, Essayes* as recorded under nos. 45 and 46. One of mine has leaves *A*2–6.

(*b*) Separate copies in contemporary bindings: Isham copy, Lamport Hall, with leaves *A*2–6; St. Augustine's College, Canterbury, copy (Sotheby's 21 December 1948, lot 354) with leaves *A*2–6; G. L. Keynes, Prideaux Place copy, with leaves *A*2–6; R. S. Pirie, St. Bartholomew's Vicarage, Dublin, copy, with leaves *A*2–6; R. S. Pirie, Jennings–Cherry–Garrard copy, lacking leaves *A*2–6.

(*c*) Separate copies in modern bindings: Worcester College, Oxford, with leaves *A*2–6; R. S. Pirie, Izaak Walton's copy, with his signature, but lacking leaves *A*2–6.

---

[1] In one of my copies of no. 46, in an elaborately tooled contemporary morocco binding with silk ties, the binder became so upset that he cancelled both *A*2–5 (the dedication) in the first book and *A*1–6, this including the title-page, in the second book.

51 ESSAYS IN DIVINITY   12° 1855

Essays in divinity by John Donne, D.D. some time Dean of St. Paul's.
Edited by Augustus Jessopp, M.A. of St. John's College, Cambridge.
London: John Tupling, 320 Strand. 1855.
    14·8 cm, 1 l. title, verso blank; 1 l. dedication to *Philip Bliss*, verso blank;
    pp. ix–lxxiv *Some notice of the author and his writings*; 1 l. facsimile of
    the title-page of no. 50, verso blank; pp. 1–245 text; 1 p. blank;
    3 ll. *A list of words . . . remarkable in their form or usage*. Purple cloth
    with paper label on spine.

Note: 2 leaves are unaccounted for in the pagination at the beginning. Six copies were
printed on thick paper. This edition is unaccountably scarce.

Copies: HCL, PUL.
    G. L. Keynes; I. A. Shapiro (Jessopp's copy, on thick paper); J. Sparrow.

51*a* ESSAYS IN DIVINITY   8° 1952

Essays in Divinity by John Donne Edited by Evelyn M. Simpson Oxford
    At the Clarendon Press 1952
    22 cm, pp. xxx, 137, [3]; black cloth.

Note: An edition of *Donne's Shorter Prose Works* was announced by a New York
publisher to appear in 1948, edited by Mrs. Simpson and Professor R. E. Bennett.
This was afterwards abandoned owing to the publisher's failure, and part of the
material was used in the above edition of *Essays in Divinity*.

Reviewed: A[llen], D. C., *Mod. Lang. Notes*, LXVIII, 1953, 280; Grierson, H. J. C.,
Mod. Lang. Rev. XLVIII, 1953, 73–4; Jenkins, C., *Rev. Eng. Stud.* N.S. IV, 1953,
287; Swansea & Brecon, Edward *Journ. Theol. Stud.* IV, 1953, 132–4.

LETTERS

BIBLIOGRAPHICAL PREFACE

THE great majority of those of Donne's letters that have survived have been preserved through the energy of his son, John Donne, D.C.L. A few had been printed by Marriot in the early editions of the poems. Later, in 1651, the younger Donne issued a volume containing 129 *Letters to severall persons of honour*; these letters were not 'edited' by him according to the standards of the present day, as, although printed with reasonable care, their arrangement is irregular and they are for the most part without dates. Nevertheless they have much literary and biographical importance and become of great interest when modern scholarship has assigned to them their proper dates and positions in relation to the events of Donne's life. This necessary editing was begun by Gosse, and in his *Life and Letters of Donne*, London, 1899 (p. 235), the letters can be read with more appreciation than had previously been possible. The younger Donne further increased our obligations to him by editing in 1660 in the same manner a collection of letters which had been made by Sir Tobie Matthew; this collection includes, among a number of letters to and from Donne, twenty-five from him which had not been printed before, and the majority of these were incorporated by Gosse in his book already mentioned. Ten new letters were printed from manuscripts at Loseley House, Surrey, in *The Loseley Manuscripts*, 1835, by A. J. Kempe, and eight of these were reprinted by Gosse. Finally Gosse himself was able to add from manuscript sources nineteen letters which had not previously been printed, so that his volumes contain the only authoritative collection of Donne's letters that has yet been made. A few more letters, also used by Gosse, have been gathered from other sources and are recorded in the entries following. The only important fresh discovery of letters from Donne made since the publication of Gosse's *Life* is in the collection of thirty-two written to Sir Henry Wotton and others found by Mr. Logan Pearsall Smith in a commonplace-book in the library of the late Mr. G. H. Finch at Burley-on-the-Hill. These were also seen by Sir Herbert Grierson, and were transcribed by order of the Clarendon Press—very fortunately, as the manuscript was destroyed not long afterwards in a fire at Burley-on-the-Hill. The letters were first printed by Mrs. Simpson in her *Study of the Prose Works*, 1924, but the authorship of most of them is questioned by Professor Shapiro (see no. 68*a*, note). Three more letters were added by Mr. John Hayward in his Nonesuch edition of the *Complete Poems and Selected Prose* (1929). One new letter was printed in *The London Mercury* (December 1925); another was privately printed at Harvard in 1930. Two others are recorded under nos. 69 *f* and 69 *g*. It is possible that other letters from Donne may yet come to light.[1]

The text of the 154 letters printed in 1651 and 1660 cannot now be verified, the original manuscripts of only two of them being known to be extant. Their dates and places can therefore be determined in many instances only by reasoning from internal evidence. This task is being undertaken by Professor I. A. Shapiro, who has published some of his preliminary results (see p. 360), and he states that a complete edition of Donne's letters is in course of preparation, in which many of Gosse's dates and attributions as given below, will have to be altered. Publication is expected in 1972.

52 POEMS   4° 1633

Title: Poems, By J. D. . . . 1633 [see no. 78]

Letters: Eleven prose letters were printed among the *Poems* of 1633 (see pp. 154–6, nos. 79, 88, and 158–66). These were reprinted in all later editions of the *Poems* up to 1719. Nos. 159–66 appear also among the *Letters* of 1651.

53 POEMS   8° 1635

Title: Poems, By J. D. . . . 1635 [see no. 79]

Letters: Four new letters were added in this edition to those already printed in the *Poems*

---

[1] Copies in a seventeenth-century hand of five letters from Donne were sold at Puttick and Simpson's on 19 December 1855, and were acquired by J. H. Anderdon. His collection was sold in 1879, and the Donne letters seem to have passed into O'Flahertie's possession. They were printed by Gosse in 1899 (see no. 67), and were stated to be 'in the possession of J. H. Anderdon Esq.', though this was certainly not so at that date. Professor Shapiro informs me that the Anderdon MS. consisted of two folio leaves, perhaps at one time conjugate. In 1897 one leaf (containing the letters printed by Gosse, I, 109; II, 16, 206) belonged to Miss Hilda Donne of Chester, and it now belongs to her niece, Miss Mary Donne of Abbey Square, Chester. The other leaf (containing the letters printed by Gosse, I, 309; II, 33) is in the possession of Mr. Roger Barrett of Chicago, whose father bought it at the sale of a collection in Syracuse, New York, before 1900. The two leaves are covered on both sides with writing in the same seventeenth-century hand, apparently that of a professional copyist.

of 1633 (see p. 160, nos. 20–3); these four appear in later editions of the *Poems* up to 1719 and among the *Letters* of 1651.

54 LXXX SERMONS   F° 1640

Title: LXXX Sermons Preached By ... Iohn Donne, ... MDCXL [see no. 29]

Letter: In Walton's *Life and Death of Dr Donne*.

    On B5*b*: [To George Garrard] January 7. 1630 (*Poems*, 1635, no. 23; *Letters*, 1651, no. 87; Walton's *Life*, 1658, no. 1; *Lives*, 1670 and 1675; Gosse, II, 268).

Note: Some passages are here omitted from the letter.

55 LETTERS [Wing D 1864] first edition   4° 1651

Title: Letters To Severall Persons Of Honour: ... London, Printed by J. Flesher, for Richard Marriot, and are to be sold at his shop in St Dunstans Church-yard under the Dyall. 1651. [*see facsimile*]

Collation: A^4 B–Z^4 Aa–Sf^4; 164 leaves.

Contents: A1 blank; A2 title; A3*a*–A4*b* The Epistle Dedicatory To the most virtuous and excellent Lady M^{ris}. Bridget Dunch[1] signed *Jo. Donne* [*jun.*]; B1*a*–Sf3*b* (pp. 1–318) text; Sf4 blank.

Frontispiece: Inserted between A1 and A2. A bust of Donne at the age of 49 within an oval, 12 × 9·5 cm, engraved by Pieter Lombart after the oil-painting now at the Deanery of St. Paul's. The whole engraving measures 15·5 × 10 cm, and is inscribed on a cloth hanging beneath the portrait:

Viri seraphici Joannis Donne Qua-
dragenarii Effigies vera, Qui post
eam ætatem Sacris initiatus Ec-
clesiæ S^{ti} Pauli Decanus obiit.

$$A\bar{n}o \begin{cases} D\bar{o}m \ 1631° \\ \textit{Ætatis suæ } 59° \end{cases}$$

The engraving is signed at the right-hand bottom corner: *Lombart sculp. A londre.*

Letters: PAGE

    1. To the worthiest Lady M^{rs}. Bridget White. Strand S. Peters day at nine.
        [29 June 1610?] (Tobie Matthew collection, no. 5; Gosse, I, 234)   1
    2. To the worthiest Lady M^{rs} B[ridget] W[hite] Strand S. Peters day at 4.
        [1610?] (Gosse, I, 235)   3
    3. To the same. Novemb. 8 [1610?] (Gosse, I, 235)   4

---

[1] Daughter of Sir Anthony Hungerford by his first marriage with Elizabeth, daughter of Sir Thomas Lucy, wife of Edmund Dunch of Wittenham, Berks. (see Gosse, I, 233).

LETTERS

TO
SEVERALL PERSONS
OF HONOUR:

WRITTEN BY

JOHN DONNE
Sometime Deane of
St Pauls London.

Published by JOHN DONNE Dr. of
the Civill Law.

LONDON,
Printed by *J. Flesher,* for *Richard Marriot,* and are
to be sold at his shop in St *Dunstans* Church-yard
under the Dyall. 1651.

Title-page of no. 55

Viri seraphici Ioannis Donne Qua=
dragenarij Effigies vera, Qui post
eam ætatem Sacris initiatus Ec=
. clesiæ Sti Pauli Decanus obijt.
Anõ { Dõm 1631°
{ Ætatis suæ 59°

Lombart Sculp Alondre

[1] The original MS., in a damaged state, was sold with the library of Edward Dalton at Hodgson's, 1 February 1934, lot 558; it was resold at Sotheby's with the Tredegar library, 1 June 1943, lot 219, and was sold by Messrs. Maggs Bros. from their cat. 597, 1943, but cannot now be traced.

[2] Gosse, 11, 122, states that 'O'Flahertie met with the original', but was evidently confusing this with the copy in O'Flahertie's MS.

[1] This letter should not have been included. It is a draft of a letter from Sir Henry Goodere to the Earl of Salisbury, 1609. See S. Johnson, *Mod. Lang. Notes*, LXIII, 1948, 38–9, where it is suggested that the draft may have been made for Goodere by Donne.

Note: The portrait by Lombart, which appears in this and the succeeding edition of the *Letters,* is very finely engraved. The same plate was used in two editions of Walton's *Lives,* 1670 and 1675, but by that time it had become worn and the impressions are poor. Pp. 182–3 are numbered 183–2. One of the copies in the BM (1086. h. 1) is on large and thick paper, 20·4 × 15·3 cm. The NYPL copy also appears to be on large paper. Also R. S. Pirie, 19·5 × 14·8 cm (Buxton–Forman–Litchfield copy).

Copies: BM (2), BLO, NLS; HCL (2), HEH (2), FSLW, NYPL, LCW, PUL, YUL.
    Cambridge Colleges: Magdalene, Pembroke, St. John's (no portrait), Trinity.
    Oxford Colleges: Christ Church, Worcester.
    Salisbury Cathedral Library (Izaak Walton's copy, with his signature in two places;[1] also that of his son, Canon Izaak Walton, dated 1683). Carlisle Cathedral Library.
    G. L. Keynes; R. S. Pirie (2, one on large paper)

56 LETTERS [Wing D 1865] first edition, second issue   4° 1654

Title: Letters To Severall Perfons Of Honour: . . . London, Printed by J. Flefher, and are to be fold by John Sweeting, at the Angel in Popeshead-Alley. 1654. [*see facsimile*]

Collation: A⁴ (±A2) B–Z⁴; 164 leaves.

Contents, Frontispiece, Letters: As in no. 55.

Note: The same sheets as in no. 55, with cancel title-page.

Copies: BM (2), BLO; HCL, HEH, FSLW (Hagen copy with notes by Malone), PUL, YUL.
    Cambridge Colleges: Corpus Christi, Trinity.
    Oxford Colleges: Jesus, Worcester.
    Chapter Library, Windsor.
    G. L. Keynes; R. S. Pirie (2nd Ld. Herbert of Cherbury—Powis copy)

57 CABALA [Wing C 184]   4° 1654

Title (within single rule): Cabala, Myfteries of State, in Letters of the great Minifters of K. James and K. Charles. Wherein Much of the publique Manage of Affaires is related. [rule] Faithfully Collected by a Noble Hand [ornament between rules].
London, Printed for M.M. G.Bedell, and T. Collins, and are to be fold at their Shop at the Middle-Temple Gate in Fleetftreet, 1654.

---

[1] Also textual alterations in his hand; see J. E. Butt in *Rev. Eng. Stud.* viii, 1932, 72–4

LETTERS

TO
SEVERALL PERSONS
OF HONOUR:

WRITTEN BY

JOHN DONNE

Sometime Deane of
St Pauls London.

Published by JOHN DONNE Dr. of
the Civill Law.

LONDON,
Printed by *J. Flesher*, and are to be sold by *John Sweeting*, at the Angel in Popeshead-Alley.
1 6 5 4.

Title-page of no. 56

Collation: A⁸ B–Z⁴ Aa–Zz⁴ Aa⁴; 196 leaves.

Contents: A1 blank; A2 title; A3*a*–A4*a* preface; A4*b* blank; A5*a*–A8*b* contents; B1*a*–Yy2*a* (pp. 1–347) text; Yy2*b* blank; Yy3*a*–Zz4*b* index; Aa1*a*–4*b Books printed for G. Bedell,* etc.

Letters: Donne's letters are as follows:

　　1. p. 314. Dr. Donne to the Marqueſſe of Buckingham. 13ᵗʰ Septemb. 1621. (Gosse, ii, 147)

　　2. p. 315. Dr. Donne to the Duke [of Buckingham] [1623–4] (Gosse, ii, 207; Tobie Matthew collection, no. 9)

Note: In the same year *A ſupplement of the Cabala* was issued, and a general title-page: *Cabala: five ſcrinia ſacra . . . 1654.,* was inserted between A1 and A2 of the present work. A second edition was published in 1663, and a third in 1691.

Copies: BM, ULC, NLS; HCL (2), HEH, FSLW, YUL.
　　Trinity College, Cambridge.
　　G. L. Keynes; J. Sparrow; R. S. Pirie.

58 WALTON'S LIFE OF DONNE   12° 1658

Title: The Life Of John Donne . . . 1658 [see no. 150]

Letters:

　　1. p. 100. [To George Garrard 7 January 1630] (*Poems,* 1635, no. 23; *80 Sermons,* 1640; *Letters,* 1651, no. 87; *Lives,* 1670 and 1675; Gosse, ii, 268)

　　2. p. 122. To all my friends: Sir H. Goodere [1612] (*Letters,* 1651, no. 17; Gosse, ii, 7)

　　3. p. 128. To Sir H. Goodere [7 September 1608] (*Letters,* 1651, no. 18; Gosse, i, 190)

　　4. p. 134. To Sir H. Goodere [1608?] (*Letters,* 1651, no. 12; Gosse, i, 195)

　　5. p. 141. To the Honᵇˡᵉ Lady, the Lady Kingsmel, upon the death of her Husband. 26 Octob. 1624. (*Letters,* 1651, no. 5; Tobie Matthew collection, no. 4; Gosse, ii, 210)

Note: Part of no. 3 was incorporated in the edition of Walton's *Lives* published in 1670; nos. 2, 4, and 5 were omitted. Walton's version of no. 3 is different from that of the *Letters* of 1651.

59 TOBIE MATTHEW COLLECTION [Wing M 1319] first edition   8° 1660

Title: A Collection Of Letters, Made By Sʳ Tobie Mathews Kᵗ· . . . London, Printed for Henry Herringman, and are to be ſold at his Shop, at the

A COLLECTION OF

LETTERS,

MADE BY

Sr Tobie Mathews

Kr.

With a Character of the most Excellent Lady,
LUCY, *Countesse of*

CARLEILE:

By the same Author.

To which are Added many Letters of
his own, to severall Persons

OF HONOUR,

who were Contemporary with him.

LONDON,
Printed for *Henry Herringman,* and are to be
sold at his Shop, at the sign of the *Anchor*
in the Lower walk in the New
Exchange. 1 6 6 o.

Title-page of no. 59

L

fign of the Anchor in the Lower walk in the New Exchange. 1660. [*see facsimile*]

Collation: π² *A–C*⁸ D–Z⁸ Aa⁸ Bb⁴; 198 leaves.

Contents: π1*a* blank; π1*b* portrait; π2 title; *A1a–A3b* dedication *To the Right Honourable Lucy, Counteffe of Carleile* signed by *John Donne* [*jun.*]; *A4a–A8b The Character of the moft excellent Lady, Lucy Counteſs of Carleile*; B1*a*–C1*b To the Reader*; C2*a–*Bb3*b* (pp. 1–356) text; Bb4 blank.

Frontispiece: A bust of the subject in an oval, 9 × 7 cm, inscribed below: *The lively Portraieture of* | *Sʳ Tobias Mathewes Knᵗ* | *James Gammon sculp.* The plate-mark measures 14 × 9·5 cm. Printed on a leaf conjugate with the title-page.

Letters to and from Donne:

---

[1] *Devotions*, 1624.
[2] *The first sermon preached to King Charles*, 1625. [3] *Devotions*, 1624.
[4] *A sermon upon the xx. verse of the v. chapter of the Booke of Judges*, 1622.

Note: This collection was edited by John Donne, jun., whose name was added to the title-page of the issue of 1692 (see no. 62). Bald (p. 143 n.) says of the *Letters:* 'pp. 1–271 seem to represent the collection originally made by Matthew, and pp. 272–356 were added by the younger Donne from his father's unpublished correspondence. Pp. 272–95 contain a series of letters to, not from, Donne, and (except for the last) may be from the same person.' The following account of Matthew is transcribed, with amendment of dates, from a note written on the fly-leaves of the ULC copy of the *Letters.*

    Sir Tobie Matthew was son of Dr. Tobie Matthew, Archbishop of York; he was born in Oxford in 1577, while his father was Dean of Christ Church. During his travels he was reduced to the Romish religion by Father Parsons. This occasioned his absence from England from 1607 to 1617, when he had leave to return. He was ordered to leave it again in Oct. 1618; but in 1622 was recalled to assist in the match with Spain, and on account of his endeavours to promote it was knighted by King James on Oct. 23 1623. He was much cultivated by Lord Bacon, and translated the *Essays* into Italian. He died at Ghent, Oct. 13, 1655.

    Three of Donne's letters (nos. 1–3) in this collection were not reprinted by Gosse. Wing's entry M 1320, is an error; both ULC copies are dated 1660 and the imprint given for the non-existent copy with date 1670 belongs to the reissue of 1692. For a full account of Sir Tobie see his *Life* by A. H. Mathew and A. Calthrop, 1907.

Copies: BM, ULC (2); HCL, HEH, FSLW, PUL, YUL.
Oxford Colleges: Jesus, Queen's, Worcester (no frontispiece).
G. L. Keynes, R. S. Pirie.

60 WALTON'S LIFE OF HERBERT [Wing W669]   8° 1670

Title: The Life Of Mr. George Herbert . . . To which are added ſome Letters . . . London, Printed by Tho: Newcomb, for Rich: Marriott, Sold by moſt Bookſellers. M.DC.LXX. [*see facsimile*]

Collation: A⁸(A1+χ1) B–I⁸ K⁴(–K3, 4, K4=χ1); 76 leaves.

Contents: A1 portrait; χ1*a* general title inserted before A2, separate title to *The Life of Mr. George Herbert* (see facsimiles); χ1*b* Imprimatur signed *Sam. Parker*, *21 April 1670*; A3*a* (with sig. A2)–A5*a* (pp. 5–9) verses *To Mr. Izaack Walton* signed *Sam: Woodforde*, *Bensted*, *Apr. 3. 1670*; A5*b*–F4*a* (pp. 10–119) *The Life*; F4*b* blank; F5*a* subtitle to *Letters Written by Mr. George Herbert to his Mother*, *Lady Herbert with others Written by John Donne* (see facsimile); F5*b* blank; F6*a*–K1*b* (pp. 123–

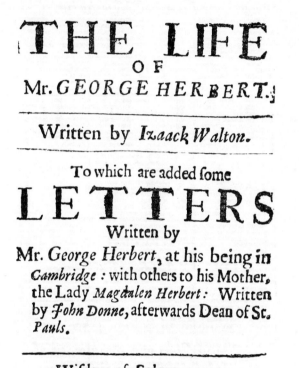

General title of no. 60

46) *Letters*; K2*a–b* verses *On Mr. George Herbert's Book The Temple by Mr Crashaw*; K3 blank.

Frontispiece: Bust of George Herbert in an oval, 9·5 × 8 cm, inscribed below: *The Effigies of Mr. George Herbert: | Author of those Sacred Poems called | The Temple.* Signed: *R. White fculp.* Platemark measures 13·6 × 7·8 cm.

Letters: Donne's letters are as follows:

1. pp. 24–6.   With the verses *To the Lady Magdalen Herbert, of St. Mary Magdalen.* Micham, July 11. 1607. [?] (Gosse, 1, 167)

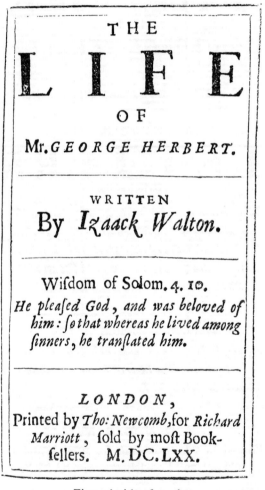

First sub-title of no. 60

2. pp. 141–2. To the worthiest Lady, Mrs. Magdalen Herbert. Michin [Micham], July 11. 1607. (Gosse, 1, 164)

3. pp. 143–4. Ditto. London, July 23. 1607. (Gosse, 1, 165)

4. pp. 145–6. Ditto. August 2d. 1607. (Gosse, 1, 166)

Note: These letters are also printed in the subsequent editions of Walton's *Lives*, 1670, etc. The general title-page was imposed with the final section K and was intended for insertion before (or replacement of) A2, but it has often been omitted altogether. In my copy it is still in its original position folded back before K1.

LETTERS
Written by
Mr. *GEORGE HERBERT*,
At his being in
CAMBRIDGE:
With others to his Mother, the Lady
MAGDALEN HERBERT.
Written by
JOHN DONNE,
Afterwards
Dean of St. PAULS.

LONDON,
Printed by *Tho: Newcomb*, for *Richard Marriott*, Sold by most Book-sellers. M.DC.LXX.

Second sub-title of no. 60

Copies: BM, BLO, ULC; HCL, HEH, FSLW, YUL.
Trinity College, Cambridge.
G. L. Keynes; R. S. Pirie; I. A. Shapiro.

61 WALTON'S LIVES [Wing W 671]   8° 1670

Title: The Lives [of] Dr. John Donne, Sir Henry Wotton, Mr. Richard
Hooker, Mr. George Herbert [rule] Written by Izaak Walton. [rule] . . .
London, Printed by Tho. Newcomb for Richard Marriott. Sold by moſt
Bookſellers. 1670. 8°.

Letters: In the life of Donne:

1. p. 29. [To Sir R. Drury] Aug. 10 [1614?] (*Letters*, 1651, no. 50; Gosse, I,
    189 and II, 36)
2. p. 29. [To Sir Henry Goodere] Sept. 7 [1608] (*Letters*, 1651, no. 18; Walton's
    Life, 1658, no. 3; Gosse, I, 190)
3. p. 69. [To George Garrard. 7 January 1603] (*Poems*, 1635, no. 23; *80 Sermons*,
    1640; *Letters*, 1651, no. 87; Walton's *Life*, 1658, no. 1; Gosse, II,
    268)
   With the life of Herbert:
4–7. Letters to Mrs. Magdalen Herbert as in no. 60.

Note: The first of these Walton says is 'an extract collected out of some few of his
many letters', part being taken from *Letters*, 1651, no. 50.[1] The second is here
incomplete though it was printed entire among the letters at the end of Walton's
Life of Donne, 1658 (see no. 58). All were reprinted in *Lives*, 1675.

62 TOBIE MATTHEW COLLECTION [Wing M 1321] second
    issue   8° 1692

Title: A collection of letters Made By Sʳ Tobie Mathews, Kᵗ· . . .
Printed for Tho. Horne, Tho. Bennet, and Francis Saunders; at the
Royal-Exchange, St. Paul's Church-yard, and the New-Exchange in the
Strand. 1692. [*see facsimile*]

Collation, Contents, Frontispiece, Letters: As in no. 59.

Note: A reissue of no. 59 with a new title-page inserted after the original title-page of
1660.

Copies: ULC; HCL, HEH.

[1] See R. E. Bennett, *Philol. Quart.* XVI, 30–4.

63 LOSELEY MSS. 8° 1835

The Loseley Manuscripts. Manuscripts, and other rare documents, . . . Preserved in the muniment room of James More Molyneux, Esq. At Loseley House, in Surrey . . . Now first edited, with notes, By Alfred John Kempe, Esq. F.S.A.

A

COLLECTION

O F

L E T T E R S,

Made By

Sr. Tobie Mathews, Kt.

WITH

A CHARACTER of the
Moft·Excellent LADY,

LUCY

Countefs of *CARLISLE*:

By the fame Author.

To which are added many Letters of his own,
to feveral Perfons of HONOUR.

Publifhed by the Revd Dr *J. DONNE.*

LONDON,

Printed for *Tho. Horne, Tho. Bennet,* and *Francis Saunders;* at the *Royal-Exchange,* St. *Paul*'s Church-yard, and the *New-Exchange* in the *Strand.* 1692.

Title-page of no. 62

London: John Murray, Albemarle Street. 1835.
22 cm, pp. xxiv, 506, [2]. Frontispiece and 4 plates.

Letters: The following letters were printed here for the first time (pp. 328–46):

1. To the Right Worshipful Sir George More, Kt. From my lodginge in ye Savoy, 2° Februar. 1600–1. (Gosse, I, 101)
2. To the right wor. S^r. Geo. More, Kt. From the Fleete, 11° Febr., 1601. (Gosse, I, 104)
3. To the right hon^ble my very good L. and Master, Sir Tho. Egerton, knt., L. keeper of the greate Seale of Englande. Fleete, 12° Febr. 1601. (Gosse, I, 105)
4. To the right wor'p^ll Sir George More, Knight. From my chamber whither by your favour I am come, 13 feb. 1601. (Gosse, I, 306)
5. To the right hon. my very good L. and Master Sr Tho. Egerton, knt. . . . 13 Feb., 1601. (Gosse, I, 107)
6. To the right honorable my very good Lord and Master Sr Tho. Egerton, knt. [February 1601]
7. To the right worshipfull Sr George More, knight. Mar. 1601. (Gosse, I, 112)
8. To the right honorable my very good L. and master, Sr Thomas Egerton, knight. 1° Martii, 1601. (Gosse, I, 114)
9. To the right wor. Sr Robert More, knight at Lothersley. 10 Aug. 1614. (Gosse, II, 47)
10. To the Honorable K^t and my most honored frinde Sr Henry Wotton, provost of Eton. From Sr John Da[n]vers house at Chelsey . . . 12 Julii, 1625

Note: Of these letters nos. 1–9 were reprinted in Walton's *Life of Donne*, ed. Tomlins (1852) (see no. 194). This reprint was used by Gosse, who omitted, however, no. 6. No. 10 I found in *The Loseley Manuscripts* in 1922; later it was found independently by Mr. John Hayward, who first reprinted it in the Nonesuch edition of the *Complete Poems and Selected Prose* (1929), p. 485. All the original documents were in the possession of Messrs. Robinson, Pall Mall, in June 1938 and were offered for purchase by the Nation, but the money was not forthcoming. They are now in the Folger Shakespeare Memorial Library, Washington, D.C., which has generously presented facsimiles to the British Museum.

64 DONNE'S WORKS 6 vols 8° 1839

The Works of John Donne, D.D. [Edited] by Henry Alford . . . 1839 [see no. 33]

Letters: In vol. VI:

pp. 299–440. Letters to Several Persons of Honour (rearranged by the editor)
pp. 440–1. Henrico Goodyere (Latin letter from *Poems*, 1633, no. 158)

65 CAMDEN SOCIETY 4° 1868

Letters and other Documents illustrating the Relations between England and Germany at the commencement of the Thirty Years' War. Second series . . . Edited by S. R. Gardiner. Printed for the Camden Society. M.DCCC.LXVIII. 4° pp. xi, 194.

Letter: No. v. pp. 5–6. To Sir Dudley Carleton. Ma[e]strich. 31 Aug. 1619, stylo vetere. (P.R.O., S.P.84 (Holland), vol. 91, fo. 219. Gosse, II, 133)

66 CAMDEN SOCIETY 4° 1871

The Fortescue Papers . . . Edited . . . by S. R. Gardiner . . . Printed for the Camden Society M.DCCC.LXXI. 4° pp. [iv], xxxv, 225.

Letter: No. CVIII, pp. 157–8. To the Right Honourable my singular good L. the Marquis of Buckingham. 8° August 1621. (*Hist. MSS. Comm.* Rep. II. App. p. 59. Gosse, II, 140. Now Bodl. MS. Add. D111, no. 370, ff. 133–4)

66a MORRISON COLLECTION 8° 1896

The Collection of Autograph Letters and Historical Documents formed by Alfred Morrison (second series, 1882–93). Volume III. D. Printed for Private Circulation. 1896. 8° pp. [iv], 318.

Letter: P. 128. To Sir Nicholas Cary [Carew] 23 July 1624.

Note: The manuscript is now in the Pforzheimer Collection, and was reprinted in *The Carl H. Pforzheimer Library, English Literature*, 1475–1700, New York, 1940, III, 1256.

67 GOSSE 8° 1899

The Life and Letters of John Donne . . . By Edmund Gosse . . . 1899 2 vols. 8° (see p. 324)

Letters: The following letters were printed here for the first time:

1. To my very honest and very assured friend Robert Cotton Esq., at his house in Blackfriars. From my prison in my chamber 20th February 1601. (I, 109. BM, Cotton MS. Jul. C. iii, f. 153)
2. [To Robert Cotton] 24 Jan: (I, facing p. 108. BM, Cotton MS Jul. C. iii, f. 154)
3. [To Sir Henry Goodere] 23rd February 1601 from my chamber at Mr. Haines' house by the Savoy. (I, 109. MS. copy in possession of Miss Mary Donne)
4. To Sir Robert Cotton, Pyrford. [1603?] (I, 123. BM, Cotton MS. Cleop. F. vii)

5. [To a brother of Mrs. Donne] Amiens, 7 Febr. here, 1611. (I, 287. From the Loseley MSS.; *Hist. MSS. Comm.* Rep. VII. App. p. 670. MS. in FSLW)

6. [To?] [1612] (I, 309. MS. copy in possession of Mr. Roger Barrett)

7. [To?] From my Hospital, July 17, 1613. (II, 16. MS. copy in possession of Miss Mary Donne)

8. [To?] Sat. 12 Feb. 1613. (II, 33. MS. copy in possession of Mr. Roger Barrett)

9. To Sir Robert Moore [More]. At my poor hospital, 28th July 1614. (II, 46. From the Loseley MSS.; *Hist. MSS. Comm.* Rep. VII, App. p. 670. MS. in FSLW)

10. [To Sir Robert More] At my poor house, 3 December 1614. (II, 60. From the Loseley MSS.; *Hist. MSS. Comm.* Rep. VII. App. p. 671. MS. in FSLW)

11. To Sir Henry Marten. At my house at S. Paul's, May 9, 1622. (II, 156. Loder-Symonds MSS., *Hist. MSS. Comm.* Rep. 13, App. 4, 383. MS. now in HCL, *42M–137F)

12. To the Right Honourable Sir Thomas Roe, Ambassador for His Majesty of Great Britain to the Grand Seignior. At my poor house at St. Paul's, London, 1st December, 1622. (II, 173. Domestic State Papers, James I, vol. cxxxiv, no. 59)

13. To the Most Honourable and my most honoured Lord, the Marquess of Buckingham [1623] (II, 176. Bodleian, Tanner MS. lxxiii, f. 305)

14. [To a lady at the Court of Bohemia] 1st February, 1623. (II, 206. MS. copy in possession of Miss Mary Donne)

15. To the Right Worshipful Sir N. Carew, at Bedington. At my house at St. Paul's, 1st September 1624. (II, 209. BM, MS. 29598, f. 13)

16. To Sir Nicholas Carew. At my house at Drury House, September 17th. [1624?] (II, 209. BM, MS. 29598, f. 15)

17. To Secretary Conway. At my poor house at Paul's, 7th December 1624. (II, 213. Domestic State Papers, James I, vol. clxxvi, no. 28)

18. [To Sir Thomas Roe] At Chelsea, 25th November, 1625. (II, 222, 310. Domestic State Papers, Charles I, vol. x, no. 28)

19. To Sir Nicholas Carew. At Paul's house, 26th June, 1626. (II, 232. MS., much damaged, in HEH, H.M. 2781)

68 LETTERS 1910

Letters to Several Persons of Honour. Edited by C. E. Merrill Jr. New York. 1910.

19·5 cm, pp. xix [i], 317 [1].

Note: This edition, limited to 600 copies, is an exact reprint of the first edition of 1651 with notes by the editor.

68*a* SIMPSON'S PROSE WORKS OF DONNE   8° 1924

A Study of the Prose Works of John Donne by Evelyn M. Simpson . . .
Oxford . . . 1924 [second edition 1948]

Letters: The following letters from the collection of transcripts formerly at Burley-
on-the-Hill were printed here for the first time (pp. 284–318) [1948, pp. 291–336]:

  1. [To?] Written frō Plymouth [August 1597]
  2. [To?, summer 1599]
  3. [To Sir Henry Wotton, autumn 1599]
  4. [Ditto, 1600]
  5. [Ditto, 1600]
  6. [Probably to Sir Henry Wotton, 1600]
  7. [Ditto, 1599–1600]
  8. [Ditto, perhaps early 1598]
  9. [Ditto, *c.* 1600]
 10. [Ditto, 1600]
 11. [Ditto, *c.* 1600]
 12. [To?, 1600 or 1601]
 13. [To?, February 1601/2]
 14. [To Sir Henry Wotton, July 1604]
 15. [To a Lady]
 16. [Probably to the Countess of Bedford] Signed *Anonimus*; perhaps not by Donne
 17. [To?]
 18. [To?, after July 1604]
 19. [To?, *c.* 1596–7]
 20. [To?]
 21. [To?]
 22. [To?]
 23. [To?]
 24. [To?]
 25. [To?, after 1603]
 26. [To?, 1605]
 27. [Probably to Sir Henry Wotton]
 28. [To?, 1607]
 29. [To Sir Henry Wotton, *c.* 1608–9]
 30. [Probably to the Countess of Bedford, *c.* 1611]
 31. [To?]
 32. [To?, *c.* 1615]

Note: In an article in *Times Lit. Sup.*, 22 August 1952, Mr. Baird W. Whitlock
questioned whether no. 1 (Donne's 'First Letter') was really written by him, and

concluded that it was not. The matter was further discussed in letters from I. A. Shapiro, B. W. Whitlock, and R. C. Bald in *Times Lit. Sup.*, 12 September, 19 September, 26 September, 3 October, and 24 October 1952. In Professor Shapiro's opinion[1] only three of these letters (nos. 11, 14, and 32) are certainly Donne's; though several others (nos. 2, 3, 6–9, 12, 21, 22, 25, 29, 30) are reminiscent of his style, none can be proved to be his.

68*b* LONDON MERCURY   4° 1925

The London Mercury. Vol. XIII. London, 1925 [see p. 334]

Letter: One letter from the Loseley MSS. was printed here for the first time (pp. 159–60):

> To the R. Wor^full Sr George More Kt. At Pauls house. 22 Jun: 1629. (MS. now in FSLW.)

68*c* SELECTED PROSE ED. HAYWARD   8° 1929

John Donne . . . Complete Poetry and Selected Prose. Edited by John Hayward The Nonesuch Press Bloomsbury 1929 [see no. 97]

Letters: The following letters were here collected for the first time:

1. No. xv. p. 462. To the Prince [of Wales] [1610] (Bath MSS. II, 59, *Hist. MSS. Comm.* Rep. III. App. 196)
2. No. XVII. p. 464. To Sir Robert Harley, 7 April 1613, Montgomery (Portland MSS. vol. III, *Hist. MSS. Comm.* Rep. XIV. App. II, p. 6)
3. No. XIX. p. 465. To the Honourable Kt. Sir Edward Herbert, 23 January 1614 (Powis MSS. Ser. II)

68*d* LETTER TO SIR NIC. CAREY [CAREW]   1930

John Donne's Letter to Sir Nicholas Carey, Written from his House in London in the early Summer of the Plague Year 1625, and Printed from the Original Manuscript which is preserved in the Charles Eliot Norton Collection of Donne's writings which is now a part of the Harvard College Library.

Colophon: This letter has been put into type at the sign of The George in December 1929

18 cm, pp. [12].

Note: The manuscript of this letter of 21 June 1625 was inserted in a copy of the *Letters*, 1651, which was sold at Sotheby's, 6 June 1929, lot 643. Now in HCL:

---

[1] Personal communication.

Nor. 4651. 3. It had not previously been printed, and is here edited, with a prefatory note, by T. Spencer. The type was composed by George P. Winship.

68e LETTER TO LORD ELLESMERE 1951

Catalogue of Books from the Bridgewater Library sold at Sotheby's auction rooms 19 March 1951.

Lot 109 [Donne, J.] Pseudo-Martyr . . . 1610 Presentation copy from the Author to Lord Chancellor Ellesmere with A.L.S. from the former to the latter [transcript of the letter follows].

Note: The original manuscript of the letter was fixed by an old pin to a blank leaf at the end of the book, which was bought by Quaritch for £450. It had already been printed by Grierson, II, p. 204, but was reprinted in the catalogue, some copies of which also contained a collotype reproduction. The book was acquired by Allerton C. Hickmott, Hartford, Conn. It is now in the collection of R. S. Pirie.

68f LETTER TO BISHOP WILLIAMS 1626

R. C. Bald, John Donne A Life. Oxford. 1970.

Letter: p. 487: To John Williams 'At my poore house at pauls 22 Aug: 1626'.

Note: Donne was writing to the Archbishop on behalf of the son of the Revd. Mr. Holney, who 'was in the quality of a chapleyne in Sir George Mores house, then when I married into that family'. The letter was discovered by Miss D. Williamson in the Lincolnshire Archives, L.T. and D. 1626/11 (J. Donne), and communicated to Dame Helen Gardner (*Divine Poems*, 1952, p. 138 n.)

68g LETTER TO THE EARL OF MIDDLESEX 1628

The Sermons of John Donne. Ed. E. M. Simpson and G. R. Potter. Vol. VIII. Berkeley and Los Angeles. 1956.

Letter: pp. 24–5: part of a letter to Lionel Cranfield, Earl of Middlesex, dated 'At Pauls House. 18 Nov. 1628', concerning Donne's illness with a squinancy, or quinzy, was first printed here, by permission of Lord Sackville (reported by Mrs. M. Prestwich). It is also mentioned by Bald, p. 512.

OCCASIONAL PIECES

BIBLIOGRAPHICAL PREFACE

IN this section I have included those few pieces which are certainly by Donne and were printed in various books during his lifetime. Some other poems by him were printed in books published between 1640 and 1675, and these are recorded in the footnotes to the section containing the collected *Poems*. Several other poems attributed to Donne, though actually spurious or of doubtful authenticity, are to be found in other publications of the seventeenth century, but I have not given these a place in this bibliography; they will, for the most part, be found recorded in Grierson's and Gardner's editions of the poems. Grierson was not aware of the musical setting by Ferrabosco (no. 69*a*). Other settings of poems wrongly attributed to Donne are in works such as Orlando Gibbons's *First Set of Madrigals & Mottets*, 1612, and Dowland's *A Pilgrim's Solace*, 1612, but no others of genuine pieces by Donne have yet been found in print.

According to Walton in *The Life*, 1670, p. 55, Donne caused 'A Hymne to God the Father' 'to be set to a most grave and solemn Tune, and to be often sung to the *Organ by the Choristers* of St. *Pauls* Church, in his own hearing, especially at the Evening Service'. The setting is assumed to be that by John Hilton (1599–1657), preserved in Egerton MS. 2013 in the British Museum. This and other musical settings found only in manuscript are listed below:

1. Song (Deerest Love, I doe not goe). Anonymous. St. Michael's College, Tenbury Wells, MS. 1018 f. 44*b*. Printed by Grierson, 1. 18; Gardner, p. 240; Shawcross, p. 100; Jacquot (*Poèmes de Donne*, 1961),[1] p. 1.

2. The same, alternative setting. Anonymous. 'Elizabeth Rogers hir Virginal Book', BM., Add. MS. 10337 f. 55*b*. Printed by Jacquot, pp. 2–3.

3. Song (Goe and catch a falling star). Anonymous. BM., Egerton MS. 2013 f. 58*b*. Printed by Grierson, 1, 8–9; Gardner, p. 241; Shawcross, p. 91; Jacquot, pp. 4–5.

[1] See p. 234 of this Bibliography.

4. The Message (Send home my longe strayde eies to mee). Giovanni Coperario. St. Michael's College, Tenbury Wells, MS. 1019 f. 1*b*. Printed by Grierson, 1, 43; Gardner, p. 241; Shawcross, p. 81; Jacquot, pp. 6–7.

5. The Expiration (So, so, breake off this last lamenting Kisse). Anonymous. BLO, MS. F575 f. 8*b* (a different setting from Ferrabosco's). Printed by Grierson, i, 68; Gardner, pp. 242–3; Jacquot, pp. 8–9.

6. A Hymn to God the Father (Willt thou forgive that sinne where I begunne). John Hilton.[1] BM., Egerton MS. 2013 f. 13*b*. Printed by Grierson, ii, 252; Gardner, p. 246, with the setting by Pelham Humfrey in *Harmonia Sacra*, q.v.

7. The Apparition (When by thy scorne foule murdress I am dead). William Lawes. Edinburgh University, MS. D. C. 1. 69, pp. 13–14. Printed by Shawcross, p. 84.

8. The Primerose (Upon this Primrose hill). Martin Peerson. Fitzwilliam Virginal Book, no. 264, pp. 381–2. Fitzwilliam Museum, Cambridge.

9. The Lamentations of Jeremy (How sits this city late most populous) Thomas Ford. Christ Church, Oxford, MS. 736–8, ff. 21a, 21a, 22a. Printed by Shawcross, p. 372.

69 JONSON'S VOLPONE [*STC* 14783]   4° 1607

Ben: Ionſon his Volpone Or the foxe . . .

Printed for Thomas Thorppe. 1607.

Collation: π² ¶⁴ A–N⁴ O²; 60 leaves (π1, O2 blank).

Poem: On A1*a. Amiciſſimo & meritiſſimo* BEN: IONSON. Signed I[ohn] D[onne]

          (*Quuod arte auſus es hic tuâ,* POETA)

Note: First printed among Donne's poems in the edition of 1650 (no. 82). Printed also in *The Workes of Beniamin Jonson*, 1616, f°, ¶6*a*.

Copies: BLO, BM; HEH.

    University Libraries: Edinburgh, Leeds, London.

    Eton College Library (2); Marsh's Library, Dublin.

---

[1] Printed also in *The Cambridge Hymnal*, edited by D. Holbrook and E. Poston, Cambridge, 1967, no. 130, pp. 196–7 (edited and inner parts added by E. P.).

69*a* FERRABOSCO'S AYRES [*STC* 10827]   f° 1609

Ayres: By Alfonſo Ferraboſco.

London: Printed by T. Snodham, for Iohn Brovvne, . . . 1609.

Collation: [A]² B–K²; 20 leaves (K2 blank).

Poem: On C2*b*, vii. So, ſo, leave off [The Expiration (So, so, breake off)]

Note: Two stanzas of the poem with two verbal alterations and a musical setting.

Copies: BM (MR K. 8. h. 4); HEH.

70 CORYAT'S CRUDITIES [*STC* 5808]   4° 1611

Engraved title: Coryat's Crudities.

Printed Title: London, Printed by W. S. Anno Domini 1611 8°.

Poems: Under *Panegyricke Verses vpon the Author and his booke.*

   1. On d3–4. *Incipit Ioannes Donne* (Oh to what height will loue of greatneſſe driue)
   2. On d4. *In eundem Macaronicon. Explicit Ioannes Donne* (Quot, dos hæc, Linguists, perfetti, Disticha fairont)
   3. On f5*b*. *Incipit Ioannes Dones* (Loe her's a Man, worthy indeed to trauell)

Note: These were also printed in the separate edition of the *Panegyricke Verses* issued in 1611 under the title *The Odcombian Banquet.* No. 1 was first printed among Donne's poems in the edition of 1649. The second and third are given by Chambers, II, 289–90, and by Grierson, I, 174, II, 129, though the third is probably not by Donne.

Copies: BLO, BM, ULC (2); HEH.

70*a* ODCOMBIAN BANQUET [*STC* 5810]   4° 1611

The Odcombian Banquet: Diſhed foorth by Thomas the Coriat and Serued in by a number of Noble Wits in prayſe of his Crudities and Crambe too. Asinus Portans Mysteria Imprinted for Thomas Thorp. 1611.

Collation: A–P⁴; 60 leaves.

Poems: The three pieces by, or attributed to, Donne first printed in *Coryat's Crudities* (no. 70) are here reprinted on E2–4 and I4.

Copies: BLO, BM; HEH.
London University Library; Manchester, Rylands Library.

71 CORKINE'S SECOND BOOKE OF AYRES [*STC* 5769]

fº 1612

The Second Booke of Ayres, Some to Sing and Play to the Bafe-Violl alone: Others, to be sung to the Lute and Bafe-Violl.
    London: Printed for M. L[ownes] I. B[rowne] and T. S[nodham]. Affigned by W. Bailey. 1612.

Collation: A–I²; 18 leaves.

Poems: On B1*b*. III. [Breake of Day] Musical setting, with three stanzas of the poem, containing verbal changes.
    On C1*b*. VIII. Musical setting for The Baite.
    The text of the poem is not printed, four stanzas of an alternative song being given ('Beware faire Maides of Mufky Courtiers oathes'). The first line of The Baite is given in *A Table of all the Songs contained in this Booke* on I2*b*.

Note: The settings were transcribed for Sir Herbert Grierson by the late Sir Barclay Squire, and were printed by him II, 55–7, but Mr. Macdonald Emslie has pointed out that these transcriptions are very inaccurate (see *Notes and Queries*, CC, 1955, 12).

Copies: BM (MR, K. 8. h. 5); HEH.

72 LACHRYMÆ LACHRYMARUM [*STC* 23578]   4º 1613

Lachrymæ Lachrymarum or The Spirit of Teares Distilled for the vn-tymely Death of The incomparable Prince, Panaretus. by Iosuah Syluester. The third Edition, with Addition of His Owne.

Colophon: London Printed by Humfrey Lownes. 1613.

Collation: A–C⁴ 'C–D'⁴ D–I⁴ (±D1); 40 leaves.

Poem: On E1*a*–2*b*. Elegie on the vntimely Death of the incomparable Prince, Henry. By Mʳ Donne.

Note: Donne's 'Elegie' was reprinted in all the editions of the collected poems (1633, no. 84, p. 154) with title 'Elegie on Prince Henry'. For a full description of the book see *Papers of the Edinburgh Bibliographical Society 1901–1904*. Edinburgh. 1906, pp. 155–6, in 'Elegies and Other Tracts issued on the Death of Prince Henry, 1612', by J. P. Edmonds. In most copies of *Lachrymæ Lachrymarum* D1 has been cancelled and the stub is preceded by a gathering of four leaves with signature C–D on the first leaf. Edmonds's article describes a copy, then in private possession, containing the leaf usually cancelled; it has a different form of C–D3*a*–*b*.
    Bald (p. 269) regarded the poem as 'almost entirely lacking in depth of feeling and manifests an aridity that is the product of mere intellectual ingenuity'. 'Ben Jonson

related that Donne told him that he wrott that Epitaph on Prince Henry Look to me Fath to match Sir Ed: Herbert in obscureness.'

Copies: BM, TCD.
University Libraries: Liverpool, London, Manchester (Chetham's Library).
Dublin, Marsh's Library, London; University College.
G. L. Keynes.

73 OVERBURIE'S CHARACTERS [*STC* 18904]   4° 1614

A Wife Novv the Widow of Sir Thomas Ouerburye . . . Wherevnto are added many witty Characters, and conceited Newes, written by himfelfe and other learned Gentlemen his friends . . .
London Printed for Lawrence Lifle, and are to bee fold at his fhop in Paules Church-yard, at the figne of the Tigers head. 1614.

Collation: A–H⁴; 32 leaves.

Prose piece: On G2*a–b*: 'Newes from the very Country', [signed] I[ohn] D[onne], followed by 'An Anfwer to the very Country Newes', [signed] A.S.

Note: First included with Donne's poems in the edition of 1650 (see no. 82). This is the second edition of Overburie's *Wife*. Donne's piece was reprinted in the subsequent editions: 3rd, 4th, 5th (1614); 6th, 1615; 7th, 8th, 9th, 1616; 10th, 1618; and later (see no. 73*a*).

Copies: BLO (2), BM; HEH.

73*a* OVERBURIE'S CHARACTERS [*STC* 18913]   8° 1622

Sir Thomas Overbury His Wife with Additions of New Characters, and many other Wittie Conceits neuer before Printed. The eleuenth Impreffion.
London, Printed for Laurence Lifle, and are to be fold by Henry Seile at the Tigers-head in Pauls Church-yard, 1622.

Collation: A–V⁸; 160 leaves.

Prose pieces: (1) On G3*a–5a*: 'The true Character of a Dunce'.
    (2) On Q6*a–9a*: 'An effay of Valour'.
    (3) On R7*b–8b*: 'Newes from the very Countrey', [signed] I[ohn] D[onne].

Note: The two additional pieces were first reprinted with other writings by Donne in the *Juvenilia* of 1652 (see no. 45). 'An effay of Valour' was also printed in Sir Robert Cotton's *Cottoni Posthuma*, 1651, with an attribution to Sir Philip Sidney, and in the later editions of *Overburie's Characters*: 12th, 1626; '12th', 1627; 13th, 1628; 14th,

1630; 15th, 1632; 16th, 1638; '16th', 1655; 17th, 1664. 'The true Character of a Dunce' has been reprinted in W. J. Paylor's edition of *The Overburian Characters*, 1936.

Copies: BLO, BM, ULC; HEH.

G. L. Keynes (also 17th, 1664)[1], R. S. Pirie (all editions).

73b HELPE TO MEMORY AND DISCOURSE [not in *STC*]

12° 1630

A Helpe to Memory and Discourse: with Table-Talke as Musicke to a Banquet of Wine. Being a Compendium of witty, and usefull Proposi-tions, Problemes, and Sentences, Extracted from the larger Volumes of Physicians, Philosophers, Orators and Poets.

London: Printed by T. B. for Leonard Becket, and are to be sold at his Shop in the Temple, neere the Church. 1630. A–H¹².

Poems: 1. On C2, pp. 45–6, 'The Lovers complaint written by a Gentleman of 'quality' [The Broken Heart, *Poems*, 1633, no. 99].

2. On G3a, p. 143 [Song, Go and catch a falling Starre, *Poems*, 1633, no. 102]. The last part of the first stanza and all of the third have been omitted.

Note: This early printing of no. 2 was first recorded by Mr. James E. Walsh, *Times Lit. Sup.*, 6 April 1956, p. 207. He did not mention the printing of no. 1. The authorship of the book is doubtful. An earlier work, *A Helpe to Discourse, or a miscellany of merriment*, 1619, etc. (*STC* 1547–54), has been attributed to William Basse and Edward Pond, and the *Helpe to Memory and Discourse* may be by the same hands. Two earlier editions of the latter are known (1620, not in *STC*; 1621, *STC* 13051), but these do not contain, according to Mr. Walsh, the section '*Table-Talke as Musicke to a Banquet of Wine*', in which Donne's poems are found. On the other hand Mr. C. J. Hindle, *Times Lit. Sup.*, 8 June 1956, p. 345, states that *Table Talke* was entered in the Stationers' Register on 16 November 1620 by Leonard Becket and was recorded in the 1635 Appendix to the Bodleian Catalogue of 1620 with the class-mark 8° D 52 [Art], though it had disappeared by the time when the 1674 Catalogue was published. It seems certain, therefore, that Donne's poems were first printed in 1620 or 1621.

Copies: HCL.

Mr. John Fleming, New York (1957).

[1] With two title-pages: *for John Playfere* (Wing O 611), and *by Peter Lillicrap for Philip Chetwin* (not in Wing).

ANNIVERSARIES

BIBLIOGRAPHICAL PREFACE

AN ANATOMY OF THE WORLD, afterwards known as *The First Anniversary*, was composed by Donne in memory of Elizabeth Drury, a child of fifteen, whom he had never seen, in the hope of securing the patronage of her father, Sir Robert Drury of Hawstead (or, sometimes, Halsted) near Bury St. Edmunds in the county of Suffolk. The book consists of three parts, 'To the Praise of the Dead and the Anatomy', 'The Anatomy of the World', and 'A Funerall Elegie'. It was implied in Ben Jonson's conversations with Drummond of Hawthornden that the first part was written by Joseph Hall, rector of Hawstead from 1601 to 1608 and afterwards Bishop of Exeter and of Norwich. This attribution has been generally accepted. It has been supposed that Donne first wrote 'A Funerall Elegie' at the time of Elizabeth's death in 1610 and 'The Anatomy' afterwards in the early part of 1611, but there is no documentary evidence of this.

The volume containing the poems was published in 1611 by Samuel Macham (working 1608–15), probably through his association with Hall. Both men were natives of Ashby-de-la-Zouche, a small place in the county of Leicester, and Macham had already published books for Hall. There is no manuscript authority for any part of the poem.[1] Only two copies of the book are known to have survived, but a facsimile edition was printed for the Roxburghe Club in 1952, so that the text is now available (see no. 77c). Frank Manley collated both copies of the original for his edition in 1963 (no. 77d). The book was not registered at Stationers' Hall and the exact date of publication is not known, but Sir Arthur Throckmorton, Sir Walter Ralegh's brother-in-law, living in Northamptonshire, received a copy, brought from London by his agent, on 21 November 1611.[2] Throckmorton was an eager book buyer, so perhaps it may be inferred that Donne's poem was published late in the year.

---

[1] BLO, MS. Eng. Poet. e. 37 is a copy of 'A Funerall Elegie' from the edition of 1621 and has no authority.

[2] A. L. Rowse, *Ralegh and the Throckmortons*, London, 1962, p. 288.

The Second Anniversarie was written early in 1612, but again only 'Of the Progres of the Soule' is by Donne, 'The Harbinger to the Progres' being presumably by Hall. '*The Second Anniversarie*' was not printed separately, the two poems being printed together in 1612. Again, the volume was not registered at Stationers' Hall, but Throckmorton received a copy on 10 May 1612 at a cost of sixpence.[1]

The Anatomy of the World is regarded by Manley as having been accurately printed; he has detected only five press corrections in the two copies examined and suggests that the proofs were read by Donne himself. Confirmation of this is furnished by the volume of 1612, printed very much less accurately while the author was in France. One copy has the unusual feature of a printed errata slip with a very large number of corrections (see facsimile) pasted in at the end. This was perhaps made by Donne himself on his return from France. Only six other copies are known, but none of these has the slip, and the later editions of 1621 and 1625 do not incorporate the corrections, implying that most of the edition was sold before the author saw the book, so that the later publisher, Thomas Dewe, was not aware of it.

Donne's name does not appear in any of the separate editions, but their authorship was no doubt well known. In a letter to George Garrard dated 14 April 1612 Donne wrote:

> Of my Anniversaries, the fault that I acknowledge in myself, is to have descended to print any thing in verse, which though it have excuse even in our times, by men who professe, and practise much gravitie; yet I confesse I wonder how I declined to it, and do not pardon my self: But for the other part of the imputation of having said too much, my defence is, that my purpose was to say as well as I could: for since I never saw the Gentlewoman, I cannot be understood to have bound myself to have spoken just truths, but I would not be thought to have gone about to praise her, or any other in rime; except I took such a person, as might be capable of all that I could say. If any of those Ladies think that Mistris *Drewry* was not so, let that Lady make her self fit for all those praises in the book, and they shall be hers.[2]

[1] Rowse, op. cit., p. 289.
[2] *Letters*, 1651, pp. 238–9.

In the First Anniuersarie,

PAg.13.lin.4.for true made, read nevv made.
p.14.l.7.for searse r.scarse. p.21.l.3.for then
r.there. p.25.l.1.for then r.there. p.25.l.4.for
towers r.townes. p.27.l.4.for peace r.pace.p.44
l.7.for same r.fame. Harb.fol.2.p.2.for by progresse r.Hy progresse.

In the Second Anniuersarie,

Pag.2.l.5.for through r.though. p.5.l.9.for till,
thou r.till thou p.5.l.10.for 'to r.t'is.p.5.l.10.for
hydroptique r. hydropique. p.7.l.7.for t'was r.
was.p.12.l.4.for right r.rite.p.13.l.vlt.for worne
r. wonne.p.17.l.10. for expausion r. expansion.
p.19.l.5.for recards r.retards. p.22.l.7. for then
r.there. p.28.l.1.for.thought r. taught. p.30.l.1.
for point r.print.p.32.l.3.for wise r.will. p.33.l.
7.for thoughts r. thought. p.36.l.1.for whether
r.whither. p.37.l.8.for row r. vow. p.39.l.5.for
to'rect r.t'erect. p.44.l.10.for reders r.redresse.
p.48.l.5.for inroque r.inuoque.p.48.l.vlt.for do
me, r.do, me.

This defence was perhaps stimulated by various criticisms such as Ben Jonson's well-known complaint recorded by Drummond of Hawthornden.

All the separate editions contain marginal glosses of unknown authorship. Some of these were omitted in 1625 and none was printed thereafter. The *Anniversaries* were reprinted in all the editions of the *Collected Poems*, the text being very much improved in the first of 1633.

Some contemporary writers took notice of them. John Webster used them in *The Duchess of Malfi*, 1613; Drummond imitated them in *The Cypress Grove*, 1623, and they were noticed by Dryden at the end of the century; Steele misunderstood them in *The Spectator* in 1712, and Fielding followed this in *Tom Jones*, 1749.

Donne's relations with Sir Robert Drury have been studied in detail by R. C. Bald in *Donne and the Drurys*, Cambridge, 1959. A contemporary portrait of Elizabeth, still in the possession of the family, is reproduced by Gosse, 1, facing p. 272, and by Bald, facing p. 68. The image was crudely reproduced on the monument in Hawstead Church, which has a Latin inscription believed to have been composed by Donne. Attention was drawn to this by John Sparrow in *The Times Literary Supplement*, 26 March 1949, 'Two Epitaphs by John Donne'. The second epitaph is on Sir Robert's monument also at Hawstead.

74 AN ANATOMY OF THE WORLD [*STC* 7022] first edition

8° 1611

Title (*within woodcut border*): An anatomy of the World. . . . London, Printed for Samuel Macham. and are to be folde at his fhop in Paules Church-yard, at the figne of the Bul-head. An. Dom. 1611. [*see facsimile*]

Collation: A–B⁸; 16 leaves.

Contents: A1 blank except for sign. A on recto; A2 title; A3*a*–A4*a* *To the praiſe of the Dead, and the Anatomy* (in roman type); A5*a*–B6*a* *An Anatomy of the World* (in italic); B7*a*–B8*b* *A Funerall Elegie* (in roman type).

Note: This book was probably printed by Humfrey Lownes I (1592–1629). The same woodcut border, printed from the same block, is found on the title-pages of Joseph Hall's *The Passion Sermon* . . . *At London Printed by H. L. for Eleazar Edgar, and Samuell Macham* . . . 1609, and *Pharisaisme And Christianitie*: . . . *London, Printed by H. L. For Samuel Macham* . . . 1609 [*Copies:* G. L. Keynes].

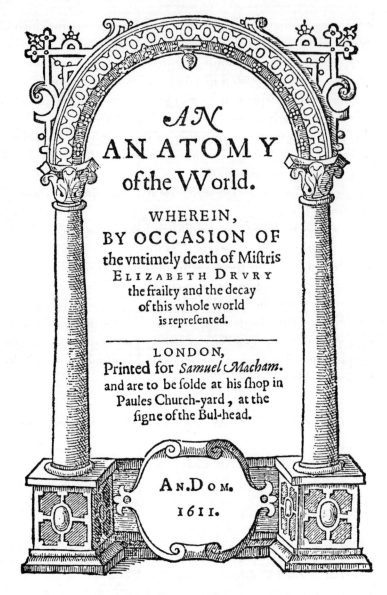

An
AN ATOMY
of the World.

WHEREIN,
BY OCCASION OF
the vntimely death of Miſtris
ELIZABETH DRVRY
the frailty and the decay
of this whole world
is repreſented.

LONDON,
Printed for *Samuel Macham.*
and are to be ſolde at his ſhop in
Paules Church-yard, at the
ſigne of the Bul-head.

AN.DOM.
1611.

Title-page of no. 74

Copies: HEH (lacks A1; Ellesmere copy from Bridgewater House).[1]

G. L. Keynes (Corser–O'Flahertie copy, Sotheby's, 10 February 1948, lot 337).

75 FIRST AND SECOND ANNIVERSARIES [*STC* 7023] second and first editions 8° 1612

First title (*within double rules*): The Firſt Anniuerſarie. An anatomie of the World. . . . London, Printed by M. Bradwood for S. Macham, and are to be ſold at his ſhop in Pauls Church-yard at the ſigne of the Bull-head. 1612.

Second title (*ditto*): The Second Anniuerſarie. . . . London, . . . 1612. [*see facsimiles*]

Collation: A⁸ B–D⁸, E–H⁸; 64 leaves.

*Contents: A*1 first title; *A2a–A4b To the praiſe of the Dead, and the Anatomy* (in italic); *A5a–D2b* (pp. 1–44) *The Firſt Anniuerſarie* (in roman type); *D3a–D7b* (pp. 45–54) *A funerall Elegie* (in italic); *D8* blank except for marginal rules; *E1* second title; *E2a–E4a The Harbinger to the Progres* (in italic); *E4b* blank except for marginal rules; *E5a–H5a* (pp. 1–49) *The Second Anniuerſary* (in roman type); *H5b–H8b* blank except for marginal rules. Errata slip, 19 lines, pasted on to H5b in my copy.

Note: The text of *The Firſt Anniuerſary* contains many variations from that of 1611. The book is considered by Grierson to have been somewhat carelessly printed. The unique errata slip was described by John Sparrow, *Times Lit. Sup.*, 29 June 1946.

Copies: HCL (from Pickering and Chatto, 1914), HEH, FLSW (Huth–Hagen–Chew–Harmsworth copy), YUL (2, Thorn-Drury copy, lacking C1, C8, D1, D8, G3, H3, H6–7 and Rosenbloom copy, also imperfect).

G. L. Keynes (Corser–Cunliffe copy, Sotheby's 13 May 1946, lot 146; formerly bound with John Hall's *Poems*, 1646). R. S. Pirie (Richard Farmer copy).

76 FIRST AND SECOND ANNIVERSARIES [*STC* 7024] third and second editions 8° 1621

First title (*within double rules*): The Firſt Anniuerſarie. . . . London, Printed by A. Mathewes for Tho: Dewe, and are to be ſold at his ſhop in Saint Dunſtons Church-yard in Fleeteſtreete. 1621.

Second title (*ditto*): The ſecond Anniuerſarie. . . . London, . . . 1621. [*see facsimiles*]

---

[1] Described by J. Payne Collier in 1837 (*Catalogue of Early English Literature in the Elles-mere Library*, pp. 9–10). A facsimile was published, Santa Barbara, *c.* 1941.

The Second Anniuersarie.

OF THE PROGRES
of the Soule.

Wherein:

BY OCCASION OF THE
Religious Death of Mistris
ELIZABETH DRVRY,
the incommodities of the Soule
in this life and her exaltation in
the next, are Contem-
plated.

LONDON,
Printed by *M. Bradwood* for *S. Macham*, and are
to be sould at his shop in Pauls Church-yard at
the signe of the Bull-head.
1612.

Second title of no. 75

The First Anniuersarie.

AN ANATOMIE
of the World.

Wherein;

BY OCCASION OF
the vntimely death of Mistris
ELIZABETH DRVRY,
the frailtie and the decay of
this whole World is
represented.

LONDON,
Printed by *M. Bradwood* for *S. Macham*, and are
to be sold at his shop in Pauls Church-yard at the
signe of the Bull-head. 1612.

First title of no. 75

8181558

N

The First Anniversarie.

AN
ANATOMIE
of the World.

Wherein,

By Occasion Of
the vntimely death of Mistris
Elizabeth Drvry,
the frailtie and the decay of
this whole World is
represented.

LONDON,

Printed by *A. Mathewes* for *Tho: Dewe*, and are
to be sold at his shop in Saint *Dunstons* Church-
yard in Fleetestreete. 1621.

First title of no. 76

The second Anniversarie.

OF
THE PROGRES
of the Soule.

Wherein,

By Occasion Of
the Religious death of Mistris
Elizabeth Drvry,
the incommodities of the Soule
in this life, and her exaltation in
the next, are Contem-
plated.

LONDON,

Printed by *A. Mathewes* for *Tho: Dewe*, and are
to be sold at his shop in Saint *Dunstons* Church-
yard in Fleetestreete. 1621.

Second title of no. 76

Collation: A^8 B–D^8, E–H^8; 64 leaves.

Contents: A1 blank; A2 first title; A3a–A5a *To the praiſe of the Dead, and the Anatomy* (in italic); A6a–D3b (pp. [1]–44) *The Firſt Anniverſary* (in roman type); D4a–D8b (pp. 45–54) *A Funerall Elegie* (in italic); E1 second title; E2a–E4a *The Harbinger to the Progreſſe* (in italic); E4b blank except for marginal rules; E5a–H5a (pp. [1]–49) *The ſecond Anniverſary* (in roman type); H5b–H8b blank.

Note: The text of this edition contains further variations.

Copies: BM, BLO (imperfect); HCL (Gosse copy).

    G. L. Keynes (H. T. Butler copy, bound with Donne's *Poems*, 1635; Hodgson's 25 June 1913, 23 July 1913, 13 June 1934, lot 135).

77 FIRST AND SECOND ANNIVERSARIES [*STC* 7025] fourth and third editions   8° 1625

First title (within woodcut border): An anatomie of the World. . . . The firſt Anniuerſarie. London Printed by W. Stansby for Tho. Dewe, and are to be ſold in S. Dunſtanes Church-yard. 1625

Second title (ditto): Of the progres of the ſoule . . . The ſecond Anniuerſarie. London . . . 1625 [*see facsimiles*]

Collation: A^8 B–H^8; 64 leaves.

Contents: A1–A2 blank; A3 first title; A4a–A6a *To the praiſe of the Dead, and the Anatomy* (in italic); A6b blank; A7a–D4b (pp. 1–44) *An Anatomie of the World* (in roman type); D5a–E1b (pp. 45–54) *A funerall Elegie* (in italic); E2 second title; E3a–E5a *The harbinger to the Progreſſe* (in italic); E5b blank; E6a–H6a (pp. [1]–49) *Of the progreſſe of the Soule* (in roman type); H6b–H8b blank.

Note: The woodcut title-page border of a compartment with a pile of books at the top and the Seven Sciences at the sides and below was copied from one first used by W. Lily and J. Colet in 1585. Copies in reverse were also used in a series of *Almanackes,* 1609–17. It was again used for the Company of Stationers in 1631 (see McKerrow and Ferguson's *Title-page Borders,* 1932, nos. 202, 240, 241, and 293). The text follows that of 1621.

Copies: BM, BLO; HCL (Britwell copy), HEH, YUL (Hoe–Hagen–Chew copy, lacks A1–2, H7–8).

    G. L. Keynes (Dowden–Meynell copy, lacks A8, C6–8, D1–2).

77a FIRST AND SECOND ANNIVERSARIES   8° 1927

The Noel Douglas Replicas. John Donne The First and Second Anniversaries.

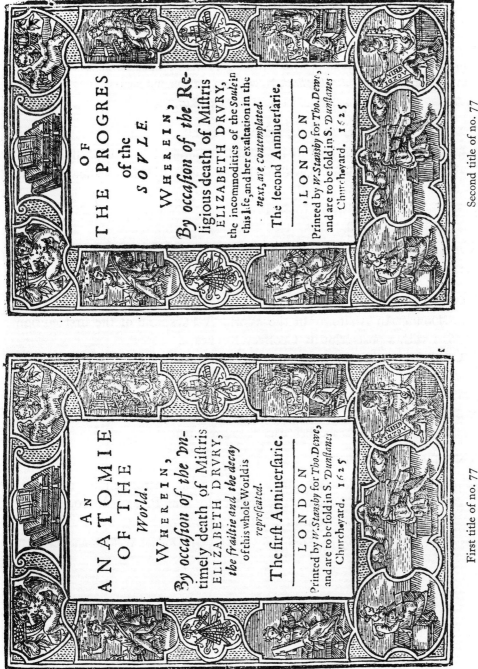

Second title of no. 77

First title of no. 77

Noel Douglas 38 Great Ormond Street London WC 1
22·5 cm, pp. [vi], [vi], 49, [1].

Note: A facsimile reproduction of the BM copy of the edition of 1621. The unsigned prefatory note is by John Sparrow. 100 copies were printed on hand-made paper. Also published in *English Replicas*, New York, Payson and Clarke, 1927.

Reviewed: Times Lit. Sup., 25 November 1926, p. 847.

77*b* AN ANATOMIE OF THE WORLD   4° 1929

John Donne An Anatomie of the World wherein by occasion of the untimely death of Mistris Elizabeth Drury the frailtie and the decay of this whole world is represented.
Shaftesbury The High House Press 1929
26 cm, pp. 32, [4].

Note: 170 copies printed.

Reviewed: Times Lit. Sup., 21 November 1929, p. 955.

77*c* AN ANATOMY OF THE WORLD   12° 1951

John Donne An Anatomy of the World A Facsimile of the first edition 1611 with a postscript by Geoffrey Keynes.
Cambridge Printed for presentation to Members of the Roxburghe Club 1951
17 cm, pp. [viii], [32] facsimile, 1 l. blank, 10 postscript.

Note: 120 copies printed, bound in one-quarter crimson mor., t.e.g. The Roxburghe Club members' copies have their names printed in red.

77*d* ANNIVERSARIES ED. MANLEY   8° 1963

John Donne: The Anniversaries Edited with Introduction and Commentary by Frank Manley The Johns Hopkins Press Baltimore 1963.
21 cm, pp. viii, [iv], 209, [1].

Reviewed: Times Lit. Sup., 6 April 1967, p. 277, 'Ill Donne: Well Donne'.

COLLECTED POEMS

VII

Madame,
Here, where by all all Saints invoked are,
T'were too much scisme to bee singulare,
And gainst a practise generall to warr;
yett turninge to Saints, should my Humilitee
To other Saint, then you directed bee,
That were to make my Scisme Heresee.
nor would I bee a Convertite so cold
As not to tell yee; If thys bee too bold,
Pardons are in thys markett cheaply sold.

where because Fayth ys in too lowe degree,
I thought yt some Apostleshipp in mee
To speak thinges wch by Fayth alone I see:
That ys, of yow, who are a firmament
Of vertues, where no one ys growen, nor spent;
Thay' are yor Materialls, not yor Ornament.

Others, whom wee call vertuous, are not so
In theyr whole Substance, but theyr vertues grow
But in theyr Humors, and at Seasons show.

For when through tastles flatt Humilitee,
In Dow-bakd men some Harmelesnes wee see,
Tis but hys fleqme that's vertuous, and not hee.
So ys the Blood sometymes, who euer ran
To Danger vninnportund, hee was than
no better then a Sanguine vertuous man.

So Cloystrall Men who in pretence of fear,
All Contributions to thys Lyfe forbear,
Haue vertu in Melancholy, and onely there.

Spirituall Cholerique Critiqs, wch in all
Religions find faults, and forgiue no fall,
Haue, through thys Zeale, vertu, but in theyr Gall.

we' are thus but parcell-gilt; To Gold we' are growen,
when vertu ys our Soules Complexione.
who knowes hys vertues Name, or place, hath none.

vertu ys but Aguishe when tis Seuerall,
By' occasion wakd, and Circumstantiall;
True vertu ys Soule, allwayes in all deeds all.

Thys vertu, thinkinge to giue Dignitee
To yer Soule, found there no Infirmitee,
for yer Soule was as good vertu, as shee.

shee therfore wrought upon that part of yow
wch ys scarse lesse then Soule, as shee could doe
And so hath made yor Beauty vertue too;

BIBLIOGRAPHICAL PREFACE

DONNE'S poems were composed at various periods of his life, the secular ones during his younger days, the Divine Poems in middle life and after he had taken orders; but before entering the Church he seems to have had the idea of having some of them put into print, though not necessarily for publication. In an often quoted passage from a letter to Sir Henry Goodere dated 20 December 1614, Donne wrote:

> ... One thing more I must tell you; but so softly, that I am loath to hear my self: and so softly, that if that good Lady were in the room, with you and this Letter, she might not hear. It is, that I am brought to a necessity of printing my Poems, and addressing them to my L. Chamberlain. This I mean to do forthwith; not for much publique view, but at mine own cost, a few Copies. I apprehend some incongruities in the resolution; and I know what I shall suffer from many interpretations: but I am at an end, of much considering that; and, if I were as startling in that kind, as ever I was, yet in this particular, I am under an unescapable necessity, as I shall let you perceive, when I see you. By this occasion I am made a Rhapsoder of mine own rags, and that cost me more diligence, to seek them, then it did to make them.[1]

There is no evidence, however, that this intention was ever carried out, no such printed text having ever been discovered, and it was left to others to collect and print the poems after the author's death.

The texts of the various editions of the collected *Poems* were exhaustively dealt with in the Oxford edition of 1912 by Sir Herbert Grierson; he gave type-facsimiles of all the title-pages, but only mentioned some of the more strictly bibliographical details, which will be found recorded under the entries following.

Until the year 1969 none of Donne's poems in English written by his own hand was known to have survived. The last edition of this Bibliography was able to record only two Latin epigrams, one of two lines, the other of four, written by Donne on fly-leaves of books.[2] In 1970 Messrs. Sotheby

---

[1] *Letters*, 1651, no. 65.   [2] See Appendix IV, L 53 and L 161.

were able to announce the discovery of Donne's original script of his well-known Verse Letter 'to the Lady Carey and Mrs. Essex Rich'. This was found by an observant cataloguer working on the muniments of the Duke of Manchester. It had lain unidentified among the Rich, and later the Montagu, family papers, deposited in the Public Record Office in 1882. The *Eighth Report of the Historical Manuscripts Commission*, Appendix (Part II), 1881, had listed it as 'Copy of verses To the honourable Lady, the Lady Carew', and said to be of doubtful date. The poem was carefully written with only two corrections on both sides of a gilt-edged sheet of thin letter paper, which Donne then folded twice and addressed on the blank side. The manuscript is of inestimable value for the guidance of Donne scholars in knowledge of exactly how the poet wished his punctuation and elisions to appear and is an object of great beauty. Nevertheless the price of £23,000 paid for it at the auction sale (lot 267) on 23 June 1970 exceeded most estimates. The manuscript was bought by a dealer on behalf of a continental collector, but its exportation was blocked by the Reviewing Committee, and it was ultimately acquired, with assistance from the government and private benefactors, for the Bodleian Library.

Very few of Donne's compositions, besides *The Anatomy of the World*, 1611, and *The Second Anniversary*, 1612, were published during his lifetime (see the section of Occasional Pieces), but a considerable number of contemporary manuscript collections were in circulation among his friends—so many that Michael Drayton was moved to complain in 1612 in the Preface to his *Polyolbion* that: 'In publishing this Essay on my Poeme, there is this great disadvantage against me; that it commeth out at this time, when Verses are wholly deduc't to Chambers, and nothing esteem'd in this lunatique Age, but what is kept in Cabinets, and must only passe by Transcription.'[1]

As already indicated, Donne's holograph manuscripts have disappeared except for one poem in English and two Latin epigrams:

Verse Letter 'to the Lady Carey and Mrs. Essex Rich', BLO (MS., Eng. Poet. d. 197). (*Poems*, 1633, no. 75.)

Epigram on Joseph Scaliger in his *Opus novum de emendatione temporum*, 1583 (see L 161, p. 275). Library of Sir Geoffrey Keynes.

[1] Drayton twice repeated his complaint in verse; see p. 282.

VIII

Should I tell what, a miracle shee was. /

The Dampe. /

When I am dead, and Doctors know not why,
      And my freinds curiositie,
Will haue me cutt vp, to suruay each part,
When they shall finde. your picture in my hart,
      You thinck a sudden damp of loue
      Will through all theire sences moue.
And works on them as mee, and so preferr
Your murder, to the name of Massacre,
Poore Victories; butt if you dare be braue
            And pleasure in yo conquest haue,
First kill th'Enormous Giant, your disdaine,
And lett th'Enchantres honnor, next be slaine.
            And like a Goth and vandall rize,
            beface reccords, and histories.
Of your owne arts, and tryumphs ouer men,
And without such aduantage kill me then. /
For I coolde muster vp as well as you,
      My Giants, and my witches too.
                              ch
                        v. /

Epigram on Richard Hooker in Covell's *Defence of Ecclesiastical Politie*, 1603 (see L 53, p. 267). Harvard University.

Other manuscripts of Donne's poems are now divided into three classes: (1) those containing large collections of the poems, subdivided into three main groups related to their priorities; (2) those with considerable collections of poems with those of other poets; (3) those containing single poems or small collections. These are set out below. A list of 105 other manuscripts comprising miscellanies or commonplace books containing one or more poems or fragments by Donne is given by John T. Shawcross in his edition of the *Complete Poetry* (see no. 105), pp. 424–7; the list is complete as at present known save for the occurrence of the epigram, 'The lame begger', in BLO (MS. Douce, f. 5) and in Huntington Library (MS. HM 116).

MANUSCRIPTS

(1) *MSS. containing important collections of Donne's poems*

Group I

C 57	Cambridge University Library, Add. MS. 5778.[1]
D	Dowden MS., BLO, MS. Eng. Poet. e. 99 (formerly in the library of Wilfred Merton).
H 49	British Museum, Harleian MS. 4955.
Lec	Leconfield, or Percy, MS. Library of Sir Geoffrey Keynes.[2]
SP	St. Paul's Cathedral Library, MS. 49. B. 43.
H 40	British Museum, Harleian MS. 4064.

Group II

A 18	British Museum, Add. MS. 18647.
N	Norton MS., Harvard College Library, MS. Eng. 966/3 (formerly MS. Nor. 4503).
TCC	Trinity College, Cambridge, MS. R. 3. 12.
TCD	Trinity College, Dublin, MS. G. 2. 21.
L 74	British Museum, Lansdowne MS. 740.
DC	National Library of Wales, Dolau Cothi MS.

[1] Bought from G. David in the market-place at Cambridge, and given by me to the Library 15 December 1916.

[2] This should really be called the Percy MS., since it undoubtedly belonged to Henry Percy, ninth Earl of Northumberland, who died at Petworth House in 1632.

Group III

Dob	Dobell MS., Harvard College Library, MS. Eng. 966/4 (formerly MS. Nor. 4506).
Lut	Luttrell MS. Library of Sir Geoffrey Keynes.[1]
O'F	O'Flahertie MS., Harvard College Library, MS. Eng. 966/5 (formerly MS. Nor. 4504).[2] Derived from the Luttrell MS.
S 96	British Museum, Stowe MS. 961.

Group IV

Westmoreland MS., Berg Collection, New York Public Library.[3]

Manuscripts associated with those of Group III

A 25	British Museum, Add. MS. 25707.
B	Bridgewater MS., Huntington Library, MS. EL 6893.
Cy	Carnaby MS., Harvard College Library, MS. Eng. 966/1 (formerly MS. Nor. 4502).
D 17	Victoria and Albert Museum, Dyce Collection, MS. D. 25. F. 17.
HK	Haslewood-Kingsborough MS. (two parts), Huntington Library MS. HM 198.
JC	John Cave MS., George Arents Tobacco Collection, New York Public Library (formerly in the library of Richard Jennings).
K	King MS., James Osborn Library, Yale University (Raphael King, catalogue 51, item 73).
O	Osborn MS., James Osborn Library, Yale University.
P	Phillipps MS., BLO MS Eng. Poet, f. 9.
S	Stephens MS. Harvard College Library, MS. Eng. 966/6 (formerly MS. Nor. 4500).

---

[1] From the library of Narcissus Luttrell, with his signature dated 1680; sold at Sotheby's, 4 May 1936.

[2] The MS. was described at some length by R. Warwick Bond in catalogue no. 93 issued by Ellis and Elvey of New Bond Street, November 1899.

[3] Formerly in the library of Sir Edmund Gosse, sold at Sotheby's, 30 July 1928, lot 35. It is accepted that the MS. is written in the hand of Rowland Woodward.

the Damp

When I am dead & Doctors know not why
        And my freinds curiosity?
Will haue me cutt vp to suruey Eache part
When they shall find your picture in my heart
        You thinke a suddaine Damp of loue
        Will through all their sinews moue
And worke on them as me, & so preferre
Your murder to the name of Massacre.

Poore victoryes, but if you dare be braue
        And pleasure in your conquest haue
First kill th'enormous Gyant your Disdaine
And lett th'Enchantresse Hono. next be slaine
        And like a Goth & Vandale rise
        Deface Recordes & Hystories
Of your owne Arts & triumphs ouer men
And, without such advantage, kill me then.

For I could muster vp as well as you
        My Gyants & my witches too
Which are vast Constancy & Secretnes
But these I neither looke for, nor professe.
        Kill me as woman, Lett me dye
        As a meere man. Doe you but try
Your passiue valour, & you shall find than
Naked y'haue odds enough of any man.

(2) *MSS. containing considerable collections of Donne's poems with those of other poets*

CCC	Corpus Christi College, Oxford, MS. CCC 327.
EH	Edward Hyde MS. Library of Sir Geoffrey Keynes.[1]
Grey	S. African Public Library, Cape Town, MS. Grey 2. a. 11.
Hd	Harvard College Library, MS. Eng. 966/7 (formerly Nor. 4620).
HN	Hawthornden MS., National Library of Scotland, MS. 2067.
Hol	Holgate MS., Pierpont Morgan Library, New York, MS. 1057.
La	Laing MS. Edinburgh University Library, MS. III. 493.
RP 117	Bodleian Library, MS. Rawl. poet. 117.
S 962	British Museum, Stowe MS. 962.
TCD (2)	Trinity College, Dublin, MS. G. 2. 21 (second collection).
Wed	Wedderburn MS., National Library of Scotland, MS. 6504.
Wel	Welbeck MS., Duke of Portland's Library, University of Nottingham, MS. P w V 37.

(3) *MSS. containing single poems or small sets of poems*

D 16	Dyce Collection, Victoria and Albert Museum, MS. D. 25. F. 16.
G	Gosse MS., Folger Shakespeare Library, Washington, MS. V. a. 241.
H	British Museum, MS. Harleian 3998.
H 51	British Museum, MS. Harleian 5110.
Q	Queen's College, Oxford, MS. 216.

Some of these manuscripts form very attractive volumes. Perhaps the most beautiful from the point of view of script and general condition is the Leconfield MS., now in my library, assigned to the group of the earliest manuscripts, written about 1620. The Leconfield MS. is a quarto volume

---

[1] At each end of the volume is the signature 'Edward Hyde'. Comparison of these with documents in the Bodleian Library and the University Archives leaves no doubt that the manuscript belonged to the future Earl of Clarendon, who contributed an Elegy to *Death's Duell* (see pp. 52 and 196 n.). Beneath one signature someone has written 'is a Knave'.

in a contemporary binding of olive-green morocco, and one page is reproduced here (plate VIII) with one from the Luttrell MS. (plate IX).

Donne died in March 1631, and the publisher, John Marriot, seems to
have entered upon the preparation of his poems for the press very shortly
afterwards, helped, it is conjectured, by Henry King, Bishop of Chichester.
The compilers of the Luttrell and the O'Flahertie MSS. both appear also
to have made their collections with a view to publication, but neither of these
is in fact the source of the printed text. The poems were registered at
Stationers' Hall on 13 September 1632, and the following entry was made:

13° Septembris 1632

John Marriot. Entred for his Copy vnder the handes of Sir Henry
Herbert and both the Wardens *a booke of verses and Poems* (the five
satires, the first, second, Tenth, Eleventh, and Thirteenth *Elegies*
being excepted) and these before excepted to be his when he bringes
lawfull authority   .   .   .   . vj^d

written by Doctor John Dunn
(Arber's *Transcripts* (1877), IV, *249)

Another entry is found shortly afterwards:

31° octobris [1632]

John Marriott. Entred for his Copy vnder the hands of Sir Henry
Herbert and Master Aspley warden *The five Satires* written by
Doctor J: Dun these being excepted in his last entrance   . vj^d

(Ibid., IV, 261)

There is no further entry, however, concerning the excepted elegies. The
first edition of the *Poems*, dated 1633, is accepted as the most trustworthy of
the original editions, though the arrangement is somewhat chaotic. In 1635
the pieces were rearranged and a considerable number were added, but the
additions contain a large proportion of spurious poems; there are also many
verbal alterations, which seem to be derived from the O'Flahertie MS., and
so are of little or no textual value,[1] and some changes of title. Two more
poems were added in 1649 and several unimportant pieces in 1650. Several
more were added in 1669, but of these only two are by Donne. In 1650 the
younger Donne had secured control of the publication and the edition of

[1] According to Dame Helen Gardner, who lists them in *The Divine Poems*, 1952, pp. 118–20.

that year contains a characteristic dedication from his pen. Of the seventeenth-century editions those of 1633 and 1669 occur most commonly. The first contains, as has been said, the best text; that of 1669 is the most complete, but it contains many very bad readings and a large number of spurious pieces. Some of Donne's poems were translated into Dutch by Sir Constantine Huygens early in the seventeenth century, though the translations were not published until 1658 (see no. 108).

The octavo editions from 1635 to 1654 contain the portrait engraved by William Marshall. This is one of the engraver's best plates, but it was never touched up and becomes progressively more worn after 1635 and by 1654 is hardly recognizable.

After Tonson's edition of 1719 very slight notice was taken of Donne's poems during the eighteenth century and, indeed, no edition of importance was published until they were edited by Grosart for the Fuller Worthies Library in 1872–3. The Grolier Club of New York issued a text edited by C. E. Norton in 1895 and an exceedingly useful edition was prepared by Sir (then Mr.) E. K. Chambers for the Muses Library in 1896. All previous editions, however, were superseded by that edited in 1912 for the Clarendon Press by Sir Herbert (then Professor H. J. C.) Grierson, whose scholarship and industry provided for readers of Donne's poems an almost final text, to which few additions have been made. Nevertheless further revisions of the text were done by John Hayward for the Nonesuch edition of 1929 (no. 97), by R. E. Bennett in 1942 (no. 103), Dame Helen Gardner (no. 187), Professor Wesley Milgate (no. 189), Professor J. T. Shawcross (no. 105), and other scholars. A number of poems not previously printed were added successively by Chambers, Gosse, and Grierson, and a new Elegy, possibly by Donne, was identified by Sir E. K. Chambers in the Holgate MS. and printed in *Rev. Eng. Stud.* 1931 (see p. 332). Latin epigrams on Scaliger and Ignatius Loyola have been more recently added to the canon (see pp. 275 and 216).

Donne's *Poems*, 1633, has been printed in facsimile by Scolar Press Ltd., Menston, Ilkley, Yorks. *A Concordance to the English Poems of John Donne* (Chicago: Packard and Company, pp. x, 418), compiled by Homer Carroll Combs and Zay Rusk Sullens, was published in 1940.[1]

[1] Reviewed by L. Cooper, *Mod. Lang. Notes*, LVII, 1942, 241–3.

78 POEMS [*STC* 7045] first edition   4° 1633

Title: Poems . . . London. Printed by M. F. for Iohn Marriot, and are to
be fold at his fhop in St Dunftans Church-yard in Fleet-ftreet. 1633. [*see
facsimile*]

Collation: A⁴ ²A² B–Z⁴ Aa–Zz⁴ Aaa–Fff⁴; 210 leaves.

Contents: A1 blank; A2 title; A3*a*–A4*a Epiftle to the Progreffe of the Soule* (*Infinitati
facrum*, 16. *Augufti* 1601. *Metempfycosis*); A4*b* blank; ²A1*a*–²A2*a The printer to the
Underftanders*; A2*b Hexaftichon Bibliopolae* signed *Jo. Mar*[*riot*]; B1*a*–Fff3*b*
(pp. 1–406) text; Fff4 blank.

Poems, satyres, letters, and elegies upon the author: PAGE

Poëms: 1. The Progresse of the Soule, [stanzas] I–LII   1
     2–8. Holy Sonnets: i. La Corona   v. Crucifying
                          ii. Annunciation   vi. Resurrection
                         iii. Nativitie   vii. Ascension
                          iv. Temple   28
    9–20. Holy Sonnets I–XII   32
   21–36. Epigrams: i. Hero and Leander¹   ix. Antiquary
                       ii. Pyramus and Thisbé   x. Disinherited
                      iii. Niobe   xi. Phryne
                       iv. A burnt ship   xii. An obscure writer
                        v. Fall of a wall   xiii. [Klockius]
                       vi. A lame beggar   xiv. Raderus
                      vii. A selfe accuser   xv. Mercurius Gallo-Belgicus
                     viii. A licentious person¹ xvi. [Ralphius]   40
     37. Elegie I [Iealousie. 1635]   44
     38. Elegie II [The Anagram. 1635]²   45
     39. Elegie III [Change. 1635]   47
     40. Elegie IV [The Perfume. 1635]   49
     41. Elegie V [His Picture. 1635]   51
     42. Elegie VI [Elegie on the L[ord] C[hamberlain].³ 1635]   52
     43. Elegie VII [Elegie VI. 1635]   53
     44. Elegie VIII [Elegie VII. 1635]   55
     45. The Storme. To Mr. Christopher Brooke   56
     46. The Calme   59

¹ Both epigrams printed in Henry Stubbe's *Deliciae Poetarum*, 1658, with Greek translations
(see no. 109, p. 220).

² Printed in A. Wright's *Parnassus Biceps*, London, 1656, 8°, p. 86.

³ i.e. Henry Carey, Baron Hunsdon, but it is doubtful if this identification by Giles Oldisworth is correct.

POEMS,

By J. D.

WITH

ELEGIES

ON THE AUTHORS

DEATH.

LONDON.
Printed by *M. F.* for Iohn Marriot,
and are to be sold at his shop in St *Dunstans*
Church-yard in *Fleet-street.* 1 6 3 3.

Title-page of no. 78

¹ Identification of this by Giles Oldisworth (see no. 80, note) is very dubious.
² See R. C. Bald, *Huntington Library Quart.* xv, 1952, 284.
³ Printed in *Reliquiae Wottonianæ*, 2nd edn. London, 1654, 8º, p. 36, and in later editions.
Also in Walton's *Lives*, 1670, etc.

[1] Printed in A. Wright's *Parnassus Biceps*, London, 1656, p. 118.

[2] First printed in *Lachrymæ Lachrymarum*, 1613; see no. 72.

[3] Not found among the *Letters* of 1651; but reprinted from a MS., probably a copy of the original, in *Epistolary Curiosities*, 1st series, ed. Rebecca Warner, London, 1818, 8o.

[4] Printed in Walton's *Compleat Angler*, London, 1653, 8o, p. 184. See also no. 71.

[5] Nos. 99 and 102 printed in *A Helpe to Memory and Discourse*, 1630 (see no. 73*b*, p. 168). No. 102 also in *Poems by Francis Beaumont*, 1653. The second stanza printed in Sir John Mennes's *Wits Recreations*, 1640.

[6] No. 100 printed in *The Harmony of the Muses*, London, 1654, pp. 97–8, in Henry Stubbe's *Deliciae Poetarum*, 1658, and in Walton's *Lives*, London, 1675, p. 33.

[1] No. 113 printed in John Cotgrave's *Wit's Interpreter*, 1655 (cf. entry p. 293).

[2] Set to music in Corkine's *Second Booke of Ayres*, London, 1612. See no. 71. Part printed in John Gough's *The Academy of Complements*, 1650, 12°. Also printed in Cotgrave's *Wit's Interpreter*, 1655 (twice, pp. 14, 25–6), and in *The Loyal Garland* by S. N., 1686, as 'A Love Song'.

[3] Nos. 133–4 printed in *The Harmony of the Muses*, London, 1654, pp. 99–100, 102–3.

[1] No. 143 printed in *The Harmony of the Muses*, London, 1654, pp. 98–9.
[2] No. 144 set to music in Ferrabosco's *Ayres*, 1609 (see no. 69a, p. 165).
[3] Printed among *Underwoods* in Ben Jonson's *Works*, London, 1640, F°, p. 204.
[4] Printed in Walton's *Life*, 1640, etc.
[5] Also in *Death's Duell*, 1632; Walton's *Life*, 1658, etc.; King's *Poems*, 1657, Playford's *Harmonia Sacra*, 1688 (see p. 221), etc.

Note: The text of this first edition of Donne's collected *Poems* does not appear to have been derived from any single source. Grierson and later editors, notably Gardner and Milgate, believe that the original compiler used two sources belonging to the two main groups of surviving manuscripts, but made changes on his own authority and by reference to yet other manuscripts. The resulting text has more authority than any other in print, but still affords many opportunities for critical emendation. The compiler's care is reflected in the many changes made while the book was passing through the press. In 1914 I made some attempt to find a method of differentiating earlier from later issues, but it became clear that such 'states' were really governed by chance according to the order in which the sheets were taken up for folding before making up the book. No importance, therefore, can be given to the various combinations in which the corrections are found.

The pagination, which is faulty, varies in different copies; the mistakes occurring in the copy of the book from which the poems, etc., were here listed are noted in square brackets in the page references. The most conspicuous irregularity in the

---

[1] This elegy is omitted from later editions of the poems. Its author was identified by Gosse with Sir Thomas Browne of Norwich (*Life of Sir T. B.* by E. Gosse, London, 1905, 8º, p. 18), and Grierson (II, 255) accepted this identification, though there is no evidence in support of it. It seems to me most improbable that the elegy is by Sir Thomas Browne, who in 1633 was an obscure medical student working in Leyden. The author of the poem is more likely to have been Thomas Browne, B.D. (1604–73), undergraduate at Christ Church, Oxford, 1620, and domestic chaplain to Archbishop Laud, 1637. He published in 1634 a sermon preached before the University of Oxford, and signed the *Imprimatur* of Donne's *LXXX Sermons*, 1640 (see no. 29).

[2] Also in *Death's Duell*, 1632.   [3] Also in Walton's *Life*, 1658, etc.; Corbet's *Poems*, 1647.
[4] Also in Walton's *Lives*, 1670, etc.   [5] Also in Carew's *Poems*, 1640.
[6] Identification supplied by Giles Oldisworth (see no. 80, note); also for no. 169 above.

printing occurs on leaf Nn1 (pp. 273-4), where there may be thirty-five lines of text on p. 273 instead of the normal thirty or thirty-one, with omission of the usual running headline, *Poems* between rules, in order to accommodate the extra lines. This is seen in one of my copies of the book, lacking the leaves, 'The Printer to the Understanders'. In a second copy, containing these leaves, the printing of the pages in question has been adjusted. The headline on p. 273 has been restored and there are thirty-three lines of text on p. 273 and thirty-three on p. 274 instead of thirty-five and thirty-one, without any verbal changes.

The prefatory address by the printer, Miles Fletcher, to the 'Understanders' assumes that the readers will understand that there is no formal 'Epistle', as is more usual, because they already know and take it for granted that the contents are 'the best in this kinde, that ever this Kingdome hath yet seene'. He then explains in a rather tortuous manner that the reader must accept the book with all its faults and take it as he finds it. Another edition might be more correct or enlarged. He ends by pointing out that he has compensated for the lack of an Epistle by providing at the conclusion so many Encomiums written by the author's friends. The *Hexastichon Bibliopolæ*, written by the bookseller and publisher, John Marriot, refers to the portrait of Donne in his shroud prefixed to his last sermon, *Death's Duel*, and to his monument in St. Paul's. These represent him dead, whereas if you buy his poems you have him eternally alive.

The first quire of the book consists of four leaves: first leaf blank, second leaf title-page, third and fourth leaves (with sig. A3 and A4) with the Epistle to 'The Progresse of the Soule'. The two leaves with 'The Printer to the Understanders' and *Hexastichon Bibliopolæ* (with sig. A and A2) are an insertion, and are placed sometimes after the Epistle, but more often in the centre of the first quire, so that the collation appears to be: π1 blank, π2 title, A1–A2 *The Printer* etc., A3–A4 *Epistle* etc., and this has misled some authorities. The correct formula is printed above. Sometimes the two leaves of *The Printer* etc. have been omitted altogether. It is evident that they were an afterthought and were inserted only in a portion of the edition, so that their absence is not a defect. The *Juvenilia* of 1633 is frequently found bound in at the end of the volume when in a contemporary binding.

This edition of the *Poems* properly contains no portrait, but the engraving by Lombart from the *Letters*, 1651, is found inserted in some copies. Lowndes recorded as occurring in one copy the engraving by Marshall printed on paper of quarto size. This was no doubt occasioned by the appearance of lot 1194, 'Donne's (John) Poems ... brilliant impression of Marshall's rare portrait, (on large paper) ... green morocco, gilt edges, 1633', in the catalogue of William Pickering's books sold by Sotheby and Wilkinson, fourth day, 10 August 1854. No other copy with this addition is known.

Copies: BM (2, one Ashley Library), BLO (2), ULC (imperfect), ULD; HCL (2), HEH, FLSW (4), LCW, NLC, NYPL (4), PUL, YUL (3).

Cambridge Colleges: Christ's, Clare, Corpus Christi, Gonville and Caius, St. John's, Trinity (2).

Oxford Colleges: All Souls, Christ Church, Corpus Christi, St. John's, Balliol, Brasenose, Queen's, Wadham, Worcester.

Cathedral Libraries: Lincoln, Winchester.

John Rylands Library, Manchester.

G. L. Keynes (2, one Duke of Beaufort copy), R. S. Pirie.

79 POEMS [*STC* 7046] second edition   8° 1635

Title: Poems . . . London Printed by M. F. for John Marriot, and are to be fold at his Shop in Sᵗ Dunſtans Church-yard in Fleet-ſtreet. 1635. [*see facsimile*]

Collation: A–Z⁸ Aa–Dd⁸; 216 leaves.

Contents: A1 title; A2*a*–A4*a The printer to the vnderſtanders*; A4*b Hexaſtichon Bibliopolae* and *Hexaſtichon ad Bibliopolam. Incerti.*; A5*a*–A6*a Epiſtle* to *The Progreſſe of the Soule*; A6*b* blank; A7*a*–Bb8 (pp. 1–388) text; Cc1*a*–Dd8*a Elegies upon the Author* (errata, 6 lines, at bottom of Dd8*a* signed, *Thine, I.M.*); Dd8*b* blank.

Frontispiece: Inserted before A1. A portrait of Donne at the age of 18, engraved by Marshall; the painting from which the engraving was done is not known.[1] A bust of the subject is shewn, within an oval, 8·5 ×6 cm. His dress is plain, but he is represented with long hair and with a large ear-ring in the shape of a cross hanging from his right ear. His right hand is grasping the hilt of his sword. Above the oval, on the left, the engraving is inscribed: *Anno Dni.* 1591. | *aetatis suae.* 18.; above, on the right, is a crest with motto: *Antes muerto que mudado.*[2] Below are eight lines of verse, specially written for this book, beginning: *This was for youth, Strength, Mirth, and wit*, and signed *Iz:Wa:* [Izaak Walton]. At the bottom, on the left, the engraving is signed: *Will: Marshall. ſculpsit.* The plate-mark measures 12·3 × 7·7 cm.

Poems, etc.: As in the edition of 1633 with the omission of nos. 87 and 166, and with the addition of the following:

PAGE

Poems: 1. Song (Soule's joy now I am gone) [*spurious*; probably by the Earl of Pembroke]   62
     2. Farewell to Love   63

[1] The late Laurence Binyon suggested that it may have been a miniature by Nicholas Hilliard, 1537–1619 (Grierson, II, 134).

[2] i.e. 'Sooner dead than changed'. This is a line of Spanish poetry, 'Antes muerta que mudada', from the last stanza of the first song in Montemayor's *La Diana Enamorada* (see T. E. Terrill in *Mod. Lang. Notes*, XLIII, 1928, 318).

X

ANNO DÑI. 1591
ÆTATIS SVÆ 18:

ANTES   MVDADO
MVRTOQVE

This was for youth, Strength, Mirth, and wit that Time
Moſt count their golden Age; but t'was not thine.
Thine was thy later yeares, so much refind
From youths Droſſe, Mirth, & wit; as thy pure mind
Thought (like the Angels) nothing but the Praiſe
Of thy Creator, in thoſe laſt, beſt Dayes.
  Witnes this Booke, (thy Embleme) which begins
  With Love; but endes, with Sighes, & Teares for ſins.

Will: Marshall ſculpſit.   IZ: WA:

POEMS,

By J.D.

WITH

ELEGIES

ON

THE AuTHORS

DEATH.

LONDON

Printed by *M.F.* for JOHN MARRIOT,
and are to be fold at his Shop in Sᵗ *Dunſtans*
Church-yard in *Fleet-ſtreet*.
1 6 3 5.

Title-page of no. 79

[1] Formerly regarded as spurious; accepted by Hayward, 1929, and by Grierson.

[2] Identified by Giles Oldisworth (see no. 80, note) as Lady Goodere, but she had died before 1611.

[3] Printed by Grierson in 1912, but rejected in 1929 (no. 98).

[4] For Tilman's poem which gave rise to this see W. H. Wood in *Essays and Studies*, 1931, p. 184 (p. 258).

[5] For a discussion of this quatrain see *Notes and Queries*, N.S. V, III, 1875, pp. 382, 433, 472–3, 494; IV, 1875, pp. 18, 27; V, 1876, p. 313; VII, 1877, pp. 111–12 (with a summary of the earlier notes, amply demonstrating that it is spurious).

[6] Printed in Walton's *Lives*, London, 1670, etc. 8°, p. 60.

PAGE

Elegies on the Author:
- 35. In obitum venerabilis viri Iohannis Donne [by] Daniel Darnelly.　　Cc2
- 36. Elegie on D. D. [by] Sidney Godolphin.　　Cc6
- 37. On Dr. John Donne, late Deane of S. Paules, London [by] I. Chudleigh.[1]　Cc7

Note: In this edition the pieces have been rearranged (see Grierson, II, lxiii) and there are some changes in the text; they include all that had appeared in 1633 with the exception of Basse's *Epitaph upon Shakespeare,* and Thomas Browne's elegy on the author. Of the thirty-seven pieces that have been added twenty-nine are poems supposed to be by Donne; of these one (no. 17) appears twice and eleven are not accepted as genuine. This edition contains therefore seventeen additional poems by Donne. The *Hexastichon ad Bibliopolam. Incerti* on A4b is also an addition.

The errata, signed *Thine, I[ohn] M[arriot],* explain that the *Epiſtle* to *The Progreſſe of the Soule* (on A5–A6) should have been printed before the poem on p. 301. There seems, however, to have been an earlier issue in which the errata do not appear. This fact was communicated to me by Miss Henrietta C. Bartlett of New York, who had herself examined an example of this issue in the Beverly Chew Library;[2] she states that the volume, which, as far as I know, is unique, is in other respects identical with the ordinary issue.

The variations in a part of the text of this edition from that of 1633 are tabulated in Dame Helen Gardner's *The Divine Poems* (1952), pp. 118–20.

Walton's *Elegie* is given in this and later editions in a revised form, with four additional lines at the end. It is no longer signed.

Copies: BM, BLO, NLS, ULC; HCL (2), HEH, FSLW (2, Arnold & Harmsworth copies), LCW, NLC, PUL, YUL.
Cambridge Colleges: Christ's, Magdalene (2, no portraits).
Wadham College Oxford.
G. L. Keynes (2, one from the library of Lord Denny), R. S. Pirie.

80 POEMS [*STC* 7047] third edition　　8° 1639

Title: Poems . . . London, Printed by M. F. for John Marriot, and are to be ſold at his Shop in St Dunſtans Church-yard in Fleet-ſtreet. 1639. [*see facsimile*]

Collation: A–Z8 Aa–Dd8; 216 leaves.

Contents: A1 title; A2a–A4a *The printer to the vnderſtanders;* A4b *Hexaſtichon* etc.; A5a–V2b (pp. 1–300) text; V3a–V4b *Epiſtle to The Progreſſe of the Soule;* V5a–Bb8b (pp. 301–88) text; Cc1a–Dd8a *Elegies upon the author;* Dd8b blank.

[1] Part is printed in Walton's *Life,* 1658, etc.
[2] Sold at the Anderson Galleries, New York, 8 December 1924, lot 129.

Frontispiece, Poems, etc.: As in the edition of 1635.

Note: The errata of 1635 have been omitted and the *Epiſtle* to *The Progreſſe of the Soule* has been printed in its proper place between pp. 300 and 301. There are a number of minor changes in the text. Nos. 87 and 166 have been restored.

A copy of this edition annotated by Giles Oldisworth (1619–1678) was described by Dr. John Sampson in 1921 in vol. VII of *Essays and Studies by Members of the English Association.* Oldisworth's notes supply several emendations and elucidations, though they are not always quite trustworthy. Dr. Sampson afterwards generously added this copy to my collection of Donne's works.

Copies: BM, BLO, NLS; HCL (2), HEH, FSLW (Corser copy), LCW, NLC, TSP, YUL.

Cambridge Colleges: St. John's, Trinity (Capell Collection).

Oxford Colleges: Christ Church, Worcester (2, no portraits).

Cathedral Libraries: Canterbury, Carlisle, Lambeth Palace.

G. L. Keynes (2, one, the Giles Oldisworth copy, lacking the portrait), R. S. Pirie.

81 POEMS [Wing D 1868] fourth edition, first issue   8° 1649

Title: Poems . . . London Printed by M. F. for John Marriot, and are to be ſold at his ſhop in Sᵗ Dunſtans Church-yard in Fleet-ſtreet. 1649. [*see facsimile*]

Collation: A⁴ B–Z⁸ Aa–Cc⁸; 204 leaves.

*Contents: A*1 blank; *A*2 title; *A*3*a–A*4*a The printer to the vnderſtanders; A*4*b Hexa-ſtichon* etc.; B1*a*–Aa8*b* (pp. 1–368) text; Bb1*a*–Cc8*a Elegies upon the Author;* Cc8*b* blank.

Frontispiece: As in the edition of 1635.

Poems, etc.: As in the edition of 1635 with the addition of the following, after the *Funerall Elegies,* pp. 262–5:

   1. Upon Mr Thomas Coryat's Crudities.[1]
   2. Sonnet. The Token.

Note: Of this edition very few copies seem to have been circulated, and it is now rare. Probably it was never actually published, the sheets of most of the copies being incorporated in the volume issued by the same publisher in 1650 under the editorship of the younger Donne (see next entry). It contains a few unimportant changes in the text.

Copies: BLO (Chew–Hagen copy, given by J. L. Lowes); HCL, HEH, YUL (lacking portrait and last 3 ll.). Univ. of Illinois.

G. L. Keynes, R. S. Pirie (lacking portrait).

[1] First printed in Coryat's *Crudities,* 1611; see no. 70.

POEMS,

By J.D.

WITH

ELEGIES

ON

THE AUTHORS

DEATH.

LONDON,

Printed by *M. F.* for John Marriot,
and are to be sold at his Shop in St *Dunstans*
Church-yard in *Fleet-street.*
1 6 3 9.

Title-page of no. 80

POEMS,

By J.D.

WITH

ELEGIES

ON

THE AUTHORS

DEATH.

LONDON

Printed by *M. F.* for John Marriot,
and are to be sold at his shop in St *Dunstans*
Church-yard in *Fleet-street.*
1 6 4 9.

Title-page of no. 81

82 POEMS [Wing D 1869] fourth edition, second issue   8° 1650

Title: Poems . . . London, Printed for John Marriot, and are to be fold by Richard Marriot at his fhop by Chancery lane end over againft the Inner Temple gate. 1650. [*see facsimile*]

Collation: A⁴ B–Z⁸ Aa⁸ (aa)⁸ (bb)⁴ Bb–Cc⁸; 216 leaves.

Contents: A1 blank; A2 title; A3*a*–A4*a To the Right Honourable William Lord Craven Baron of Hamfted Marfham* signed *John Donne* [*jun.*]; A4*b Hexaftichon Bibliopolae, Hexaftichon ad Bibliopolam. Incerti,* and *To John Donne by B[en] Jons[on]*); B1*a*–(bb)4*b* (pp. 1–392) text; Bb1*a*–Cc8*a Elegies upon the Author;* Cc8*b* blank.

Frontispiece: As in the edition of 1635.

Poems, etc.: As in the edition of 1649, with the addition of the following on the extra leaves, (aa)1–(bb)4 (pp. 369–92):

1. Newes from the very Countrey¹
2. Amiciffimo, & meritiffimo Ben. Jonson. In Vulponem²
3. Aevum fortiti fumus . . . [preface to no. 4]
4. Catalogus Librorum³
5. In Sacram Anchoram Pifcatoris [by] G. Herbert⁴
6. To Mr George Herbert, with one of my Seal, of the Anchor and Christ
7. A fheafe of Snakes ufed heretofore to be my Seal, the Creft of our poore Family⁵
8. Ut primum per literas . . .
9. Tranflated out of Gazæus, Vota Amico facta. fol. 160.
10. To Lucy, Counteffe Of Bedford, with M. Donnes Satyres [by] Ben. Jon[son]
11. To John Donne [by] Ben. Jon[son]
12. [No title] (The heavens rejoyce in motion; why fhould I) [Elegy XVII. Variety. 1669]
13. [No title] (He that cannot chufe but love) [Self-love. Chambers]

Note: The sheets B–Aa and Bb–Cc are those of the preceding entry or at least were printed from the same type, but the first quire of four leaves was changed; in addition to the alterations on the title-page the younger Donne's dedication to Lord Craven was substituted for *The printer to the underftanders,* and a third poem, by Ben Jonson, was added on A4*b.* Furthermore, the additional sheets (aa), (bb) were inserted

¹ First printed in Overburie's *Characters,* 1614; see no. 73.

² First printed in Ben Jonson's *Volpone,* 1607; see no. 69.

³ Reprinted in the editions of 1654, 1669, and 1719, but not included in later editions of the poems. Edited by Mrs. E. M. Simpson in 1930 (see no. 135).

⁴ Printed in Walton's *Life,* 1658, p. 84, and on D6*b* of Herbert's *Jacula Prudentum,* 1651, usually found bound up with *A Priest to the Temple,* 1652, under a general title-page, *Herbert's Remains,* London, T. Garthwait, 1652.

⁵ Printed in Walton's *Life,* 1658, p. 83.

after Aa8, or, sometimes, in error, after Cc8, so that this volume is very variously composed.

Copies: BM, DWL; HCL (2, one Walton's copy),[1] HEH, FSLW, LCW, NLC (O'Flahertie copy), PUL, YUL.

Emmanuel College, Cambridge (sheets A, (aa), and (bb) only).

Christ Church, Oxford. Canterbury Cathedral Library.

G. L. Keynes, J. Sparrow, R. S. Pirie.

[1] Izaak Walton's copy is inscribed after his signature, *Given me by Mr Maryot the 7° of nouember 1650.* He has made notes and emendations in the text on 8 ll.

POEMS,

By J. D.

WITH

ELEGIES

ON THE

AᴜTHORS DEATH.

TO WHICH

Is added divers Copies under his own hand never before in print.

LONDON,

Printed for *John Marriot* , and are to be sold by *Richard Marriot* at his shop by *Chancery* lane end over against the Inner Temple gate. 1 6 5 0.

Title-page of no. 82

83 POEMS [Wing D 1870] fourth edition, third issue   8° 1654

Title: Poems . . . London, Printed by J. Flefher, and are to be fold by John Sweeting, at the Angel in Popeshead-Alley. 1654. [*see facsimile*]

Collation, Contents, Frontispiece, Poems, etc.: As in the edition of 1650.

Note: A reissue of the last edition with cancel title-page.

Copies: BM, BLO; HCL, HEH, FSLW (with notes by Malone), YUL.
Cambridge Colleges: Gonville and Caius, Jesus (no portrait), Pembroke, St. John's, Peterhouse.

POEMS,

By J.D.

WITH

ELEGIES

ON THE

AUTHORS DEATH.

TO WHICH

Is added divers Copies under his own hand never before in Print.

LONDON,

Printed by *J. Flefher*, and are to be fold
by *John Sweeting*, at the Angel in
Popeshead-Alley. 1654.

Title-page of no. 83

Oxford Colleges: Christ Church, Queen's (2), Jesus.

Trinity College, Dublin.

G. L. Keynes, R. S. Pirie (2, one the Norton–Lowell copy, sheet A from the 1649 edn.).

84 POEMS [Wing D 1871] fifth edition　　　　　　　　　　　8° 1669

Title: Poems, & . . . In the Savoy, Printed by T. N. for Henry Herringman, at the fign of the Anchor, in the lower-walk of the New-Exchange. 1669. [*see facsimile*]

Collation: A⁴ B–Z⁸ Aa–Dd⁸; 212 leaves.

Contents: A1 blank; A2 title; A3*a*–A4*a* dedication to Lord Craven; A4*b Hexaftichon* etc.; B1*a*–Dd7*b* (pp. 1–414) text; Dd8 blank.

Poems, etc.: As in the edition of 1650 with the addition of the following:　　PAGE

1. Break of day, stanza 1 [*spurious*; probably by John Dowland]　　　　17
2. Elegie XIIII, ll. 5–44, 57–66, and 83–94　　　　　　　　　　86–9
3. Elegie XVIII [Love's Progrefs. MS.]¹　　　　　　　　　　　94
4. To his Miftrefs going to bed [Elegy XIX. Going to bed. Bridgewater MS.]²　97
5. Satyre VI (To Sir Nicholas Smyth) [*spurious*; probably by Sir John Roe]　138

Note: Printed by Thomas Newcomb (1649–81). There are numerous changes in the text of this edition. Hazlitt states that pp. 95–8, containing the additional elegies, were suppressed, but I have not yet seen a copy in which this was the case. This edition does not, as is sometimes stated,³ contain a portrait. Pp. 121, 123, 221 are numbered 221, 213, 291, but with these exceptions the pagination is correct up to p. 304 (U8*b*); it then becomes very erratic, and the remaining quires are numbered as follows: sign. X is paginated 307–22; sign. Y, 321–36; sign. Z, 377–92; and sign. Aa–Dd, 353–414.

*Copies*⁴: BM, BLO; HCL (2), HEH, FSLW (3), NLC, PUL, YUL.⁵

Cambridge Colleges: King's, St. John's, Magdalene (Pepys Library), Trinity.

Oxford Colleges: All Souls, Christ Church, Merton, Wadham, Worcester.

Trinity College, Dublin.

G. L. Keynes (3, one in red morocco with the arms of the Duke of Buckingham on the sides); R. S. Pirie (contemp. red morocco).

---

¹ First printed in *The Harmony of the Muses*, London, 1654, pp. 36–9, and later in *Wit and Drollery*, London, 1661, pp. 237–40.

² First printed in the *Harmony of the Muses*, pp. 2–3.

³ This mistake appears to have been originated by Lowndes.

⁴ Horace Walpole's copy, shelfmark K. 7. 30, was sold in 1842, but has not yet been recovered by Mr. Wilmarth S. Lewis.

⁵ Coleridge's copy with his notes is in the Beinecke Rare Book Collection.

POEMS, &c.

BY

JOHN DONNE,

late Dean of St. Pauls.

WITH

ELEGIES

ON THE

AUTHORS DEATH.

To which is added

Divers Copies under his own hand,

𝔑𝔢𝔳𝔢𝔯 𝔟𝔢𝔣𝔬𝔯𝔢 𝔓𝔯𝔦𝔫𝔱𝔢𝔡.

In the SAVOY,

Printed by *T. N.* for *Henry Herringman*, at the sign of the *Anchor*, in the lower-walk of the *New-Exchange.* 1669.

Title-page of no. 84

85 [formerly 86] POEMS[1] sixth edition 12° 1719

Title: Poems On Several Occaſions. . . . London: Printed for J. Tonſon, and
    Sold by W. Taylor at the Ship in Pater-noſter-Row. 1719. [*see facsimile*]

Collation: A–Q¹² R–S²; 196 leaves.

Contents: A1 title; A2*a*–A3*b* dedication to Lord Craven; A4*a*–A9*a* *Some account Of*
    the life of Dr. John Donne; A9*b Hexaſtichon*, etc.; A10*a*–A12*b* contents; B1*a*–S1*a*
    (pp. 1–365) text; S1*b*–S2*b Books Printed for Jacob Tonſon.*

[1] No. 85 of the earlier editions has been transferred to the Section of Selected Poems; see p. 219.

POEMS

ON SEVERAL

OCCASIONS.

Written by the Reverend

JOHN DONNE, D.D.

Late Dean of St. PAUL'S.

WITH

ELEGIES on the Author's Death.

To this Edition is added,

Some ACCOUNT of the LIFE
of the AUTHOR.

————————————

LONDON:

Printed for J. TONSON, and Sold by
W. TAYLOR at the *Ship* in
Pater-noſter-Row. 1719.

Title-page of no. 85

Poems, etc.: As in the edition of 1669, with the omission of Satyre VI (addition no. 5, 1669).

Note: The account of Donne's life is abridged from Walton. A copy in the Emerson Collection at Harvard, printed on thick paper, has a variant title-page, both publishers' names being given in full. The book was advertised at 3*s.* in the *London Gazette*, 11 July 1719 (*Notebook of Bennet and Clements*, Oxf. Bib. Soc., 1956, p. 138).

Copies: BM, ULC; HCL, NLC, PUL.
    Trinity College, Cambridge.
    Cathedral Library, Durham.
    G. L. Keynes (3, one in original boards, untrimmed and unopened, Britwell Court copy), R. S. Pirie.

86 POEMS. BELL'S EDITION.   3 vols. 12° 1779

Engraved title: Bell's Edition: The Poets of Great Britain Complete from Chaucer to Churchill. [*vignette, engraved by Delattre after Stothard*] Donne. Vol. I. [II, III] [*quotation from Donne*] Printed for John Bell, near Exeter Exchange Strand, London, Septr 24.th 1779 [vol. II, 1778; vol. III, 17 August 1779]

Printed title: The Poetical Works of Dr. John Donne, Dean of St. Paul's, London, with the Life of the Author [from Walton] [*quotation, 10 lines, from Ben Johnson* (Donne! the delight of Phoebus and each Muse)] Vol. I [II, III] Edinberg: At the Apollo Prefs, by the Martins. Anno 1779.

Collation: Vol. I. Engraved frontispiece and title, A–O⁶, pp. cvi, 107–65, [3, blank]; vol. II. Engraved title, A–O⁶, pp. 168; vol. III. Engraved title, A–Q⁶, pp. 192. The volumes are dated at the end: July 29, Aug. 5, Aug. 12, 1779.

Frontispiece to vol. I. Portrait of Donne engraved by Cook (after the engraving by Lombart).

Contents: Vol. I. Satires and Epithalamions. Vol. II. Songs, Sonnets, Divine Poems, and Epigrams. Vol. III. Elegies, Funeral Elegies, Letters, etc.

Note: Donne comprises vols. XXIII–V of Bell's Edition. Each engraved title has a different vignette after Stothard with a quotation from Donne below. The volumes are also found with the imprint: *London, G. Cawthorn, 1779–1800.*

87 POEMS ED. ANDERSON   8° 1793

A Complete Edition of the Poets of Great Britain. Volume the Fourth London: . . . and . . . Edinburgh. [1793] [Ed. by R. Anderson] 8°

pp. 1–107. The Poetical Works of Dr. John Donne, with short life.

88 POEMS ED. CHALMERS 8° 1810

The works of the English poets, . . . including the series edited, . . . by Dr. Samuel Johnson: . . . The additional lives by Alexander Chalmers, F.S.A. In twenty-one volumes. Vol. v. . . . London: . . . 1810. 8°.

pp. 116–218. Poems of John Donne, with life by Chalmers.

89 POEMS ED. LOWELL 8° 1855

The Poetical Works of Dr. John Donne, with a memoir. Boston: Little, Brown and Company . . . M.DCCC.LV. 8°. pp. xxii, 431.

Frontispiece: Portrait of Donne, drawn and engraved by S. A. Schoff (after the engraving by Merian).

Note: A copy sold at the Parke–Bernet Galleries, New York, on 12 January 1948, carried a pencil note in the hand of James Russell Lowell stating that the volume was edited by him. This copy, bound in original cloth with a paper label on the spine, had a publisher's catalogue, 8 pp., at the front of the volume. Reissued in 1864 and 1866. The book is vol. xxxix of *The Complete Collection of British Poets*, ed. F. J. Child.

90 POEMS ED. LOWELL 8° 1855

The Poetical Works of Skelton and Donne with a memoir of each Four volumes in two
Boston Houghton, Mifflin and Company The Riverside Press, Cambridge [1855] 8°

Note: Donne's poems are printed from the same setting of type as no. 89, the sheets being bound up in the second volume of the combined Skelton and Donne. Eight pages of preliminary matter have been omitted. The engraved portrait of Donne is used as frontispiece to this volume.

91 POEMS ED. GROSART 8° 1872

The Fuller Worthies Library. The complete poems of John Donne, D.D. Dean of St. Pauls. For the first time fully collated with the original and early editions and MSS. and enlarged with hitherto unprinted and in-edited poems from MSS. etc. and portraits, facsimiles, and other illustrations in the quarto form. Edited with preface, essay on life and writings, and notes, by the Rev. Alexander B. Grosart, . . . In two volumes. Vol. I.

[II.] Printed for private circulation. 1872. 8°. Vol. I, pp. xiv, 278, [2]. Vol. II, pp. [ii], lvi, 358.

Illustrations in l.p. copies: 1. Vol. I. Frontispiece. A bust of Donne in an oval 5·5 × 4·2 cm, 'Engraved by W. J. Alais from a miniature painted in 1610 by Isaac Oliver, in the possession of Mr. Samuel Addington' (see *Iconography*, no. 1).

2. Vol. II. Frontispiece. A reproduction of the engraving by Marshall.

3. Vol. II. Facing p. ix. Reproduction of Droeshout's engraving of Hollar's engraving of the effigy in St. Paul's, and of Donne's autograph and seals.

Note: A number of poems were printed here for the first time from MSS., but none of them is accepted by critics as genuine. 100 copies were printed on large paper (4°). Vol. I of the 8° edition has a portrait previously used in vol. I of Alford's edition of Donne's *Works* (see *Iconography*, no. 14).

92 POEMS ED. LOWELL   8° 1895

The Poems of John Donne from the text of the edition of 1633 revised by James Russell Lowell with the various readings of the other editions of the seventeenth century, and with a preface, an introduction, and notes by Charles Eliot Norton. Volume I. [II.] New York: The Grolier Club, 1895. 8°. Vol. I, pp. xxxviii, [ii], 253, [5]. Vol. II, pp. x, [ii], 282, [8].

Frontispieces: Portraits of Donne etched by S. J. Ferris (after the engravings by Marshall and Lombart).

Note: 380 copies on hand-made paper, and three on vellum (one in the collection of R. S. Pirie).

93 POEMS ED. CHAMBERS   8° 1896

The Poems of John Donne. Edited by E. K. Chambers. With an Introduction by George Saintsbury. Vol. I. [II.] London: Lawrence & Bullen . . . 1896. [The Muses' Library] 8°. Vol. I, pp. [ii], lii, 252. Vol. II, pp. xi, 326, [2].

Note: Chambers printed for the first time the Verse Letter 'written by Sir H. G[oodere] and J. D. *alternis vicibus*' (see Milgate's *Satires, Epigrams and Verse Letters*, 1967, pp. 7–8). 100 copies were printed on large paper with a photogravure frontispiece after the portrait ascribed to Jansen.

94 GOSSE: LIFE AND LETTERS   8° 1899

The Life and Letters of John Donne . . . revised and collected by Edmund Gosse In two volumes London 1899 (see p. 324)

Verse letters first printed. Vol. 1, p. 82. To Mr E[verard] G[uilpin].
                    Vol. 2, p. 318. To Mr R[owland] W[oodward].

Note: Gosse transcribed the first poem from the Westmoreland MS. Grierson, II, 169, preferred to think that the recipient was 'a Goodyere', but it seems more probable that Gosse's conjecture was correct (see R. E. Bennett, *Rev. Eng. Stud.* XV, 1939, 66).

95 POEMS ED. CHAMBERS   8° [1926]

The Muses' Library. Poems of John Donne. Edited by E. K. Chambers. With an Introduction by George Saintsbury. Vol. I. [II.] London: George Routledge & Sons, Limited. New York: E. P. Dutton & Co. [n. d.] 8° Vol. I, pp. lii, 252. Vol. II, pp. ix, 326.

Note: Printed from the same setting of type as no. 93.

96 POEMS ED. GRIERSON   8° 1912

The Poems of John Donne. Edited from the old editions and numerous manuscripts with introduction & commentary by Herbert J. C. Grierson M.A. Chalmers Professor of English Literature in the University of Aberdeen. Vol. I. The text of the Poems with Appendices [Vol. II. Introduction and Commentary] Oxford: At the Clarendon Press. 1912. 8°. Vol. I. pp. xxiv, 474, [2]. Vol. II. pp. cliii, [iii], 276.

Reviewed: Belden, H. M., *Journ. Eng. Germ. Philol.* XIV, 1915, 135–48.
  Chambers, E. K., *Mod. Lang. Rev.* IX, 1914, 269–71.
  Times Lit. Sup., 30 January 1913, 37–8.
  Spectator, CX, 1913, 102–3.

97 POEMS, ETC. ED. HAYWARD   8° 1929

John Donne Dean of St. Paul's Complete Poetry and Selected Prose Edited by John Hayward The Nonesuch Press Bloomsbury 1929 19 cm, pp. [iv], xxiii, [i], 793, [3].

Contents: Poems: complete.
  Selected Prose: Paradoxes and Problemes.
             Ignatius his Conclave.
             Miscellaneous Prose.
             Letters (selected). (See no. 68c.)
             Meditations from Devotions.
             Sermons (selections, with *Death's Duell* in full).

Note: Of this edition 675 copies were printed on special paper and bound in whole niger morocco. The text of the Poems is necessarily based upon that of Professor Grierson, but the editor has collated independently all the printed texts and most of the MSS.

Reviewed:

Beachcroft, T. O., *New Criterion*, IX, 1930, 747–50.
Cogan, I., *Poetry Rev.* 1930, pp. 183–94.
Dalatte, F., *Rev. belge philol. & d'hist.* IX, 1931, 3–4.
Koszul, A., *Rev. Anglo-Améric.* IX, 1932, 548–9.
MacCarthy, D., *Sunday Times* (Lond.), 27 January 1929.
Marshall, H. P., *Edinb. Rev.* CCXLIX, 1929, 375.
Porter, A., *Spectator*, CXLI, 1929, 289.
Quennell, P., *New Statesm.* XXXII, 1929, 568.
R., *Sat. Rev. Lit.* V, 1929, 817.
Sackville-West, V., *Nat. & Athen.* XLIV, 1929, 846–7.
Smith, G. C. Moore, *Mod. Lang. Rev.* XXIV, 1929, 104–5.
Sparrow, J., *Lond. Mercury*, XX, 1929, 93–7.
Times Lit. Sup., 26 March 1931, pp. 241–2.
Welby, T. E., *Sat. Rev.* CXLVII, 1929, 358.

98 POEMS ED. GRIERSON 8° 1929

The Poems of John Donne Edited by H. J. C. Grierson Professor of Rhetoric and English Literature in the University of Edinburgh London Oxford University Press Humphrey Milford 1929 18·5 cm, pp. lvi, 404.

Note: The text of this edition is based upon the editor's larger edition of 1912 (see no. 96), and contains a few corrections and improvements. There is a new introduction, and the *apparatus criticus* is abbreviated. Part of the edition was printed on India paper. This edition was the basis for *A Concordance to the English Poems of John Donne by H. C. Combs and Z. R. Sullens.* Chicago. Packard and Co. 1940. 25·8 cm, pp. x, 418.

Reviewed:

B., A., *Arch. Stud. neueren Sprach.* CLXIV, 1933, 301–2.
Beachcroft, T. O., *New Criterion*, IX, 1930, 747–50.
Bruel, A., *Rev. Angl. Amer.* XII, 1934, 152–3.
C., H. B., *Manch. Guard. Weekly*, XXIX, 1933, 452.
Cazamian, L., *Rev. Anglo-Améric.* VIII, 1931, 355–6.
Fischer, W., *Anglia Beiblatt.* XLV, 1934, 208–9.
Liljegren, S. B., *Englische Stud.* LXVI, 1931, 274–5.
Praz, M., *Eng. Stud.* XII, 1930, 117–19.

Richter, H., *Anglia Beiblatt.* XLII, 1931, 71–4.
Robbie, H. J. L., *Rev. Eng. Stud.* VI, 1930, 475–6.
Schirmer, W. F., *Deutsche Literaturz.* LII, 1931, 455–6.
Sisson, C. J., *Mod. Lang. Rev.* XXV, 1930, 246–7.
Times Lit. Sup., 6 February 1930, p. 96; 26 March 1931, pp. 241–2.

99 POEMS, ETC. ED. HAYWARD   8° 1930

John Donne Dean of St. Paul's Complete Poetry and Selected Prose Edited by John Hayward London: The Nonesuch Press New York: Random House Inc. 1930 19 cm, pp. [iv], xxiii, [i], 794, [2].

Contents: As in no. 97, with the addition of a Latin epigram and a passage from *Six Sermons*, and with some changes in the text. Ninth impression revised, 1962. Tenth impression, 1967.

100 POEMS ED. FAUSSET   8° 1931

The Poems of John Donne [Edited with an introduction by Hugh I'Anson Fausset] London & Toronto Published by J. M. Dent & Sons Ltd. In New York by E. P. Dutton & Co [1931] 17 cm, pp. xxx, 290.

Note: Everyman's Library, no. 867. The text is modernized throughout. Reprinted 1938.
Reviewed: Times Lit. Sup., 26 March 1931, pp. 241–2.

101 POEMS ED. GRIERSON   8° 1933

The Poems of John Donne Edited by Sir Herbert Grierson . . . Geoffrey Cumberlege Oxford University Press London [1933]

Note: Printed from the same setting of type as no. 98, though machined, according to the imprint on the last page, by J. and J. Gray, Edinburgh, instead of by the Oxford University Press. Reprinted in 1937, 1939, 1942, 1945, 1949, 1951, 1953, and 1966.

102 POETRY AND SELECTED PROSE   8° 1941

The Complete Poetry and Selected Prose of John Donne & The Complete Poetry of William Blake with an Introduction by Robert Silliman Hillyer . . . Random House New York [1941] 22·8 cm, pp. lv, 1045, [3].

Note: The text of Donne follows that of no. 99. Reprinted in *The Modern Library*, N.Y., 1946.

103 POEMS ED. BENNETT   8° 1942

The Complete Poems of John Donne Edited by Roger E. Bennett Packard
and Company Chicago [1942] 18 cm, pp. xxix, [i], 306.

Note: In the University Classics series. The text is modernized and embodies emenda-
tions based on fresh research, though the *apparatus* at the end is greatly abbreviated.
The epigram 'Manliness' from W (Westmoreland MS.) is first printed here (see
Milgate's *Satires, Epigrams and Verse Letters*, 1957, p. 52).

Reviewed: Botting, R. E., *Mod. Lang. Notes*, LIX, 1944, 141–2.
Allen, D. C., *Journ. Eng. Germ. Philol.* XLI, 1942, 548–9.

104 POETRY AND SELECTED PROSE   8° 1952

The Complete Poetry and Selected Prose of John Donne Edited, with an
Introduction by Charles M. Coffin . . . The Modern Library New York
[1952] 18 cm, pp. xliv, 594, [2].

Note: The text follows that of no. 99. Published by Random House Inc.

105 COMPLETE POETRY ED. SHAWCROSS   8° 1967

The Complete Poetry of John Donne With an introduction notes and
variants by John R. Shawcross Anchor Books Doubleday & Company
Inc. New York [1967] 20·8 cm, pp. xxv, [ii], 521, [1] (paperback
edition).

Note: The editor adds three items for the first time to Donne's *Collected Poems:* 1. No.
102 *Faustus* (a couplet of little value from the Hawthornden MS.).
     2. No. 104 *Ad Autorem* (the four-line epigram to Joseph Scaliger (see p. 275).
     3. *Ignatii Loyolae* ἀποθέωσις[1] (in an Appendix).
He prints also at the end an elaborate Apparatus, an Index of Textual Differences from
Gardner's Text, and a Table for Use with Combs and Sullens's *Concordance*.

106 COMPLETE ENGLISH POEMS ED. SMITH   1971

John Donne The Complete English Poems Edited by A. J. Smith Penguin
Books [Harmondsworth, Middx., Baltimore, Victoria. Penguin Education Poetry ISBN 0 14 080 236 3].

Note: Nearly half the book (pp. 352–666) is occupied by the editor's notes. The cover
has a reproduction of the Lothian portrait with lipstick and other colouring added.

---

[1] Durham Cathedral Library, Hunter MSS., XXVII.

SELECTED POEMS AND PROSE
INCLUDING TRANSLATIONS
AND MUSICAL SETTINGS

107 HARMONY OF THE MUSES [Wing C 105]   8° 1654

The harmony of the Muses: or, The Gentlemans and Ladies Choifeſt
Recreation; . . . Heretofore written by thoſe unimitable Maſters of
learning and Invention,

Dr. Joh. Donn	Sr. Kenelm Digby	J. Cleveland
Dr. Hen. King	Mr. Ben. Johnſon,	T. Randolph
Dr. W. Stroad	Mr. Fra. Beamont	T. Carew.

. . . Never before Publiſhed.

London, Printed by T. W. for William Gilbertſon . . . 1654.

Collation: A–G⁸; 56 leaves, with an engraved frontispiece.

Poems not previously printed: Elegie XVIII [Loves Progress, 1669], pp. 36–7. Elegie
XIX [Going to bed, 1669],[1] pp. 2–3.

Already printed in 1633: A Valediction forbidding mourning, pp. 97–8. Loves diet,
pp. 99–100. The Prohibition, pp. 98–9. The Will, pp. 102–3.

Attributed, but probably spurious: Dr. Dun's answer to a Lady, p. 75.[2]

Certainly spurious: On Black eyes by J.D., pp. 39–40.

Copy: HEH.

108 *HUYGENS'S KORENBLOEMEN*   4° 1658

Title: Koren-bloemen. Nederlandſche gedichten Van Constantin Huygens
Ridder, . . . In XIX Boecken.

In's Graven-Hage By Adriaen Vlack M.DC.LVIII. . . .

Collation: *–***⁴ ****² A–Z Aa–Zz Aaa–Zzz Aaaa–Zzzz Aaaaa–Zzzzz Aaaaaa–
Zzzzzz Aaaaaaa–Zzzzzzz Aaaaaaaa–Kkkkkkkk⁴; 698 leaves.

Translations: Pp. 1089–120 *Uyt Engelſch Dicht Van Doctor John Donne*

1. De Vloy [1633, no. 127]
2. De verſchijning [1633, no. 98]
3. Toovery door een' Schildery [1633, no. 96]
4. Den Hof te Twichnam [1633, no. 118]
5. Liedt [1633, no. 102]

---

[1] Printed again in *Wit and Drollery*, London, for Nath. Brook, 1661, p. 237.

[2] MS. V. a. 170 in the Folger Shakespeare Library contains among copies of poems by Donne
a couplet headed 'A Lady to Dr. Donne' with 'His answere to the Lady', of which there is a
variant form in MS. V. a. 345 headed 'Dr Donne to his Mrs'. These lines were printed by
Prof. R. G. Howarth in his *A Pot of Gillyflowers*, Cape Town, 1964.

6. De dry-dobbele geck [1633, no. 109]
7. Schreyens affcheit [1633, no. 125]
8. De Droom [1633, no. 124]
9. De Verftelling [1633, no. 38]
10. Aen fijn Lief [1633, part of no. 43]
11. De Vervoering [1633, no. 131]
12. De Bloeffem [1633, no. 136]
13. Vrouwen ftandvaftigheit [1633, no. 103]
14. Affcheit, met verbot van treuren [1633, no. 100]
15. De opgaende Son [1633, no. 105]
16. Dagheraet [1633, no. 115]
17. Godheit der Minne [1633, no. 132]
18. De Dood-gift [1633, no. 112]
19. Goede Vrydagh. Rijdende Weftwaert [1633, no. 92]

Note: The translations are preceded by one leaf *Tot den leser*, and two poems, *Aen Teffelfchade* and *Aen ein' fchoone Weduwer*. Huygens explains in the note *Tot den leser* that 'Charles I having heard of his intention to translate Dr. Donne, "declared he did not believe that anyone could acquit himself of that task with credit" ' (Grierson, II, lxxvii). This is also referred to by Morhof in his *Polyhistor* (see p. 303) where he writes: 'Quorum [*Poemata*] aliquot in Linguam Belgicam vertit Constantius Hugonius a Carolo secundo Rege sollicitatus, qui inimitabilem Germanis et Belgis hujus viri stylum putabat.' For Huygens's opinion of Donne expressed in a letter to Hooft in 1630 see Grierson (loc. cit.). The translations are also referred to in M. Llewellyn's *Men-Miracles*, 1646, in a passage the last two lines of which run:

> Thus we climbe downwards, and advance as much
> As He that turn'd Donne's Poems into Dutch.
> (J. B. to my Ingenious Friend Captaine LL.)

The second edition (BM) was published in 1672, with the translations from Donne as before (pt. II. pp. 533–57).

Further interesting references to Donne will be found in the section of Biography and Criticism under Huygens and in Rosalie Colie's book, *Some Thankfulness to Constantine*, The Hague, 1956.

Copies: BM, BLO (presentation copy with inscription by Huygens); HCL.
G. L. Keynes.

109 STUBBE'S DELICIÆ POETARUM [Wing S 6040]

8° 1658

Title: Deliciæ Poetarum Anglicanorum in Græcum versæ. Quibus accedunt Elogia Romæ & Venetiarum. Authore H. Stubbe A.M. ex æde Christi.

Oxoniæ, Excudebat H. Hall, Aacademiæ Typographus, impensis
Edvardi Forrest. 1658.

Collation: A–C⁸ D²; 26 leaves.

Translations: pp. 36–41, English and Greek versions on opposite pages.
1. A Valediction forbidding mourning [1633, no. 100]
2. Hero and Leander. [1633, no. 21]
3. A licentious person [1633, no. 28]

Copies: BM, BLO; HEH, YUL.
Trinity College, Cambridge. Worcester College, Oxford.

110 HARMONIA SACRA   f° 1688

Harmonia Sacra: or, Divine Hymns and Dialogues, [Edited by Henry
Playford] London: E Jones for H. Playford. 1688. f°.

Poem: 'Wilt thou forgive that Sin where I begun' ('A Hymn to God the Father', *Poems*,
1633, p. 350). The Words by Dr. Dunn. Set by Mr. Pelham Humphreys.

Note: In *The Second Part*, 1693, fº, pp. 23–4, is an unsigned setting for Sir Thomas
Browne's Evening Hymn, 'The night is come like to the day'. In the third edition,
1714, Donne's and Browne's poems are placed together at pp. 67–8.

Copies: BLO, BM, TCC; HEH, HCL.

111 THE GROVE   8° 1721

The Grove; or, A Collection of Original Poems, Translations, &c. By W.
Walsh, Esq; Dr. J. Donne. Mr. Dryden. . . . London: Printed for
W. Mears, at the Lamb without Temple-Bar. 1721. A⁸b⁸B–Z⁸.

Poem: pp. 37–9. 'Absence. By Dr. Donne. This Poem was found in an old Manuscript
of Sir John Cotton's of Stratton in Huntingdon-Shire.'

Note: The poem is of doubtful authorship. Grierson, 1, 428, regarded it as being probably
by John Hoskyns. *The Grove* was reissued in 1732 with a cancel title: *A Miscellany of
Original Poems, Translations, &c. Collected and Published by Mr. Theobald.*

Copies: BM, etc.
G. L. Keynes (on large paper, 22·5 × 13·5 cm).

112 POPE'S WORKS   8° 1735

The Works Of Alexander Pope Efq.; Vol. II . . . London: Printed for L.
Gilliver, 1735. 8°

Poems: pp. 131–61. Satires of Dr. John Donne [the second and fourth, versified by
A. Pope, with the original versions on the left-hand pages].

Note: The Fourth Satire was first printed as *The Impertinent, Or A Visit to the Court.
London: Printed for John Wileord [Wilford].* 1733. fº. The Second Satire was
printed for the first time in vol. II. of the *Works* (1735), both folio and octavo.

113 POPE'S WORKS [PARNELL]   8º 1738

The Works Of Alexander Pope, Esq; Vol. II. Part II. . . . London: Printed
  for R. Dodsley . . . 1738. 8º.

Poem: pp. 151–63. 'Third Satire of Dr. John Donne. Versifyed by Dr. Parnell', with
  the original lines and Parnell's versification on opposite pages.

Note: Parnell's versification of Donne's satire was not included in any edition of his
  works and was first printed here, although the volume contains nothing else that is not
  by Pope. It was not printed again until 1751 in Warburton's edition of Pope's *Works*.

114 MORAVIAN HYMNS   8º 1754

A Collection of Hymns . . . Designed chiefly for the Use of the Congregations In Union with the Brethren's Church. London. 1754. 8º.

A3. Reference to Donne in the Preface.
pp. 222–4. No. 383. [four Holy Sonnets]
  No. 384. The Litany [abridged]

115 TWO POEMS ED. WALDRON   4º 1802

The Shakespearean miscellany: . . . Printed chiefly from Manuscripts . . . by
  F. G. Waldron, . . . London: . . . 1802. 4º.

Poems: Among *Miscellaneous Poetry.*
pp. 1–5. Two Elegies by Dr. Donne
  1. (Till I have peace with thee, warre other men) [Love's War]
  2. (Is death so great a gamester that he throws)

Note: The first is also printed by Waldron in his *Collection of Miscellaneous Poetry* (1802),
  and, later, by Simeon (see no. 121). The second is by William Browne.

116 SELECTED POEMS ED. CAMPBELL   8º 1819

Specimens of the British Poets; with biographical and critical notices, . . .
  By Thomas Campbell. In seven volumes. Vol. III. . . . London: John
  Murray, . . . 1819. 8º.

pp. 73–9. Four poems by Donne, with biographical notice.

117 SELECTED POEMS ED. SANFORD   12° 1819

The work of the British poets. With lives of the authors, by Ezekiel Sanford. Vol. IV. . . . Philadelphia: . . . 1819. 12°.

pp. 133–95. Select Poems of Donne, with life by Sanford.

118 SELECTED POEMS ED. SOUTHEY   8° 1831

Select works of the British poets, . . . with biographical sketches by Robert Southey Esqr. LL.D. London . . . 1831. 8°.

pp. 714–31. Poems of John Donne, with life by Southey.[1]

119 SACRED POEMS   8° 1835

The Sacred Classics: or, Cabinet Library of Divinity . . . [London] MD CCC XXXV [etc.] 8°. Vol. XXVI Sacred Poetry of the seventeenth century, pt. ii, 1836.

pp. 53–78. John Donne (eight poems).

120 SELECT WORKS   12° 1840

Selections from the Works of John Donne, D.D. . . . Oxford: D. A. Talboys. 1840. 14·8 cm, pp. vi (numbered viii), 280.

Note: This consists chiefly of prose extracts, with a small selection from the poems at the end (pp. 269–80). Published in blind stamped cloth, with architectural gold block on spine lettered *Donne's | Select | Works*. The title is printed within a gothic architectural design, and there are other embellishments on pp. v, vi, 1, 280.

121 UNPUBLISHED POEMS ED. SIMEON   1856

Miscellanies of the Philobiblon Society. Vol. III. . . . London: . . . 1856–7.

Poems: Unpublished Poems of Donne, 31 pp., with a prefatory note by Sir John Simeon, Bart.

Note: Simeon prints here seventeen poems and three epigrams, all of which are spurious or doubtful except one (Till I have peace with thee, warre other men), which had already been printed by Waldron (see no. 115). One epigram, 'The Lier', is accepted by Milgate (*Satires, Epigrams and Verse Letters*, 1967, p. 53).

[1] For a list of other anthologies of the nineteenth century containing poems by Donne see R. B. Botting, p. 142 (p. 329 of this Bibliography).

122 SELECTED POEMS ED. GILFILLAN   8° 1860

Specimens with memoirs of the Lesser-known British Poets. Ed. George
Gilfillan. Edinburgh. 1860. 3 vols. 8°.

I, pp. 201–29. Memoir of Donne ('a great genius ruined by a false system') with Holy
Sonnets and The Progress of the Soul.

123 SELECTED POEMS ED. PALGRAVE   8° 1889

The Treasury of Sacred Song. Ed. F. T. Palgrave. Oxford. 1889. 8°.

pp. 19–20. John Donne (four poems); p. 333, a brief note on Donne's life and poems.

124 SELECTED POEMS   16° 1897

The Bibelot. Vol. III. No. 4. Selections from Dr. John Donne. Thomas B.
Mosher, Portland, Maine, April, 1897. 16°. pp. [10], 109–35, [6].

125 SELECTED POEMS   8° 1904

The Orinda Booklets V. John Donne: Selected Poems. Henry King:
Elegies, etc. Izaak Walton: Verse-Remains. J. R. Tutin, Cottingham
near Hull. 1904. Limited to 1000 copies. 8°. pp. 63, [1].

126 LOVE POEMS ED. NORTON   12° 1905

The Love Poems of John Donne selected and edited by Charles Eliot
Norton Boston Houghton, Mifflin & Company MDCCCCV 19 cm, pp. xii,
[ii], 85, [1].

Note: 535 copies printed at the Riverside Press, Cambridge, Mass. Designed by Bruce
Rogers.

127 SELECTED POEMS ED. BABBOTT   4° 1905

Poems of John Donne selected from his Songs, Sonnets, Elegies, Letters,
Satires, and Divine Poems . . . The Marion Press, Jamaica, Queens-
borough, New-York. 1905. 25·5 cm, pp. xiii, [iii], 133, [3].

Frontispiece: Portrait of Donne engraved on wood by Henry Wolf (after the painting in
the Deanery of St. Paul's).

Note: 100 copies printed on hand-made paper. There is a short introduction by Mr.
Frank L. Babbott, for whom the volume was printed.

128 SEVEN SONNETS MUSIC BY FUSNER 1912

La Corona (The Crown)—Seven Sonnets of John Donne set to music by
Henry Fusner. For tenor solo, mixed chorus, oboe, harp, and strings.
Vocal score with organ accompaniments [Roselle Park. New Jersey.
c. 1912].

129 SELECTION 12° 1922

Selection from John Donne The Medici Society Ltd London: 7 Grafton
Stteet [*sic*], W. 1 [1922] 12·5 cm, in fours; pp. 30, [2].

130 SELECTION 12° 1923

Selections from John Donne The Medici Society Ltd. London 7 Grafton
Stteet [*sic*] W. 1 [1923] 12·8 cm, pp. 29, [3].

131 LOVE POEMS 8° 1923

Love Poems of John Donne With some account of his life taken from the
writings in 1639 of Izaak Walton Soho The Nonesuch Press 30 Gerrard
Street 1923 26 cm, in fours, pp. xxiii, [i], 91, [7].

Note: 1,250 numbered copies were printed at the Oxford University Press in Fell types
on Vidalon hand-made paper. Collotype frontispiece after the engraving in *LXXX
Sermons* (1640). The first publication of the Nonesuch Press. 'A few *ad personam*
copies' were issued in stained vellum (*Nonesuch Century*, p. 51).

Reviewed:

Eliot, T. S., *Nat. & Athen.* XXXIII, 1923, 331–2.
Strachey, J. St. L., *Spectator*, CXXX, 1923, 969.
Times Lit. Sup., 10 May 1923, p. 319.

132 SELECTION 12° 1926

Selections from John Donne The Medici Society Ltd. London: 7 Grafton
Street, W.1 Boston, U.SA.: 755 Boylston Street also Liverpool,
Bournemouth, and Harrogate [1926] 12.8 cm, pp. 27, [3], first and
last leaves blank used as paste-downs.

133 AUGUSTAN BOOK ED. WOLFE 8° 1927

The Augustan Books of English Poetry Second Series Number One John
Donne [with brief introduction by Humbert Wolfe] London: Ernest
Benn. 22 cm, pp. iv, 5–31, [1]. 24 poems.

134 SELECTED POEMS ED. COLE   8° 1928

John Donne Selected Shorter Poems Edited by G. D. H. & M. I. Cole
London Noel Douglas 1928 16·5 cm, pp. 61, [3].

Note: The Ormond Poets, No. 7.

135 COURTIER'S LIBRARY ED. SIMPSON   12° 1930

The Courtier's Library, or *Catalogus Librorum Aulicorum incomparabilium et
non vendibilium* By John Donne Edited by Evelyn Mary Simpson with
a translation 1930 The Nonesuch Press 16 Great James Street, W.C.
16 cm, pp. [iv], 93, [i].

Note: This is the first separate reprint of the *Catalogus Librorum,* which was among
the prose pieces added by the younger Donne to the *Poems* of 1650 (see no. 82).
It was reprinted in the editions of 1654, 1669, and 1719, but not afterwards. The
editor has collated the printed texts with a MS. copy in a commonplace-book now in
the library of Trinity College, Cambridge. 950 copies were printed at Oxford in Fell
types on Auvergne hand-made paper. Enclosed in slip-case lettered on side.

136 POEMS ED. FAUSSET   8° 1931

The Poems of John Donne London & Toronto J. M. Dent New York
E. P. Dutton & Co. [1931] 17 cm, pp. xxx, 290.

Note: With introduction by H. I'A. Fausset. Acknowledgements to Grierson and
others. No. 867 of Everyman's Library.

137 SONGS AND SONETS   8° 1932

John Donne Songs and Sonets The Peter Pauper Press Mount Vernon
New York [1932] 23·5 cm [not seen].

Note: Reprinted in 1941 and probably at another date before that, but Mr. Beilenson,
the publisher, is unable to remember and has no record.

138 SELECTED POEMS TRANSL. INTO FRENCH   1936

In Revue de Littérature Comparée. Vol. XVI. October 1936. pp. 710–16.
'Aubade; Chansonne; Constance féminine; Infini d'amour; Ta fièvre;
Message; Sorcellerie par image; Le gage.' Translations by F. Baldeune.

139 LOVE POEMS 8° 1937

The Love Poems of John Donne Dean of St. Paul's 1937 Chatto and
Windus London 18·2 cm, pp. lx, [i].

Note: Zodiac Books no. 3. Reprinted 1941, 1950.

140 HOLY SONNETS ED. FAUSSET 8° 1938

Introduction by Hugh l'A. Fausset Engravings by Eric Gill [*rule*] The
Holy Sonnets of John Donne [*rule*] London: J. M. Dent & Sons Ltd
for Hague & Gill Ltd [1938] 26 cm, pp. xiv, [26].

Note: Four wood engravings and a final decoration by Gill. 550 copies printed in
October 1938 signed by the artist.

Reviewed: Times Lit. Sup., 24 December 1938, p. 812.

141 POETRY AND PROSE ED. HAWKINS 16° 1938

Poetry and Prose of John Donne Selected and Edited by A. Desmond
Hawkins Thomas Nelson & Sons Ltd London. . . . [1938] 15·5 cm,
pp. vi, 7–479, [1].

Note: Nelson Classics. Reprinted 1950, 1955.

142 LA CORONA DUTCH TRANSLATION 8° 1939

John Donne Dean of St. Paul's 1573–1631 De wonderbare Tweestrijd La
Corona—Gewijde Sonnetten MCMXXXIX Marnix-Pers Amsterdam 22·5
cm, pp. 35, [5].

Note: Translations into Dutch by Hein de Bruin, Fedde Schurer, Gabriel Smit, Peter
Venemans, and Theun de Vries, with G. K. v. d. Heijden. 50 copies clandestinely
printed and published *c.* 1944.

143 SELECTED POEMS 8° 1941

Some Poems and A Devotion of John Donne The Poet of the Month New
Directions Norfolk, Connecticut 1941 23 cm, 16 ll., unnumbered.

Note: Printed from Caslon type by D. B. Updike, The Merrymount Press, Boston,
U.S.A.

144 LOVE POEMS   8° [before 1943]

The Love Poems of John Donne Late Dean of St. Paul's b. 1573 d. 1631 The Peter Pauper Press New Rochelle 23·5 cm, pp. [ii], 70, [2].

Colophon: The present volume contains the complete group of lyrics known as *Songs & Sonets*. This edition consists of one hundred copies, handset in Deberny roman and printed on ivory Shadowmould paper by the Walpole Printing Office, New Rochelle.

145 POESIE ITALIAN TRANSLATION   8° 1944

Poesie con testo a fronte, traduzione e prof. di Franco Giovannelli. Modena, Guanda 1944 19 cm, pp. 111.

Note: Collectione Fenice, 7. Poems in English and Italian.

146 THREE SONNETS WITH MUSIC   1944

Three Sonnets of John Donne set to Music for high voice and piano by Douglas Moore New York G. Schirmer inc. 1944

147 THE FANTASTICKS   8° 1945

The Fantasticks Donne Herbert Crashaw Vaughan by W. S. Scott John Westhouse London 1945 21·5 cm, pp. 170 (pp. 10–53, 'John Donne', with selected verse).

148 SELECTED POEMS TRANSLATED INTO CZECH
                                                 8° 1945

O Pilgrim Soul: Ó Duše Poutniku. Czechoslovak P.E.N. 1945 17·5 cm, pp. 32.

Note: Evergreen Series. Thirteen poems translated into Czech with a comment, also translated, by Sir Herbert Read.

149 HENGIVELSEN [The Ecstacy *sic*]   8° 1945

John Donne Hengivelsen Oversættelse: Ove Abildgaard Træsnit: Povl Christensen København H. Hirschsprungs Forlag 1945 19 cm, pp. 21, [3].

Note: 1,000 numbered copies. English and Danish texts on opposite pages. Illustrated with wood engravings. Printed by Branco Luno's Printing House on imitation Japanese vellum. Sent as a New Year's gift to friends of the publisher.

150 HOLY SONNETS MUSIC BY BRITTEN 1946

The Holy Sonnets of John Donne, op. 35 By Benjamin Britten. High voice and piano. London. New York. Boosey & Hawkes [*c.* 1946, reprinted 1951] 31 cm, pp. 40.

151 LOVE POEMS 8° 1946

Donna mia: a group of Love Poems by John Donne with drawings by Kurt Roesch. Mount Vernon, New York. The Golden Eagle Press. 1946. 26 cm, 8 plates, pp. 44.

152 SELECTED POEMS ED. DELATTRE 8° 1946

John Donne Poems (1633) Texte établi par F. Delattre Paris Société d'Edition 'Les Belles Lettres' 1946 20 cm, pp. 60.

153 SELECTED POEMS AND PROSE ED. GARROD 8° 1946

John Donne Poetry & Prose with Izaac Walton's Life Appreciations by Ben Jonson, Dryden, Coleridge and others With an Introduction and Notes by H. W. Garrod Oxford At the Clarendon Press 1946 18·5 cm, pp. lviii, 126. Portrait after Marshall.

154 SELECTED POEMS ED. EGGINK 8° 1946

John Donne Poems selected from his Songs and Sonets Elegies Epithalamions Verse Letters Divine Poems Amsterdam A. A. Balkema 1946 19·2 cm, pp. [iv], 80, [4 blank].

Note: The poems selected by Clara Eggink from Hayward's edition; the portrait and title engraved by S. L. Hartz; the book designed by J. van Krimpen and printed by Joh. Enschedé en Zonen, Haarlem.

155 LOVE POEMS WITH A DEVOTION 8° 1946

Love Poems of John Donne Together with the Devotion: 'For whom the Bell Tolls' Peter Pauper Press Mount Vernon New York [1946] 23·5 cm, pp. [ii], 73, [6].

156 SELECTED POETRY AND PROSE ED. SCOTT 8° 1946

Poetry and Prose of John Donne selected by Walter Sydney Scott John Westhouse London [1946] 18·5 cm, pp. [viii], 9–444.

Note: With foreword by Adam Fox.

157 A HYMNE MUSIC BY HUMPHREY   1947

A Hymne to God the Father (music by) Pelham Humphrey [Humfrey] from the figured base by Michael Tippett and Walter Bergmann London: Schott. New York: Associated Music Publishers. 1947 (see no. 110).

158 A PRAYER   8° 1947

A Prayer by John Donne. The Banyan Press [1947] 20 cm, pp. 6, [2].

Note: 120 copies privately printed by Claude Fredericks and Milton Saul at the Banyan Press, New York, Christmas Eve, 1947.

159 THREE SONGS WITH MUSIC   1948

Three Songs: The words by John Donne Music by Barnard Stevens. London. Oxford University Press. 1948.

160 LOVE POEMS ED. UNTERMEYER   8° 1948

The Love Poems of Robert Herrick and John Donne Edited with an introduction by Louis Untermeyer New Brunswick Rutgers University Press [1948] 20 cm, pp. xvi, 254.

161 SELECTED POEMS ED. HAYWARD   16° 1950

John Donne A Selection of his Poetry Edited with an Introduction by John Hayward Penguin Books Harmondsworth Middlesex [1950] Baltimore [1955] 18 cm, pp. 182, [10].

Reviewed: Times Lit. Sup., 22 September 1950, p. 597: Poets and Editors.

162 LOVE POEMS   8° 1951

John Donne Love Poems including 'Songs and Sonets' and 'Elegies' The Peter Pauper Press Mount Vernon New York [1951] 23·5 cm, pp. [ii], 93, [1].

Note: Printed in Janson types on ivory wove paper with decorations after John Pine.

163 SELECTED PRAYERS ED. UMBACH   8° 1951

The Prayers of John Donne Selected and Edited from the earliest sources, with an Essay on Donne's Idea of Prayer by Herbert H. Umbach, Ph.D.

Professor of English Valparaiso University Bookman Associates New York [1951] 21·2 cm, pp. [ii], 109, [1].

164 DONNE'S POETRY 8° 1952

The Poetry of John Donne Norfolk Va. Printed and published at the Signe of the ink-well by Vincent Torre 1952 31 cm, 2 p. 1, 31 f., il. 50 copies printed 'aboard the USS Orion, a submarine tender; the decorations cut in oak-wood' (US Union Catalogue).

165 DIVINE POEMS ED. GARDNER 8° 1952

John Donne The Divine Poems Edited with Introduction and Commentary by Helen Gardner Fellow of St Hilda's College, Oxford Oxford At the Clarendon Press 1952 22 cm, pp. xcviii, 147, [1]. Frontispiece from the head of the effigy in St Paul's.

Reviewed:

A[llen], D. C. *Mod. Lang. Notes*, LXVIII, 1953, 437.
Bethell, S. L., *Theology*, LVI, 1953, 198–9.
Legouis, P., *Études Angl.* VII, 1954, 118.
Leishman, J. B., *Rev. Eng. Stud.* N.S. V, 1954, 74–83.
Murphy, R., *Spectator*, CXC, 20 March 1953, 352, 354: Donne and Milton.
Powicke, F. M., *Journ. Theol. Stud.* IV, 1953, 280–1.
Shapiro, I. A., *New Statesman*, 21 February 1953, p. 210.
Times Lit. Sup., 7 January 1953, p. 24.

166 SELECTED POEMS ED. REEVES 8° 1952

John Donne Selected Poems Edited with an Introduction Notes and Commentary by James Reeves William Heinemann Ltd Melbourne London Toronto [1952] 17 cm, pp. xviii, 104, [2].

Note: 'The Poetry Bookshelf'. Reprinted in a larger format in 1957, 1958, 1967.

Reviewed: Legouis, P., *Études Angl.*, VI, 1953, 359.

167 SEVEN SONNETS SET TO MUSIC 4° 1952

'La Corona' Seven Sonnets by John Donne Set for Mixed Chorus a capella by A. Didier Graeffe Seventeenth Century News, Vol. X, No. 1, March 1952 Special Supplement 28 cm, pp. [1], 30, [1].

168 DIVINE POEMS ETC. 8° 1953

John Donne Divine Poems Devotions Prayers The Peter Pauper Press Mount Vernon New York [1953] 23 cm, pp. [vi], 7–115, [1].

Note: The *Devotions* consist of the twenty-three Meditations only, with five Prayers from *Essays in Divinity*. Printed in Janson types on paper by the Curtis Paper Company.

169 POEMAS SPANISH TRANSLATION BY GIRRI 8° 1953

Poemas: versiones de William Shand y Alberto Girri Buenos Aires Ediciones Botella al Mar 1953 19 cm, illustrated.

170 RIME SACRE ITALIAN TRANSLATION 8° 1953

John Donne Rime Sacre precedente da 'La Vita e la Morte del Dottor Donne' di Izaak Walton A Cura di Enzo Giachino [Torino] Giulio Einaudi Editore [1953] 21·5 cm, pp. 117, [3].

Note: With editor's dedication to A. D. P., Walton's *Life* in Italian, 19 Holy Sonnets and 3 Hymns with English and Italian on opposite pages, and notes. (Advertised as containing a frontispiece of Donne in his shroud, but this is not found in the copy examined—given by the translator to Sir Herbert Grierson).

171 POEMES CHOISIS ED. LEGOUIS 8° 1955

Donne Poèmes Choisis Traduction, introduction et notes par Pierre Legouis Professeur à l'université de Lyon Aubier Éditions Montaigne, Paris [1955] 19 cm, pp. 224.

Note: 'Collection bilingue des classiques étrangers'.

Reviewed:

Allen, D. C., *Mod. Lang. Notes*, LXX, 1955, 530–1.
Leishman, J. B., *Rev. Eng. Stud.* N.S. VII, 1956, 310–16.
Simon, I., *Études Angl.* IX, 1956, 54–5.

172 SONGS AND SONETS ED. REDPATH 8° 1956

The Songs and Sonets of John Donne An *Editio minor* with Introduction and Explanatory Notes by Theodore Redpath Fellow of Trinity College Cambridge . . . Methuen and Co. Ltd . . . [1956] 20 cm, pp. li, [i], 155, [1]. (Fifth impression, 1967. Paperback edn. fourth impr. 1971.)

Reviewed: *Times Lit. Sup.*, 14 December 1956, p. 750: Passport to Donne.
  See also J. Sparrow, 21 December, p. 765: The Text of Donne.
  Wright, D., *Time and Tide*, 22 December 1956, p. 1593.

173 POEMS OF LOVE   8° 1958

John Donne Poems of Love Introduction by Kingsley Hart 1958 Folio
  Society 18·5 cm, pp. 208. (Text taken from the Oxford Standard
  Authors.)

174 SELECTED POEMS ED. SHAABER   1958

Selected Poems Edited by Mathias A. Shaaber (Croft's Classics) New York:
  Appleton-Century-Crofts 1958

175 SELECTED POEMS ITALIAN TRANSLATION   1958

Poesie seelte di John Donne S. Rosati Naples 1958

176 SELECTION ED. BALD   8° 1959

Seventeenth Century English Poetry. Edited by R. C. Bald New York
  Harper & Bros. 1959, pp. 600 (Harper's English Series).

Note: Donne is fully represented and is discussed in the introduction.

177 SONGS AND SONNETS   8° 1959

Songs and Sonnets with illustrations by June Wayne Los Angeles: Zeitlin
  and Verbrugger 1959 28 cm.

Note: The type set in Walbaum-Antiqua with 15 signed lithographs (3 in colour).
  Printed and bound in West Berlin by Bruder-Hartmann. 110 copies on Rives paper,
  3 copies on Japanese vellum.

178 THREE VERSIONS IN ITALIAN   1960

Tre versioni da John Donne. By C. Campo. *Paragone*, IX, no. 128, 1960,
  pp. 91–3.

179 LOVE POEMS   8° 1961

The Pocket Poets John Donne Love Poems London: Vista Books [1961]
  18·4 cm, pp. 48.

180 METAPHYSICAL POETS ED. GARDNER　　　　8° 1961

The Metaphysical Poets Selected and Edited by Helen Gardner Oxford
University Press 1961 18·2 cm, pp. xxvi, 309, [1]. (First published by
Penguin Books Ltd., 1957; repr. 1959.)

180a METAPHYSICAL POEMS IN GERMAN　　　　8° 1961

Metaphysische Dichtungen [translated by Werner Vortriede] Wiesbaden
1961 [not seen]

181 POEMES DE DONNE WITH MUSIC　　　　4° 1961

Poèmes de Donne Herbert et Crashaw mis en musique par leurs con-
temporains G. Coperario, A. Ferrabosco, J. Wilson, W. Corkine, J.
Hilton Transcription et réalisation par André Souris d'après des re-
cherches effectuées sur les sources par John Cutts Introduction par Jean
Jacquot Editions du Centre National de la Recherche Scientifique 15,
Quai Anatole-France Paris VIIᵉ 1961 31·5 cm, pp. xix, [i], 26, [2].

Contents: Seven settings for poems by Donne, two by Crashaw and one by Herbert. For
a list of those by Donne see above pp. 163–4.

182 METAPHYSICAL POEMS GERMAN TRANSLATION
　　　　　　　　　　　　　　　　　　　　8° 1961

Metaphysische Dichtungen aus dem Englischen übertragen von Werner
Vortriede. Frankfurt am Main 1961

183 POEMS FRENCH TRANSLATION　　　　1962

Poèmes, traduction de J. Fuziet et Yves Denis. Paris: Gallimard. 1962.

184 SELECTED POEMS ED. MELCHIOR　　　　1962

Selected Poems a cura di Giorgio Melchiori. Bari Adriatica Editrice [1962],
pp. 200 (Biblioteca Italiana di testi Inglesi II)

185 POEMS SPANISH TRANSLATION BY GIRRI　　8° 1963

Poemas de John Donne Selección prologo y notas de Alberto Girri Buenos
Aires Ediciones Culturales Argentinas [p. 963] 21 cm, pp. 94. (Biblioteca
del sesquicentenario) Poems in English and Spanish.

186 SELECTED POEMS   8° 1964

The English Poets Chaucer to Yeats Donne Oxford University Press in Association with the British Council [1964] 18·2 cm, printed wrappers, pp. [32] (the text of the poems recorded by Argo Record Company on RG 403).

187 ELEGIES SONGS & SONNETS ED. GARDNER   8° 1965

John Donne The Elegies and The Songs and Sonnets Edited with Introduction and Commentary by Helen Gardner Fellow of St. Hilda's College, Oxford. Oxford At the Clarendon Press 1965 22 cm, pp. xcix, 272. With two portraits.

Reviewed: Anon., *Times Lit. Sup.*, 6 April 1965, pp. 277–80. For the subsequent discussion see under Curtis, L. P., Gardner, H., Holloway, J., Le Comte, E., Roberts, M., Bradbrook, M. C., *New Statesman*, 16 July, 1965, pp. 87–8.
Ellrodt, R., *Études Angl.* xx, 1967, 282–8.
Empson, W., *Crit. Quart.* IX, 1967, 89 ff.
Hardison, O. B., *Mod. Philol.* LXV, 1967, 67–70.
Holloway, J., *Spectator*, 6 August 1965, pp. 181–2.

188 SELECTED POETRY ED. BEWLEY   8° 1966

John Donne Selected Poetry Edited by Marius Bewley The Signet Classic Poetry Series General Editor John Hollander The New American Library New York and Toronto The New English Library Series London [1966] 18 cm, pp. l, 51–288 (Paperback Signet no. CQ 343)

189 SATIRES EPIGRAMS & VERSE LETTERS ED. MILGATE
                                                  8° 1967

John Donne The Satires Epigrams and Verse Letters Edited with Introduction and Commentary by W. Milgate Reader in English The Australian National University Oxford At the Clarendon Press 1967 21·5 cm, pp. lxxvii, 296 (errata slip, 13 lines). With two portraits.

Reviewed:
Sylvester, R. S., *Erasmus*, xx, 165–7.
Legouis, P., *Rev. Eng. Stud.*, N.S., XIX, 437–9.
Maxwell, J. C., *Notes and Queries*, CCXIII, 112–15.

190 POETRY AND SELECTED PROSE ED. WARNKE   8° 1967

John Donne: Poetry and Selected Prose. Edited by F. J. Warnke. Modern Library. New York. 1967.

191 SELECTED PROSE ED. SIMPSON   8° 1967

John Donne Selected Prose Chosen by Evelyn Simpson Edited by Helen Gardner and Timothy Healy Oxford At the Clarendon Press 1967 20·7 cm, pp. xvi, 197, [3].

192 SELECTED POEMS ED. KERMODE   8° 1970

The Poems of John Donne, Selected, introduced and annotated by Frank Kermode. Wood engravings by Imre Reiner. The Heritage Press. New York. 1970. pp. xxvi, 198. (The text based on Hayward's edition, 1929.)

WALTON'S 'LIFE OF DONNE'

BIBLIOGRAPHICAL PREFACE

WALTON'S *Life of Donne*, though written with an extraordinary grace and spontaneity, is not to be relied upon for accuracy of detail, in spite of the fact that the author declared in his note *To the reader* in the edition of 1658: 'My desire is to inform and assure you, that shall become my Reader, that in that part of this following discourse, which is onely narration, I either speak of my own knowledge, or from the testimony of such as dare do anything rather than speak an untruth.' The *Life* appeared in its first form in the prefatory matter to *LXXX Sermons*, 1640, which was edited by the younger Donne. Though considerable additions were made in later issues, this original form of the *Life* remained, except in detail, unaltered. The first separate issue of the *Life* was published in 1658 and contained, as Walton says in the dedication, 'fewer blemishes and more ornaments than when 'twas first made publique'. The dedication was addressed to Sir Robert Holt, grandson of John King, Bishop of London, and nephew of Henry King, Bishop of Chichester, friend and executor of Donne, who warmly commended Walton's *Life of Donne* in a letter printed as a preface to the *Life of Hooker*, 1665. The chief additions made to the *Life* in 1658 are noted under the entry following.

In 1670 Walton included the *Life of Donne* in the well-known volume of *Lives*,[1] which passed through two editions in the seventeenth century and has been so many times reprinted since; I have made no attempt to deal with the bibliography of this volume.[2] The account of the facts of Donne's life underwent little change, but Walton introduced a large number of verbal alterations in order to make his statements more explicit. The *Epistle Dedicatory* and the greater part of the note *To the reader* were omitted, these being replaced by an *Introduction* derived from the first part of the *Life* and a passage from *To the reader*. Walton omitted the letters printed at the end of the edition of 1658, but made free with passages from these and other

---

[1] *The Lives of Dr. John Donne, etc.... Written by Izaak Walton ... London, Printed by Tho. Newcomb for Richard Marriott ... 1670. 8°.* Contains portrait by Lombart.

[2] For full details see J. E. Butt's *Bibliography of Izaak Walton's Lives*, Oxford Bibliographical Society, Proceedings and Papers, vol. II, pt. IV, 1930.

letters printed in 1651, putting together a 'synthetic' letter in order, as R. E. Bennett wrote,[1] 'to illustrate Donne's state of mind during the Mitcham period', quoting and paraphrasing freely. There were also added 'An hymn to God, my God, in my sickness. March 23, 1630', and Walton's 'Elegy on Dr. Donne. April 7, 1632'. A detailed study of Walton's method of biographical presentation and of his artistic licence is provided in David Novarr's *The Making of Walton's Lives*, 1958.

The second edition of the *Lives*, called on the title-page the *Fourth edition*,[2] and published in 1675, contains several alterations and additions, including a long account of Donne's vision of his wife seen while he was in Paris in 1612, together with the verses entitled 'A Valediction forbidding mourning' (*Poems*, 1633, no. 100), which he had given her at parting.

An edition of the *Lives* was edited with important annotations by Thomas Zouch in 1796.[3] Further annotations, useful though sometimes rather prolix, were added by T. E. Tomlins to an edition of the *Life of Donne* published in 1852, which is the only separate reprint of this *Life* known to me and is therefore described under entry no. 194.

Walton, no doubt, according to his custom gave a number of copies of his *Life of Donne* to his friends. It will be noticed that three of the copies recorded below have corrections in his hand. Two others carry inscriptions —'For Mr. Comerford from I. Wa.', and 'Unus ex libris Edmi Pytt ex dono Authoris Isaaci Walton'.[4]

193 WALTON'S LIFE [Wing W 668]   12° 1658

Title (within ornamental border): The Life Of John Donne, . . . London, Printed by J. G. for R. Marriot, and are to be fold at his fhop under S. Dunftans Church in Fleet-ftreet. 1658. [*see facsimile*]

Collation: A–G¹²; 84 leaves.

Contents: A1 blank; A2 title; A3a–A9a dedication *To my Noble & honoured Friend Sir Robert Holt of Afton, in the County of Warwick, Baronet* signed *Ifaac Walton*;

---

[1] *Philol. Quart.* xvi, 1937, 30–4.

[2] No edition between those of 1670 and 1675 has ever been recorded; presumably the latter was called the *fourth* because it contains the fourth editions of the lives of Donne and Hooker.

[3] *The Lives of Dr. John Donne, etc. By Isaac Walton. With notes and the Life of the Author. By Thomas Zouch M.A. York.* 1796, 4° and 1807, 8°.

[4] Both sold with William Pickering's library, Sotheby's, 24 March 1854, lots 1145–6.

A9*b* blank; A10*a–b To the Reader* signed *I. W.*; A11*a*–F11*b* (pp. 1–122) *The Life of Dr. Donne* signed *J.W.*; F11*b*–G11*a* (pp. 122–45) four letters from Donne; G11*a*–G12*b* (pp. 145–8) *An Epitaph written by Dr. Corbet, Bishop of Oxford, on his friend Dr. Donne*, and *To the Memory of my ever desired Dr. Donne. An Elegy by H. King, B.C.*

Frontispiece: Inserted between A1 and A2. A bust of Donne within an oval as in the frontispiece to *LXXX Sermons*, 1640 (no. 29), but without any of the surrounding design; it is printed from the same plate, which has not been retouched, though it shews signs of wear.

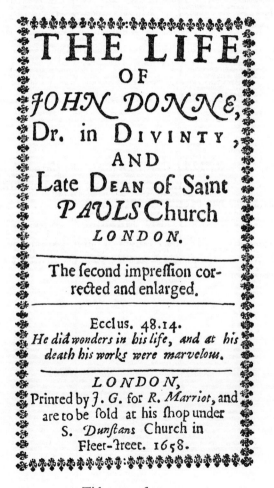

Title-page of no. 193

Note: Printed by John Grismond II (1639–66). This edition, which is now rare, is a reprint of the *Life*, which had been printed at the beginning of *LXXX Sermons* (1640), but it contains, among many others, the following important additions: (i) An extended account of Donne's marriage (pp. 15–18); (ii) An account of Morton's attempt to persuade Donne to take orders (pp. 24–33); (iii) Part of Chudleigh's Funeral Elegie (pp. 48–9); (iv) Donne's grief at his wife's death (pp. 52–5); (v) An account of the friendship of Henry King, Bishop of Chichester, and his proffered benefaction (pp. 67–72); (vi) A relation of Donne's pleasure at hearing his Hymn sung; his seal; an enumeration of his friends; George Herbert and the lines that passed between them (pp. 77–85); (vii) Donne's bequests (pp. 90–2); (viii) An account of the making of the portrait of Donne in his shroud and of the stone effigy in St. Paul's (pp. 111–13); (ix) Four letters from Donne, printed together at the end (see no. 58).

Copies: BM (2, with corrections in Walton's hand), BLO (no portrait); HCL (no portrait), HEH (2), FSLW, NYPL, YUL.

Trinity College, Cambridge (no portrait).

G. L. Keynes; R. S. Pirie (2 both lacking portrait, one with corrections apparently in Walton's hand).

194 WALTON'S LIFE   8° 1852

The Life of John Donne, D.D. Late Dean of St Paul's Church, London. By Izaak Walton. With some original notes, by An Antiquary. London: Published by Henry Kent Causton, . . . [1852]. (The Contemplative Man's Library for the Thinking Few) 8°. pp. iv, 164.

Note: The annotations are by Thomas Edlyne Tomlins, an antiquary well known at that period (see *Notes and Queries*, N.S. X, VI, 228 and 338); they include nine letters from the Loseley MSS. (see no. 63). This edition is scarce.

APPENDICES I–VI

APPENDIX I

WORKS BY JOHN DONNE, D.C.L

PREFACE

JOHN DONNE the younger was born while his father was living at Pyrford in Surrey in 1604. He was sent to Westminster School, and in 1623 was elected an undergraduate at Christ Church, Oxford. While there he contributed some Latin lines to *Carolus Redux*, to *Camdeni Insignia*, and to *Parentalia*, all of which were published at Oxford (see nos. 202 to 205). Nothing is known of his life during the next ten years except that in 1629 his father had destined him for the Church, as appears from a passage in a letter to Mrs. Cockain, in which he tries to console her for the death of her son by writing: 'Since I am well content to send one son to the Church, the other to the Wars, why should I be loth to send one part of either son to heaven and the other to earth?'[1] In 1634 the younger Donne was still at Oxford and a somewhat unpleasant incident is said to have taken place there; it is related[2] that in a fit of temper he struck a small boy with his riding whip, the child afterwards dying as the result of his injuries. He was tried at Oxford in August 1634 for manslaughter, but was acquitted owing to the uncertainty of the medical evidence. He proceeded soon afterwards to Padua and there took the degree of D.C.L. He returned in 1637 and was incorporated a D.C.L. at Oxford on 30 June 1638.[3] Already some years before this he had fulfilled his father's wishes by taking orders. He first held the living of Tillingham, Essex (1631), and later those of High Roding, Essex (10 July 1638), Ufford, Northants. (1638), Polebrooke, Northants. (1639), and Fulbeck, Lincs. (1639). It seems that Ufford was an exchange for that of Tillingham, but in a letter to Sir Edward Hyde, 14 January 1640/1, Donne complained that he was 'cozened' by a trick out of the living of Tillingham by Thomas Nicholson, previous rector of Ufford, and the Revd. Michael Hudson. Legal proceedings followed, the rectory of Ufford

---

[1] Tobie Matthew collection, no. 37.   [2] Gosse, **II**, 308.
[3] Gosse, **II**, 311.

being claimed by Richard Titlor or Titley, vicar of Bourne, Lincs.[1] In spite of this he continued to rise in the Church and in 1648 was chaplain to the Earl of Denbigh, to whom he dedicated the *Fifty Sermons* of 1649. From about the year 1640 he lived in Covent Garden and he may have been incumbent of some church in that district. His petition of 1661 on behalf of the inhabitants of Covent Garden is recorded here under entry no. 198. He died at the age of 58 in 1662, and his will (see no. 200) was printed as a broadside in February of the same year.

Meanwhile, from the year 1640 to the time of his death, he had been shewing considerable literary activity, and it is owing to his energy that the greater portion of his father's writings has been preserved for us. There is evidence that the elder Donne had early thought of his son as his future literary executor, for he had written to a friend from Chelsea on 25 November 1625: 'I have revised as many of my sermons as I have kept any note of, and I have written out a great many, and hope to do more. I am already come to the number of eighty,[2] of which my son, who, I hope will take the same profession, or some other in the world of understanding, may hereafter make some use.'[3] On the other hand, Henry King, Bishop of Chichester, in a long letter written in 1640 to Izaak Walton, which was prefixed to the *Lives* in 1670, states that Donne professed before several witnesses on his death-bed 'that it was by my restless importunity, that he had prepared them [the sermons] for the press'; he declares also that three days before his death Donne had made him his executor and given him the sermons, his sermon notes, 'and his other papers, containing an extract of near Fifteen hundred Authors'. He further hints that the younger Donne, using Walton as a go-between, had filched these papers from his keeping, and this was, indeed, probably the case, for in his will Donne makes the following bequest: 'To the Reverend Bishop of Chichester I return that Cabinet that was my Father's . . . and all those Papers which are of Authors analysed by my Father.' Donne states in his preface to the *XXVI Sermons* of 1660 that 'upon

---

[1] See article by M. A. Beese, *Mod. Lang. Rev.* xxxiii, 1938, 356.

[2] This does not refer to *LXXX Sermons* of 1640, since twenty-six of the sermons in that collection are dated later than 1625, the year in which this letter was written. This was first pointed out by Mr. F. E. Hutchinson in the *Camb. Hist. of Eng. Lit.* iv, 240–1.

[3] Gosse, ii, 225, 310.

the death of my father ... I was sent to by His Majesty of Blessed Memory to recollect and publish his Sermons'; this may or may not have been true. It is, in any case, difficult not to suspect Donne of sharp practice. In 1648 litigation took place between Donne and Francis Bowman, bookseller and printer in London and Oxford, 1634–47, regarding the printing of the *LXXX* and *Fifty Sermons*. The documents relating to this were found in the Public Record Office by J. Milton French and, although the final decree in the case has not come to light, it does not appear that Donne's dealings in the matter were particularly honourable, if we may judge from French's summary.[1]

Donne's petition of 1637 to the Archbishop of Canterbury shews that already before 1640 he had made an attempt to gain control of those others of his father's writings which had been published without his authority. The petitioner states 'that since ye death of his Father there hath bene manie scandalous Pamflets printed, and published, under his name, which were none of his, by severall Boocksellers, withoute anie leave or Autoritie; in particular one entitoled Juvenilia, printed for Henry Seale; another by John Marriot and William Sheares, entitoled Ignatius his Conclave, as allsoe certaine Poems by ye sayde John Marriote, of which abuses thay have bene often warned by your Pe^{tr} and tolde that if thay desisted not, thay should be proceeded against beefore your Grace, which they seeme soe much to slight, that thay profess soddainly to publish new impressions, verie much to the greife of your Pe^{tr} and the discredite of ye memorie of his Father.'[2] The Archbishop granted Donne's petition by calling upon those concerned to desist from their illegal practices, but his authority was ineffectual, and it was only in 1650 that Donne acquired control of his father's poems, in which year he published an edition with a dedication to Lord Craven. In 1647 he published his father's *Biathanatos*, and his presentation copies of this book with the letters contained in them have already been noticed (see pp. 112–16). In 1647 he seems to have edited Corbet's *Poems* and to have dedicated them to Lady Teynham.[3] In 1649 he issued the second volume

---

[1] See 'Bowman *v.* Donne' by J. Milton French, *Times Lit. Sup.*, 12 December 1936.
[2] Printed in full by Grierson, ii, lxvi. The petition is preserved in the Public Record Office.
[3] *Certain Elegant Poems written by Dr Corbett Bishop of Norwich. London, Printed by R. Cotes for Andrew Crooke* ... 1647. 12º. In HCL is a copy of the first issue of this volume containing a

of *Fifty Sermons*, and in an address to the Lords Commissioners of the Great Seal he indicates that he had not undertaken the publication of the sermons without some official reward. In a letter already quoted (p. 114) of about 1644 he shews that he had had these sermons ready and entered at Stationers' Hall, but that he had kept them back from fear of persecution by the Commonwealth government. In 1651 he published his father's *Letters to several persons of honour*, and in the same year he prepared the *Essayes in Divinity*, which he incorporated in 1652 in the volume of *Juvenilia* together with a reprint of *Ignatius his Conclave*. In 1660 he issued the final volume of *XXVI Sermons*, this time at his own expense. In the same year he also edited both Sir Tobie Matthew's *Collection of Letters* (see no. 59), and a collection of poems by the Earl of Pembroke and Sir Benjamin Ruddier.[1] A work attributed to him, entitled *Donne's Satyr* (no. 199), and consisting of 'merry conceits' and apothegms in verse was published in 1662, but in Professor Shapiro's opinion it is by a Shrewsbury man of the same name. A 'Satire on Sir W. Davenant' may be another piece of verse by Donne. It was ascribed to him by Thomason[2] and was printed in *Merry Drollery*, 1661, among *Certain Verses written by severall of the Author's Friends, to be reprinted with the second edition of Gondibert*, 1653. It was answered in *The Incomparable Poem Gondibert vindicated from the Wit Combats of Four Esquires, Clinias, Demetus, Sancho, and Jack Pudding*, 1655.[3] Donne is referred to more than once as Jack Pudding or Jack Straw, but it seems possible that the satire is really by Denham, who was the author of most of the poems, according to Aubrey.[4]

The younger Donne's character has usually been held somewhat in contempt, and it is certain that he gives no particular sign of intellectual distinction and does not appear to have been remarkable either for honesty

MS. dedication written and signed by John Donne, who appears to be also the signatory of the printed dedication under the letters N.N. See C.'s *Poems*, ed. Bennett and Trevor-Roper, Oxford, 1955.

[1] *Poems, Written by the right honourable William Earl of Pembroke . . . Many of which are answered by way of Repartee, by Sr Benjamin Ruddier, Knight. With several distinct poems . . . London, Printed by Matthew Inman, and are to be sold by James Magnes . . .* 1660. 8⁰.

[2] Thomason Tracts, BM 669, f. 15 (82).

[3] See M. A. Beese, loc. cit.

[4] *Aubrey's Brief Lives*, ed. Clark, II, 221.

or for morality.[1] Anthony Wood has characterized him as 'an atheistical buffoon, a banterer, and a person of over free thoughts, yet valued by Charles II'. Such letters to his friends as are known all have an unpleasant flavour,[2] but we must leave him with gratitude for his labours on behalf of the memory of his father.

195 CAROLUS REDUX [*STC* 19027]   4° 1623

Title: Carolus Redux [*woodcut device*]
   Oxoniae, Excudebant Iohannes Lichfield, & Iacobus Short, Academiae Typographi. 1623

Collation: π² ¶⁴ ¶¶² A–I⁴ K²; 46 leaves.

Note: On G4 are fourteen Latin lines beginning:

   Ecce procus virtutis adest: quæ Fœmina digna est?
   They are signed *Iohannes Donne Æd. Christi alumnus.*

Copy: BM, BLO, ULC; HCL, HEH.
   John Rylands Library, Manchester.
   G. L. Keynes.

196 CAMDENI INSIGNIA [*STC* 19028]   4° 1624

Title: Camdeni Infignia
   Oxoniae. Excudebant Iohannis Lichfield, & Iacobus Short, Academiae Typographi. 1624.

Collation: π² ¶–¶¶⁴ ¶¶¶² A–F⁴ G²; 38 leaves.

Note: On E2*a* are seventeen Latin lines beginning:

   An nos invidiâ ferociori,
   and a couplet headed, *In obitum* Camdeni *Regi Fecialis.*
   They are signed *Ioh. Donne Ædis Christi Alumnus olim Westm.*

Copies: BM, BLO, ULC; HEH.
   G. L. Keynes.

---

[1] John Beresford sought to rehabilitate his memory in *Gossip of the Seventeenth and Eighteenth Centuries*, 1923, pp. 59–91. M. A. Beese, loc. cit. also cited letters from Miles Woodshaw to Lord Conway in which he refers to Donne's love of birds. In his will Donne left 'all my Doves' to his friend Thomas Killigrew.

[2] See extracts in *Notes and Queries*, N.S. III, vol. IV, p. 19 (reprinted in the first two editions of this Bibliography); in Dobell's cat. 15, January 1936, to Lord Conway; in Dobell's cat. 52, October 1939, to the same.

197 OXON. ACAD. PARENTALIA [*STC* 19030]   4° 1625

Title: Oxonienſis Academiae Parentalia, Sacratiſsimae Memoriae potentiſ-
simi Monarchae Iacobi . . . [*device*]
Oxoniae, Excudebant Iohannes Lichfield, & Guilielmus Turner. Anno
Dom. 1625.

Collation: ¶⁴ ¶¶² A–K⁴ L²; 48 leaves.

Note: On D4*a* are 21 Latin lines beginning:

    Raptura Regem Fata quaerebant Virum.

They are signed *Io. Donne Æd. Chriſti alumnus.*

Copies: BM, BLO, ULC; HCL, HEH.
John Rylands Library, Manchester.

198 DONNE'S PETITION [Wing D 1875]   1661

To the Right Honorable, the Lord Chancellor, the humble Petition of
Covent Garden. [1661.] *Broadside,* 31 × 21 cm.

Note: A petition for the removal of one, Dr. Babre, from a position of authority, by
reason of his unjust persecutions. It is signed by *Bedford Berry, St. An. Shandois,
Piazza King, Henrietta Bedford, James Ruſſel, Charles York, Bridges Bowſtreet,
Amen Manto, Todos Autros.*[1] The copy described is inscribed below in a contemporary
hand:

    Authore D. Dʳᵉ. Donne Jun. 1661.

Donne lived at an unknown address in Covent Garden.

Copy: BLO.

199 DONNE'S SATYR [Wing D 1877]   8° 1662

Title: Donne's Satyr. Containing
   1. A ſhort Map of mundane Vanity
   2. A Cabinet of Merry Conceits
   3. Certain pleaſant Propoſitions, and Queſtions, with their merry
      Solutions and Anſwers.
Being very Uſeful, Pleaſant, and Delightful to all; and Offenſive to none.
[rule] By Jo. Donne. [ornament between rules]
London, Printed by R. W. for M. Wright, at the Kings Head in the
Old-Bailey, 1662.

---

[1] i.e. 'All the rest'; the other names are evidently fictitious, several of them being made up
from the names of various streets round Covent Garden.

Collation: A–I⁸; 72 leaves.

Contents: A1 frontispiece (a satyr); A2 title; A3a–A7b *The Epiftle Dedicatory*; A8a–I8a (pp. 1–129) text; 18b *Books printed for M. Wright.* Folding sheet inserted between B6 and B7.

Note: Printed by (?) Robert White (1639–67). Probably by another John Donne of Shrewsbury.

Copy: BM; HCL.

200 DONNE'S WILL [Wing D 1875]   1662

Dr. Donne's Laft Will and Teftament. July 21. 1657 . . . Printed, February 23. 1662. *Broadside, with black border,* 39 × 26 cm.

Note: Donne makes *Jerome, Earl of Portland,* his executor, and the will was witnessed by the *Earl of Marleburgh* and *Will. Glascocke, November* 2, 1661. The following extract is of interest:

To Mr. *Isaac Walton,* I give all my writings under my Father's hand, which may be of some use to his Son, if he makes him a Scholar. To the Reverend *Bishop of Chichester,* I return that *Cabinet* that was my Father's, now in my Dining-Room, and all those Papers which are of *Authors Analysed* by my Father; many of which he hath already received with his *Common-Place Book,* which I desire may pass to Mr. *Walton's* Son, as being more likely to have use for such a help, when his age shall require it.

Copies: BM, BLO; HCL, YUL.
Trinity College, Cambridge.

201 DONNE'S WILL [Wing D 1876]   4° 1663

The Laft Will and Teftament of Dr. John Donne, who Dyed at his Houfe in Covent Garden, 1° Febr. 1662. Publifhed to prevent the mifunder-ftanding his Religion. [*quotation*]
London, Printed in the Year, 1663.

Collation: A⁴; 4 leaves.

Copies: HCL.
G. L. Keynes.

APPENDIX II

WORKS BY JOHN DONE

PREFACE

THE two dull and unimportant works by John Done called *Polydoron* and *The Ancient History of the Septuagint* have been persistently attributed to Donne, some colour being lent to this attribution by the fact that the publishers have falsely described Done on the title-page of the second edition of *The History of the Septuagint* as 'the Learned and Reverend Dr John Done, late Dean of St Pauls'. An inquiry concerning Done, which was made in *Notes and Queries* (N.S. VI, VI, 47), elicited from the late Dr. Augustus Jessopp the following reply:

> It is one of the 'curiosities of literature' that this latter volume [*The History of the Septuagint*] should have been attributed to the Dean of St Paul's by every editor of Walton's *Lives* till the mistake was pointed out by me in 1855. It is a trumpery production, and could never be set down to the great dean by any one at all familiar with his writings. I tried to find out something about the man Done twenty-five years ago, but I cannot lay my hands on my notes; my impression is that he was a needy schoolmaster, who was employed by the booksellers. (*Notes and Queries*, N.S. VI, VI, July 1882, 95.)

A long letter from a John Done on alchemy is preserved in the Bodleian (Ashm. MS. 1415, f. 19*b*), and he is probably the same individual (see Simpson, p. 359).

The authorship of the books was discussed in a long letter from Professor S. G. Dunn in *The Times Lit. Sup.* for 7 July 1921. He was inclined to believe that both are by John Donne the younger, who might even have used some early writings of his father's in compiling *Polydoron*. These suggestions were further examined, and rejected, by Mrs. Simpson in her *Study of the Prose Works*, pp. 357–60.

202 POLYDORON [*STC* 7020]   12° 1631

> *Title:* Polydoron: or a miſcellania of Morall, Philoſophicall, and Theo-
> logicall ſentences. [rule] By Iohn Done. [rule and device]
> Printed at London by Tho. Cotes, for George Gibbes dwelling in Popes-
> head Alley at the ſigne of the Flower de Luce. 1631.

> *Collation:* A–I¹² K⁴; 112 leaves.

> *Contents:* A1 blank except for sign.; A2 title; A3*a*–A4*a To the Reader* signed *I. Done*;
> A4*b* blank; A5*a*–K4*b* (pp. 1–216) text (errata, 4 lines, at bottom of K4*b*).

> *Note:* In the BM copy and in one of the two in FSLW the leaf A3 has been cancelled
> and a sheet of two leaves, with a dedication to the Earl of Dover and the first leaf of
> *To the Reader*, has been substituted. These two leaves have signatures A3 and A4,
> so that A4 appears twice. The device on the title-page of a fleur-de-lis within a
> border of leaves and berries is recorded as no. 415 in McKerrow's *Printers' and
> Publishers' Devices*, London, 1913.

> *Copies:* BM, ULC; HCL, HEH, FSLW (2, one being another state as above,
> Willoughby–Harmsworth copy).
> Emmanuel College, Cambridge.
> Innerpeffray Library, Perthshire.

203 POLYDORON [Wing D 1857]   12° 1650

> *Title (within ornamental border):* A miſcellanea of morall, theologicall,
> and philoſophicall ſentances; [rule] Worthy obſervation. [ornament
> between rules]
> Printed for Iohn Sweeting, At the Angel in Popes-head-alley, 1650.

> *Collation:* A¹²(–A1, 2, 3+A1, A3.4) B–I¹² K⁴.

> *Contents:* A1 title; A2*a*–*b* (with sign. A3) dedication *To the Right Honourable Henry,
> Earl of Dover, &c.* signed *Iohn Donne*; A3–K4 as in preceding entry.

> *Note:* This is a reissue of the preceding entry. A1 and A2 are both cancel leaves, consist-
> ing of a new title-page and a dedication, which had been inserted in some copies of the
> first issue.

> *Copy:* BLO.

204 HISTORY OF THE SEPTUAGINT [*STC* 750]   8° 1633

> *Title (within double rules):* The Auncient Hiſtory of the Septuagint. Written
> in Greeke, by Ariſteus 1900. Yeares since. . . . Newly done into English
> [rule] By I. Done. [rule] *Tempora, Tempera, Tempore.* [rule]
> London: Printed by N. Okes. 1633.

Collation: A–O⁸; 112 leaves.

Contents: A1 blank; A2 title; A3a–A6a *To the Intelligent General Reader*; A6b–A8b *The Elenchus, or Contence of the Following Booke*; B1a–O8b (pp. 1–80, 89–184, 189–219) text, pp. 1–10 being headed: *Certaine Præcognita.*

Note: A number of pages, as noted above, are omitted from the pagination.

Copies: BM, BLO, ULC; HCL, HEH, FSLW (Britwell–Harmsworth copy), PUL, YUL.
   G. L. Keynes; J. Sparrow (imperfect); R. S. Pirie.

205 HISTORY OF THE SEPTUAGINT [Wing A 3682]

12° 1685

Title (within double rules): The ancient hiftory of the Septuagint. Written in Greek by Arifteus near two thoufand years ago. . . . [rule] Firft Englifh'd from the Greek, by the Learned and Reverend Dr. John Done, late Dean of St. Pauls. [rule] Now Revifed, and very much Corrected from the Original. [rule]
London, Printed for W. Henfman, and Tho. Fox, Bookfellers in Weft-minfter-Hall. 1685.

Collation: A–I¹²; 108 leaves.

Contents: A1 blank; A2 title; A3a–A5b *To the Reader*; A6a–A7b *The Elenchus*; A8a–A12b (pp. 1–10) *Certain Præcognita*; B1a–I12b (pp. 1–192) text.

Note: Done is falsely described on the title-page of this edition (see my preface).

Copies: BM, ULC; HCL.
   Jesus College, Cambridge.
   Balliol College, Oxford.
   G. L. Keynes, R. S. Pirie.

APPENDIX III

BOOKS DEDICATED TO DONNE

206 TISDALE'S LAWYER'S PHILOSOPHY [*STC* 24090]

8° 1622

Title: The lawyers Philosophy: or, law brought to light. Poetized In a
Diuine Rhapſodie or Contemplatiue Poem. By Roger Tiſdale, Gent.
Sat Serò. [device]
At London printed for I. T. and H. G. and are to bee ſold at the Widdow
Goſſons in Pannier Alley. 1622.

Collation: A–C⁸ D⁴; 28 leaves.

Contents: A1 blank; A2 title; A3*a*–A5*b* *The Epiſtle Dedicatorie To the learned and
reuerend Iohn Donne, D. of Diuinitie, Deane of the Cathedrall Church of Sᵗ Paule
London, Roger Tiſdale wiſheth peace of Conſcience in this world, and the ioy of the world
to come;* A6*a–b* *To the learned and conſiderate Reader;* A7*a*–D2*b* *The Lawyers
Philoſophy;* D3*a–b* *To the deſire of my Youth, and hope of mine Age, my young ſonne
Roger;* D4 blank.

Note: The publishers were John Trundle (1603–26) and Henry Gosson (1601–40).
Nevertheless, the device on the title-page of *The Lawyer's Philosophy* is the same as
that used by Elizabeth Purslowe on the title-pages of both editions of Donne's
Juvenilia, 1633 (nos. 43, 44), and is said to have been first used in England by George
Purslowe in 1618. Roger Tisdale also wrote *Pax Vobis, or Wit's changes,* 1623, 4°,
but little further is known of him, and he is not mentioned in the *DNB*. In the
Dedication of his poem he writes to Donne: 'To your friends I was heretofore bound
in dutie, and (in our youthfull societie) to your selfe in love', which might mean that
they had been friends in early days. No copies of *The Lawyer's Philosophy* are known
to me besides the four recorded below.

Copies: BM; HCL.
G. L. Keynes (O'Flahertie–Gosse copy).
Britwell Court Library (sold at Sotheby's, 8 April 1927, lot 1956).

207 ADAMS'S BARREN TREE [*STC* 106]

4° 1623

Title (within double rules): The Barren Tree. A Sermon Preached at Pauls
Croſſe October 26. 1623. [rule] By Tho: Adams. [ornament between
rules]

London, Printed by Aug: Mathewes for Iohn Grifmand, and are to be fold at his Shop in Pauls Alley, at the figne of the Gunne. 1623.

Collation: A–H⁴; 32 leaves.

Contents: A1 blank; A2 title; A3*a–b* dedication *To the reverend and learned, Doctor Donne, Deane of St. Pauls, together with the Prebend-Refidentiaries of the fame Church, my very good Patrons;* A4*a–b To the Reader;* B1*a*–H4*b* (pp. 1–56) text.

Note: Thomas Adams, vicar of Wingrave, Bucks., 1614–36, held the preachership of St. Gregory's under St. Paul's Cathedral, 1618–23. He published many sermons between 1612 and 1632. His *Workes* were published in 1629.

Copies: BM; HCL, HEH.
Cosin Library, Durham.
Marsh Library, Dublin.
G. L. Keynes, R. S. Pirie.

208 PETLEY'S ROYALL RECEIPT [*STC* 19801]   4° 1623

Title: The Royall Receipt: or, Hezekiahs Physicke. A sermon Delivered At Pavls-Croffe, on Michaelmas Day, 1622. [rule] By Elias Petley. [rule, quotation from Deut. 30: 19.]
London, Printed by B.A. for Edward Blackmore, and are to be fold at his Shop, at the great South Doore, going vp into S. Pavles. 1623.

Collation: A² B–G⁴ H²; 28 leaves.

Contents: A1 title; A2*a–b The Epistle etc. to the Reverend and Right Worshipful, M.ʳ Doctor Donne, Dean of the Cathedrall Church of S. Paul. London.;* B1*a*–H2*a* text; H2*b* errata.

Note: The printer was Bernard Alsop, or Allsopp (1617–1650). Elias Petley published also a Greek version of the Book of Common Prayer (Δειτουργία βρεττανικὴ, *STC* 16432), but is not mentioned in the *DNB*.

Copies: BM, BLO, ULC.
G. L. Keynes.

209 DAN. DONNE'S SUB-POENA [*STC 7021*]   8° 1623

Title: A Sub-poena from the Star-chamber of Heaven. A Sermon preached at Paul's Croffe the 4. of Auguft 1622. With fome particular Enlargements which the limited time would not then allow. By Dan. Donne, Mafter of Arts, and Minifter of the Word [*rule*] Auguft. Confeff. lib. 8. cap. 12. *Tolle, Lege: Tolle, Lege.* [*rule*]

London, Printed by Auguſtine Mathewes for John Grifmond, and are to be ſold at his Shop in Pauls Alley at the Signe of the Gunne. 1623.

Collation: [A]⁴ B–I⁸; 68 leaves.

Contents: [A]1 title; [A]2a dedication to Viscount Haddington and Sir Henry Hobart; [A]2b blank; [A]3a dedication to VIRO VERE REVERENDO MULTIS QUE NOMINIBUS COLENDO IOHANNI DONNE DOCTORI IN SACRA THEOLOG. ET DECANO ECCLESIÆ DIVI PAVLI LONDON. DANIEL DONNE HAS SVAS QVALEE CVNQVE MEDITATIONES HVMIL-LIME, D.D.D. [A]3b blank; [A]4a–b *To the Reader*; B1a–18b *A Sub-poena.*

Note: The Revd. Daniel Donne 'is thought to have been the son of John Donne, rector of St. Bennet's, Gracechurch Street, and to have succeeded there after his father's death in 1636'. He may possibly have been a connection of Sir Daniel Dun (see Bald, p. 395).

Copies: BLO (2), BM.
Trinity College, Cambridge.
Cathedral Libraries: Lincoln, St. Paul's.

APPENDIX IV

BOOKS FROM DONNE'S LIBRARY

PREFACE

DONNE'S erudition and virtuosity in ecclesiastical polemics can only have been founded on hard reading and familiarity with contemporary writings.[1] He is likely, therefore, to have possessed a considerable library, and the chief evidence of its contents is described in this appendix, where are recorded 213 works associated with evidence of his ownership. It is noticeable that the great majority of them were published before the appearance of *Pseudo-Martyr* in 1610, the work for which Donne first applied himself seriously to controversial theology. It is still more remarkable that very few of the books were published after 1615, the year in which he took orders. It seems, therefore, that he collected a good part of his library while at work on *Pseudo-Martyr* and that he bought fewer books after entering the Church. Sixty-one of these books were described in the second edition of this *Bibliography*, these including twenty identified by John Sparrow among Selden's 8,000 books in the Bodleian Library. Twenty more came to light from various sources during the next seventeen years and these I listed in 1949.[2] Shortly after this the attention of the late Professor R. C. Bald was drawn to the fact that there are a considerable number of Donne's books in the Middle Temple Library among those bequeathed by Robert Ashley[3] in 1641. At Professor Bald's suggestion these were investigated by John Sparrow, who published in *The Times Lit. Sup.*, 29 July, 5 August 1955, two articles summarily describing the sixty-one

---

[1] According to Walton Donne left at his death 'the resultance of 1400. Authors, most of them abridged and analysed with his own hand'. (*Life*, 1658, p. 88.)

[2] *Trans. Camb. Bib. Soc.* I, 1949, 64.

[3] Robert Ashley (1565–1641), of a Dorset family, was educated at Oxford (Hart Hall and Magdalen), but left without a degree and was called to the bar by the Middle Temple. He practised law, but found more interest in knowledge of languages, translating works from French and Spanish. He lived for many years in the Middle Temple, where he died unmarried. He could have been acquainted with Donne and evidently acquired a portion of his library after his death. All these books can now be seen in the Rare Book Room of the Middle Temple Library.

volumes thus brought to light. Not all the books in this library were then available and eight in the list of 1958 were marked 'not verified'. These have recently been seen and described by John Sparrow with the exception of one (L182 *Vallederius*), which cannot now be found. During this re-examination five additional books belonging to Donne's library were found and, by Mr. Sparrow's kindness, have been added to the appended list of books identified since 1958. One last-minute addition brings the total number of titles to 213. A short list of books given by Donne to friends, but not proved to have been part of his library, has also been added.

An inscription by a later owner in one of the books (L135) records that it was bought in Duck Lane in December 1633, suggesting that most of Donne's library was sold soon after his death and was thus dispersed gradually through the booksellers. Part, however, was probably not sold, since Donne mentioned his books in his will as follows: 'All which legacies being so paid . . . my will is that my plate and books (such books only being excepted as by a schedule signed with my hand I shall give away) and all my other goods being praised and sold all my poor estate of money left . . . may be distributed in manner and form following.' Friends such as Henry King, whose books are now in Chichester Cathedral Library, may have acquired some of Donne's books by virtue of the 'schedule' signed by him.

Recognition of Donne's books is usually easy because he made a practice of writing his name with a terminal flourish on the lower right-hand corner of the title-page and an Italian motto at the top. In more than one instance he has carefully erased a former owner's name in order to do this, and usually the inscription is so near the top of the page that often it has been almost wholly removed by trimming during later binding. Some years ago John Sparrow recorded his discovery in Bishop Joseph Hall's *The Remedy of Prophaneness*, 1637, of the following reminiscence of Donne: 'It was the motto of that witty and learned Doctor Donne, the late Dean of Paul's, which I have seen more than once written in Spanish in his own hand, *Blessed be God that he is God, divinely like himself.*' Hall did not necessarily mean to imply that Donne wrote this Spanish motto in his books, and no book of his containing it has yet been discovered, but the passage is interesting in its relation to the motto that Donne ordinarily used:

Per Rachel ho seruito, & non per Lea.

This is a line from Petrarch (*Canz.* XIX, st. 7, l. 1) and is founded on Gen. 29: 25: 'And it came to pass, that in the morning, behold, it was Leah: and he said to Laban, What is this thou hast done unto me? did I not serve with thee for Rachel? wherefore then hast thou beguiled me?' Donne's reason for using this motto was obscure until Percy Simpson made the suggestion[1] that he was referring to the medieval symbolism whereby Rachel represented the contemplative life and Leah the active. He implied in this way that circumstances had forced on him a life of action though his inclination was for study and contemplation.[2] The use of a motto in books was not infrequent in the seventeenth century, but usually it took the form of a somewhat sententious Greek or Latin tag. Thus among Donne's contemporaries Ben Jonson was in the habit of writing *Tanquam explorator* in his books, Selden put περὶ παντὸς τὴν ἐλευθερίαν, Lancelot Andrewes often wrote *Et aratrum et ad aram*,[3] and at a later date John Evelyn used the motto *Omnia explorate: Meliora retinete*. Donne's friend Rowland Woodward introduced a variation by using a Spanish motto, which he put in his copy of *Pseudo-Martyr* (see p. 7). Donne's own choice is thoroughly in keeping with his character if the suggested explanation is correct. In one volume (L102) Donne has erased Ben Jonson's motto and has pasted a slip with his own name over Jonson's, though he has not added his motto.

So many of Donne's books are still in their covers of limp vellum that it seems likely that this was his favourite form of binding. Obviously a limp vellum binding, which is characteristic of the period, is of very little value by itself as evidence of ownership, but fortunately there is often other evidence when the motto and signature are absent. It was Professor I. A. Shapiro who first noticed that many of the signed volumes also shewed additional evidence in having pencil markings in the margins, which are undoubted signs of the care with which Donne read his books. I have now seen them in very many of his books and find that they take several forms—

---

[1] *Bodl. Lib. Rec.* I, 1940, 148.

[2] The same motto may have been used by others. The late Raphael King shewed me a book, *Detti Memorabili di Personaggi Illustri del Signor Giovanni Botero*, Turin, 1608, 4º, with marginal notes and the motto on a fly-leaf in the form: *per Rachaell ho feruito & non per Lea*, but neither notes nor motto were in Donne's hand.

[3] D. D. C. Chambers, 'A Catalogue of the Library of Lancelot Andrewes', *Trans. Camb. Bib. Soc.* V, 1970, 100.

vertical or slanting ticks, a wavy line or a bracket close to the edge of the type, or occasionally a vertical line labelled NB. These marks have proved to be of great value in identifying as Donne's many tracts themselves unsigned, though bound together with one or more signed works. Professor R. E. Bennett has argued that the eight unsigned tracts accompanying two signed ones and forming the composite volume in limp vellum covers now in Harvard College Library must be regarded with great suspicion.¹ I have satisfied myself, however, that all these tracts have Donne's characteristic markings, so that there can be no doubt that all belonged to him and must have been bound for him, since the motto in one has been mostly trimmed away and was therefore certainly written before the tract was bound. The same argument applies to all the other composite volumes that I have examined in the Bodleian Library, Cambridge University Library, and the library of Chichester Cathedral. In all these most of the tracts, signed or unsigned, carry clear evidence of having been read by Donne and, moreover, conform in their subjects to his interests.

The dispersal of Donne's books not long after his death has ensured that the listing of his books will never be completed; they will continue to turn up here and there, either in the sale rooms or from hiding places on library shelves where their provenance has long remained unnoticed. One book listed here, Minsheu's *Ductor in Linguas*, 1617, is included on the evidence of the list of subscribers, one of the earliest of such lists yet recorded. Donne's name appears here as 'Doctor *Dunne* Chaplaine *to the* K. Majest.', in the fifth column of the list. John Sparrow, who first drew attention to the book,² noted that Minsheu excused his seeming neglect of reverence for rank and quality by explaining that he put the subscribers' names in 'the order he used *in delivery of the Bookes to them*, which was not according to their degrees, but promiscuously as they took them'. It may be assumed, therefore, that Donne did actually have the book on his shelf, and perhaps one day it may be identified. Another book of Donne's is mentioned in the will of Bishop Henry King, who bequeathed to his sister, Mrs. Anne Dutton, 'my great French Bible with prints, which once belonged to my honored Friend Doctor Donne'. When Donne resigned the office of Reader at Lincoln's Inn on 11 February 1622, he presented to the

¹ *Rev. Eng. Stud.* XIII, 1937, 333.   ² *Times Lit. Sup.*, 3 March 1946.

Society a copy of the Bible in six volumes folio printed at Douai, 1617, with the commentary of Nicholas de Lyra. This contains a long presentation inscription in Donne's hand, but it is not included in the main list, as it cannot be said to have formed part of his library.

Donne directed in his Will, proved 5 April 1631,[1] that 'my Plate & Bookes (such Bookes only being excepted as by a Scedule signde wth my hand I shall give away)' should be sold for the benefit of his heirs. The list of excepted books has not survived but, according to the testimony of Izaak Walton, it contained the three volumes of Bellarmine's *Disputationes de controversiis Christianae Fidei, adversus huius temporis haereticos*, published in 1586, 1588, and 1593. Walton related (*Lives*, 1670, pp. 14–16) that Donne, having been admitted to Lincoln's Inn, in his nineteenth year 'begun to survey the Body of Divinity', and so, 'being to undertake this search, he believed the *Cardinal Bellarmine* to be the best defender of the *Roman cause*, and therefore he took himself to the examination of his Reasons . . . and before the twentieth year of his age, did shew the then Dean of Gloucester . . . all the Cardinals works marked with many weighty observations under his own hand; which works were bequeathed by him at his death as a Legacy to a most dear Friend'. These annotated volumes still remain to be discovered. That there may be others is suggested by a letter written by Donne to the Duke of Buckingham in 1623. The Duke was then in Madrid with Charles, Prince of Wales, and Donne began his letter thus (Gosse, II, 176): 'I can thus far make myself believe that I am where your Lordship is, in Spain, that, in my poor library, where indeed I am, I can turn mine eye towards no shelf, in any profession from the mistress of my youth, Poetry, to the wife of mine age, Divinity, but that I meet more authors of that nation than of any other.' The books listed here in fact include only one Spanish text, but many others are by Spanish authors, though in Latin. Again, in his first Satyre Donne described his library in the lines:

> Away thou fondling motley humorist,
> Leave mee, and in this standing wooden chest,
> Consorted with these few bookes, let me lye
> In prison, and here be coffin'd, when I dye;

[1] Bald, p. 565.

Here are God's conduits, grave Divines; and here
Nature's Secretary, the Philosopher;
And jolly Statesmen, which teach how to tie
The sinewes of a cities mistique bodie;
Here gathering Chroniclers, and by them stand
Giddie fantastique Poëts of each land.

Yet it is to be noticed that the great majority of Donne's books are concerned with theological controversy. One of the lighter books is an Italian translation of Virgil's *Aeneid*, Venice, 1538. The book with the latest date, 1629 (L89), is a moving relic of Donne's friendship with Izaak Walton, their two signatures appearing on the title-page one above the other. Perhaps Donne gave the book to Walton not long before his death, his failing powers being shewn by the shaky writing.

[The names are arranged in alphabetical order and are not included in the general index]

L1 A., G.S. *Confutatio Causarum, quibus Elisabeth Angla Classiarios suos adductos fuisse, libello in lucem edito, declarat, ad naues non paucas onerarias Hanseaticorum in Oceano Occidentali intercipiendas* [No place], 1590, 8°.
No motto or signature, but pencil markings in the margins. Bound with L53 and eight other tracts.

L2 ABBOT, GEORGE, Archbishop of Canterbury. *Explicatio sex illustrium Quaestionum. . . . Oxoniæ anno 1597 in schola Theologica proposita*, Frankfurt, 1616, 4°.
Donne's motto and signature on the title-page. Many marginal pencil markings. Bound in contemporary limp vellum. DWL (2012. D. 19).

L3 [BACON, SIR FRANCIS] *A Declaration of the Practices & Treasons attempted and committed by Robert late Earle of Essex and his complices*, London, 1601, 4°. [*STC* 1133].
No motto and no signature now visible and no pencil markings in the margins, but inscribed on the title-page in Donne's hand: *Sinite eum maledicere, nõ Dominus iuſsit & reg* . . . This gives the sense of 2 Sam. 16: 10, but is paraphrased, not

quoted, from the Vulgate. In an old binding, not contemporary, with five other tracts (L17, 48, 147, 156, 173), all of which are much trimmed. From the library of Bishop John Moore (1646–1714) acquired by George I and given to Cambridge in 1717. ULC (Syn. 7. 60. 26 (6)).

L4 ANON. *Dialogue du fou et du sage* [1510?].
Donne's motto and signature on the title-page. BM (C. 22. a. 42). It is suggested by Mr. Ian R. Maxwell in *Times Lit. Sup.*, 11 July 1935, that this book may have belonged to Donne's grandfather, John Heywood, who is believed to have used the *Dialogue* as his model.

L5 ANON. *Lettres d'un Francois, sur certain discours faict n'agueres, pour la preseance du roy d'Hespagne* [No place], 1587, 8°.
No motto or signature, but many marginal pencil markings on the early leaves. Bound with L39, and eight other tracts.

L6 ANON. *Theologica Mystica a pio quodam Ordinis Dominorum Teutonicorum Sacerdote, . . . a Ioanne Theophilo in Latinum translata.* [with] *Ludovici Blosii Enchiridion Parvulorum*, Lyons, 1580, 12°.

Donne's motto and signature on the title-page. His signature also on the verso of a fly-leaf at the end of the volume. Middle Temple Library.

L7 AQUINAS, THOMAS. *De Summi Pontificis Auctoritate, De Episcoporum Residentia, et Beneficiorum Pluralitate, Gravissimorum Auctorum Complurium Opuscula ad Apostolicæ Sedis dignitatem maiestatemque tuendam spectantia*, Venice, 1562, 2 vols, 4°.

Donne's motto and signature on the first title-page. Pencil marks in margins of vol. 2. Middle Temple Library.

L8 ARNISÆUS, HENNINGUS. *De Subjectione Clericorum*, Frankfurt, 1612, 4°.

Donne's motto and signature on the title-page. Pencil markings in the margins. Bound in contemporary limp vellum, with fragments of a MS. as end papers, with L28 and L169. From Selden's library. BLO (4°. A. 9. Jur. Seld.).

L9 ARREST & *Declaration du Roy, contenant la dispense des quarante iours, accordée par sa Majesté, en faueur de tous les Officiers de ce Royaume qui en voudront iouir, en payant par chacun au quatre deniers pour liure de la valeur & estimation de leurs Office, suiuant les Estats qui en seront arrestez au Conseil de sa dite Majesté*, Paris, 1604, 8°.

No motto or signature, but many pencil markings in the margins. Bound with L53, and eight other tracts.

L10 ARTICLES *of Peace, Entercourse, and Commerce, concluded by James I. with Philip III of Spaine*, 1605, 4°.

No motto or signature, but many of Donne's pencil markings in the margins. Bound in contemporary limp vellum with L53 and eight other tracts.

L11 AB ASSONLEVILLA, GULIELMUS. *Atheomastix sive Adversus Religionis Hostes Universos (politicos maxime) Dissertatio*, Antwerp, 1598, 8°.

Donne's motto and signature on the title-page. In contemporary limp vellum. Middle Temple Library.

L12 AUCTORES LATINÆ LINGUÆ *in unum redacti corpus* [Geneva?], 1595, F°.

Donne's signature and motto on the title-page. On the fly-leaf, probably in the hand of a seventeenth-century librarian, *Ex dono Johannis Donne Armigeri*. Library of Sidney Sussex College, Cambridge (E. 5. 36).

L13 AVIGNON, BERTRAND. *Declaration presenté en la faculté de Theologie & Sorbonne. Par laquelle il deduict les raisons qui l'ont meu de quitter la Religion Romaine, pour embrasser la verité de l'Euangile* [No place], 1605, 8°.

No signature or motto, but with Donne's pencil markings. Bound with L53, and eight other tracts.

L14 BALDVINUS, FRANCISCUS. *Constantinus Magnus, sive de Constantini Imperatoris Legibus Ecclesiasticis atque Civilibus*, Strassburg, 1612, 8°.

The title-page only, with Donne's signature and motto. BLO (Rawl. MS. D 1386, fo. 193).

L15 BALDUINUS, FRIDERICUS. *Passio Typica seu liber unus typorum veteris Testamenti*, Wittenberg, 1614, 8°.

Donne's motto and signature on the title-page. Bound in contemporary limp vellum. Chichester Cathedral Library.

L16 BARCLAY W. *De Regno et Regali Potestate adversus Buchananum, Brutum, Boucherium, et reliquos Monarchomachos, Libri Sex*, Paris, 1600, 4°.

Donne's motto and signature on the title-page. In contemporary limp vellum. Formerly in the Bridgewater Library, sold at Sotheby's, 19 March 1951, lot 21 (Maggs).

L17 BARLOW, WILLIAM. *The Summe and Substance of the Conference in his Maiesties Privy-Chamber, at Hampton Court. Ianuary 14, 1603*, London, 1604, 4° [*STC* 1456].

No signature or motto, but many of Donne's pencil markings in the margins. Bound (see L3) with five other tracts. ULC (Syn. 7. 60. 26 (5)).

L18 BENEDICT, S. *Regula Sancti Patris Benedicti cum declarationibus et constitutionibus Congregationis Montis Casini, alias S. Iustinae de Padua*, Paris, 1604, 8°.

This consists of three distinct works, but with a general title, which carries Donne's motto and signature. Pencil markings in the margins. Middle Temple Library.

L19 BESSAEUS, PETRUS. *Democritus Christianus, id est, Contemptus Vanitatum Mundi,* Cologne, 1616, 8⁰.

Donne's signature and motto on the title-page. Middle Temple Library.

L20 BEZA THEODORUS. *Tractatio de polygamia,* Geneva, 1568, 8⁰.

Donne's motto and signature on the title-page. Also carries Selden's motto. Bound in contemporary limp vellum with L21. BLO (8⁰. B. 6. Th. Seld.).

L21 BEZA, THEODORUS. *Tractatio de repudiis et divortiis,* Geneva, 1569, 8⁰.

No signs of ownership, but bound in contemporary limp vellum with L20. There are marginal annotations, but not in Donne's hand.

L22 BIGNON, HIEROSME. *Traicté Sommaire de l'Election des Papes,* Paris, 1605, 8⁰.

No motto or signature, but many pencil markings in the margins. Bound with L53, and eight other tracts.

L23 BINDER, CHRISTOPHER. *De Bonis Ecclesiæ ante legem, sub lege, ac sub evangelio,* Tübingen, 1615, 8⁰.

No signature, motto, or marginal marks, but bound between L112 and L192. Some of the pages have not been opened. Chichester Cathedral Library.

L24 BINSFELDIUS, PETRUS. *Exactum Examen Ordinandorum, seu Theologiæ Pastoralis, et Doctrinæ Necessariæ Sacerdotibus curam animarum administrantibus Enchiridion,* Douay, 1611, 12⁰.

Donne's motto and signature on the title-page. Pencil markings in the margins towards the end. Middle Temple Library.

L25 BISHOP, WILLIAM. *An answer unto M. Perkins Advertisement* [?Douay], [1607], 4⁰.

No motto or signature, but has Donne's pencil markings in the margins. Bound with nine other tracts in contemporary limp vellum (see L53). HCL. This tract is stated by R. E. Bennett (*Rev. Eng. Stud.* XIII, 1937, 333) to be the preface

to the next by Bishop; the two are catalogued as separate works in *STC* (3093, 3097), but will be treated as one in the new *STC*.

L26 BISHOP, WILLIAM. *The Second Part of the Reformation of a Catholike Deformed by M. W. Perkins* [?Douay], 1607, 4⁰.

No motto or signature, but Donne's pencil markings in the margins. Bound with nine other tracts in contemporary limp vellum (see L53). On Aa4*b* is a line supplied from Calvin's *Harmony of the Gospels,* which may be in Donne's hand (see R. E. Bennett, *Rev. Eng. Stud.* XIII, 1937, 334). HCL.

L27 BLACKWOOD, ADAM. *Adversus Georgii Buchanani dialogum, de jure regni apud Scotos,* Poitiers, 1581, 4⁰.

Donne's signature and motto on the title-page. In the possession of John Sparrow.

L28 BORNITIUS, IACOBUS, *Aerarium,* Frankfurt, 1612, 4⁰.

No name or motto, but bound with L8 and L169. His pencil markings in the margins.

L29 BOYER, PHILIBERT. *Le Stile de la Cour de Parlement, et forme de proceder en toutes les Cours souueraines du Royaume de France,* Paris, 1602, 12⁰.

Donne's motto and signature on the title-page. Pencil markings in the margins. Middle Temple Library.

L30 BRIDGEWATER, JOHN. *Concertatio Ecclesiæ Catholicæ in Anglia,* Trier, 1594, 8⁰.

Donne's motto and signature on the title-page. Chapter Library, Windsor Castle.

L31 BRIDGEWATER, JOHN. *Confutatio virulentæ disputationis theologicæ in qua G. Sohn conatus est,* Treves, 1589, 4⁰.

Donne's motto and signature on the title-page. Numerous pencil markings in the margins of the first part. BM.

L32 BRUNUS, ANTONIUS. *Entelecheia seu De Animæ Immortalitate Disputatio,* Venice, 1597, 4⁰.

Donne's motto and signature on the title-page. Middle Temple Library.

L33 BURHILL, ROBERT. *De Potestate Regia, et Usurpatione Papali, pro Tortura Torti,* Oxford, 1613, 8⁰ [*STC* 4117].

Donne's signature and motto on the title-page. ULC (Syn. 8. 61. 157). From Bishop Moore's library, presented by George I in 1717.

L34 BUTEON, JOHANNES. *De Quadratura Circuli Libri Duo*, Lyons, 1559, 8°.
Donne's motto and signature on the title-page. Pencil marks in the margins. Middle Temple Library.

L35 DE CASARUBIOS, ALFONSO. *Compendium Privilegiorum Fratrum Minorum et aliorum Mendicantium et non Mendicantium*, Venice, 1603, 8°.
Donne's motto and signature on the title-page. Much damaged by damp. Middle Temple Library.

L36 CAMPION, THOMAS. *Poemata. Ad Thamesin. Fragmentum Umbræ. Liber Elegiarum. Liber Epigrammatum*, London, 1595, 8° [*STC* 4544].
Donne's signature, mutilated, and motto on the title-page. Pierpont Morgan Library, New York.

L37 CANINIUS, ANGELUS. Ἑλληνισμός, London, 1613, 8° [*STC* 4566].
Donne's signature and motto on the title-page. From Selden's library. Bound in contemporary limp vellum. BLO (C. 8. Art. Seld.).

L38 [CAOULT, WALRANDUS (translator).] *Miracula Quæ Ad Invocationem Beatissimæ Virginis Mariæ, apud Tungros, Camberones, et Servios in Pannonia . . . effulsere*, Cologne, 1607, 12°.
Donne's motto and signature on the title-page. Middle Temple Library.

L39 CASMANNUS, OTTO. *Biographia, sive De Vita Hominis Naturali, quam Homo vi animæ suæ viventis, et corpus suum animantis, naturaliter vivit*, Frankfurt, 1602, 8°.
Donne's motto and signature on the title-page. Middle Temple Library.

L40 CEPARIUS, VIRGILIUS, S.J., *De Vita Beati Aloysii Gonzagæ e Societate Iesu . . . Libri Tres*, Cologne, 1608, 8°.
Donne's motto and signature on the title-page. Much damaged by damp. Middle Temple Library.

L41 CERTOSINO, DIONISIO. *Infiammatorio dell'Amor Divino*, Venice, 1575, 12°.
Donne's motto and signature on the title-page. In contemporary limp vellum. Middle Temple Library.

L42 CHEIRONUS, ISAACUS. *Ignorantia Iesuitarum*, Geneva, 1613, 8°.
Donne's motto and signature on the title-page. Middle Temple Library.

L43 CLAVASIO, ANGELUS DE. *Summa Angelica de Casibus Conscientiae*, Nuremberg, 1492, F°.
Donne's signature and motto on the verso of the title-page. In the Codrington Library, All Souls College, Oxford, presented by Sir Dudley Digges (S.R. 36, b. 10).

L44 COCHELET, ANASTASIUS. *Palaestrita Honoris D. Hallensis Pro Justo Lipsio adversus Dissertationem mentiti idoli Hallensis Anonymi cuiusdam Hæretici*, Antwerp, 1607, 4°.
Donne's motto and signature on the title-page. Middle Temple Library.

L45 COCHLAEUS, IOANNES. *Historia de Actis et Scriptis Martini Lutheri*, Paris, 1565, 8°.
Donne's motto and signature on the title-page. Pencil marks in the margins. Middle Temple Library.

L46 COLVILLE, JOHN. *The Palinod of J. Colvill wherein he doth recant his former offences*, Edinburgh, 1600, 8° [*STC* 5587].
Lacks the title-page, and no signs of ownership, but bound in limp vellum with ten other tracts. ULC (Bb*. 11. 42 (2)). From Bishop Moore's library, presented by George I in 1717.

L47 COMITOLUS, PAULUS. *Responsa Moralia*, Lyons, 1609, 4°.
Donne's signature and motto on the title-page. Pencil markings in the margins. From Selden's library. BLO (Z. 6. Th. Seld.).

L48 CONSTITUTIONS *and Canons Ecclesiasticall Treated upon by the Bishop of London and the rest of the Bishops and Clergie*, London, 1604, 4° [*STC* 10069].
No signature or motto, but Donne's pencil markings in the margins. Bound with

five other tracts (see L3). ULC (Syn. 7. 60. 26 (1)). From Bishop Moore's library, presented by George I in 1717.

L49 COPE, ALAN [HARPSFIELD, NICHOLAS]. *Dialogi Sex contra summi pontificatus monasticae vitae, sanctorum, sacrarum imaginum oppugnatores*, Antwerp, 1573, 4°.

Motto and signature on the title-page. Pencil marks (?Donne's) on pp. 400–7. Rebound in 1958. Middle Temple Library.

L50 COPPENSTEIN, J. A. *Dispositiones ex D. Thomae de Aquino Commentariis in Matthaeum et Ioann. et ex S. Bonaventurae Comment. in Lucam. Tomus Secundus*, Mainz, 1616, 8°.

Donne's motto and signature on the title-page. In old calf, lacking the back-strip. In my library.

L51 CORVINUS *contra Bogermann*, 1614.

A page with Donne's signature and motto, stated to have been torn out of a copy of this book, is in BLO (Rawl. MS. D 1386).

L52 COVELL, WILLIAM. *A Briefe Answer unto certaine Reasons by way of an Apologie delivered to the L. Bishop of Lincolne by Mr. John Burges*, London, 1606, 4° [*STC* 5880].

Donne's signature on the title-page, the motto mostly removed by trimming. Many pencil markings in the margins. ULC (Bb*. 11. 42 (3)). From Bishop Moore's library, presented by George I in 1717.

L53 COVELL, WILLIAM. *Defence of the five books of Ecclesiastical Policie: written by Mr. Richard Hooker*, London, 1603, 4° [*STC* 5881].

On the leaf opposite the title Donne has written a Latin epigram as follows:

Ad Autorem

Non eget Hookerus tanto tutamine; Tanto Tutus qui impugnat sed foret Auxilio

J. Donne

Bound in contemporary limp vellum with nine other tracts, one of which contains Donne's signature and motto (L132),

and all the others his marginal pencil markings. HCL.[1]

L54 CRASHAWE, WILLIAM. *The Iesuites Gospel*, London, 1610, 4° [*STC* 6016].

No signature or motto, but many of Donne's pencil markings in the margins. Bound in limp vellum with ten other tracts. ULC (Bb*. 11. 42 (1)).

L55 CRECCELIUS, JOANNES. *Collectiones ex historiis, de origine et fundatione omnium fere monasticorum ordinum in specie*, Frankfurt, 1614, 4°.

Donne's motto and signature on the title-page. Bound in vellum with L136. The shelf mark on the spine shews that this book was formerly in Chichester Cathedral Library. Now in the possession of J. H. P. Pafford.

L56 CUFFE, HENRIE. *The Differences of the Ages of Man's Life. Together with the Originall causes, Progresse, and End thereof*, London, 1607, 8° [*STC* 6103].

Donne's signature and motto on the title-page. Both have been partly removed by trimming. HCL, among the books given to the University by Thomas Hollis in 1767.

L57 CUPERS, RUDULPHUS. *Tractatus de sacrosancta universali ecclesia*, Venice, 1588, 4°.

Donne's signature and motto on the title-page, and some vertical pencil markings in the margins. Bound in contemp. vellum. Chichester Cathedral Library.

L58 D'ALUIN, STEPHANUS. *Tractatus de Potestate Episcoporum, Abbatum, &c.* Paris, 1607, 4°.

Donne's signature and motto on the title-page. William Pickering's library, sold at Sotheby's, 8 August 1854, lot 1141. Afterwards in the library of Dr. Augustus Jessopp. Now in HEH.

L59 DANTE ALIGHIERI. *L'Amoroso Convivio*, Venice, 1531, 8°.

[1] The volume was sold with William Pickering's books, Second Portion, eleventh day, 18 August 1854, lot 3467. The epigram to Hooker was noted in the catalogue.

Donne's signature on the title-page, and his motto on the blank leaf facing it. Three earlier inscriptions on the title-page— *Di Thomaso Langtono egli amici*, *Di Tomaso Langstono*, and *Thomas Langton*— have been deleted. From Selden's library. Bound in contemporary limp vellum. BLO (D. 19. Art. Seld.).

L60 D'AVEROULTIUS, ANTONIUS. *Catechismus Historicus, sive Flores Exemplorum Collecti ex Sacra Scriptura, Sanctis Patribus, aliisque Ecclesiæ Doctoribus, ac Historicis*, Cologne, 1614, 2 vols, 8°.

Donne's motto and signature on the title-page of the first of two volumes bound together. Middle Temple Library.

L61 DELOMMEAU, PIERRE. *Les Maximes Generalles du Droict François Diuisees en Trois Liures*, Rouen, 1612, 8°.

Donne's motto and signature on the title-page. A few pencil markings in the margins. Middle Temple Library.

L62 DE SANCTA FIDE, HIERONYMUS. *Hebræomastyx, Vindex Impietatis, ac Perfidiæ Iudaicæ*, Frankfurt, 1602, 8°.

Donne's motto and signature on the title-page. Middle Temple Library.

L63 DRUSIUS, I. *Miscellanea Locutionum Sacrarum*, Franeker, 1586, 8°.

Donne's motto and signature on the title-page. Bound with L64, 65. Middle Temple Library.

L64 DRUSIUS, I. *Ad Minerval Serarii Responsio*, Franeker, 1606, 8°.

No signs of ownership, but bound with L63, 65. Middle Temple Library.

L65 DRUSIUS, I. *Tetragrammata sive de Nomine Dei proprio quod Tetragrammata vocant*, Franeker, 1604, 8°.

No signs of ownership, but bound with L63, 64. Middle Temple Library.

L66 DUDITH, ANDREAS. *Orationes in Concil. Trident. habitae*, Offenbach, 1610, 4°.

Donne's motto and signature on the title-page. Some pencil markings in the margins. Bound in contemporary limp vellum. DWL (2008. D. 4).

L67 [DU PUY, PIERRE.] *Traictez des Droicts et Libertez de L'Eglise Gallicane*, Paris, 1609, 4°.

Donne's motto and signature on the title-page. Middle Temple Library.

L68 DURANDUS, GULIELMUS, Mimatensis Episcopus. *Rationale Divinorum Officiorum. Tomus Primus*, Lyons, 1605, 8°.

Donne's signature and motto on the title-page. No marginal marks by him. Bound in old vellum. Formerly in the possession of Dr. Chr. Wordsworth, Master of Trinity College, Cambridge, and of Dr. Chr. Wordsworth, Bishop of Lincoln. Afterwards in the library of the late Dr. Chr. Wordsworth, Canon of Salisbury, and now in Liverpool Cathedral Library.

L69 ECLOGE *Bullarum et Motupropriorum Sanctissimorum Patrum*, Lyons, 1582, 8°.

Donne's signature and motto on the title-page. Also carries Selden's motto. BLO (B. 32. Jur. Seld.).

L70 [EGERTON, THOMAS.] *The Speech touching the Post-nati*, London, 1609, 4° [*STC* 7540].

Contains marginal notes, some trimmed by the binder, probably in Donne's hand. Many pencil markings in the margins. Bound in limp vellum with ten other tracts. ULC (Bb*. 11. 42 (7)).

L71 FENTON, R. *Answere to William Alablaster, his Motives*, London, 1599, 4° [*STC* 10799].

No motto or signature, but many of Donne's pencil markings in the margins. Bound in contemporary limp vellum with L53 and eight other tracts. HCL.

L72 FERRIUS, PAULUS. *Scholastici Orthodoxi Specimen Hoc est Salutis nostræ Methodus Analytica*, Gotstad, 1616, 8°.

Donne's motto and signature on title-page. Middle Temple Library.

L73 FILESACUS, JOANNES. *De Sacra Episcoporum auctoritate comment.*, Paris, 1606, 8°.

Donne's signature and motto on the title-page. From William Pickering's library, sold at Sotheby's, 8 August 1854, lot 1140. Afterwards in the library of Lord

Crewe. Offered by Messrs. Maggs in January, 1943 (*Mercury*, no. 77).

L74 FitzSimon, Henricus, S.J. *Britanno-machia Ministrorum, in plerisque et fidei fundamentis, et fidei articulis dissidentium*, Douay, 1614, 4°.
Donne's motto and signature on the title-page. Middle Temple Library.

L75 Florentinus, F. Ricoldus. *Propugna-culum Fidei, Toti Christianæ Religioni adversum mendacia et deliramenta Sara-cenorum, Alchorani præcipue, maxime utile*, Venice, 1607, 4°.
Donne's motto and signature on the title-page. Middle Temple Library.

L76 Forgemont, Ioachim. *Repliques aux pretendues responses faictes par Maistre Pierre du Moulin . . . sur XXXII demandes à luy proposees*, Paris, 1615.
Donne's motto and signature on the title-page. Middle Temple Library.

L77 Freher, M. *Sulpitius; sive de æquitate commentarius, etc.*, 1608. 4°.
Donne's signature on the title-page. BM (501. e. 10 (3)).

L78 De Gallemart, Joannes. *Decisiones et Declarationes Illustrissimorum Cardinalium sacri Concilii Tridentini Interpretum*, Douay, 1615. 8°.
Donne's motto and signature on the title-page. Middle Temple Library.

L79 Gentilis, Albericus. *In Titulum Digestorum De Verborum Significatione Commentarius*, Hanover, 1614, 4°.
Donne's signature and motto on the title-page. In contemporary limp vellum. ULC (Q*. 11. 56). From the library of Henry Lucas of St. John's College be-queathed in 1664.

L80 Gentilis, Albericus. *Regales Disputa-tiones tres*, London, 1605, 4° [*STC* 11741].
Donne's motto and signature on the title-page, both much trimmed by the binder. Some pencil markings. Formerly in the library of Leonard Woolf. Sold at Sotheby's 27 July 1970, lot 143 (Dawson £480).

L81 Gentilis, Scipio. *De Conjurationibus Libri Duo*, Hanover, 1602, 8°.

Donne's motto and signature on the title-page, both cropped by the binder. Pencil markings in the margins. Royal College of Physicians.

L82 Gesner, Salomon. *Papismi Calvinia-norum XXV. dogmatici & XX. practici*, Frankfurt, 1598.
Title-page only, with Donne's motto and signature, mounted in a copy of *Poems*, 1633. Wellesley College, Mass.

L83 Gillet, Didiere ('simple femme de village'). *La Subtille et Naifre Recherche de l'Heresie*, Paris, 1609, 8°.
Donne's motto and signature on the title-page. Pencil markings in margins. In contemporary limp vellum. Middle Temple Library.

L84 Goclenius, Rodolphus. *Physiologia Crepitus Ventris et Risus*, Frankfurt, 1607, 8°.
Donne's signature and motto on the title-page. Pencil markings in the margins. Also carries Selden's motto. Bound in contemporary limp vellum. BLO (G. 4°. Art. Seld.).

L85 Goldastus, Melchior. *Imperialia decreta de cultu imaginum*, Frankfurt, 1608, 8°.
Motto and signature on the title-page. Pencil markings in margins. Rebound in 1958. Middle Temple Library.

L86 Goulart, S. *Considerations sur Divers Articles de la doctrine Chrestienne*, Saumur, 1608, 12°.
Donne's motto and signature on the title-page. Middle Temple Library.

L87 Gracian, Geronimo. *Iosephina*, Brus-sels, 1609, 4°.
Donne's motto and signature, mutilated, on the title-page. Pencil markings in the margins. BM (486. b. 23).

L88 de Graffiis, Iacobus. *De Arbitrariis Confessariorum, quæ ad Casus Conscientiæ attinent, Libri Duo*, Cologne, 1616, 8°.
Donne's motto and signature on the title-page. Middle Temple Library.

L89 Gregorius Magnus, Episcopus Ro-manus. *De Cura Pastorali. Ed. a Jer. Stephano*, London, 1629, 8° [*STC* 12348].

Signatures of Donne and Izaak Walton on the title-page,[1] William Salt Library, Stafford, having been presented by the daughter of the late Revd. W. Beresford of Leak. It is bound with another book, which carries the signature Merrywether, a family connected by marriage through Canon Merrywether of Salisbury with the Hawkins family, and so with Walton's son-in-law, Dr. Hawkins of Winchester.

L90 GRETSERUS, JACOBUS, S.J. *De Modo Agendi Iesuitarum cum Pontificibus, Prælatis, Principibus, Populo, Iuventute, et inter se mutuo . . .*, Ingolstad, 1600, 4°.

Donne's motto and signature on the title-page. Middle Temple Library.

L91 GRETSERUS, JACOBUS, S.J. *Libri Duo De Benedictionibus et Tertius De Maledictionibus*, Ingolstad, 1615, 4°.

Donne's motto and signature on the title-page. Middle Temple Library.

L92 GRETSERUS, JACOBUS, S.J. *Mysta Salmuriensis seu Mysterium Iniquitatis, editum quidem a Philippo Mornayo Plessiaci Domino etc. nunc autem a Iacobo Gretsero S.J. revelatum et dilucide explanatum*, Ingolstad, 1614, 4°.

Donne's motto and signature on the title-page. Middle Temple Library.

L93 GRETSERUS, JACOBUS, S.J. *Summula Casuum Conscientiæ de Sacramentis . . . ex Luthero, Calvino, et Beza fideliter collecta*, Ingolstad, 1611, 4°.

Donne's motto and signature on the title-page. Middle Temple Library.

L94 GUERRERO, ALPHONSUS ALVAREZ. *Utriusque Dignitatis. Tam Ecclesiasticæ quam Politicæ. Speculum*, Cologne, 1607, 8°.

Donne's motto and signature on the title-page. Pencil markings in the margins. From Selden's library. BLO (8°. Art. 5. Jur. Seld.).

L95 GUICCARDINI, Fr. *Piu consigli et avvertimenti in materia di republica et di privata*, Paris, 1576, 4°.

Donne's signature and motto on the title-

[1] Reproduced in the second edition of this *Bibliography*, 1932.

page; also those of a previous owner, whose name has been disguised by Donne by altering the letters in ink and adding his terminal cipher. Numerous marginal notes by the other owner, Herbert, and on interleaves. Bound in limp vellum. HCL.

L96 GULIELMUS, JANUS. *Plautinarum Quæstionum Commentarius*, Paris, 1583, 8°.

Donne's signature and motto on the title-page. A few pencil markings in the margins. From Selden's library. Bound in contemporary limp vellum. BLO (G. 10. Art. Seld.).

L97 HELVICUS, CHRISTOPHERUS. *Tractatus historicus et Theologicus, de Chaldaicis bibliorum paraphrasibus*, Giessen, 1612, 4°.

Donne's motto and signature on the title-page. His pencil markings in the margins. Bound in contemporary limp vellum with L98–100. Middle Temple Library.

L98 HELVICUS, CHRISTOPHERUS. *Synopsis Historiæ Universalis*, Giessen, 1612, 4°.

No signs of ownership, but bound with L97, 99, 100. Middle Temple Library.

L99 HELVICUS, CHRISTOPHERUS. *Epelenchus sive Appendix Elenchorum Judaicorum*, Giessen, 1613, 4°.

No signs of ownership, but bound with L97, 98, 100. Middle Temple Library.

L100 HELVICUS, CHRISTOPHERUS. *Systema controversiarum theologicarum, quæ Christianis cum Judæis intercedunt, octo elenchis comprehensum*, Giessen, 1612, 4°.

No signs of ownership, but bound with L97–9. Middle Temple Library.

L101 [HENRY VIII, King, and FISHER, Bishop.] *Assertio Septem Sacramentorum*, Paris, 1562, 8°.

Donne's signature and motto on the title-page. Pencil markings in the margins. From Selden's library. Bound in contemporary limp vellum. BLO (H. 15. Th. Seld.).

L102 HILL, NICOLAUS. *Philosophia Epicurea, Democritiana, Theophrastica proposita simpliciter, non edocta*, Paris, 1601, 8°.

A motto at the head of the title-page has

been deleted, and a slip bearing Donne's signature (evidently cut down after it was written) has been pasted over a deleted inscription half-way down the page. John Sparrow has determined that the inscription under the slip runs: *Ben Jonsonij liber*, and that the deleted motto is: *Tamquā Explorator*, habitually used by Jonson. (*Times Lit. Sup.*, 5 August 1955, p. 451.) Bound in contemporary calf, with device of a rose and wreath surmounted by a crown stamped in gold on the covers. Contemporary interleaving. Recently rebacked. Middle Temple Library.

L103 HOBY, EDWARD. *A Letter to Mr T[heoph.] H[iggons]*, London, 1609, 4° [*STC* 13541].

No signature or motto, but has Donne's pencil markings in the margins. Bound in limp vellum with ten other tracts. ULC (Bb*. 11. 45 (5)).

L104 HOLLAND, T. *Panegyris D. Elizabethæ Reginæ, a Sermon in Paul's Church, 17th November, 1599*, Oxford, 1600, 4° [*STC* 13597].

No motto or signature, but with Donne's pencil markings in the margins. Bound in contemporary limp vellum with L53 and eight other tracts. HCL.

L105 HYLL, A. *Defence of the Article, Christ Descended into Hell, against one Alexander Humes*. London, 1592, 4° [*STC* 13466].

No motto or signature, but with Donne's pencil markings in the margins. Bound in contemporary limp vellum with L53 and eight other tracts. HCL.

L106 [JESUITS.] *Answere made by one of our Brethren, a Secular Priest, now in Prison, to a Fraudulent Letter of M. George Blackwels, in commendation of the Jesuites in England*, 1602, 4°.

No evidence of Donne's ownership except one marginal pencil mark, but bound in contemporary limp vellum with L53 and eight other tracts. HCL.

L107 KEPPLERUS, JOANNES. *Eclogæ Chronicæ*, Frankfurt, 1615, 4°.

Donne's motto and signature on the title-page. In contemporary limp vellum. Middle Temple Library.

L108 KING, JOHN. *A Sermon preached at Whitehall the 5. day of November. ann. 1608*, Oxford, 1608, 4° [*STC* 14986].

No signature or motto, but has Donne's pencil markings in the margins, some marked NB. Bound in contemporary limp vellum with ten other tracts. ULC (Bb*. 11. 42 (9)).

L109 KIRCHNERUS, HERMANNUS. *Legatus: Ejusque Jura Dignitas & Officium Duobus libris explicata*, Marburg, 1614, 4°.

Donne's signature on the title-page. William H. Arnold Library, sold at the Anderson Galleries, New York, 10 November 1924, lot 282. Bought by the Rosenbach Co.

L110 DE L['ALLOUETTE], E[DMOND]. *Apologia Catholica ad Famosos et Seditiosos Libellos Conjuratorum*, [Paris?], 1584, 8°.

Donne's signature and motto on the title-page. Bound in contemporary limp vellum. ULC (Syn. 8. 58. 170). From Bishop Moore's library presented by George I in 1717.

L111 LAMPUGNANUS, POMPEIUS. *Iusti Lipsi in C. Cornelium Tacitum Notæ cum Manuscripto Cod. Mirandulano Collatæ* Bergamo, 1602, 8°.

No evidence of ownership, but bound with L139, and eight other tracts.

L112 LOCMAN. *Fabulæ et selecta quædam Arabum adagia*, Leyden, 1615, 8°.

No signature or motto, but with some of Donne's marginal marks. Bound with L23 and L192. Chichester Cathedral Library.

L113 LULLUS, REMUNDUS. *Duodecim Principia Philosophiæ*, Paris, 1516, 8°.

Donne's signature and motto on the title-page. Pencil markings in margins. In contemporary limp vellum. Middle Temple Library.

L114 LYDIAT, THOMAS. *Recensio et Explicatio Argumentorum productorum libello Emendationis Temporum compendio factæ* [No place], 1613, 8° [*STC* 17045].

Donne's motto and signature on the title-page. Middle Temple Library.

L115 MANUTIUS, ALDUS. *Epitome Orthographiæ*, Antwerp, 1579, 8º.

Donne's signature and motto on the title-page. From Selden's library. Bound in contemporary limp vellum, with L195; fragments of a MS. as end-papers. BLO (8º M. 75. Art. Seld.).

L116 MARCOBRUNI, PAOLO EMILIO. *Raccolta di Lettere di diversi Principi, & alti Signori*, Venice, 1595, 4º.

Donne's motto and signature on the title-page, and a few pencil markings in the margins. Bound in contemporary limp vellum. Queen's College, Oxford.

L117 MARCULFI MONACHI *formularum Libri duo. Hieronymus Bignorius ed.*, Paris, 1613, 8º.

Donne's signature and motto (cropped by the binder) on the title-page. Royal College of Physicians.

L118 MASSONUS, PAPIRIUS [editor]. *Gesta Collationis Chartageni Habitæ Honorii Cæsaris Iussu inter Catholicos et Donatistas*, Paris, 1588, 8º.

Donne's motto and signature on the title-page. Middle Temple Library.

L119 MATTHÆUS, PETRUS. *Septimus Decretalium Constitutionum Apostolicarum Post Sextum*, Frankfurt, 1590, 8º.

Donne's signature on the title-page, with the motto almost entirely trimmed away by the binder. Pencil markings in the margins. Royal College of Physicians.

L120 MENGUS, HIERONYMUS. *Flagellum Dæmonum, Exorcismos Terribiles, Potentissimos, et Efficaces, Remediaque probatissima . . . complectens*, Lyons, 1604, 8º.

Donne's motto and signature on the title-page. Pencil markings in the margins. Bound in contemporary limp vellum with L121. Marsh's Library, Dublin, from Bishop Stillingfleet's books.

L121 MENGUS, HIERONYMUS. *Fustis Dæmonum*, Lyons, 1604, 8º.

No motto or signature, being bound in contemporary limp vellum with L120. Pencil markings in the margins. Marsh's Library, Dublin, from Bishop Stillingfleet's books.

L122 MESUA, JOANNES. *De Re Medica Libri Tres* (transl. by Jacobus Sylvius), Paris, 1562, 8º.

Donne's motto and signature on the title-page. Some old ink underlinings. Bound in nineteenth-century half-calf with L157. Middle Temple Library.

L123 MINSHEU, JOHN. *Ductor in Linguas. The Guide into Tongues*, London, 1617, Fº [*STC* 17944].

The book contains one list, or sometimes two, of subscribers, both containing Donne's name.

L124 MOLINÆI *Opuscula* [No place], 1610, 8º.

Donne's signature and motto on the title-page. From Selden's library. Bound in contemporary limp vellum. BLO (M. 13. Jur. Seld.).

L125 [MONIPENNIE, JOHN.] *Certayne Matters concerning the Realme of Scotland, composed together*, London, 1603, 4º. [*STC* 18017].

Donne's motto on the title-page. The signature has probably been removed by trimming. Bound in contemporary limp vellum with ten other tracts. ULC (Bb*. 11. 42 (4)).

L126 [MOORE, ROBERT.] *Diarium Historico-Poeticum*, Oxford, 1595 [*STC* 18061].

Donne's signature and motto on the title-page. Also the signature of Sir J. Wolley, Latin Secretary to Queen Elizabeth. The title-page is mounted and the writing rather faint. FSLW.

L127 MORE, SIR THOMAS. *Lucubrationes*, Basel, 1563, 12º.

Donne's signature and motto on the title-page, cropped. With his marginal notes. In San Francisco Univ. Libr. (See J. B. Gleason, *Journ. Eng. Germ. Philol.*, 69 (1970) 599–612.) In old calf, incomplete.

L128 MORE, SIR THOMAS. *The Workes, written by him in the Englishe tonge*, London, 1557, Fº [*STC* 18076].

Donne's motto and signature on the title-page. His pencil markings in the margins

XI

Richardus *per Rachel hò seruito & non*
per Lea.

PREDICHE

di Bernardino Ochino da Siena.

Nouellamente ristampate & con grande
diligentia riuedute & corrette.

Parte Prima.

Con la sua Tauola
nel fine.

of the first part of the book. In a modern binding. Library of the Catholic University of America, Washington, D.C.

L129 MORTON, THOMAS. *A Direct Answer to the Scandalous Exceptions, which Theophilus Higgons hath lately objected against D. Morton*, London, 1609, 4° [*STC* 18181]. No signs of ownership, but bound for Donne in limp vellum with ten other tracts. ULC (Bb*. 11. 42. (6)).

L130 OCHINO DA SIENA, Bernardino. *Prediche* [No place or date], 8°. Donne's signature and motto on the title-page. He has partially erased a former owner's name to make room for the motto (see facsimile). In my library. In an Oxford binding of stamped calf with MS. paste-downs at each end. (The decorations are the stamped roll MW. b(1) and ornament 26. See N. R. Ker, *Publ. Oxf. Bib. Soc.* N.S. v, 1954.)

L131 OCHINUS, BERNARDINUS. *Sermones de Fide* [No place], 1544, 8°. Donne's signature and motto on the title-page. Signature of 'Cha: Blount'[1] on a2. Middle Temple Library.

L132 ORMEROD, O. *Picture of a Puritane, or a Relation of the Opinions, Qualities and Practices of the Anabaptists in Germany, and of the Puritans in England, and discovery of Puritan-Papisme*, London, 1605, 4° [*STC* 18851]. Donne's signature on the title-page, the motto mostly trimmed away by the binder. Bound in contemporary limp vellum with L53 and eight other tracts. HCL.

L133 P., C.L. *Discours de l'abus des justices de village*, Paris, 1605, 8°. Motto and signature on the title-page. Pencil markings throughout. Originally bound with L134 and rebound with it in 1958. Presumably a second edition since it is of later date than the *Suitte*. Middle Temple Library.

L134 P., C.L. *Suitte du discours de l'abus des justices de village*, Paris, 1605, 8°.

[1] Presumably Lord Mountjoy, later Earl of Devonshire (1563–1606).

Frequent pencil marks. Rebound, as before, with L133. Middle Temple Library.

L135 PARACELSUS, PHILIPPUS AUREOLUS THEOPHRASTUS. *Chirurgia Magna, in duos tomos digesta. Nunc recens a Iosquino Dalhernio Ostofranco donata*, Strassburg, 1573, 4°. Donne's signature and motto on the title-page. These have been lightly crossed out by a later owner, who has added his own initials, *G. P.*, with the inscription, *bought in Duck Lane 13. 10ᵇʳ. 1633 preciū. 7s. 6d.* R. B. Adam Library, Buffalo, N.Y. A facsimile is given in the catalogue, 111, 86. Now in the Donald F. Hyde Library. Title-page only.

L136 PARÉ, DAVID. *Irenicum: sive, De unione et synodo evangelicorum concilianda*, Heidelberg, Frankfurt, 1614, 4°. Bound in vellum with Creccelius, *Collectiones* (L55). No signature or motto, but pencil marks in the margins. J. H. P. Pafford.

L137 [PARKER, MATTHEW.] *De Antiquitate Britanniae Ecclesiae*, Hanover, 1605, F°. Donne's signature and motto on the title-page. Oriel College, Oxford (F. d. 12).

L138 PASCHALUS, CAROLUS. *Legatus Opus*, Rouen, 1598. Donne's signature and motto on the title-page. HEH.

L139 [PERIER, IEREMIE.] *Histoire remarquable et veritable de ce qui s'est passé par chacun iour au siège de la ville d'Ostende, de part & d'autre iusques à present*, Paris, 1604, 8°. Donne's motto and signature on the title-page, but mostly cut away by the binder. A few pencil markings in the margins of the early leaves. Bound with L140 and eight other tracts. From Selden's Library. BLO (8°. 45. Art. Seld. (7)).

L140 [PERIER, IEREMIE.] *Continuation des Sièges d'Ostende, et de l'Escluse*, Paris, 1604, 8°. No evidence of ownership, but bound with L139, and eight other tracts. BLO.

L141 PERSONA, J. B. *Noctes Solitaræ*, Venice, 1613, 4°.

Donne's signature and motto on the title-page. Also carries Selden's motto. Bound in contemporary limp vellum. BLO (P. 35. Art. Seld.).

L142 PETREUS, THEODORUS. *Confessio Tertulliniana et Cypriana in Quatuor digesta libros . . .*, Paris, 1603, 8⁰.

Donne's motto and signature on the title-page. Middle Temple Library.

L143 PIGGHE, ETIENNE WYNANTE. *Annales Magistratuum et Provinciarum SPQR*, Antwerp, 1599. F⁰.

Donne's motto and signature were on the title-page, but have been cut out, leaving only enough of the descenders for identification. His signature was probably also on the top right-hand corner of the fly-leaf before the title, but has also been removed. His pencil markings are in the margins of the first thirty pages. Bound in contemporary limp vellum. From the Bridgewater Library. Now in the collection of John Sparrow (see his letter, *Times Lit. Sup.*, 13 March 1953).

L144 [PITHOU, PIERRE, ed.] *Epigrammata et Poematia Varia*, Paris, 1590, 8⁰.

Donne's signature and motto on the title-page. His signature also appears on a fly-leaf, and there are several notes in his hand on that leaf and in the text with pencil markings in the margins. The volume also carries Selden's motto. BLO (8⁰. E. 4. Art. Seld.). The annotations are the subject of an article by John Sparrow in *The London Mercury*, December 1931.

L145 [PITHOU, PIERRE.] *Traicté des Libertez de l'Eglise Gallicane*, Paris, 1608, 12⁰.

Donne's motto and signature on the title-page. Middle Temple Library.

L146 A POLITIO, HIERONYMUS. *Expositio [Regulæ Seraphici S. Francisci]*, Naples, 1606, 8⁰.

Donne's motto and signature on the title-page. Pencil markings in margins of preliminary pages. Middle Temple Library.

L147 POWEL, GABRIEL. *A consideration of the deprived and silenced Ministers arguments*, London, 1606, 4⁰ [*STC* 20142].

Donne's signature and motto on title-page, but mostly removed by trimming. His pencil markings in the margins. Bound with five other tracts (see L3). ULC (Syn. 7. 60. 26 (4)).

L148 PRIEUR, CLAUDE. *Dialogue de la Lycanthropie ou Transformation d'Hommes en Loups, vulgairement dit Loups-garous et si telle se peut faire*, Louvain, 1596, 8⁰.

Donne's signature with traces of motto, cut by binder, on the title-page. Middle Temple Library.

L149 PROPHESIE. *A Prophesie that hath lyen hid, above these 2000 yeares*, London, 1610, 4⁰ [*STC* 20441].

No signature or motto, but many of Donne's pencil markings in the margins, and a note (trimmed) in his hand on the end fly-leaf. Bound in limp vellum with ten other tracts. ULC (Bb*. 11. 42 (10)).

L150 DE PUTEO, Paris. *De Syndicatu Tractatus Elegantissimus et Absolutissimus*, Frankfurt, 1605, 8⁰.

Donne's motto and signature on the title-page. In vellum boards. Marsh's Library, Dublin, from Bishop Stillingfleet's books.

L151 RADERUS, MATTHÆUS. *De Vita Petri Canisii de Societate Iesu Libri Tres*, Munich, 1614, 8⁰.

Donne's motto and signature on the title-page. Middle Temple Library.

L152 RAMUS, PETRUS, & RISNERUS, FRIDERICUS. *Opticæ Libri Quatuor*, Cassel, 1606, 4⁰.

Donne's motto and signature on the title-page, Middle Temple Library.

L153 RENSINCK, JOANNES. *Manuale Franciscanorum, Regulæ Expositonem aliaque ad eius observantiam, ac monasticæ vitæ disciplinam spectantia, breviter complectens*, Cologne, 1609, 12⁰.

Donne's motto and signature on the title-page. Middle Temple Library.

L154 REUSNERUS, NICOLAUS. *Aenigmatographia Sive Sylloge Aenigmatum et Griphorum conuiuialium*, Frankfurt, 1599, 12⁰.

Donne's motto and signature on the title-page. Pencil markings in margins. Middle Temple Library.

L155 RICCOBONIUS, ANTONIUS. *De Gym-*

nasio Patavino Commentariorum Libri Sex, Padua, 1598, 4°.

Donne's motto and signature on the title-page. Pencil markings in margins. Middle Temple Library.

L156 [ROGERS, THOMAS.] *The Faith, Doctrine, and religion professed & protected in the Realme of England: Expressed in 39 Articles*, Cambridge, 1607, 4° [*STC* 21228].

Donne's signature, trimmed, on the title-page; the motto almost completely removed. No pencil markings. Bound with five other tracts (see L3). ULC (Syn. 7. 60. 26 (2)).

L157 RONDELET, GUILLAUME. *Traité De Verole* (transl. by Estienne Maniald), Bordeaux, 1576, 8°.

No evidence of ownership, but bound with L122. Middle Temple Library.

L158 a SACROBOSCO, CHRISTOPHORUS, S.J. *Defensio Decreti Tridentini et Sententiæ Roberti Bellarmini SRE Cardinalis De authoritate vulgatæ editionis Latinæ adversus sectarios, maxime Whitakerum.* Antwerp, 1604, 8°.

Donne's motto and signature on the title-page. Bound with L159. Middle Temple Library.

L159 a SACROBOSCO, CHRISTOPHORUS, S.J. *De Investiganda Vera ac Visibili Christi Ecclesia*, Antwerp, 1604, 8°.

No evidence of ownership, but bound with L158. Middle Temple Library.

L160 SARNANUS, CARDINAL CONSTANTIUS. *Conciliatio Dilucida Omnium Controversiarum quæ in doctrina duorum summorum Theologorum S. Thomæ, et subtilis Ioannis Scoti passim leguntur*, Lyons, 1590, 8°.

Donne's motto and signature on the title-page. Middle Temple Library.

L161 SCALIGER, JOSEPH. *Opus novum de emendatione temporum in octo libros tributum*, Paris, 1583, F°.

Donne's signature and motto on the title-page, both much faded; also a presentation inscription, possibly to Donne, but mostly erased and illegible. On the fly-leaf facing the title-page are four lines of Latin verse *Ad Autorem* in Donne's hand with his signature:

*Emendare cupis Joseph qui tempora, Leges
præmia, Supplicium, Religiosa cohors
Quod tam conantur frustra, Conabere frustra;
Si per te non sunt deteriora sat est.*
              J: Donne.

Pencil markings on many leaves. Bound in contemporary limp vellum. Discovered in Ireland in 1958 and now in my collection.[1]

L162 [SCIOPPIUS, GASPAR.] *Nicodemi Macri Senioris Civis Romani cum Nicolao Crasso Juniore civi Veneto, Disceptatio*, Munich, 1607, 4°.

Donne's motto and signature on the title-page. A note on the author in his hand on the fly-leaf facing the title and many pencil markings in the margins. Bound with five other tracts. ULC (Syn. 7. 60. 185). From Bishop Moore's library, presented by George I in 1717.

L163 SEDULIUS, HENRICUS. *Apologeticus adversus Alcoranum Franciscanorum, pro Libro Conformitatum Libri Tres*, Antwerp, 1607, 4°.

Donne's motto and signature on the title-page. Pencil markings in margins. Middle Temple Library.

L164 SERARIUS, NICOLAUS, S.J. *Minerval Divinis Hollandiae, Frisiæque Grammaticis, Ios. Scaligero et Io. Drusio defensum*, Mainz, 1605, 8°.

Donne's motto and signature on the title-page. Middle Temple Library.

L165 SERARIUS, NICOLAUS, S. *Trihaeresium*, Mainz, 1604, 8°.

Motto and signature on the fly-leaf. Bound in contemporary limp vellum with L203 and L208. Middle Temple Library.

L166 SERARIUS, NICOLAUS, S.J. *Rabbini, et Herodes, Seu De Tota Rabbinorum Gente … maximè De Herodis Tyranni natalibus, Judaismo, uxoribus, liberis & regno, Libri Tres*, Mainz, 1607, 8°.

---

[1] Reproduced facing p. 220 in the third edition, 1958, of this bibliography. See *Times Lit. Sup.*, 21 and 28 February 1958, for full description.

Donne's signature and motto on the title-page. In contemporary limp vellum with L211. In the Harold Greenhill collection, Chicago.

L167 SICCAMA, SIBRANDUS. *De Veteri Anno Romano* ... Kampen, 1599, 4°.
Bound with L168.

L168 SICCAMA, SIBRANDUS. *Fastorum Kalendarium Lib.* 11, Amsterdam, 1600, 4°.
Donne's signature and motto on the title-page. Also carries Selden's motto. BLO (H. 26. Art. Seld.). Bound with L167.

L169 SIMONIA *Curiae Romanae*, Frankfurt, 1612, 4°.
No motto or signature, but bound with L8 and L28. Pencil markings in the margins.

L170 SOCOLOVIUS, STANISLAUS. *Censura Orientalis Ecclesiæ De præcipuis nostri seculi hæreticorum Dogmatibus*, Paris, 1584, 8°.
Donne's motto and signature on the title-page. Middle Temple Library.

L171 DE SOTO, DOMINGO. *Institucion de como se a de euitar el abuso de los juramentos*, Antwerp, 1569, 12°.
Donne's motto and signature on title-page. Frequent pencil markings in margins. Middle Temple Library.

L172 STENGELIUS, CAROLUS. *Sacrosancti nominis Iesu cultus et miracula.* Augsburg, 1613, 8°.
Donne's signature and motto (cropped by the binder) on the title-page. Bound with another book in old vellum. BLO (8° B. 114. Th.). Recorded in the Bodleian catalogue of 1635.

L173 SUTCLIFFE, MATTHEW. *An Answere unto a certaine calumnious letter published by M. Job Throckmorton*, London, 1595, 4° [*STC* 23451].
Donne's signature and motto on the title-page, part of the signature and almost the whole of the motto removed by trimming. A few pencil markings in the margin. Bound with five other tracts (see L3). ULC (Syn. 7. 60. 26 (3)). From Bishop Moore's library, presented by George I in 1717.

L174 SUTCLIFFE, MATTHEW. *Subversion of Robert Parsons, his confused and worthlesse*

work, entituled a Treatise of Three Conversions of England*, London, 1606, 4° [*STC* 23469].
No motto or signature, but Donne's pencil markings in the margins. Bound in contemporary limp vellum with L53 and eight other tracts. HCL.

L175 SUTOR, PETRUS. *De Vita Cartusiana Libri Duo*, Cologne, 1609, 8°.
Donne's motto and signature on the title-page. Middle Temple Library.

L176 SYLVIUS, AENEAS. *Opera Omnia*, Basel, 1571, f°.
Motto and signature on the title-page. Rebound in 1958. Middle Temple Library.

L177 SYMONDS, WILLIAM. *Virginia. A Sermon preached at White-Chappel In the presence of many, Honourable and Worshipfull, the Adventurers and Planters for Virginia. 25. April. 1609*, London, 1609, 4° [*STC* 23594].
No signs of ownership, but bound in limp vellum with L46 and nine other tracts. ULC. (Bb*. 11. 42 (8)).

L178 TANNERUS, ADAMUS, S.J. *Defensionis Ecclesiasticæ Libertatis Libri Duo contra Venetæ Causæ Patronos, Ioannem Masilium Neapolitanum et Paulum Venetum Servitam etc.* Ingolstad, 1607, 4°.
Donne's motto and signature on the title-page. Middle Temple Library.

L179 THYRAEUS, PETRUS, S.J. *De Demoniacis Liber Unus Inquo Dæmonum obsidentium conditio; obsessorum hominum status; rationes item et modi, quibus ab obsessis dæmones exiguntur, discutiuntur et explicantur*, Cologne, 1594, 4°.
No motto or signature, but bound (and probably issued) with L180. Pencil markings in margins. Middle Temple Library.

L180 THYRAEUS, PETRUS, S.J. *De Variis tam Spirituum quam Vivorum Hominum prodigiosis Apparitionibus, et nocturnis Infestationibus Libri Tres*, Cologne, 1594, 4°.
Donne's motto and signature on the title-page. Pencil markings in the margins. Bound with L179. Middle Temple Library.

L181 UGOLINUS, BARTHOLOMÆUS. *Responsiones*, Bologna, 1607, 4°.

Donne's signature and motto on the title-page. Pencil markings in the margins. From Selden's library. Bound in contemporary limp vellum. BLO (V. 9. Jur. Seld.).

L182 VALLADERIUS, ANDREAS. *Speculum sapientiæ matronalis ex vita Sanctæ Franciscæ Romanæ*, Paris, 1609, 4°.

[Not verified and cannot now be found.] Middle Temple Library.

L183 VANINUS, JULIUS CÆSAR. *Amphitheatrum Æternæ Providentiæ Divinomagicum*, Lyons, 1615, 8°.

Donne's signature and motto on the title-page, both partly removed by trimming. Given to me by Charles Edmund Merrill jr., 1936. There is the signature of another early owner, *Th. Bride* [?] *è soc. med. Lond.*, on title-page.

L184 VELASCUS, J. F. *Hispaniorum Vindiciae*, Louvain, 4°.

Motto on the title-page; the signature trimmed away. Pencil markings. Rebound in nineteenth-century half-calf. Middle Temple Library.

L185 [DU VERGIER DE HANRANNE, JEAN.] *Apologie pour Messire Henry-Lovys Chastaignier de la Rochepozay Euesque de Poictiers* [no place], 1615, 8°.

Donne's motto and signature on the title-page. Middle Temple Library.

L186 VICUS, HENRICUS. *De descensu Jesu Christi ad inferos*, Antwerp, 1586, 4°.

Motto and signature on the title-page. Pencil markings. Rebound in nineteenth-century half-calf. Middle Temple Library.

L187 VIGNIER, NICOLAS. *Concerning the Excommunication of the Venetians. A Discourse against Cæsar Baronius, Cardinall of the Church of Rome*, London, 1607, 4°. [*STC* 24719].

Donne's signature and motto, both trimmed, on the title-page. His pencil markings in the margins, some marked NB. Bound in limp vellum with L46 and nine other tracts. ULC (Bb*. 11. 42 (11)).

L188 VILAGUT, ALPHONSUS. *Tractatus de Rebus Ecclesiae non Rite alienatis recuperandis, atque in integrum restituendis*, Bologna, 1606, 4°.

Donne's signature and motto on the title-page and with some marginal marks. Bound in contemporary limp vellum. Chichester Cathedral Library.

L189 DE VINEUS, PETRUS. *Epistolarum libri vi*, Hamburg, 1609, 12°.

Donne's signature and motto on the title-page. HCL.

L190 VIRGIL. *La Eneide tradotta in Terza Rima per M. Giovanpaolo Vasio*, Venice, 1538, 8°.

Donne's signature and motto on the title-page. Bound in contemporary limp vellum. HCL.

L191 VORSTIUS, CONRADUS. *Responsio ad Mathæi Sladi scholasticæ disceptationis partem primam*, Gouda, 1615, 4°.

Donne's motto and signature on the title-page. From the library of Lord Herbert of Cherbury. Jesus College, Oxford (H. 15. 15).

L192 WILDE, JEREMIAS, *Augustanus*. *De Formica*, Hamburg, 1615, 8°.

Donne's motto and signature on the title-page. Bound in contemporary limp vellum with L23 and L112. Pencil marks are found in the first and third of the books in this volume. Chichester Cathedral Library.

L193 WILLOT, HENRICUS. *Athenæ Orthodoxorum sodalitii Franciscani*. Liége, 1598, 8°.

[Not verified.] Middle Temple Library.

L194 WINDECK, J. P. *De Theologia Iurisconsultorum*, Cologne, 1604, 4°.

Donne's signature and motto on the title-page. A few pencil markings in the margins. Also carries Selden's motto. BLO (T. 3. Th. Seld.).

L195 WINTZLER, C. *Observationes de Collectis seu Contributione Imperii*, Frankfurt, 1612, 8°.

Donne's signature and motto on the title-page. Also carries Selden's motto. Bound in contemporary limp vellum with L115. BLO (8° W. 1. Jur. Seld.).

L196 WOLDERUS, JOHANNES. *Hæreseologiæ Synopsis*, Wittenberg, 1609, 8°.

No evidence of ownership, and some leaves unopened, but bound with L139 and eight other tracts. BLO.

L197 ZEHNERUS, IOACHIMUS. *Pythagoræ Fragmenta*, Leipzig, 1603, 8°.

No motto or signature. Text in Greek and Latin. Many marginal pencil markings in the Latin portion. Bound with L139 and eight other tracts. BLO.

Books from Donne's library discovered since 1958

L198 AMBROSE, ST. *Confessio Ambrosiana in libros quatuor digesta . . . Opera et studio Dn. Ioannis Nopelii*, Cologne, 1580, 8°.

Donne's motto on the title-page, the bottom right-hand corner torn away. No pencil markings. Bound in nineteenth-century calf. Middle Temple Library.

L199 ANON. *De Summi Pontificis Auctoritate . . . Gravissimorum auctorum opuscula*, Venice, 1561, 4°.

Donne's signature and motto on the title-page. No pencil markings. Rebound in 1958. Middle Temple Library.

L200 BELLOY, PIERRE DE. *Examen du Discours publié contre la Maison Royalle de France*, [no place], 1587, 8°.

Donne's motto half-way down the title-page, top outer corner torn away. No pencil markings. Rebound in nineteenth-century half-calf. Middle Temple Library.

L201 BENI, PAOLO. *Qua tandem ratione dirimi possit controversia quae in præsens de efficaci Dei auxilio et libero arbitrio inter nonnullos Catholicos agitatur*, Padua, 1603, 4°.

Donne's motto and signature on the title-page. Bequeathed to Corpus Christi College, Oxford, by John Rosewell, an Eton Master, in 1684. Reported by Paul Morgan (*Times Lit. Sup.*, 13 January 1966).

L202 BORDONI, GIOVANNI FRANCESCO. *De rebus præclare gestis a Sixto V. Pont. Max. . . . Carminum liber primus*. Rome, 1588, 4°.

Donne's motto and signature on the title-page. Bound in contemporary limp vellum. Identified by Miss H. M. Black in the Hunterian Collection, University of Glasgow (see Clifford Dobb, *Times Lit. Sup.*, 30 December 1965).

L203 C., I.D. *La Cabale des Reformez*. Montpellier, 1597, 8°.

Donne's signature and motto on the title-page, and many pencil markings. Bound in eighteenth-century calf. From the library of the Earl of Pembroke. Now in the collection of R. S. Pirie (1967).

L204 DRUSIUS, IOHANNES. *De Tribus Sectis Iudaeorum*, Franeker, 1605. 8°.

No motto or signature, but bound with L165 and L208. With Donne's pencil markings. Middle Temple Library.

L205 MENGHI, GIROLAMO. *Compendio dell'Arte Essorcistica*. Venice, Appresso Paolo Ugolini, 1599, 8°.

Donne's motto and signature on the title-page. No pencil markings. Bound in contemporary limp vellum with L201. In the library of John Sparrow (see *Times Lit. Sup.*, 6 January 1966).

L206 MENGI, GIROLAMO. *Parte seconda del Compendio dell'Arte Essorcistica*. Venice, Appresso Georgio Varisco, 1601, 8°.

No motto or signature, but bound with L200 and probably acquired by Donne in that form, though published separately.

L207 MESUA, JOANNES. *Textus Mesue Doctorum celeberrimum*. Lyons, 1540, 8°.

Donne's motto and signature on the title-page and his pencil markings in the margins of the first 54 pages. Rebound in boards c. 1800. From the library of Richard Holdsworth, Master of Emmanuel College, Cambridge (d. 1649). ULC (N*. 13.40).

L208 PAMELIUS, IACOBUS. *Missale SS. Patrum Latinorum*. 2 vols. Cologne, 1609, 4°.

Donne's motto and signature on the title-page. Bound in contemporary calf. Each volume has the bookplate of John Hall, Master of Pembroke College, Oxford, 1664–1710. Now in the college library. Reported by Paul Morgan (see *Times Lit. Sup.*, 25 November 1965, letter from John Sparrow).

L209 SCALIGER, JOSEPH. *Elenchus Trihaeresii Nicolai Serarii*, Franeker, 1605, 8°.

No motto or signature, but bound with L165 and L203. With Donne's pencil markings. Middle Temple Library.

L210 SCHLUESSELBURG, CONRAD. *Haereticorum catalogus*. Vol. XIII. Frankfurt, 1599, 8°.

Donne's motto and signature on the title-page and his pencil markings in the margins. Now in the Chapter Library, Windsor Castle. Reported by the Librarian, J. Callard (*Times Lit. Sup.*, 23 December 1965).

L211 SERARIUS, NICOLAUS. *Lutherus Theodotos*. Mainz, 1607 (colophon dated 1605), 8°.

No motto or signature, but bound in contemporary limp vellum with L166 by the same author. Now in the Harold Greenhill Collection, Chicago. First noticed by Professor R. C. Bald (*Life*, p. 537).

L212 SYLVIUS, ANTONIUS CLARUS. *Commentarius ad leges . . . Romani iuris antiqui*. Paris, 1603, 4°.

Donne's motto and signature on the title-page and many pencil markings, with some annotations, in the margins. Bound in eighteenth-century calf, signed on the fly-leaf by George Royce, Provost of Oriel College, Oxford, 1691–1708. Now in the college library. Reported by Paul Morgan (see *Times Lit. Sup.*, 25 November 1965, letter from John Sparrow).

L213 CODEX CANONUM *vetus ecclesiæ Romanæ*. Lutetiæ Parisorum. 1609, 8°.

Donne's signature and motto on the title-page. In the possession of B. Weinreb, London, 1971. Annotations on two pages, but not in Donne's hand. No pencil markings. Bound in contemporary vellum.

Books given by Donne to friends, but not proved to have been part of his library

L214 LUSIGNANO, STEFANO DI, of Lemasus, Ferè. [sic] *Affinitates omnium principum Christianitatis, cum Serenissimo Francisco Medices*. Paris, 1587, f°. Donne's signature and motto on the title-page. No pencil

markings. Bound in contemporary limp vellum, lettered in gold on the cover *Edward Gwynn*. Reported by Mr W. A. Kelly to be now in NLS.

L215 LLOYD, or LHUYD, JOHN. *Peplus. Illustrissime Viri D. Philippi Sidnaei Supremis Honoribus Dicatus*. Oxford, 1587, 4° [STC 22552].

Edited by John Lloyd, or Lhuyd, who signed the dedication to Lord Pembroke. Bound in contemporary limp vellum. Inscribed on the title-page, *Donum cognati mei Johannis Donne*, and this is the only evidence that it passed through Donne's hands. It was stated by Paul Morgan that the remains of Donne's motto and signature, removed by trimming, appear on the title-page, but the fragments visible do not correspond with these. The book is now in the library of Balliol College, Oxford.

L216 MONTAGU, RICHARD. *A gagg for the new gospell? No. A new gagg for an old goose, Or, an answer to a late abridger of controversies*. London, 1624, 4° [STC 18038].

Inscribed within the ornament at the top of the second leaf: *Izaak Walton given me by Doc Don 1625*. There are also marginalia in Walton's hand. Now in the library of R. S. Pirie.

L217 MUNSTER, SEBASTIAN. *Cosmographia*. Basel, 1578, f°. Inscribed on the fly-leaf: *Liber Ed Parvyshe ex dono J. Donne*.

Reported by E. J. S. Parsons of the Bodleian staff to John Sparrow, who thought that the whole inscription was in Donne's hand, but that there is no evidence that the book, bound in continental stamped pigskin, was ever part of his library. (See *Times Lit. Sup.*, 25 November 1965 and a letter from Professor I. A. Shapiro on the identity of Parvish, 20 January 1966.)

L218 VULGATE BIBLE, commentary by *Nicholas de Lyra*, Douai, 6 vols., f°, 1617, with a long inscription by Donne, given by him to the library of Lincoln's Inn when he resigned the Office of Reader, 11 February 1622.

APPENDIX V

BIOGRAPHY AND CRITICISM

A CHECK-LIST UNNUMBERED

PREFACE

IN 1958 this section was greatly enlarged from the lists given in earlier editions, mainly owing to the contributions made by Professor Wesley Milgate with others added by Professor William White. In the present edition my debt to them is further increased. For the past year (1970–1) I have worked in close collaboration with Professor Milgate and the result has been a very great extension of the record of the literature of Donne's influence during the period of nearly three centuries since other writers became aware of him. The most surprising part of this is the large number of entries relating to the eighteenth century, formerly believed to provide very few references to Donne. It is true that they express almost uniform disapproval of his poetic form, but his distinction was such that it could not be ignored.

As before, the entries for the seventeenth, eighteenth, and nineteenth centuries have been arranged, as a matter of historical interest, in chronological order. Professor Howarth's contributions, mainly for the seventeenth century, printed formerly as a stop-press addendum, have been incorporated in their proper places in the lists. The enormously swollen list for the present century has again been printed in alphabetical order of authors' names (chronological under any one name), these not being given in the General Index. Many articles written as reviews have been included, but I have not attempted to make these exhaustive—the list is surely already as long as anyone can wish.

The book has necessarily gone to the printer in June 1971, so that few entries for this year could be included.

1594–1700

[Arranged chronologically]

LINCOLN'S INN, RECORDS OF THE HONOURABLE SOCIETY OF. *The Black Books*, vol. II, 1586 to 1660, Lincoln's Inn, 1898. References to Donne: p. 38, as Steward of Christmas, 1594–5; p. 57, as Master of the Revels (Mr. Deone,? Donne); pp. 187, 195, 212, 220, as preacher; pp. 229–30, 234, 243 n., 255, 273, 333 n., 444, 445, as Dean of St. Paul's.

[HALL, JOSEPH]. *Virgidemiarum*, London, 1597, 8° [*STC* 12716], pp. 32–5: Book IV, Satire 4, ll. 84 ff., seem to contain an answer to passages in Donne's 'Elegie xx, Love's War' (see R. E. Bennett, *Rev. Eng. Stud.* xv, 1939, 71).

BASTARD, THOMAS. *Chrestoleros*, London, 1598, 8° [*STC* 1559], p. 29, Lib. 2, epigr. 4. Reference to Donne in *Ad Henricum Wottonum* (see Grierson, II, 140–1).

GUILPIN, EDWARD. *Skialetheia*, London, 1598, 8° [*STC* 12504]. Sig. B8, *Satyre Preludium*, and sig. C8*b*ff., *Satyra tertia*, contain apparent allusions to Donne. Sig. D4*a*, *Satyra quinta*, begins with a paraphrase of Donne's first Satire (see R. E. Bennett, *Rev. Eng. Stud.* xv, 1939, 66–72).

WEEVER, JOHN. *Epigrammes in the Oldest Cut and Newest Fashion*, London, 1599, 8° [*STC* 25224], p. 50: Possible reference to Donne in *Ad D. Mounteagle*.

DONNE, JOHN. *Historical Manuscripts Commission*, 7th Report, Appendix, London, 1879. More-Molyneux MSS., p. 629 a, b: letters to Sir George More, 1601, concerning his marriage; p. 660: a decree attesting his lawful marriage to Anne More, 1601; pp. 670a, b, 671a, 676a: other letters to More; p. 673b: epitaph on Anne Donne, 1617; p. 31b: petition from John Donne, jr., for discharge from improper arrest.

MANNINGHAM, JOHN (1602–3). *Diary, ed. J. Bruce*, London, Camden Soc., 1868, 8°, pp. 99, 130, 154: Reference to Donne and extracts from *Paradoxes* and *Poems*.

CORNWALLIS, SIR WILLIAM. In transcribing an early MS. entitled 'The Encomium of Richard the Third' in the Devonshire Collection Cornwallis addressed it to 'his worthy friend Mr. John Donne'. See W. G. Zeefeld, 'A Tudor Defence of Richard III', *Publ. Mod. Lang. Assoc. Am.* LV, 1940, 450. A verse letter from Cornwallis to Donne is printed by Grierson, *Poetical Works*, II, pp. 171–2 (Bald, *Life*, p. 117).

[DONNE, JOHN] (1605–9). *Calendar of State Papers, Domestic*, 1603–10, London, 1857, p. 196 (1605): Licence to Donne to travel for three years; p. 492 (4 February 1609): 'John Donne desires to be Secretary of Virginia'.

SHAKESPEARE, WILLIAM (1605). *King Lear*. Act III, sc. iv, ll. 89–100. Edgar loqu. '. . . Let not the creaking of shoes nor the rustling of silks betray thy poor heart to woman. . . .' Possible reminiscence of Donne's 'Elegy IV. The Perfume', esp. ll. 51–2, 'I taught my silks, their whistling to forbeare, | Even my opprest shoes, dumbe and speechlesse were', composed between 1593 and 1598 (see A. Davenport, *Notes and Queries*, CXCVIII, 1953, 21).

DEKKER, THOMAS. *A Knights conjuring done in earnest*, London, 1607, 4° [*STC* 6508]. B2*a*: Reference to two lines (71–2) from Donne's 'The Storme'.

DELONEY, THOMAS. *Strange Histories, or Songes and Sonets*, London, 1607, 8° [*STC* 6567]. E6*a* 'An Epigram', appropriates in the first two lines Donne's epigram, 'A lame beggar', in an altered form.

DAVISON, FRANCIS (*c.* 1608). *Poetical Rhapsody, ed. N. H. Nicholas*, London, 1826, 8° (and by *A. H. Bullen*, London, 1890). 1826, I, pp. xlii–xlv, 1890, I, pp. l–lv. References in Davison's *memoranda* to Donne's Satyres, Elegies, Epigrams.

HALL, JOSEPH. *Characters of Vertues and Vices*, London, 1608, 8° [*STC* 12648], p. 95:

'The Profane—he never names God but in his oathes.' Perhaps derived from Donne's 'The Perfume', l. 32: 'That oft names God in oathes, and onely than'.

WYBARNE, JOSEPH. *The New Age of Old Names*, London, 1609, 4° [*STC* 26055], p. 113: Quotation of ll. 18–23 from Donne's 'Satyre IV'.

BOYS, JOHN. *An exposition of the Dominicall Epistles and Gospels*, London, 1610, 4° [*STC* 3458]. *The Spring-part*, p. 118. A reference to Donne's *Pseudo-Martyr* (see p. 6 of this bibliography).

DAVIES, JOHN, of Hereford. *Scourge of Folly*, London, [1611], 8° [*STC* 6341], p. 45, epigr. no. 97: 'To the no lesse ingenious then ingenuous Mr John Dun.'

HOSKYNS, JOHN (*c.* 1611). In *Aubrey's Brief Lives*, ed. *Andrew Clark*, Oxford, 1898, 2 vols, 8°, vol. II, p. 50: In 'Mr Hoskins his Convivium Philosophicum', Macaronic verses, second stanza, is a reference to 'Johannes *Factus*', i.e. John Donne.

DAVIES, JOHN, of Hereford. *The Muses Sacrifice or Divine Meditations*, London, 1612, 8° [*STC* 6338], ff. 117*b*–118*a*: Allusion, in a funeral elegy to Mistress Elizabeth Dutton, to Donne's *Anniversaries*. (Printed in Grosart's *Complete Poems of J. D.*, 1872, I, p. 104.)

DRAYTON, M. *Polyolbion*, London [1612], f° [*STC* 7226]. A1*a To the Generall Reader:* 'In publishing this Essay of my Poeme, there is this great disadvantage against me; that it commeth out at this time, when Verses are wholly deduc't to Chambers, and nothing esteem'd in this lunatique Age, but what is kept in Cabinets, and must only passe by Transcription.' This has been thought to refer to the circulation of Donne's poems only in MSS. Drayton makes similar references in *Polyolbion*, pt. II, 1622, p. 23, l. 21, and in *The Battaile of Agincourt*, 1627, p. 208 (Elegy to Henery Reynolds Esq.):

For such whose poems, be they nere so rare,
In private chambers, that incloistered are,
And by transcription daintly must goe, . . .

DRUMMOND, WILLIAM. *A Character of Several Authors*, MS. [between 1612 and 1616]: Donne, among the Anacreontic lyrics, is second to none, and far from all second; but as Anacreon doth not approach Callimachus, though he excels in his own kind, nor Horace to Virgil, no more can I be brought to think him excel either Alexander's or Sidney's verses. They can hardly be compared together, treading diverse paths; the one flying swift, but low; the other, like the eagle, surpassing the clouds. I think, if he would, he [Donne] might easily be the best epigrammatist we have found in English; of which I have not yet seen any come near the ancients.

TAYLOR, JOHN. *Laugh and Be Fat: or, A Commentary upon the Odcombyan Banket* [1612], 8° [*STC* 23769], pp. 17–19, 27, Iohannes Donne: comment in verse on Donne's verses to Coryate prefixed to *Coryates Crudities*, 1611.

[FITZHERBERT, THOMAS.] *A supplement to the Discussion of M. D. Barlowe's Answere to the Judgement of a Catholike Englishman* [St Omer], 1613, 4° [*STC* 11021], pp. 86–110: A reply to Donne's *Pseudo-Martyr* (see p. 5 of this bibliography, and Simpson, pp. 190–1).

WEBSTER, JOHN. *A monumental column erected to the memory of Henry late Prince of Wales*, London, 1613, 4° [*STC* 25174]: References to Donne's *Anniversaries* (see C. Crawford's *Collectanea*, 2nd ser., 1907).

FREEMAN, THOMAS. *Rubbe, and a great cast.* (*Runne and a great cast. The second book*), London, 1614, 4° [*STC* 11370]. Epigr., no. 84, beginning:

Thy *Storme* described hath set thy name afloat,
Thy *Calme* a gale of famous winde hath got.

In *The Second book*, references to seven poems by Donne.

SCOTT, Sir MICHAEL. *The Philosophers Banquet*, London, 1614, 8° [*STC* 22062]: Twice quotes l. 144 of Donne's *An Anatomie of the World* (pp. 331, 340 in the third edition of 1633).

CHAMBERLAIN, JOHN (1615–23). *The Letters of John Chamberlain*, ed. N. E. McClure, Am. Philosoph. Soc., Philadelphia, 1939, 2 vols.: References to Donne, *passim* (see index), but especially vol. II, pp. 451, 518 for references to his sermons (see no. 12).

CAREW, GEORGE LORD. *Letters from George Lord Carew to Sir Thomas Roe*, Camden Society, London, 1860, p. 2: 'Mr John Don is a Minister, the King's Chaplaine, and a Doctor of Divinitie.' 18 April 1615 (Donne was ordained in January).

CHAMBERLAIN, JOHN. *Calendar of State Papers, Domestic*, 1611–18, London, 1858, p. 282 (1615): Donne made Doctor at Cambridge by the King's command; p. 284: Donne made a King's Chaplain and a Doctor; p. 454 (1617): a sermon by Donne in which 'he did Queen Elizabeth great right' (see Bald, p. 323).

[CORYATE, THOMAS, 1615]. In *Purchas his Pilgrimes*, Part I, London, 1624–5, f° [STC 20509], pp. 595–7: 'Pray remember the recommendations of my dutifull respect; to all those whose names I have heere expressed, being the Lovers of Vertue, and Literature; and so consequently the welwillers (I hope) of a pro[s]perous issue of my designements, in my laborious pedestriall perambulations of Asia, Africa, and Europe. ... In primis, to the two Ladies Varney, ... '5 Item, to Master John Donne, . . .'

CORYATE, THOMAS. *T. Coriate Traveller for the English VVits: Greeting*, London, 1616, 4° [STC 5811], p. 45: 5. Item, to M. Iohn Donne, the author of two most elegant Bookes, *Pseudo-Martyr* and *Ignatii Conclave*, of his abode either in the Strand, or elsewhere in London: I thinke you shall bee easily informed by the meanes of my friend, M. L. W[hitaker] ... 9 Item, to George Garrat of whose beeing you shal understand by Master Donne aforesaide.' Reprinted in *Purchase his Pilgrime*, London, 1625, f° [STC 20509], IV, ch. xvi, p. 597.

JONSON, BEN. *Workes*, London, 1616, f° [STC 14751], p. 775. Epigrammes, no. xxiii 'To Iohn Donne'; p. 796. Ditto, no. xciiii 'To Lucy, Countesse of Bedford, with Mr

Donne's Satyres'; p. 797. Ditto, no. xcvi 'To Iohn Donne'.

SOMERSET, EARL OF (1616). In *Cabala, Mysteries of State*, London, 1654, 4° [Wing C 184], p. 3: Letter from Somerset to King James: 'As I took from *Dr. Donne* in his Sermon, that the goodnesse of God is not so much acknowledged by us in our being our Creator, as in being our Redeemer'. The same passage is referred to by Richard Gibson in a letter to Pepys, 1671 (see Bald, p. 412 n.).

CHAMBERLAIN, JOHN. *Letters*, ed. E. McC. Thomson, New York, 1965, pp. 141 (29 March 1617), 290–1 (1 July, 25 September 1622): References to Donne's sermons; p. 297 (20 December 1623) reference to Donne's daughter's Marriage to Alleyn; pp. 164–5 (16 March 1615) references to Donne's degree at Cambridge; p. 321 (21 February 1624): '... Dr. Donne's *Devotions* in his sickness newly come abroad, wherein are many curious and dainty conceits, not for common capacities, but surely full of piety and true feeling'.

CLIFFORD, Lady ANNE (1617). *The Diary*, ed. V. Sackville-West, London, 1923, 8°, p. 74: Reference to Donne's visit to Knole on 20 July 1617 and his preaching on 27 July in the Chapel.

FENNOR, WILLIAM. *The Compter's Commonwealth*, London, 1617, 4° [STC 10781], pp. 3, 14, 20: Three passages make it quite evident that Fennor had read Donne's fourth *Satyre*. (See A. Davenport, *Notes and Queries*, CC, 1955, 12. References identified from A. V. Judges, *The Elizabethan Underworld*, 1930, pp. 429, 437, 441, which reprints *The Compter's Commonwealth*.)

ANON. *The Mirrour of Majestie*, London, 1618, p. 55: *Emblem*, no. 28, resembles Donne's 'Satyre III', ll. 78–82. (Sometimes attributed to Sir Henry Goodere, but see letter from Mr. I. A. Shapiro, *Times Lit. Sup.*, 5 February 1949.)

BOLTON, EDMUND. *Hypercritica*, c. 1618: Reference to Donne's poems (probably the *Anniversaries*): 'The English poems of Sr Walter Raleigh, of John Donn, of Hugh

Holland, but especially of Sr Foulk Greville in his matchless *Mustapha*, are not easily to be mended', but these poets are excelled by Jonson (see J. E. Spingarn, *Critical Essays of the Seventeenth Century*, I, p. 111).

[COFFIN, EDWARD]. *A Refutation of M. Joseph Hall His Apologeticall Discourse for the Marriage of Ecclesiasticall Persons directed unto M. John Whiting. By C. E. a Catholike Priest*. Permissu Superiorum. 1619, 8⁰ [*STC* 5475], p. 240 (P8*b*): A reference to *Iohn Dunns Pseudomartyr, nec pes, nec caput uni reddatur formæ* (as being a disioynted gall-ma-frey of many things hudled up togeather, whereof no one part or patch agreeth with another) so it seemeth to have fared with M. Hall. [in the margin] Dunns Pseudo-martyr a meere bundle of rotten rags ill favouredly bound together.

DRUMMOND, WILLIAM. *A Midnights Trance*, London, 1619, 12⁰. Drummond is thought to have owed some debt to Donne's *Anniversaries* in his *A Midnights Trance*, afterwards printed in a revised form as 'A Cypress Grove' in *Flowers of Sion*, 1623 (see Luttrell Society's reprint of *A Midnight's Trance*, ed. R. Ellrodt, Oxford, 1951).

DRUMMOND, WILLIAM, of Hawthornden (1619), *Works*, Edinburgh, 1711, f⁰, pp. 224–6: 'Heads of a Conversation betwixt the Famous Poet Ben Johnson, and William Drummond of Hawthornden, January 1619.' Quoting Jonson's opinions of Donne's poems, and some by Drummond, who also included a MS. book of 'Jhone Done's lyriques' in a list of books read by him in 1613 (MS. 2059, Hawthornden MSS., vol. VII, f. 336*a*, in NLS). See also *Conversations of Ben Jonson with William Drummond*, ed. Philip Sidney, London, 1906; ditto, ed. R. F. Patterson, London, 1923; and Jonson's *Works*, ed. Herford and Simpson, I, 128–51. According to *Auctarium Bibliothecæ Edinburgenæ*, 1627, Drummond gave the University a copy of Donne's *First Sermon preached to King Charles*, 1625 (see no. 19), and MS. copies of two poems, 'A Satyre' and 'An Hymne to the Saints, and Marquis Hamilton'.

GOODYER, SIR HENRY (1619). *Historical Manuscripts Commission*, Fourth Report, Lord Sackville's MSS., London, 1874, p. 284: A letter, 24 February 1619, to the Marquis of Buckingham relating his history, his services, his misfortunes, his family descent, and requests to the King. This letter borrows the sense of a long passage in a letter from Donne to Goodyer of September 1608 (*Letters*, 1651, pp. 50–1). See S. Johnson, *MLN*, LXIII (1948), 41–2.

KEPLER, JOHANN. *Gesammelte Werke*, ed. Caspar, Munich, 1954, vol. XVI, p. 215. In an undated letter to an unnamed friend Kepler wrote that he had recently spoken with '*Doctore Theologo* Namens *Donne*', who had arrived in Linz on 23 October with the ambassador, Lord Doncaster. Donne had agreed to carry a letter to Kepler's London agent about a book for King James. The editor suggests 1608 as the date, assuming that the book was Kepler's *De Stella Nova*; but see W. Applebaum's 'Donne's Meeting with Kepler', *Philol. Quart.*, L. 1971, 132–4, suggesting that the book was his *Harmonice Mundi*, and the date October 1619, when Donne is known to have been with Doncaster's embassy (for which see *Calendar of State Papers, Venetian*, London, 1910, vol. XVI, under James Hay, Lord Doncaster).

CHAMBERLAIN, JOHN. *Calendar of State Papers, Domestic*, 1623–5, London, 1859, p. 132 (1623): Chamberlain on Constance Donne's marriage to Edward Alleyn; p. 168 (1624): Chamberlain on Donne's *Devotions*, 'contains curious conceits, but much piety'; p. 177; grant to Donne of the rectory of Burnham [Blunham]; p. 393: a letter from the King about the admission of Smith to the cure of St. Faith's; p. 403: letter from Donne to Sec Conway on the same; p. 423: letter from the King to Donne thanking for the same. See also *The Chamberlain Letters*.

ALLEYN, EDWARD (1618–25). In *The History of Dulwich College with a Life of the Founder*, by William Young, 2 vols., 4⁰, Edinburgh and London, 1889, references, I, pp. 35–8: Alleyn's marriage to Constance Donne, with letter from Alleyn to Donne 24 January

1625; p. 187: Donne preaching at Camberwell 20 August 1620; p. 120: 30 December 1618; p. 244: 14 July 1622; p. 249: dined with Donne 21 September 1622. See also J. P. Collier, *Memoirs of Edward Alleyn*, London, 1841, pp. 172–6.

TAYLOR, JOHN. *The Praise of Hemp-seed*, London, 1620, 4° [*STC* 23788], p. 26: ... And many there are living at this day, Which doe in paper their true worth display. As *Davis, Drayton*, and the learned *Dun*, ... Must say their lines, but for the paper sheet, Had scarcely ground whereon to set their feet.

BURTON, ROBERT. *The Anatomy of Melancholy*. Oxford, 1621, 4° [*STC* 4159]. Part 2. Sect. 2. Memb. 3. X1*b*: A reference to 'Ignatius parler', with sidenote: *Conclave Ignatii*.

CHAMBERLAIN, JOHN. *Calendar of State Papers, Domestic*, 1619–23, London, 1858, p. 298 (1621): Donne made Dean of St. Paul's; p. 310: Chamberlain writes, 'so that if Ben Jonson could be Dean of Westminster, St. Paul's, Westminster, and Christchurch would each have a poetical Dean'; p. 438: presentation of Donne to be a prebend of Chiswick, Chamberlain on Donne's sermon of preachers and preaching; p. 461 (16 November 1622): Donne's sermon to the Virginia Company; p. 466: letter from Donne to Sir Thomas Roe, death of Lady Jacob and Sir Wm. Killigrew.

DRUMMOND, WILLIAM of Hawthornden (*c.* 1621). In *Archeologia Scotica. Trans. of the Soc. of Antiqu. of Scotland*, vol. IV, Edinburgh, 1857, 4°. Extracts from Hawthornden Manuscripts, p. 81: 'J. Done gave my Lord Ancrum his picture in a melancholic posture with the words about it De tristitia ista libera me Domine' (see under Iconography). Concerning Donne's promotion to the Deanery of St. Paul's: 'Bishop Billie [Williams] falling out in termes with Doctor Done, said None save some Popish fellowes as hee thought otherwayes, to which Done [replied], I would not give so much to be a Pope as ye did to be Bishop. Hold your peace, said Billie. I know better how

to hold my peace than yee how to speake. Yee are a foule. That, my Lord, said Done, is your owne; yee may give it to whom yee please' (see Bald, pp. 378–9).

GOODYER, SIR HENRY. *Calendar of State Papers, Domestic*, 1619–23, London, 1858, p. 585: A letter, 17 May 1623, to Sec. Conway, enclosing a congratulatory poem to the Prince of Wales on his journey to Spain, paraphrasing ll. 1–2 of Donne's 'To Mr. E. G.', and a prose letter from Donne to Goodyer. See S. Johnson, *MLN*, LXIII, 1948, 38–43.

WEBSTER, JOHN. *The tragedy of the Duchess of Malfy*, London, 1623, 4° [*STC* 25176]. Influence of Donne's *Anniversaries*, noted in C. Crawford's *Collectanea*, 2nd ser., 1907.

GOODYER, SIR HENRY (*c.* 1624). *Calendar of State Papers, Domestic*, 1623–5, London, 1859, vol. CLXXX, no. 15, p. 427: Letter from Goodyer to the Marquis of Hamilton, borrowing a passage from Donne's letter to himself, *Letters*, 1651, pp. 27–8, erroneously headed: To Sir H. R. (see S. Johnson, *MLN*, LXIII, 1948, 41–2).

BACON, SIR FRANCIS. *The Essayes or Counsels Civil and Morall*. London, 4°, 1625 [*STC* 1147], p. 70, in Essay XII, 'Of Goodnesse And Goodnesse of Nature': 'And that his Heart, is no Island, cut off from other Lands; but a Continent, that ioynes to them', borrowed from *Devotions*, 1624, Meditation 17, pp. 415–16, 'No Man is an Island, intire of it selfe; euery man is a peece of the *Continent*, a part of the *maine*' (See John Crossett, *Notes and Queries*, N.S. VII, 1960, 252). This passage was first added by Bacon in 1625.

CHAMBERLAIN, JOHN. *Calendar of State Papers, Domestic*, 1625–6, London, 1858, p. 12 (1625): Copy by Chamberlain of verses by Donne on the death of the Marquis Hamilton (see Bald, p. 467); p. 158: letter from Donne to Sir Thomas Roe, Ambassador at Constantinople, 25 November 1625 (Gosse, II, 222, 310).

[DONNE, JOHN] (1626). In *Concilia Magnae Britanniae et Hiberniae*, ed. David Wilkins, 1646–1717, vol. IV, London, f°, 1737,

p. 469: under date 18 May 1626, reference to Donne's election as prolocutor.

COMMISSION TO DONNE (1627). *Calendar of State Papers, Domestic*, 1627–8, London, 1859, p. 208 (1627): A commission to Donne and others to re-examine the proceedings in the Prerogative Court of Canterbury *re* will of Thomas Payne of Plymouth; p. 586 (1628): a report on the dispute.

HAYMAN, ROBERT. *Quodlibets, lately come over from New Britaniola, Old Newfoundland*, London, 1628, 4° [STC 12973]. Book IV, no. 9, pp. 58–9, epigr. 'To the Reverend and divinely witty, Iohn Dun, Doctor in Divinity, Deane of Saint Pauls, London' (first discovered by Prof. F. P. Wilson).

BURRELL, PERCI. *Sutton's Synagogue, or, The English Centurion*, London, 4°, 1629 [STC 4126]. On sig. E2a, A Catalogue of the names of the Governors of King James his Hospitall, founded by Thomas Sutton, including 'Doctor Dunne, Deane of Pauls'.

CALENDAR OF STATE PAPERS, DOMESTIC, 1629–31, London, 1860, p. 336 (1630): Benefices which might fall to Donne if he is promoted to a Bishopric.

CROSFIELD, T. (*c.* 1630). *The Diary of Thomas Crosfield M.A., B.D., Fellow of Queen's College, Oxford. Ed. F. S. Boas*, London, 1935, 8°, p. 43. Reference to Donne as preacher. 'Dr. Donne deane of Pauls, his powerfull kinde of preaching by his gesture & Rhetoriquall expression.'

HUYGENS, C. *Die Briefwisseling*, 1608–87, ed. J. A. Worp, 's Gravenhage, 1903: References to Donne, I, pp. 288, 289 (letters to Hooft), 290, 335, 447, 452 (*c.* 1630).

HUYGENS, C. In *Bijdragen en Mededeelingen der Hist. Genootschap*, XVIII, 1897, Fragment eener autobiographie van Constantijn Huygens, ed. J. A. Worp, pp. 57–8: Huygens on Donne as a preacher (*c.* 1630). See Colie, R. L., 1956, pp. 53–4.

JONES, JOHN. *London's looking-backe to Jerusalem.* London, 4°, 1633 [STC 14722], p. 1, in a Paul's Cross Sermon delivered on 7 August 1630: '. . . but God alwayes speakes before he striks, lightens before he thunders, warnes before he wounds', with marginal note, 'D. Donne'. Jones was paraphrasing a passage from *A Sermon Preached before the King, 24 Feb. 1625.* London, 1626, p. 7 (Potter and Simpson, VII, 76. See MacClure, *The Paul's Cross Sermons*, 1958, p. 150).

DRUMMOND, WILLIAM. *Letter to Sir William Alexander, Earl of Stirling*, on Drayton's death, second draft, 1631: 'Of all the good race of poets who wrot in the tyme of Queen Elizab your L. now alone remaines. Daniel Sylvester King James Done and now Drayton' (published by D. Laing among Drummond's 'Unpublished Letters' in *Archaeologia Scotica*, IV, 1859, 93).

CHARLES I. *To the Memory of My ever Desired Friend, Dr Donne*, ?1631 (not located):
At common graves we have poetic eyes
Can melt themselves in easy elegies . . .
But at thine, poem or inscription
(Rich soul of wit and language) we have none.
Indeed, a silence does that tomb befit,
When is no herald left to blazon it.

CALENDAR OF STATE PAPERS, DOMESTIC, 1631–3, London, 1862, p. 437 (1632): Sir Henry Herbert to give an account of why he warranted the book of Dr. Dun's Paradoxes to be printed, 'By the King's Command delivered by the Bishop of London'.

COLMAN, WALTER. *La Dance Machabre, or Death's Duell*, London, [1633], 8° [STC 5569]. G1a Verses alluding to the title of Donne's *Death's Duell* (see p. 53 of present work).

HERBERT, GEORGE. *The Temple*, Cambridge, 1633, pp. 177–8: 'A Parodie'. A recasting of the Song, 'Souls joy, now I am gone', attributed to Donne.

HOLLAND, HENRY. *Ecclesia Sancti Pauli Illustrata*, London, 1633, 4° [STC 13584]. A description of Donne's monument, on E2b–3a: And to come backe to the South Ile, betweene the doore and Deane Colet's Monument, is newly errected a Monument for Deane Donne which is, his face appearing out of his winding sheete, done in white Marble, standing upon an Urne, and this Inscription following: all done according to the will of the sayd Deane Donne (see Bald, p. 534).

STOW, JOHN. *The Survey of London*, London, f°, 1633 [*STC* 23345], p. 776b: Donne's epitaph in St. Paul's.

VONDEL, JOOST VAN DEN. *Werken*, ed. Sterck, Moller, etc. Amsterdam, 1927–40, III, 415: lines on Huygens's translation of Donne's poems, *c.* 1633. See Colie, R. L., 1956, p. 67.

GARRARD, GEORGE. In *Strafford's Letters and Dispatches*, ed. W. Knowler, London, 1739, f°, vol. I, p. 338, letter to Strafford, 10 November 1634: 'I send your Lordship Verses made in the Progress. I that never had Patience in all my life to transcribe Poems, except they were very transcendent, such as Dean *Donn* writ in his younger Days, did those with some Pain.'

HABINGTON, WILLIAM. *Castara* [two parts]. London, 1634, 4° [*STC* 12583]. In the second part, pp. 73–4 (L1a–b): *Against them who lay unchaſtity to the ſex of Women*, an answer to 'Goe and catche a falling starre', four stanzas beginning,

They meet but with unwholeſome Springs,
And ſummers which infectious are:
They heare but when the Meremaid ſings
And onely ſee the falling ſtarre,
    Who ever dare
Affirme no woman chaſte and faire.

See also the second edition, London, 1635, 12°, pp. 112–13.

HOWELL, JAMES. *Epistolæ Ho-Elianæ*, London, 1645, 4° [Wing H 3071]. [Bk. I] Sect. 6, letter xxxii [25 July 1635], p. 50, probable echo of 'Good Friday. Riding Westwards'; letter xli, [1 February 1638], p. 63, possible echo of 'The Canonization'. See *Howell's Letters*, ed. J. Jacob, London, 1890, I, 335, and F. Kermode, *Notes and Queries*, CXCIX, 1954, 357.

STAFFORD, ANTHONY. *The Femall Glory: or, The Life and Death of the holy Virgin Mary*, London, 1635, 8° [*STC* 23123], p. 148: 'You who have vow'd virginity mentall and corporall, you shall not onely have in-gresse here, but welcome. Approach with Comfort and kneele downe before the Grand white Immaculate Abbesse of your snowy Nunneries and present the all-saving

Babe in her Armes with due veneration', quoting Donne's The Litany XII, *Poems*, 1633, p. 177, ll. 100–101, 'The cold white snowie Nunnery, / Which, as thy mother, their high Abbesse, sent / Their bodies backe againe to thee'.

THIMELBY, KATHERINE (*c.* 1635). In *Tixall Letters*, ed. A. Clifford, London, 1815, p. 147, letter to Herbert Aston: 'How infinite a time will it seem till I see you: for lovers' hours are full eternity. Doctor Dun sayd this, but I think it', with quotation from 'The Legacie', l. 4.

PAMAN, CLEMENT (*c.* 1635). In Jonson's *Works*, ed. Herford and Simpson, XI, pp. 481–5: *Upon Elegies to Ben Jonson's Memory*, ll. 41–4:
        Else what ist to Doune
Though I crie twenty times, Hee's not the sonne
Of noyse and schisme, nor did he compose
His sermons to be sung unto the nose.

CAMDEN, WILLIAM. In *Remaines of a Greater Worke concerning Britaine*, London, 1636, 4° [*STC* 4526], pp. 417–18: 'Impossibilities', beginning,
        Embrace a Sun-beame, and on it
        The shadow of a man beget.
Apparently indebted to Donne's 'Goe and catche a falling starre'; ascribed in MS. Ashmole 47, no. 132 (BLO) to 'John Coventry'.

JORDAN, THOMAS. *The Poeticall Varieties: or, Varietie of Fancies*, London, 1637, 4° [*STC* 14788], pp. 8–9: To Leda his coy Bride, on the Bridall Night (Why art thou coy (my *Leda*) ar't not mine), an imitation of Donne's 'To his Mistress going to bed'. Repr. in *Roxburghe Ballads*, ed. J. W. Ebsworth, VII, 458.

HALL, JOSEPH. *The Remedy of Prophanenesse*, London, 1637, 8° [*STC* 12710], p. 247: 'It was the motto of that witty and learned Doctor *Donne*, the late Deane of *Paules*, which I have seene, more then once, written in Spanish with his owne hand, *Blessed bee God that hee is God, divinely, like himselfe*' (see John Sparrow, *Times Lit. Sup.*, 30 March 1946).

WHITING, NATHANIEL. *Il Insonio Insonadado, or a sleeping-waking Dreame, vindicating the divine breath of Poesie from the tongue-lashes of some Cynical Poet-quippers, and Stoicall Philo-prosers*, London, 1637–8 [not in *STC*], H 8*b*, ll. 429–32:
Dunn was a poet, and a grave Divine,
Highly esteemed for the sacred Nine
That aftertimes shall say whilst there's a sun
'This verse, this Sermon, was compos'd by Dun.'

BRIDEOAKE, RALPH. In *Jonsonus virbius*, London, 1638, 4° [*STC* 14784]. Elegy on Jonson, ll. 55–9, reference to 'learned *Donne*, *Beaumont* and *Randolph*' whose 'notes' would have been 'too lowe' to write an appropriate elegy on Jonson.

STRAFFORD, EARL OF (1638). In *Letters and Dispatches*, ed. William Knowler, London, 1739, f°, vol. ii, p. 158, letter from Strafford to Archbishop Laud: 'The Lady Astrea, the Poet tells us, is long since gone to Heaven, but under Favour I can yet find Reward and Punishment on Earth; indeed sometimes they are like Doctor *Donn's* Anagram of a good Face, the ornaments mis-set, a yellow Tooth, a red Eye, a white lip or so . . .', Dublin, 10 April 1638. The reference is to Elegie II, *Poems*, 1633, p. 45: Though all her parts be not in th'usuall place, / She hath yet an Anagram of a good face.

DOORT, ABRAHAM VAN DER. *Catalogue of the Collections of Charles I.* Windsor MS. (1639–40), f. 19. In return for the gift of a picture sent to the King by Mons. de Lyon Court, two others were sent. One was Holbein's portrait of Erasmus, 'And the other of yor Ma^ts Pictures was done by Tichin, being our Lady and Christ and St. John half figures as bigg as Life, wch was placed in y^r Ma^ts midle privy lodging roome being in a Carv'd gilded frame, and was given heeretofore to yor Matie by my lord of Carlile who had it of Docto^r Dunn painted upon the right lighte' (see *Doort's Catalogue*, ed. Oliver Millar, Glasgow, for the Walpole Society, 4°, 1960, p. 89).

BANCROFT, THOMAS. *Two Bookes of Epigrammes, and Epitaphs*, London, 1639, 4° [*STC* 1354], D 3*a*, No. 136:
To Doctor *Donne*
Thy Muses gallantry doth farre exceed
All ours; to whom thou art a *Don* indeed.

CAREW, THOMAS. *Poems*, London, 1640, 8° [*STC* 4620], pp. 121–5: 'An Elegie upon the death of Doctor Donne, Deane of Pauls'. First printed in Donne's *Poems*, 1633, p. 384; p. 126: 'In answer of an Elegiacall Letter upon the death of the King of Sweden from Aurelian Townsend'. ll. 11–15:
Virgill, nor Lucan, no, nor Tasso more
Then both, not Donne, worth all that went before,
With the united labour of their wit
Could a just poem to this subject fit.
(See G. C. Moore Smith, *Mod. Lang. Rev.* xii, 1917, 422 for Townsend's 'Elegiacall Letter' with a reference to Carew's Elegie on 'devine Donne'.)

DANIEL, GEORGE (*c.* 1640). *The Poems* ed. A. B. Grosart, privately printed, 1878, 4 vols, 4°, vol. i, p. 29, stanzas 13–14 of 'A Vindication of Poesie', beginning:
The reverent Donne, whose quill God purely fill'd.

GOSTELOW, R. In Randolph's *Poems, with the Muses Looking-Glass and Amyntas*, 2nd edn., Oxford, 1640, 8° [*STC* 20695]. B1*b*. *On the death of Mr. Randolph*:
When *Donne*, and *Beaumont* dyed, an Epitaph
Some men (I well remember) thought unsafe;
And said they did *presume to write, unlesse They could their teares in their expression dresse.*

JONSON, BEN. *The Workes. The Second Volume*, London, 1640, f° [*STC* 14754]. On P4*b*, p. 116, in 'Timber: or, Discoveries', reference to Donne: 'And as it is fit to reade the best Authors to youth first, so let them be of the openest and clearest. Livy before Sallust, Sydney before Donne.' In 'Underwoods', pp. 204–6, reprints Elegie XV.

[MENNES, SIR JOHN]. *Witt's Recreations*, London, 1640, 8° [*STC* 25870]. L2*a*: Epigram 464 is the second stanza of Donne's Song 'Goe, and catche a falling starre'.

L7, No. 486, 'On a Picture':

> The face here pictur'd time shall longer have,
> Then life the substance of it, or the grave,
> Yet as I change from this by death I know,
> I shall like death, the liker death I grow.

(Suggested by Donne's 1591 portrait and motto. Cf. also Randolph, 'Upon his Picture'.)

LING, W. In John Tatham's, *The Fancies Theater*, London, 1640, 8° [STC 23704], A4*b*:

> To his Friend the Author
> Had I *Chapmans* Line or Learning, *Iohnsons* Art,
> *Fletchers* more accurate Fancie, or that part
> Of *Beaumont* that's divine, *Dun's* profound skill,
> Making good Verses live, and damning ill:
> I then would prayse thy Verses, which sho'd last
> Whilst *Time* ha's sands to run, or Fame a blast. . . .

STANHOPE, CHARLES, Second Baron. *Marginalia* (*c.* 1640) in Ben Jonson's *Works*, 1640:

> 'Jack Dunne yᵉ father
> Jack Dunne yᵉ sonne',

suggesting that Donne was the 'better Verser . . . Or *Poet*' who had supplanted Jonson in the favour of Lucy Countess of Bedford. Other references. See James M. Osborn, *Times Lit. Sup.*, 4 January 1957, p. 16.

WALTON, IZAAK. In *The Compleat Walton*, ed. G. Keynes, London, 1929, 8°, pp. 579–80, 627: Notes for the Life of Donne (1640).

BEEDOME, THOMAS. *Poems: Divine and Humane*, London, 1641, 8° [Wing B 1689], pp. 34–6: 'To the Memory of his honoured friend Master *John Donne*, an Anniversary' (after Donne's own *Anniversaries*).

OXINDEN, HENRY (1641). In *The Oxinden Letters*, ed. D. Gardiner, London, 1933, 8°, pp. 245–6: Reference to Donne's Song, 'Goe, and catche a falling starre.'

STRAFFORD, EARL OF. *Verses Lately written by Thomas Earle of Strafford*, 1641, broadside [Wing S 5803] with the lines:

> But O! how few there ar'
> (Though danger from that act be far)
> Will stoop and catch a falling star.

See A. Alvarez, *The School of Donne*, 1961, p. 50.

WECKERLIN, G. R. *Gaistliche und Weltliche Gedichte*, Amsterdam, 1641. Contains, *inter alia*, forty epigrams, 'five of which may with certainty be traced to Donne': W. Böhm, *Englands Einfluss auf G. R. Weckerlin*, 1893.

KYNASTON, SIR FRANCIS. In *Cynthiades, or Amorous Sonets*, 1642 [not in *STC*], 'To Cynthia, On a Mistress for his Rivals', an imitation of Donne's 'The Anagram'. Printed in *Minor Poets of the Seventeenth Century*, ed. G. Saintsbury, Oxford, 1906, 8°, pp. 157–8.

STANHOPE, CHARLES, Second Baron. *Marginalia* (*c.* 1642) in *The Life and Death of Sir Thomas More*, 1642:

> Fulke & Jhon, Fulke & Jhon,
> you shall rise anon,
> when better wits are gone.

(Refers to Fulke Greville, Lord Brooke, and Donne?)

See G. P. V. Akrigg in *Joseph Quincy Adams Memorial Studies*, 1948, pp. 785–802.

BAKER, SIR RICHARD. *A Chronicle of the Kings of England*, 1643, f° [Wing B 501]. 'The Raigne of King James', p. 156. Reminiscences of Donne.

[GLAPTHORNE, HENRY]. *White-Hall. A Poem*. Written 1642, London, 1643, 4° [Wing G 840], B2*b*:

> The Muses then did flourish, and upon
> My pleasant mounts planted their Helicon.
> Then that great wonder of the knowing age,
> Whose very name merits the amplest page
> In Fames faire book, admired *Iohnson* stood
> Up to the chin in the Pierian flood,
> Quaffing crownd bowles of Nectar, . . .
> *Beaumont* and *Fletcher* . . .
> . . . . .

And noble *Donne* (borne to more sacred use)

Exprest his heavenly raptures; As the juice

Of the Hyblean roses did distill

Through the Alembeck of his nectard quill.

ANON. *Vindex Anglicus; or the Perfections of the English Language defended and asserted*, Oxford, 1644, 4° [Wing V 461]: 'There is no sort of verse either ancient, or modern, which we are not able to equal by imitation: we have our English Virgil, Ovid, Seneca, Lucan, Juvenal, Martial, and Catullus: in the Earl of Surry, Daniel, Johnson, Spencer, Don, Shakespear, and the glory of the rest, Sandys and Sydney.'

BULWER, JOHN. *Chirologia: or the Naturall Language of the Hand*. London, by Tho. Harper for R. Whitaker, 1644, 8° [Wing B 5467], pp. 25–6: Eusebius hath left a memoriall, that *Constantine* was wont to be figur'd in Coines and painted Tables with his Hands holden abroad, and his eyes lift up to Heaven, which he calls *The habit and composition of Prayer*. Doctor *Donne* in reference to the Symbolicall signification of the Gesture calls it *Constantines* Catechistic-all Coyne (*LXXX Sermons*, no. 13, on Job 16: 17, p. 131A). Also a reference to Donne's remarks in the same sermon (p. 129 D) on cleanness of hands.

BROWNE, WILLIAM (before 1645). In *The Poems*, ed. G. Goodwin, London, 1894, 12°, II, p. 197: 'Poor silly fool! thou striv'st in vain to know / If I enjoy or love whom thou lov'st so', an answer to Donne's 'The Curse'.

CAVENDISH, WILLIAM, Marquis of Newcastle [1645]. In *The Phanseys addressed to Margaret Lucas*, London, 1956, p. 63: Reference in 'The Unexpressible love',

'Love, forty years agoe, serv'd Doctor Dunn.'

MENNES [MENNIS], SIR JOHN. *Recreation for ingenious head-peeces*, 3rd edn., London, 1645, 8° [Wing M 1712]. O6*b* Epitaphs, 177, 'On Doctor Donnes death', 18 ll.

LLEWELLYN, MARTIN. *Men-Miracles, with other Poemes* [London], 1646, 8° [Wing L 2624].

A4*a* 'To my Ingenious Freind Captaine LL;' signed J.B. Lines referring to the translations of Donne's poems into Dutch (see no. 108).

SUCKLING, SIR JOHN. *Fragmenta Aurea*, London, 1646, 8° [Wing S 6126]. *To my Friend Will Davenant: On his other Poems*:

Thou hast redeem'd us, *Will*; and future Times

Shall not account unto this Age's crimes

Dearth of pure Wit: since the great Lord of it

(*Donne*) parted hence, no Man has ever writ

So neere him, in's owne way:

Also printed in Davenant's *Madagascar; with other Poems*, London, 1648, 8°, A4*b*.

VAUGHAN, HENRY (1646–55). For probable borrowings by Vaughan from Donne see *The Works of Henry Vaughan*, ed. L. C. Martin, Oxford, 1914, notes to *Poems*, 1646; *Olor Iscanus*, 1651; *Silex Scintillans*, 1655.

BROWNE, WILLIAM, of Tavistock. *The Poems*, ed. G. Goodwin, 2 vols. 1894, vol. II, p. 197: A poem beginning 'Poore silly soule, thou striv'st in vayne to know' is stated to be found in BLO, MS. Rawl. Poet. 147, fol. 83 (1647), with title: 'An Answer to Dr. Donnes curse'. See A. Alvarez, *The School of Donne*, 1961, p. 196.

CORBET, RICHARD. *Certain Elegant Poems*, London, 1647, 8° [Wing C 6270]. 'On Doctor Donne'. First printed in Donne's *Poems*, 1633, p. 378.

COWLEY, ABRAHAM. *The Mistresse*, London, 1647, 8° [Wing M 6674]: Many poems imitating Donne's.

(For list see *The Mistress*, ed. J. Sparrow, London, 1926, Introduction, p. xvi.)

HARRIS, JOHN. In Beaumont and Fletcher's *Comedies and Tragedies*, London, 1647, f° [Wing B 1581]. On the Death and Workes of Mr John Fletcher: [h]2*a* 'the intelligence that did move that Spheare' (the stage) echoes l. 52 of Donne's 'The Extasie'.

DRYDEN, JOHN. In: B., R. *Lachrymæ Musarum; The Tears of the Muses: Exprest in Elegies Upon the death of Henry Lord Hast-

ings, London, 1649, 8°, pp. 88–92: 'Upon the death of the Lord Hastings'. By John Dryden. Draws on Donne's *Anniversaries*. Also:

> 'Time's offals, only fit for the hospital!
> Or to hang an antiquary's rooms withal.'

(may allude to Donne's Epigram, 'Antiquary').

GOODWIN, JOHN. *The Obstructors of Justice, Or A Defence of the Honourable Sentence passed upon the late King by the High Court of Justice*, London, 4°, 1649. With a reference to *Biathanatos* in relation to a political issue. Not identified, but see S. E. Sprott, *The English Debate on Suicide*, 1961, pp. 57–9.

HAMMOND, HENRY. *To the Right Honourable the Lord Fairfax and His Councell of Warre: The Humble Addresse*, London, 4°, 1649, pp. 9–10: A passage concerning suicide related to Donne's *Biathanatos*, which is specifically mentioned in *A Vindication of Dr. Hammond's Adresse*, London, 4°, 1649 (see Sprott's *The English Debate on Suicide*, 1961, pp. 57–9).

ANON (*c.* 1650). In *Seventeenth Century Songs from a Bodleian MS*, ed. J. P. Cutts and F. Kermode, University of Reading, 1956, 8°, pp. 25–6: xiii, 'Laugh not fond fool, cause I a face', an imitation of Donne's 'Elegie VIII. The Comparison' (1635).

COWLEY, ABRAHAM. *The Guardian; a comedie*, London, 1650, 4° [Wing C 6673]. C2*b*, Act III, sc. i. Dogrel: 'thou'dst be a rare wife for me, I should beget on thee *Donnes*, and *Johnsons*: but thou art too witty.'

DAVIES, JOHN. In John Hall's *Paradoxes*, London, 1650, 12° [Wing H 353], Epistle Dedicatory: '*Tully* himself was not asham'd to appear in this kind, . . . the Authour may well be justified by the example of Sir Will. *Cornwallis, Dr Donne & Carpenter* in our Nation.'

[GOUGH, JOHN.] *The Academy of Complements. The Last Edition*, London, 1650, 12° [Wing G 1402], p. 195: 'Breake of day'. The first stanza with alterations is printed as the second stanza of 'A Song'. Not in the first edition of the same year.

PESTELL, THOMAS (*c.* 1650). *Poems, ed. Hannah Buchan*, London, 1940, pp. 7, 12, 26, 28, 36, 84: References to Donne (see also *Bodl. Quart. Rec.* VII, 1933, 329–32).

POWEL, EDWARD (1650). In Walton's *Compleat Angler*, London, 1676, B1*b*: Reference to Walton's *Life* of Donne in verses 'To the Readers of my most ingenious Friend's Book'.

BARKSDALE, CLEMENT. *Nympha Libethris: or the Cotswold Muse*, London, pr. at Worcester, 1651, 8° [Wing B 804], p. 96: Reference to Donne's poetry in *To the Readers*:

> My verses, because they are not hard and rare,
> As some of Dav'nant's, Don's and Cleveland's are,
> You censure. Pray Sir, must all men write so? . . .
> I write, just as I speak, to be understood.

[BELL, WILLIAM.] In *Comedies Tragi-Comedies with other Poems, by William Cartwright*, London, 1651, 8° [Wing C 709]. Sig. ***2*b*: Reference to Donne in the commendatory poem by Wil. Bell:

> With Donne's Rich Gold, and Johnson's silver mine.

CARTWRIGHT, WILLIAM. *Comedies*, London, 1651, [add]: 'On the Great Frost, 1634': echoes of Donne's 'The Calm' (so too in H.C., 'On the Hott Summer following the Great Frost, in imitation of the Verses made upon it by W:C:', Harl. MS. 6931, ff. 80–1.

CARY, LUCIUS, VISCOUNT FALKLAND (d. 1643). *Discourse of Infallibility with An Answer to it. And his Lordship's Reply. Together with Mr. Walter Mountague's Letter concerning his changing his Religion*, London, 4°, 1651 [Wing F 317], p. 107: Misquotation of ll. 41–2 of Donne's 'Satyre II': p. 288 in Cary's reply to Mountague: '. . . which would be a glosse not much unlike to that which one of the most wittie, and most eloquent of our Modern Divines, Doctor Donne, notes of Statuimus (i) abrogamus'. The reference is to *Pseudo-martyr*, pp. 111–12.

See also K. B. Murdock, *Harvard Stud. and Notes in Philol. and Lit.* xx, 1938, 38, for a reference to Donne in Cary's 'An Elegie on Sir Henry Morison' (MS.).

CARTWRIGHT, WILLIAM. *Comedies, Tragi-comedies, with other poems*, London, 1651, 8° [Wing C 709]. a5*b* 'To the Reader'. Reference to Donne, 'The highest Poet our Language can boast of . . .'.

CONWAY, VISCOUNT EDWARD. *Historical Manuscripts Commission*, 14th Report, Appendix, Part II, MSS. of the Duke of Portland. Vol. III, London, 1894, p. 195, letter, 10 June 1651, from Conway to his nephew, Col. Edward Harley: 'The happyness which Doctor Donne found out when his wife lay inne, to be a widower and his wife alive, was but poetike in respect of what my Lord Brooke, that is old Brooke, did wish for to have a sonne living and a wife dead.' See Donne's *Letters*, 1651, p. 179, letter to Sir Henry Goodyer.

COSIN, JOHN. *The Works*, 5 vols., Oxford, 8°, 1843, I, pp. 276–90: Sermon XX. John I: 9, 10. *Evangelium Diei. Coram Rege Carolo* (The Christmas Sermon, Paris, 1651). With extensive borrowings from Donne's sermon Preached at St. Paul's upon Christmas Day, 1621, John I: 8 (*Fifty Sermons*, 1649, no. 36; Potter and Simpson, III, p. 348).

HOWELL, JAMES. *Cottoni Posthuma Divers Choice Pieces of Sir Robert Cotton*, ed. J. Howell, London, 1651 [Wing C 6485]. On pp. 323–7, with subtitle: *Valour Anatomized in a Fancie by Sir Philip Sidney* 1581, is part of Donne's 'An Essay of Valour', beginning at the passage, 'Valour towards Men, is an Emblem of an ability towards women'. The attribution to Sir Philip Sidney is unexplained. The *Essay* was first printed in Overburie's *Wife*, 1622 (see no. 73*a*).

BEAUMONT, FRANCIS. *Poems*, London, 1653, 8° [Wing B 1602]: Reprints stanzas 1 and 2 of Donne's song, 'Goe, and catch a falling starre'.

BULWER, JOHN. *Anthropometamorphosis: Man Transform'd*, London, 1653, 4° [Wing B 5461]. On ****3*b* Donne is listed among the authorities quoted. P. 265: 'Have ye

not seene (saith a learned wit) a compleat beauty made worse by an artificiall addition, because they have not thought well enough before ?', with marginal reference to 'Doctor Donne Serm. 70' [*LXXX Sermons*, p. 714A]; p. 271: 'And to take in what a grave and learned Divine hath, in concurring with the purpose of God in dignifying the Body, we may exceed and go beyond God's purpose. God would not have the Face mangled and torne', with marginal reference to 'Dr. Donne Serm. 20' [*LXXX Sermons*, p. 194D].

DENNY, SIR WILLIAM. *Pelecanicidium or the Christian Adviser against Self-Murder*, London, 1653, 8° [Wing D 1051]: A challenge to Donne's *Biathanatos*; see p. 116.

[SHEPPARD, SAMUEL]. *Merlinus Anonymus. An Almanack, And no Almanack. A Kalendar, And no Kalendar. An Ephemeris (between jest, and earnest) for the year*, 1653. By Raphael Desmus, Philologist, London, 1653, 8° [Wing A 1588]: Many quotations, adaptations, and paraphrases from Donne ('Upon Mr. Coryats Crudities'), Satires I, II, III, IV, V, 'The Calm', 'To Sir Edward Herbert', 'The First Anniversary', 'To the Countess of Bedford', II, III, 'To Sir Henry Wotton', 'The Countess of Salisbury', Elegy 16, 'To Mr. Rowland Woodward', III, 'Epithalamion Made at Lincoln's Inn', 'Obsequies to the Lord Harrington'.

WALTON, IZAAK. *The Compleat Angler*, London, 1653, 12° [Wing W 661], p. 184: Reference to Donne.

GATAKER, THOMAS. *A discours apologetical*, London, 4°, 1654 [Wing G 319], p. 52, reference to Donne as his successor as Reader at Lincoln's Inn (see W. Gifford, *Notes and Queries*, XIII, 1966, p. 14, and Bald, p. 412).

GAYTON, EDMUND. *Pleasant Notes upon Don Quixot*, London, 1654, f° [Wing G 415]: Quotation of ll. 3–5 of Donne's 'The Storme' (page reference not identified).

WALTON, IZAAK. *Reliquiæ Wottonianæ*, London, 1654, 12° [Wing W 3649], p. 22: Wotton's friendship with Donne; p. 36: Donne's verse letter to Wotton.

The first passage is on b7*b* of the first edition, 1651. The second was added in the second edition, 1654.

WHITLOCK, RICHARD. *Zwotomia, or, observations*, London, 1654, 8º [Wing W 2030], p. 218: Reference to Donne's Satyre III with quotation; p. 313: 'Doctor Donnes high Praise of *Ben Johnsons* Works, in one expression *extolleth* them, and justly enough *depresseth* our *Admiration* of the Worlds businesse.

> *The State, and mens Affaires are the best Playes*
> *Next yours: Tis nor more, nor lesse then due Praise.'*

('To Ben. Iohnson, 6 Jan. 1603.' *Poems*, 1635, no. 13, not by Donne, but by Sir John Roe.); pp. 322, 339 (misnumbered 336), 350: References to Donne's *Anniversaries*, with quotations; p. 471: Reference to Donne's *Essays in Divinity*, 1652, p. 204: 'And God himself in that last peice of his, which he commanded Moses to record, that Heavenly Song which onely he composed. . . .'

WOTTON, SIR HENRY. In Walton's *Reliquiae Wottonianae*, London, 1654, 'Letters to Severall Persons'. Bb6*b*, 'To *Iz. Wa.* In answer of a Letter requesting him to perform his promise of Writing the Life of *Dr. Donne'*: 'in saying somewhat of the Life of so deserving a man, I may perchance over-live mine own'; Bb7*a*, 'To the same': 'a short *Hymn'*, composed in his sickness; Bb7*b*, 'A Hymn to my God in a Night of my late Sickness' (?after Donne).

[C, R.]. *The Harmony of the Muses, or the Gentlemans and Ladies Choicest Recreation; Full of various pure and transcendent Wit, containing severall excellent Poems, Some Fancies of Love, some of Disdain, &c. written by those unimitable Masters of Learning and Invention, Dr. Joh. Donn, Dr. H. King, . . .*, London, 1654, 8º [Wing C 105].

[COTGRAVE, JOHN.] *Wit's Interpreter, The English Parnassus*, London, 1655, 8º [Wing C 6370]. In the fourth part, *Apollo and Orpheus*, pp. 15–16: 'A Lover's Passions',

related to Donne's 'A Feaver'; pp. 25–6: 'Two loath to depart', related to Donne's 'Breake of day'.

FULLER, THOMAS. *The Church History of Britain*, London, 1655, fº [Wing F 2416], Book x, sect. VIII, par. 15–16, p. 112: 'As for the *Convocation* [October 1623] . . . I am informed Doctor *Joseph Hall* preached the *Latine Sermon*, and *Doctor Donne* was the *Prolocutor'*, followed by a short account of Donne. See also David Wilkins, *Concilia Magnæ Britanniæ et Hiberniæ*, London, 1737, IV, 469–71, quoted by Bald, pp. 481–2 n.

[SHEPPARD, SAMUEL]. *The Marrow of Complements*, London, 1655 [MS. correction, B.M. copy, 1654], 12º [Wing M 719], B11: 'The Lover finding himself abus'd by her who promis'd him Marriage (she deserting him and electing another) may thus vent himselfe.

'*Mistresse,*

'To make the doubt clear that no Woman can be constant, was it my fate to prove it folly in you?' . . . (Elegie XV, 'The Expostulation', ll. 1–2, adapted).

W[INSTANLEY,] W[ILLIAM]. *The Muses Cabinet, Stored with variety of Poems, Both pleasant and profitable*, London, 1655, 8º [Wing W 3067], B8*b*: 'To one who enquired the Name of her whom I loved':

> Yet sure I think, and think I think aright,
> Beauty was not alone given to delight.
> The wanton eye, but as a note or sign,
> Fair outsides inwardly are most divine,
> Men do not Marble put to uses foul,
> Nor God give beauty with an impure soul;
> It seldome is we see together joyn'd,
> A fair complexion, and a vicious mind.

(Suggested by Holy Sonnets, XIII, l. 11?)

ANON. *Klioos Kraam*, Leewarden, 1656. A Dutch anthology including Huygens's translation of 'Go and catch a falling star' under the date 1626.

CHAPPELL, WILLIAM. *The Preacher or the Art and Method of Preaching*, London, 1656, 12º [Wing C 1957]: List of 'Elaborate Sermons' contains the name of 'Dr Donn'.

COLLOP, JOHN. *Poesis Rediviva*, London, 1656,

Appendix V

8º [Wing C 5395]. A3a *The Epistle Dedicatory* 'Nor is Poesie unworthy of your Patronage, which a Sir Philip Sidney has prais'd, our seraphick Donne us'd . . .'.

COWLEY, ABRAHAM. *Poems*, London, 1656, fº [Wing C 6683]. (a)3b 'And I think *Doctor Donnes Sun Dyal in a grave* is not more useless and ridiculous then *Poetry* would be in that *retirement*.'

[KING, PHILIP]. *The Surfeit*, London, 1656, 8º [Wing K 513]. In § 1 'For Bishop *Andrews* and Dr. *Donne* I could never conceive better of them, then as a voluntarie before a lesson to the lute, which is absolutely the best pleasing to the eare; but after finished absolutely forgotten, nothing to be remembered or repeated.' (Quoted in *Reliquiæ Hernianæ*, ed. P. Bliss, Oxford, 1857, II, 930–1.)

PHILLIPS, JOHN. *Sportive Wit: The Muses Merriment*, London, 1656, 8º [Wing P 2113]. Address to the Reader. '. . . we shall see Ballads inserted shortly, to as much dishonour of our English Wit, as if Don's Poems were turned into Dutch.'

OSBORN, FRANCIS. *Advice to a Son*, Oxford, 1656, 8º [Wing O 508], p. 12: Reference to 'the incomparable Dr. D.' and his employment by Lord Chancellor Egerton.

[WRIGHT, ABRAHAM]. *Parnassus Biceps*, London, 1656, 8º [Wing W 3686]. A3b *To the Ingenuous Reader*: Reference to Donne's Elegy IX. Elegies II and IX are printed in the text (pp. 86, 118) with titles 'On the praise of an ill-favoured Gentlewoman' and 'On an aged Gentlewoman'.

BELASYE, HENRY. *An English Traveler's First Curiosity, or The Knowledge of his owne Countrey* (MS.), 1657: 'What nation can shew more refined witts then those of our Ben, our Shakespeare, our Baumont, our Fletcher, our Dunn, our Randol, our Crashaw, our Cleveland, our Sidney, our Bacon, &c.' (*The Jonson Allusion-Book*, J. F. Bradley and J. Q. Adams, 1922, p. 313).

DRUMMOND, SIR WILLIAM, OF HAWTHORNDEN. In *The Diary of Sir William Drummond*, ed. H. W. Meikle, Miscellany of the Scottish History Society, vol. VII, 1941, p. 19: 'A

Booke of Memorandums 10 [May 1657]. Sabboth: there was no preachinge in Lasswad, Mr James Fairlie beinge seeke; red at hom Donn's Devotions.'

KING, HENRY. *Poems, Elegies, Paradoxes, and Sonnets*, London, 1657, 8º [Wing K 501], pp. 101–3: 'Upon the death of my ever desired friend Doctor Donne Dean of Pauls'. First printed in Donne's *Poems*, 1633, p. 373.

POOLE, JOSHUA. *The English Parnassus*, London, 1657, 8º [Wing P 2814], p. 42: Quotations from 'Dunn's Poems'.

ANON. *In Wit Restored* (Sir John Mennes), London, 1658, 8º [Wing M 1719], pp. 90–1: 'On a Good Legg and Foot', an imitation of Donne's 'Love's Progress'; printed in *The Poetical Works of William Strode*, ed. B. Dobell, London, 1907, pp. 108–10. Attributed by the editor to Strode or Corbett, more probably the latter.

[AUSTIN, SAMUEL]. In Thomas Flatman's *Naps upon Parnassus*, London, 1658, 8º [Wing F 1140]. B4b 'To his ingenuous Friend, the Author, on his incomparable Poems. Carmen Jocoserium. . . . *Once again*'.

. . . .

To thee compar'd, our English Poets all stop,
And vail their Bonnets, even *Shakespear's Falstop*,
Chaucer the first of all wasn't worth a farthing, . . .
Beaumont, and *Fletcher*, *Donne*, *Jeremy Candish*,
Herbert, and *Cleeveland*, and all the train noble
Are *Saints-bells* unto *thee*, and *thou* great *Bow-bell*,
Ben Johnson . . . .

CHARLES, KING. *Witty Apothegmes Delivered At Severall Times and upon Severall Occasions, by King James, King Charles, The Marques of Worcester, Francis Lord Bacon and Sir Thomas Moore*, London, 12º, 1658 [Wing W 3236], p. 26: Apothegms of King Charles. Upon a Discourse of the singular past which Doctor Donne was indowed withall . . . John Donne, Anne Donne, undone.

COKAYNE, SIR ASTON. *Small Poems of Divers sorts*, London, 1658, 8º [Wing C 4898], H8 'To my learned friend Mr. Thomas Bancroft upon his Book of Satyres' (after mention of satirists of ancient and modern times):

'(But all in one t'include) So our prime wit
(In the too few short *Satyres* he hath writ)
Renowned *Don* hath so rebuk'd his times,
That he hath jear'd vice-lovers from their crimes.'

Epigrams, The Third Book, R2, No. 3: 'Look
Upwards, that towards her. . . .'
(Donne, 'The Second Anniversary', l. 65).
P. 234 (misnumbered 134): Second Book of Epigrams, no. 99, reference to his acquaintance with Donne, in lines addressed to Charles Cotton. MS. *Epigrams*, sold at Sotheby's 31 January 1956, lot 47, also contains a reference to Donne, perhaps the same.

DUGDALE, WILLIAM. *The History of St Pauls Cathedral in London*, London, 1658, fº [Wing D 2482], p. 62: Full-page engraving of the effigy of Donne, with inscription above and coats of arms; p. 63: The inscription transcribed. (Above the effigy on the right is an inscription recording that the engraving was paid for by Margaret Clapham, wife of Christopher Clapham of Bramesley, Yorks.)

LONDON, WILLIAM. A *Catalogue of The most vendible Books in England*, London, 1658, 4º [Wing L 2849]. M2a, V2b, Ee4b list many of Donne's works. On Gg1a is included 'D. Donn. Fasciculus Poematum & Epigrammatum Miscelaneorum. 12º' (see p. 94 n. in this bibliography).

[MOSELEY, HUMPHREY]. SUCKLING, SIR JOHN. *Fragmenta Aurea*, 3rd edn. London, 1658, 8º [Wing S 6128]. Moseley, in the address prefixed to Suckling's unfinished tragedy, *Mortimer*, quotes ll. 3–5 of Donne's 'The Storme'.

CAPEL, RICHARD. *Tentations. The Sixth Edition*

[with] *The Fourth Part*, London, 1659, 8º [Wing C 475], p. 279: a reference to Donne's *Biathanatos* in a discussion of suicide.

CHAMBERLAYNE, WILLIAM. *Pharonnida*, London, 1659, 8º [Wing C 1866], Bk. ii, canto i, ll. 161 ff.: Plagiarizes Donne's 'The Flea'. See A. Alvarez, *The School of Donne*, 1961, p. 131.

ANON. In *A Collection of Letters made by Sʳ Tobie Mathews Kᵗ.*, London, 1660, 8º [Wing M 1319], p. 203: 'A most humble Servant in the Country, to a great Noble Lady at Court; written at New-Years-tide. I wish . . . that all the raggs of time, as *Dunne* calls them, may prove no worse than fair Embroideries to you.' See Donne's 'The Sunne Rising', l. 10.

BUTLER, SAMUEL (*c.* 1660–70). In *The Genuine Remains in Prose and Verse*, ed. R. Thyer, London, 1759, 2 vols., 8º, ii, p. 498: 'Dr Don's writings are like Voluntary or Prelude in which a man is not tyd' to any particular Designe of Air, but may change his key or moode at pleasure: So his compositions seeme to have been written without any particular Scope.' Repr. in *Characters and Passages from Notebooks*, ed. A. R. Waller, Cambridge, 1908, p. 402.

FORDE, THOMAS. *Faenestra in Pectore. Or, Familiar Letters*, London, 1660 [not in Wing], 'To the Reader': 'I know no better Interpreter of the *Heart*, than the *hand*; especially in *Familiar Letters*, whereby friends mingle souls, and make mutual discoveries *of*, and *to* one another' (allusion to Donne's verse letter to Sir Henry Wotton beginning 'Sir, more than kisses, letters mingle Soules').

FORDE, THOMAS. *A Theatre of Wits. Ancient and Modern. Represented in a Collection of Apothegmes*, London, 1660, 8º [Wing F 1548], C8b 'To the Reader': 'I have waived my particular *Dedication*, as not willing to intitle any man to the *Patronage* of my weaknesses; nor am I of that vain humour of *Appian* the grammarian, who promised immortality to those to whom he dedicated any of his Works.'

And they who write to Lords rewards to get,

Are they not like fingers at doors for meat?'
(in margin, 'Donnes Sat.', i.e. Satire II, ll. 21–2).

WINSTANLEY, WILLIAM. *England's Worthies*, London, 1660, 8º [Wing W 3058]. Reference on a2*b*: 'Don's and Cleaveland's *Poems, how they have whipt and Pedantized the other locusts of Poetry?*'. In 'The Life of Lancelot Andrewes', p. 293: 'Doctor Dun renders an excellent reason, why some are so tedious and long-winded in their holding forth; For that, saith he, their ware is course, they can afford the larger measure'; pp. 298–308: 'The Life of Doctour Donne Deane of Pauls', from Walton's *Life*. Also in the second edition, 1684, pp. 377–88. Each edition has an engraved title-page containing a miniature head of Donne, numbered 86, with many others, resembling the engraving by Lombart.

ASTRY, SIR JAMES (after 1661). Donne's epigram 'Raderus' (*Poems*, 1633, p. 43) transcribed by Sir James Astry, or his son James, with a four-line note on the fly-leaf of a copy of *Martial, Epigrammata cum notis, Lugd. Batavorum, Hackius*, 1661, now in the Univ. of London Library (see J. H. P. Pafford, *Notes and Queries*, ccxi, 1966, p. 377).

BARKSDALE, CLEMENT. *Memorials of Worthy Persons. Two Decads*, London, 1661, 12º [Wing B 800], pp. 5–22: Dr John Donne (*out of his Life, written by Jerem. Walton*) [*sic*]; pp. 23–31: Sir William Cockayne (out of his Funeral Sermon by Dr Donne Dec. 23 1626) [*LXXX Sermons*, no. 80; see also Wilford, J., 1741].

SIDNEY, ROBERT, 2nd EARL OF LEICESTER. *Letters and Memorials of State*, ed. A. Collins, London 1746, fº, p. 723, letter to Algernon, Earl of Northumberland, Penshurst, 17 February 1661, referring to the recent death of Elizabeth, Queen of Bohemia: 'It is a pitty that she lived not a few Houres more to dye upon her Wedding-day, and that there is not as good a Poet to make her Epitaph as Doctor *Donne*, who

wrote her *Epithalamium* upon that Day unto *St. Valentine.*'

FULLER, THOMAS. *Worthies*, London, 1662, fº [Wing F 2440]. Fff1*a* (p. 221): Worthies of London 'John Donne' (refers the reader to Walton's *Life*).

CAVENDISH, MARGARET, Duchess of Newcastle. *Plays written*, London, 1662, fº, p. 219: Lady Ward, in 'The Lady Contemplation', pt. 11, exclaims—'Prethee Nurse, lest thou should'st become mad, goe sleepe to settle thy thoughts, and quiet thy mind, for I remember a witty Poet, one Doctor Don, saith, Sleep is pains easie salve, and doth fulfil

All offices, unless it be to kill.'
(from The Storme, ll. 35–6, with changes).

BUTLER, SAMUEL. *Hudibras*, London, 1663, 8º [Wing B 6296–6302], Part I, Canto I, ll. 649–50:

As we find in sullen writs,

And cross-grained works of modern wits. . . .
(*The Progress of the Soul*, last stanza).

BOLD, HENRY. *Poems Lyrique Macaronique Heroique, &c.*, London, 1664, 8º [Wing B 3473], B4*b*, Song V:

I'le *Swear* they *Lye*, who say they *love*,

One onely Beauteous *Face*,

He's *Mad* (or *Honest*) does not prove

A *Score* in three days space. . . .
(from Suckling, 'Out Upon It!', after Donne, 'The Broken Heart'? See also Songs VI, VII, VIII, IX for influence from Donne).

KILLIGREW, THOMAS. *Comedies and Tragedies*, London, 1664, fº [Wing K 450], 11, i:

'*Jolly.* Dear, do not too fast pour in my joys, lest I too soon reach my heaven.

Love-all. Be gone, then, lest we prove (having gain'd that hight) this sad truth in Love. The first minute after noon is night' [quotes from Donne, 'A Lecture upon the Shadow', last lines].

11, vii: 'I'de be a Traytor etc I'de look on, and see Beauty thus go to wrack: it is enough custom has made us suffer them to be enclos'd; I am sure they were created common, and for the use of Man, and not intended to be subject to jealousie and choler, or to be bought or sold, or let for terms of lives or years, as they are now, or else sold at Outcrys; Oh Yes! who'le give most, take her' (Donne, 'Confined Love' or, after Donne, Carew, 'The Rapture').

WALTON, IZAAK. *The Life of Mr. Rich. Hooker*, London, 1665 [Wing W 670]. In a letter from Dr. Henry King to Walton dated 13 November 1664 references on A2*b*–3*a* to King's relations with Donne.

HERBERT OF CHERBURY, EDWARD. *Occasional Verses*, London, 1665, 8⁰ [Wing H 1508], pp. 9–13: 'The State-progress of Ill. Aug. 1668 [1608]. A Merlow in France', and pp. 14–17: 'Of Travellers from Paris May 1608'. Both poems are closely related to Donne's poem: 'To Sr Edward Herbert at Iuliers', *Poems*, 1633, p. 82 (see D. A. Keister, *MLQ*, VIII, 1947, 430–4). Also pp. 57–9: 'Elegy for Doctor Dunn'.

MAGALOTTI, LORENZO (1667–8). *Un' inedita relazione di un viaggio in Inghilterra nel 1667–68*, Florence, 1936. Donne's name occurs in a list of English poets.

ANON (*c.* 1668). *Inedited Poetical Miscellanies 1584–1700* [ed. W. C. Hazlitt, for Henry Huth], Chiswick Press, 1870. S2*b*. In 'Elegy on Sir William Davenant', stanza 7:

He out of breath himself did run,
When with high rapture he begun,
By emulating Doctor Dunne——
I mean the father, not the son.

Written on the fly-leaves of a copy of Denham's *Poems*, 1668, in a contemporary hand. Attributed to Sir John Denham in *Dramatists of the Restoration*, Davenant, vol. 1, ed. Maidment and Logan, p. lxxxvii.

DRYDEN, JOHN. *Of Dramatick Poesie, an Essay*, London, 1668, 4⁰ [Wing D 2327], p. 23: Donne's Satires compared with Cleveland's.

EVELYN, MARY (1668). In *Evelyn's Diary and Correspondence*, ed. H. B. Wheatley, London, 1906, 4 vols. 8⁰, IV, p. 55: Letter to Mr. Bohun. Reference to Donne's reputation as a letter writer.

LLOYD, DAVID. *Memoires of the Lives of the Personages that Suffered for the Protestant Religion*, London, 1668, f⁰ [Wing L 2642], p. 521: 'Dr. Mathew Griffith, born in

London, bred in *Brazen-nose* Colledge in Oxford, Lecturer at St. *Dunstan's in the West*, under Dr. *Donnes* inspection, whose favourite he was'. Bald, p. 393, notes that he was appointed lecturer 31 October 1631, after Donne's death. Lloyd's statement is repeated by Wood, *Athenae Oxonienses*, 1721, I, p. 363.

PEPYS, SAMUEL. *Diary*, 27 May 1668 [ed. *Wheatley*, London, 1924, VIII, 29]: Reference to Donne's entering into Orders.

BADILEY, RICHARD. *The Life of Dr. Thomas Moreton late Bishop of Duresme. Begun by R.B. Secretary to his Lordship. And Finished by J.N.D.D. his Lordships Chaplain*. York, 1669, 12⁰ [Wing B 387], pp. 97–104, an account of Donne derived from Bishop Moreton: Donne's misfortunes after his marriage; urged by Moreton to take orders and offered the Rectory of Long Marston in Yorkshire; his journey to France; advised not to continue the study of the law, ministry in the Church much safer; a description of the picture 'taken in Shaddowes' (see p. 373 in Iconography); an 'instance of his ripe and sudden wit' when given by the Bishop 'a good quantity of gold (then a usefull token) saying, *Here Mr Donne, take this, Gold is restorative*: He presently answered, *Sir, I doubt I shall never restore it back again*: and I am assured he never did'.

ETHEREGE, GEORGE. *The Comical Revenge, or, Love in a Tub*, London, 1669, 4⁰ (Licensed 8 July 1664) [Wing E 3367], reference p. 48, Act IV, sc. v, l. 41, Gracian speaking to Lord Beaufort, 'Blasted with sighs, and almost drown'd in tears', misquoted from 'Twicknam Garden', l. 1, 'Blasted with sighs, and surrounded with tears'. Grierson, II, 25, notes that 'surrounded' here means 'overflowed'.

PHILLIPS, EDWARD. *Compendiosa Enumeratio Poetarum* (appended to Johannes Buchler's *Sacrarum Profanarumque Phrasium Poeticarum Thesaurus*, seventeenth edition, London, 1669, 12⁰ [Wing B 5303]), R7*b*: 'Joannes Donnius qui annis juvenilioribus prima Erotica, deinde Satyras & Metricas Epistolas, tandem senectute appropinquante, sacra & divina Carmina protulit, in quibus omnibus summum Ingenii acumen eminet, postremis annis sacerdotale Munus obiit, Diaconatum Templi Paulini obtinuit, & Celeberrimus Concionator evasit.'

PLAYFORD, JOHN. *The Treasury of Musick: containing Ayres and Dialogues To Sing to the theorbo-lute of Basso Viol Composed by Henry Lawes. In Three Books*. London, 1669, f° [Wing D 2504], p. 11: On Womans Inconstancy, 'Catch me a Star that's falling from the Skie . . . Then hast thou found Faith in a Womans mind.' Signed by John Playford. Adapted from Donne's poem.

WALTON, IZAAK. *The Life of Mr George Herbert*, London, 1670, 12° [Wing W 669], p. 21: Herbert's friendship with Donne. See also no. 60.

BRUNE DE JONGHE, JOHAN DE. *Alle Volgeestige Werken*, Harlingen, 1672, p. 145: Reference to Huygens's translations of Donne's poems.

HOWELL, JAMES. *Epistolæ Ho-Elianæ*, London, 1673, 8° [Wing H 3074], bk. 1, sect. vi, letter xxxii, 25 July 1635. Possible allusion to Donne's 'Good Friday, 1613. Riding Westward'; bk. 1, sect. vi, letter xli, 1 February 1638. Possible allusion to Donne's 'The Canonization' (see F. Kermode, *Notes and Queries*, CXCIX, 1954, 337).

MARVELL, ANDREW. *The Rehearsal Transpos'd: The Second Part*, London, 1673, 8° [Wing M 882], p. 63: 'In so much that upon consideration of so various an identity, methings [*sic*] after so many years I begin to understand Doctor *Donn's* Progress of the Soul, which pass'd through no fewer revolutions, and had hitherto puzzled all its Readers.' [There follows a summary of the poem with quotations.] 'This was the Sum of that witty fable of Doctor *Donne's*, which if it do not perfectly suit with all the transmigrations of mine Answerer, the *Author of the Ecclesiastical Politie*, as equal the Progress of so great a Prince, yet whoever will be so curious as himself to read that Poem, may follow the parallel much farther than I have done, lest I should be tedious to the Reader by too long and exact a similitude.'

PHILIPOT, THOMAS. *Self-Homicide-Murther, some Antidotes and Arguments*, London, 1674 [Wing P 2001]: A reference in the Epistle Dedicatory to 'a learned but unfortunate Treatise, stil'd *Biathanatos*, wherein Self-killing in several Cases is concluded not to be Murder'.

SPEED, SAMUEL. *Fragmenta Carceris: or, The Kings-Bench Scuffle; with the Humours of the Common-Side*, London, 1674, 4° [Wing W 4900]. F1*b*. In 'The Legend of Duke Humphrey', ll. 37–8:
And drink they must; I never yet knew one
Could quench his thirst, with reading Doctor
Donne.

PHILLIPS, EDWARD. *Theatrum Poetarum, or a compleat collection of the poets*, London, 1675, 12° [Wing W 2075], pp. 106–7: A short account of Donne.

DUPORT, JAMES. *Musae Subsecivae, seu Poetica Stromata*, Cambridge, 1676, 8° [Wing D 2652], A3*a*: 'Ad Virum optimum, & Piscatorem peritissimum, Isaacum Waltonum': (also prefixed, with others, to *The Compleat Angler or, The Contemplative Men's Recreation, The first part*. . . . The Fifth Edition much corrected and enlarged. . . . 1676).
Dum tu profundum scribis *Hookerum*, & pium
Donnum ac disertum, sanctum et *Herbertum*, sacrum
Vatem: hos videmus nam penicillo tuo
Graphicà, & perità, *Isace*, depictos manu.

RAINBOW, EDWARD, Bp. of Carlisle. *A Sermon Preached At the Funeral of Anne Countess of Pembroke. With some Remarks on the Life of that Eminent Lady*, 4°, London, 1677 [Wing R 142]: Reference, p. 38, to Lady Pembroke's converse with Divines and others, thought by Bald to refer to Donne.

HUYGENS, CONSTANTIJN (1678). *De Gedichten*, ed. J. A. Worp, 8 vols., Groningen, 1892–8, VIII, pp. 203–36: *De vita propria sermonum inter liberos, lib. II*, ll. 65–144, an account of the embassy that brought him to London in 1622–3; ll. 145–220, the friends he met there (see especially p. 208, ll. 170–5, his pleasure in Donne's company. Bald, p. 442).

VON HOFFMANNSWALDAU, CHRISTIAN HOF-MANN. *Deutsche Übersetzungen und Gedichte*, 1679, preface: 'The English have at all times shown themselves to be lovers of poetry, though not always with equal felicity, for the poems of merit are mostly by modern writers. In Chaucer, the English Homer, as his countrymen call him, and Robert of Gloucester we do not meet with the same learning, art and elegance as in Edmond Spencer's faerie Queene and Michael Draiton's Poly-Olbion, Johnson's comedies and tragedies, and the religious poems of Quarles and Don' (G. Waterhouse, *The Literary Relations of England and Germany in the Seventeenth Century*, 1914, p. 119).

TUCKNEY, ANTHONY. *Prælectiones Quæstionum variorum insignium Scholis Academicis Cantabrigiensibus habitæ*, Amsterdam, 4°, 1679. In the second part, *Theses & Prælectiones Theologicæ*, pp. 159–60: a discussion of Donne's *Biathanatos*. See J. E. Sprott, *The English Debate on Suicide*, Le Salle, 1961, pp. 63–4 for a translation of Tuckney —'The earliest attempt to examine Donne's relativist reasoning for suicide'.

AUBREY, JOHN (c. 1680). In Aubrey's *Brief Lives*, ed. Andrew Clark, Oxford, 1898, 2 vols., 8°, i, 59, 68, 307, 308, 313, 418: References to Donne's lines in 'Loves diet':

> For what doeth it availe
> To be the twentieth man in an entaile?

and to his friends (Bacon, Edward Herbert, Richard Herbert, John Hoskyns). He also quotes the first stanza of Donne's 'The Primrose'.

BLOUNT, CHARLES. The *Two First Books of Philostratus Concerning the Life of Apollonius Tyraneus*, London, f°, 1680 [Wing P 2132], p. 154: a reference to Donne's *Biathanatos*.

LEE, NATHANIEL. *Theodosius: or, The Force of Love. A Tragedy*, London, 1680, 4° [Wing L 877]. A2a Epistle Dedicatory to the Duchess of Richmond. Quotations from 'The First Anniversary', ll. 112–14, 117–20. A3a Ditto. Quotations from 'The Second Anniversary', ll. 244–6, 'To the Countesse of Bedford', ll. 22–4.

ANON. *A Paradox Against Life. Written By the Lords in the Tower. An Heroick Poem*, London, 1681, f° [Wing P 331], p. 6, ll. 18, 19, plagiarized from Donne's Nocturnall upon S. Lucies day, stanza 2; p. 9, ll. 10, 11: 'He falls upon, An Ominous Precipitation', alludes to Donne's 'First Anniversary', ll. 97–8.

BORRICHIUS, DR OLAUS. *Dissertationes Academicæ de Poetis*, Frankfurt, 1683, 4°, p. 161: Donne's name in a list of recommended English poets.

SHIPMAN, THOMAS. *Carolina: Or, Loyal Poems*, London, 1683, 8° [Wing S 3440] I4b–5: 'Gratitude. 1667. *Some grateful Acknowledgments to that most excellent Poet*, Mr. A. C. [Abraham Cowley]':

> Hail *God of Wit*! *England's Apollo*, hail!
> . . . .
> The *Muse's Empire* bears so great a Name.
> Thou hast two *Rivals* in thy *Lady-Fame*;
> *Waller* and *Donne*. You are the only three
> Who justly can pretend that *Monarchy*.
> *Donne's* Judgment, Fancy, Humour, and his Wit,
> Strong, searching, happy, and before ne're hit,
> Gives him a fair pretence to climb the Throne;
> But *Waller* rather stops than plucks him down.
> Rich he appears; his courtly Vesture grac'd
> With golden *Similes* all over lac'd.
> But Cowley (like the *Infant* of the *Sun*)
> Out-glitters *Waller*, and ev'n dazzles *Donne*.
> Both of 'em, to *Augustus*, leave the Field;
> Like *Lepidus* and *Anthony*, they yield.
> He triumphs! their triumv'racy of Rays
> Unite in *Cowley* and compound his blaze.

N2b: 'Wit and Nature' 1677. *A Pindaric Ode* to Sr. Edw. Rich':

> . . . .
> *Nature*—I cannot yet define;
> More fit for some *seraphical Divine*:
> Tho they but *Graces* three, and we have
> [*Muses* nine. . . .

Priests we are both alike, and both alike
[are fir'd
With sacred heat: *Poets* have been
[inspir'd,
Shar'd in their gifts of *Prophecy*,
As they in ours of *Poetry*,
And both have *Lawrels* won;
They have their *Doctor Sprat*, & had their
[*Doctor Donne*.
Q2: 'Built with *Mud-walls* of *Flesh* and thatcht with *Hair*' (cf. 'The Litanie', stanza III, ll. 1–2).

C., J. *An Elegie, Upon the Death of the most Incomparable, Mrs Katharine Philips, The Glory of Her Sex*. [London] [1684], f°, broadside [Wing C 53]. Reprinted in *A Little Ark*, ed. G. Thorn-Drury, London, 1921, pp. 26–9. The editor suggests that the author may be John Crouch. The *Elegie* draws heavily on Donne's *Anniversaries*.

OLDHAM, JOHN. *Works*, London, 1684, 8° [Wing O 225]. On a2b, reference to Donne.

FISHER, PAYNE. *The Tombs, Monuments, And Sepulchral Inscriptions, Lately Visible in St Pauls Cathedral . . . Compleatley Rendred In Latin and English*, London [1684], 4° [Wing F 1041], pp. 55–8: An account of Donne's tomb with a translation of the inscription and a brief life.

WOLSELEY, ROBERT. In Rochester's *Valentinian*, London, 1685, 4° [Wing F 1354], b3b Preface: Reference to Donne's versification: verses are not given feet 'to stand stock-still like *Dr. Donne's*'.

WINSTANLEY, WILLIAM. *The Lives of the most Famous English Poets, or the Honour of Parnassus*, London, 1687, 8° [Wing W 3065], pp. 117–21: Doctor John Donne.

WALKER, JOSEPH. *A Discourse upon Monsieur Pascalls Thoughts*, London, 1688, 8° [Wing P 645]. *S2a. Dedicatory Epistle to Sir John Hewet. 'I desire as Dr Donn did, to swim like a Fish, quietly to my Long Home.' (In *Monsieur Pascall's Thoughts, Meditations, and Prayers . . . Done into English by Jos. Walker*, London, 1688, dedicated to the Hon. Robert Boyle.)

WHITE, H. *Diarium Biographicum*, Dantzig,

1688, 4°. Dd1a–b. Short notice of Donne, with list of books.

COTTON, CHARLES, the Younger. *Poems on Several Occasions*, London, 1689, 8° [Wing C 6389]: 'To my old and most Worthy Friend Mr. Izaak Walton, on his Life of Dr. Donne, etc.', with many references to Donne.

EVELYN, JOHN (1689). In *Diary and Correspondence*, ed. H. B. Wheatley, London, 1906, 8°, vol. III, p. 435, letter to Lord Spencer, remarking on the fewness of volumes of English letters: 'Sir Fr. Bacon, Dr. Donne, and I hardly remember any else who have publish'd any thing of considerable, and they but gleanings of cabbal men, who have put many things in a heape, without much choice or fruits, especially as to the culture of the style or language'; p. 444, letter to Samuel Pepys, including Donne's portrait among those that should be hung in the nation's state rooms. For list of Donne's works in Evelyn's library see Keynes, *Bibliogr. of Evelyn*, 1937, 1968, p. 17.

TEMPLE, Sir WILLIAM. *Miscellanea. In Two Parts*, London, 1690, 8° [Wing T 652]. Second part, p. 127: Upon the Gardens of Epicurus (reference to Donne).

WALLER, EDMUND. *The Second Part of Mr. Waller's Poems*, London, 1690, 8° [Wing W 521]. A6, reference to Donne in the Preface.

LANGBAINE, GERARD. *An Account of the English Dramatic Poets*, Oxford, 1691, 8° [Wing L 373], pp. 277–8: References to Donne.

WOOD, ANTHONY. *Athenæ Oxonienses*, London, 1691–2, 2 vols. f° [Wing W 3382], I, pp. 474–5, 'John Donne'. Also London, 1721, 2 vols., f°, I, pp. 554–6; *Fasti*, 187, incorporated M.A. 18 April 1610. Ed. Philip Bliss, London, 1815, 4°, II, pp. 502–5.

DRYDEN, J. *Eleanora: A Panegyrical Poem Dedicated to the Memory of the Late Countess of Abingdon*, London, 4°, 1692 [Wing D 2270]: Reference on the third leaf of The Dedication: 'Doctor Donn, the greatest Wit, though not the best Poet of our Nation, acknowledges that he had never seen Mrs. Drury, whom he has made immortal in his admirable Anniversaries; I have had the same fortune; though I have not succeeded to the same Genius. However, I have follow'd his footsteps in the Design of his Panegyrick, which was to raise an Emulation in the living, to copy out the Example of the dead.'

BLOUNT, Sir THOMAS POPE. *Essays on Several Subjects*, London, 1692, p. 61: 'if learning happens to be in the possession of a Fool, 'tis then but a Bawble, and like Dr. Donne's *Sun-Dial in the Grave*, a trifle, and of no use.' (Reference to 'The Will': see Cowley, 1656.)

[DUNTON, J.]. *The Young-Students-Library*, London, f°, 1692 [Wing D 2635], p. xiii: in 'An Essay Upon all sorts of Learning', under 'Poetry', Dr. Donne is listed without comment among English Poets.

PIERCE, EZRA. *A Discourse of Self-Murder. In a Letter to R.F.*, London, 1692, 4° [Wing P 2162], pp. 10, 14: References to Donne's *Biathanatos*.

[WALSH, WILLIAM]. *Letters and Poems, Amorous and Gallant*, London, 1692, 8° [Wing W 647]. Preface, A4*b*–5*a*: 'There are no Modern Writers, perhaps, who have succeeded better in Love-Verses than the English . . . Never was there a more copious Fancy or greater reach of Wit, than what appears in Ðr. Donne. &c.'

BROWN, EDWARD. *The Letters of the Renowned Father Paul* [Sarpi] *Written to Monsieur Del Isle Groslot, the Learned Monsieur Gillot, and others. Translated out of Italian. By Edward Brown, Rector of Sunridge in Kent*, London, 1693, 8° [Wing S 698], pp. 9–10: '. . . though a very excellent Person [*footnote*: Dr. Donne, in his Advertisement to the Reader, before his *Pseudo-martyr*] and a very good friend of Father Paul's, was once of the Mind, that a Man could not well be called a Reader, till he had read a Book over; and did therefore design, he says, to have met his Reader at the End of his Book, and there tell him what he had to say about it.' There is another reference at p. 115.

DRYDEN, JOHN. *The Satires of Juvenal Trans-lated by Mr. Dryden and other Eminent Hands*, London, 1693, f° [Wing J 1288], in Dedication to Charles, Earl of Dorset, p. iii: *Donn* alone, of all our Countrymen, had your Talent; but was not happy enough to arrive at your Versification. And were he Translated into Numbers, and English, he wou'd yet be wanting in the Dignity of Expression. . . . He affects the Metaphysicks, not only in his Satires, but in his Amorous Verses, where Nature only shou'd reign. . .; p. xlvi: Wou'd not *Donns* Satires, which abound with so much Wit, appear more Charming, if he had taken care of his Words, and of his Numbers? But he follow'd *Horace* so very close, that of necessity he must fall with him: And I may safely say it of this present Age, that if we are not so great Wits as *Donn*, yet, certainly we are better Poets. Repr. in *Essays*, ed. W. P. Ker, Oxford, 1900, ii, pp. 19, 102 (Original and Progress of Satire). Dryden here first introduced the idea of 'Metaphysicks' in Donne's poetry.

[DUNTON, JOHN?]. *The Athenian Mercury*, London, Tues., 24 October 1693: 'Question 4. What Books of Poetry wou'd you Advise one that's Young, and extremely delights in it, to read, both Divine and other? Answ. . . . Spencer's Fairy Queen, etc. Tasso's Godfrey of Bulloign, Shakespear, Beaumont and Fletcher, Ben Johnson, Randal, Cleaveland, Dr. Donne, Gondibert, *Waller*, all *Dryden*, Tate, Oldham, Flatman, the Plain Dealer. . . .'

HACKET, JOHN. *Scrinia Reserata. A Memorial of John Williams, D.D.*, London, f°, 1693 [Wing H 171]. Part 1, p. 63: Reference to Donne's appointment as Dean of St. Paul's, 'a laureate Wit; neither was it possible that a vulgar Soul should dwell in such promising Features'.

WILKINS, JOHN. *Ecclesiastes: or a Discourse concerning the Gift of Preaching*, London, 1693, 8° [Wing W 2188], pp. 251: Listing sermons on the subject of Friendship, Wilkins includes: Dr. Donne's Sermon Rom. 12: 20. (*LXXX Sermons*, no. 10.)

BENTHEM, H. L. *Engeländischer Kirch Und Schulen-Staat*, Lüneberg, 1694, 8°, p. 612,

§ 29. The name of John Dunne occurs in a list of English *Gelehrte.*

BLOUNT, Sir THOMAS POPE. *De Re Poetica: or, Remarks upon Poetry. With Characters and Censures of the Most Considerable Poets, whether Ancient or Modern. Extracted out of the Best and Choicest Criticks,* London, 1694, 4° [Wing B 3347], pp. 67–9. John Donne.

LAUD, WILLIAM, ARCHBISHOP. *The History of the Troubles and Tryal of William Laud. To which is prefixed The Diary of his Own Life.* Ed. Henry Wharton, London, f°, 1695 [Wing L 586]. Diary, p. 41: Referring to slips made by Donne in a sermon preached before the King on 1 April 1627; p. 44: concerning a paper threatening Laud himself, found in Donne's yard at St. Paul's and sent by him to the King in 1629. History, p. 146, sidenote: Donne's name in a list of persons present at the sentencing of Lady Purbeck for adultery (see Bald, p. 420).

WERNICKE, CHRISTIAN. *Auf die Schlesischen Poeten,* 1697, note to one of his epigrams: 'Of the English writers he [Hofmannswaldau, q.v.] mentions with admiration Donne and Quarles, whom no Englishman ever reads, and has not a word for Milton, Cowley, Denham and Waller, whom they justly regard as their best poets' (G. Waterhouse, *The Literary Relations of England and Germany in the Seventeenth Century,* 1914, p. 119).

ADAMS, J. *An Essay Concerning Self-Murther,* London, 1700, 8°: Contains a full examination of *Biathanatos* (see p. 117 of present work).

DRYDEN, JOHN. *Fables Ancient and Modern,* London, 1700, f° [Wing D 2278], pp. 537–8: 'The Monument of a Fair Maiden Lady, who dy'd at *Bath,* and is there Interr'd'. The poem shews evidence of influence by Donne's *Anniversaries.*

1701–1800

[Arranged chronologically]

DICTIONARY. *Historical, Geographical, Genealogical and Poetical Dictionary.* Ed. *Jer. Collier,* London, 1701, f°. Ddd2a. 'Donne', a short account.

[DUNTON, JOHN]. *The Post-Angel,* 4°, May 1701, pp. 324–7: Notes by 'The Spiritual Observer' refer on p. 325 to *Biathanatos:* 'But I do believe the Scenes of those Tragedies which have been lately acted by several misguided Persons upon themselves, have had their Original extraction from a learned Pamphlet call'd *Biathanatos,* wherein SELF-MURDER in many cases, is concluded not to be Murder.'

ANON. *A Comparison Between the Two Stages,* London, 1702, pp. 43–4:

> *Critick* . . . Wit and Sense are no more the same than Wit and Humour; nay there is even in Wit an uncertain Mode, a variable Fashion, that is as unstable as the Fashion of our Cloaths: This may be prov'd by their Works who writ a hundred Years ago,

compar'd with some of the modern; Sir *Philip Sidney, Don, Overbury,* nay *Ben* himself took singular delight in playing with their Words: Sir *Philip* is every where in his *Arcadia* jingling, which certainly by the example of so great a Man, proves that sort of Wit then in Fashion; now that kind of Wit is call'd Punning and Quibbling, and is become too low for the Stage, nay even for ordinary Converse. . . .

[DUNTON, J.]. *The Athenian Oracle.* Second edition, vol. II, London, 8°, 1704. Q[uery]. What books of Poetry wou'd you Advise one that is Young, and extreamly delights in it, to read both Divine and other? A[nswer]. (A list of names) including Dr. Donne.

POPE, ALEXANDER. *The Correspondence,* ed. George Sherburn, Oxford, 8°, 1956, I, 16. Letter to William Wycherley, 10 April 1706: 'Donne (like one of his Successors [i.e. Wycherley]) had infinitely more Wit than he wanted Versification: for the great dealers in Wit, like those in Trade, take least Pains to set off their Goods; while the Haberdashers of small Wit, spare for no Decorations or Ornaments.' First printed in *The Posthumous Works*, London, vol. ii, 1729.

SPENCE, JOSEPH. *Quelques Remarques Hist: sur les Poëts Anglois, 17—*

(Of lyric poetry in the seventeenth century):

Tout étoit plein de jeux de mots, de pensées brillantes, détranges Comparaisons & de Metaphores outrées. *Donne* étoit universellement declaré le Prince de l'Esprit, dans cet Interregne de bons Sens. En verité, il s'y trouve beaucoup de sentimens judicieux dans ses Satyres, & dans quelq'unes de ses Epîtres: mais ces sentimens sont toûjours embarassés d'une puerile affectation de dire quelque chose de beau. De là il vient que la plupart de ses Piéces ne sont qu'un Tissu d'Epigrammes. Sa versification, comme celle des autres Poëtes de son temp, est très mauvoise.

See James M. Osborn, 'The First History of English Poetry', in *Pope and his Contemporaries*, ed. James L. Clifford and Louis A. Landa, O.U.P., 1949, pp. 230–50.

[DUNTON, J.]. *Athenian Sport*, London, 8°, 1707. pp. 409: in Paradox xciv,

Then steal from *Cowley*, or from *Done*
(Since none will miss'em when they're gone)
Two Hundred thousand Stanzas on
                    Her Shoo-ty.

HEARNE, THOMAS. *Remarks and Collections*, ed. C. E. Doble. Oxford, 8°, 1886, vol. ii, pp. 191–2, 2 May 1709: Reference to the MS. of Donne's *Biathanatos* given by him to Lord Herbert of Cherbury. Vol. iii, p. 46, 7 September 1710: Note of Donne's copy of *Epigrammata et Poemata vetera* [*varia*] by Pierre Pithou in BLO. See L144 in list of Donne's library. Vol. iii, p. 326, 30 March 1712: Reference to John Adams's 'book against Self-Murder against Dr. Donne'. See p. 117 of present work.

PRINCE, JOHN (Vicar of Berry-Pomeroy in the County of Devon). *Self-Murder*, London,

8°, 1709: References to passages in *Biathanatos* on pp. 9, 31, 40, 41.

[STEELE, SIR R.]. *The Lucubrations of Isaac Bickerstaff*, vol. iv, London, 8°, 1711. *The Tatler*, no. 264, 14–16 December 1710, p. 425: This *Guicciardin* is so very prolix and circumstantial in his Writings, that I remember our Countryman Dr. Don, speaking of that Majestick and Concise Manner in which Moses has described the Creation of the World adds 'That if such an Author as *Guicciardin* were to have written on such a subject, the World it self would not have been able to have contained the Books that gave the History of its Creation' (*Fifty Sermons*, no. 28, preached to the King, April 1629. Potter and Simpson, ix, 47–8).

[STEELE, SIR R.]. *The Spectator*, vol. i, London, 8°, 1712, no. 41, Tuesday 17 April, p. 231: How like is this Lady, and how unlike is a *Pict*, to that Description Dr. Donne gives of his Mistress? (*The Second Anniversary*, ll. 244–6). See *The Spectator*, ed. D. F. Bond, 1965, i, 176.

ANON. *The Guardian*, vol. i, London, 8°, 1714, no. 16, Monday 30 March, pp. 96–7, in a letter to Mrs. Annabella Lizard: 'But of all our Countrymen, none are more defective in their Songs, through a redundancy of Wit, than Dr. *Donne* and Mr. *Cowley*. In them one Point of Wit flashes so fast upon another, that the Reader's Attention is dazled by the continual sparkling of their Imagination; you find a new Design started almost in every Line, and you come to the end, without satisfaction of seeing any one of them executed.'

MORHOF, DANIEL GEORGE. *Polyhistor Literarius Philosophicus et Practicus. Editio Secunda*, Lubecae, 1714, 4°. Tome i, p. 81 (Lib. i, cap. ix, §14): Reference to Donne's Latin letter and his catalogue of books; Tome i, p. 994 (Lib. vi, cap. iv, §18): A short account of Donne, mentioning his *Poems*, *Devotions*, and *Biathanatos*. Quoted in full by Zouch in his edition of Walton's *Lives*, 1796, 4°. See also pp. 82 and 220 of the present work.

COCKBURN, J., D.D. *A Discourse of Self-Murder*.

In which the Heinousness of the Sin is expos'd, London, 1716, 8°, pp. 29–30: References to Donne's *Biathanatos* and the answer by Adams.

LE NEVE, JOHN. *Fasti Ecclesiæ Anglicanæ*, London, 1716, F°, p. 185: The date of Donne's appointment to the Deanery of St. Paul's, 27 November 1621.

PRIOR, MATTHEW. *Poems on Several Occasions*, London, f°, 1718, p. [389], in Preface to 'Solomon on the Vanity of the World. A Poem in Three Books': I would say one Word of the Measure, in which This, and most Poems of the Age are written. Heroic with continued Rhime, as DONNE and his Contemporaries use it, carrying the sense of one Verse most commonly into another, was found too dissolute and wild, and came very often too near prose.

JACOB, GILES. *An Historical Account of the Lives and Writings of English Poets*, E. Curll, London, 8°, 1720, pp. 46–8: John Donne D.D., with Henry King's 'Elegie' (also in *The Poetical Register: or, The Lives and Characters of All the English Poets*, London, 2 vols., 8°, 1723, ii, 46–8).

STRYPE, JOHN. *A Survey of the Cities of London and Westminster*, 2 vols., London, f°, 1720. Vol. i, Book 3, p. 168a: In the South side of the Quire of St. Paul's Church, stands a white marble Statue on an Urn, with this Inscription over it (quoting Donne's epitaph).

[SEDLEY, SIR CHARLES]. In *The Works*, 2 vols., 8°, 1722, ii, pp. 1–2: 'The Lover's Will' (Let me not sigh my last, ere I bequeath), 5 stanzas. An adaptation of Donne's 'The Will' (Collected *Poems*, pp. 283–5); regarded by Pinto as spurious (*Works*, ed. Pinto, 1928, ii, xxv).

POPE, ALEXANDER. *Miscellanea. In Two volumes*. Printed in the year 1727, 8°, p. 78, in 'An Epistle to Henry Cromwell Esq.'
    Just as a Still, with Simples in it,
    Betwixt each Drop stay half a Minute.
    (That Simile is not my own,
    But Lawfully belongs to Donne).
Also in *Mr. Pope's Literary Correspondence*, vol. ii, London, E. Curle, 1735, 8°, Part ii,

p. 131. See also *Minor Poems*, ed. N. Ault and J. Butt, London, New Haven, 1954, pp. 25, 28.

OLDMIXON, JOHN. *The Arts of Logick and Rhetorick Illustrated from Father Bouhours*, London, 8°, 1728, pp. 309, 332–3: References to Cowley's imitations of Donne and mentioning Donne's 'metaphysical gallantry', the first adjectival use of the term.

FENTON, ELIJAH. *The Works of Edmund Waller in Verse and Prose. Published by Mr. Fenton*, London, 4°, 1729, p. xxxv, in 'Observations on some of Mr. Waller's Poems, on 'Song. Stay Phoebus, Stay!': Dr. Donne and Mr. Cowley industriously affected to entertain the fair sex with such philosophical allusions, which Mr. Waller as industriously avoided. Also in *The Works*, etc., London, 12°, 1730, p. lxi. This is obviously derived from Dryden, *A Discourse*, 1693 (see above).

NICERON, J. P. *Memoires pour servir à l'Histoire des Hommes Illustres dans la République des Lettres*, Tome viii, Paris, 1729, 8°, pp. 138–53: 'Jean Donne', with a list of his works.

HARTE, WALTER. *An Essay on Satire, Particularly on the Dunciad*. London, 8°, 1730, p. 9: A reference to Donne's 'Progresse of the Soul' as a mock-epic in the lines:
    As thinking makes the Soul, low things exprest
    In high-rais'd terms, define a *Dunciad* best.
    Books and the Man demands as much, or more,
    Than *He* who *wander'd to the Latian shore*:
    For here (eternal Grief to *Dun's* Soul,
    And B——'s thin Ghost!) the Part contains the *Whole*:
    Since in Mock-Epic none succeeds, but he
    Who tastes the Whole of Epic Poesy.
Reprinted by The Augustan Reprint Society, no. 132, 1968, ed. T. B. Gilmore, Clark Memorial Library, Los Angeles.

POPE, ALEXANDER (1730–6). In Joseph Spence's *Observations Anecdotes and Characters of Books and Men. Collected from the Conversation of Mr. Pope and Other Eminent Persons*. Ed. James M. Osborn, 2 vols., Oxford At the Clarendon Press, 1966, i, pp. 187–9: nos. 434–6, 439, 440 (1730–6), Pope's opinions of Donne, comparing him with Herbert, Randolph, Davenant, and Cowley, with annotations by the editor. (First edited by S. W. Singer, London, 1820; see pp. 22, 136, 144, 170, 173.)

ANON. *The Barbados Gazette*, 18 July 1733. 'On reading Dr. Donne's Poems', a poem professing to have been written by a woman suffering from unrequited love. See p. 337 of this *Bibliography* under R. C. Fox.

ANON. *The Universal Spectator*, London, f°, 1733–4. Five poems based on originals by Donne. (i) No. 258, 15 September 1733: 'To Sir Gimcrack Noddy' (6 lines) from Donne's 'Antiquary'. (2) No. 260, 29 September 1733: 'The Man of Business no Lover! A Morning Dialogue varied from Dr. Donne' ('Break of Day'). (3) No. 278, 2 February 1734: 'The Oxonian's Trip to The Drawing Room', from Donne's 'Satyre IV'. (4, 5) No. 280, 16 February 1734: The General Lover (34 lines) from Donne's 'The Indifferent' and 'The Lover's Curse' (19 lines) from Donne's 'The Curse'. Both printed also in *The Gentleman's Magazine*, IV, February 1734, p. 102. (See Brijraj Singh, *Notes and Queries*, XVIII, 1971, 50, with editor's note added.)

SINCERUS, THEOPHILUS (i.e. Schwindel, G. J.). *Neue Sammlung von lauter alten und raren Buchern*, Frankfurt and Leipzig, 1733, 8°, pp. 37–9: Notices of *Conclave Ignati*, 1638, and *Biathanatos*, with reference to Denny's *Pelicanicidium*, 1653 (q.v.)

THEOBALD, L. *The Works of Shakespeare*, London, 1733, seven vols., 8°, vol. I, p. xlvi. Theobald's Preface. 'Thus became the Poetry of Donne (tho' the wittiest Man of That Age) nothing but a continued Heap of Riddles.'

ZEDLER, J. H. *Grosses vollständiges universal Lexicon*, vol. VII, Halle and Leipzig, 1734, f°, p. 1279: Biographical account of Donne.

BAYLE, J. *A General Dictionary*, vol. IV, London, 1736, f°, pp. 631–7: 'Donne', with extensive notes. Thomas Birch is presumed to have been the writer.

ROBECK, JOHN. *Exercitatio Philosophica de*

Morte Voluntaria, Rintelii, 4°, 1736, p. 18: A reference in a footnote to Donne's *Biathanatos*.

[COOPER, ELIZABETH]. *The Muses Library*, London, 8°, 1738 [also with cancel title-page, 1741], p. xii: 'Donne, and Corbet added Wit to Satire, and restor'd the almost forgotten Way of making Reproof it self entertaining.' Also p. 332, in an account of Sir John Davis: 'The joint Applauses of Cambden, Sir John Harrington, Ben Johnson, Selden, Donne, Corbet, &c! These are great and unquestionable Authorities in Favour of this Author.'

WESLEY, JOHN. *An Extract of the Journal From his Embarking for Georgia To his Return to London*. Second edn., Bristol, 12°, 1743, p. 67, 24 January 1738: Wesley quotes Donne's Hymne to God the Father, stanza III, ll. 1–2,

> I have a Sin of Fear, that when I've spun
> My last Thread, I shall perish on the
> Shore.

HAWKINS, SIR JOHN (1719–89). In P. A. Scholes's *The Life and Adventures of Sir John Hawkins*, Oxford, 8°, 1953, pp. 262–3: in BLO MS. Eng. poet. e. 9, *Miscellanies*, 1741, compiled by Thomas Phillibrown, f. 12, is 'Sonnet (The Canonization) imitated from Dr. Donne by Mr. J. Hawkins', with a letter from Moses Browne, 23 November 1741, commending it. Professor Milgate has noted that the MS. has a second imitation, 'Paraphrased from Dr. Donne by Mr. Foster Webb 1741'. There is another (remote) allusion to the poem in verses by Hawkins called 'On Purgatory', pp. 9–10.

THE LONDON MAGAZINE. London, 8°, 1741, June, p. 301: Prints *Song*, 'Go, catch a falling star' [*sic*], altered and adapted in 24 lines.

WILFORD, JOHN. *Memorials and Characters, Together with the Lives of Divers Eminent and Worthy Persons*, London, 1741, f°, pp. 292–3: The Character of Sir Willm Cockayne, Kt. and Alderman of London, by John Donne, D.D. and Dean of St. Paul's. With footnote: From the Sermon preach'd at St. Paul's December 12 1626; and printed with his other Sermons in Folio [*LXXX*

Sermons, no. 80, Preached at the funerals of
Sir William Cockayne Knight, Potter and
Simpson, VII, 257–78]. These extracts, in-
accurately printed, had already been used in
Clement Barksdale's *Memorials*, 1661, q.v.

BROWN, JOHN, the Revd. In Robert Dodsley's
A Collection of Poems by Several Hands,
London, 8º, 1748, 1751, vol. III, p. 333, in
'An Essay on Satire, occasioned by the Death
of Mr. POPE':

> 'Twas then plain DONNE in honest
> vengeance 'rose,
> His wit refulgent, tho' his rhyme were
> prose:
> He 'midst an age of puns and pedants
> wrote
> With genuine sense, and Roman strength
> of thought.

MASON, JOHN. In Robert Dodsley's *A Collection
of Poems by Several Hands*, London, 8º,
1748, 1751, vol. III, p. 311; in 'Musaeus a
Monody to the Memory of Mr. Pope':

> Come then that honest fame: whose sober
> ray
> Or gilds the satire, or the moral lay;
> Which dawns tho' thou, rough DONNE!
> hew out the line,
> But beams, sage HORACE! from each
> strain of thine.

FIELDING, HENRY. *The History of Tom Jones a
Foundling*, London, 1749, 6 vols., 12º,
vol. II, p. 11: The heroine, Sophia Western, is
described by a quotation from 'the celebrated
Donne's' *Second Anniversary*, ll. 244–6.

BROWNE, MOSES. In Preface, p. vi, to Walton's
Compleat Angler, London, 1750: Reference
to Donne's popularity and wit.

FREYTAG, F. G. *Analecta Literaria*, Leipzig,
1750, 8º, p. 296: Donne's *Biathanatos*, and
references.

GRAY, THOMAS. In *Essays and Criticism*, ed.
C. S. Northup, Boston and London, 1911,
pp. 37 n., 48, 175 with note on 342: Brief
references to Donne.

KIPPIS, A. *Biographica Britannica*, vol. III,
London, 1750, pp. 1724–9: Donne.

WARBURTON, WILLIAM. *The Works of Alexander Pope Esq.*, vol. IV, London, 8º, 1751,
pp. 191–227: The Satires of Dr. John

Donne Versified. With notes by Warburton
referring to Donne's text on pp. 202, 208–9,
210–11, 214.

CIBBER, THEOPHILUS. *The Lives of the Poets*,
London, 12º, 1753, I, 202–11: Dr. John
Donne. Derived largely from Walton;
quotes 'A Hymn to God the Father'.

HILL, A. *The Works of the late Aaron Hill*,
London, 1753, 8º, vol. IV, p.58: To a Lady,
who lov'd Angling, from a Hint out of Dr.
Donne [The Bait]. (See P. A. Tasch, *Notes
and Queries*, CCXVI, 1971, 464.)

MASON, WILLIAM (*c.* 1753). 'First Satire of
Dr Donne Versified' (159 lines), first printed
by D. A. Low (q.v., p. 349, *Rev. Eng. Stud.*
XVI, 1965, pp. 293–7), with annotations,
from Mason's *Commonplace Book* now in
the library of York Minster. Records in
Pembroke College, Cambridge, shew that
Mason borrowed Donne's *Poems*, 1635,
from the college library in 1753.

GAMBOLD, JOHN. *A Collection of Hymns . . . for
the Use of the Congregations In Union with
the Brethren's Church*, London, 8º, 1754.
This collection of Moravian hymns contains
two adapted from Donne: no. 383, from
Holy Sonnets I, II, XI, XIII; no. 384, from
The Litanie, stanzas 1–3. (See *Hymns Un-
bidden, Donne, Herbert, Blake, Emily
Dickinson and the Hymnographers*, by M. W.
England and John Sparrow. New York
Public Library, 1966, pp. 19–26.)

PILKINGTON, LETITIA (1712–50). *Memoirs*, 3
vols., Dublin, 12º, 1748–54. Vol. III, 1754,
pp. 150–2: Account of a mock trial convened
by Dean Swift, who invented a story of
Dr. Donne's finding a skull in a church-
yard with a nail fixed in the temple. By
means of this evidence he convicted a woman
of murdering her drunken husband. (See the
edition in The English Library with introduction by Iris Barry, London, 8º, 1928,
p. 412. See also Dr. Wordsworth in *Eccles.
Biogr.* 3rd edn. III, p. 647; J. C. Robertson,
Gent. Mag. N.S. XVI, 1841, 156, shewing
that the original authority for the story is
Heywood's *Apology for Actors*, 1612; J.
Yeowell, *Notes and Queries*, N.S. II, v, 1858,
68–9, 'Dr. Donne's discovery of a murder';

ibid. vi, 1858, 18. W. D. Macray, note on a version of the same story in BLO Rawl. MS. B. 258, where the anecdote is attributed to Dr. Airy, Provost of Queen's, 1594–1616.) The story had been repeated in *The Christian Recorder and British and Foreign Religious Intelligencer* (Glasgow), II, 1821, p. 144, 'Remarkable Discovery of a Murder'.

ANON. *The World*. No. cxxxvii. By Adam Fitz-Adam. Thursday, August 14, London, f°, 1755: Will not every man of taste admire the gaiety and good sense of Horace, the gallantry and genteel carelessness of Ovid, the fire and energy of Juvenal, and the passion of Tibullus, in paraphrases of and translations of Donne, Dryden, Garth, Congreve, and Hammond? See *Harrison's British Classics*, London, 8°, 1778, VII, p. 307.

JOHNSON, SAMUEL. *A Dictionary of the English Language*, 2 vols., London, f°, 1755. Johnson has used 384 quotations ascribed to Donne, though often misquoted or abbreviated, from Songs and Sonets (89), Elegies (56), Epithalamions (16), Satyres (51), Verse Letters (88), Anatomie of the World (36), Second Anniversary (21), Epicedes and Obsequies (17), Divine Poems (1). See A. D. Atkinson, *Notes and Queries*, CXCVI, 1951, 387–8, and W. B. C. Watkins, *Johnson and English Poetry before 1660*, Princeton, 1936, p. 80.

BIRCH, THOMAS. In *The Works of Dr. John Tillotson*, 3 vols., London, f°, 1752, with the Life of the Author by Birch, now first prefixed. Vol. I, p. vi: all the wit and learning of Dr. DONNE cannot secure his sermons from universal neglect; p. viii: His predecessors had been generally men of the greatest eminence for learning, and among these were Mr. THOMAS GATAKER . . . and Dr. JOHN DONNE, Dean of *St. Paul's*, whose *Pseudo-Martyr*, the most valuable of his prose writings, contains an unanswerable confutation of the Papal supremacy, and whose poetical works shew a prodigious fund of genius under the disguise of an affected and obscure style, and a most inharmonious versification.

GOLDSMITH, OLIVER [?]. *The Literary Magazine*, London, vol. ?, January 1758, p. ?, in an unsigned article, 'A Poetical Scale': Dr. Donne was a man of wit, but he seems to have been at pains not to pass for a poet. (Reprinted only in Goldsmith's *Works*, ed. J. W. M. Gibbs, 5 vols., London (Bohn's Standard Library), vol. IV, 1885, p. 423. Gibbs believed the article to be by Goldsmith.)

GOLDSMITH, OLIVER (?). *The Critical Review*, London, vol. VIII, August 1759, p. 91, in a review of Guicciardini's *History of Italy*, tr. by A. P. Goddard, second edn. The writer quotes a passage from Donne's *Fifty Sermons*, no. 28 (1629) on the prolixity of Guicciardini. The review was ascribed to Goldsmith in *Essays and Criticisms*, 1798, and is reprinted in Goldsmith's *Collected Works*, ed. A. Freeman, Oxford, 1966, I, 192. See Steele's *Tatler*, 1710, where the same passage was used. There is no proof of Goldsmith's authorship.

WALPOLE, HORATIO. *Book of Memoranda*, 1759. The MS., now among the Walpole collections in the library of Wilmarth S. Lewis, Farmington, Conn., contains the following notes: p. 26, 'A poem called Twickenham-gardens in Donne's, p. 22' (the reference is to Donne's *Poems*, 1650 or 1654); p. 35, 'Christiana, Countess of Devonshire. The poems of Wm. E. of Pembroke were dedicated to her, on whom many of them were written, so I think were some of Dr. Donne's'[1]; p. 66, 'Life of Dr. Donne in Winstanley's [*England's Worthies*], 377'; p. 107, 'Character of Dr. Donne. Baker's Chron. 156'.

BIRCH, T. *The Life of Henry Prince of Wales*, London, 8°, 1760, p. 367: A reference to Donne's 'Elegy on Prince Henry'.

LONDON MAGAZINE, THE, AND MONTHLY CHRONICLE MDCCLXI. London, Printed for T. Astley. June, p. 301: Song (Goe and catch a falling starre) is quoted in an altered form without comment (Go, catch a falling star . . . Prove false to *two* or *three*).

---

[1] Donne had addressed her daughters, Lady Carey and Miss Essex Rich.

STERNE, LAURENCE. *The Life and Opinions of Tristram Shandy*, vol. v, London, 8º, 1762, chapter XII, pp. 62–3: A reference to 'Eleazer's oration as recorded by *Josephus (de Bell. Judaic.)*'. This is derived from Donne's *Biathanatos*, [1647], p. 54. Chapter XVI, p. 78: 'In short, my father . . . advanced so very slow with his work, that . . . I verily believe I had put by my father, and left him drawing a sundial, for no better purpose than to be buried under ground.' The idea is derived from Donne's 'The Will',

And all your graces no more use shall have
Then a Sun dyall in a grave.

See John Ferrier, 'Comments on Sterne', *Manchester Lit. and Philos. Trans.*, 1793, repr. in *The Annual Register*, 1793, pp. 379–98, and in *Illustrations of Sterne*, London, 1798, p. 170.

[DIDEROT, DENIS]. *Encyclopédie ou dictionnaire raisonné des sciences*. Tome 15 SEN-TCH, Neufchatel, fº, 1765, pp. 640–1: In article on 'Suicide', a summary of Donne's *Biathanatos*.

GRANGER, J. *A Biographical History of England*, 2 vols., London, 4º, 1769. Vol. I, pp. 186–7: Donne as a poet, with quotation from Brown's *Essay on Satire*; p. 246: an account of Donne's *Pseudo-Martyr*, sermons and the monument in St. Paul's; p. 288: a description of the (Lothian) portrait of Donne, inscribed *Domine illumina tenebras meas* [*sic*], derived from R. B's (i.e. Badiley's) *Life of Bishop Morton*; p. 390: a reference to Donne's monument.

HURD, RICHARD. *Select Works of Mr. A. Cowley*, 2 vols., London, 8º, 1772. Vol. II, p. 117, note to 'Ode upon Liberty': Or to the sweetness of the sound or greatness of the sense. Intimating, that these two things cannot, or should not, be united in poetry. It is certain that Donne and Jonson (Cowley's great models) seemed to think so, who when they had a better thing than ordinary to say, were sure to say it in the roughest and harshest metre.

L., W. In *The Gentleman's Magazine*. By Sylvanus Urban, vol. XLII, December 1772, p. 565 n., in 'A Short Account of the several sorts of Organs used for Church Service, signed, 'Leicester, Dec. W. L.': The old organ at Lynn had on it a figure of King David playing on the harp cut in solid wood, larger than the life; likewise several moving figures which beat time &c. This is an old practice and alluded to by Dr. Donne,

As in some organs, puppets dance above
And bellows pant below, which them do
move (Satyre II, lines 15–16).

WALPOLE, HORACE. In *The Letters*, ed. Mrs. Paget Toynbee, 16 vols., Oxford, 8º, 1904. Vol. IX, 26 December 1774, letter to Hon. Henry Seymour Conway, p. 111: I am always delighted with all the honours that you receive . . . For the glorious part, I am always like the man in Pope's Donne

Then happy he who shows the tombs, said
I (The happy Man who shows the tombs!
said I. Pope's Sat. VIII, l. 102, Donne's
Sat. IV, l. 75).

JOHNSON, SAMUEL. *The Life, by James Boswell*, 2 vols., London, 4º, 1791. Vol. I, under 18 April 1775, p. 487: He [Dr. Johnson] talked of Walton's Lives, which was one of his favourite books. Dr. Donne's Life, he said, was the most perfect of them; vol. II, under 20 March 1776, p. 26: In a conversation about doing a new edition of Walton's Lives, Johnson said that, by way of adapting the book to the taste of the present age, they have, in a later edition, left out a vision which he relates Dr. Donne had, but it should be restored.

HUME, DAVID. *The History of England. A New Edition with the author's Corrections and Improvements*, 8 vols., London, 8º, 1778. Vol. VI, Appendix to the reign of James I, p. 193: In Donne's satires, when carefully inspected, there appear some flashes of wit and ingenuity; but these totally suffocated and buried by the harshest and most uncouth expression, that is any-where to be met with.

ENCYCLOPAEDIA BRITANNICA. The Second Edition, vol. IV, Edinburgh, 4º, 1779, pp. 2515b–2516a: Donne (Dr. John). An excellent poet and divine of the 17th. century . . . He had a prodigious richness of fancy, but his thoughts were much debased by his versification (reprinted in the third edition, vol. VI, Edinburgh, 1797, p. 89a–b).

JOHNSON, SAMUEL. *Prefaces, Biographical and Critical to the Works of the English Poets*, 10 vols., London, 12°, 1779, vol. I, in Preface to Cowley, p. 49: This kind of writing, which was, I believe, borrowed from Marino and his followers, had been recommended by the example of Donne, a man of very extensive and various knowledge, and by Jonson, whose manner resembled that of Donne more in the ruggedness of his verse than in the cast of his sentiments; vol. III, in Preface to Dryden, p. 203: Dryden very early formed his versification: there was in this early production no traces of Donne's or Jonson's ruggedness; but he did not so soon free his mind from the ambition of forced conceits.

REVIEWED: *Monthly Rev.* LXI, 1780, with references to Donne on p. 4.

NICHOLS, JOHN. *A Select Collection of Poems with Notes Biographical and Historical*, 8 vols., London, 8°, 1780. Vol. I, pp. 282–3, note on Thomas Carew: Wood says that he was adored by the poets of the time . . . that Donne, D'Avenant and May loved him.

WARTON, THOMAS. *The History of English Poetry*, ed. Richard Price from the edition of 1824, 3 vols., London, 8°, 1840. Vol. III, section li, p. 231: The English Poems of Sir Walter Raleigh, of John Donne, of Hugh Holland, are not easily to be mended; section lxvi, p. 456: Thomas Freeman, a student in Magdalen College, Oxford, about the year 1609, who appears to have enjoyed the friendship and encouragement of Shakespeare, Daniel, Donne, Chapman, and Heywood, the dramatist, printed in quarto *Rub and a Great Cast* . . . London, 1614 (with a note on the references to Donne; see p. 282 of the present work); p. 465: a note on Donne's Satires, with a reference to Wood's attribution of John Davies's *A Scourge for paper-persecutors*, by I. D., 4°, 1625, to Donne. (These sections were not included in the first edition, 3 vols., 4°, 1775–81, but were added in the edition of 1824.)

KNOX, VICESIMUS. *Essays Moral and Literary*. New Edition, 2 vols., London, 12°, 1782, in no. clxxiii, 'On the merits of Cowley as a poet', p. 366: He [Cowley] as well as they whom he imitated, Donne and Jonson, were unquestionably possessed of great learning and ingenuity, but they all neglected the graces of composition, and will, therefore, soon be numbered among those once celebrated writers, whose utility now consists in filling in vacancies on the upper shelf of some dusty and deserted library.

WARTON, JOSEPH. *An Essay on the Genius and Writings of Pope*, London, 1782, 2 vols., 8°, vol. I, pp. iv, xii: References to Donne in the dedication to Dr. Young; vol. II, pp. 421–5: Criticisms of Donne, with quotations from Drummond's Conversation with Ben Jonson.

Vol. I was first published in 1756.

REVIEWED: *Monthly Rev.* XIV, 1756, 535, with references to Donne.

GRAY, THOMAS. In *The Gentleman's Magazine*, vol. LIII. London, 8°, 1783, pp. 100–1, a letter from Gray to Thomas Warton concerning a design for a history of English Poetry: Part IV, Spenser, his character . . . Drayton, Fairfax . . . A Third Italian School full of conceit, begun in Queen Elizabeth's reign, continued under James and Charles the first, by Donne, Crashaw, Cleveland, carried to its height by Cowley, and ending perhaps in Sprat.

RITSON, JOSEPH. *A Select Collection of English Songs*, 3 vols., London, J. Johnson. 1783. Vol. I, pp. 257–8: Donne's 'The Message', with extensive adaptations; vol. III, 18a: a musical setting for the poem (there is no indication of the date of the setting).

OWEN, W., and JOHNSTON, W. *A New and general Biographical Dictionary*. A New Edn., 12 vols. Vol. IV, London, 8°, 1784, pp. 469–78: Donne (John). The article is derived chiefly from Walton and Wood.

BOSWELL, JAMES. *The Journal of a Tour to the Hebrides with Samuel Johnson*, London, 8°, 1785, pp. 432–3 under 23 October 1773 in a discussion of Johnson's use of the word *Quotidian*, meaning *every-day*: I imagined it

to be a word of Dr. Johnson's own invention;
but I have since found it in Dr. Young's
Night Thoughts . . . and in my friend's
Dictionary supported by the authorities of
Charles I and Dr. Donne. (Donne used the
word once only, in his Elegie on Prince
Henry, l. 7.)

HEY, RICHARD. *A Dissertation on Suicide*,
Cambridge, 8°, 1785, pp. 64–5: A discussion of Donne's *Biathanatos*, summed up as
'a confusion of ideas'.

HEADLEY, HENRY. *Select Beauties of Ancient
English Poetry*, London, 8°, 1787: References, p. xv: Introduction, with tabulation of
poets, includes Donne under 'Satyrical';
p. lvi: Biographical Sketches, Herbert, 'He
who takes up the poems of Herbert would
little suspect that he . . . had received flattery
and praise from Donne and from Bacon.'
Donne is not included among the *Select
Beauties*.

DICTIONARY. *Nouveau Dictionnaire Historique
Septième ed.* Caen & Lyon, vol. III, 1789,
pp. 331–2: Account of Donne with references to *Pseudo-Martyr* and *Biathanatos*.

COWPER, WILLIAM. *Correspondence*. Ed. T.
Wright, 4 vols., London, 8°, 1904, vol. III,
p. 435: To Mrs. Bodham, 27 February
1790, 'Add to all this, I deal much in poetry
as did our venerable ancestor, the Dean of
St. Paul's, and I think I shall have proved
myself a Donne at all points'; p. 478: To
John Johnson, 31 July 1790, 'If you have
Donne's poems bring them with you, for
I have not seen them many years, and should
like to look them over.'

ELLIS, GEORGE. *Specimens of the Early English
Poets*, London, 8°, 1790, pp. 140–1:
Donne's Song (Go and catch a falling star),
Song [Negative Love] (I never stoop'd so
low as they).

MOORE, C. *A full enquiry into the subject of
suicide*, London, 1790, 4°, vol. I, pp. 83–
103; vol. II, pp. 1–41: An examination of
Biathanatos.

BLAKE, WILLIAM. *The Note-Book of William
Blake* [facsimile edition], ed. Geoffrey
Keynes, London, The Nonesuch Press,
1935, p. 85 of the facsimile: an 'Emblem'

drawing (*c.* 1793) of the figure of Destiny,
below which is inscribed, 'Whose changeless
brow / Ne'er smiles nor frowns. / Donne.'
('The Progresse of the Soule', st. 4, ll.
35–6).

COWPER, WILLIAM. *The Poems*. Ed. J. C.
Bailey, London, 8°, 1905, in Sonnet (July
1793). To John Johnson on his presenting
me with an antique bust of Homer, p. 495:
    Be wiser thou!—like our forefather
    DONNE,
    Seek heavenly wealth, and work for God
    alone.

KIPPIS, ANDREW. *Biographia Britannica*, London, f°, 1793, v, 331–7: Donne (signed K).

RITSON, JOSEPH. *The English Anthology*, 3 vols.,
London, 8°, 1793. Vol. I, pp. 20–1: The
Baite (with note that it is 'an imitation of a
still more beautiful one by Christopher
Marlowe, beginning with the same line').

COLERIDGE, S. T. *The Notebooks*, ed. K.
Coburn, 4 vols., London, 8°, 1957. Vol. I,
no. 171 n., under ? October 1796. A pro-
jected work: A satire on Monthly Reviewers
in the manner of Donne; a proposal to write
on Dryden and the History of the witty
Logicians . . . B. Johnson, Donne, Cowley,
Pope. No. 1786 n. C. reading Donne's
'Obsequies to the Lord Harrington'; no.
1787 n. C. quotes from 'The Progress of the
Soul' and 'The Second Anniversary', l. 171;
no. 1788, cf. Donne's Verse Letter to the
Countess of Bedford; no. 1789, cf. Donne's
'To Mr. T. W.'.

MASON, WILLIAM. In *The Works*, 4 vols.,
London, 8°, 1811, I, p. 452, in a note to
'Religio Clerici . . . written in imitation of
Mr. Dryden's *Religio Laici*, 1796: I lately
re-examined it [Dryden's poem on the Death
of Lord Hastings] and find it of that species
of poetry, which Dr. Johnson calls Metaphysical, but which I should rather term
Pseudo-physical (if I had as great a licence to
coin words as the Doctor); for the Poets in
vogue at that time thought it a test of excel-
lence to combine true and natural images in
a forced, a false, and unnatural manner. In
this style Dr. Donne appears to have been
Dryden's archetype. With respect to the

Poem in question he appears to aim at rivalling him not only in false wit and false thoughts, but in prosaic phrase and unmetrical or ill-accented verse. In the former he even outstrips his master, as a young hound, got upon a wrong scent, is said by huntsmen to throw himself more out of chace than an old one.

[Gilpin, William]. *Three Dialogues on the Amusements of Clergymen. Second Edition*, London, 1797, pp. 68–73: A *jeu d'esprit* concerning a fictitious MS. of dialogues in the hand of Dr. Joseph Frampton dated 23 September 1686. In the first dialogue with Dean Stillingfleet Dr. Frampton observed, 'That skilful casuist, and able divine, Dr. Donne, I have heard was once an able angler.' Stillingfleet replied that, 'Donne you know was esteemed in the early part of his life an *incorrect* man; and I suppose you are not much acquainted with his opinion on the subject after he became a *pious divine* . . . If you could assure me that Dean Nowel or Dr. Donne (who was still an acuter man) had ever considered the art of angling with any attention in a moral light, their *Opinions* at least might have had some weight.' Not in the first edition of the *Dialogues*.

Warton, Joseph and others. *The Works of Alexander Pope* 9 vols. Vol. iv. London, 8°, 1797, pp. 251–93: The Satires of Dr. Donne Versified; the original Satires, with modernized spelling, are printed with Pope's versions opposite. There are many footnotes, some by Warton, mostly derogatory of Donne's versification—e.g. p. 290, '. . . he need not have left his numbers so *much more rugged* and *disgusting*, than many of his contemporaries' (printed also in *The Critical Review*, xxii, 1797, 16). On p. 263 *Pseudomartyr* is characterized by Warton as 'this adsurd and blasphemous trash'.

Drake, Nathan. *Literary Hours*, Sudbury and London, 8°, 1798, p. 452, in no. xxvi, following Headley's tabulation of poets (1787): As to Donne, if it be true, that the purpose of poetry should be to please, no author has written with such utter neglect of the rule. It is scarce possible for a human ear to endure the dissonance and discord of his couplets, and even when his thoughts are clothed in the melody of Pope, they appear to me hardly worth the decoration.

Cary, H. F. *Memoir by Henry Cary with his Literary Journal and Letters*, 2 vols. London, 8°, 1847. Vol. i, p. 159, under 1 March 1800: 'Read Donne's Satires &c., and Ben Jonson's translation of Horace *Ad Pisones* (no comment).'

Wordsworth, William. *Lyrical Ballads*, second edn., 2 vols., London, 8°, 1800. Vol. i, Preface, p. xi: Reference to 'the metrical language' employed by Donne and others in different eras.

1801–1900
[Arranged chronologically]

[Bliss, Phillip]. *The Gentleman's Magazine*, lxxvii, 1802 (April), 313: a note on Donne's seal of Christ crucified on an anchor, with an engraving, fig. 7, on plate II facing. Repeated in vol. iv, December 1835, p. 623.

Jeffrey, Francis. Edinburgh Review, i, 1802, 64, in a review of Southey's *Thalaba the Destroyer*, a reference to 'the quaintness of Quarles and Dr. Donne'.

Malcolm, James Peller. *Londinium Redivivum*, [?] vols., London, 4°, 1803. Vol. iii, p. 59, reference to the effigy of Donne in St. Paul's; pp. 61–2, description of the effigy 'carved by Nicholas Stone for 120 l. It stands erect, in a window, without its niche and deprived of the urn on which the feet are placed, with a further description of the state of this and other monuments. Facing p. 61 is a plate with a crude engraving of the figure. Pp. 453, 455: References to Donne as vicar of St. Dunstan's, 1624.

[Lamb, Charles] (c. 1805). *Mrs Leicester's School and Other Writings in Prose and*

Verse. Ed. Alfred Ainger, London, 1885, pp. 358–9. Criticism of Donne and Cowley (in Table-talk and Fragments of Criticism).

BOWLES, WILLIAM LISLE. *The Works of Pope*, ed. Bowles, 10 vols., London, 8°, 1806. Vol. 1, in Memoir of Pope, p. xcii: 'The obsolete satires of Donne were now versified, with the same view with which the satires of Horace were imitated, as a vehicle for personalities.'

SOUTHEY, R. *Specimens of the Later English Poets*, London, 1807, 3 vols., 8°, vol. 1, p. xxiv: 'Donne could never have become a Poet, unless Apollo, taking his ears under divine care, would have brought as miraculous a change in their internal structure, as of old he wrought in the external of that of Midas.'

WHITE, HENRY KIRKE. *Life by Robert Southey*, 2 vols., London, 1807. Vol. II, p. 284, Melancholy Hours: Donne had not music enough to render his broken rhyming couplets sufferable, and neither his wit, nor his pointed Satire were sufficient to rescue him from that neglect which his uncouth and rugged versification speedily superinduced.

LAMB, CHARLES. *Specimens of English Dramatic Poets who lived about the Time of Shakespeare. With notes*, London, 1808, 8°, pp. 363–5, in a note upon Beaumont and Fletcher's *Philaster*: Donne has a copy of verses addressed to his mistress . . . It is so earnest, so weighty, so rich in poetry, in sense, in wit and pathos that I have thought fit to insert it, as a solemn close in future to all such sickly fancies as he there deprecates (followed by Donne's *Elegie* XVI). Reprinted in a revised form in Lamb's *Works*, London, 1818. See *Works*, ed. T. Hutchinson, Oxford, 1908, I, 71–2.

SCOTT, SIR WALTER. *The Works of Dryden*, ed. Scott, with Life of the Author, 18 vols., London, 8°, 1808. Vol. 1, pp. 10–17: Remarks on the metaphysical poets with references to Donne's relations with James I and Charles I; pp. 46–8: references to the poetry of Donne and Cowley and their gradual superseding by the Restoration poets.

COLERIDGE, S. T. In *Inquiring Spirit. A New*

Presentation of Coleridge, by K. Coburn, London, 1951. Memoranda by Coleridge, pp. 29–30, with quotation from Donne's 'Eclogue, 1613', and editor's note on p. 415 pointing out that the quotation does not appear with the same passage in *The Friend*, 1809–10; p. 153, memorandum about 'a History of English Poetry', and on 'Dryden and the History of the witty Logicians—Butler, B. Johnson, Donne, Cowley, Pope', with editor's note on p. 424.

COLERIDGE, S. T. *Miscellaneous Criticism*, ed. T. M. Raysor, London, 1936. Passages on Donne, pp. 131–2: marginalia from *Literary Remains*, 1836–8; pp. 133–45: marginalia from *The Literary World* on poems and letters; p. 67: in notes on Beaumont and Fletcher, 'Read even Donne's Satires as he meant them to be read and as the sense and passion demand, and you will find in the lines a manly harmony'; p. 184: a reference to an image in Milton's *Ode on the Morning of Christ's Nativity*, 'Dante would have written it, tho' it is most in the spirit of Donne.'

COLERIDGE, S. T. *On the Seventeenth Century*, ed. R. F. Brinkley, Duke University Press, 1955. Including Coleridge's notes and marginalia on Donne (see index).

COLERIDGE, S. T. *The Literary Remains*, ed. H. N. Coleridge, 4 vols., London, 8°, Pickering, 1836–8. Vol. 1, pp. 148–50: 'Lecture X, on Donne, Dante, Milton', but nothing remains of this lecture. The editor gives instead Coleridge's notes on Donne's poetry written in a volume of Chalmers's *English Poets*, 1810, belonging to Gilman, preceded by Coleridge's quatrain on Donne ('With Donne, whose muse on dromedary trots, etc.'), and 9 lines by another hand. Vol. III (1838), pp. 92–156, Coleridge's notes on Donne written in a copy of *LXXX Sermons*, now in HCL. See also Coleridge, Derwent, 1853, *Literary World*, 1853, and Brinkley, R. F., 1955.

COLERIDGE, S. T. In *The Literary World*, vol. XII, New York, 1853. Coleridge's Marginalia were printed at pp. 349–50 (30 April), 393 (14 May), 433 (28 May). Except for a few short passages they had already appeared in *Notes Theological, Political and Miscellaneous*, 1853. See *Coleridge's Miscellaneous Criticism*, ed. T. M. Raysor, 1936.

COLERIDGE, S. T. *The Literary World*, vol. xii, January–July 1853, N.Y., 1853. Pp. 349–50, 393, 433: MS. notes of S. T. Coleridge in Charles Lamb's books, sold at auction in New York 'a few years ago [4 October 1848] now for the first time published', Notes in Donne's *Poems* dated at the end 2ᵈ May 1811.

LAMB, CHARLES. *The Reflector*, 2 vols., London, 8°, 1811. No. lv, article xiii, specimens from the writings of Fuller, p. 349, in a note on an extract from *Church History*: 'Thus Donne and Cowley, by happening to possess more wit and faculty of illustration than other men, are supposed to have been incapable of nature or feeling, ... in the very thickest of their conceits,—in the bewildering maze of their tropes and figures, a warmth of soul and generous feeling shines through ... I think the injustice which has been done to [Fuller] in the denial that he possesses any other qualities than those of a quaint and conceited writer, is of the same kind as that with which those two great Poets have been treated.'

BRYDGES, SIR EGERTON. *The Poems of Sir Walter Raleigh*, Lee Priory Press, 4°, 1813, p. 67, note on Raleigh's poem, 'Come, live with me, and be my dear': Dr. Donne has also given an imitation of this poem, which he calls 'The Bait' ... It is full of pitiful conceits, which shew that Donne had no taste for fine poetry, nor any conception wherein the beauty of this piece consisted.

BRYDGES, SIR EGERTON. *Restituta*, London, 1814, 4 vols., 8°, vol. I, pp. 225–6: Reference to the Miscellany Epigrams (see p. 94 of the present work); vol. II, pp. 9–10, vol. III, p. 2: Opinions of Donne's poetry; vol. II, pp. 426–7: Extracts from Lord Herbert's 'Elegy for Doctor Dunn'.

DISRAELI, ISAAC. *Quarrels of Authors*, 3 vols., London, 1814, 8°. Pp. 231: Reference to Davenant's 'The Incomparable Poem of Gondibert vindicated from the Wit-Combats of Four Esquires: Clinias, Dametus, Sancho and Jack-Pudding', with footnote: It is said there were four Writers. The Clinias and Dametus were probably Sir John Denham and Dr. Donne: Sir Allan Broderick and Will Crofts appear to be the Sancho and Jack-Pudding.

LOFFT, CAPEL, the Elder. *Laura: or An Anthology of Sonnets*, 5 vols., London, 12°, 1814. Vol. v, sonnets nos. 830 (To E. of D.), 831 (To Mr. S.B.), 916 (Holy Sonnet I). The index in vol. I erroneously lists no. 922 as Donne's.

EMERSON, R. W. *The Letters*, ed. R. L. Rusk, 6 vols., New York, 1939. Vol. I, p. 10, in a letter of 1815 to William Emerson, a reference to lines by Donne quoted in Johnson's Life of Cowley with comment, 'This is old fashioned Poetry. I should like to see the Poem it was taken from.'

FERRIAR, J. *An Essay towards a Theory of Apparitions*, London, 8°, 1813, p. 63: Donne's vision of his wife attributed to his writing the farewell poem.

G., A. F. *Bibliotheca Anglo-Poetica, a Catalogue of a Collection of Early English Poetry*, London, roy. 8°, 1815, pp. 78–9 (nos. 197–204), a list of editions of Donne's poems; pp. 27–8 (no. 63), *Donne's Satyr*, 1662 (J.D., jr.).

GIFFORD, W. *The Works of Ben Jonson*, 9 vols., London, 1816. Vol. I, pp. lxv–vi, gives the first (probably erroneous) reference to Jonson's meeting at the Mermaid in Friday-street with 'Shakespeare, Martin, Donne, and many others, whose names, even at this distant period, call up a mingled feeling of reverence and respect'. Repr. in 1853.

COLERIDGE, S. T. *Biographia Literaria*, 2 vols., London, 8°, 1817. Vol. I, p. 23, reference to the pure English of Donne and Cowley; vol. II, p. 75, reference to Donne's Style; pp. 87–8, reference to, and quotation from, his 'Progress of the Soul'.

DRAKE, NATHAN. *Shakespeare and his Times*, 2 vols., London, 4°, 1817. Vol. I, p. 615: John Donne D.D.—a brief account. 'Wit he has in abundance, and even erudition, but they are miserably misplaced; and even his amatory pieces exhibit little else than cold conceits and metaphysical subtleties', etc. Cf. pp. 667, 734.

AUSTEN, HENRY. *Northanger Abbey and Persuasion*, by Jane Austen, 4 vols., London, 12º, 1818. Vol. I, p. 10 in 'Biographical Notice of the Author', unsigned, but by Henry Austen, the author's brother: 'It might with truth be said, that her eloquent blood spoke through her modest cheek.' Cf. Donne's *Second Anniversary*, 1612, ll. 244–5, '. . . her pure, and eloquent blood / Spoke in her cheekes.'

COLERIDGE, S. T. *Collected Letters*, ed. E. L. Griggs. Vol. IV, p. 824: in a letter to H. F. Cary, 30 January 1818, a reference to his 'lecture on Donne, Dante and Milton' on 27 February.

HAZLITT, WILLIAM. *Lectures on the English Poets*, London, 8º, 1818. Lecture IV, On Dryden and Pope, p. 163: 'Of Donne I know nothing but some beautiful verses to his wife, dissuading her from accompanying him on his travels abroad, and some quaint riddles in verse, which the Sphinx could not unravel.' See *Works*, ed. P. P. Howe, vol. V, 1930, p. 83.

HAZLITT, WILLIAM. *Lectures on the English Comic Writers* [delivered 1818], London, 8º, 1819. Lecture III, On Cowley, Butler, Suckling, Etheredge, etc., pp. 93–100, 108, references to Donne: 'Donne, Davies, Crashaw, and others, not merely mistook learning for poetry—they thought anything was poetry that differed from ordinary prose and the natural impression of things, by being intricate, far-fetched, and improbable', etc. See *Works*, ed. P. P. Howe, vol. VI, 1931, pp. 49–53.

CAMPBELL, THOMAS. *Specimens of the British Poets and an Essay on English Poetry*, 7 vols., London, 8º, 1819. Vol. I, in 'An Essay', pp. 201, 233: References to Donne. Vol. III, pp. 73–9: a brief account of Donne ('The life of Donne is more interesting than his poetry'), with four poems.

HUNT, LEIGH. *The Correspondence*, ed. Thornton Hunt, 2 vols., London, 1862. Vol. I, pp. 148–9: In a letter to P. B. Shelley, 20 September 1819, describing Donne's relations with his wife and quoting parts of Elegie XVI, On his Mistris, '[Donne] was one of those over-mystical-headed men, who can find out connections between everything and anything, and allowed himself at *last* to become a Clergyman, after he had (to my convictions at least) been as free and deep a speculator in morals as yourself.'

COLLIER, J. PAYNE. *The Poetical Decameron*, London, 1820, 2 vols, 8º, vol. I, pp. 153–60: In the Third Conversation, discussion of Donne and his poetry; vol. II, p. 108: Donne's reference to fishing in 'The Progresse of the Soule'.

AIKIN, LUCY (Mrs. Barbauld). *Memoirs of the Court of King James the First*, 2 vols., London, 8º, 1822. Vol. I, p. 76, refers to 'the occasional pieces of Spenser, of Jonson, of Donne'.

D., M. M. *The European Magazine*, vol. LXXXII, London, 1822, pp. 44–8, 108–12: Essay on the Genius of Cowley, Donne and Clieveland.

[SPENCE, J.]. *Retrospective Rev.* VIII, 1823, 31–55: Donne's Poems (with many specimens).

LAMB, CHARLES. *Letters*, ed. E. V. Lucas, 3 vols., London, 1935. Vol. II, p. 421, in a letter to Bernard Barton, 24 March 1824, is a reference to Donne's 'admirable poem on the Metempsychosis' (The Progress of the Soule, l. 55).

HAZLITT, WILLIAM. *The Plain Speaker*, London, 8º, 1826, Essay IV, [On the Conversation of Authors] The Same Subject Continued, pp. 80–1: 'But with what a gusto would he [Lamb] describe his favourite authors, Donne, or Sir Philip Sidney, and call their most crabbed passages *delicious!*' See *Works*, ed. P. P. Howe, vol. XII, 1931, p. 36.

HAZLITT, W. *New Monthly Mag.* part I, 1826, p. 33. In the essay 'Of persons one would wish to have seen', reference to Donne with quotations from 'Epithalamion on St Valentine's Day', st. VII, and 'On his Mistris'. Reprinted in *Literary Remains*, II, 1836, pp. 337–9. The essay was based on a conversation held with Lamb and others about 1805. See *Works*, ed. P. P. Howe, vol. XVII, 1931, pp. 124–5.

[HARE, J. and A.] *Guesses at Truth by Two Brothers*, 2 vols., London, 8⁰, 1827. Vol. I, p. 4, quotes from Donne's Satyre III, ll. 5–11.

HOOD, THOMAS. *Whims and Oddities*. Second Series, London, 8⁰, 1827, p. 128: In 'A Marriage procession', Hood quotes Donne's line, 'Here lyes a shee Sunne, and a hee Moone here' (An Epithalamion or marriage Song on the Lady Elizabeth, l. 85) in the form 'a he-moon here and a she-sun there', without acknowledgement.

MONTGOMERY, JAMES. *The Christian Poet*, Glasgow, 8⁰, 1827, pp. 116–17: Three poems by Donne, 'Author of many heterogenous compositions in verse, so harsh as to be scarcely readable and so obscure as to be scarcely intelligible, yet abounding with shrewd remarks, elaborate wit, and caustic sarcasm'.

DE QUINCEY, T. *Blackwood's Edinburgh Magazine*, XXIV, July–December 1828. Edinburgh and London, 1828. In an unsigned review of Richard Whateley's *Elements of Rhetoric*, Oxford, 1828 (pp. 885–908), pp. 892–3: '. . . the first very eminent rhetorician in English is Donne . . . Few writers have shewn a more extraordinary compass of powers than Donne, for he combined what no other man has ever done—the last sublimation of dialectical subtlety and address with the most impassioned majesty.'

EMERSON, R. W. *The Journals and Miscellaneous Notebooks*, ed. W. H. Gilman (and others), 7 vols., Cambridge, Mass., 1963. Vol. III, pp. 165, 180, 181 (1829): References to, and quotations from, Donne's Sermons; vol. IV, p. 337 (1834): quotation from *An Anatomy of the World*, ll. 317–18; p. 291: quotations from Eclogue, 26 December 1613; vol. V, p. 148: reference to Sermons; pp. 339–41 (1837): quotations from poems; p. 342: reference to Donne as a philosopher; vol. VI, pp. 88, 103, 386: references to Donne; vol. VII, pp. 5, 53, 151 n., 163, 501: references to Donne.

LANDOR, W. S. *Imaginary Conversations. The fifth volume*, London: James Duncan, 1829, 8⁰, pp. 525–48. Conversation XII. 'Izaac Walton, Cotton, and William Oldways'. Walton gives an account of Donne's love affairs and marriage. (In Landor's *Works*, 2 vols., 1853, vol. I, pp. 274–6.)

WOOD, WILLIAM PAGE, BARON HATHERLEY. *A Memoir*, ed. W. R. W. Stephens, 2 vols., London, 1883. Vol. I, p. 175, under 29 June 1829: 'In the evening with B. Montagu to Coleridge's. He had been siezed with a fit of enthusiasm for Donne's poetry, which I think somewhat unaccountable. There was great strength, however, in some passages which he read. One stanza . . . on the "Progress of the Soul" struck me very much; it was, I think, the fourth in which he addresses "Destiny" as the "Knot of all Causses". The rest of the poem seemed the effusion of a man very drunk or very mad.'

WORDSWORTH, W. *The Letters. The Later Years*, 1821–30, 2 vols., ed. E. de Selincourt, London, 1939. Vol. I, p. 469: 'I have been trying my skill upon one of Dr. Donne's [sermons], which I hope to make something of'; vol. II, p. 652: in a letter to Alexander Dyce, urging him to include in his book Donne's Sonnet, 'Death be not proud', 'so weighty in thought and vigorous in the expression'. See under Dyce, p. 316.

COLLIER, J. PAYNE. *The History of English Dramatic Poetry*, 3 vols., London, 1831. Vol. II, pp. 431–3, footnote concerning a MS. containing 'Divine Meditations', seventeen sonnets by Dr. Alablaster, together with sermons by Donne, King, etc. (This is now identified as the Merton MS. as in the list on p. 29 of the present work, though it no longer contains Alablaster's sonnets.)

GODWIN, W. *Thoughts on Man*, London, 8⁰, 1831, p. 4: 'I cannot avoid quoting here the most deep-thinking and philosophical of our poets', with Donne's *Second Anniversarie*, ll. 243–6; pp. 83–4: an account of Donne's poetry—'One of the most admired of our English poets about the close of the sixteenth century. . . . not one in an hundred even among persons of cultivation, can give any account of him, if in reality they ever heard of his productions.'

HUNT, LEIGH. *The Tatler*, no. 24, London, 26 February 1831. In a review of Alfred Tennyson's *Poems, Chiefly Lyrical*, 1830, Hunt compares the poem, 'Tears of Heaven', with Donne's writing. See *Leigh Hunt's Literary Criticism*, ed. L. H. Houtchens and others, New York, 1956, p. 358.

JAMESON, Mrs. A. M. *Memoirs of the Loves of the Poets*, London, 1831, 8º, vol. II, pp. 94–109: The Story of Dr Donne and his Wife.

COLERIDGE, S. T. *Notes, Theological, Political and Miscellaneous*, ed. Derwent Coleridge, London, Moxon, 1833. Pp. 249–61: Notes on Donne's Poems (Versification, The Triple Fool ver. 15, Songs and Sonnets, The Good Morrow, Woman's Constancy, The Sun's Rising, The Indifferent, Canonization, A Fever, The Extasy, The Primrose), notes on Donne's Letters, notes on the Elegies upon Dr. Donne.

DYCE, ALEXANDER. *Specimens of English Sonnets*, London, Pickering, 16º, 1833, p. 108: Donne's Sonnet, 'Death be not proud', with comment on p. 214, 'Deep-thoughted and forcible'.

PHILLIPS, SIR THOMAS, R. A. *Lectures on the History and Principles of Painting*, London, 8º, 1833, p. 40: In Lecture I at the Royal Academy, Phillips compares the paintings by Giotto at Assisi and Padua with poetry: 'It is as the poetry of Chaucer or of Donne, with their uncouth phraseology, full of sense and sentiment.'

STEINMAN, G. S. *The Gentleman's Magazine*, N.S., vols. I, III, and IV, London, 1834–5. Vol. I, p. 512: A letter signed G. S. S. concerning Alleyn's marriage to Constance Donne; vol. III, pp. 610–11: a letter on 'The Family of Dr. Donne'; vol. IV, p. 150, a letter on the same.

TAYLOR, SIR HENRY. *Autobiography*, 2 vols., London, 1885: Reference to Donne's poems with quotations, vol. I, p. 183 (1834), pp. 273, 288 (1838).

BARKER, E. H. *The Constitutional Magazine and Literary Review*, August–November 1835. Nos. I–IV, pp. 156–7, Specimens of Wit and Wisdom, Eloquence and Learning from the Old Vintage: Donne's Paradoxes, IV and IX (from the edn. of 1652, pp. 13, 26).

COLERIDGE, S. T. *Specimens of the Table Talk*, 2 vols., 2nd edn., London, 1836. Vol. I, p. 88: 'Compare [Taylor] in this particular with Donne, and you will feel the difference in a moment. Why are not Donne's volumes reprinted at Oxford?' With editor's footnote in support.

HOUSMAN, R. F. *A Collection of English Sonnets*, London, [1835]. With two sonnets by Donne.

NEWMAN, J. H. *Tracts for the Times*, vol. III for 1835–6, new edn., London, 1839. No. 76, pp. 12–13: 'The water of baptism', referring to Donne's sermon xxi, i.e. *LXXX Sermons*, 1640, p. 201 (Simpson and Potter, *Sermons*, vol. VII, Berkeley, 1954, p. 94).

ST. JOHN, J. A. In *Friendship's Offering*, London, 12º, 1835, p. 321, quotes Donne's Elegie XVI, 'On his Mistris', ll. 53–4, as motto for a story, 'Hell's Hollow'.

CUNNINGHAM, G. G. *Lives of Eminent and illustrious Englishmen*, London, 1836, 8º, vol. III, p. 242: John Donne.

HALL, S. C. *The Book of Gems. The Poets and Artists of Great Britain*, 3 vols., London, 8º, 1836. Vol. I, pp. 122–3: An account of Donne; pp. 123–31: a selection of 10 poems, headed by an engraved vignette by W. Miller after S. Prout illustrating 'The Storm'. On p. [xix] is a facsimile of Donne's signature with those of other poets.

LANDOR, WALTER SAVAGE. *A Satire on Satirists*, London, 8º, 1836, p. 15: Churchmen have chaunted satire, and the pews / Heard good sound doctrine from the sable Muse. / Frost-bitten and lumbaginous, when Donne, / With verses gnarl'd and knotted, hobbled on. See *Landor's Complete Works*, ed. S. Wheeler, vol. XVI, London, 1936, p. 220.

[WILMOTT, R. A.]. *Conversations at Cambridge*, London, 1836, 8º, pp. 15–16: 'Langhorne and Donne' (I think you will find the original of Langhorne's celebrated line—

The child of misery baptized in tears,

in Donne's Sermon on the First Epistle to

the Thessalonians . . . Donne's poetry must be sought in his prose . . .).

See Sermon 50, Thes. 5. 16, *Fifty Sermons*, 1649, p. 466.

ANON. In *The Penny Cyclopaedia of the Society for the Diffusion of Useful Knowledge*, London, 1837, vol. IX: Article 'John Donne'.

ANON. *The Quarterly Review*, vol. LIX, London, 1837. On p. 6, in a review of Coleridge's *Literary Remains*, there are remarks on Coleridge's criticism of Donne's poetry and sermons, with a plea for an Oxford reprint of the sermons.

HALLAM, H. *Introduction to the Literature of Europe*, 4 vols., London, 8º, 1837–9. Vol. II, p. 316: References to Donne's Satires; vol. III, pp. 124–5: comments on Donne's sermons and opinions; pp. 491–3: Donne as founder of the metaphysical poetry, 'the most inharmonious of our versifiers, etc.'.

BARRETT, E. B. [BROWNING]. *The Seraphim and other poems*, London, 8º, 1838, p. 354: The author uses Donne's Holy Sonnet XII, l. 9 (Weaker I am, woe's me) as motto for her poem, 'The Weakest Thing'.

[LEWES, G. H.]. *The National Magazine and Monthly Critic*, London, 1838, vol. II, pp. 373–8: Unsigned article, 'Retrospective Reviews, no. vii. Donne's Poetical Works'— 'That Donne's poems are not poems at all, may be very readily granted, but they are a very pleasant repertory of thought, wit, fancy and conceits, and therefore worthy to be read.' He mentions borrowing from Leigh Hunt his annotated copy of Donne's poems.

BELL, ROBERT. *Cabinet of Biography. Eminent Literary and Scientific Men. English Poets*, 2 vols., London, 8º, 1839. Vol. I, pp. 50–2, in an account of Cowley, there is criticism of Donne, and quoting Theobald (see p. 305).

ANON. *The Gentleman's Magazine*, N.S. XVI, London, 1841, 15–18: references to Alleyn's marriage to Constance Donne in a review of J. P. Collier's *Memoirs of Edward Alleyn*, London, 1841.

[CATTERMOLE, R.]. *Gems of Sacred Poetry.* (*British Sacred Poets*), 2 vols. [London, 8º, 1841]. Vol. I, pp. 86–90: a brief account of Donne, with four Sacred Sonnets and three other poems.

[CATTERMOLE, R.]. *Gems of Sacred Literature*, 2 vols. [London, 8º, 1841]. Vol. I, pp. 14–18: A short note on Donne with quotations from three sermons.

DUYCKINCK, E. A. *Arcturus*, N.Y., II, 1841, pp. 19–26: Dr. Donne.

EMERSON, R. W. *Essays*, ed. T. Carlyle, London, 1841. In the essay 'Love' quotes, p. 176, the Palatine Epithalamion, ll. 202–3; p. 185, The Second Anniversarie, ll. 244–6. Reprinted from the original American edition. See *Works*, ed. E. W. Emerson, 1903, II, 175, 184.

ROBERTSON, J. C. *The Gentleman's Magazine*, N.S. XVI, London, 1841, pp. 25–32: 'Notes on the Life and Works of Dr. Donne', an interesting attempt to correct some of the mistakes in Walton's *Life*; on p. 30 is a note that Walton's image of Donne preaching 'like an angel from a cloud' is derived from Donne's poem 'To Mr. Tilman after he had taken orders' (As Angels out of clouds from Pulpits speak); pp. 154–6: a supplementary note on Alleyn's marriage to Constance Donne and on the Pilkington anecdote (see p. 306).

ANON. *Book of the Poets*, 2 vols., London, 1842, I, p. xxiii, in 'Essay on English Poetry': Dr. Donne also, who was contemporary with Davies, was a poet of great strength and deep piercing wit, but of studied obscurity, who seems to have delighted in puzzling his readers, and setting all their faculties upon the stretche; pp. 49–50: '. . . His poems, which are of a miscellaneous character, suggested by the impulse of the moment rather than the result of systematic study, consist chiefly of satires, elegies, songs and sonnets; and although his versification is frequently harsh, and his language pedantic, yet his productions possess an innate vigour and freshness which will always secure them a high rank in our English poetry.' Followed by three poems: 'His Picture', 'The Dissolution', 'Sonnet' (Holy Sonnet XIII). (Reviewed by Eliz. B. Browning, *Athenaeum*, June–August 1842, but no mention of Donne; p. 797: 'We have said nothing of the metaphysical poets because we disclaim the classification.')

BROGDEN, JAMES. *Illustrations of the Liturgy and Ritual of the Church of England*, 3 vols., London, 8º, 1842. Vol. III, p. ix: Brief biographical details of Donne; pp. 161–82: his sermon on Hosea 2: 19 (*Fifty Sermons*, no. 3).

BROWNING, E. B. *The Greek-Christian Poets and the English Poets*, London, 1863. Reference in the section headed 'The Book of the Poets', p. 145: 'Donne, who takes his place naturally in this new class, having a dumb angel, and knowing more noble poetry than he articulates'. The essay was first printed in *The Athenaeum*, 1842, being 'occasioned by publication of *The Book of the Poets*, a compilation of the day'.

THOREAU, H. D. *Life*, by F. B. Sanborn, Boston and New York, 1917, p. 274, Thoreau's view of Donne: 'Not a poet, but a man of strong sense, etc.', from his Journal, 1843 (see Thoreau's *Writings*, Boston, 1906, VII, 467).

CATTERMOLE, R. *The Literature of the Church of England*, 2 vols., London, 8º, 1844. Vol. I, pp. 118–45: An account of Donne, with a list of his works and Sermon on Acts 28: 6 (*LXXX Sermons*, no. 48).

CHAMBERS, ROBERT. *Cyclopaedia of English Literature*, 2 vols., London, roy. 8º, 1844. Vol. I, pp. 109–12: An account of Donne and a selection from the poems and Satires, with a wood engraving of his effigy in a state of neglect in St. Paul's (as described by Malcolm, 1803). Ed. of 1876, vol. I, pp. 97–9: the same with some revision and changes in the selection of poems.

CRAIK, G. L. *Sketches of the History of Literature and Learning in England*, London, 1845, vol. III, pp. 168–74: Donne.

HALLAM, H. *Introduction to the Literature of Europe. Second edition*, London, 1845, 8º, vol. II, pp. 129, 358, vol. III, pp. 20, 32. References to Donne.

[PATMORE, COVENTRY]. *Lowe's Edinburgh Magazine*, vol. I, June–October, Edinburgh. 1846, pp. 228–36. Unsigned article: Gallery of Poets. No. I. John Donne. Biographical and critical, probably by Patmore.

FARR, E. *Select Poetry Chiefly Sacred of the Reign of James I*, Cambridge, 8º, 1847. P. xii: A short note on Donne; pp. 8–22: the Holy Sonnets and other poems.

ROGERS, W. H. *Spiritual Conceits, Illustrated*, London, 1847. An anthology with emblematic drawings. Quotes, p. 26: The Present (Holy Sonnets, v); p. 128: The Crosse, ll. 15 ff.; p. 208: a brief note on Donne's poetry.

HUNT, LEIGH. *The Town*, 2 vols., London, 1848, II, pp. 45–50: Donne and the Drurys.

LANGFORD, J. A. *The Literature of Working Men* (a supplement to *The Working Man's Friend*), London, 1850–1, December 1850, pp. 18–21: 'An Evening with Donne', with quotations. Reprinted in *Discussions of John Donne*, ed. F. Kermode, 1967.

DE QUINCEY, T. *Collected Writings*, ed. D. Masson, Edinburgh, 1890, p. 110, in an essay, 'Lord Carlisle on Pope': 'In Marston and Donne (a man yet unappreciated) Satire first began to respire freely.' This first appeared in *Tate's Magazine*, vol. for April–July, 1851 (not verified).

GILFILLAN, G. *The Book of British Poesy*, London, 1851, p. xx: Donne and the metaphysicals; pp. 147–9: two poems (Valediction, The Will).

DON, LOUIS. *Notes and Queries*, VI, 1852, 273–4: A query about Donne's family.

COLERIDGE, DERWENT. *Notes on the English Divines by S. T. Coleridge*, 2 vols., London, 1853. Vol. I, pp. 65–120: Notes on Donne [from *LXXX Sermons*].

LITERARY WORLD, New York, XII, 1853, pp. 349–50: Coleridgiana II [on Donne's sermons]; pp. 393: Coleridgiana III: Coleridge on Donne's Letters; p. 435: Coleridgiana IV [on Donne's poems].

SIMPSON, W. SPARROW. *Notes and Queries*, N.S. II, I, 1856, 205: Under 'Suffolk Notes', Local Tradition. Epitaph by Dr. Donne for Elizabeth Drury. See *Proc. of Suffolk Inst. of Archeol.*, Bury St. Edmunds, 1855.

ANON. *Putnam's Monthly Magazine*, vol. VII, April 1856: Reference in a review of books by Robert Browning, p. 372: 'Browning's poetry is certainly very hard reading, like Cowley's or Donne's. But the difference between him and such obscurists is, that with the earlier poets, both the style and the sentiment were equally conceits—while Browning's style is the naturally quaint form of a subtle and sinewy thought' (this is probably the first comparison of Donne with Browning).

EMERSON, R. W. *English Traits*, London, 1911, pp. 176, 179: References to Donne's prose and verse style (1856).

GILFILLAN, G. *The Poetical Works of Richard Crashaw*, Edinburgh and London, 1857, pp. xv–xvii: References to Donne.

Y., J. *Notes and Queries*, n.s. II, IV, 1857, 49: A query about the whereabouts of Donne's Will. Answered, pp. 175–6, by J. O., but giving the Will of John Donne jr.

B., B. *Notes and Queries*, n.s. II, VIII, 1859, 170: A query as to the owner of Donne's seal given to George Herbert, with an editorial footnote saying that it belonged to Walton and later to H. A. Merewether and Dr. Bliss of Oxford. Answered, p. 216, by M. T. Ellacombe, giving a letter from Phillip Bliss, who saw the seal and wrote about it in *The Gentleman's Magazine* (see under 1802); he also knew of one belonging to Mr. Domeville Wheeler of Badham, from which Tassie of Leicester Square had made a glass seal.

[PALGRAVE, F. T.]. *The Passionate Pilgrim or Eros and Anteros*, by Henry J. Thurstan, London, 1858, p. 68, quotes inaccurately 'A Funeral Elegie', ll. 61–2. Palgrave's opinions of Donne are collected in K. Tillotson's 'Donne's Poetry in the Nineteenth Century', q.v.

DONE, LOUIS ap. *Notes and Queries*, n.s. II, VII, 1859, 36: A query about families named Donne. Answered, p. 241, by letters from T. Jones and J. Donne about the Donnes of Radnorshire and Norfolk.

GILFILLAN, G. *Specimens with Memoirs of the Lesser-known British Poets*, 3 vols., Edinburgh and London, 1860, I, pp. 201–29: Memoir of Donne, with Holy Sonnets and The progress of the Soul.

ALFRED, LORD TENNYSON. *A Memoir by His Son* [H. Tennyson], 2 vols., London, 1897. Vol. II, p. 503, in 'Personal Recollections by F. T. Palgrave and Criticisms on Books': 'From Donne he would quote the "Valediction forbidding Mourning", the last four stanzas . . . where the poet compares himself to the moving leg, his love to the central, of the compass when describing a circle: praising its wonderful ingenuity.'

CRAIK, G. L. *Compendious History of English Literature*, London, 1861, 8°, vol. I, pp. 551–6, 584: Donne.

FITZGERALD, E. *Letters & Literary Remains*, ed. W. A. Wright, 7 vols., London, 1903. Vol. II, p. 132, in a letter to E. B. Cowell, 7 December 1861: 'I always said about Cowley, Donne, &c., whom Johnson calls the metaphysical Poets, that their very Quibbles of Fancy showed a power of Logic which could follow Fancy through such remote Analogies.'

PALGRAVE, F. T. *The Quarterly Review*, vol. cx, London, 1861. In an unsigned review of *Bell's British Poets*, 29 vols., London, pp. 449–50: References to 'the far-sought conceits and allusions, the strange phraseology are no peculiarities of Donne and Cowley'; p. 456: 'Donnes [fancies are] the frost-work ingenuities of the intellect.'

THOMPSON, Mrs. K. B. *Celebrated Friendships*, London, 1861, vol. I, pp. 297 ff.: Magdalene Herbert and Dr. Donne.

ANON. *Temple Bar*, III, 1861, pp. 78 ff.: The metaphysician.

ARNOLD, T. *A Manual of English Literature*, London, 1862: References, pp. 88, 103, to Donne and Andrewes as 'the chief writers of the Episcopalian party' and 'deeply versed in ecclesiastical literature'; pp. 116–18: 'Donne and Cowley gave in to the prevailing fashion and instead of simple natural images, studded their poems with *conceits* (concetti).'

CLOUDESLEY: *Notes and Queries*, n.s. III, I, 1862, 370: A query about the portrait of Donne in his shroud, given to Henry King.

SAGE, E. J. *Notes and Queries*, n.s. III, II, 1862, 344–5: Entries relating to clergymen in the parish registers of Barking, co. Essex—'1631

Jan. 28. Widdow Ranford, Dr. Donne's mother', with editorial note on Donne's relations with his mother (Elizabeth Rainsford).

G., A.B. *Notes and Queries*, N.S. III, II, 1862, p. 295: A note on the copy of *Biathanatos* given by John Donne, jr., to Sir Constantine Huygens with a letter of 'Julie 29 1649' (see p. 115).

CHESSBOROUGH. *Notes and Queries*, N.S. III, III, 1863, 308: Query on the date of Donne's *Collected Poems*, Chambers's *Cyclopaedia of Eng. Lit.* having stated that Tonson's edition of 1719 was the first, with editorial note on the editions, including 1633 with portrait by Lombart.

COLLIER, J. P. *Notes and Queries*, N.S. III, III, 1863, 336: Note on editions of Donne's poems. He believed that some of Donne's Satires had been printed by 1614 from a passage in a letter, but knew of no such edition. He had never seen Lombart's portrait prefixed to the *Poems* of 1633, but owned a print of Marshall's portrait struck off in quarto in that edition.

CPL. [T. R. O'Flaherty]. *Notes and Queries*, N.S. III, III, 1863, 307: A query whether John Donne, jr., ever held the Rectory of Martinsthorpe, co. Rutland, with editorial note that Ufford, co. Northants., was probably meant.

CPL. [T. R. O'Flaherty]. *Notes and Queries*, N.S. III, IV, 1863, 149: A query about the letters of John Donne, jr., with an editorial note about letters sold at Puttick & Simpson's, 19 December 1853 (lot 36, 5s.) and Sotheby's, 3 August 1858 (lot 39, 4s.); the latter resold by Puttick & Simpson's, 28 April 1859. By the same, p. 150: a reference to Jonson's 'Pucelle of the Court', who was perhaps Mrs. Bulstrode, a lady in waiting, with editorial note that it had been surmised that she was 'the concealed subject of much of Donne's light verse', and references to the letters and poems (see Bald, p. 178).

G[ROSART], A. B. *Notes and Queries*, N.S. III, IV, 1863, 295: Note on a copy of *Biathanatos* in his possession given by John Donne, jr., to Huygens with a letter dated 29 Julie 1649. See under *Biathanatos*, p. 115.

CUNNINGHAM, G. G. *The English Nation*, 5

vols., Edinburgh and London, 1863–8. Vol. II, pp. 428–30: John Donne (biographical and critical).

HARPER, J. A. *Notes and Queries*, N.S. III, IV, 1863, 198–9: A note on the identity of Mrs. Bulstrode, with a reference to the Farmer-Chetham MS. (Chetham Library, Manchester), with many poems by Donne.

RIMBAULT, E. F. *Notes and Queries*, N.S. III, IV, 1863, 415: Note on Mrs. Cockayne of Ashbourne, to whom Donne addressed letters, with a reference to the tradition of 'Dr. Donne's chamber' at Ashbourne.

ANON. *The Leisure Hour*, XIII, 1864, pp. 555–8: Dr. Donne (biographical sketch).

COLNAGHI's *Photographic Historical Portrait Gallery*, London, P. and D. Colnaghi, 1864, pl. XLI. 'Dr Donne', from a miniature in the collection of C. S. Bale (see p. 372); p. 82. Biographical notice.

CPL. [T. R. O'Flaherty]. *Notes and Queries*, N.S. III, V, 1864, 21: Notes on John Donne, jr., and his letters.

CPL. [T. R. O'Flaherty]. *Notes and Queries*, N.S. III, VI, 1864, 535: A query as to the meaning of Donne's suffering from the *vurbah* (*Letters*, 1651, p. 317), with an editorial note suggesting that it was a *verber* or wheal, perhaps nettle-rash, referring also to his letter to Mrs. Cockaine (*Tobie Matthew Collection*, 1660, p. 342) when he was suffering from a 'violent falling of the uvula' about the same time.

COLLIER, J. PAYNE. *A Bibliographical and Critical Account of the Rarest Books in the English Language*, 2 vols., London, 1865. Vol. I, pp. 22–3: A description of the Ellesmere copy of *An Anatomy of the World*, 1611, mentioning the recent discovery of a second copy (see p. 322 of the present work). On p. 1*, Additions and Corrections, Collier mentions Davison's memorandum that he had lent a copy of 'J. Dun's Satyres' to his brother, Christopher, i.e. MS. Harley 298, BM, f. 159 (see Milgate's *Satires*, 1967, p. xlviii n.) and alludes to Freeman's *Rubbe and a great Cast*, 1614 (see p. 282).

CPL. [T. R. O'Flaherty]. *Notes and Queries*, N.S. III, VII, 1865, 77: Charles I and Donne's

Sermons. A query as to the King's having offered a large reward for printing the sermons, with editorial note referring to passages in the Advertisements by John Donne, jr., in *Fifty Sermons* and *XXVI Sermons*. By the same, p. 84: asking for an explanation of the lines by Donne, *In eundem Macaronicum*, in *Coryat's Crudities*. (A reply by R.S.Q., p. 145.) By the same, p. 439: asking for identification of the initials of persons addressed in Donne's poems. Suggesting Christopher and Samuel Brooke, Rowland Woodward, and Magdalen Herbert for C.B., S.B., R.W., and M.H.

HUNT, LEIGH, and LEE, S. A.: *The Book of the Sonnet*, 2 vols., Boston, 1867. In 'An Essay on the Sonnet' a reference, p. 39, to 'Cowley's and Donne's worst condescensions to conceit'; p. 78, reference to Donne's 'Crown of Sonnets' (La Corona). 'Donne's piety though sincere was not healthy.' Nothing by Donne is quoted in the anthology.

BELLEW, J. C. M. *Poet's Corner. A Manual for Students in English Poetry*, London, 1868, 8º, pp. 188–95: An account of Donne, with a small selection of poems.

CPL. [T. R. O'Flaherty]. *Notes and Queries*, N.S. IV, II, 1868, 35: Asking for names of owners of books from Heber's library sale, Pt. IV, no. 617, *Poems*, 1635, with notes by Park; Pt. VIII, no. 728, *Biathanatos*, given to J. Marckham.

FITZGERALD, E. *Rubaiyat of Omar Khayyam*. 2nd edn., London, 1868, p. 28: note on a mathematical Quatrain of Omar's paralleled by Donne's verses on the compass image ('A Valediction forbidding Mourning').

HAZLITT, W. C. *Notes and Queries*, N.S. IV, II, 1868, 483: A note on readings in a MS. 'already described elsewhere', with a reference to Harleian MS. 5110. (A note on these readings, p. 614, by CPL.)

MACDONALD, G. *England's Antiphon*, London [1868], 8º, pp. 113–24: Dr. Donne.

MILMAN, H. H. *Annals of St. Paul's Cathedral*, London, 1868, 8º, pp. 322–30: Dean John Donne.

TRENCH, R. C. *A Household Book of English Poetry*, London, 1868, quotes, p. 59: Lecture upon the Shadow; pp. 141–2: Holy Sonnets, II, X. Pp. 403–4: a critical note on Donne.

LANDOR, W. S. *A Biography*, J. Forster, 2 vols., London, 1869. Vol. II, p. 183, in the section on *Imaginary Conversations*, Bk. V, 1822–8, remarks on the effect of Donne's early love-pieces, with footnote on lines shewing Donne's influence.

WHIPPLE, E. P. *The Literature of the Age of Elizabeth*, Boston, 1869, pp. 229–38: references, biographical and critical, to Donne; p. 237: 'Donne's published sermons are in form nearly as grotesque as his poems, though they are characterized by profounder qualities of heart and mind.'

BAILEY, J. E. *Notes and Queries*, N.S. V, v, 1870, 313: 'Royal Authors. Queen Elizabeth on Dr. Donne'. Lines in a common-place book.

GROSART, A. B. *Notes and Queries*, N.S. IV, v, 1870, 504: Asking for information about editions and MSS. of Donne's poems; p. 565: a reply from CPL [T. R. O'Flaherty]; p. 587: a further query about the Latin Epigrams.

HALLIWELL, J. O. *Notes and Queries*, N.S. IV, v, 1870, 148: Asking about an apparent reference to Shakespeare in a letter to Sir Robert Carr, with an editorial note that the reference is to the accompanying poem to Marquis Hamilton.

JORISSEN, T. *Nederland*, 1870: John Donne en Constantin Huygens.

ALPHA. *Notes and Queries*, N.S. IV, VII, 1871, 536: A query about a letter of Donne's in Walton's *Life* referring to Spring under a date in September, with an editorial note explaining that the letter was a conflation of several.

ELIOT, GEORGE. *Middlemarch*, 4 vols., Edinburgh and London, 1871. Vol. II, p. 299: Motto for chap. xxxix, stanzas 5–7 of 'the Undertaking'; vol. IV, p. 312: motto for chap. lxxxiii, stanza 2, ll. 1–4 of 'The Goodmorrow'.

GROSART, A. B. *Notes and Queries*, N.S. IV, VII, 1871, 494: Requesting help in identifying persons addressed by their initials in Donne's verse letters. Also asking about a Dutch translation of Donne's poems mentioned in Llewellyn's *Men-Miracles*.

JORISSEN, T. *Constantin Huygens. Studien*. Arnhem, 1871: References to Donne, pp.230 ff.

TAINE, H. *A History of English Literature*, 2 vols., Edinburgh, 1871, pp. 203–4: criticism of Donne: 'A pungent prose style of terrible crudeness, a powerful poet, of a precise and intense imagination, who still preserves something of the energy and thrill of the original inspiration. But he deliberately abuses all these gifts, and succeeds with great difficulty in concocting a piece of nonsense', etc., with two quotations.

MINTO, W. *A Manual of English Prose Literature*, London, 1872, pp. 294–5: An account of Donne's prose style with quotations from the sermon on St. Paul at Malta.

ALFORD, H. A. *Life, Journals and Letters*, London, 1873, pp. 75, 112, 173: A reference to a new edition of the Works of Dr. Donne, at the request of Mr. Parker of Cambridge.

CORSER, T. *Collecteana Anglo-Poetica. Part V*, Chetham Society (Manchester), 4°, 1873, pp. 219–28: Descriptions of his copies of *The Anatomy of the World*, 1611, *The First* and *Second Anniversaries*, 1612, *Poems*, 1633, 1719; pp. 228–32: *Donne's Satyr*, 1662. Extensively annotated, with quotations.

JESSOPP, A. *The Athenæum*, London, 1873 (2), pp. 81–2: Donne's Epigrams (by A. Jessopp); pp. 148, 179–80, 210–11: Further articles by R. D., A. B. Grosart, A. Jessopp, Brinsley Nicholson.

MORLEY, H. *Illustrations of English Religion*, London, [1875] (Cassell's Library of English Literature), 8°, pp. 232–7: Donne (with quotations from his writings).

ANON. *Temple Bar*, XLVII, 1876, pp. 377 ff.: First of the English satirists.

B., A.R. *Notes and Queries*, N.S. V, v, 1876, 242–3: Drawing attention to the MS. of a poem attributed to Donne, addressed to Lord Craven; the text is printed (spurious).

H., H. *Notes and Queries*, N.S. V, VII, 1877, 148–9: A query about the descent of Anne Donne, Cowper's mother; p. 215: reply by

C. R. Manning, shewing that the relationship was collateral.

LIGHTFOOT, J. B. *The Classic Preachers of the English Church*. London, 1877, 8°, pp. 1–26: Donne, the poet-preacher.

DIXON, J. *Notes and Queries*, N.S. VI, ii, 1880, 8: A query about a reading (*glare* for *glaze*) in Satire IV, l. 8; p. 90: replies by E. Solly and A. Jessopp attributing the error to the edition of 1650.

HALES, J. W. In *English Poets*, ed. A. W. Ward, London, 1880, 8°, vol. I, pp. 558 ff.: Donne.

MINTO, W. *The Nineteenth Century*, VII, 1880, pp. 845–63: John Donne.

ROSSETTI, D. G. *His Family Letters*, ed. W. M. Rossetti, with a Memoir, 2 vols., London, 1895. Vol. II, p. 356: Reference to Donne in a letter to W.M.R., 22 February 1880, 'I have been much enjoying Donne, who is full of excellences, and not brimming, but rather spilling, with quaintnesses.'

KING, ALICE. *The Argosy*, XXXII, 1881, pp. 299–305: John Donne.

WELSH, A. H. *Development of English Literature*, Chicago, 1882, pp. 412–13: A note on Donne's poems—'We find little to admire and nothing to love.'

GOSSE, E. W. *Seventeenth Century Studies*, London, 1883, 8°, pp. viii–ix: Reasons why Donne is not included.

PLUMPTRE, E. H. *Notes and Queries*, N.S. VI, X, 1884, 426: A query about a ring left by Donne to Walton; p. 456: a reply by J. Pickford referring to Major's edn. of Walton's *Angler*, 1824, p. xxx, with description of Donne's anchor seal; p. 473, a note by 'Tiny Tim' referring to the younger Walton's will bequeathing his rings to his sister; p. 526: a note by C. Elkin Mathews on Donne's seals and stating that his ring was in the keeping of H. A. Merewether (probably the same ring that is now in the library of Salisbury Cathedral).

GOSSE, E. *From Shakespeare to Pope*, Cambridge, 1885: References to Donne *passim* (see index).

P., J. *Notes and Queries*, N.S. VI, XII, 1885, 350: A query about sermons preached at Donne's funeral.

ROBERTS, W. *Notes and Queries*, N.S. VI, XII, 1885, 307: A query as to the identity of persons addressed by Donne—the E. of D. (with six Holy Sonnets), and Mrs. Essex Riche (A Letter); p. 391: reply about the latter by F. W. Cosens.

THOMPSON, FRANCIS. *Literary Criticism*, ed. T. L. Connolly, New York, 1948: Several references to Donne (see index).

THOMPSON, FRANCIS. *The Life*, by E. Meynell, London, 1913: Several references to Donne (see index).

COTMORE, C. *Notes and Queries*, N.S. VII, I, 1886, 508: A query about the will of George Donne, the Dean's second son.

WARD, G. A. *Notes and Queries*, N.S. VII, I, 1886, 227: A query about musical settings of Donne's 'Hymne to God the Father'.

JESSOPP, A. *Dictionary of National Biography*, London, 1888, vol. xv, pp. 223–34: John Donne.

WHIPPLE, E. P. *The Literature of the Age of Elizabeth*, London, 1888, 8º, pp. 229–38: References to Donne.

JEWETT, SARA ORME. *Letters*, ed. A. Fields, London, Boston and N.Y., 1911, p. 60: in a letter to Mrs. Fields, 1889: 'I have been reading an old copy of Donne's poems with perfect delight. They seem new to me just now, even the things I knew best. We must read many of them together.'

POLAK, H. J. *De Gids*. 1889, I, II: Constantin Huygens, references to Donne.

SWINBURNE, A. C. *A Study of Ben Jonson*. London, 1889: References to Donne, pp. 99 ('Donne is rugged, Jonson is stiff'), 106, 129, 142.

COLLIER, W. F. *A History of English Literature in a Series of Biographical Sketches*, London, 1890, pp. 168 ff.: John Donne.

DOWDEN, E. *Fortnightly Rev.*, O.S. LIII, 1890, 791–808: Poetry of John Donne.
Repr. in *Eclectic Rev.* LII, 1890, 234–44; *Littell's Living Age*, CLXXXVI, 1890, 195 ff. Also in *New Studies in Literature*, Boston and New York, 1895 (pp. 90–120).

LOWELL, J. R. *The Writings*, 10 vols., London, 1890: References to Donne, vol. I, p. 381; vol. II, pp. 79, 160; vol. III, pp. 35, 171; vol. V, p. 108.

BAYNE, T. *Notes and Queries*, N.S. VII, XI, 1891, 427: A query as to the correct reading of a couplet used by Sir J. Millais as motto to his painting, 'Lingering Autumn' (Elegy IX, ll. 1–2); p. 493: replies by E. H. Marshall and C. L. Thompson. See also W. F. Prideaux, vol. XII, 1891, p. 274, quoting the reading of *Poems*, 1633, and T. R. O'Flaherty, N.S. VIII, vol. I, 1892, p. 440, on MS. readings of the lines and Grosart's errors.

GOSSE, E. W. *Gossip in a Library*, London, 1891, 8º, pp. 55–64: 'Death's Duel' (an essay on).

NICHOLSON, B. *Notes and Queries*, N.S. VII, XII, 1891, 365: A note on the editions of *Letters*, 1651 and 1654, shewing that they contain the same sheets; p. 495: a note by M. Buxton Forman on the presence or absence of Lombart's portrait in each edition.

BRADFORD, GAMALIEL. *A Naturalist of Souls*, Boston and N.Y., 1926, pp. 63–96: 'The Poetry of Donne', Lowell and Swinburne both emphasize the merit of Donne by a comparison with Gray, with quotations in illustration (written in 1892).

BRUMBAUGH, M. G. 'A Study of the Poetry of John Donne' (1893): An unpublished dissertation, Univ. of Pennsylvania.

GOSSE, E. W. *The New Rev.* IX, 1893, pp. 236–47: The Poetry of John Donne.
Also printed in *Littell's Living Age*, CXCIX, 1893, 429 ff.

GOSSE, E. W. *Jacobean Poets*, London, 1894, 8º, pp. 47–67: John Donne.

LOWELL, J. R. *Letters*, ed. C. E. Norton, 2 vols., London, 1894: References to Donne, vol. II, pp. 319, 364, 305–6, 430, 480.

[SAINTSBURY, G. E. B.].*English Prose Selections*. Ed. Henry Craik, London, 1894, 2 vols., 8º, vol. II, pp. 83–94: John Donne (prose selections with introduction by George Saintsbury).

DOWDEN, E. *New Studies in Literature*, London, 1895: References to Donne, pp. 92–5.

LIGHTFOOT, J. B. *Historical Essays*, London, 1895, 8º, pp. 221–45: Donne—the Poet-Preacher.

SCHELLING, F. E. *A Book of Elizabethan Lyrics*, Boston, 1895, pp. vii–lxix: Introduction with many references to Donne (see index); pp. 97–105, 142: Selection of Donne's poems.

CRAWFURD, O. *Lyrical Verse*, London, 1896, pp. 78–80: xciii, 'The Will'; pp. 105–6: cxxix, 'The Message'; p. 426: a note on 'The Will'—'probably the wittiest and the bitterest lyric in our language'.

CRAWLEY-BOEVEY, A. W. *Notes and Queries*, N.S. VIII, ix, 1896, 41–3: 'Dr. Donne's Seals', a description with a P.S. describing the pendent seal then in the possession of the Revd. Wyndham Merewether.

FURST, C. B. *The Citizen*, Philadelphia, II, 1896, pp. 229–37: The Life and Poetry of Dr. John Donne.

JOHNSON, LIONEL. *Post Liminium. Essays and Critical Papers*, ed. T. Whittemore, London, 1911, pp. 112–20: 'The Soul of Poetry', with refs. to Donne. First published in *The Academy*, December 1896.

MEYNELL, A. *The Flower of the Mind*, London, 1897, pp. 53–6: 'The Funeral', 'The Dreame', 'Death be not proud' (attributed), 'Hymne to God the Father'; p. 334: a note on 'The Funeral'—'a poet of fine onsets'.

NORTON, C. E. *Studies and Notes in Philology and Literature*, vol. v, Child Memorial Volume, Boston, 1897, pp. 1–19: The Text of Donne's Poems.

ANON. *The Quarterly Review*, CLXXXV, 1897, 173 ff.: Fathers of Literary Impressionism (Rev. of *Donne's Poems*, ed. Chambers, with Sterne's *Works* and Poems of Keats).

FURST, C. B. *Mod. Lang. Notes*, XII, 1897, 318: Notes on Donne.

JESSOPP, Dr. AUGUSTUS. *John Donne, Sometime Dean of St. Paul's*, London, 1897 [Leaders of Religion Series], 8°, pp. x, [ii], 239, [i]; two portraits.

REVIEWED:
Anon. *The Academy*, LII, 1899, 474–5.
Furst, C. B. *Mod. Lang. Notes*, XIV, 1899, 61–2.

HANNAY, D. *The Later Renaissance* (Periods of European Literature), Edinburgh and London, 1898, pp. 220–2: References to Donne.

ALDEN, R. M. *The Rise of Formal Satire in England under Classical Influence*, Philadelphia, 1899, pp. 75–90: John Donne (for other references see index).

BEECHING, H. C. *Athenæum*, 1899 (2), p. 802: The Life of Donne.

FURST, C. B. *A Group of Old Authors*, Philadelphia, 1899, ch. 1: A Gentleman of King James' Day. Dr. John Donne.

REVIEWED:
Child, C. G. *Mod. Lang. Notes*, xv, 62–3.

GOSSE, E. W. *The Life and Letters of John Donne Dean of St. Paul's. Now for the first time revised and collected. With portraits &c.*, London, Heinemann, 1899, 8°, vol. I, pp. xxii, 318, [2]; vol. II, pp. viii, 391, [1] (Reissued 1959).

REVIEWED:
Athenæum, 1899 (2), 645–6.
Academy, LVII, 1899, 505–6.
Bookman (N.Y.), x, 1899, 582–4.
Dial. Chadwick, J. W., xx, 1896, p. 280: Briefs on new books.
Littell's Living Age, CCXXIII, 1900, 726–31.
Nation (N.Y.), LXX, 1899, 111–13, 133–5.

GOSSE, E. W. *Athenæum*, 1899 (2), p. 802: The Life of Donne.

PHELPS, W. L. *Mod. Lang. Notes*, XIV, 1899, 258: Donne's 'Anyan' [in 'Hymn to God, my God in my Sicknesse'].

SYMONS, A. *Fortnightly Rev.* N.S. LXVI, 1899, 734–45: John Donne.
Repr. in *Figures of Several Centuries*, London, 1916, pp. 80–108.

STEPHEN, SIR LESLIE. *Nat. Rev.* XXXIV, 1899, 595–613: John Donne.
Repr. in *Studies of a Biographer*, 1907, III, 33–77.

VINCENT, A. *Athenæum*, 1899 (2), p. 836: The Life of Donne.

ANON. *Quart. Rev.* CXCII, 1900, 217–40: John Donne and his Contemporaries. (Rev. of Gosse, *Life and Letters*, Jessopp, *John Donne*, and other poets—Carew, Crashaw, Herbert, and Vaughan.)

1901–1971

[The names are arranged in alphabetical order and are not included in the general index]

ABRAHAMOWITZ, I. *Great Prisoners*, N.Y., 1946, pp. 174–6: John Donne—Anne Donne—Undone.

ADAMS, R. M. *Kenyon Rev.* XVI, 1954, 278–91: Donne and Eliot. Metaphysicals. Repr. in *Strains of Discord in Literary Openness*, Ithaca, N.Y., 1958.

ADDLESHAW, S. *Church Quart. Rev.* CXIII, 1931, 38–54: Famous Dean: Dr John Donne of St Paul's.

ALDEN, R. M. *Stud. Philol.* XIV, 1917, 129–52: The Lyrical Conceits of the Elizabethans.

ALDEN, R. M. *Stud. Philol.* XVII, 1920, 183–98: The Lyrical Conceits of the Metaphysical Poets.

ALEXANDER, H. *Queen's Quart.* XLII, 1935–6, 471–81: John Donne, Poet and Divine.

ALLEN, D. C. *Mod. Lang. Notes*, LVI, 1941, 129–33: Donne's suicides.

ALLEN, D. C. *Mod. Lang. Notes*, LVI, 1941, 609–11: Donne and the Bezoar.

ALLEN, D. C. *Journ. Eng. Lit. Hist.* X, 1943, 208–29: Dean Donne sets his text.

ALLEN, D. C. *Journ. Eng. Germ. Philol.* XLII, 1943, 322–42: John Donne's knowledge of renaissance medicine.

ALLEN, D. C. *Mod. Lang. Notes*, LVIII, 1943, 610–12: John Donne and Pierio Valeriano.

ALLEN, D. C. *Mod. Lang. Notes*, LX, 1945, 54–5: Two annotations on Donne's verse; pp. 398–400: John Donne's Paradise and Calvarie.

ALLEN, D. C. *Mod. Lang. Notes*, LXI, 1946, 63–4: Donne's 'Specular Stone'; pp. 65: Donne, Butler, and ?; pp. 257–60: Donne among the giants.

ALLEN, D. C. *Mod. Lang. Notes*, LXII, 1947, 340–2: Donne's Phoenix.

ALLEN, D. C. *Journ. Eng. Lit. Hist.* XV, 1948, 167 ff.: Style and certitude.

ALLEN, D. C. *The Legend of Noah: Renaissance Rationalism in Art, Science and Letters*, Illin. Stud. Lang. Lit. XXXIII, Urbana, 1949. Refs. to Donne *passim*.

ALLEN, D. C. *Mod. Lang. Notes*, LXIV, 1949, 481–3: John Donne and the Tower of Babel.

ALLEN, D. C. *Mod. Lang. Notes*, LXV, 1950, 102–6: Three Notes on Donne's Poetry with a glance at *Othello*.

ALLEN, D. C. In *A Tribute to G. C. Taylor*, Univ. of N. Carolina, 1952, pp. 83–99: The double journey of John Donne.

ALLEN, D. C. *Mod. Lang. Rev.* LXVIII, 1953, 288–9: A note on Donne's Elegy VIII.

ALLEN, D. C. *Mod. Lang. Notes*, LXIX, 1954, 559–60: Donne's 'The Will'.

ALLEN, D. C. *Mod. Lang. Notes*, LXXI, 1956, 256–7: Donne's Compass Figure.

ALLEN, D. C. *Mod. Lang. Notes*, LXXIV, 1959, 393–7: Donne on the Mandrake.

ALLEN, D. C. *Mod. Lang. Notes*, LXXIV, 1959, 485–6: Love in a Grave.

ALLEN, D. C. *Image and Meaning: Metaphoric Traditions in Renaissance Poetry*, Baltimore, 1960.

ALLEN, D. C. *Mod. Lang. Notes*, LXXV, 1960, 293–5: The Genesis of Donne's Dreams.

ALLEN, D. C. *Mod. Lang. Notes*, LXXVI, 1961, 308–12: Donne and the Ship Metaphor.

ALLEN, D. C. *Eng. Lang. Notes*, Columbia Univ., I, 1964, 188–91: Donne's Sapho to Philaenis.

ALPHONSE, SISTER MARY. *Explicator*, XXV, 1967, item 43: Donne's 'Love's Growth'.

ALVAREZ, A. *Listener*, LVII, 1957, 827–8: John Donne and his Circle.

ALVAREZ, A. *The School of Donne*, London, 19.5 cm, 1961, pp. 202, [1].
REVIEWED:
Matie, M. R. *Seventeenth Cent. News*, XIX, Autumn 1961, 41.

Anon. *Va. Quart. Rev.* XXXVIII, XLIX.

Archer, S. *Renaissance News*, XVI, 1963, 36–8.

Crutwell, P. *Hudson Rev.* XV, 1962, 450–1.

Williamson, C. F. *Rev. Eng. Stud.* XIII, 1962, 196–8.

ANDREASEN, N. J. C. *Stud. Eng. Lit.* III, 1963, 59–75: Theme and Structure in Donne's Poems.

ANDREASEN, N. J. C. *Diss. Abstr.* XXIV, 1964, 3320: Donne and the Correlative Traditions: The Poetry in the Ovidian and Petrarchan Contents.

ANDREASEN, N. J. C. *Mod. Philol.* LXII, 1965, 207–16: Donne's *Devotions* and the Psychology of Assent.

ANDREASEN, N. J. C. *John Donne: Conservative Revolutionary*, Princeton Univ. Press, 1967, pp. vii, 249.
REVIEWED:
P. Legouis. *Etudes Angl.* XXI, 195–6.
P. A. Rathburn. *Seventeenth Cent. News.* XXVI, 38.
Anon. *Times Lit. Sup.,* 25 March 1935, p. 182: The School of Donne.

ANON. *Quart. Rev.* CXCVI, 1902, 438–46: The Elizabethan Lyric.

ANON. *Times Lit. Sup.,* 20 October 1921, pp. 669–70: The Metaphysical Poets. See also pp. 698, 716, 734, 27 Oct., 3 Nov., 10 Nov., letters from G. Saintsbury.

ANON. *Times Lit. Sup.,* 5 November 1925, pp. 725–6: The margins of philosophy.

ANON. *Scotsman,* Edinburgh, 23 October 1929: The Gloomiest Dean. Donne Manuscript found in Edinburgh.

ANON. *Times Lit. Sup.,* 26 March 1931, pp. 241–2: John Donne (leading article).

ANON. *The Times,* 31 March 1931, John Donne (leading article on the tercentenary of Donne's death); John Donne. Preacher and Bencher of Lincoln's Inn.

ANON. *Times Lit. Sup.,* 25 March 1935, p. 182: The School of Donne.

ANON. *Times Lit. Sup.,* 24 December 1938, pp. 814–16: Devotional Poetry: Donne to Wesley.

ANON. *Times Lit. Sup.,* 26 August 1939, p. 502: John Donne's disdain.

ANON. *Bodl. Libr. Rec.* I, 1939–41, Oxford, 1941, pp. 147–8: A Book from Donne's Library (see L139); p. 205: Donne *desiderata*, a list.

ANON. *Yale Univ. Libr. Gaz.* XV, 1940, pp. 47–8: John Donne *Desiderata*.

ANON. *Time.* XXVII, 13 January 1941, p. 76: John Donne O. P. Repr. in *Essay Annual,* ed. E. A. Walter, N.Y., 1941, p. 153.

ANON. *Times Lit. Sup.,* 22 September 1950, p. 597: Poets and Editors.

ANON. *Times Lit. Sup.,* 6 April 1967, pp. 277–9: Ill Donne: Well Donne. A review of F. Manley's *Anniversaries,* A. Stein's *Donne's Lyrics* and H. Gardner's *Elegies and Songs and Sonnets.*

ANON. *Times Lit. Sup.,* 25 May 1967, p. 436: Donne and others. A review of J. Sparrow's *Hymns Unbidden,* D. L. Guss's *Donne Petrarchist,* and M. Clive's *Jack and the Doctor.*

ANON. *Cambridge Evening News,* 5 May 1971: 'Testing time for Donne', announcing that Donne's Sermon on Psalm 63 (*LXXX Sermons,* no. 66) would be read by Oliver Neville in King's College Chapel at the morning service on 9 May.

ARCHER, S. *Journ. Eng. Lit. Hist.* XXVIII, 1961, 137–47: Meditation and the Structure of Donne's Holy Sonnets.

ARMITAGE, C. M. *Stud. Philol.* XLIII, 1967, 697–707: Donne's Poems in Huntington Manuscript 198: New Light on 'The Funeral'.

ARMS, G. W. *Explicator,* I, February 1943, Item 29: Donne's song, 'Go and catch a falling star'.

ARMS, G. W., and KUNTZ, J. M. *Poetry Explication: A Checklist of Interpretation since 1925 of British and American Poets Past and Present.* N.Y., 1950.

ARONSTEIN, P. *Englische Studien,* XLIX, 1916, pp. 360–76: John Donne und Francis Bacon.

ARONSTEIN, P. *John Donne als Dichter: Ein Beitrag zur Kenntnis der Englischen Renaissance,* Halle, 1922. First printed in *Anglia,* June 1920.
REVIEWED:
Ackermann, R. *Literaturbl. germ. und rom. Philol.* XLIV, 1923, 174–5.
Brunner, K. *Neueren Sprach.* XXXI, 1923, 85–6.
Keller, W. *Jahrb. deutsch. Shakesp. Gesell.* LVII, 1921, 109–10.

L., M. *Lit. Zentralbl.* LXXXIV, 1923, 317–18.

Times Lit. Sup., 28 September 1922, p. 616.

van Kranendonk, A. G. *Neophilologus*, II, 1921, 4.

ATKINS, A. H. *Notes and Queries*, CLXVII, 1934, p. 39: Mr Banks and his horse (ref. in Donne's Satyre I, ll. 79–82).

ATKINS, S. *Times Lit. Sup.*, 22 May 1937, pp. 396, 412: Donne's Satires.

ATKINSON, A. D. *Notes and Queries*, CXCVI, 1951, pp. 387–8: Donne quotations in Johnson's *Dictionary*.

ATTAL, J. P. *Critique* (Paris), XV, 1959, 682–707: Qu'est-ce que la poésie métaphysique?

B., R.S., and MAXWELL, H. *Notes and Queries*, CLXVIII, 1935, 104: All Tincture. See also J., p. 346.

BACHRACH, A. G. H. *Neophilologus*, XXXV, 1952, 120–9: Sir Constantine Huygens and Ben Jonson.

BACHRACH, A. G. H. *Sir Constantine Huygens and Britain, 1596–1687*, Leiden and London, 1962: References to Donne, pp. 5, 6, 15, 42, 70, 208.

BAILEY, J. *Quart. Rev.* CCXXXIII, 1920, 317–28: The Sermons of a Poet. A review of L. P. Smith's *Donne's Sermons*, Oxford, 1919.

BAKER-SMITH, D. *Engl. Miscell.* XIX, 1968, pp. 65–82: John Donne and the Mysterium Crucis.

BALD, R. C. *Donne's Influence in English Literature*, Morpeth, 1932, 8º, p. 62.

BALD, R. C. *Philol. Quart.* XVI, 1937, pp. 402–5: Three Metaphysical Epigrams (by Donne, Cowley, Beedome).

BALD, R. C. *Notes and Queries*, CXCIII, 1948, 302: A Spanish book of Donne's.

BALD, R. C. *Rev. Eng. Stud.* XXIV, 1948, 321–3: William Milbourne, Donne and Thomas Jackson.

BALD, R. C. *Times Lit. Sup.*, 1949, p. 313: Donne's activities.

BALD, R. C. *Seventeenth Cent. News*, VII, 1949: Donne's Travels.

BALD, R. C. *Huntington Libr. Quart.* XV, 1952, 283–9: Donne's early Verse-Letters.

BALD, R. C. *Times Lit. Sup.*, 24 October 1952, p. 700, 19 December, p. 837: Donne's Letters.

BALD, R. C. (ed.). *An Humble Supplication to Her Maiestie, by Robert Southwell*, Cambridge, 1953: Contains many references to Donne.

BALD, R. C. *Essays in Eng. Lit. Renais. to Vict. Age presented to A. S. P. Woodhouse*, 1964, pp. 69–84: Historical Doubts Respecting Walton's *Life of Donne*.

BALD, R. C. *Mod. Philol.* LXI, 1964, 198–203: A Latin Version of Donne's Problems.

BALD, R. C. *Donne & the Drurys*, Cambridge, 1959, 21·5 cm, pp. x, 176.

REVIEWED:

Barnes, T. G. *Journ. Econom. Hist.* XX, 1960, 94 ff.

Eccles, M. *Mod. Lang. Rev.* IV, 1960, 624–5.

Fowler, A. D. S. *Notes and Queries*, VII, 1960, 79–80.

Hill, C. *Spectator*, 19 June 1959, 900.

Leishman, J. B. *Journ. Eng. Germ. Philol.* LIX, 1960, 293–5.

Mahl, M. R. *Seventeenth Cent. News*, XVII, 1959, 21.

Manley, F. *Mod. Lang. Notes*, LXXV, 1960, 515–17.

Milgate, W. *Austr. M. L. A.*, no. 13, 1960, 77–9.

Shapiro, I. A. *Rev. Eng. Stud.* XIII, 1962, 301–3.

BALD, R. C. *Stud. Bibliogr.* XVIII, 1965, 69–80: Dr. Donne and the Book-sellers.

BALD, R. C. *John Donne. A Life*, Oxford, Clarendon Press, 1970, 21·5 cm, pp. xiv, 627, [1]. With 8 plates and errata slip. Completed and seen through the press by W. Milgate. Bald has four *Appendices*: A. Chronology of Donne's Life. B. Donne's Children. C. Donne's Library. D. Appendix of Documents: (i) The Will of Donne's Father. (ii) Donne's Will. (iii) Donne's Complaint against Christopher Danby. (iv) A Cypher Entrusted to Donne. (v) Draft of Sir Henry Martin's Judgement on Henry Scyliard's Claim to Keyston Rectory. (vi) Minutes of a Vestry Meeting at St. Dunstan's-in-the-West. (vii) Donne's Address to Convocation, 1626. (viii) Statement by John

Donne the younger. (ix) Pleadings in the Suit of Sir George Grymes against John Donne the Younger. Most of these are not printed elsewhere, but the list omits Donne's holograph inscription taken from the *Album Amicorum* of *Michael Corvinus*, signed and dated *Sept: 17 1623* (library of G. L. Keynes).

REVIEWED:

Alvarez, A. *Observer*, 22 March 1970.

Bush, D. *Bost. Sund. Herald*, 19 April 1970.

Byatt, A. S. *Times*, 7 March 1970.

Elrodt, R. *Études Angl.*

Gardner, H. L. *New Statesm.*, 13 March 1970.

Hodge, A. *Financ. Times*, 19 March 1970.

Lask, T. *N.Y. Times*, 16 May 1970.

BALL, L., jr. *Explicator*, VIII, April 1950, item 44: Donne's 'The Computation'.

BAMBOROUGH, J. B. *The Little World of Man*, London, 1952: References to Donne *passim*.

BARUCH, F. R. *Times Lit. Sup.*, 30 May 1952, p. 361: Donne and Herbert.

BATESON, F. W. *English Poetry and the English Language*, Oxford, 1934, see pp. 34–46.

BATTENHOUSE, R. W. *Church Hist.* XI, 1942, pp. 217–48: The Grounds of Religious Toleration in the Thought of John Donne.

BAUER, R. J. *Diss. Abstr.* XXVIII, 1967, 618A: John Donne and the Schoolmen.

BAUERLE, R. F. *Notes and Queries*, VII, 1960, 386: John Donne Redone and Undone (a revision of 'Go and Catch a Falling Star' in *The London Mag.* June 1741).

BECK, R. *Rev. Eng. Stud.* XIX, 1968, 166–9: A Precedent for Donne's Imagery in 'Goodfriday 1613, Riding Westward'.

BEECHING, CANON H. C. *Cornhill Mag.* N.S. VIII, 1900, 249–68: Izaak Walton's Life of Donne—An Apology. Repr. in *Religio Laici*, London, 1902, pp. 89–123. A defence of Walton against criticisms by Gosse and Leslie Stephen.

BEERS, H. A. *The Connecticut Wits*, New Haven, 1920, in 'Abraham Cowley', pp. 200–1, a reference to Donne.

BEESE, M. A. *Mod. Lang. Rev.* XXXIII, 1938, 356–9: John Donne the Younger: Addenda and Corrections to his Biography.

BELDEN, H. M. *Mod. Lang. Notes*, XIX, 1904, pp. 76–8: Donne's Compasses and Wither's Compass.

BELL, A. H. *Cresset* (Valparaiso U.), XXXII, 1969, II, pp. 15–16: Donne's Atonement Conceit in the Holy Sonnets.

BELL, C. *Times Lit. Sup.*, 1 July 1939, p. 389: Donne's 'Farewell to love'.

BELLETTE, A. F. *Diss. Abstr.* XIX, 1969, 3571A–2A: Form and Vision in Four Metaphysical Poets [Donne, Herbert, Traherne, Vaughan].

BENDER, T. K. *Times Lit. Sup.*, 12 August 1965, p. 704: The Platan Tree in Donne, Horace and Theocritus.

BENHAM, A. R. In *Renaissance Studies in Honor of Hardin Craig*. Ed. B. Maxwell *et al.*, Stanford Univ., 1941, pp. 273–81: The myth of John Donne the Rake. A reprint from *Phil. Quart.* XX, iii, 1941.

BENJAMIN, E. B. *Notes and Queries*, XV, 1968, pp. 92–4: Donne and Bodin's *Theatrum*.

BENNETT, J. *Four Metaphysical Poets*, London, 1934 (second edn., 1953). Repr. with an anthology of their works. Vintage Books, N.Y., 1960. Incorporated (as revised 1957) in *Five Metaphysical Poets*, Cambridge and N.Y., 1964.

REVIEWED:

Hutchinson, F. E. *Rev. Eng. Stud.* XI, 1935, 484–6.

Sisson, C. J. *Mod. Lang. Rev.* XXX, 1935, 374–5.

Dublin Mag. XXX, 1954, 45.

Notes and Queries, N.S. I, 1954, 43.

Sisson, C. J. *Mod. Lang. Rev.* XLIX, 1954, 542–3.

BENNETT, J. In *Seventeenth Century Essays presented to Sir H. J. C. Grierson*, Oxford, 1938, pp. 85–104: The love poetry of John Donne. A Reply to Mr. C. S. Lewis.

BENNETT, J. *Rev. Eng. Stud.* XVII, 1941, 285 ff.: An aspect of the evolution of seventeenth-century prose.

BENNETT, J. A. W. *Rev. Eng. Stud.* V, 1954, 168–9: A note on Donne's 'Crosse'.

BENNETT, J. A. W. *Notes and Queries*, XIII (CCXI), 1966, 254: Donne's Elegy XVI, 31.

BENNETT, R. E. *Mod. Lang. Notes*, XLVI, 1931,

309–13: John Manningham and Donne's Paradoxes.

BENNETT, R. E. *Mod. Lang. Rev.* XLVIII, 1933, 167–8. Addition to Donne's *Catalogus Librorum*.

BENNETT, R. E. *Times Lit. Sup.*, 31 January 1935, p. 62: Donne and Sir Thomas Roe. See also Shapiro, I. A., 7 February, p. 76.

BENNETT, R. E. *Times Lit. Sup.*, 29 August 1936, p. 697: Donne and 'the Queen'. Concerning Donne's letter of 17 July 1613.

BENNETT, R. E. *Philol. Quart.* XVI, 1937, 30–4: Walton's use of Donne's Letters.

BENNETT, R. E. *Rev. Eng. Stud.* XIII, 1937, 333–5: Tracts from Donne's Library.

BENNETT, R. E. *Rev. Eng. Stud.* XV, 1939, 66–72: John Donne and Everard Gilpin.

BENNETT, R. E. *Philol. Quart.* XIX, 1940, 66–78: Donne's letters from the continent in 1611–12.

BENNETT, R. E. *Publ. Mod. Lang. Assoc.* LVI, 1941, 120–40: Donne's *Letters to Several Persons of Honour*.

BENNETT, R. E. *Mod. Lang. Quart.* III, 1942, 603–4: John Donne and the Earl of Essex.

BENSLEY, E. *Notes and Queries*, CLXI, 1931, answer to 'A Query on Donne's Sermon XXX' (*Notes and Queries*, CLXI, 1931, 156–7).

BENTLEY, N. E. *Mod. Lang. Notes*, LXI, 359 f.: In defence of Butler.

BERRY, L. E. *A Bibliography of Studies in Metaphysical Poetry*. Madison, Univ. of Wisconsin Press, 1964 (a continuation of Spencer and Van Doran's *Studies in Metaphysical Poetry*, 1939). Contains 521 entries for Donne.

BETHELL, S. L. *The Cultural Revolution of the Seventeenth Century*, London, 1951: References to Donne *passim*.

BETHELL, S. L. *North. Misc. of Lit. Crit.* I, 1953, pp. 19–40: Gracián, Tesauro and the nature of Metaphysical Wit. Repr. in Kermode, F., *Discussions of John Donne*, Boston, 1962.

BEWLEY, M. *Kenyon Rev.* XIV, 1952, 619–46: Religious cynicism in Donne's poetry. Repr. enlarged as the Introduction to *The Selected Poems of Donne*, 1967, and again with further additions as 'The Mask of John Donne' in *Masks and Mirrors*, N.Y., 1970, pp. 3–49.

BINYON, L. *Bookman*, London, LXVII, January 1925, 201–2: A Study of Donne.

BIRRELL, T. A. *Times Lit. Sup.*, 4 November 1949, p. 715: Donne's Letters.

BISHOP, J. P. *New Repub.* XCVII, 1938, 198: John Donne's Statue (poem).

BLACKBURN, W. S. *Atlant. Quart.* L, 1951, 378–88: Lady Magdalen Herbert and her son, George.

BLANCHARD, M. M. *Renaissance*, XVII, 1964, 38–50: The Leap into Darkness: Donne, Herbert and God.

BLANDA, E. *Mod. Lang. Rev.* LVI, 1966, 357–68: The Background of Donne's Elegies.

BLOCK, H. M. *Compar. Lit. Stud.* IV, 1967, pp. 147–59: The Alleged Parallel of Metaphysical and Symbolist Poetry (with many examples from Donne).

BOASE, A. M. *Rev. des Sciences Hum.*, nos. 55–6, 1949, pp. 155–84: Poètes Anglais et Français de l'Epoque Baroque.

BOGGS, W. A. *The N.Y. Times*, CIX, 8 August 1960, p. 20, col. 3: Upon his secret marriage. John Donne to his father-in-law, Sir George More. (5 stanzas, with much play upon the words 'more' and 'done'.)

BOLLIER, E. P. *Tulane Stud. Eng.* IX, 1959, 103–18: T. S. Eliot and John Donne. A Problem in Criticism.

BOLTON, J. S. G. (ed.), *Melanthe, a Latin Pastoral Play written by Samuel Brooke*, Yale, 1928: Relations of Brooke with Donne.

BOORMAN, S. C. *Trivium*, I, 1966, pp. 184–7: A Possible Allusion in Donne's 'A Tale of a Citizen and his Wife'.

BOTTING, R. B. *Nineteenth Century Research Stud. of the State Coll. of Washington*, IX, 1941, no. 3, pp. 139–88: The Reputation of John Donne during the Nineteenth Century.

BOURNE, R. *Poetry Rev.* XXVIII, 1947, 460–1: John Donne and the Spiritual Life.

BOWERS, F. T. *Mod. Lang. Notes*, LIV, 1939, 280–2: An interpretation of Donne's Tenth Elegy.

BRADBROOK, F. W. *Notes and Queries*, n.s. IV (ccii), 1957, 146–7: John Donne and Ben Jonson.

BRADFORD, G. *South-west Rev.* x, 1924, 40–8: Little Glimpses of Great People.

BRANDENBURG, A. S. *Publ. Mod. Lang. Assoc.* LVII, 1942, see pp. 1039–45.

BRANTS, J. *Kronick van Kurst en Kultmer*, IX, 1959, no. 6, pp. 68–76.

BREDVOLD, L. I. *Journ. Eng. Germ. Philol.* Urbana, Ill. xxii, 1923, 471–502: The Naturalism of Donne in relation to some Renaissance Traditions.

BREDVOLD, L. I. *Times Lit. Sup.*, 13 March 1924, p. 160: Sir T. Egerton and Donne.

BREDVOLD, L. I. *Studies in Shakespeare, Milton, and Donne*, Univ. of Michigan Publications, I, New York and London, 1925. The religious thought of Donne in relation to medieval and later traditions.

REVIEWED:

B., C. R. *Mod. Phil.* xxiv, 1926, 244–5.

Gilbert, A. H. *Mod. Lang. Notes*, XLI, 1926, 264–8.

Greenlaw, E. *Journ. Eng. Germ. Phil.* xxv, 1926, 423–7.

Eichler, A. *Englische Studien*, LXIII, 1928, 114–19.

Wilson, J. D. *Rev. Eng. Stud.* II, 1926, 475–9.

Times Lit. Sup., 4 February 1926, p. 82.

BREDVOLD, L. I. *Comp. Lit.* II, 1950, pp. 253–68: The Rise of English Classicism: Study in the Methodology.

BRETT, R. D. *Diss. Abstr.* xxii, 1962, 2783–4: Ironic Harmony: Poetic Structure in Donne, Marvell and Dryden.

BRETT-SMITH, H. F. B. *Mod. Lang. Rev.* x, 1915, 86–8: A Crux in the Text of Donne.

BRILLI, A. *Stud. Urbin. Stor. Filos. Lett.* XXXVIII, 1964, 100–39: Gli Amores Ovidiani e la poesia di J. Donne.

BRINKLEY, R. F. *Coleridge on the Seventeenth Century*. Introd. by L. I. Bredvold. Duke University Press, N.C., 1955, pp. 163–205: John Donne, Sermons; 428–31: Letters; 519–30: Poems.

BRITTIN, N. A. *Amer. Lit.* VIII, 1936, 1–21: Emerson and the Metaphysical Poets.

BROOKE, RUPERT. *Nation*, XII, 1913, 825–6: John Donne the Elizabethan. *Poetry and Drama*, I, 1913, pp. 185–8: John Donne. Reviews of *Poems*, ed. Grierson, 1912. Both repr. in *The Prose of R.B.*, ed. C. Hassall, London, 1956, pp. 85–98.

BROOKS, C. *South. Rev.* I, 1936, 151–63, 328–38, 568–83: Three Revolutions in Poetry.

BROOKS, C. and WARREN, R. P. *Understanding Poetry: An Anthology for College Students*, New York, 1938: Containing critiques of some poems by Donne.

BROOKS, C. *Yale Rev.* n.s. XXXIV, 1945, 642–65: Shakespeare as a Symbolist Poet.

BROOKS, C. *The Well Wrought Urn. Studies in the Structure of Poetry*, New York, 1947, [London, 1949]: References to Donne *passim* (see index). The essay entitled 'The Language of Paradox' had already appeared in *The Language of Poetry*, ed. A. Tate (Princeton U.P. 1942), and was reprinted elsewhere.

BROOKS, C. *Modern Poetry and the Tradition*, Chapel Hill and London, 1948: References to Donne *passim*.

BROOKS, C. *Sewan. Rev.* LIX, 1951, 1–22: Milton and the New Criticism.

BROOKS, H. *Times Lit. Sup.*, 16 August 1934, p. 565: Donne and Drant.

See further correspondence by J. Lindsay, 23 August; V. Scholderer, 30 August; E. G. Lewis, 6 September; J. Lindsay and A. Werner, 20 September; E. G. Lewis, 27 September.

BROSS, A. C. *Xavier Univ. Stud.* v, 1966, 133–52: Alexander Pope's Revisions of John Donne's Satyres.

BROWER, R. A. *The Fields of Light*, N.Y., 1951. For references to Donne see index.

BROWN, A. *Dublin Mag.*, April 1933, pp. 20–31: Scientific criticism in connection with the Clarendon edition of Donne.

BROWN, M. *Notes and Queries*, CLXXVIII, 1940, 12: Query as to author of 'Verses on Donne's burial'.

BROWN, N. P. *Mod. Lang. Rev.* LXVIII, 1953, 324–7: A note on the imagery of Donne's 'Love's Growth'.

BRUCE, G. H. *Diss. Abstr.* XXIII, 1963, 3350: John Donne and the Anglican Faith.

BRYAN, R. A. *Seventeenth Cent. News*, Summer 1954, p. 21: A Sidelight on Donne's Seventeenth Century Literary Reputation. Repr. in *S. Atlant. Bull.* XIX, no. 3, p. 11.

BRYAN, R. A. *Diss. Abstr.* XXI, 1961, 2702–3: The Reputation of John Donne in England, 1600–1832.

BRYAN, R. A. *Engl. Stud.* XLIII, 1962, 170–4: John Donne's Poems in Seventeenth Century Commonplace Books.

BRYAN, R. A. *Journ. Eng. Germ. Philol.* LXI, 1962, 305–12: John Donne's Use of the Anathema.

BRYAN, R. A. In *All These to Teach: Essays in Honor of C. A. Robertson*. Gainsville, 1965, pp. 120–9: Translatio Concepts in Donne's 'The Progress of the Soul'.

BRYSON, J. *The Times*, 13 October 1959, pp. 13, 15: Lost Portrait of Donne (the rediscovered Lothian portrait at Newbattle Abbey). See also letter from Geoffrey Keynes, 17 October 1959.

BUCHAN, H. A. *Bodl. Quart. Rec.* VII, 1933, 329–32: Thomas Pestell's poems in MS. Malone 14 (contains references to Donne).

BUCKLEY, V. *Crit. Rev.* (Melb.), no. 8, 1965, pp. 19–31: John Donne's Passion.

BUNTON, N. D. *Diss. Abstr.* XIV, 1954, 1841–2: A Rhetorical Analysis of Representative Sermons of John Donne [State Univ. of Iowa].

BUSH, D. *English Literature in the Earlier Seventeenth Century*, Oxford, 1945 (Oxford History of English Literature). Ch. iv, pp. 104–69. Jonson, Donne, and their successors (other references *passim* (see index)).

BUSH, D. *Science and English Poetry. A Historical Sketch. 1590–1950*, N.Y., 1950. For references see index.

BUTER, M. *Cahiers du Sud.* XXVIII, 1954, 276–83: Le Progrès de l'Âme de John Donne.

BUTT, J. E. *Times Lit. Sup.*, 10 April 1930, p. 318: John Donne and Lincoln's Inn. See also Shapiro, I. A., 16, 23 October.

BUTT, J. E. *Rev. Eng. Stud.* VIII, 1932, 72–4: Walton's copy of Donne's Letters.

BUTT, J. *Times Lit. Sup.*, 15, 29 December 1932, pp. 963, 989: Donne's Mr. Tilman.

BUTT, J. E. *Essays & Studies by Members of the Eng. Assoc.* XIX, 1933, 67–84: Izaak Walton's methods in biography.

BUXTON, J. *Elizabethan Taste*, London, 1963, pp. 317–38.

BYATT, A. S. *Times Sat. Rev.* 7 March 1970, p. iv: The Behaviour of John Donne. Review of Bald's *Life of Donne*.

C., S. *Explicator*, XVIII, 1959, item 1: Donne's 'The Legacie'.

CAIN, T. H. *Diss. Abstr.* XX, 1959, 2285: The Poem of Compliment in the English Renaissance.

CALLARD, I. *Times Lit. Sup.*, 23 December 1965: Donne's Books.

CAMERON, A. B. *Discourse*, XI, 1968, 252–6: Donne and Dryden: Their Achievement in the Verse Epistle.

CAMPBELL, H. M. *College English*, V, 1944, 192–6: Donne's 'Hymn to God, my God, in My Sickness'.

CAMPBELL, H. M. In *Readings for Liberal Education*, ed. L. G. Locke *et al.*, N.Y., II, 1948, pp. 500–4; 1952 edn., pp. 32–6: Donne's Hymn to God my God in My Sickness.

CANDELARIA, F. H. *Ren. Notes.* XIII, 1960, 294–7: Ovid and the Indifferent Lovers.

CAREY, J. *Times Lit. Sup.*, 27 March 1959, p. 177: 'Clement Paman', suggesting a date for the poem recorded in this *Bibliography*, 1958, p. 226, and drawing attention to further imitations of Donne's style in Paman's poems (Rawlinson MSS., BLO).

CAREY, J. *Rev. Eng. Stud.* XVI, 1965, pp. 50–3: Notes on two of Donne's Songs and Sonets ('A Valediction forbidding Mourning' and 'The Extasie').

CARLETON, P. D. *Mod. Lang. Notes*, LVI, 1941, 366–8: John Donne's 'Bracelet of bright hair about the bone'.

CAROLINE, SISTER MARY. *Xavier Univ. Stud.* VII, 1968, 37–50: The Existentialist Attitude of John Donne.

CARPENTER, F. I. *English Lyrical Poetry*, London, 1909, pp. xlvii ff., 113–19.

CATHCART, C. D. jr. *Diss. Abstr.* 1969, 29,

3092A: Doubting Conscience: John Donne and the Tradition of Casuistry (Vanderbilt).

CAUTHEN, I. B. ?unpublished paper, Univ. of Va.: Donne's Sweare by thy selfe (see *Seventeenth Cent. News*, 1958, 22).

CAZAMIAN, L. *Development of English Humour.* Durham, N. C., 1952, pp. 362–6: Donne.

CHADWICK, J. W. *New World*, IX, 1900, 35 ff.: John Donne, Poet and Preacher.

CHAMBERS, A. B. *Journ. Eng. Germ. Philol.* LIX, 1960, 212–17: The Meaning of the 'Temple' in Donne's 'La Corona'.

CHAMBERS, A. B. *Journ. Eng. Lit. Hist.* XXVIII, 1961, 31–53: Good Friday, 1613, Riding Westward: the Poem and the Tradition.

CHAMBERS, A. B. *Journ. Eng. Germ. Philol.* LXV, 1966, 252–9: The Fly in Donne's 'Canonization'.

CHAMBERS, E. K. *Mod. Lang. Rev.* V, 1910, 492–3: John Donne, Diplomatist and Soldier.
See also *Mod. Lang. Rev.* VI, 153, 397, for further notes by Grierson and Chambers.

CHAMBERS, E. K. *The Spectator*, CX. 1913, p. 102: The Poetry of John Donne.

CHAMBERS, E. K. *Mod. Lang. Rev.* IX, 1914, 269–71: The Poems of John Donne (Rev. of Grierson, 1912).

CHAMBERS, E. K. *Rev. Eng. Stud.* VII, 1931, 69–71: An Elegy by John Donne. (Lines from the Holgate MS. in the Pierpont Morgan Library.)

CHATMAN, S. *Kenyon Rev.* XVIII, 1956, 443–51: Mr. [Arnold] Stein on Donne.

CHIARI, J. In *The Harrap Anthology of French Poetry*, London, 1958, pp. 165–8: Relating Donne with Du Bartas.

CHIARI, V. K. *Ind. Journ. Eng. Stud.* VI, 1965, 19–32: The Dramatic in Donne.

CHITANAND, T. P. *Ind. Journ. Eng. Stud.* IV, 1963, 48–68: Donne's The progress of the Soul.

CHRISTENSEN, G. J. *Explicator*, VII, October 1948, item 3: Donne's 'The Sunne rising'.

CIRILLO, A. R. *Stud. Eng. Lit.* IX, 1969, 81–95: The Fair Hermaphrodite. Love Union in the Poetry of Donne and Spenser.

CLAIR, J. A. *Publ. Mod. Lang. Assoc.* LXXX, 1965, 300–2: Donne's 'The Canonization'.

CLEMENTS, A. L. *Mod. Lang. Notes.* LXXVI, 1961, 484–9: Donne's Holy Sonnet xiv.

CLEMENTS, A. L. ed. *John Donne's Poetry: Authoritative Texts, Criticism* (A. Norton, Crit. Ed.), N.Y., 1966.

CLEVELAND, E. D. *Explicator*, VIII, October 1949, item 4: Donne's 'The Primrose'.

CLINE, J. M. *The Poetry of the Mind.* Univ. Calif. Publ. Eng. IV, 1934, see pp. 27–47.

CLIVE, Lady MARY. *Jack and the Doctor*, London and N.Y., 21·5 cm, 1966, pp. [xiv], 216, [2]. Fully illustrated.
REVIEWED:
Times Lit. Sup., 25 May 1967, p. 436.

CLOUGH, B. C. *Mod. Lang. Notes*, XXXV, 1920, 115–17: Notes on the Metaphysical Poets.

CLUTTON-BROCK, A. *Essays on Books.* London [1920], pp. 78–91: Donne's Sermons.

COANDA, R. *Renascence.* IX, 1957, 180–7: Hopkins and Donne. Mystic and Metaphysical.

COBB, L. S. *Explicator*, XIV, 1956, item 40: Donne's Satyre II, 1–48.

COBB, L. S. *Explicator*, XV, 1956, item 8: Donne's Satyre II, 49–57.

COBB, L. S. *Diss. Abstr.* XVII, 1957, 1082: John Donne and the Common Law (Washington Univ.).

COFFIN, C. M. *Times Lit. Sup.*, 2 August 1934, p. 541: Bibliography of Donne.

COFFIN, C. M. *John Donne and the New Philosophy*, New York, 1937, 8º, pp. xii, 311.
REVIEWED:
Ashley-Montagu, M. F. *Isis*, XXVIII, 1937, 473–5.
Budd, F. E., *Rev. Eng. Stud.* XV, 1939, 101–3.
Flewelling, R. T. *Personalist*, XIX, 1938, 315–18.
Garrison, W. E. *Christ. Cent.* LIV, 1937, 1329.
Hutchison, P. *N.Y. Times*, 26 September 1937, p. 9.
Johnson, F. R. *Mod. Lang. Notes*, LIII, 1938, 290–3.
Jones, R. F. *Sewanee Rev.* XLVI, 1938, 261–3.
Legouis, P. *Études Angl.* II, 1938, 46–8.

Maude, Mother M. *Living Church*, xcvii, 1937, 198.

McColley, G. *Ann. Science*, ii, 1937, 475–6.

McNeil, J. T. *Journ. Relig.* xvii, 1937, 306–9.

Metz, R. *Englische Stud.* lxxiii, 1939, 397–401.

Shapiro, I. A. *Mod. Lang. Rev.* xxxiii, 1938, 280–1.

Times Lit. Sup., 21 August 1937, p. 604.

Van Doren, M. *Nation* (N.Y.), cxliv, 1937, 442–3.

Coffin, C. M. *Kenyon Rev.* xvi, 1954, 292–8: Donne's Divinity.

Coffin, R. P. T., and Witherspoon, A. M. *A Book of Seventeenth Century Prose*, London, 1929, see introduction and pp. 56–123.

Cogan, I. *Poetry Rev.* May 1929, pp. 183–94: John Donne: Poet and Metaphysician.

Cohen, J. M. *The Baroque Lyric*, London, 1963, ch. 6: Donne's Elephant and Donne's Courtier.

Coleridge, S. T. *Miscellaneous Criticism*, ed. T. M. Raysor, 1936, pp. 131–45: Marginalia on John Donne.

Colie, R. L. *Some Thankfulness to Constantine. A Study of English Influence upon the Early Works of Constantijne Huygens*, The Hague, 1956: Contains an account of Donne's relations with Huygens and of his translations of Donne's poems in *Korenbloemen*, 1672 (q.v., no. 108). For references see index.

Colie, R. L. *Philol. Quart.* xliii, 1964, pp. 145–70: i. The Rhetoric of Transcendence. ii. John Donne's Anniversary Poems and the Paradoxes of Epistemology. Repr. in her *Paradoxia Epidemica*, 1966.

Collins, C. *Explicator*, xii, October 1953, item 3: Donne's 'The Canonization'.

Collmer, R. G. *Diss. Abstr.* xii, 1953, 804–5: The Concept of Death in the Poetry of Donne, Herbert, Crashaw and Vaughan.

Collmer, R. G. *Mississ. Quart.* xiv, 1961, 51–7: The Background of Donne's Reception in Holland.

Collmer, R. G. *Humanitas*, no. 5, 1964, 297–307: John Donne, la Clave de la poesia inglese moderna.

Collmer, R. G. *Compar. Lit. Stud.* ii, 1965, 25–39: Donne's Poetry in Dutch Letters.

Collmer, R. G. *Rev. Litt. Comp.* xliii, 1969, 219–32: Donne and Borges.

Colvin, Sir S. *Eng. Assoc. Pamph.* no. 32, 1915, pp. 17–19: On Concentration and Suggestion in Poetry.

Combecher, H. *Neu. Sprach*, 1960, pp. 488–92: John Donne's 'Annunciation': Eine Interpretation.

Combellack, F. M. *Explicator*, xvii, 1958: Jonson's 'To John Donne'.

Conlon, Sister Mary Samuel. *Diss. Abstr.* xxiv, 1964, 2890: John Donne's Divine Poems: Another Dimension.

Coon, A. M. *Times Lit. Sup.*, 12 August 1939, p. 479: [Donne's] Farewell to Love.

Cooper, H. *Mod. Lang. Notes*, lvii, 1942, 661–3: John Donne and Virginia in 1610.

Corin, F. *Eng. Stud.* l, 1969, 89–93: A Note on Donne's 'Canonization'.

Cornelius, D. K. *Explicator*, xxiv, 1965, item 25: Donne's Holy Sonnet xiv.

Courthope, W. J. A. *A History of English Poetry*, London, 1903, vol. iii, ch. viii, pp. 147–68: The School of Metaphysical Wit: John Donne.

REVIEWED:

Quart. Rev. cc, 1904. Anon. The Meaning of Literature, p. 18.

Cowan, S. A. *Explicator*, xix, 1961, item 58: Donne's The Legacie, ll. 17–20.

Cox, G. H., III. *Diss. Abstr.* xxix, 1969, 3970A: Tradition and Devotion; The Prose Meditations of John Donne, Jeremy Taylor and Thomas Traherne (Stanford).

Cox, R. G. *Guide to Eng. Lit.* iii, 1956, pp. 98–115: The Poems of John Donne.

Cox, R. G. In *From Donne to Marvell*, ed. B. Ford, Penguin Books, 1956, pp. 43–85: Survey of literature from Donne to Marvell; pp. 98–115: The poems of Donne.

Crawford, C. *Notes and Queries*, 10th ser., 1905–6, iv, 41, 121, 201, 302; v, 301, 382; vi, 22: Montaigne, Webster, and Marston: Dr. Donne and Webster.

CRAWFORD, C. *Collectanea.*, ser. II, 1907, pp. 58–63.

CROFTS, J. E. V. In *Nelson's History of English Literature*, ed. J. Buchan, London, 1923, pp. 231–6: John Donne.

CROFTS, J. E. V. In *Essays and Studies by Members of the Eng. Assoc.* XXII, 1937, 128–43: John Donne.

CROSS, K. G. *Mod. Lang. Notes*, XXI, 1956, 480–2: 'Balm' in Donne and Shakespeare: Ironic Intention in 'The Extasie'.

CROSS, K. G. *Notes and Queries*, V (CCIII), 1958, 532–3: Another Donne Allusion (in Etherege's *Comic Revenge*).

CROSSETT, J. *Boston Univ. Stud. Engl.* IV, 1960, 121–4: Did Johnson mean 'Paraphysical'?

CROSSETT, J. *Notes and Queries*, VII (CCV), 1960, 386–7: Bacon and Donne (see p. 285 of this Bibliography).

CRUM, M. *Library*, XVI, 1961, 121–32: Notes on the Physical Characteristics of some MSS. of the Poems of Donne and King.

CRUM, M. *The Poems of Henry King*, Oxford, 1965. For references to Donne see index, especially pp. 45–6 for echoes of Donne.

CRUM, R. B. *Scientific Thought in Poetry*, New York, 1931, 8°, see pp. 42–8: References to Donne.

CRUTTWELL, P. *The Shakespearean Moment and its Place in the Poetry of the 17th Century*. London, 1954, N.Y., 1955, pp. 39–72: Donne and the 'New-found Methods'; pp. 73–106: The Poetry of the Shakespearian Moment (Donne's 'Anniversaries' and Shakespeare's Last Plays).

CRUTTWELL, P. In *Metaphysical Poetry. Stratford upon Avon Studies*, XI, London, 1970: John Donne. Pedantique Weeds or Fresh Invention.

CUNNINGHAM, J. S. *Durham Univ. Journ.* XVIII, 1958, 28: At Donne's Death Bed.

CUNNINGHAM, J. V. *Mod. Philol.* LI, 1954, 33–41: Logic and Lyric. Ref. to Donne, p. 36.

CURTIS, L. P., jr. *Times Lit. Sup.*, 18 May 1967: Letter on the review 'Ill Donne Well Donne' (6 April), with reply 25 May from the reviewer.

DAICHES, D. *A Critical History of English Literature*, 4 vols., London, 1960 (repr. 1961, 1963, 1968). For references to Donne see index.

DANBY, J. F. *Elizabethan and Jacobean Poets*, London, 1952: Many references to Donne (first pr. in *Poets on Fortune's Hill*, London, 1952).

DANIEL, E. R. *Anglic. Theolog. Rev.* XLVIII, 1966, 14–30: Reconciliation, Covenant and Election. A Study in the Theology of John Donne.

DANIELS, E. *The Art of Reading Poetry*, New York, 1941.

DANIELS, E. F. and WANDA, J. D. *Explicator*, XXIV, 1965, item 34: Donne's Elegy VII, l. 22.

DANIELS, R. B. *Some Seventeenth Century Worthies in a Twentieth Century Mirror*, Chapel Hill, 1940.

DARK, S. *Five Deans*, London, [1928], pp. 54–108: John Donne.

DAVENPORT, A. *Notes and Queries*, CC, 1955, 12: An early reference to John Donne (see Fennor, W. 1617).

DAVIES, H. S. *Rev. Eng. Lit.* VI, 1, 1965, 93–107: Text or Context? (reply by Helen Gardner, pp. 108–10).

DAVIS, B. H. *Diss. Abstr.* XXII, 1962, 3643: Studies in Donne by Ruth C. Wallerstein.

DAVIS, K. *Notes and Queries*, X (CCVIII), 1963, 187–9: Unpublished Coleridge Marginalia in a Volume of Donne's Poetry.

DAY, W. G. *Notes and Queries*, XVII (CCXV), 1970, p. 94: Sterne, Josephus and Donne (some borrowings from *Biathanatos*).

DEAS, M. C. *Rev. Eng. Stud.* VII, 1931, 454–7: A note on Rowland Woodward, the friend of John Donne.

DE HAVILLAND, M. *London Mercury*, XIII, 1925, 159–62: Two Unpublished Manuscripts of John Donne (including one letter, see no. 68*b*).

DE LA MARE, W. J. *Edinb. Rev.* CCXVII, 1913, 372–86: An Elizabethan poet and modern poetry.

DELATTRE, F. *Mod. Lang.* XXVIII, 1947, 91–6: De la Chanson Elizabéthaine ou Poème Métaphysique.

DE MARAY, J. G. *Personalist.* XLVI, 1965, pp. 366–81: Donne's Three Steps to Death.

DE MOURGUES, O. *Metaphysical Baroque & Précieux Poetry*, Oxford, 1953: References to Donne *passim* (see index).

DENONAIN, J. J. *Thèmes et formes de la poésie 'métaphysique'*, Paris, 1956: References to Donne, esp. pp. 99–184, 410–25.

DICKER, H. *Centenn. Rev.* XI, 1967, pp. 53–64: The Bell of John Donne.

DIONISOTTI, C. *Times Lit. Sup.*, 2 November 1967, p. 1037: A Donne Discovery (see under P. G. Stanwood).

DOBB, C. *Times Lit. Sup.*, 30 December 1965, p. 1213: Donne's Books.

DOEBLER, B. A. V. *Diss. Abstr.* XXI, 1961, 3096: Death in the Sermons of John Donne.

DOEBLER, B. A. V. *Anglia*, LXXXV, 1967, 15–33: Donne's Debt to the Great Tradition. Old and New in the Testament of Death.

DOGGETT, F. A. *Sewanee Rev.* XLII, 1934, 274–92: Donne's Platonism.

DORSTEN, J. A. van, *Tijdschr. nederland Taalen-Letter kunde*, Leyden, LXXVI, 1959, 111–25: Huygens en de Engelse 'metaphysical poets'.

DOUDS, J. B. *Cornell Abstr. of Theses*, 1936, p. 3: Poetry of Donne, Herbert, Cowley, and Marvell.

DOUDS, J. B. *Publ. Mod. Lang. Assoc. Am.* LII, 1937, 1051–61: Donne's technique of dissonance.

DOUGHTY, W. L. *Studies in Religious Poetry of the Seventeenth Century*, London, [1946].

DOUGLAS, N. *Times Lit. Sup.*, 23 December 1926, p. 949: Donne's Anatomie.

DOWDEN, E. *Essays Modern and Elizabethan*, London, 1910, pp. 308–33: Elizabethan Psychology (with indirect bearing on Donne's poetry).

DRINKWATER, D. J. *Notes and Queries*, CXCIX, 1954, 514–15: More references to John Donne.

DUCKLES, V. *7th. Internat. Musicolog. Conf. Bericht.* Kessel and London, 1959, pp. 91–3: The Lyrics of John Donne as set by his Contemporaries.

DUNCAN, E. H. *Bull. Vanderbilt Univ.* XLI, 1941, 16–17: Alchemy in the Writings of Chaucer, Jonson, and Donne [abstr. of diss.].

DUNCAN, E. H. *Journ. Eng. Lit. Hist.* IX, 1942, 257–85: Donne's alchemical figures.

DUNCAN, E. H. *Explicator*, I, June 1943, item 63: Donne's 'A valediction forbidding mourning'.

DUNCAN, J. E. *Stud. Philol.* L, 1953, 81–100: The intellectual kinship of John Donne and Robert Browning.

DUNCAN, J. E. *Publ. Mod. Lang. Assoc.* LXVIII, 1953, 658–71: The revival of metaphysical poetry.

DUNCAN, J. F. *Stud. Philol.* L, 1953, 81–110: The Intellectual Kinship of John Donne and Robert Browning. Repr. in *The Revival of Metaphysical Poetry, 1800 to the Present.* Minneapolis, Univ. of Minnesota Press, 1959, pp. 236. See esp. 'Donne and Browning', 'Yeats, Donne and the Metaphysicals'. Most of Browning's references to Donne will be found here.

DUNCAN-JONES, E. E. *Notes and Queries*, VII, 1960, 53: The Barren Plane-Tree in Donne's 'The Autumnal'.

DUNCAN-JONES, E. E. *Mod. Lang. Rev.* LVI, 1961, 213–15: Donne's Praise of Autumnal Beauty. Greek Sources.

DUNLAP, R. *Times Lit. Sup.*, 28 December 1946, p. 643: Donne as Navigator.

DUNLAP, R. *Mod. Lang. Notes*, LXIII, 1948, 258–9: The date of Donne's 'The Annunciation'.

DUNN, E. C. *The Literature of Shakespeare's England*, New York, [1936], pp. 158–63: A Note on John Donne (and other references (see index)).

DUNN, S. G. *Times Lit. Sup.*, 7 July 1921, p. 436: The Authorship of *Polydoron* (letter, suggesting that the younger Donne was the author).

DURAND, L. G. *Comp. Lit.* XXI, 1969, 319–36: Sponde and Donne. Lens and Prism.

DURR, R. A. *Journ. Eng. Germ. Philol.* LIX, 1960, 218–22: Donne's 'The Primrose'.

EASTMAN, M. *The Literary Mind*, N.Y., 1931: References to Donne pp. 135 ff.

EATON, H. A. *Sewanee Rev.* XXII, 1914, 50–72: Songs and Sonnets of John Donne.

ELDREDGE, F. *Journ. Eng. Lit. Hist.* XIV, 1952, 214–28: Further allusions and debts to John Donne.

ELIOT, T. S. *New Statesman*, VIII, 1915, 518: Reflections on Vers Libre.

ELIOT, T. S. *The Sacred Wood*, London, [1920], p. 20: Chapman's affinity to Donne.

ELIOT, T. S. *Times Lit. Sup.*, 20 October 1921, pp. 669–70: The Metaphysical Poets (unsigned). Repr. in *Selected Essays*, London, 1932, and elsewhere. Reviewing Grierson's *Metaphysical Lyrics and Poems of the Seventeenth Century*, Oxford, 1921.

ELIOT, T. S. *Nation and Athen.* XXXIII, 1923, 331–2: John Donne.

ELIOT, T. S. *The School of Donne*, Clark Lectures, Cambridge, 1926, never printed (see H. Gardner, *A Collection of Seventeenth Century Essays*, 1962, p. 7 n.)

ELIOT, T. S. In *Nouv. Rev. Franc.* XXVII, 1926, 524–6: Note sur Mallarmé et Poe (references to Donne).

ELIOT, T. S. *Chroniques*, no. 3, 1927: Deux Attitudes Mystiques. Dante et Donne.

ELIOT, T. S. *The Listener*, III, 1930, 552–3: The Devotional Poets of the Seventeenth Century. Donne, Herbert, Crashaw.

ELIOT, T. S. *The Listener*, 19, 26 March 1930, Talks on Donne's poetry (broadcast).

ELIOT, T. S. In *A Garland for John Donne*, ed. T. Spencer, Cambridge, Mass., 1931, pp. 3–19: Donne in Our Time.

ELIOT, T. S. *Essays Ancient & Modern*, London, [1936], pp. 11–29: Lancelot Andrewes. References to Donne (first printed in *For Lancelot Andrewes*, 1928).

ELLIOTT, G. R. *The Bookman*, LXXIII, 1931, 337–46: John Donne, the middle phase.

ELLRODT, R. *English*, VII, 1949, 228–31: Drummond's debt to Donne.

ELLRODT, R. *Études Angl.* XIII, 1960, 452–63: Chronologie des poèmes de Donne.

ELLRODT, R. *L'Inspiration Personnelle et l'esprit du temps chez les Poètes Métaphysiques Anglais*, 3 vols., Paris, 1960. Vol. 1 is entitled: John Donne et les poètes de la tradition chrétienne (pp. 460).

ELLRODT, R. *Mod. Philol.* LXI, 1964, 180–97: Scientific Curiosity and Metaphysical Poetry in the Seventeenth Century.

ELLRODT, R. *Études Angl.* XX, 1968, 282–9: Nouvelle édition de Donne.

ELMEN, P. *Papers Bibliogr. Soc. Am.* XLIX, 1955, 181–6: John Donne's Dark Lantern (in 'A Litanie').

ELTON, O. *The English Muse*, London, 1933, pp. 208–12: Survey of Donne's poetry. For other references see index.

EMMERSON, K. T. *Mod. Lang. Notes*, LXXII, 1957, 93–5: Two Problems in Donne's 'Farewell to Love'.

EMPSON, W. *Seven Types of Ambiguity*, London, 1930, see pp. 175–86, etc.: References to Donne.

EMPSON, W. *Some Versions of Pastoral*, London, 1938 [pub. in U.S.A. as: *English Pastoral Poetry*].

EMPSON, W. *Kenyon Rev.* XI, 1949, pp. 571–87: Donne and the rhetorical tradition.

EMPSON, W. *Kenyon Rev.* XIX, 1957, 337–99: Donne the Space Man.

EMPSON, W. *Crit. Quart.* VIII, 1966, 255–80: Donne in the New Edition.

EMPSON, W. *Crit. Quart.* IX, 1967, 89: Donne.

EMSLIE, M. *Notes and Queries*, CXCVIII, 1953, 495: A Donne setting.

EMSLIE, M. *Notes and Queries*, CC, 1955, 12–13: Barclay Squire and Grierson's Donne.

ENGLAND, M. W., and SPARROW, J. *Hymns Unbidden. Donne, Herbert, Blake, Emily Dickinson and the Hymnographers*, New York, N.Y. Publ. Libr., 1966.

REVIEWED:

Times Lit. Sup., 25 May 1967, p. 436.

ESCH, A. *Englische religiöse Lyrik des 17. Jahrhunderts: Studien zu Donne, Herbert, Crashaw, Vaughan*, Tübingen, 1955.

REVIEWED:

Ellrodt, R. *Études Angl.* IX, 1956, 55–7.

Leishman, J. B. *Rev. Eng. Stud.* N.S. VII, 1956, 310–16.

Martin, L. C. *Mod. Lang. Rev*, LI, 1956, 101–2.

Martz, L. L. *Mod. Philol.* LIV, 1957, 278–80.

ESCH, A. *Anglia*, LXXVIII, 1960, 74–7: Paradise and Calvary.

ESCOTT, H. *Congregational Quart.* January 1940, pp. 57–64: The Modern Relevance of John Donne.

ESDAILE, K. A. *English Church Monuments 1510–1840*, London, 1946: References to Donne's monument, pp. 20, 82, 104–5.

ESDAILE, K. A. *Times Lit. Sup.*, 23 August 1947, p. 427: Monuments resembling Donne's.

EVANS, B. I. *Tradition and Romanticism: Studies in English Poetry from Chaucer to W. B. Yeats*, London and New York, 1940, pp. 44–60: Donne to Milton.

EVANS, E. W. P. *Welsh Outlook*, 1931, pp. 208–10: John Donne.

EVANS, G. B. *Mod. Lang. Rev.* LVII, 1962, 60–2: Two Notes on Donne: 'The Undertaking', 'A Valediction of my Name in the Window'.

EVANS, M. *English Literature in the Sixteenth Century*, London, 1955, pp. 161–75: Donne and the Elizabethans.

EVERSON, W. *Explicator*, IV, June 1946, item 56: Donne's 'The Apparition'.

FAERBER, H. *Das paradoxe in der Dichtung von John Donne*, Zürich, 1950.
REVIEWED:
Conkin, G. S. *Journ. Eng. Germ. Philol.* LI, 1952, 105–6.
Leishman, J. B. *Mod. Lang. Rev.* LXVIII, 1952, 575.
Times Lit. Sup., 20 July 1951, p. 452.

FALK, R. E. *Explicator*, XVII, 1959, item 24: Donne's 'Resurrection Imperfect'.

FAUSSET, H. I'A. *John Donne. A Study in Discord*, London, [1924], 8°, pp. 318, [2], with four portraits.
REVIEWED:
Aldington, R. *Nation and Athen.* XXXVI, 1924, 220.
Binyon, L. *Bookman* (Lond.), LXVII, 1925, 201–2.
Bredvold, L. I. *N.Y. Her. Trib.*, 15 March 1925, p. 5.
Coppard, A. E. *Sat. Rev.* CXXXVIII, 1924, 449.
Lucas, F. L. *New Statesman*, XXIV, 1924, 112.
Morley, C. *Sat. Rev. Lit.* I, 1925, 613.
Porter, A. *Spectator*, CXXXIV, 24 January 1925, p. 122.
Read, H. *Criterion*, III, 1925, 315–20.

Schriftgiesse, K. *Bost. Transcr.*, 21 February 1925, p. 5.
Turner, A. R. *N.Y. Ev. Post*, 25 April 1927, p. 7.
Times Lit. Sup., 16 October 1924, p. 647.
Zeitlin, J. *Nation*, CXXI, 1925, 235–6.

FAUSSET, H. I'A. *Bookman*, London, LXXIX, 1931, 341–2: In Memory of John Donne. The Poet and his Vision.

FAUSSET, H. I'A. *The Holy Sonnets of John Donne*, 1938.

FAUSSET, H. I'A. *Poets and Pundits*, London, [1947], pp. 130–4: Donne's 'Holy Sonnets'.

FEDDEN, H. R. *Suicide*, London, [1938]. See pp. 135–6, 142, 178–85, etc.

FIEDLER, L. A. In *Summaries of Doctoral Diss.*, *Univ. of Wisconsin*, VI, 1942, pp. 281–2: John Donne's 'Songs and Sonnets': A Reinterpretation in the Light of Their Traditional Backgrounds.

FIELD, G. C. *Anglic. Theolog. Rev.* XLVIII, 1966, 307–9: Donne and Hooker.

FIELDING, E. *The Month*, CCXXVIII, 1969, pp. 194–202: John Donne and the New Christianity.

FINKELPEARL, P. J. *Rev. Eng. Stud.* XIV, 1963, 164–7: Donne and Everard Gilpin. Additions, Corrections and Conjectures.

FLEISSNER, R. F. *Mod. Lang. Notes*, LXXVI, 1961, 315–20: Donne and Dante. The Compass Figure Reinterpreted.

FLOWER, R. *The Times*, 2 November 1938, pp. 15–16: A Poet's Love Story. (Article on the Loseley MSS.)

FOGLE, R. H. *Journ. Eng. Lit. Hist.* XII, 1945, 221: Romantic bards and metaphysical reviewers.
Repr. in *The Imagery of Keats and Shelley*, 1949.

FORSTER, L. *Times Lit. Sup.*, 9 December 1965, p. 1159: Donne's Books (see also 23 December, p. 1204, and 27 January 1966).

FOSTER, T. *Month*, CLVII, 1931, 404–9: The Tragedy of John Donne.

FOX, R. C. *Hist. Ideas News Letter*, V, 1960, pp. 77–80: Donne in the British West Indies.

FRANCIS, H. E. *Diss. Abstr.* xxv, 1964, 1891: The Adjectives of Donne and Wordsworth. The Key to a Poetic Quality.

FRANCIS, W. N. *Explicator*, XIII, 1955, 21: Donne's 'Good Friday 1613. Riding Westward'.

FRANCON, M. *Publ. Mod. Lang. Assoc.* LVI, 1941, 307–36: Un motif de la poésie amoureuse au xvie siècle ('The Flea').

FRECCERO, J. *Journ. Eng. Lit. Hist.* xxx, 1963, 335–76: Donne's 'Valediction Forbidding Mourning'.

FREEMAN, R. *English Emblem Books*, London, 1948.
For references to Donne see index.

FRENCH, A. L. *Essays in Crit.* (Oxford), XVII, 1967, pp. 115–20: Dr. Gardner's Dating of the Songs and Sonnets.

FRENCH, J. M. *Times Lit. Sup.*, 12 December 1936, p. 1035: Bowman *v.* Donne [jr.].

FRERE, W. H. *A History of the English Church, 1558–1625*, London, 1904, p. 349: Donne and *Pseudo-Martyr*.

FRIEDMAN, D. M. *Marvell's Pastoral Art*, Berkeley, 1970: References to Donne.

FRITZ, H. *Lock Haven Rev.* IX, 1967, 16–38: Drummond's Authentic Voice.

FROST, A. C. *Cambridge Rev.* 1929, pp. 449–50: Donne and a Modern Poet [T. S. Eliot].

FRYE, NORTHROP. *Anatomy of Criticism. Four Essays*, Princeton, 1957: References to Donne, pp. 12, 18, 143, 258, 298, 299.

FRYE, R. M. *Notes and Queries*, CXCVII, 1952, 495–6: John Donne junior on *Biathanatos*.

FURST, CLYDE B. *Mod. Lang. Notes*, XII, 1897, 159–60: Notes on Donne.

GALE, R. L. *Explicator*, XV, 1956, item 14: Donne's 'The Sunne Rising', 27–30.

GAMBERINI, S. *Poeti Metafisici e Cavalieri in Inghilterra*, Florence, 1959.

GAMBERINI, S. *Saggio su John Donne*, Genova, Inst. di lingua e lett. inglese e anglo-amer., 1967.

GARDNER, H. L. *Mod. Lang. Rev.* XXXIX, 1944, 333–7: John Donne; A Note on Elegie V, 'His Picture'.

GARDNER, H. L. *Mod. Lang. Rev.* XLI, 1946, 318–21: Notes on Donne's verse letters.

GARDNER, H. L. *Brit. Afr. Monthly*, I, 1948, 31–2.

GARDNER, H. L. *Sobornost*, III, 1953, pp. 7–12: 'None Other Name'.

GARDNER, H. L. *Times Lit. Sup.*, 30 January 1953, p. 73: Letter on Donne's 'Divine Poems'.

GARDNER, H. L. *The Limits of Literary Criticism*, London, 1956. Repr. in *The Business of Criticism*, Oxford, 1959, pp. 62–75: 'Air and Angels'; also pp. 136–42.

GARDNER, H. L. *Mod. Lang. Rev.* LII, 1957, 564–5: Another Note on Donne's 'Since She whome I Lov'd'.

GARDNER, H. L. *The Metaphysical Poets, selected and edited*, Penguin Books, London, 1957.
REVIEWED:
Seventeenth Cent. News, 1958, 21.

GARDNER, H. L. In *Elizabethan and Jacobean Studies Presented to F. P. Wilson*, Oxford, 1959, pp. 279–306: The Argument about the Extasy.

GARDNER, H. L. *Times Lit. Sup.*, 11 March 1960, p. 168: Donne MSS. for the Bodleian (concerning the gift of the Wilfred Merton MSS. by Dr. E. S. de Beer).

GARDNER, H. L. (ed.). *John Donne A Collection of Critical Essays*, Englewood Cliffs, N.J., 1962 (Twentieth Century Views). With contributions by G. Saintsbury, H. J. C. Grierson, P. Legouis, W. Empson, M. Praz, J. E. V. Crofts, C. S. Lewis, C. Brooks, J. B. Leishman, H. Gardner, E. M. Simpson, L. L. Martz, A. J. Smith.
REVIEWED:
H. Maclean. *Univ. Toronto Quart.* XXIII, 89–97.

GARDNER, H. L. *Times Lit. Sup.*, 26 August 1965, p. 740: Donne's Platan Tree.

GARDNER, H. L. *Crit. Quart.* VIII, no. 4, 1966, 374–7: Letter in defence of Empson's criticism of her edition of *Elegies Songs and Sonnets*, 1966.

GARDNER, H. L. In *Friendship's Garland. Essays Presented to Mario Praz*, Rome, 1966, 2 vols. I, pp. 189–207: The Titles of Donne's Poems.

GARDNER, H. L. *Times Lit. Sup.*, 24 August 1967, p. 772: On Editing Donne (see also 8 June, p. 509).

GARDNER, H. L., and LEISHMAN, J. B. *Times Lit. Sup.*, 11 May 1956, p. 283: Poetic Tradition in Donne.

GARDNER, H. L., and SIMPSON, E. *Times Lit. Sup.*, 25 May 1956, p. 320: Donne and the Church.

GARNETT, R., and GOSSE, E. W. *English Literature, An Illustrated Record in Four Volumes*, London, Heinemann, 1903, vol. II, pp. 292–6: John Donne (illustrated).

GARROD, H. W. *Times Lit. Sup.*, 30 December 1944: The date of Donne's birth.

GARROD, H. W. *Rev. Eng. Stud.* XXI, 1945, 38–42: The Latin poem addressed by Donne to Dr. Andrews; pp. 161–73: Donne and Mrs. Herbert.

GARSTANG, A. H. *Fortnightly Rev.* LXXX, 1903, 976–7: Poetry of John Donne.

GARVIN, K. *Times Lit. Sup.*, 23 November 1953, p. 770: Looking babies.
See also Tillotson, G., 7 December, p. 338; Wilson, F. P., Waller, R. D., Lindsay, J., 14 December, p. 859.

GEGENHEIMER, A. F. *South Atlantic Quart.* XLVI, 1947, 511–23: They Might Have Been Americans.

GERALDINE, SISTER M. *Stud. Philol.* LXI, 1964, pp. 41–63: Erasmus and the Tradition of Paradox (Donne's Paradoxes).

GERALDINE, SISTER M. *Stud. Eng. Lit.* V, 1965, 115–131: John Donne and the Mindes Indeavours.

GERALDINE, SISTER M. *Univ. Toronto Quart.* XXXVI, 1966, 24–36: Donne's Notitia: the Evidence of the Satires.

GÉRARD, A. *Publ. de l'Univ. de l'État à Élisabethville*, I, 1961, pp. 27–37: Mannerism and the Scholastic Structure of Donne's 'Extasie'.

GIBBS, A. M. *Rev. Eng. Stud.* XVIII, 1967, 45–8: A Davenant Imitation of Donne?

GIERASCH, W. *Explicator*, VI, May 1948, item 47: Donne's 'The Sunne rising'.

GIERASCH, W. *Explicator*, IX, November 1950, item 13: Donne's 'Negative love'.

GIFFORD, W. *Hunt. Libr. Quart.* XXIX, 1966, 235–44: John Donne's Sermons on the Grand Days.

GIFFORD, W. *Notes and Queries*, XIII, 1966, 14: A Donne Allusion (in Gataker's *Discours Apologetical*, 1654).

GIFFORD, W. *Publ. Mod. Lang. Assoc.* LXXXII, 1967, 388–98: Time and Place in Donne's Sermons.

GIFFORD, W. *Notes and Queries*, XVI, 1969, 370–1: Donne on Candlemas at St. Paul's.

GILBERT, A. H. *Explicator*, IV, June 1946, item 56: Donne's 'The Apparition'.

GILPATRICK, N. *Cath. World*, CLIX, April. 1944, 52–7: Autobiographies of Grace.

GLECKNER, R. F. *Explicator*, VIII, April 1950, item 43: Donne's 'Love's Usury'.

GOHN, E. S. *Papers Mich. Acad. Sci. Arts Lett.* XLVIII, 1963, 609–19: Dating Donne and Scholarly Sentimentality.

GOLDBERG, M. A. *Explicator*, XIV, 1956, item 50: Donne's 'A Lecture upon the Shadow'.

GORLIER, C. *Paragone*, XVI, 1965, CLXXXII, pp. 55–78; CLXXXIV, pp. 43–80: Il poeta e la nuova alchimia.

GOSSE, Sir E. *Seventeenth Century Studies*, 1913.

GOSSE, Sir E. *Sunday Times*, London, 12 October 1919: The Sepulchral Dean.

GOSSE, Sir E. *More Books on the Table*, London, 1923, pp. 307–13: Metaphysical Poetry.

GRANSDEN, K. W. *John Donne* (Men and Books Series), London, 1954, 18·5 cm, pp. VIII, 197, [1].
REVIEWED:
Times Lit. Sup., 19 November 1954, p. 740.
Davenport, A. *Year's Work in Eng. Stud.* XXXV, 1954, 130: Reviews several articles and books on Donne.
Heuer, H. *Shakespeare Jahrbuch*, XCI, 1955, 318–19.
Lawlor, J. *Time & Tide*, 20 November 1954, 1554.
Legouis, P. *Études Angl.* VIII, 1955, 156–7.
Michie, J. *Lond. Mag.* II, March 1955, 86–9.

GRAY, M. MURIEL. *Times Lit. Sup.*, 8 April 1920, p. 225: Drummond's borrowings from Donne.

GRAZIANI, R. *Rev. Eng. Stud.* XIX, 1968, 121–36: John Donne's 'The Extasie' and Ecstasy.

GREENE, G. S. *Philol. Quart.* XI, 1932, 26–38: Drummond's borrowings from Donne.

GREGORY, E. R., jr. *Univ. Rev.* (Kansas), XXXV, 1968, 51–4: The Balance of Parts: Imagistic Unity in Donne's 'Elegie xix'.

GRENANDER, M. E. *Explicator*, XII, 1955, item 42: Donne's 'Holy Sonnets xii'.

GRENANDER, M. E. *Bost. Univ. Stud. Eng.* IV, 1960, pp. 95–105: Holy Sonnets viii and xvii, John Donne.

GRENMAN, J. E. *The Poetry of John Donne and the Metaphysical Poets*, N.Y., 1965 (Monarch Notes and Study Guide).

GRETTON, G. H. In *Arbeiten aus dem Seminar für Englische Sprache und Kultur an der Hansischen Universität*, Hamburg, 1936: John Donne: the spiritual background.
REVIEWED:
Brunner, K., *Literaturblatt*, LX, 1939, 21.

GRETTON, G. H. *John Donne: seine Beziehung zu seiner Zeit und seine Einfluss auf seine 'nichtmetaphysischen' Nachfolger*, Düsseldorf, 1938.

GRIERSON, Sir H. J. C. In *Periods of English Literature*, Edinburgh and London, 1906, vol. VII, pp. 152 ff.: The First Half of the Seventeenth Century.

GRIERSON, Sir H. J. C. *Camb. Hist. of Eng. Lit.* IV, Cambridge, 1909, ch. xi, pp. 196–223: John Donne (Bibliography, pp. 488–90).

GRIERSON, Sir H.J. C. *Notes and Queries*, N. S. II, 1910, 7–8: A Query on O'Flaherty's copy of the *Anniversaries*, etc. See also W. Scott, pp. 75–6.

GRIERSON, Sir H. J. C. *Mod. Lang. Rev.* VI, 1911, 145–56: Bacon's poem 'The World': its date and relation to certain other poems. Repr. in *Essays and Addresses*, 1940, pp. 221–37.

GRIERSON, Sir H. J. C. *Mod. Lang. Rev.* VI, 1911, 383–6: The authorship of 'Absence, Hear Thou My Protection'.

GRIERSON, Sir H. J. C. *Mod. Lang. Rev.* IX, 1914, 237–9: Donniana.

GRIERSON, Sir H. J. C. *Metaphysical Lyrics and Poems of the Seventeenth Century*, Oxford, 1921, 8°, pp. 1–23: Selection of Donne's poems, with general introduction and notes.

GRIERSON, Sir H. J. C. *The Background of Metaphysical Poetry*, London, 1924, pp. 115–66: The Metaphysical Poets.

GRIERSON, Sir H. J. C. *New Statesman*, XXVI, 1925, 108; Reply to Donne's poems: Concerning the authorship of Absence, Hear thou my Protestations.

GRIERSON, Sir H. J. C. *Cross-currents in English Literature of the Seventeenth Century*, London, 1929.

GRIERSON, Sir H. J. C. *Times Lit. Sup.*, 5 December 1929, p. 1032: Donne and Lucretius (letter).

GRIERSON, Sir H. J. C. *Times Lit. Sup.*, 6 March 1930, p. 190: Donne's Satyres, II, ll. 71–3.
See also Sisson, C. J., 13 March, p. 214.

GRIERSON, Sir H. J. C. *Times Lit. Sup.*, 26 February 1931, p. 154: Donne and the Roman Poets (letter).

GRIERSON, Sir H. J. C. *Spectator*, 26 March 1943: A Spirit in Conflict (letter; see Hardy, E.).

GRIERSON, Sir H. J. C. *Mod. Lang. Rev.* XLIII, 1948, 305–14: John Donne and the *Via Media*.
Repr. in *Criticism and Creation*, London, 1949.

GRIERSON, Sir H. J. C., *Criticism and Creation*, London, 1949, pp. 35–45: The Metaphysics of Donne and Milton.

GRIERSON, Sir H. J. C., and SISSON, C. J. *Times Lit. Sup.*, 20 February 1930, p. 142: The Oxford Donne (letters).

GRIERSON, Sir H. J. C., and SMITH, J. C. *A Critical History of English Poetry*, New York, 1946 [1944], pp. 99–109: The Jacobeans.

GRINDIN, J. J. *Diss. Abstr.* XIV, 1954, 2066–7: Renaissance and Modern Theories of Irony. Their Application to Donne's 'Songs and Sonnets'.

GRØNBECH, V. *Mystikere i Europa og Indien. 4. Del. Donne, Wordsworth, Herder*, Copenhagen, 1934.

GROOM, B. *The Diction of Poetry from Spenser to Bridges*, Toronto, 1956.

GROS, LÉON G. *Cahiers du Sud*, 1936, pp. 785–802: Présentation de John Donne (with translations).

Gros, L. G. *Cahiers du Sud*, XXIX, 1949, 3–30: Métaphysique Anglais, du raisonnement en poésie.

Gros, L. G. *John Donne. Étude et traduction*, Paris, Seghers, 1964. 15·3 cm, pp. 214, [2]. Illustrated.
REVIEWED:
Ellrodt, R. *Études Angl.* XIX, 303–4.

Grundy, J. *Times Lit. Sup.*, 27 April 1956, p. 253: Donne's Poetry.

Guss, D. L. *Diss. Abstr.* XXII, 1961, 1998–9: Donne's Songs and Sonnets and Italian Courtly Love Poetry.

Guss, D. L. *Notes and Queries*, X, 1963, 57–8: Donne and the Greek Anthology.

Guss, D. L. *Publ. Mod. Lang. Assoc.* LXXVIII, 1963, 308–14: Donne's Conceit and Petrarchan Wit.

Guss, D. L. *Hunt. Libr. Quart.* XXVIII, 1964, 79–82: Donne's 'The Anagram'. Sources and Analogues.

Guss, D. L. *Journ. Eng. Germ. Philol.* LXIV, 1965, 17–28: Donne's Petrarchism.

Guss, D. L. *John Donne Petrarchist. Italianate Conceits and Love Theory in the 'Songs and Sonets'*, Detroit, Wayne State U.P., 1966, pp. 231.
REVIEWED:
Colie, R. L. *Mod. Lang. Quart.* XXVIII, 1967, 496–7.

Daniels, E. F. *Seventeenth Cent. News*, XXVI, 1968, 38–9.

Grant, P. *Journ. Eng. Germ. Philol.* LVI, 1967, 582–4.

Marenco, F. *Notes and Queries*, CCXIII, 1968, 111–12.

Redpath, T. *Rev. Eng. Stud.* XIX, 1968, 193–6.

Smith, A. J. *Renaiss. Quart.* XXI, 1968, 230–2.

Warnke, F. J. *Mod. Philol.* LXVI, 1968, 77–9.

Hacker, M. *Bookman*, LXXX, 1931, 140: To John Donne (poem).

Haddow, G. C. *Queen's Quart.* XL, 1933, 87–98: Donne's Prose.

Haefner, G. *Neuer. Spracher.* XVIII, 1969, 169–75: John Donne. 'The Canonization'. Eine Interpretation.

Hagopian, J. V. *Diss. West. Res. Univ.*, 1955: The Morphology of John Donne. Including a Pun Index, Rhyme Index and Studies in the Relations between Linguistics and Literature.

Hagopian, J. V. *Notes and Queries*, IV (CCII), 1957, 500–2: Some Cruxes in Donne's Poetry.

Hagopian, J. V. *Explicator*, XVII, 1958, item 5: Donne's 'Love's Diet', ll. 20–4.

Hagopian, J. V. *Mod. Lang. Notes*, LXXIII, 1958, 255–7: A Difficult Crux in Donne's Satyre II (ll. 71–3).

Halewood, W. H. *Donne to Milton*, Yale Univ. Press, New Haven and London, 1970.

Hall, V., jr. *Explicator*, XV, 1957, item 24: Donne's Satyre II.

Hamburger, —. *Transformation*, II, 1940: Some Aspects of Donne.

Hamer, E. *The Metres of English Poetry*, London, [1930], see pp. 50, 199–202, 237.

Hamilton, C. H. *Diss. Abstr.* XXIX, 1968, 262A–63A: A Study of Imagery in John Donne's Sermons (Univ. of Arkansas).

Hamilton, G. Rostrevor. *Lond. Mercury*, 1926, pp. 606–20: Wit and Beauty. A study of metaphysical poetry [Donne and Francis Thompson].

Hamilton, G. R. *The Tell-Tale Article: A Critical Approach to Modern Poetry*, London, 1949 (ch. i uses Donne's poetry to explain absence of the definite article).

Hanford, J. H. *Studies in Shakespeare, Milton and Donne*, Univ. of Mich. I, 1925.

Harding, D. W. *Kenyon Rev.* XIII, 1951, 427–44: Coherence of theme in Donne's poetry. Repr. in *Experience into Words*, London, 1963, pp. 11–30.

Hardison, O. B. *The Enduring Monument. A Study of the Idea of Praise in Renaissance Literary Theory and Practice*, Univ. of N. Carol., 1962 (Donne's *Anniversaries*).

Hardy, E. *Donne: A Spirit in Conflict*, London, 1942, 18 cm, pp. xii, [2], 274, [2].
REVIEWED:
Times Lit. Sup., 27 March 1943, p. 154.

Harper, G. McL. *Literary Appreciations*, Indianapolis, 1937, pp. 21–6: John Donne.

HARRINGTON, D. V. *Explicator*, XXV, 1966, item 22: Donne's 'The Relique'.

HARRIS, B. In *Shakespeare Survey*, XVII, ed. A. Nicoll, Cambridge, 1964, 120–37: Dissent and Satire (with references to Donne).

HARRIS, V. *All Coherence Gone*, Chicago, 1949: References to Donne and Du Bartas (on the background of 'The First Anniversarie').

HARRIS, V. *Philol. Quart.* XLI, 1962, 257–69: John Donne and the Theatre.

HARRISON, C. T. *Harvard Stud. in Classical Philol.* XLV, 179: The Ancient Atomists and English Literature of the Seventeenth Century.

HARRISON, G. B. *Nicholas Breton Melancholike Humours. Edited with an Essay on Elizabethan Melancholy*, London, 1929, p. 74: Reference to Donne.

HARRISON, G. B. *Times Lit. Sup.*, 29 May 1937, p. 412: Donne's Satires.

HARRISON, J. S. *Platonism in English Poetry of the 16th and 17th centuries*, Columbia Univ. Press, New York, 1903: References to Donne's conceptions of Love and Women.

HARRISON, R. *Explicator*, XXV, 1967, item 33: Donne's 'To the Countess of Huntingdon'.

HART, E. F. *Rev. Eng. Stud.* N.S. VII, 1956, pp. 19–29: The Answer-poem of the Early Seventeenth Century ('The Bait').

HATHAWAY, C. M. *Mod. Lang. Notes*, XIX, 1904, 192: The Compass Figure again.

HAYDN, H. *The Counter-Renaissance*, N.Y., 1950: References to Donne *passim*.

HAYWARD, J. In *A Garland for John Donne*, ed. T. Spencer, Cambridge, Mass., 1931, pp. 75–97: A Note on Donne the Preacher.

HAYWARD, J. *Times Lit. Sup.*, 5 July 1947, p. 337: The Nonesuch Donne.

HAZO, S. *Essays and Studies in Literature*, XXIII, 1964, pp. 38–43: Donne's Divine Letter (on 'The Crosse').

HEATHERINGTON, M. E. *Texas Stud. Lit. Langu.* IX, 1967, 307–16: 'Decency' and 'Zeal' in the Sermons of John Donne.

HEBEL, J. W. *Publ. Mod. Lang. Assoc.* XXXIX, 1924, 814–36: Drayton's *Sirena*. See also Jenkins, R.

HEBEL, J. W., and HUDSON, H. H. *Poetry of the English Renaissance, 1509–1660*, New York, 1929, pp. 455–94: Selection from Donne's poems; p. 906: Extracts from critical essays; pp. 985–9: Introduction and notes.

HEBEL, J. W. *et al. Prose of the English Renaissance*, New York, [1952], pp. 630–43: Selection of Donne's prose; pp. 856–8: Introduction and notes.

HEIST, W. W. *Papers Mich. Acad. Sci. Arts Lett.* LIII, 1968, 311–20: Donne on Divine Grace. Holy Sonnet xiv.

HELTZEL, V. B. *Mod. Lang. Notes*, LIII, 1938, 421–2: An early use of Donne's Fourth Satire (see Wyburne, J., 1609).

HENDERSON, H. *Explicator*, VII, June 1949, item 57: Donne's 'The Will'.

HENNECKE, H. *Die Lit.* XLI, 1938, 21–4: John Donne und die metaphysische Lyrik Englands.

HENRY, N., and MOODY, P. R. *Explicator*, XX, 1962, item 60: Donne's 'A Lecture upon the Shadow'.

HERFORD, C. H. *Contemp. Rev.* CXXVII, 1925, 669–71: John Donne.

HERMAN, G. *Explicator*, XII, December, 1953: Donne's Holy Sonnets XIV.

HERMAN, G. *Explicator*, XIV, 1956, item 60: Donne's 'Good Friday Riding Westward'.

HEUER, H. *Englische Studien*, LXXII, 1938, 227–44: Browning und Donne (Hintergründe einer Wortentlehnung).

HEYWOOD, T. *Horizon*, II, 1942, 267–70: Some Notes on English Baroque.

HICKEY, R. L. *Philol. Quart.* XXVI, 1947, 181–92: Donne and Virginia.

HICKEY, R. L. *Tennessee Stud. Lit.* I, 1956, 65–74: Donne's Art of Preaching.

HICKEY, R. L. *Tennessee Stud. Lit.* III, 1958, 29–36: Donne's Art of Memory.

HICKEY, R. L. *Tennessee Stud. Lit.* IX, 1964, 39–47: Donne's Delivery.

HIJIKATA, T. *Stud. Eng. Lit.* (Tokyo), XX, 1940, 336–47: John Donne's 'Songs and Sonets'.

HILBERRY, C. *Notes and Queries*, CCII, 1957, 336–7: The First Stanza of Donne's 'Hymne to God My God in My Sicknesse'.

HILL, D. A. *Diss. Abstr.* XXIII, 1963, 3026: The Modus Prædicandi of John Donne. A Rhetorical Analysis of Selected Sermons.

HINDLE, C. J. *Times Lit. Sup.*, 8 June 1956, p. 345: A Poem by Donne.

HINMAN, R. B. In *The Apotheosis of Faust: Poetry and New Philosophy in the Seventeenth Century* (Palmer, D. J., and Bradbury, M.). 1970.

HOKOFF, C. *Hochland*, XLI, 1949, 138–47: John Donne.

HOLLANDER, J. *The Untuning of the Sky: Ideas of Music in English Poetry, 1500–1710*, Princeton, 1961: References to Donne.

HOLLOWAY, C. J. *The Charted Mirror*, London, 1960, pp. 53–72: Patmore, Donne and the Wit of Love.

HOLMES, E. *Aspects of Elizabethan Imagery*, Oxford, 1929.

HOOPER, J. *Notes and Queries*, N.S. IX, XII, 1903, 24, 131: Notes on Donne's Ancestry.

HÖLTGEN, K. J. *Arch. Stud. Neu. Sprach. Lit.* CC, 1963, 347–52: Eine Emblemfolge in Donne's Holy Sonnet xiv.

HOTSON, L. *Times Lit. Sup.*, 16 April 1949, p. 249: A Crux in Donne ('Farewell to Love').

See also Maxwell, J. C., 6 May, p. 297; Gardner, H., 10 June, p. 381.

HOUSMAN, A. E. *The Name and Nature of Poetry*, Cambridge, 1933, see pp. 13–15.

HOUSMAN, LAURENCE. *Cornered Poets. A book of Dramatic Dialogues*, London, [1929], pp. 237–56: John Donne.

HOWELL, A. C. *Notes and Queries*, CLXI, 1931, 156–7: A Query on Donne's Sermon XXX, folio of 1640.

See also Bensley, E., 1931.

HOWELL, A. C. *Religion in Life*, XVI, 1947, 216–33: John Donne's Message for the Contemporary Preacher.

HUGHES, M. Y. *Mod. Lang. Rev.* XXVII, 1932, 1–5: Lineage of 'The Extasie'.

HUGHES, M. Y. *Univ. of California, Essays in Criticism*, 2nd ser., 1934, pp. 61–89: Kidnapping Donne.

HUGHES, M. Y. *Contemporary Literary Scholarship* (1456), 1958, pp. 67–82: Donne and Milton.

HUGHES, M. Y. *Publ. Mod. Lang. Assoc.* LXXV, 1960, pp. 509–18: Some of Donne's Ectasies.

HUGHES, R. E. *Cithara*, IV, II, 1965, 60–8: John Donne's 'Nocturnall upon S. Lucie's Day'. A Suggested Resolution.

HUGHES, R. E. *Journ. Eng. Lit. Hist.* XXXIV, 1967, 307–26: The Woman in Donne's 'Anniversaries'. (Enlarged to form ch. iv of the author's *Progress of the Soul*, London, 1969.)

HUGHES, R. E. *The Progress of the Soul. The Interior Career of John Donne*, N.Y. and Toronto, 1968.

HUNT, C. *Donne's Poetry. Essays in Literary Analysis*, Yale Univ. Press, 1954, pp. 270. 2nd impr. 1956.

REVIEWED:

Benjamin, E. B. *College Eng.* XVII, 1955, 61–2.

Coffin, C. M. *Yale Rev.* XLIV, 1955, 623–32: Religious Poetry of the Seventeenth Century.

Davenport, A. *Year's Work in Eng. Stud.* XXXV, 1954, 130–1.

Leishman, J. B. *Rev. Eng. Stud.* N.S. VII, 1956, 310–16.

Seventeenth Cent. News, XIII, 1955, 9–10.

Times Lit. Sup., 16 March 1956, p. 164.

See also Grundy, J., 27 April, p. 253; Gardner, H., and Leishman, J. B., 11 May, p. 283; Gardner, H., 25 May, p. 320; Simpson, E. M., ditto.

HUNTER, G. K. *Essays in Criticism*, III, 1953, pp. 152–64: The Dramatic Technique of Shakespeare's Sonnets [compared with Donne and others].

HUNTLEY, F. L. *Explicator*, VI, June 1948, item 53: Donne's 'Aire and Angels'.

HUSAIN, I. *Theology*, XXVII, 1936, 299–301: John Donne on Conversion.

HUTCHINSON, Revd. F. E. *Camb. Hist. of Eng. Lit.* IV, Cambridge, 1909, ch. xii, pp. 224–41: The English Pulpit from Fisher to Donne.

HUTCHINSON, Revd. F. E. *Theology*, XXII, 1931, 155–63: Donne the Preacher.

HUTTON, W. H. *Theology*, IX, 1924, 149–65: John Donne, Poet and Preacher.

HUXLEY, A. *On the Margin*, London, 1923, pp. 34–8: Subject-matter of Poetry; pp. 184–202: Ben Jonson (with references to Donne).

HUXLEY, A. *Texts and Pretexts. An Anthology with Commentaries*, London, 1932, see pp. 91, 116, 119, 121, 122, 226, specimens from Donne with notes.

HYNES, S. L. *Mod. Lang. Rev.* XLVIII, 1953, pp. 179–81: A Note on Donne and Aquinas ('The First Anniversary').

INCE, R. *Angel from a Cloud*, London, 1939.
REVIEWED:
Times Lit. Sup., 29 July 1939, p. 455: A Novel of John Donne.

ING, C. *Elizabethan Lyrics*, London, 1951: References, pp. 18–20: Donne compared with Spenser; p. 148: Donne's 'Confined Love'; pp. 208–9: Donne and Spenser; pp. 231–6: Donne's poems and their suitability for musical settings, the influence of Shakespeare on 'The Canonization'.

IRVING, W. H. *The Providence of Wit in the English Letter Writers*, Duke Univ. Press, 1955: References to Donne; see esp. pp. 91–4.

ISER, W. *German. Roman. Monat-Schrift*, X, 1960, 266–87: Manieristische Metaphorik in der Englischen Dichtung.

ITRAT-HUSAIN. *Theology*, May 1936: John Donne on Conversion.

ITRAT-HUSAIN. *The Dogmatic and Mystical Theology of John Donne*. Preface by Sir H. J. C. Grierson, London, 1938, 8°, pp. xv, 149.
REVIEWED:
Demillière, A. *Études Angl.* III, 1939, 146.
Spectator, 18 March 1938, p. 488.
Times Lit. Sup., 5 March 1938, p. 148.

ITRAT-HUSAIN. *The Mystical Element in the Metaphysical Poets of the Seventeenth Century*, Edinburgh, 1948, pp. 37–119: John Donne (other references *passim* (see index)).

ITRAT-HUSAIN. *Notes and Queries*, CXCIII, 1948, 567: John Donne's seals.

ITRAT-HUSAIN. *Times Lit. Sup.*, 12 June 1953, p. 381: An Enquiry for King James's copy of *Pseudo-Martyr*.

J. *Notes and Queries*, CLXVIII, 1935, 62: All Tincture (see also notes by Maxwell, H., and B., R.S., p. 104).

JACK, I. *Publ. Mod. Lang. Assoc.* LXVI, 1951, 1009–22: The weighty bullion of Dr. Donne's Satires.

JACKSON, H. *Expository Times*, February 1917, pp. 216–20: The Bookshelf by the Fire: V. John Donne.

JACKSON, R. S. *Cithara*, N.S. VIII, I, 1968, 39–46: John Donne's Christian Skepticism.

JACKSON, R. S. *John Donne's Christian Vocation*, Northwestern Univ. Pr., Evanston, 1970.

JACOBSEN, E. *Classic. et Mediaev.* XIII, 1952, 1–37: The Fable is invented, or Donne's Aesop.

JACOBSEN, E. *Eng. Stud.* XLV, 1964, suppl. pp. 190–6: Donne's Elegy VII.

JAMES, E. *Texas Stud. Eng.* XXIII, 1943, 26–50: The Emblem as an Image-Pattern in some Metaphysical Poets. (See also *Univ. of Wiscon. Summ. of Doct. Diss.* VII, 1942, pp. 291–3.)

JENKINS, R. *Public. Mod. Lang. Assoc.* XXXVIII, 1923, 557–87: Drayton's relation to the school of Donne, as revealed in *The Shepherd's Sirena* (see also Hebel, J. W.).

JOHNSON, BEATRICE. *Public. Mod. Lang. Assoc.* XLIII, 1928, 1098–1109: Classical allusions in the poetry of Donne.

JOHNSON, C. H. *Reason's Double Agents*, Chapel Hill, Univ. of N.C.P., 1966: Reason in Donne, Jonson, Pope, Tate, Winters, Berryman.

JOHNSON, ELEANOR A. *Congregational Quart.* 1932, 41–9: John Donne.

JOHNSON, S. *Journ. Eng. Lit. Hist.* XIV, 1947, 127–38: John Donne and the Virginia Company.

JOHNSON, S. *Mod. Lang. Notes*, LXIII, 1948, 38–43: Sir Henry Goodere and Donne's Letters.

JOHNSON, S. F. *Explicator*, XI, June 1953, item 53: Donne's 'Satire I'.

JONAS, L. *The Divine Science*, N.Y., Columb. Univ. Press, 1940, ch. x, pp. 201–10: John Donne (his remarks on poetry).

JONES, H. W. *Times Lit. Sup.*, 20 July 1946, p. 343: John Donne (a note on 'The Extasie').

JORDAN, J. *Univ. Rev.* (Dublin), II, x, 1962, pp. 3–24: The Early Verse-Letters of John Donne.

JOSEPH, BRO. *Explicator*, XVI, 1958, item 43: Donne's 'A Valediction forbidding Mourning', 1–8.

JUDD, B. H. *Diss. Abstr.* XXVIII, 1967, 633A: Donne's Positivism. Views of Nature and Law in the Sermons and other Prose.

JUSSERAND, J. J. *A Literary History of the English People*, London, 1906, vol. I, pp. 420–32.

KAWASAKI, T. V. *Diss. Abstr.* XVIII, 1958, 1047: John Donne's Religious Poetry and the New Criticism.

KAWASAKI, T. V. *Stud. Eng. Lit.* (Tokyo), XXXVI, 1960, 229–50: John Donne's Microcosm. Some Queries to Prof. Simpson.

KAWASAKI, T. V. *Stud. Eng. Lit.* (Tokyo), XXXIX, 1963, 11–31: From Southwell to Donne.

KEAST, W. R. *Journ. Eng. Lit. Hist.* XVII, 1950, 59–70: Johnson's criticisms of the metaphysical poets.

KEAST, W. R. *Mod. Lang. Rev.* XLV, 1950, 512–15: Killigrew's Use of Donne in 'The Parson's Wedding'.

KEAST, W. R. *Seventeenth Century English Poetry*, N.Y. and Oxford, 1962: Incl. essays concerning Donne by Grierson, H. J. C., Eliot, T. S., Leavis, F. R., Gardner, H., Mazzeo, J. A., Leishman, J. B., Lewis, C. S., Bennett, J., Williamson, G., Martz, L. L. (all recorded elsewhere).

KEEBLE, S. E. *Lond. Quart. Rev.* CXLVII, 1927, 221–32: Devotions (musings of a memorable Dean).

KEEN, G. *The Times*, 5 June 1970, p. 2: Expert finds poem in Donne's hand.

KEISTER, D. A. *Mod. Lang. Quart.* VIII, 1947, 430–4: Donne and Herbert of Cherbury: an exchange of verses.

KEISTER, D. A. *Explicator*, VIII, May 1950, item 55: Donne's 'The Will'.

KENNER, H. *Seventeenth Century Poetry. The Schools of Donne and Jonson*, N.Y., 1964 (pp. xxiv, 508): An anthology, including Donne, with introductory sections.

KERMODE, F. *Kenyon Rev.* XIX, 1951, pp. 169–74: The Dissociation of Sensibility.

KERMODE, F. *Notes and Queries*, N.S. I, 1954, 337: Donne allusions in Howell's 'Familiar Letters'.

KERMODE, F. *John Donne* (Writers and their Work, no. 86). Brit. Council and Nat. Bk. League. Longmans Green, 1957 (pp. 48, with portrait).

KERMODE, F. *Discussions of John Donne*, Boston, 1962: An Anthology of Donne Criticisms.

KERMODE, F. *The Metaphysical Poets*, N.Y., 1969.

REVIEWED:

R. W. French, *Seventeenth Century News*, autumn 1970, p. 48.

KERNAN, A. *The Cankered Muse*, New Haven, 1959, p. 67: Donne's 'Anniversaries'; pp. 117–18: Satires.

KEYNES, G. L. *A Bibliography of the Works of Dr. John Donne*, Cambridge, 1914, 25 cm, pp. xii, 168, 4 collotype plates, 12 reproductions of title-pages, 300 copies for the Baskerville Club.

KEYNES, G. L. *A Bibliography of Dr. John Donne*, 2nd edn., Cambridge, 1932, 25 cm, pp. xiv, [2], 196. 10 collotype plates, 17 reproductions of title-pages, 350 copies.

REVIEWED:

D., E. A. *Libr. Assoc. Rec.* 3rd ser. III, 1933, 51–2.

Flower, D. *Book Coll. Quart.* pt. VII, 1932, 85–9.

Jones, H. S. V. *Journ. Eng. Germ. Philol.* XXXII, 1933, 134–5.

Pollard, A. W. *Library*, N.S. XIII, 1932, 107–8.

Praz, M. *Engl. Stud.* XVI, 1934, 68.

Simpson, E. M. *Rev. Eng. Stud.* IX, 1933, 105–11.

KEYNES, G. L. *Times Lit. Sup.*, 24 Sept. 1938, p. 620: Death's Duell.

See also James, P., *Times Lit. Sup.*, 8 Oct., p. 652, 15 Oct., p. 668.

KEYNES, G. L. *Trans. Camb. Bib. Soc.* I, 1949, pp. 64–8: Books from Donne's library. (Twenty titles added to those previously known.)

KEYNES, G. L. *Times Lit. Sup.*, 28 May 1954, p. 351: John Donne's sermons. (Description of the Ellesmere MS.)

KEYNES, G. L. *A Bibliography of Dr. John Donne*, 3rd edn. Cambridge, 1958, 25 cm, pp. xviii, [ii], 285, [1]. Twelve collotype plates, 40 reprod. of title-pages. 750 copies.

REVIEWED:

Anon. *Times Lit. Sup.*, 27 June 1958.

Bald, R. C. *The Library*, s.v. xiv, 1959, 54–8.

Gardner, H. *Book Collector*, winter 1958.

Kirschbaum; L. *Libr. Quart.*, N.Y., 1959.

White, W. *Bull. Bibliogr.* xxii, 1959: A review with additions.

KEYNES, G. L. *Times Lit. Sup.*, 21 February 1958, p. 108: Dr. Donne and Scaliger (with facs. of epigram). See also J. Sparrow, 28 February, p. 115, for his correction of his own rendering of Donne's lines.

KEYNES, G. L. *Times Lit. Sup.*, 13 January 1966, p. 25: Donne's Books (see also 20 January, p. 48; 27 January, p. 68).

KEYNES, G. L. *The Life of William Harvey*, Oxford, 1966: References to Donne, pp. 115, 121–2, 413.

KHANNA, U. *Notes and Queries*, xvii, 1970, 404–5: Donne's 'A Valediction forbidding Mourning'—some possible alchemical allusions.

KILEY, F. *CEA Crit.* XXX, vii, 1968, 16–17: A Larger Reading of Donne's 'A Lecture upon the Shadow'.

[KING, HENRY]. Goodspeed's Catalogue 500, Boston, 1961, no. 44, offers a copy of Donne's Poems, 1635, in which the concluding part of King's 'Exequy' has been written out by a contemporary hand on the final blank leaf with the heading: 'Donne's good-night'. The passage begins: 'So close the ground about her shade.' The same hand has written on the front blank a description of Donne's tomb in St. Paul's, written before 1666. With a reproduction of the MS. of the poem. No early provenance. The writer also added the 'Klockius' and 'Ralphius' titles to the epigrams XII and XVI, these being known only in the Hawthornden MS., Soc. of Antiqu., Edinburgh.

KIRBY, J. P. *Explicator*, i, February 1943, Item 29: Donne's Song 'Go and catch a falling star.'

KIRSCHBAUM, L. *Shakespeare and the Stationers*, Columbus, 1955: Gives accounts of the publication of some of Donne's works, pp. 43–4: *Poems*; pp. 53–4: *Paradoxes and Problemes*; pp. 133–8: J. Donne, jr., and *Juvenilia, Poems* and *Ignatius*; pp. 152, 176: Donne's poems in *Volpone*; pp. 374–6: sermon in *Sapientia Clamitans*, and pp. 394–5.

KLAMMER, E. *Cresset* (Valparaiso), XXXII, 1968, 14–15: Cosmography in Donne's Poetry.

KLINE, G. L. *Rus. Rev.* XXIV, 1965, 341–53: Joseph Brodsky's 'Elegy for John Donne' (introd. and translation).

KNIGHTS, L. C. *Scrutiny*, XIII, 1945, 37–52: On the social background of metaphysical poetry.

KNOX, G. *Explicator*, xv, 1956, item 2: Donne's Holy Sonnet xiv.

KOCH, W. A. *Linguistica*, XXXIII, 1967, pp. 68–81: A Linguistic Analysis of a Satire (Satyre II).

KOPPENFELS, W. von. *Anglia*, LXXXVII, 1969, 167–200: Donne's Liebesdichtung und die Tradition von Tottel's Miscellany.

KORTEMME, J. *Das Verhältnis John Donnes zur Scholastik und zum Barock Eine Untersuchung zu den Anfängen des Englischen Barock*, Münster (Westf.), 1933, 8°.

KRIEGER, M. *The New Apologists for Poetry*, Minneapolis, 1956: Refs. to Donne, pp. 12–17, 25, 26, 205. Repr. 1963.

KRUEGER, R. *Rev. Eng. Stud.* xv, 1964, 151–60: The Publication of John Donne's Sermons.

KRUPPA, J. E. *Diss. Abstr.* XXVII, 1967, 3013A: John Donne and the Jesuits.

KUHLMANN, H. *Die Neue Sprach.*, N.S. III, 1954, 452–8: John Donne. Betrachtungen über Elend und Grösse der Menschen.

KUHNE, W. W. *Diss. Abstr.* XXIX, 1968, 1514A: Natural Law and Prose Works of the English Renaissance.

KUHNRE, W. W. *Lutheran Quart.* XII, 1960, 217–34: Exposition of Sin in the Sermons of John Donne.

LABRANCHE, A. *Mod. Lang. Rev.* LXI, 1966, 357–68: *Blanda Elegia*. The Background to Donne's Elegies.

LANDER, C. *Stud. Eng. Lit.* xi, 1971, 89–108:

A Dangerous Sickness which turned to Spotted Fever.

LANGSTON, B. *Times Lit. Sup.*, 18 January 1936, p. 55: A Donne Poem overlooked (letter concerning commendatory verses signed *Io. Done* in Capt. John Smith's *Generall Historie of Virginia*, 1624).

See also letters from J. Hayward and B. H. Newdigate, 25 January; I. A. Shapiro and E. K. Chambers, 1 February; B. H. Newdigate, 8 February.

LAWNICZAK, D. A. *Serif.* VI, 1969, 1, 12–19: Donne's Sainted Lovers—Again.

LEA, K. M. *Mod. Lang. Rev.* xx, 1925, 389–406: Conceits.

LEAVIS, F. R. *Bookman* (Lond.), LXXIX, 1931, 346–7: The influence of John Donne on modern poetry.

LEAVIS, F. R. *Scrutiny*, IV, 1935, 236–56: English Poetry in the seventeenth century.

LEAVIS, F. R. *Revaluation. Tradition and Development in English Poetry*, London, 1936: References to Donne, pp. 11–17.

LECOCQ, L. *La Satire en Angleterre de 1588 à 1603*, Paris, 1970.

LECOMTE, E. *Grace to a Witty Sinner. A Life of Donne*, London, 1965, 21·5 cm, pp. [iv], 307, [3].

LECOMTE, E. *Times Lit. Sup.*, 11 May 1967: a letter on the review, 'Ill Donne. Well Donne', 3 April. See also Curtis, L. P.

LECOMTE, E. *Études Angl.* xxi, 1968, 168–9: The Date of Donne's Marriage (January 1602).

LEDERER, J. *Rev. Eng. Stud.* XXII, 1946, 182–200: John Donne and the Emblematic Practice.

LEDERER, J. *Diss. Univ. Lond.*, 1951: The Manifestations of the Baroque in the Works of John Donne.

LEES, F. N. *Notes and Queries*, CXCV, 1950, 195, 482: References to Donne.

LEGOUIS, P. *Donne the Craftsman*, Paris, 1928, 8º, pp. 98, [4]. Repr. 1962.
REVIEWED:
Aronstein, P. *Englisch. Stud.* LXIII, 1929, 430–1.
Bredvold, L. I. *Mod. Lang. Notes*, XLV, 1930, 61–2.

Douady, J. *Rev. Anglo-Améric.* VI, 1929, 439–40.
Grierson, H. J. C. *Rev. Eng. Stud.* VI, 1930, 214–16.
Hague, R. *Lond. Merc.* XIX, 1928, 211.
Praz, M. *Eng. Stud.* XI, 1929, 33–40.
Smith, G. C. M. *Mod. Lang. Rev.* XXIV, 1929, 104–5.
Times Lit. Sup., 27 June 1929, p. 510.
Life and Letters, I, 1928, 525–6.

LEGOUIS, P. *Rev. Anglo-Améric.* X, 1932, 1933, 49–50, 228–30: Sur un vers de Donne. [Second Anniversary, ll. 197–8.]

LEGOUIS, P. *Studia neophilologica*, XIV, 1942, 184–96: Some lexicographical notes on Donne's Satires.

LEGOUIS, P. *Rev. Hist. du Théâtre*, II, 1951, no. 2: Le thème du rêve dans le *Clitandre* de Corneille, et *The Dreame* de Donne. (Supplemented in no. IV, 1952.)

LEGOUIS, P. *Études Angl.* V, 1952, 97 ff.: L'état présent des controverses sur la poésie de Donne.

LEGOUIS, P. *Études Angl.* VI, 1953, 39–40: Éditions savantes d'Outre-Atlantique et d'Outre-Manche.

LEGOUIS, P. *Notes and Queries*, CXCVIII, 1953, 111–12: The Epistolary Past in England. (Donne's prose letter to Sir Edward Herbert.)

LEGOUIS, P. *Études Angl.* X, 1957, 115–22: Donne, l'Amour et les Critiques.

LEGOUIS, P. *Anglia*, LXXVI, 1958, 536–8: John Donne and William Cowper.

LEGOUIS, P. *Études Angl.* XVI, 1963, 134–9: Sur une traduction en vers de Donne (review).

LEISHMAN, J. B. *The Metaphysical Poets. Donne Herbert Vaughan Traherne*, Oxford, 1934.
REVIEWED:
Bennett, J. *Mod. Lang. Rev.* XXX, 1935, 372–4.
Williamson, G. *Mod. Lang. Notes*, LI, 1936, 197.

LEISHMAN, J. B. *Listener*, 24 April 1950, p. 747: Was John Donne a metaphysician?

LEISHMAN, J. B. *The Monarch of Wit. An Analytical and Comparative Study of the*

Poetry of John Donne, London, 1951, 23 cm, pp. 278. Sixth edn. 1962.

REVIEWED:

Bennett, J. *Rev. Eng. Stud.*, N.S. III, 1952, 289–90.

Martin, L. C. *Mod. Lang. Rev.* LXVII, 1951, 220–1.

Mayhead, R. *Scrutiny*, XVIII, 1951–2, 241–4.

Pinto, V. de S. *English*, IX, 1951, 25–6.

Times Lit. Sup., 20 July 1951, p. 452.

Ure, P. *Camb. Journ.* V, 1951, 434–40.

Adelphi, XXVIII, 1951, 448–9.

Dobrée, B. *Spectator*, CLXXXVII, 17 August 1951, 218: Donne the Outrageous.

Durham Univ. Journ. N.S. XIII, 1951, 31–2.

Fausset, H. I'A. *Manchester Guard. Weekly*, LXV, 12 July 1951, p. 11: Transition.

Notes and Queries, CXCVI, 1951, p. 506.

Leishman, J. B. *Times Lit. Sup.*, 13 June 1952, p. 391: Donne and Herbert.

Levenson, J. C. *Explicator*, XI, March 1953, item 31: Donne's 'Holy Sonnets xiv'.

Levenson, P. C. [*sic*], *Explicator*, XII, April 1954, item 36: Donne's 'Holy Sonnets xiv'.

Levine, J. A. *Journ. Eng. Lit. Hist.* XXVIII, 1961, pp. 301–15: 'The Dissolution'. Donne's Twofold Elegy.

Levtow, W. H. *Diss. Abstr.* XIX, 1959, 2338–9: The Convention of Revolt. Origins of the Renaissance Realistic Lyric.

Lewis, C. S. In *Seventeenth Century Essays presented to Sir H. J. C. Grierson*, Oxford, 1938, pp. 64–84: Donne and Love Poetry in the Seventeenth Century. (Repr. with modifications in *English Literature in the Sixteenth Century*, Oxford, 1954, and in Gardner's *A Collection of Critical Essays*, 1962.)

Lewis, C. S. *Oxford History of English Literature*, Oxford, 1954, pp. 546–51: English literature in the sixteenth century.

Lewis, E. G. *Mod. Lang. Rev.* XXIX, 1934, 436–40: An Interpretation of Donne's Elegy, the Dreame.

Lewis, E. G. *Times Lit. Sup.*, 13, 27 October 1934, pp. 604, 655: Donne's Third Satyre. See also Lindsay, J., 20 October 1934, p. 636.

Lewis, E. Glyn. *Mod. Lang. Rev.* XXXIII, 1938, 255–8. The question of toleration in the works of John Donne.

Lewis, J. C. *Diss. Abstr.* (Univ. of Wash.), XXV, 1964, 2963–4: The Rhetoric of Faith. A Study of Donne's Use of the Conceit in the Divine Poems.

Lindon, J. B., Q.C. *The Times*, 10 May 1960: Announcing the bequest to the Society of Lincoln's Inn of 'a portrait of Donne by an Elizabethan artist'. (The portrait is, in fact, of an unknown individual.)

Lindsay, J. *Times Lit. Sup.*, 19 February 1931, p. 135: Donne and the Roman poets. See also Grierson, Sir H. J. C., 26 February.

Lindsay, J. *Times Lit. Sup.*, 19 March 1931, p. 234: The date of Donne's 'Autumnal Elegy'. See also Johnson, S., 30 April.

Lindsay, J. *Times Lit. Sup.*, 20 June 1936, p. 523: Donne and Giordano Bruno. See also letters from Ince, R., 27 June, p. 544; Yates, F. A., 4 July, p. 564; Lindsay, J., 11 July, p. 580.

Lindsay, J. *Times Lit. Sup.*, 1937, p. 544: Donne and Blake.

Linneman, Sister M. R. A. *Xavier Univ. Stud.* I, 1961, 264–72: Donne as Catalyst in the Poetry of Elinor Wylie, Wallace Stevens, Herbert Read, and William Empson.

Locke, J. D. *Diss. Abstr.* XIX, 1959, 1743: Images and Image Symbolism in Metaphysical Poetry with special reference to Unworldliness.

Locke, L. G. *Explicator*, I, February 1943, item 29: Donne's Song, 'Go and catch a falling star.'

Lorca, J. G. *Insula*, no. 86, February 1953, suppl., p. 3: Un aspecto de John Donne: su originalidad.

Louthan, D. *Philol. Quart.* XXIX, 1950, 375 ff.: The Tome-Tomb pun in renaissance England (refers to four poems by Donne).

Louthan, D. *The Poetry of John Donne*, New York, 1951, pp. 194.

REVIEWED:

Bennett, J. *Mod. Philol.* L, 1952, 277–8.

P., J. M. *Seventeenth Cent. News*, X, 1952, 20.

Clancy, W. P. *Commonweal*, LIV, 1951, 604.

Garrison, W. E. *Christ. Cent.* LXVIII, 1951, 1223: The two John Donnes.

Mandel, S. *Sat. Rev.* XXXV, 29 March 1952, 32.

Times Lit. Sup. 4 April 1952, p. 238: About Donne.

U.S. Quart. Book Rev. VII, 1951, 353–4.

Love, H. *Mod. Philol.* LXIV, 1966, 125–31: The Argument of Donne's *First Anniversary*.

Love, H. *Explicator*, XXVI, 1967, item 33: Donne's 'To his Mistress going to Bed'.

Low, D. A. *Rev. Eng. Stud.* XVI, 1965, 291–8: An Eighteenth Century Imitation of Donne's First Satire. (See under Mason, William, p. 306.)

Lowe, I. *Diss. Abstr.* XVIII, 1958, 590–1: Both Centers One. The Reason-Faith Equation in Donne's Sermons.

Lowe, I. *Journ. Hist. Ideas*, XXII, 1961, pp. 389–97: John Donne. The Middle Way. The Reason-Faith Equation in Donne's Sermons.

Lowe, R. L. *Notes and Queries*, CXCVIII, 1953, pp. 491–2: Browning and Donne.

Lucas, F. L. *Authors Dead and Living*, London, 1926, 8°, pp. 54–61: John Donne. (Review of Fausset's *Study in Discord*.)

Lucas, F. L. *Decline and Fall of the Romantic Ideal*, Cambridge, 1936, see pp. 86–9, 176–7.

Lucas, P. *The Blood of Song*. Pt. I. London, 1914, 4°, pp. 4–5: The lineal descendants of John Donne.

Lynd, R. *Lond. Mercury*, I, 1920, 435–47: John Donne.

Lynd, R. *The Art of Letters*, London, [1920], pp. 29–48: John Donne.

Mabbott, T. O. *Mod. Lang. Notes*, LX, 1945, 358: John Donne and Valeriano.

Mabbott, T. O. *Explicator*, VIII, February 1950, item 30: Donne's 'The Will', ll. 40–1.

Mabbott, T. O. *Seventeenth Cent. News*, IX, 2, 1951: Forms, Moods, Shapes of Grief.

Mabbott, T. O. *Explicator*, XVI, 1957, item 19: Donne's 'Satyre II', 71–72. [See Cobb and Hall above.]

Macaulay, R. *Some Religious Elements in English Literature*, London, 1931, see pp. 84–92: References to Donne.

McCanles, M. F. *Diss. Abstr.* (Kansas Univ.), XXV, 1964, 5932–3: Analogy and Paradox in the Love Poetry of John Donne.

McCanles, M. F. *Stud. Eng. Lit.* VI, 1966, 59–75: Distinguish in order to Unite. Donne's 'The Extasie'.

McCanles, M. F. *Stud. Renaiss.* XIII, 1966, 266–87: Paradox in Donne.

McCann, E. *Huntington Lib. Quart.* XVII, 1953–4, 125–32: Donne and St. Teresa on the Ecstasy.

MacCarthy, Sir D. *New Statesman*, XX, 1923, 660: Books in General. (Affable Hawk.)
Repr. in MacCarthy's *Criticism*, New York, 1932, pp. 36–60.

MacCarthy, Sir D. *New Statesman*, XXI, 1923, 143: Books in General. (Affable Hawk.)
See also *New Statesman*, XXII, 1923, 17.

MacCarthy, Sir D. *Life and Letters*, 1928, pp. 156–60, 433: Reader's Bibliography.

MacColl, A. *Rev. Eng. Stud.* XIX, 1968, 293–5: A New MS. of Donne's Poems. (The Wedderburn MS. 6504 in NLS, containing over 40 poems by Donne. Closely related to the Hawthornden MS.)

MacColl, A., and Roberts, M. *Ess. Crit.* (Oxford), XVII, 1967, 258–78: The New Edition of (Gardner's) *Donne's Love Poems*.

McGuire, P. C. *Diss. Abstr.* XXIX, 1968, 1515A: The Soul in Paraphrase. A Study of the Devotional Poems of Jonson, Donne and Herbert.

Macleane, D. *Sat. Rev.* 21 August 1915: Donne.

McClure, N. E. *Times Lit. Sup.*, 17 January 1942, p. 31: King James on Bacon. [See P. Simpson, 25 October 1941, p. 531: King James on Donne.]

Macklem, M. *The Anatomy of the World: Relations between Natural and Moral Law from Donne to Pope*, Minnes., Univ. of Minnes. Press, 1958 (pp. 150).

Maclure, M. *The Paul's Cross Sermons 1534–1642*. Univ. of Toronto Dept. of Engl. Stud. and Texts, no. 6, Toronto, 1958 (including Donne's Sermons).

McNaron, T. A. H. *Diss. Abstr.* XXV, 1964,

2496–7: John Donne's Sermons approached as Dramatic 'Dialogues of One' (Ann Arbor Univ. 1964).

McQueen, W. A. *Milton Newsletter*, ii, 1968, pp. 63–4: Prevent the Sun. Milton, Donne and the Book of Wisdom.

Madison, A. L. *Notes and Queries*, ccii, 1957, 60–1: Explication of John Donne's 'The Flea'.

Mahoney, J. L. *Coll. Lang. Assoc. Journ.* (Morgan St. Coll.), v, 1962, 203–12: Donne and Greville. Two Christian Attitudes toward the Renaissance Idea of Mutability and Decay.

Mahoney, P. J. *Diss. Abstr.* xxiv, 1964, 3339: A Study of Donne's Anniversaries.

Mahoney, P. J. *Journ. Eng. Germ. Philol.* lxviii, 1969, 407–13: The Anniversaries. Donne's Rhetorical Approach to Evil.

Mahood, M. M. *Poetry and Humanism*, London, [1950], pp. 87–130: Donne: The Progress of the Soul; pp. 131–68: Donne: The Baroque Preacher. (Other references *passim* (see index).)

Main, C. E. *Stud. in Bibliography*, Bibliogr. Soc. of Univ. of Virginia, ix, 1957, 225–33: New texts of Donne (Harvard MSS., MS. Eng. 686).

Main, W. W. *Explicator*, x, November 1951, item 14: Donne's 'Elegie XIX, Going to bed'.

Mais, S. P. B. *Why We Should Read*, London, 1921, pp. 51–7: John Donne.

Malloch, A. E. *Coll. Engl.* xv, 1953, 95–101: The Unified Sensibility and Metaphysical Poetry.

Malloch, A. E. *Mod. Lang. Notes*, lxx, 1955, 174–5: Donne's *Pseudo-martyr* and *Catalogus Librorum Aulicorum*.

Malloch, A. E. *Stud. Philol.* liii, 1956, 191–203: The Techniques and Function of the Renaissance Paradox.

Malloch, A. E. *Mod. Lang. Notes*, lxxii, 1957, 332–5: The Definition of Sin in Donne's *Biathanatos*.

Malloch, A. E. *Stud. Eng. Lit.* ii, 1962, 57–76: John Donne and the Casuists.

Manley, F. *First Anniversary of Wisdom's Death*, Johns Hopkins Univ., 1959.

Manley, F. *Mod. Lang. Notes.* lxxiv, 1959, 385–8: Chaucer's Rosary and Donne's Bracelet. Ambiguous Coral.

Manley, F. *Mod. Lang. Notes*, lxxvi, 1961, 13–15: Walton's *Angler* and Donne. A Probable Allusion.

Manley, F. *John Donne: The Anniversaries*, Baltimore, 1963, 21 cm, pp. x, 209.
REVIEWED:
Times Lit. Sup., 6 April 1967, pp. 277–9.

Mann, L. A. *Diss. Abstr.* xxvi, 1966, 5440–1: John Donne's Doctrine of Marriage in its Historical Context.

Mann, L. A. *Notes and Queries*, xvii, 1970, 403–4: A Note on the text of Donne's Sermon preached at Paul's Cross, 24 March 1616/17. (*XXVI Sermons* 1660/1, no. 24, p. 324E.) This corrects an error not noticed by Potter and Simpson.

Marenco, F. *Notes and Queries*, xv, 1968, 111–12: Review of D. L. Guss's *John Donne. Petrarchist*, 1966.

Marion, St. Thomas. (Unpublished Essay) Donne's Casuistry: A Study of *Biathanatos* and *Pseudo-Martyr*, Cornell Univ., 1956.

Marotti, A. F. *Engl. Lang. Notes* (Univ. Color.), vi, 1968, 24–5: Donne's 'Love's Progress', ll. 37–8, and Renaissance Bawdry.

Marsh, T. N. *Engl. Misc.* xiii, 1962, 25–9: Elizabethan Wit in Metaphor and Conceit: Sidney, Shakespeare, Donne.

Marshall, J. *Hound and Horn*, iii, 1929, 121–4: 'The Extasie'.

Marshall, W. H. *Notes and Queries*, s.v. cciii, 1958, 533–4: Elizabeth Drury and the Heathens; pp. 540–1: A Possible Interpretation of Donne's 'Second Anniversary', ll. 33–6.

Martin, S. *Notes and Queries*, n.s. ix, ix, 1902, 28: A note asking who was the unknown friend, who according to Walton [in the *Lives*, 4th edn. 1675] wrote a four-line epitaph in charcoal on the wall above Donne's grave. Was it, perhaps, Walton himself? (The question remained unanswered.)

Martz, L. L. *Journ. Eng. Lit. Hist.* xiv, 1947, 247–73: John Donne in Meditation: 'The Anniversaries'.

MARTZ, L. L. *The Poetry of Meditation*, New Haven, Yale Univ. Press, 1954, ch. 6, pp. 211–18: John Donne in Meditation: The Anniversaries; Appendix 2, pp. 353–6: The Dating and Significance of Donne's Anniversaries. Revised edn. 1962.

MARTZ, L. L. *Thought*, XXXIV, 1959, 269–78: Donne and the Meditative Tradition.

MARTZ, L. L. *Massach. Rev.* I, 1960, 326–42: John Donne. The Meditative Voice.

MARTZ, L. L. *The Poem of the Mind. Essays on Poetry, English and American*, N.Y., Oxford Univ. Press, 1960 (On Donne and others).

MARTZ, L. L. *The Action of the Self. Devotional Poetry in the Seventeenth Century* (see Palmer, D. J., and Bradbury, M., 1970).

MARTZ, L. L. *The Wit of Love. Donne, Carew, Crashaw, Marvell*, Ward Phillips Lectures in Eng. Lang. and Lit., vol. 3, Notre Dame, 1970, pp. xv, 216.
REVIEWED:
K. Koller, *Seventeenth Century News*, autumn 1970, 48–9.

MASOOD-AL-HASAN. *Donne's Imagery*, Aligarh, Muslim Univ., India, 1958.
REVIEWED:
E. Morgan. *Rev. Eng. Stud.* XI, 1960, 233–4.

MASSINGHAM, H. J. *A Treasury of Seventeenth Century English Verse*, London, 1919, pp. ix–xxiii: References to Donne; pp. 74–89: Selection of Donne's poems.

MATCHETT, W. H. *Rev. Eng. Stud.* XVIII, 1967, 290–2: Donne's 'Peece of Chronicle'.

MATHEW, A. H., and CALTHROP, A. *The Life of Sir Tobie Matthew, Bacon's Alter Ego*, London, 1907, pp. 125, 155, 157, 158, 170, 344: References to Donne; pp. 21, 185, 188, 317, 351–2, 362: References to John Donne, jr.

MATHEWS, C. ELKIN. *Times Lit. Sup.*, 6 October, 1921, p. 644: Elegiac lines on Dr. Donne.

MATHEWS, E. G. *Times Lit. Sup.*, 12 September 1936, p. 729: A Spanish proverb [in a letter from Donne to Goodere].

MATHEWS, E. G. *Mod. Lang. Notes*, LVI, 1941, 607–9: John Donne's 'Little Rag'.

MATSUURA, K. *Stud. in Eng. Lit.* (Tokyo), XV, 1935, 58–67: Lyrical Poems of John Donne.

MATSUURA, K. *Stud. in Eng. Lit.* (Tokyo), XXVI, 1949, 125–84: A Study of Donne's Imagery.

MATSUURA, K. *A Study of Donne's Imagery*, Tokyo, 1953.

MATTHEWS, W. R. *A History of St. Paul's Cathedral*, London, 1957: References to Donne, pp. 154–62.

MAUD, R. *Bost. Univ. Stud. Eng.* XI, 1956, 218–25: Donne's 'First Anniversary'.

MAXWELL, H. *Notes and Queries*, CLXVIII, 1935, 62, 104: John Donne's 'All Tincture'.

MAXWELL, I. R. *Times Lit. Sup.*, 11 July 1935, p. 448: John Donne's library.

MAXWELL, J. C. *Notes and Queries*, CXCIII, 1948, 4: A note on Donne.

MAXWELL, J. C. *Durham Univ. Journ.*, N.S. XII, 1951, 61–4: John Donne and the new philosophy.

MAXWELL, J. C. *Rev. Eng. Stud.*, N.S. V, 1954, 168–9: A note on Donne's Crosse.

MAXWELL, J. C. *Notes and Queries*, XV, 1958, 112–15: Review of W. Milgate's *Satires, Epigrams and Verse Letters*, 1967.

MAXWELL, J. C. *Notes and Queries*, XVI, 1969, 208: A Donne Echo in 'The Ring and the Book', ll. 89–90: Give it me back! The thing's restorative / I'the touch and sight. (See Donne's Elegie XII, 'The Bracelet', l. 112: Gold is restorative, restore it then.)

MAYCOCK, H. *Camb. Rev.* LXIII, 1942, 164–5, 180–1: John Donne, Dean of St. Paul's.

MAYNARD, B. A. *Diss. Abstr.* XXVIII, 1967, 1789A–90A: The 'Songs and Sonnets' of John Donne. An Essay on Mutability. (Louisiana St. Univ.)

MAZZEO, J. A. *Romanic Rev.* XLIII, 1951, 245–55: A Seventeenth Century Theory of Metaphysical Poetry.

MAZZEO, J. A. *Mod. Philol.* I, 1952, 88–96: A Critique of Some Modern Theories of Metaphysical Poetry.

MAZZEO, J. A. *Journ. Hist. Ideas*, XIV, 1953, 221–34: Metaphysical Poetry and the Poetry of Correspondence.

MAZZEO, J. A. *Isis*, XLVIII, 1957, pp. 103–23: Notes on Donne's Alchemical Imagery.

MAZZEO, J. A. *Renaissance and Seventeenth Century Studies*, N.Y. and London, 1964:

Containing reprints of the three articles preceding.

MEGROZ, R. L. *Dublin Mag.*, N.S. I, 1926, 47–51: The Wit and Fantasy of Donne.

MEGROZ, R. L. *Francis Thompson*, London, 1927, ch. 8: References to Thompson and Donne.

MELLER, H. S. *Times Lit. Sup.*, 22 April 1965, p. 320: The Phoenix and the Well-wrought Urn.

MELTON, W. F. *The Rhetoric of John Donne's verse*, Baltimore, 1906, 8°, pp. viii, 209.
REVIEWED:
Wauchope, G. A. *Mod. Lang. Notes*, XXIV, 1908, 114–16.
Smith, G. C. Moore. *Mod. Lang. Rev.* III, 1908, 80.

MELTON, W. F. *Mod. Lang. Notes*, XXIII, 1908, 95–6: Coleridge's lines on Donne.

MEMORABILIST. *Notes and Queries*, CLXXXIV, 1943, 77, 165–6: Some notes on Donne.

MEMORABILIST. *Notes and Queries*, CLXXXVIII, 1945, 257. Sir Richard Baker on John Donne.

MENASCE, E. In *Studi di Letteratura e Filosofia, in Onore de Bruno Revel*, Florence, 1965. Contribution: Donne, l'ultimo poeta del Mediaevo. (Also in *Stud. Revel.* (75) 1966, 393–414.)

MERRILL, T. F. *Diss. Abstr.* XXV, 1964, 2497: The Christian Anthropology of John Donne.

MERRILL, T. F. *Neuphilol. Mitteil.* LXIX, 1968, 597–616: John Donne and the Word of God.

MILCH, W. *Trivium*, V, 1947, pp. 65–73: Deutsche Barocklyrik und 'Metaphysical Poetry' in England.

MILCH, W. *Compar. Lit. Stud.* XXIII–IV, 1959, 16–22: Metaphysical Poetry and the German 'Barocklyrick'.

MILES, J. *Publ. Mod. Lang. Assoc.* LX, 1945, 766–74: From *Good* to *Bright*: A Note in Poetic History.

MILES, J. *The Primary Language of Poetry in the 1640's*, Univ. of California Press, 1948.

MILES, J. *Kenyon Rev.* XIII, 1951, 37–49: The language of the Donne tradition.

MILES, J. *Eras & Modes in English Poetry*, Berkeley, 1957, pp. 20–32: The Language of the Donne Tradition.

MILGATE, W. *Times Lit. Sup.*, 1 August 1942, p. 379: Donne the lawyer.

MILGATE, W. *Notes and Queries*, CXCI, 1946, 206–8: The date of Donne's birth.

MILGATE, W. *Notes and Queries*, CXCIV, 1949, 318–19: Dr. Donne's art gallery.

MILGATE, W. *Notes and Queries*, CXCV, 1950, 229–31, 246–7, 290–2, 381–3: The early references to Donne.

MILGATE, W. *Notes and Queries*, CXCVIII, 1953, 421–4: References to Donne.

MILGATE, W. *Notes and Queries*, N.S. XIII (CCXI), 1966, 12–14: A Difficult Allusion in Donne and Spenser (mice destroying elephants).

MILGATE, W. *Études Angl.* XXII, 1969, 66–7: The Date of Donne's Marriage. A Reply (see Lecomte, 1968).

MILLER, C. H. *Stud. Eng. Lit.* VI, 1966, 77–86: Donne's 'A Nocturnall upon S. Lucie's Day' and the Nocturns of Matins.

MILLER, C. W. *Explicator*, IV, February 1946, item 24: Donne's 'The Apparition'.

MILLER, H. K. *Mod. Phil.* LIII, 1956, 145–78: The paradoxical encomium with special reference to its vogue in England, 1600–1800.

MILLS, J. L. *Notes and Queries*, XV, 1968, 368: Donne's Bracelets of Bright Hair. An Analogue.

MIMS, E. *The Christ of the Poets*, New York and Nashville, 1948, pp. 48–64: John Donne: Preacher and Poet.

MINER, E. *The Metaphysical Mode from Donne to Cowley*, Princeton Univ. Press, 1969.

MINTO, W. *Nineteenth Cent.* VII, 1880, 845–63: John Donne.
Also in *Argosy*, XXXII, 1881, 299 ff.

MINTON, A. *Explicator*, IV, May 1946, item 50: Donne's 'The Perfume'.

MITCHELL, C. *Stud. Eng. Lit.* VIII, 1968, 91–101: Donne's 'The Extasie'. Love's sublime Knot.

MITCHELL, F. L. *Bookman's Journ.*, London, XIV, 1926, 15–18: Jack Donne, the Pagan. Doctor John Donne, the Divine.

MITCHELL, W. F. *English Pulpit Oratory from Andrewes to Tillotson*, London, 1932: Ref. to Donne *passim* (see index).

MIZENER, A. *Sewanee Rev.* LI, 1943, 27–51: Some notes on the Nature of English Poetry.

MOLELLA, L. *Thoth.* III, 1962, 69–77: Donne's 'A Lecture upon the Shadow'.

MOLONEY, M. F. *Cath. World*, CLII, 1940, 189–95: The End of the Renaissance.

MOLONEY, M. F. *Univ. of Illinois Stud. in Lang. and Lit.* XXIX, 1944, nos. 2, 3: John Donne: his flight from mediævalism. Repr. 1965.

REVIEWED:

Frederick, J. T. *Book Week* (Chicago Sun), 24 December, 1944, p. 2.

Perkinson, R. H. *Thought*, XXI, 1946, 322–3.

Spencer, T. *Mod. Lang. Notes*, LX, 1945, 131–3.

Williams, M. *Cath. World*, CLX, October 1944, 89–90.

MOLONEY, M. F. *Mod. Lang. Quart*, VIII, 1947, 426–9: John Donne and the Jesuits.

MOLONEY, M. F. *Publ. Mod. Lang. Assoc.* LXV, 1950, 232–9: Donne's metrical practice.

MONTGOMERY, R. L. *Kerygma*, IV, 1964, no. 2, 3–14: Donne's 'Ecstasy'. Philosophy and the Renaissance.

MOORE, A. K. *Philol. Quart.* (Iowa), XLII, 1963, 102–5: Donne's 'Love's Deitie' and *De Planctu Naturae*.

MOORE, J. F. *Rev. Anglo-Améric.* XIII, 1935, 289–96: Scholasticism, Donne, and the Metaphysical Conceit.

MOORE, T. V. *Mod. Philol.* LXVII, 1969, pp. 41–9: Donne's Use of Uncertainty as a Vital Force in Satyre III.

MOORMAN, F. W. *Robert Herrick*, London, 1910, see pp. 174–83: References to Donne, and others *passim* (see index).

MOORMAN, F. W., *et al. Cambridge History of English Literature*. Vol. VII. *Cavalier and Puritan*, Cambridge, 1911: References to Donne *passim* (see index).

MORAN, BERNA. *Eng. Dept. Studies*, Istambul Univ. III, 1952, 69–76: Some notes on Donne's attitude to the problem of body and soul.

MORAN, BERNA. *Litera*, VI, 1959, 31–3: Donne's Poem 'The Dream'.

MORE, P. E. *George Herbert. Shelburne Essays*, S. 4, N.Y., 1905, pp. 74–5: Reference to Donne.

MORGAN, B. Q. *Publ. Mod. Lang. Assoc.* LXXV, 1960, pp. 634–5: Compulsory Patterns in Poetry.

MORILLO, M. *Tulane Stud. Eng.* XIII, 1963, pp. 33–40: Donne's 'Farewell to Love'.

MORILLO, M. *Eng. Lang. Notes* (Univ. Colorado), III, 1966, 173–6: Donne's Compasses. Circles and Right Lines.

MORLEY, C. *Sat. Rev. Lit.* XVI, 1937, 10, 16: Courting John Donne.

MORRIS, B. 'Satire from Donne to Marvell'. (See under Palmer, D. J., and Bradbury, M.)

MORRIS, D. *The Poetry of Gerard Manley Hopkins and T. S. Eliot in the light of the Donne Tradition. A Comparative Study*, Bern, [1953] (Swiss Studies in English).

MORRIS, H. *Tulane Stud. Eng.* XI, 1961, 23–37: In Articulo Mortis.

MORRIS, W. E. *Notes and Queries*, N.S. X (CCVIII), 1963, 414–15: Donne's Early use of the Word Concoction.

MORRIS, W. E. *Explicator*, XXIII, 1965, item 45: Donne's 'The Sunne Rising', l. 30.

MORTIMER, R. *New Statesm. and Nat.* XXI, 1941, 534: The Metaphysical School of Poetry (Books in General).

MOSES, W. R. *The Metaphysical Conceit in the Poems of John Donne*, Vanderbilt Univ., Abstracts of Theses, 1939.

MOULTON, C. W. *The Library of Literary Criticism of English and American Authors*, New York, 1901, I, 710–19: John Donne (quotations from various writers).

MUELLER, J. M. Donne's *Ars Praedicandi. The Development of the Methods and Themes of his preaching*, Ph.D. Thesis, Harvard Univ., 1965.

MUELLER, J. M. *Huntington Libr. Quart.* XXX, 1967, 207–16: A Borrowing of Donne's Christmas Sermon of 1621 (by John Cosin, Bishop of Durham. See p. 292).

MUELLER, J. M. *Journ. Eng. Germ. Philol.* LXVII, 1968, 1–19: The Exegesis of Experience. Dean Donne's *Devotions*.

MUELLER, W. R. *Mod. Lang. Notes.* LXXVI, 1961, pp. 312–4: Donne's Adulterous

Female Town ('Batter my heart . . .' Holy Sonnet XIV).

MUELLER, W. R. *John Donne Preacher.* Princeton Univ. Press, 1962 (pp. 288).
REVIEWED:
Anon. *Times Lit. Sup.*, 14 June 1963, p. 448.
R. Ellrodt, *Études Angl.* XIX, 1963, 302–3.
H. Gardner, *Rev. Eng. Stud.* XV, 1963, 59, 341.
J. M. Patrick, *Seventeenth Cent. News*, XXI, 1963, 11–12.
H. M. Sikes, ibid. 12.
A. J. Smith, *Renaiss. News*, XVI, 1963, 241–2.
P. G. Stanwood, *Anglian. Theol. Rev.* XLV, 1963, 428–32.
L. Unger, *College Eng.* XXV, no. 6, 1963, 474–5.

MULLIK, B. R. *Studies in Poets. Vol. V. Donne.* S. Chand & Co., Delhi, 1965 (third edn.; first publ. 1955), pp. [vi], 56, [2].

MUÑOZ ROTAS, J. A. *Rivista de Filol. Españ.* XXV, 1941, 108–11: Un libro Español en la biblioteca de Donne (on Donne's copy of Gracian's *Iosephina*, 1609; see L87).

MUÑOZ ROTAS, J. A. *Papales de Son Armadans* (Mallorca), XXVII, 1962, pp. 23–48: Encuentro con Donne.

MURAOKA, J. *Stud. Eng. Lit.* (Tokyo), XXXVI, 1960, 49–64: The Historical Background of Metaphysical Poetry.

MURPHY, J. *Bull. Rocky Mountains Mod. Lang. Assoc.* XXIII, 1969, 163–7: The Young Donne and the Senecan Amble.

MURRAY, W. A. *Rev. Eng. Stud.* XXV, 1949, 115–23: Donne and Paracelsus: an essay in interpretation.

MURRAY, W. A. *Mod. Lang. Notes*, LXXIII, 1958, 329–30: Donne's Gold-leaf and his Compasses.

MURRAY, W. A. *Rev. Eng. Stud.* X, 1959, 141–55: What was the Soul of the Apple? (The Progresse of the Soule, l. 83).

NANCE, J. *Poet. Rev.* XXXIX, 1948, 91–2: John Donne and the Spiritual Life.

NATHANSON, L. *Notes and Queries*, CCII, 1957, 56–9: The context of Dryden's criticism of Donne's and Cowley's love poetry.

NATHANSON, L. *Notes and Queries*, CCII, 1957, 197–8: Dryden, Donne and Cowley.

NEILL, K. *Explicator*, VI, November 1947, item 8: Donne's 'Aire and Angels'.

NELLIST, B. F. *Mod. Lang. Rev.* LIX, 1964, 511–15: Donne's 'Storm' and 'Calm' and the Descriptive Tradition.

NELLY, UNA. *The Poet Donne. A Study in his Dialectic Method*, Cork Univ. Press [1969], 21 cm, pp. [vi], 165, [1].

NELSON, L. *Baroque Lyric Poetry*, New Haven and London, 1961 (discusses four of Donne's love poems).

NETHERCOT, A. H. *Sewanee Rev.* XXX, 1922, 1–12, 463–74: The reputation of John Donne as a metrist.

NETHERCOT, A. H. *Mod. Lang. Notes*, XXXVII, 1922, 11–17: The Term 'Metaphysical Poets' before Johnson.

NETHERCOT, A. H. *Journ. Eng. Germ. Philol.* XXIII, 1924, 173–98: The reputation of the Metaphysical Poets during the seventeenth century (on p. 178 is the statement that 'Donne's Satires were brought out in 1662').

NETHERCOT, A. H. *Philol. Quart.* IV, 1925, 161–79: The Reputation of the Metaphysical Poets during the Age of Pope.

NETHERCOT, A. H. *Stud. in Philol.* XXII, 1925, 81–132: The reputation of the Metaphysical Poets during the Age of Johnson and the Romantic Revival.

NETHERCOT, A. H. *Mod. Lang. Rev.* XXV, 1930, 152–64: The reputation of native *versus* foreign Metaphysical Poets in England.

NEWBOLT, Sir HENRY. *Studies Grave and Gay*, London, 1926, p. 271: Alice Meynell's poems compared with Donne's.

NEWBOLT, Sir H. *Devotional Poets of the Seventeenth Century*, London, 1929, see pp. 1–52.

NEWDIGATE, B. H. *Lond. Mercury*, XXXIII, 1936, 425–6: An overlooked poem of John Donne?
See also Langston, B.

NEWDIGATE, B. H. *Notes and Queries*, CLXXX, 1941, 441: Donne's 'Letters to Several Persons of Honour'.

NEWTON, W. *Angl. Theol. Rev.* XLI, 1956, 10–12: A Study of John Donne's Sonnet XIV.

NICHOLLS, N. *Bookman* (Lond.), LXXIX, 1931, 370–1: The early editions of John Donne.

Nicolson, M. H. *Stud. in Philol.* XXXIII, 1935, 428–62: New Astronomy and the English literary imagination. Repr. in *Science and Imagination*.

Nicolson, M. H. *Journ. Hist. Ideas*, I, 1940, 259–80: Kepler, the *Somnium*, and John Donne. Repr. in *Science and Imagination*.

Nicolson, M. H. *Voyages to the Moon*, N.Y., 1948, pp. 49–82: *Ignatius his Conclave*.

Nicolson, M. H. *The Breaking of the Circle. Studies in the Effects of the New Science upon Seventeenth Century Poetry*, N.Y., London, 1960 (first published 1950): References to Donne *passim* (see index).

Norton, D. S. *Explicator*, IV, February 1946, item 24: Donne's 'The Apparition'.

Novak, M. *Notes and Queries*, CC, 1955, 471–2: An unrecorded reference in a poem by Donne (a reference to Campion's *Lorde's Mask* in 'An Epithalamion or Marriage Song On The Lady Elizabeth And Count Palatine').

Novarr, D. *Times Lit. Sup.*, 24 October 1952, p. 700: Donne's Letters.

Novarr, D. *Rev. Eng. Stud.* VII, 1956, 250–63: Donne's 'Epithalamion made at Lincoln's Inn', context and date.

Novarr, D. *Philol. Quart.* XXXVI, 1957, 259–65: The Dating of Donne's 'La Corona'.

Novarr, D. *The Making of Walton's Lives*, N.Y., Cornell Univ. Press, 1958, pp. 19–126: The Earliest Life (Donne) and its Revisions; pp. 503–6: Walton and the poems about Donne's seal (for other references see index).
REVIEWED:
Times Lit. Sup., 24 October 1958, p. 608.

Novarr, D. *Mod. Philol.* LXII, 1964, 142–54: The Two Hands of John Donne (review).

Oake, R. B. *Mod. Lang. Notes*, LVI, 1941, 114–15: Diderot and Donne's *Biathanatos*.

Ochojski, P. M. *Amer. Benedict. Rev.* I, 1940, 535–48: Did John Donne repent his apostasy?

O'Connor, W. van. *College Eng.* IX, 1948, 180–7: The Influence of the Metaphysicals on Modern Poetry.

O'Connor, W. van. *Sense and Sensibility in Modern Poetry*, Minneap., 1948: References to Donne.

Onizuka, K. *F29* (Japan), pp. 65–78: The Evolution of Love and its Limitation. On John Donne's 'Heavenly Love'.

Ornstein, R. *Journ. Eng. Germ. Philol.* LV, 1956, 213–29: Donne, Montaigne, & Natural Law.

Osborn, J. M. *Times Lit. Sup.*, 4 January 1957, p. 16: 'Ben Jonson and the eccentric Lord Stanhope', with references to his marginalia alluding to Donne in Jonson's *Works*, 1640.

Osborn, L. B. *The Life, Letters, and Writings of John Hoskyns, 1566–1638*, New Haven, 1937: Various references to Donne (see index). Hoskyns was a friend of Donne's.

Osmond, P. H. *Mystical Poets of the English Church*, London, 1919, pp. 42–66: Davies, Donne, and Heywood.

P., R. *Explicator*, XVI, 1957, item 5: Jonson's 'To John Donne'.

Pafford, J. H. P. *Times Lit. Sup.*, 2 September 1949, p. 569: John Donne's library.

Pafford, J. H. P. *Notes and Queries*, N.S. VI, 1959, 131–2: Donne: an early Nineteenth Century Estimate (John Fry's *Pieces of Ancient Poetry*, Bristol, 1814; from unpublished manuscripts and rare books).

Pafford, J. H. P. *Notes and Queries*, XIII, 1966, 377: An Early Donne Reference (see Astry, James).

Pafford, M. K. *Explicator*, XXII, 1963, item 13: Donne's 'The Extasie', ll. 57–60, 68.

Pagnini, M. *Linga e Stile* (Bologna), II, 1967, pp. 159–78: Sulle funzioni semilogiche della poesia di John Donne.

Palmer, D. J. 'The Verse Epistle' (see Palmer, D. J., and Bradbury, M., 1970).

Palmer, D. J., and Bradbury, M., eds. *Metaphysical Poetry*, Stratford upon Avon Studies, XI. London, 1970 (essays by Cruttwell, P., Hinman, R. B., Martz, L. L., Morris, B., Palmer, D. J., Saunders, J. W., and Warnke, F. J.).

Palmer, G. H. *The English Works of George Herbert*, Boston and New York, 3 vols., 1905: References to Donne *passim* (see index).

PARISH, J. E. *Notes and Queries*, CCII, 1957, 377–8: Donne as a Petrarchan.

PARISH, J. E. *College. Eng.* XXIV, 1963, 299–302: No. 14 of Donne's 'Holy Sonnets'.

PARISH, J. E. *Explicator*, XXII, 1963, item 19: Donne's 'Holy Sonnets XIII'.

PARISH, J. E. *Xavier Univ. Stud.* IV, 1965, 188–92: The Parley in 'The Extasie'.

PATRIDES, C. A. *Harvard Theol. Rev.* LI, 1958, 169–85: Renaissance and Modern Thought on the Last Things. A Study in Changing Conceptions.

PATRIDES, C. A. *Mod. Lang. Notes*, LXXIII, 1958, 257–60: Milton and his Contemporaries on the Chains of Satan.

PATTERSON, R. F. *Six Centuries of English Literature*, 6 vols., London, 1933. Vol. II, pp. 292 ff.

PAYNE, F. W. *John Donne and his Poetry*, London, 1926, 8°, pp. 167 [Poetry and Life Series].
REVIEWED:
Legouis, P. *Rev. Anglo-Améric.* V, 1928, 173–5.

PEARSON, L. E. *Elizabethan Love Conventions*, Berkeley, 1933: References pp. 223–30.

PELLEGRINI, G. *Barocco Inglese*, Messina, 1953.

PERKINS, D. *Journ. Eng. Lit. Hist.* XX, 1953, pp. 200–17: Johnson on Wit and Metaphysical Poetry.

PERRINE, L. *Explicator*, XXI, 1963, item 40: Donne's 'A Lecture upon the Shadow'.

PERRY, H. T. E. *Explicator*, V, November 1946, item 10: Donne's 'The Perfume'.

PETER, H. W. *Thoth*. IX, 1968, 48–57: Donne's 'Nocturnall' and the *Nigredo*.

PETERSON, D. L. *Stud. Philol.* LVI, 1959, 504–18: John Donne's 'Holy Sonnets' and the Anglican Doctrine of Contrition.

PETERSON, D. L. *The English Lyric from Wyatt to Donne. A History of the Plain and Eloquent Styles*, Princeton, 1967 (pp. 420).
REVIEWED:
Guss, D. L., *Criticism*, X, 81–3.

PHELPS, G. In *From Donne to Marvell*, ed. B. Ford, Penguin Books, 1956, pp. 116–30: The prose of Donne and Browne.

PHELPS, W. L. *Mod. Lang. Notes*, XVIII, 1903, 161: Donne's First Satire.

PICAVET, F. *Mind*, N.S. XXVI, 1917, 385–92: The mediæval doctrines in the works of Donne and Locke.

PIRIE, R. S. *Times Lit. Sup.*, 23 December 1965: Donne's Books.

PITTS, A. W., jr. *Diss. Abstr.* XXVII, 1967, 3016A: John Donne's use of Proverbs in his Poetry.

PLOWMAN, M. *Everyman*, 14 February 1929, pp. 9–10: An appreciation of the poems of John Donne.

POMEROY, E. *Explicator*, XXVII, 1968, item 4: Donne's 'The Sunne Rising'.

PONCELLA, S., segundo. *Insula*, XXI, 1966, 12: John Donne e la sensualidad.

PORTER, A. *Spectator*, CXLVI, 1931, 539–40: Dean Donne.

POTTER, G. R. *Philol. Quart.* VI, 1927, 396–400: Milton's early poems, the School of Donne, and the Elizabethan sonneteers.

POTTER, G. R. *Univ. of Calif. Essays in Crit.* 2nd ser. IV, 1934, 3–23: John Donne's discovery of himself.

POTTER, G. R. *Philol. Quart.* XV, 1936, 247–54: Donne's *Extasie*, contre Legouis.

POTTER, G. R. *Mod. Lang. Notes*, LV, 1940, 53: Donne's Paradoxes in 1707 [in Dunton's *Athenian Sport*] (see no. 46a).

POTTER, G. R. *Journ. Eng. Germ. Philol.* XLIV, 1945, 28–35: Hitherto undescribed MS. versions of three sermons by Donne.

POTTER, G. R. *Seventeenth Cent. News*, X, 1952, 13: Donne's development in pulpit oratory.

POTTER, G. R. In *Five Gayley Lectures*, Univ. of California Press, Berkeley and Los Angeles, 1954, pp. 105–26: John Donne: Poet to Priest.

POTTER, G. R., and BUTT, J. *Editing Donne and Pope*, Los Angeles [1953]. A paper on editing Donne's sermons delivered by Prof. Potter at the first Clark Library Seminar, 22 November 1952.

POTTER, M. *Notes and Queries*, N.S. XIII (CCXI), 1966, 376–7: A Note on Donne (the title of 'Love's Infiniteness').

POTTS, L. J. *English Studies 1949 (Eng. Assoc.)*, N.S. II, 7–24: Ben Jonson and the Seventeenth Century.

POWELL, A. C. *Times Lit. Sup.*, 23 September 1949, p. 617: John Donne's library.

POWER, H. W. *Diss. Abstr.* XXVII, 1967, 4228A–29A: The Speaker in the Secular Poetry of John Donne.

POWERS, D. C. *Rev. Eng. Stud.* IX, 1958, 173–5: Donne's Compass.

POYNTER, F. N. L. *Journ. Hist. Med.* XV, 1960, 233–46: John Donne and William Harvey.

PRAZ, M. *Seicentismo e Marinismo in Inghilterra. John Donne. Richard Crashaw*, Firenze, La Voce, 1925.
REVIEWED:
Greenlaw, E. *Mod. Lang. Notes*, XLIII, 275–6.
Grierson, Sir H. J. C. *Rev. Eng. Stud.* II, 1926, 467–71.
Hübner, W. *Arch. Stud. neu. Sprach.* CL, 1926, 258–9.
Hughes, M. V. *Univ. Calif. Chron.* XXIX, 1927, 225–9.
Legouis, P. *Mod. Lang. Rev.* XXI, 1926, 313–19.
Pompen, F. A. *Eng. Stud.* VIII, 1926, 24–7.
Wolf, M. S. *Eng. Stud.* LXI, 1926, 92–5.
Times Lit. Sup., 17 December 1925, p. 878.

PRAZ, M. In *A Garland for John Donne*, ed. T. Spencer, Cambridge, Mass., 1931, pp. 53–72: Donne's relation to the poetry of his time. Repr., revised and enlarged, in *The Flaming Heart*, N.Y., Anchor Books, 1958, and in H. Gardner's *Collection of Critical Essays*, 1962. See also a translation in his *Machiavelli in Inghilterra*, Rome, 1942.

PRAZ, M. *Studies in Seventeenth Century Images*, London, Warburg Inst., 1939, I, p. 150: A reference to Donne's images. 2nd edn., Rome, 1964.

PRAZ, M. *La Poesia Metafisica Inglese del Seicento—John Donne*, Rome, 1945.
REVIEWED:
Pompen, Fr. A. *Eng. Stud.* XXVIII, 1947, 49.

PRAZ, M. *Studi sul Concettismo: John Donne*, Firenze, 1946.
REVIEWED:
Pellegrini, G. *Rivista di Letteratura Moderne*, II, 1947, 86–7.
Pompen, Fr. A. *Eng. Stud.* XXVIII, 1947, 49 ff.

PRAZ, M. In *English Studies Today*, Oxford, 1951, pp. 158–66: 'The Critical Importance of the Revived Interest in 17th Century Metaphysical Poetry'.

PRAZ, M. *John Donne*, Torino, 1958.

PRAZ, M. *Times Lit. Sup.*, 20 February 1959, p. 97: Donne and Dickens.

PROSKY, M. *Explicator*, XXVII, 1968, item 27: Donne's 'Aire and Angels'.

QUENNELL, P. *Aspects of Seventeenth Century Verse*, London, 1933.

QUILLER-COUCH, Sir A. T. *Camb. Daily News*, 8 November 1917: Q. on Dr. John Donne.

QUILLER-COUCH, Sir A. T. *Studies in Literature*, ser. I, Cambridge, 1918, pp. 96 ff.: John Donne; ser. III, Cambridge, 1929; pp. 29–30: Donne's Elegies.

QUINN, D. B. *Diss. Abstr.* XVIII, 1958, 2131–2: John Donne's Sermons on the Psalms and the Tradition of Biblical Exegesis (Univ. of Wisconsin).

QUINN, D. B. *Journ. Eng. Lit. Hist.* XXVII, 1960, 276–97: Donne's Christian Eloquence.

QUINN, D. B. *Mod. Lang. Notes.* LXXV, 1960, 643–4: 'Tyr.' is Lucretius Tiraboscus. (The reference occurs in Donne's Lincoln's Inn Sermon on Ps. 38: 4, Potter and Simpson, II, 131, and note p. 397.)

QUINN, D. B. *Journ. Eng. Germ. Philol.* LXI, 1962, 326: John Donne's Principles of Biblical exegesis.

QUINN, D. B. *Stud. Eng. Lit.* IX, 1969, 97–105: Donne's *Anniversaries* as Celebration.

QUINN, D. B. *Journ. Eng. Lit. Hist.* XXXVI, 1969, 626–47: Donne and the Wane of Wonder.

RAINE, K. *Horizon*, XI, 1945, 371–95: John Donne and the Baroque Doubt.

RAIZISS, S. *The Metaphysical Passion*, Philadelphia, Univ. Penn. Press, 1952: References *passim* (see index).

RAMSAY, M. P. *Les Doctrines médiévales chez Donne*, London, 1917, 8°, pp. xii, 338, 2nd edn., 1922.
REVIEWED:
Bredvold, L. I. *Journ. Eng. Germ. Philol.* XXI, 1922, 347–53.

Burdett, O. *Lond. Mercury*, XII, 1922, 101–2.

Grierson, H. J. C. *Mod. Lang. Rev.* XVI, 1921, 343–50.

Janelle, P. *Rev. Anglo-Améric.* III, 1926, 252–4.

Smith, G. C. Moore. *Mod. Lang. Rev.* XX, 1925, 371–2.

Anon. *Times Lit. Sup.*, 25 December 1924, pp. 877–8.

RAMSAY, M. P. In *A Garland for John Donne*, ed. T. Spencer, Cambridge, Mass., 1931, pp. 101–20: Donne's relation to philosophy.

RANSOM, J. C. *South. Rev.* III, 1938, pp. 531–53: Shakespeare [and Donne] at sonnets.

RANSOM, J. C. *The World's Body*, New York and London, 1938, see pp. 78–91, 128–42, 285–303: References to Donne.

RANSOM, J. C. *Accent*, I, 1941, 148–56: Eliot and the Metaphysicals.

RASPA, A. *Journ. Eng. Lit. Hist.* XXXII, 1965, 478–89: Theology and Poetry in Donne's *Conclave*.

RATHBURN, P. A. *Seventeenth Cent. News*, summer 1968, p. 38: review of N. J. C. Andreasen's *Donne. Conservative Revolutionary*, 1967.

READ, Sir H. *The Criterion*, I, 1923, 246–66: The Nature of Metaphysical Poetry. Repr. in *Collected Essays in Literary Criticism*, 1938, pp. 69–88, and in *The Nature of Literature*, N.Y., 1956.

READ, Sir H. *Phases of English Poetry*, London, 1928, see pp. 62–8.

REED, A. W. *Early Tudor Drama*, London, 1926, p. 90: A reference to Donne and his Heywood ancestry.

REED, E. B. *English Lyrical Poetry*, 1912, pp. 233–42.

REEVES, G. B. *Univ. of Pittsburgh. Bull.* X, 1934, 554–5: The microcosm in the works of John Donne. (Abstract of theses.)

RIAZIS, M. B. *Wichita State Univ. Bull.* XLII, iv, 1966, 3–15: The Epithalamion Tradition and John Donne.

RICHARD, L. H. *Diss. Abstr.* XXVIII, 1968, 4186A–7A: Man's Middle Nature. Studies in the Poetry of John Donne.

RICHARDS, I. A. *Practical Criticism*, London, 1929, pp. 42–50, etc.

RICHARDS, I. A. In *The Language of Poetry*, ed. A. Tate, Princeton Univ. Press, 1942: The Interaction of Words.

RICHMOND, H. M. *Notes and Queries*, N.S. V (CCIII), 1958, 535–6: Donne and Ronsard (a parallel in Holy Sonnet XIII and elsewhere).

RICHMOND, H. M. *Mod. Philol.* LVI, 1959, 217–33: The Intangible Mistress.

RICHTER, R. *Beitr. zur. Neu. Philol.* 1902 (Jacob Schipper Festschrift), pp. 400 ff.: Über den Vers bei Dr. John Donne.

RICKEY, M. E. *Explicator*, XXII, 1964, item 58: Donne's 'The Relic', ll. 27–8.

RICKS, D. M. *Stud. Philol.* LXIII, 1967, 187–95: The Westmorland MS. and the order of Donne's 'Holy Sonnets'.

RINGLER, R. N. *Philol. Quart.* XLII, 1963, 423–9: Two Sources for Dryden's 'The Indian Emperor' ('The First Anniversary').

RINGLER, R. N. *Mod. Lang. Rev.* LX, 1965, 333–9: Donne's Specular Stone.

ROBBIE, H. J. L. *Rev. Eng. Stud.* III, 1927, 415–19: An undescribed MS. of Donne's poems [in Camb. Univ. Libr. Add. MS. 5778] (C 57).

ROBBIE, H. J. L. *Rev. Eng. Stud.* IV, 1928, 214–16: Two more undescribed MSS. of John Donne's poems [BM Harl. 3998, and Do.].

ROBERTS, D. R. *Publ. Mod. Lang. Assoc.* LXII, 1947, 958–76: The death wish of John Donne.

ROBERTS, M. *Ess. Crit.* (Oxford), XVI, 1966, 309–29: If it were Donne when 'tis Done (review).

ROBERTS, M. *Times Lit. Sup.*, 7 October 1967, p. 804: a letter 'On Editing Donne'.

ROCKETT, G. W. *Diss. Abstr.* XXX, 1969, 1149A: Ovidian and Naturalistic Themes in Donne's *Elegies* (Univ. Wiscons.).

ROCKWOOD, H. S. *Diss. Abstr.* XXVII, 1967, 2134A: A Reconciliation of the Poetry of Edward, Lord Herbert of Cherbury, and of its supposed conformity to the Poetry of Donne.

ROONEY, W. J. *Journ. Eng. Lit. Hist.* XXIII,

1956, 36–47: 'The Canonization': The language of paradox reconsidered.

Rooney, W. J. *Texas Stud. Lit. Lang.* IV, 1962, 24–34: John Donne's Second Prebend Sermon. A Stylistic Analysis.

Rosenthal, M. L., *et al. Effective Reading*, New York, 1944, pp. 406–13 (Donne).

Ross, M. M. *Hudson Rev.* VI, 1953, 106–13: A Note on the Metaphysicals.

Ross, M. M. *Poetry and Dogma*, New Brunswick, 1954. For references see index.

Roth, R. *Gifthorse*, 1946–7, pp. 15–18: Donne and Sonnets IX and X.

Rowe, F. A. *I Launch a Paradise: A Consideration of John Donne, Poet and Preacher*, London, Epworth Press, [1964].

Rowland, D. B. *Mannerism-Style and Mood. An Anatomy of Four Works in Three Art Forms*, New Haven, 1964 (incl. 'The First Anniversary').

Rudd, N. *Times Lit. Sup.*, 22 March 1963, p. 208: Donne and Horace (Satyre IV).

Rugoff, M. A. *Philol. Quart.* XVI, 1937, 85–8: Drummond's debt to Donne [in *A Cypresse Grove*].

Rugoff, M. A. *Donne's Imagery. A Study in Creative Sources*, New York, 1939, 23·5 cm, pp. 270, [2]. Repr. 1962.
REVIEWED:
Heywood, T. *Life and Letters Today*, XXIV, 1940, 88–9.
Williamson, G. C. *Mod. Lang. Notes*, LVI, 1941, 626–8.

Rukeyser, M. *The Traces of Thomas Hariot*, Random House, N.Y., 1970: With many references to Donne, especially in his relations with Hariot (or Harriot) and the 9th Earl of Northumberland.

Ruotolo, L. P. *Journ. Hist. Ideas*, XXVII, 1966, pp. 445–6: The Trinitarian Framework of Donne's Holy Sonnet XIV.

Russell, J. D. *Explicator*, XVII, 1958, item 9: Donne's 'A Lecture upon the Shadow'.

Rylands, G. *Essays & Studies by Members of the Engl. Assoc.* XVI, 1930, 53–84: English Poets and the Abstract Word.

Rylands, G. *Camb. Rev.* XXVI, 1934, 46–7: The metaphysical poets.

S., A. *Notes and Queries*, 9th ser., VII, 1901, 183: References in early English Literature to Dr. Donne.

Sackton, A. *Stud. Eng. Lit.* VII, 1967, 67–82: Donne and the Privacy of Verse.

Saintsbury, G. E. B. *The Earlier Renaissance*, Edinburgh and London, 1901, p. 275: A reference to Donne—'Presumed on the licence of the Satire to be rough'.

Saintsbury, G. E. B. *A History of Elizabethan Literature*, London, 1907, pp. 144–50.

Saintsbury, G. E. B. *A History of English Prosody*, 2 vols., London, 1908, vol. II, pp. 159–62.

Saintsbury, G. E. B. *A History of English Prose Rhythm*, London, 1912: References to Donne *passim* (see index).

Saintsbury, G. E. B. *A Short History of English Literature*, London, 1913, pp. 279, 365–8, 385–6, 411–12.

Saintsbury, G. E. B. *Prefaces and Essays*, London, 1933, pp. 273–91: The poetry of Donne (a reprint of the introduction to *Poems*, ed. Chambers, 1896; see no. 93).

Saito, T. *Stud. in Eng. Lit* (Tokyo), IX, 1929, 79–106: John Donne, his later life and works.

Saltmarshe, S. *Bookman* (Lond.), LXXIX, 1931, 343–4: John Donne: the man and his life.

Sampson, A. *Lond. Mercury*, XXXIII, 1936, 307–14: The resurrection of Donne.

Sampson, J. *Essays and Studies by Members of the English Association*, vol. VII, Oxford, 1921, pp. 82–107: A Contemporary Light upon John Donne. (An account of a copy of the *Poems*, 1639, annotated by Giles Oldisworth.)

Samson, P. *South. Rev.* (Univ. of Adelaide), I, 1963, pp. 46–52: Words for Music. (Musical arrangements of poems by Donne and Campion.)

Sanders, H. M. *Temple Bar*, CXXI, 1900, 614–28: John Donne.

Saunders, J. W. *Essays in Criticism*, I, 1951, pp. 150–5: The Stigma of Print.

Saunders, J. W. *Essays in Criticism*, III, 1953, 109–14: Donne and Daniel.

Saunders, J. W. 'The Social Situation of Seventeenth Century Poetry' (see Palmer, D. J., and Bradbury, M., 1970).

Sawin, L. *Mod. Lang. Notes*, LXIX, 1954, 558–9: The earliest use of 'Autumnall'.

Sawin, L. *Explicator*, XIII, 1955, 31: Donne's 'The Canonization'.

Schelling, F. E. *Publ. Mod. Lang. Assoc.* XIII, N.S. VI, 1898, 221–49: Ben Jonson and the Classical School.

Schelling, F. E. *English Literature during the Lifetime of Shakespeare*, London, 1910, ch. XIX, pp. 357–77: Donne and his place among lyrical poets.

Schelling, F. E. *The English Lyric*, London and Boston, 1913: References to Donne *passim* (see index). See also the same author's *A Book of Elizabethan Lyrics*, Boston, 1895, and *A Book of Seventeenth Century Lyrics*, Boston, 1899.

Schleiner, W. *Diss. Abstr.* XXX, 1969, 299A: The Imagery of Donne's Sermons (Brown Univ.). Printed as *The Imagery of John Donne's Sermons*, Brown Univ. Press, 1970, pp. x, 254.

Schoeck, R. J. *Notes and Queries*, XIII, 1952, 398–9: William Rastell and the Prothonotaries (Donne's ancestry).

Schwartz, E. *Explicator*, XIX, 1961, item 67: Donne's 'Elegie X' (The Dreame).

Schwartz, E. *Explicator*, XXVI, 1967, item 27: Donne's 'Holy Sonnet XIV'.

Scott, R. I. *Notes and Queries*, VI, 1959, 208–9: Donne and Kepler (on the metaphor at the beginning of 'Elegie on Prince Henry').

Scott, W. S. *The Fantasticks* (Donne, Herbert, Crashaw, Vaughan—selections), London, 1946.

REVIEWED:
Times Lit. Sup., 30 March 1946, p. 153.
Stonier, G. W. *New Statesm. & Nat.* XXXI, 23 March 1946, 215.

Scott, W. S. *Bermuda Hist. Quart.* VI, 1949, 77–8: John Donne and Bermuda.

Seccombe, T., and Allen, J. W. *The Age of Shakespeare. Vol. I. Poetry and Prose*, London, 1903, pp. 65–74: John Donne.

Seldon, R. *Mod. Lang. Rev.* LXIV, 1969, 726–7: Donne's 'The Dampe', ll. 22–4.

Sen, S. K. *Metaphysical Tradition and T. S. Eliot*, Calcutta, 1965: References to Donne.

Sencourt, E. de. *Hibbert Journ.* XXXVII, 1939, pp. 225–45: The Interplay of Literature and Science during the last Three Centuries.

Sencourt, R. *Outflying Philosophy. A Literary Study of the Religious Element in the Poems and Letters of John Donne and in the Works of Sir Thomas Browne and of Henry Vaughan.* [Hildesheim, 1924], pp. 27–84: The Supernatural Complexion of the Writer's General Work in Donne (see also pp. 127–31, 230–4, 286–91, 333–40, 347, 352–3).

Seng, P. J. *Notes and Queries*, N.S. V (CCIII), 1958, 214–15: Donne's Compass Image (see also under Fitzgerald, E., and Tennyson, A.).

Serrano Poncella, S. *Insula*, 21 October 1966: John Donne e la Sensualidad.

Seymour-Smith, M. *Poets through their Letters*, London, 1969, I, pp. 84–122: Donne.

Shapiro, I. A. *Times Lit. Sup.*, 16, 23 October 1930, pp. 833, 861: John Donne and Lincoln's Inn, 1591–1594.

Shapiro, I. A. *Rev. Eng. Stud.* VII, 1931, 291–301: The text of Donne's *Letters to Severall Persons*.

Shapiro, I. A. *Times Lit. Sup.*, 10 March 1932, p. 172: John Donne and Parliament [in 1601 and 1614].

Shapiro, I. A., *Times. Lit. Sup.*, 3 July 1937, p. 492: John Donne, the astronomer: the date of the eighth Problem.
See also Mitchell, W. F., 10 July, p. 512; Mitchell, W. F., Ashley-Montagu, M. F., 7 August, p. 576; Shapiro, I. A., 17 July, p. 528; Lindsay, J., 24 July, p. 544; Legouis, P., 31 July, p. 560; Shapiro, I. A., 14 August, p. 592; Coffin, C. M., 18 September, p. 675.

Shapiro, I. A. *Times Lit. Sup.*, 21 October 1949, p. 681: Donne Letters.

Shapiro, I. A. *Notes and Queries*, CXCIV, 1949, 473: The date of Donne's poem 'To Mr George Herbert'.

Shapiro, I. A. *Times Lit. Sup.*, 9 April 1949, p. 233: Two Donne poems.

Shapiro, I. A. *Mod. Lang. Rev.* 1950, 6–17: The Mermaid Club. See also ibid. XLVI, 1951, 58–63, Simpson, P., and Shapiro, I. S.: An Answer and A Rejoinder.

SHAPIRO, I. A. *Notes and Queries*, CXCVII, 1952, 310–13: Donne's birth-date.

SHAPIRO, I. A. *Times Lit. Sup.*, 6 February 1953, p. 96: Publication dates before 1640 (incl. *Conclave Ignati, Devotions, Pseudo-Martyr*, and *Sermon on Judges 5: 20*).

SHAPIRO, I. A. *Rev. Eng. Stud.* IX, 1958, 18–22: Walton and the Occasion of Donne's *Devotions*.

SHAPIRO, I. A. *Times Lit. Sup.*, 20 January 1966: Donne's Books (Edward Parvish and Donne).

SHAPIRO, I. A. *Notes and Queries*, XIII, 1966, 243–8: Donne, the Parvishes, and Munster's *Cosmography*.

SHAPIRO, I. A. *Times Lit. Sup.*, 26 January 1967, p. 76: Donne in 1605–6.

SHARP, R. L. *Stud. in Philol.* XXXI, 1934, 497–518: Some light on metaphysical obscurity and roughness.

SHARP, R. L. *Mod. Lang. Notes*, XLIX, 1934, 503–5: The pejorative use of 'Metaphysical'.

SHARP, R. L. *Sewanee Rev.* XLIII, 1935, 464–78: Observations on metaphysical imagery.

SHARP, R. L. *From Donne to Dryden: the Revolt against Metaphysical Poetry*, Chapel Hill, North Carolina, 1940, pp. 3–33: Donne and Elizabethan Poetry. (Other references *passim* (see index).) Reissued London, 1955.
REVIEWED:
J[ones], H. S. V. *Journ. Eng. Germ. Philol.* XL, 1941, 456.
Warren, A. *Mod. Lang. Notes*, LVI, 1941, 312–13.
Wellek, R. *Philol. Quart.* XX, 1941, 90–2.
Times Lit. Sup., 25 March 1955, p. 182.

SHARP, R. L. *Mod. Lang. Notes*, LXIX, 1954, 493–5; Donne's 'Good-morrow' and cordiform maps.

SHARP, R. L. *Notes and Queries*, IX, 1962, 210–12: Donne's 'Autumnall' and the Barren Plane Tree.

SHAWCROSS, J. T. *Seventeenth Cent. News*, autumn 1962, p. 33: review of *Sermons*, ed. Potter and Simpson, vol. X.

SHAWCROSS, J. T. *Eng. Lang. Notes*, I, 1964, pp. 187–8: Donne's 'A Lecture upon the Shadow'.

SHAWCROSS, J. T. *Explicator*, XXIII, 1965, item 56: Donne's 'A Nocturnall upon St. Lucies Day'.

SHAWCROSS, J. T. *Amer. Notes and Queries*, V, 1967, 104–5: John Donne and Drummond's Manuscripts.

SHAWCROSS, J. T. *Journ. Rutgers Univ. Libr.* XXXII, 1968, 1–32: An Early Nineteenth Century Life of John Donne. An Edition with Notes and Commentary.

SIBLEY, A. M. *Univ. of Oklahoma Bull.* 1939, p. 116: A comparative study of John Donne and T. S. Eliot.

SICHEL, E. *The Renaissance*, London, 1914, pp. 243–4: References to Donne.

SICHERMAN, C. M. *Bucknell Rev.*, XVII, 1969, II, 32–46: The Mocking Voices of Donne and Marvell.

SICHERMAN, C. M. *Univ. Toronto Quart.* XXXIX, 1970, 127–43: Donne's Timeless Anniversaries.

SICHERMAN, C. M. *Stud. Eng. Lit.* XI, 1971, 69–88: Donne's Discoveries.

SIEGEL, P. N. *Philol. Quart.* XXVIII, 1949, 507–11: Donne's 'Paradoxes and Problems'.

SIEGEL, P. N. *Seventeenth Cent. News*, X, 1952, 12–13: Donne's cynical love-poems and Spenserian idealism.

SILHOL, R. *Études angl.* XV, 1962, 329–46: Réflexions sur les sources et la structure de 'A Litanie' de John Donne.

SILK, C. E. B. *Cornhill Mag.* CLVII, 1938, 218: To John Donne (poem).

SIMON, I. *Some Problems of Donne Criticism*, Brussels, 1952 (Langues Vivantes, no. 40).
REVIEWED:
Legouis, P. *Études Angl.* VII, 1954, 327–8.

SIMPSON, A. L., jr. *Explicator*, XXVII, 1969, item 75: Donne's 'Holy Sonnets XII'.

SIMPSON, E. *Rev. Eng. Stud.* XVI, 1965, 140–50: 'Donne and the Serpent' and 'Donne the Seafarer'.

SIMPSON, E. M. [*née* SPEARING]. *Mod. Lang. Rev.* VII, 1912, 40–53: Donne's sermons and their relation to his poetry.

SIMPSON, E. M. *Mod. Lang. Rev.* VIII, 1913, 468–83: A chronological arrangement of Donne's sermons.

SIMPSON, E. M. *Mod. Lang. Rev.* XVIII, 1923, 410–15: John Donne and Sir Thomas Overbury's *Characters*.

SIMPSON, E. M. *A Study of the Prose Works of John Donne*, Oxford, 1924, 8°, pp. viii, 367, [1], with facsimile of letter. Containing 32 letters printed for the first time; see no. 68*a*. 2nd edn., 1948.

REVIEWED:

Aronstein, P. *Englische Stud.* LX, 1926, 348–52.

Clough, B. C. *Sat. Rev. Lit.* I, 1925, 522.

Greenlaw, E. *Mod. Lang. Notes*, XLIII, 1928, 275–8.

Janelle, P. *Rev. Anglo-Améric.* III, 1926, 252–4.

McLaughlin, J. J. *N.Y. Ev. Post*, 2 May 1925, p. 10.

Porter, A. *Spectator*, CXXXIV, 1925, 122.

Read, H. *Criterion*, III, 1925, 315–20.

Roberts, R. E. *Obs.*, 4 January 1925.

Saintsbury, G. *Nat. & Athen.* XXXVI, 1924, 473.

Smith, G. C. Moore. *Mod. Lang. Rev.* XX, 1925, 347–9.

Zeitlin, J. *Nation* (N.Y.), CXXI, 1925, 235–6.

Times Lit. Sup., 25 December 1924, p. 877.

SIMPSON, E. M. *Times Lit. Sup.*, 21 January 1926, p. 44: Donne's Essays in Divinity (the cancelled dedication to Sir Harry Vane, jr.). See also 4 February, p. 80, with correction.

SIMPSON, E. M. *Rev. Eng. Stud.* III, 1927, 129–45: Two manuscripts of Donne's Paradoxes and Problems.

SIMPSON, E. M. *Rev. Eng. Stud.* IV, 1928, 295–300: A note on Donne's punctuation.

SIMPSON, E. M. In *A Garland for John Donne*, ed. T. Spencer, Cambridge, Mass., 1931, pp. 23–49: Donne's Paradoxes and Problems.

SIMPSON, E. M. *Rev. Eng. Stud.* X, 1934, 288–300, 412–16: More MSS. of Donne's Paradoxes and Problems.

SIMPSON, E. M. *Rev. Eng. Stud.* XV, 1939, 274–82: Jonson and Donne: a problem in authorship.

SIMPSON, E. M. In *Essays and Studies by Members of the English Association*, XXVI, 1940, 88–105: The text of Donne's Divine Poems (a study of MS. Do.).

SIMPSON, E. M. *Notes and Queries*, CLXXXII, 1942, 64: Queries from Donne.

SIMPSON, E. M. *Philol. Quart.* XXI, 1942, 237–9: A Donne MS. in St. Paul's Cathedral Library.

SIMPSON, E. M. *Rev. Eng. Stud.* XX, 1944, 223–7: Notes on Donne.

SIMPSON, E. M. *Mod. Lang. Rev.* XLI, 1946, 9–15: The date of Donne's 'Hymne to God, my God, in my Sicknesse'.

SIMPSON, E. M. *Times Lit. Sup.*, 14 March 1947, p. 115: Donne's Sermons.

SIMPSON, E. M. *Mod. Lang. Rev.* XLIII, 1948, 182–5: Donne's Spanish authors.

SIMPSON, E. M. *A Study of the Prose Works of John Donne*, 2nd edn., Oxford, 1948, 8°, pp. viii, 371, [1], with facsimile of letter.

REVIEWED:

A[LLEN], D. C. *Mod. Lang. Notes*, LXV, 1950, 572–3.

Shapiro, I. A. *Rev. Eng. Stud.*, N.S. I, 1950, 262–4.

SIMPSON, E. M. *Rev. Eng. Stud*, N.S. II, 1951, 339–57: The biographical value of Donne's sermons.

SIMPSON, P. *Oriel Rec.*, January 1935: A book from the library of John Donne.

SIMPSON, P. *Times Lit. Sup.*, 28 October 1941, 531: King James on Donne.

SIMPSON, P. *Mod. Lang. Rev.* XXXVIII, 1943, 127 ff.: The rhyming of stressed and unstressed syllables in English verse.

SINCLAIR, VEN. W. M. *Trans. Roy. Soc. Lit.*, N.S. II, XXIX, 1909, 179–202: John Donne. Poet and Preacher.

SINGH, B. *Notes and Queries*, N.S. XVIII (CCXVI), 1971, 70: Two hitherto Unrecorded Imitations of Donne in the Eighteenth Century (poems in *The Universal Spectator*, 16 February 1734. The Editor draws attention to other imitations in the same periodical; see p. 305).

SISSON, C. J. *Mod. Lang. Rev.* XXV, 1930, 216–17: Notice of Grierson's *Poems*, 1929, with suggestions for further research.

SISSON, C. J. *Times Lit. Sup.*, 20 February

1930, p. 142: The Oxford 'Donne'. See also Grierson, Sir H. J. C., same date.

SISSON, C. J. *Times Lit. Sup.*, 13 March 1930: Donne's Satyres II, ll. 71–3.

SKELTON, R. *Elizabethan Poetry. Stratford-upon-Avon Studies*, 1960, ch. x: The Poetry of John Donne. Repr. 1961.

SKINNER, M. *Notes and Queries*, CXCVII, 1952, 134: John Donne not in Germany in 1602.

SLEIGHT, R. I. *Interpretations. Essays on Twelve English Poems*, ed. J. Wain, London, 1955, pp. 31–58: Donne, 'A Nocturnall on S. Lucie's Day'.

SLOAN, T. O., jr. *Diss. Abstr.* XXI, 1961, 1557: The Rhetoric in the poetry of John Donne. Pr. in *Stud. Eng. Lit.* III, 1963, 31–44.

SLOAN, T. O., jr. *Quart. Journ. Speech*, XLVIII, 1962, 38–45: A Rhetorical Analysis of John Donne's 'The Prohibition'.

SLOAN, T. O., jr. *Quart. Journ. Speech*, LI, 1965, 14–27: The Persona as Rhetor: An Interpretation of Donne's 'Satyre III'.

SMALLEY, D. A. *Times Lit. Sup.*, 10 October 1935, p. 631: Browning and Donne.

SMITH, A. J. *Mod. Lang. Rev.* LI, 1956, 405–7: Two notes on Donne ('Aire and Angels', the Crucial Analogy; 'Since she whom I lov'd', a note on punctuation).

SMITH, A. J. *Rev. Eng. Stud.*, N.S. VII, 1956, 348–59: An Examination of some Claims for Ramism (References to Donne's processes of thought).

SMITH, A. J. *Letterat. Mod.* (Bologna), VII, 1957, 182–90: Sources of Difficulty and of Value in the Poetry of Donne.

SMITH, A. J. *Rev. Letterat. Mod. Compar.*, X, 1957, 260–75: Donne in his Time. A Reading of 'The Extasie'.

SMITH, A. J. *Rev. Eng. Stud.* IX, 1958, 362–75: The Metaphysic of Love (Repr. in *A Mirror for Modern Scholars*, ed. L. A. Beaurline, N.Y., 1966).

SMITH, A. J. *English*, XIII, 1960, 49–53: New Bearings in Donne, 'Aire and Angels' (Repr. in *John Donne. Twentieth Century Views*, ed. Gardner, N.Y., 1962).

SMITH, A. J. *John Donne. The Songs and Sonets*, Arnold, London, 1964, 18·5 cm (pp. 72). Studies in Eng. Lit. no. 17.

SMITH, A. J. *Times Lit. Sup.*, 13 May 1965, p. 376: The Phoenix and the Urn.

SMITH, A. J. In *The Sphere History of Literature in English* II Sphere Books. 1970: Donne's Poetry.

SMITH, G. *Notes and Queries*, CXC, 1946, 203: The Tennis-ball of Fortune—examples of the metaphor, one being in Donne's letter to Wotton, *c.* 1600 (Simpson, *Prose Works*, p. 313).

SMITH, G. *Explicator*, VIII, April 1950, item 43: Donne's 'Love's Usury'.

SMITH, G. C. MOORE. *Mod. Lang. Quart.* IV, 1901, 91–3: Donniana.

SMITH, G. C. MOORE. *Mod. Lang. Quart.* VII, 1904, 100: Donne *v.* Dodsley ('The Blind Beggar of Bethnal Green' expanded from three lines of Donne's 'Woman's Constancy').

SMITH, G. C. MOORE. *Elizabethan Critical Essays*, 1904, 2 vols.

SMITH, G. C. MOORE. *Mod. Lang. Rev.* VIII, 1913, 47–52: Donniana.

SMITH, G. C. MOORE. *Mod. Lang. Rev.* XV, 1920, 303: Isaac Walton and John Donne.

SMITH, G. C. MOORE. *The Poems of Lord Herbert of Cherbury*, Oxford, 1923, pp. xviii–xx: Herbert's relation to Donne; pp. 57–9: Elegy for Doctor Dunn.

SMITH, H. W. *Scrutiny*, XVIII, 1951–2, 175–88: The dissociation of sensibility.

SMITH, J. *Scrutiny*, II, Cambridge, 1933–4 (repr. 1963), pp. 222–39: Metaphysical Poetry. (Also in *Determinations*, ed. F. R. Leavis, London, 1934, pp. 10–45.)

SMITH, L. PEARSALL. *The Life and Letters of Sir Henry Wotton*, 2 vols., London, 1907: References to Donne *passim* (see index).

SMITH, L. PEARSALL. *Reperusals and Recollections*, London, 1936, pp. 222–55: Donne's Sermons.

SMITH, R. G. *Theology*, XLV, 1942, pp. 147–59: Augustine and Donne: A Study in Conversion.

SOENS, A. L. *Times Lit. Sup.*, 2 May 1958, p. 241: Casaubon and Donne—recording a letter from John Harrington, Baron Exton, to Isaac Casaubon accompanying a copy of *Pseudo-Martyr* (BM, Burney MS. 36, f.

224) written in 1610 and referring to Donne in the second paragraph. Donne referred twice to Casaubon in *Pseudo-Martyr*, which is listed among books belonging to Casaubon (BLO, Cas. MS. 22, f. 107).

SOMMERLATTE, K. *Sat. Rev. Lit.* xxv, 5 December 1942, 27: Churchill and Donne.

SORLIEN, R. P. *Diss. Abstr.* xv, 1955, 1391: John Donne and the Christian Life: An Anthology of Sermons Preached by Donne, Edited with Introductions and Critical and Textual Notes [Brown Univ. diss.].

SORRENSON, F. S. *Diss. Abstr.* xii, 1951: The Nature of the Cursus Pattern in English Oratorical Prose as studied in Forty-three Cadences of John Donne and the Collects (Univ. of Michigan).

SOWTON, J. *Canad. Journ. Theol.* vi, 1960, 179–90: Religious Opinion in the Prose Letters of John Donne.

SPARROW, J. *Mod. Lang. Rev.* xix, 1924, 462–6: On the date of Donne's Hymne to God, my God, in My Sicknesse.

SPARROW, J. *Lond. Mercury*, xviii, 1928, 39–46: Donne's table-talk.

SPARROW, J. In *Essays and Stud. by Memb. of the Eng. Assoc.* xvi, 1930, 144–78: John Donne and contemporary preachers: their preparation of sermons for delivery and for publication.

SPARROW, J. *Theology*, xxii, 1931, 144–55: Donne's Religious Development.

SPARROW, J. *Lond. Merc.* xxv, 1931, 171–80: A Book from Donne's library [*Epigrammata et Poemata Varia*, L144].

SPARROW, J. In *A Garland for John Donne*, ed. T. Spencer, Cambridge, Mass., 1931, pp. 123–51: The date of Donne's travels.

SPARROW, J. *Times Lit. Sup.*, 30 March 1946, p. 151: A motto of John Donne. (A Spanish motto recorded by Bishop Joseph Hall, see p. 259.)

SPARROW, J. *Times Lit. Sup.*, 29 June 1946, p. 312: Donne's 'Anniversaries'. (A note on the unique *errata* slip, in the Corser copy of *Anniversaries*, 1621; see no. 75.)

See also letter by Grierson, Sir H. J. C., 20 July.

SPARROW, J. *Times Lit. Sup.*, 26 March 1949,

p. 208: Two epitaphs by John Donne. (Inscriptions on monuments in the Church at Hawstead, Suffolk; see p. 173.)

SPARROW, J. *Times Lit. Sup.*, 13 March 1953, p. 169: More Donne (letter).

SPARROW, J. *Times Lit. Sup.*, 29 July, 5 August 1955, pp. 436, 451: Donne's Books in the Middle Temple.

SPARROW, J. *Times Lit. Sup.*, 21 December 1956, p. 765: The Text of Donne.

SPARROW, J. *Times Lit. Sup.* 11 January 1963, p. 32: Hymns and Poetry (see also Sternfeld, F. W., 1 February, p. 77).

SPARROW, J. *Bull. N.Y. Pub. Libr.* lxviii, 1964, pp. 625–53: George Herbert and John Donne among the Moravians.

SPARROW, J. *Times Lit. Sup.*, 6 January 1966, p. 9: Donne's Books.

SPARROW, J. *Times Lit. Sup.*, 25 November 1966, p. 1060: Donne's Books in Oxford.

SPENCER, T. In *A Garland for John Donne*, ed. T. Spencer, Cambridge, Mass., 1931, pp. 179–202: Donne and his age.

SPENCER, T. Ed. *A Garland for John Donne*, Cambridge, Mass., 1931. Repr. 1958.

See under authors: Eliot, T. S.; Hayward, J.; Praz, M.; Ramsay, M. P.; Simpson, E. M.; Sparrow, J.; Spencer, T.; Williamson, G.

REVIEWED:

Belden, H. M. *Journ. Eng. Germ. Philol.* xxxii, 1933, 107–9.

Bredvold, L. *J. Mod. Philol.* xxix, 1932, 506.

Burgum, E. B. *Symposium*, iii, 1932, 402–6.

Butt, J. E. *Rev. Eng. Stud.* ix, 1933, 228–9.

Clough, B. C. *Mod. Lang. Notes*, xlviii, 1933, 200–1.

Dahlberg, E. *N.Y. Ev. Post*, 26 March 1932, p. 7.

Deutsch, B. *N.Y. Her. Trib.*, 3 April 1932, p. 14.

Freemantle, A. *Lond. Merc.* xxvi, 1932, 275.

Gregory, H. *Nation* (*N.Y.*), cxxxiv, 1932, 316–17.

Potter, G. R. *Univ. Calif. Chron.* xxxiv, 1932, 482–4.

Tate, A. *New Republ.* lxx, 1932, 212–13

Tillotson, G. *Mod. Lang. Rev.* XXVII, 1932, 477–8.

Witherspoon, A. M. *Yale Rev.* XXI, 1932, 636–8.

Times Lit. Sup., 10 March 1932, p. 168.

SPENCER, T. *Sat. Rev. Lit.* XII, 4 May 1935: Poets in their Fame.

SPENCER, T., and VAN DOREN, M. *Studies in Metaphysical Poetry: Two essays and a bibliography*, New York, 1939.

SPENS, J. *Two Periods of Disillusion*, Glasgow, 1909, see pp. 3–8, 13–17, 29–41, etc.: References to Donne.

SPINGARN, J. E. *Critical Essays of the Seventeenth Century*, Oxford, 1908, 3 vols.: Many references to Donne (see index).

SPITZER, L. *A Method of Interpreting Literature*, Northampton, 1949.

SPORRÉ, E. *Liebe und Tod in John Donne's Dichtung*, Sieben, 1949.
REVIEWED:
Mod. Lang. Rev. XLVI, 1951, 136–7.

SPROTT, E. *Univ. Toronto Quart.* XIX, 1949–50, pp. 235–53: The Legend of Jack Donne the Libertine.

SPROTT, S. E. *The English Debate on Suicide from Donne to Hume*, Le Salle, Ill., 1961: References to Donne and *Biathanatos passim*.

SPURGEON, C. F. E. *Quart. Rev.* CCVII, 1907, 450–2: Mysticism in English poetry.

SPURGEON, C. F. E. *Mysticism in English Literature*, Cambridge, 1913, pp. 72–6, etc.: References to Donne.

SQUIRE, J. C. ['Solomon Eagle']. *Books in General*, 2nd ser., London, 1920, pp. 114–18: Dr. Donne's Tomb.

STAMPFER, J. *John Donne and the Metaphysical Gesture*, N.Y., 1970 (pp. xx, 290): Discussed in *Seventeenth Cent. News*, autumn 1970, pp. 46–8.

STANWOOD, P. G. *Times Lit. Sup.*, 19 October 1967, p. 984: A Donne Discovery (see also 2 November, p. 1037): On a Latin epigram on St. Ignatius Loyola attributed to Donne in a MS. at Durham Cathedral. See p. 216 of this Bibliography.

STAPLETON, L. *Stud. Philol.* LV, 1958, pp. 187–200: The Theme of Virtue in Donne's Verse Epistles.

STAUFFER, D. A. *The Nature of Poetry*, New York, 1946.

STEBBING, W. *The Poets, Chaucer to Tennyson, 1340–1892. Impressions.* Vol. I. Chaucer to Burns, Oxford, 1907, pp. 69–78: John Donne (with quotations).

STEIN, A. *Publ. Mod. Lang. Assoc.* LVII, 1942, 676–96: Donne and the couplet.

STEIN, A. *Journ. Eng. Lit. Hist.* XI, 1944, 266–82: Donne and the satiric spirit.

STEIN, A. *Publ. Mod. Lang. Assoc.* LIX, 1944, 373–97: Donne's prosody.

STEIN, A. *Sewanee Rev.* LII. 1944, 288–301: Meter and meaning in Donne's verse.

STEIN, A. *Stud. Philol.* XLI, 1944, 390 ff.: Donne's harshness and the Elizabethan tradition.

STEIN, A. *Journ. Eng. Lit. Hist.* XIII, 1946, 98–118: Donne's obscurity and the Elizabethan tradition.

STEIN, A. *Kenyon Rev.* XIII, 1951, 20–36, 256–78: Structures of sound in Donne's verse.

STEIN, A. *Kenyon Rev.* XVIII, 1956, pp. 439–43: Donne's Prosody. (See Chatman, above.)

STEIN, A. *Journ. Stud. Eng. Lit.* XXVII, 1960, 16–29: Donne and the 1920's. A Problem in Historical Consciousness.

STEIN, A. *John Donne's Lyrics. The Eloquence of Action*, Minneapolis and London, 1962, 21·5 cm, pp. viii, [ii], 244, [2].
REVIEWED:
Carey, J. *Rev. Eng. Stud.* XVI, 1965, 309–11.
Kermode, F. *Eng. Lang. Notes*, I, 223–6.
Legouis, P. *Études Angl.* XVII, 1964, 189–90.
Novarr, D. *Mod. Philol.* LXII, 1964, 142–54.
Anon. *Times Lit. Sup.*, 6 April 1967, pp. 277–80.

STEPHENS, J. In *The Saturday Book*, 1941–2, London, 1941, pp. 310–29: About Love Songs. References to Donne, esp. pp. 327–8.

STEPHENS, J. *The Listener*, XXXVII, 1947, 149–50: The Prince of Wits.

STEPHENSON, A. A., S.J. *Downside Rev.* LXXII, 1959, 300–20: G. M. Hopkins and John Donne.

STEVENS, D. In *Internat. Musicol. Soc. 17th Internat. Congr. Bericht. Köln*, 1958, Kassel, London, N.Y., 1959, Article:

Improvisation in the execution of musical works of the 16th. and 17th. centuries. References to musical settings for Donne's poems.

STEVENSON, D. L. *Seventeenth Cent. News*, XII, 1954, 7: Among his Private Friends. John Donne.

STEWART, J. F. *Discourse*, XII, 1969, 193–9: Irony in Donne's 'The Funeral'; 465–76: Image and Idea in Donne's 'The Good-Morrow'.

STRACHEY, Sir C. *Times Lit. Sup.*, 24 July 1930, p. 611: William Strachey. (Includes a transcript of a letter from Donne to Wotton supposed to be unpublished—a mistake corrected by Simpson, E. M., 31 July.)

SULLENS, Z. R. *Ann. Instit. Univ. Orient*, Napoli. Sezione Germ. VII, 1964, 175–271: Neologisms in Donne's English Poems.

SULTAN, S. *Explicator*, XI, 1953, item 6: Donne's 'Satire I'.

SUMMERS, J. H. *George Herbert. His Religion and Art*, London, 1954.
  REVIEWED:
  Times Lit. Sup., 4 June 1954, p. 358.

SUMMERS, J. H. *Univ. Toronto Quart.* XXXIX, 1970, 107–26: The Heritage of Donne and Jonson.

SUMMERS, J. H. *The Heirs of Donne and Jonson*, Oxford, 1970.

SUNNE, R. *New Statesm. & Nation*, N.S. I, 1931, 222: Books in general (John Donne).

SVENSDEN, K. *Explicator*, II, June 1944, item 62: Donne's 'A hymne to God the Father'.

SWEENEY, J. L. *Kenyon Rev.* V, 1943, 55–9: Basic in Reading ('Love's Deity').

SWINBURNE, A. C. *Autobiographical Notes, with Critical Comments upon Donne's Anniversaries and Shakespeare's Comedy of Errors*, London, 1920, 4° (30 copies).

SYMES, G. *English*, VIII, 1950, 69–73: The paradoxes of poetry.

SYMONS, A. *A Pageant of Elizabethan Poetry*, London, 1906: The anthology includes 24 poems by Donne, and a note on him, pp. 391–2: . . . Donne is one of the worst and greatest poets in English literature, a poet unlike any other.

SYMONS, A. *Dramatist Personae*, London,

1925: Reference to Donne in 'Confessions and Comments', p. 146: Browning stole from Donne. Other references, pp. 159–84, in 'Francis Thompson'.

SYPHER, W. *Partisan Rev.* XI, 1944, 3–17: The Metaphysicals and the Baroque.

SYPHER, W. *Four Stages of Renaissance Style*, N.Y., Anchor Books, 1955: References to Donne, esp. p. 151.

TAGGART, G. *Scholastic*, XXIV, 1924, 11–12: John Donne, a link between the seventeenth and the twentieth centuries.

TATE, A. *Reason in Madness*, N.Y., 1935 (repr. 1936, 7, 8), pp. 73–5: An appreciation of 'Valediction forbidding Mourning', regarding the idea of 'gold to ayery thinnesse beate' as 'intension and extension'.

TATE, A. *Kenyon Rev.* XI, 1949, 379–94: Johnson on the Metaphysicals. Repr. in *Forlorn Demon: Didactic and Critical Essays*, Chicago, 1953, pp. 112–30; also includes, pp. 171–6: The Point of Dying: Donne's 'Virtuous Men'.

TATE, J. O. A. *Sewanee Rev.* XXXV, 1927, 41–8: Poetry and the Absolute.

TATE, J. O. A. *Reactionary Essays on Poetry and Ideas*, New York and London, 1936, pp. 64–82: A note on Donne (and) A note on Elizabethan satire.

TATE, J. O. A. *On the Limits of Poetry*. New York, [1948], pp. 325–32: A note on Donne, and other references *passim* (see index).

TATE, J. O. A. *Sewanee Rev.* LXI, 1953, 76–81: The point of dying. Donne's 'Virtuous Men'.

TAYLOR, R. A. *Aspects of the Italian Renaissance*, London, 1923, pp. 286–8: References to Donne.

TEAGER, F. S. *Philol. Quart.* XV, 1936, 408–13: Patronage of Joseph Hall and John Donne [by Sir Robert Drury].

TEN EYCK, H. *Explicator*, V, 1946, item 10: 'The Perfume'.

TERRILL, T. E. *Mod. Lang. Notes*, XLIII, 1928, 318–19: Notes on John Donne's early reading.

TERRILL, T. E. *Harvard Univ. Summary of Theses*, 1931, pp. 172–8: Spanish influence on John Donne.

THOMAS, P. E. *The Tenth Muse*. London, [1912], pp. 21–8: John Donne.

THOMPSON, E. N. S. *Stud. Philol.* XVIII, 1921, 170–231: Mysticism in seventeenth century literature.

THOMPSON, E. N. S. *The Seventeenth Century English Essay* (Iowa Humanistic Studies, III, no. 3), 1926.

THOMSON, P. *Mod. Lang. Rev.* XLIV, 1949, 329–40: John Donne and the Countess of Bedford.

THOMSON, P. *Essays in Criticism*, II, 1952, 267–84: The literature of patronage, 1580–1630.

THOREAU, H. In *American Renaissance*, by F. O. Matthiessen, 1941, p. 98: Quotes Thoreau on Donne.

THORNTON, R. H. *Notes and Queries*, N.S. IX, 1901, 212: a note on Donne's *Catalogus librorum*, to which Donne referred in a Latin letter to Sir Henry Goodere (2 July 1611, *Poems*, 1633, p. 352; Bald, p. 241).

THUMBOO, E. *Explicator*, XXVII, 1968, 113–14, item 14: Donne's 'The Bracelet' (Elegie XI).

TILLOTSON, G. *Mod. Lang. Rev.* XXVII, 1932, 381–91: The commonplace book of Arthur Capell (variants in Donne's poems).

TILLOTSON, K. In *Elizabethan and Jacobean Studies Presented to F. P. Wilson*, Oxford, 1959, pp. 307–26: Donne's Poetry in the Nineteenth Century (providing many references added to the present survey).

TILLYARD, E. M. W. *Rev. Eng. Stud.* XIX, 1943, 67–70: A note on Donne's 'Extasie'.

TILLYARD, E. M. W. *The Metaphysicals and Milton*, Cambridge, 1956.

TITUS, O. P. *Scientific Monthly*, LIV, February 1942, 176–8: Science and John Donne.

TOMKINSON, C. *Bookman* (Lond.), LXXIX, 1931, pp. 345–6: A note on the personal religion of John Donne.

TRACI, P. *Discourse*, XI, 1968, 98–107: The Supposed New Rhetoric of Donne's Songs and Sonets.

TREDEGAR, Viscount. In *Essays by Divers Hands. Trans. Roy. Soc. Lit.* XV, 1936, 161–202: John Donne. Lover and Priest (The Tredegar Memorial Lecture).

TROST, WILHELM. *Beiträge zur Kenntniss des Stils von John Donne in seinen 'Poetical Works'*. Inaugural Dissertation, Marburg, 1904, 8º, pp. [iv], 62, [2].

TURNELL, M. *19th Cent. and After*, CXLVII, 1950, 262–74: John Donne's quest for unity.

TURNELL, M. *Commonweal*, LVII, 10 October 1952, 15–18: John Donne's Quest for Unity.

TUVE, R. T. M. *Elizabethan and Metaphysical Imagery*, Chicago, [1947]. References to Donne *passim* (see index).

ULREY, P. *Renaiss. Papers*, 1958–60, pp. 76–83: The 'One' in Donne's Poetry.

UMBACH, H. H. *The Easter Sermons of John Donne*, New York (Cornell Univ.), 1934, with introduction, commentary, textual notes and a bibliography. Abstract of thesis.

UMBACH, H. H. *Publ. Mod. Lang. Assoc. Am.* LII, 1937, 354–8: The rhetoric of John Donne's sermons.

UMBACH, H. H. *Journ. Eng. Lit. Hist.* XII, 1945, 108–29: The merit of the metaphysical style in Donne's Easter sermons.

UMBACH, H. H. *The Prayers of John Donne*, selected and edited, New York, 1951.
REVIEWED:
Clancy, W. P. Commonweal, LIV, 1951, 604.
Ferling, L. *San Francisco Chron.*, 23 September 1951, p. 18.
Garrison, W. E. *Christ. Cent.* LXVIII, 1951, 1223: The two John Donnes.
Hiltner, S. *Journ. Relig.* XXXIV, 1954, 145–6.
P., J.M. *Seventeenth Cent. News*, X, 1952, 20.
School & Society, LXXIV, 1951, 160: Brief note.
Times Lit. Sup., 4 April 1952, p. 238: About Donne.

UMBACH, H. H. *Cresset*, Valparaiso, XVII, 1954, 15–23: When a poet prays.

UNGER, L. H. *Doctoral Diss.: Abstr. & Ref.* [Univ. of Iowa, 1940 & 1941], IV, 1944, 221–2: Donne's Poetry and Modern Definitions of 'Metaphysical': A Critical Study.

UNGER, L. H. *Donne's Poetry and Modern Criti-*

cism, Chicago, 1950. Repr. in *Man in the Name: Essays on the Experience of Poetry*, Minneapolis, 1956, pp. 30–104. Repr. 1962.

REVIEWED:

Deutsch, B. *N.Y. Her. Trib.* XXVII, 4 February 1951, p. 4: Metaphysician for Our Day.

Hardy, J. E. *Poetry*, LXXVII, 1950, 175–8.

Martz, L. L. *Yale Rev.* XL, 1951, 562–5.

U.S. Quart. Booklist, VI, 1950, 415.

UNGER, L. H. *The Man in the Name. Essays on the Experience of Poetry*, Minneapolis, 1956: References to Donne *passim* (see index.)

UNTERMEYER, L. *Lives of the Poets*, London, 1960, pp. 122–36: The Metaphysical Man. John Donne (for other references see index).

UPHAM, A. H. *The French Influence in English Literature*, New York, 1908, see pp. 178–85. References to Donne.

URE, P. *Notes and Queries*, CXCIII, 1948, 269: The 'Deformed Mistress'. Theme and Platonic Convention'. (Donne's Elegy II.)

VALLETTE, J. *Le Monde*, 20 juin 1946, p. 3: Un Précurseur Anglais des Poètes Contemporains.

VAN DE WATER, C. *Scholastic*, XXXVII, 1940, 20: First of the moderns.

VINING, E. G. *Take Heed of Loving Me*, Philadelphia, 1964 (a novel on Donne's life).

W., E. W. *Times Lit. Sup.*, 11 December 1919, p. 750: Donne's Puns.

WAGNER, G. A. *Poetry Rev.* XXXVIII, 1947, 253–8: John Donne and the Spiritual Life.

WAGNER, L. W. *Lock Haven Rev.* no. 7, 1965, pp. 13–22: Donne's Secular and Religious Poetry.

WALKER, H. *English Satire and Satirists*, London, 1925, pp. 68–72: Donne's Satires.

WALLERSTEIN, R. C. *Studies in Seventeenth Century Poetic*, Univ. of Wisconsin, Madison, 1950: References to Donne *passim* (see index). Incorporating: 'Rhetoric in the English Renaissance: Two Elegies', Columbia Univ. Press, 1949.

REVIEWED:

Notes and Queries, CXCV, 1950, 528.

Times Lit. Sup., 15 September 1950, p. 582: Learned Obsequies.

WALLERSTEIN, R. C. *Journ. Eng. Germ. Philol.* LIII, 1954, 410–34: Sir John Beaumont's *Crowne of Thornes* (see pp. 432–4, a comparison with Donne).

WALLERSTEIN, R. C. *Studies in Donne*, ed. B. H. Davis, Ann Arbor, Michigan, 1962.

WALSH, J. E. *Times Lit. Sup.*, 6 April 1956, p. 207: A poem by Donne (in *A Helpe to Memory and Discourse*, 1630; see no. 73*b*). See also Hindle, C. J., 8 June, p. 345.

WANNINGER, M. T. *Explicator*, XXVIII, 1969, item 37: Donne's Holy Sonnet XIV.

WARD, E. *English 'A' Analyst*, no. 12, *c.* 1948, pp. 1–4: Death be not proud. . . .

WARNKE, F. J. *Explicator*, XVI, 1957, item 12: Donne's 'The Anniversarie'.

WARNKE, F. J. *Journ. Aesthet. Arts Crit.* XXII, 1964, 455–64: Sacred Play. Baroque Poetic Style.

WARNKE, F. J. 'Metaphysical Poetry and the European Context' (see Palmer, D. J., and Bradbury, M., 1970).

WARREN, A. *Rage for Order. Essays in Criticism*, Chicago, 1948: References to Donne *passim*, esp. in 'George Herbert', pp. 32–6.

WARREN, A. *Kenyon Rev.* XVI, 1954, 268–77: The very Reverend Dr. Donne.

WARREN, A. *Stud. Philol.* LV, 1958, 472–80: Donne's 'Extasie'.

WASILIFSKY, A. M. *John Donne, the Rhetor, A study of the Tropes and Figures of the St. Paul's Sermons*. Ithaca (Cornell Univ.), 1935.

WEBBER, J. M. *Diss. Abstr.* XX, 1960, 4117: 'Contrary Music'. A Study of the Prose Styles of John Donne. Printed as *Contrary Music. The Prose Style of John Donne*, Univ. Wisconsin, Pr. 1962 (pp. xii, 227).

REVIEWED:

Bush, D. *Journ. Eng. Germ. Philol.* lxiii, 1963, 168–9.

Carey, J. *Notes and Queries*, XII, 1965, 395–6.

Fogle, F. *Renaiss. News*, XVI, no. 2, 1963, 132–3.

Stanwood, P. G. *Anglic. Theol. Rev.* XLVI, 1963, 123–4.

Anon. *Times Lit. Sup.*, 16 January 1964, p. 48.

WEBBER, J. M. *Anglia*, lxxix, 1962, 138–52: The Prose Style of John Donne's *Devotions*.

WEBBER, J. M. *The Eloquent I. Style and Self in Seventeenth Century Prose*, Madison, 1968 (see esp. ch. 2).

WEDGWOOD, C. V. *Seventeenth-Century English Literature*, London and New York, 1950, pp. 66–89: John Donne and Caroline Poetry.

WELLS, H. W. *Poetic Imagery. Illustrated from Elizabethan Literature*. New York, 1924, pp. 121–37: The Radical Image (Donne).

WENDELL, B. *The Temper of the Seventeenth Century in English Literature*, London, 1904, pp. 119–27, 164: References to Donne.

WENDELL, J. P. *Mod. Lang. Notes*, LXIII, 1948, 480–1: Two cruxes in the poetry of Donne.

WENDELL, J. P. *Diss. Abstr.* xv, 1955, 595: The Poems and Sermons of Donne. A Study of the Parallels between the two forms of Donne's Art. (Princeton Univ.)

WEST, B. C. *Summ. Doct. Diss. Northwest. Univ.* XVIII, 1950, 35–7: Anti-Petrarchism. A Study of the Reaction against the Courtly Tradition in English Love-poetry from Wyatt to Donne.

WHIPP, L. T. *Diss. Abstr.* XXVII, 1967, 3436A: John Donne's 'A Litanie' and Mediaeval Exegesis.

WHITE, H. C. *English Devotional Literature [Prose]*, Madison (Univ. of Wisconsin), 1931, pp. 152–7: Donne's *Devotions*. Other references *passim* (see index).

WHITE, H. C. *The Metaphysical Poets. A Study in Religious Experience*, New York, 1936: References to Donne *passim* (see index). Repr. 1956.

WHITE, H. C. In *The Seventeenth Century. Bacon to Pope*, Stanford, see pp. 355–68.

WHITE, W. *Bull. Bibliogr. Pamph.* no. 37, Boston, 1942, pp. [vi], 23: John Donne since 1900. A Bibliography of Periodical Articles.
REVIEWED:
Greever, G. *Personalist*, xxv, 1944, 106–7.
Tannenbaum, S. A. *Shakespeare Assoc. Bull.* XVIII, 1943, 143–4.
Tillotson, G. *Mod. Lang. Rev.* XXXIX, 1944, 195–6.

WHITE, W. *Bull. Bibliogr.* XXII, 1959, 186–9: Keynes's Bibliography of Donne. A Review

with Addenda (reviews and criticism, incorporated here).

WHITESELL, J. E. *Explicator*, 1, February 1943, item 29: Donne's Song, 'Go and catch a falling star'.

WHITLOCK, B. D. *Notes and Queries*, N.S. VI (CCIV), 1959, 257–62, 348–53: The Heredity and Childhood of John Donne.

WHITLOCK, B. D. *Notes and Queries*, N.S. VII (CCV), 1960, 380–6: The Family of John Donne, 1588–91.

WHITLOCK, B. D. *Eng. Stud.* XLIII, 1962, 1–20: Donne's University Years.

WHITLOCK, B. D. *Renaiss. News*, XVIII, 1965, 9–11: Notice of two MSS. containing Donne's 'Hymn to the Saints' and 'Elegy IV', giving variants.

WHITLOCK, B. D. *Bucknell Rev.* XV, 1967, 46–60: From the Counter-Renaissance to the Baroque.

WHITLOCK, B. W. *Times. Lit. Sup.*, 22 August 1952, p. 556: Donne's 'First Letter'.
See also 19 September, 30 October, 14 November; Bald, R. C., 24 October, 19 December; Shapiro, I. A., 12 September, 26 September; Novarr, D., 24 October. Correspondence summarized in *Seventeenth Cent. News*, 11 January 1953.

WHITLOCK, B. W. *Notes and Queries*, CXCVIII, 1953, 152–3: 'Cabal' in Donne's sermons.

WHITLOCK, B. W. *Notes and Queries*, CXCIX, 1954, 374–5: The Dean and the yeoman.

WHITLOCK, B. W. *Notes and Queries*, CXCIX, 1954, 421–4, 465–7: John Syminges, a poet's [Donne's] stepfather. (See also CC, 1955, 132–3. A reply.)

WHITLOCK, B. W. *The Guildhall Miscellany*, no. 4, London, 1955, pp. 22–9: The Orphanage Accounts of John Donne, Ironmonger. (Material gathered for an appendix to a thesis on the life of Donne, the poet, presented to the University of Edinburgh.)

WHITLOCK, B. W. *Rev. Eng. Stud.*, N.S. VI, 1955, 365–71: Ye Curioust Scooler in Christendom. (Gives Edward Alleyn's letter to Donne, January 1624/5.)

WHITLOCK, B. W. *Times Lit. Sup.*, 16, 23 September 1955, pp. 548, 564: Donne at St. Dunstan's.

WHITLOCK, B. W. *Rev. Eng. Stud.* VIII, 1957, 420–1: Correspondence [on Edward Alleyn's letter to Donne, published in *Rev. Eng. Stud.*, VI, 1955, 365–71].

WIGGINS, E. L. *Stud. Philol.* XLII, 1945, 41–60: Logic in the poetry of John Donne.

WILCOX, J. *Huntington Lib. Quart.* XIII, 1950, 191–200: Informal Publication of Late Sixteenth-Century Verse Satire.

WILD, F. *Anglia*, LIX, 1935, 414–22: Zum Problem des Barocks in der englischen Dichtung.

WILDER, M. L. *Mod. Lang. Rev.* XXI, 1926, 431–5: Did Jonson write 'The Expostulation' attributed to Donne?

WILEY, M. L. *Hibbert Journ.* XLVIII, 1950, 163–72: John Donne and the poetry of scepticism.

WILEY, M. L. *The Subtle Knot. Creative Scepticism in Seventeenth Century England*, London, 1952, see ch. 4, pp. 120–36: John Donne and the poetry of scepticism.

WILLEY, B. In *Major British Writers*, ed. C. W. Dunn [and others], New York, 1954, I, pp. 357–65: John Donne.

WILLIAMS, A. *The Common Expositor: An Account of the Commentaries on Genesis, 1527–1633*, Chapel Hill, 1948: References to Donne.

WILLIAMS, M. E. *Diss. Abstr.* XXIV, 1964, 4203: John Donne's 'Orbe of Man'. A Study of Donne's Use of Archetypal Images in the Round.

WILLIAMSON, G. *Sewanee Rev.* XXXV, 1927, 284–95: The Talent of T. S. Eliot (Eliot compared with Donne). Repr. as *Univ. of Washington Chapbooks*, no. 32, 1929, and again, The Curwen Press, 1969, with a Bibliogr. by J. Williamson.

WILLIAMSON, G. *Stud. in Philol.* XXV, 1928, 416–38: The nature of the Donne tradition.

WILLIAMSON, G. *The Donne Tradition A Study in English Poetry from Donne to the Death of Cowley*, Cambridge, Mass., London, 1930, 8º, pp. xii, 264.
REVIEWED:
Bredvold, L. I. *Mod. Lang. Notes*, XLVI, 1931, 349.

Croll, M. W. *Mod. Philol.* XXVIII, 1931, 490–1.

Hughes, M. V. *Univ. Calif. Chron.* XXXII, 1930, 507–10.

Legouis, P. *Rev. Anglo-Améric.* VIII, 1930, 152–4.

Nethercot, A. H. *Jour. Eng. Germ. Philol.* XXX, 1931, 293–5.

Praz, M. *Eng. Stud.* XII, 1930, 195–8.

Sisson, C. J. *Mod. Lang. Rev.* XXVI, 1931, 233–4.

W., T. W. *Cath. World*, CXXXII, 1931, 502.

Walton, E. L. *New York Times*, 31 August 1930, p. 2.

Warren, A. *Bookman* (N.Y.), LXXI, 1930, 463–4.

St. Louis Libr. Bull. XXVIII, 1930, 268.

Times Lit. Sup., 31 July 1930, p. 625.

WILLIAMSON, G. In *A Garland for John Donne*, ed. T. Spencer, Cambridge, Mass., 1931, pp. 155–76: Donne and the poetry of today.

WILLIAMSON, G. *Eng. Lit. Hist.* II, 1932, 121–50: Mutability, decay, and seventeenth century melancholy.

WILLIAMSON, G. *Times Lit. Sup.*, 18 August 1932, p. 581: The Donne Canon. (MS. notes in a copy of *Poems*, 1639.)

WILLIAMSON, G. *Philol. Quart.* XIII, 1934, 276–91: Libertine Donne: Comments on *Biathanatos*.

WILLIAMSON, G. *Eng. Stud.* XVIII, 1936, 152–8: Strong Lines in English Poetry of the first half of the Seventeenth Century. Repr. in *Seventeenth Century Contexts*, London, 1962.

WILLIAMSON, G. *Mod. Philol.* XXXVI, 1939, 301–3: Donne's 'Farewell to Love'.

WILLIAMSON, G. *Mod. Philol.* XXXVIII, 1940, 37–72: Textual Difficulties in the Interpretation of Donne's Poetry. Repr. in *Seventeenth Century Contexts*, 1962.

WILLIAMSON, G. *The Proper Wit of Poetry*. Univ. Chicago Pr. 1961, pp. 136 (analyses of wit in Donne and others).

WILLIAMSON, G. The Convention of 'The Extasie', in *Seventeenth Century Contexts*, 1962. Repr. in *Seventeenth Century English Poetry*, ed. W. R. Keast (Paperback, U.K. and U.S.A.), 1962.

WILLIAMSON, G. *Mod. Philol.* LX, 1963, 183–91: The Design of Donne's 'Anniversaries'. Repr. in *Milton and Others*, London, 1965. Tr. into Italian by R. Zelocchi, *Convivium*, N.S. XXXI, 1963, 436–47.

WILLIAMSON, G. *Milton and Others*, London, 1965: References to Donne *passim*, esp. pp. 150–64, 'Anniversaries'; 150–62, 'Ignatius his Conclave'; 154–64, 'Metempsychosis'.

WILLIAMSON, G. *Six Metaphysical Poets. A Reader's Guide* (Donne, Herbert, and others), N.Y., 1967.

WILLIAMSON, G. *Journ. Eng. Lit. Hist.* XXXVI, 1969, 250–64: Donne's Satirical 'Progresse of the Soule'.

WILLMORE, M. O. *Lond. Quart. Rev.* CLIII, 1930, 109–11: John Donne.

WILLY, M. *Essays and Studies by Members of the Eng. Assoc.* VII, 1954, 78–104: The Poetry of Donne. Its Interest and Influence Today.

WILSON, E. M. *Journ. Eccles. Hist.* IX, 1958, 38–63: Spanish and English Religious Poetry of the Seventeenth Century.

WILSON, F. P. *Rev. Eng. Stud.* III, 1927, 272–9: Notes on the early life of John Donne. Cf. *Notes and Queries*, CLIII, 1927, 56.

WILSON, F. P. *Elizabethan and Jacobean*, Oxford, 1945. For references to Donne see index.

WILSON, F. P. *Seventeenth Century Prose*, Cambridge, 1960, Ewing Lectures (pp. [xii], 130). Many references to Donne.

WILSON, G. R., jr. *Stud. Eng. Lit.* IX, 1969, 107–21: The Interplay of Perception and Reflection. Mirror Imagery in Donne's Poetry.

WINNY, J. *A Preface to Donne* (Preface Books), Longman, London, 1970.

WINTERS, Y. *Hudson Rev.* I, 1948, 457–60: The Poetry of Gerard Manley Hopkins (discussion of Donne's Holy Sonnet I).

WOLFE, R. H., and DANIELS, E. F. *Amer. Notes and Queries*, V, 1967, 116–17: Rime and Idea in Donne's 'Holy Sonnet X'.

WOOD, H. H. In *Essays and Stud. by Memb. of the Eng. Assoc.* XVI, 1931, 179–90: A seventeenth-century manuscript of poems by Donne and others, including a transcript of 'Mr. Tilman of Pembroke Hall in Cambridge, his motives not to take orders' (see *Poems*, 1635, no. 31).

WOOD, H. H. *Times Lit. Sup.*, 9 July 1931, p. 547: Donne's Mr. Tilman: A Postscript (see also J. E. Butt, *Times Lit. Sup.*, 15 December 1932).

WOOLF, V. *The Second Common Reader*, London, 1932, pp. 20–37: Donne after Three Centuries.

WOOLLAM, D. H. M. *Med. Hist.* V, 1961, 144–53: Donne, Disease and Doctors.

WRIGHT, H. G. In *Essays and Studies*, N.S. VI, 1953, 47 (Writers on the Plague), describing Donne in London in 1625, with quotations from a sermon.

WRIGHTSON, R. *Bookman's Journ.* XVI, 1928, 373–9: Note on Donne's poetry.

YARRINGTON, E. N. *Diss. Abstr.* XXIII, 1963, 2906–7: The Metaphysical Drama. A Study of Similarities between the Poems of Donne and Plays, particularly Webster's.

YEATS, W. B. In *The Letters*, ed. A. Wade, London, 1954: References to Donne, pp. 570, 571, 710 (letters to H. J. C. Grierson), 902 (letter to Dorothy Wellesley), *c.* 1912–25.

YEATS, W. B. *Autobiographies*, London, 1955, p. 326, in 'The Tragic Generation', sect. xiii, references to Donne. First pr. in *The Trembling of the Veil*, London, 1922.

YOKLAVITCH, J. *Philol. Quart.* (Iowa), XLIII, 1964, 283–8: Donne and the Countess of Huntingdon.

ZIMMERMAN, D. E. *Emporia State Research Stud.* VIII, 1960, no. 3 (Kansas St. Teachers' Coll.): The Nature of Man. John Donne's 'Songs and Holy Sonnets'.

ZIVLEY, S. *Stud. Eng. Lit.* VI, 1966, 87–95: Imagery in John Donne's *Satyres*.

ZUBERI, I.-H. *Univ. Windsor Rev.* (Ontario), I, 1966, 147–58: John Donne's Concept of Toleration in Church and State.

ZYPHERS, D. *Univ. N.Y. Unpubl. Master's Thesis*: John Donne's Use of Numbers in 'Songs and Sonnets', 1954.

APPENDIX VI

ICONOGRAPHY

THIS list does not deal exhaustively with Donne's iconography, but is intended to be a brief guide to the original sources as far as they are known.

A. *Miniatures:*

[1. Bust, looking slightly to the right. Youthful beard and moustache, hair long, lace collar. Oval, 5·5 × 4 cm. Signed: .ф. 1610, that is, Isaac Oliver. This miniature was engraved by Alais as a frontispiece to Grosart's edition of Donne's *Poems* (1872) (see no. 91). It was stated to be then in the possession of Samuel Addington. The portrait cannot be accepted as representing Donne, who was 38 in the year 1610, considerably more than the apparent age of the subject of the miniature.]

2. Bust, looking to the left. Ruff and pointed beard. Oval, 4·5 × 3·5 cm. Signed at right .ф., that is, Isaac Oliver, and dated on the left 1616. This miniature was reproduced in Colnaghi's *Photographic Historical Portrait Gallery* (1864) (see p. 320), and was then in the collection of C. S. Bale. It is now in the collection at Windsor Castle, and has been reproduced in this volume by the gracious permission of Her Majesty the Queen. It was reproduced in colours in Garnett and Gosse's *English Literature* (1903), II, 308 (see p. 339).

There can be no doubt as to the authenticity of the portrait. It was probably the source of the oil painting now in the National Portrait Gallery (see no. 3 below) and also of Merian's engraving in *LXXX Sermons* (1640) (see no. 12 below).

B. *Oil Paintings:*

3. Bust, looking to the left. Ruff and pointed beard. Dark background. Size, *c.* 54 × 44 cm. This painting closely resembles the miniature by Isaac Oliver (no. 2 above), and is likely to have been copied from it or done at the same time. It therefore represents Donne at the age of 44. An engraving was made from it by A. Duncan in 1822 (see no. 14 below), the picture being then in the possession of the Revd. Dr. Barrett. It is now in the National Portrait Gallery and was first reproduced in the *Devotions*, edited by John Sparrow (Cambridge, 1923) (no. 42*a*).

XII

John Duns.

VLTIMA · TENEBRÆ

NOSTRAS DOCTRINA

4. 1620. Bust, full face, with bare neck and a cloak round the shoulders. Inscribed: AETATIS SUAE 49 1620. Circular, diameter 58 cm. Painter unknown. Now in the dining-room at the Deanery of St. Paul's Cathedral.

An engraving seemingly after this portrait was made by Lombart in 1651, but the engraver either ignored or misread the inscription, and implied that his age was 40 (see no. 9 below). Attention has been drawn to this by Professor I. A. Shapiro, *Notes and Queries*, CXCVII, 1952, 310–13. The painting is reproduced in Gosse, frontispiece to vol. II.

5. A replica or copy of no. 4. Now in the Dyce collection at the Victoria and Albert Museum, where it is ascribed to Cornelius Janssen.

6. *c.* 1595. Three-quarter profile in an oval on an oak panel $30\frac{1}{2} \times 24\frac{1}{2}$ in. inscribed ILLUMINA TENEBR NOSTRAS DOMINA. Painter unknown. Property of the Trustees of the 11th Marquess of Lothian.

In his will Donne included the clause: 'Item I give to my honourable & faithful freinde Mr Robert Karr of his Majesties Bedchamber that Picture of myne wch is taken in Shaddowes and was made very many yeares before I was of this profession.' Dr. Thomas Morton, Bishop of Durham, recalled this picture in connection with Donne's taking orders: 'For doubtless the Holy Spirit had the greatest stroak and power to incline, and draw him to that sacred Profession: For my selfe have long since seen his Picture in a dear friends Chamber of his in Lincolnes Inne all envelloped with a darkish shaddow, his face & feature hardly discernable, with this ejaculation and wish written thereon: *Domine illumina tenebras meas*; which long after was really accomplished, when (by King *James* his weighty and powerful perswasions) he took holy Orders' (see Richard Badiley's *Life of Morton*, 1669, p. 101). William Drummond of Hawthornden confirmed that the picture passed to the beneficiary, Robert Karr, or Carr, later Earl of Ancrum, when he wrote in his memoranda: 'J. Done gave my Lord Ancrum his picture in a melancholic posture, with this word about it *De tristitia ista libera me Domine*' (see J. Bryson, *The Times*, 13 October 1959, p. 15). It was therefore certain that the picture existed and must have passed to Ancrum's descendants, the successive Marquesses of Lothian, and should have been kept at Newbattle Abbey. In 1956 I made an earnest attempt to find the picture, but was repeatedly assured by the authorities at the National Gallery of Scotland that no such picture could be found at Newbattle. Nevertheless three years later the picture was recognized from a photograph taken at Newbattle for John Bryson of Balliol College and was described by him in *The Times*, 13 October 1959. Donne's description of the picture as 'taken in Shaddowes' was now explained, since it is seen to represent a young lover in a melancholic pose with the inscription recorded above. This seems to be an irreverent parody (differently recalled by Morton and Drummond) of the third Collect for Evening Prayer: 'Illumina quaesumus Domine Deus tenebras nostras.' The sitter's face is immediately recognizable as Donne's from its resemblance to Marshall's engraving in the *Poems* of 1635. He is wearing a huge black hat turned up from his face and is posed in three-quarter profile to the right with folded arms. His left hand with long thin fingers is bare; his right wears a fur-lined glove and is holding a book, the rough edges of which suggest that it is a manuscript (of his poems?) rather than a printed book. The lower edge of the volume rests on a pewter standish with an inkpot and a quill pen. His open-necked doublet is dark with an embroidered collar and underlying lace. A thin cord hangs from beneath the collar. When the picture was found under the stairs in the basement at Newbattle Abbey the frame was labelled in large lettering; DUNS SCOTUS, thus explaining how it had been so long overlooked, though the elegant costume was clearly not that of a medieval scholar. Slight overpainting has been removed and the picture, of high quality, is in fair condition. It was for some time on exhibition at the National Portrait Gallery and is now in the keeping of the 11th Marquess of Lothian.

Reproduced opposite (before cleaning), in *The Times* (loc. cit.), in Gardner's *Elegies, Songs and Sonnets*, Oxford, 1965, p. 29 and in Bald's *Life*, 1970, p. 76. Also in Roy Strong's *The English Icon. Elizabethan and Jacobaean Portraits*, London, Paul Mellon Foundation, 1970, p. 37, with a note on the picture, p. 353.

C. *Stone Effigy:*

7. Full-size effigy of Donne in his shroud; at his feet is an urn and above his head is a marble tablet with an epitaph written by himself. Carved in Italian marble by Nicholas Stone assisted by Humphrey Mayer (or Moyer) in 1631 after the portrait, which had been drawn on a board by an unnamed artist shortly before Donne's death. The effigy was originally within the choir in the south aisle of old St. Paul's, and was the only monument which was saved intact from the fire of 1666; it is now in corresponding position in the present Cathedral. For further particulars of this effigy, see Walton's *Life of Donne*, 1658, pp. 111–14, and Gosse, 11, 280–8.

Engravings of the effigy were made by Marshall (no. 11 below) and by Hollar (no. 13 below). Photographs of it are reproduced in Gosse, vol. 11, facing p. 280, and of the head only in Dame Helen Gardner's *The Divine Poems* (see no. 165) and in this *Bibliography*, third edition, 1958, plate 12.

D. *Engravings:*

8. 1591. *Aet.* 18. Bust, three-quarter face to right, in an oval 8·4 × 6·4 cm. Engraved in line and stipple by Marshall after an unknown painting done

between January and June 1591 (see I. A. Shapiro, *Notes and Queries*, CXCVII, 1952, 312); lines by Walton below. Used as frontispiece to the second edition of the *Poems*, 1635, and to several subsequent editions (see nos. 79–83). Reproduced as frontispiece to Gosse, vol. I, facing p. 199 of the present work, and elsewhere. The late Laurence Binyon suggested that the original portrait was painted by Nicholas Hilliard (1537–1619).

9. 1612. *Aet.* 40. Bust in an oval, 10·2 × 8·5 cm. Engraved in line by Pierre Lombart (1620–81) after no. 4 or 5 above. Used as frontispiece to the *Letters*, 1651 and 1654 (see nos. 55, 56); also in Walton's *Lives*, 1670 and 1675. Reproduced in Gosse, vol. II, facing p. 80, in the present work facing p. 136, and elsewhere. The description of Donne on this plate as *quadragenarius* implies that his age was 40, but this is probably incorrect (see no. 4 above).

10. Donne's head in a shroud, within an oval, 11·4 × 8·5 cm. Engraved in line by Martin Droeshout (1596–1652) after the stone effigy (no. 7 above) or the original drawing on a board. Used as frontispiece to *Death's Duell*, 1632 (see nos. 24–6). Copied by Skelton for Walton's *Lives*, ed. Zouch, 1796, etc. Reproduced in Gosse, vol. II, facing p. 360, in the present work, facing p. 51, and elsewhere.

11. Full-length in shroud, measuring, with decorations, 9·5 × 5 cm. Engraved by William Marshall (fl. 1630–50) after the effigy in St. Paul's. Used as frontispiece to the fourth and fifth editions of the *Devotions*, 1634 and 1638 (see nos. 39 and 40). Reproduced in Pickering's edition of the *Devotions*, 1840 (see no. 41), and facing p. 87 of the present work (enlarged).

12. 1616. *Aet.* 44. Bust, three-quarter face to right, dressed in gown and ruff, within an oval, 9 × 6·5 cm. Engraved in line and stipple by Merian in the centre of the frontispiece to *LXXX Sermons*, 1640 (see no. 29), after the miniature by Oliver (no. 2 above). The portrait alone was also used as a frontispiece to Walton's *Life of Donne*, 1658 (see no. 150). Copied by Skelton for Walton's *Lives*, ed. Zouch, 1796, etc. Reproduced in Gosse, vol. II, facing p. 144, and facing p. 63 of the present work.

13. Full-length in shroud, 30 × 10 cm. Engraved in line by Hollar after the effigy in St. Paul's for Dugdale's *History of St Paul's*, 1658, p. 62.

14. Bust, three-quarter face to left, dressed in gown and ruff; rectangular, 9·6 × 7·6 cm. Engraved in line by A. Duncan after a drawing by G. Clint, A.R.A., 'from an original picture in the possession of the Rev[d] Dr Barrett'.
    A plate from *Effigies Poeticæ*, London, W. Walker, 1822, 8°; also india paper proofs on large paper. The original painting is no. 3 above. Reproduced in Gosse, vol. I, facing p. 304.

15. Bust, full-face, dressed in gown and broad linen collar, in an oval, 10·6 × 8·6 cm. Engraved in line and stipple by W. Holl, 'from the original picture by Vandyke in the possession of F. Holbrooke, Esq.'. Used as frontispiece to Donne's *Works*, ed. Alford, 1839, vol. 1 (see no. 33*a*), and in Grosart's *Donne*, vol. 1, 8° edition (see no. 91). The head closely resembles that of the two oil paintings, nos. 4 and 5 above; the 'original picture' is perhaps to be identified with no. 5, the dress having been slightly altered in the engraving.

LIBRARIES CONSULTED

A. GENERAL LIST

(The numbers refer to the entries in the bibliography)

Aberdeen
  Public Library, 40
  University Library (AUL), 29

Baltimore
  Johns Hopkins University Library (BJ), 9
Breslau, Stadtsbibliothek, 3

Cambridge Colleges
  Caius, 1, 78, 83
  Christ's, 27, 30, 31, 49, 78, 79
  Clare, 48, 78
  Corpus Christi, 56, 78
  Emmanuel, 1, 4, 19, 28*a*, 29, 30, 43, 47, 82, 202
  Jesus, 14, 16, 18, 19, 21, 22, 24, 27, 44, 83, 205
  King's, 7, 29, 30, 31, 48, 84
  Magdalene, 1, 14, 15, 19, 27, 48, 55, 79, 84
  Pembroke, 14, 16, 18, 19, 21, 26, 27, 29, 39, 44, 48, 55, 83
  Peterhouse, 29, 83
  Queens', 1
  St. Catharine's, 48
  St. John's, 1, 16, 19, 23, 24, 29, 40, 44, 47, 55, 78, 80, 83, 84
  Trinity, 1, 2, 13, 14, 16, 17, 17*a*, 19, 24, 27, 29, 34, 39, 43, 45, 48, 50, 55, 56, 57, 60, 78, 80, 84, 85, 106, 110, 150, 200, 209
Cambridge University Library (ULC), 1, 3, 4, 7, 8, 13, 15, 16, 21, 23, 27, 28, 28*a*, 29, 30, 31, 32, 34, 36, 43, 47, 57, 59, 60, 62, 70, 73*a*, 78, 79, 85, 195, 196, 197, 202, 204, 205, 208
Cathedral Libraries
  Canterbury, 80, 82
  Carlisle, 4, 12, 29, 30, 32*a*, 55, 80
  Cashel, 46
  Durham, 29, 30, 34, 85

Exeter, 1, 14, 18, 19, 21, 24, 26, 29, 30, 38
Gloucester, 29
Hereford, 1, 24, 29
Lincoln, 24, 27, 29, 37, 43, 48, 78, 209
Peterborough, 1, 8, 9, 29, 30, 34, 47
St. David's, 29
St. Paul's, 1, 12, 14, 19, 21, 25, 27, 30, 31, 36, 43, 48, 209
Salisbury, 1, 11, 29, 55
Winchester, 29, 30, 31, 43, 47, 78
Worcester, 29, 30, 31
York, 9
Chicago, Newberry Library (NLC), 9, 14, 16, 19, 28, 29, 31, 36, 43, 44, 46, 47, 50, 78, 79, 80, 82, 84

Dublin
  Marsh Library, 1, 38, 69, 72, 207
  Trinity College (TCD), 9, 14, 15, 22, 48, 70, 83, 84
Durham
  Cosin Library, 164
  University Library (ULD), 1, 14, 16, 29, 43, 49, 78

Edinburgh
  National Library of Scotland (NLS), 1, 2, 8, 12, 19, 21, 24, 29, 30, 40, 46, 48, 49, 55, 57, 79, 80
  New College, 45, 47, 50
  University Library (ULE), 7, 11, 19, 29, 69

Fleming, John, 73*b*

Glasgow University Library (GUL), 27

Harvard College Library (HCL), 1, 2, 4, 8, 9, 12, 13, 14, 15, 16, 18, 19, 21, 22, 23, 24, 26, 27, 29, 30, 31, 34, 36, 37, 38, 39, 43,

Princeton, N.J.
    Theological Seminary (TSP), 1, 9, 26,
        27, 47, 80
    University Library (PUL), 15, 16, 21,
        29, 30, 37, 38, 47, 49, 51, 55, 56, 59,
        78, 79, 82, 84, 85, 204

St. Andrews University Library, 34, 43
Shapiro, I. A., 9, 32*a*, 44, 51, 60
Sheffield University Library, 38
Sparrow, John, 1, 13, 27, 28, 30, 34, 37, 39,
    49, 51, 57, 82, 150, 204

Taylor, R. H., 23
Texas, Wren Library, 9

Washington, D.C.
    Folger Shakespeare Memorial Library
        (FSLW), 1, 8, 9, 12, 13, 14, 15, 16,
        18, 19, 20, 21, 22, 23, 24, 26, 27, 28*a*,
        34, 36, 38, 39, 43, 44, 46, 49, 50, 55,
        56, 57, 59, 60, 75, 78, 79, 80, 82, 83,
        84, 150, 202, 204
    Library of Congress (LCW), 14, 15, 16,
        18, 19, 21, 22, 29, 30, 43, 47, 48, 55,
        78, 79, 80, 82
Williamstown, Mass., Chapin Library, 47
Windsor
    Chapter Library, Windsor Castle, 1, 4, 5,
        9, 29, 56
    Eton College, 69

B. BOOKS FROM DONNE'S LIBRARY OR GIVEN BY HIM
(The numbers refer to the separate list, pp. 263–79)

All Souls College, Oxford, 43

Balliol College, Oxford, 215
Bodleian Library, Oxford (BLO), 5, 8, 14,
    20, 21, 28, 37, 47, 51, 59, 69, 84, 94, 96,
    101, 111, 115, 124, 139, 140, 141, 144,
    167, 168, 169, 172, 181, 194, 195, 196,
    197, 217
British Museum (BM), 4, 31, 77, 87

Cambridge University Library (ULC), 3, 17,
    33, 46, 48, 52, 54, 70, 79, 103, 108, 110,
    125, 129, 147, 149, 156, 162, 173, 177,
    187, 207
Catholic University of America, Washington,
    128
Chichester Cathedral, 15, 23, 57, 112, 188,
    192
Corpus Christi College, Oxford, 201

Dr. Williams's Library, London (DWL), 2, 66

Folger Shakespeare Memorial Library,
    Washington (FSLW), 126

Greenhill (Harold) Collection, Chicago, 166,
    211

Harvard College Library (HCL), 1, 9, 10, 13,
    22, 25, 26, 53, 56, 71, 95, 104, 105, 106,
    132, 174, 189, 190
Huntington Library, California, 58, 138
Hunterian Collection, Glasgow University,
    202
Hyde (Donald F.) Library, Somerville, New
    Jersey, 135

Jesus College, Oxford, 191

Keynes, G. L., 50, 130, 161, 183

Lincoln's Inn Library, London, 218
Liverpool Cathedral Library, 68

Marsh's Library, Dublin, 120, 121, 150
Middle Temple Library, London, 6, 7, 11, 18,
    19, 24, 29, 32, 34, 35, 38, 39, 40, 41, 42,
    44, 45, 49, 60, 61, 62, 63, 64, 65, 67, 72,
    74, 75, 76, 78, 83, 85, 86, 88, 90, 91, 92,
    93, 97, 98, 99, 100, 102, 107, 113, 114,
    118, 122, 131, 133, 134, 142, 145, 146,
    148, 151, 152, 153, 154, 155, 157, 158,
    160, 163, 164, 165, 170, 171, 175, 176,
    178, 179, 180, 182, 184, 185, 186, 193,
    198, 199, 200, 204, 206, 209

PRINTERS AND PUBLISHERS *1607–1719*

(The numbers refer to the entries in the bibliography)

INDEX